PUBLIC SPEAKING: PRINCIPLES AND PRACTICE

PUBLIC SPEAKING:

GILES WILKESON GRAY

and

WALDO W. BRADEN

Louisiana State University

HARPER & ROW, PUBLISHERS,

PRINCIPLES AND PRACTICE

second edition

NEW YORK, EVANSTON, AND LONDON

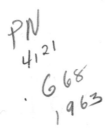

PN
4121
.G68
1963

Public Speaking: Principles And Practice, Second Edition

Copyright 1951 by Harper & Row, Publishers, Incorporated
Copyright © 1963 by Giles W. Gray and Waldo W. Braden

Library of Congress Catalog Card Number: 63-7109

H-Q

Contents

Preface

It has been just eleven years since the first edition of this textbook appeared on the academic scene. The authors claimed no high degree of originality in either the subject matter or the organization of that book, the only possible claim to uniqueness being in the emphasis placed on the ethical point of view, an emphasis made by Quintilian almost two thousand years ago.

The events that have taken place during the past eleven years on both the domestic and the international scenes have given little encouragement to any tendency to soften or reduce that emphasis. It is just as vital today as it was eleven years ago that attention be called sharply, as we pointed out then, to the fact, sometimes overlooked, that speech is a terrific force in human relations for either good or ill; that because of its potentialities, acquiring ability in any of the forms of communication carries with it a deep responsibility for its ethical use; that in scarcely any period of our history has the need existed as it exists today, even more than eleven years ago, for a type of honest thinking and speaking that is motivated by a genuine and consistent concern for the well-being of humanity.

For more than a century and a half we have been committed to a democratic principle of self-government, in which speech has always played a vital role. Government by talk, instead of being a target for slurs, has in fact been one of our most valuable contributions to civilization. So vital to democracy is the function of speech that it can be used even to destroy the societal forms which make it possible! Whereupon it ceases at once to exist.

It is the belief of the authors that a course in public speaking should therefore offer more than an understanding of the psychological and rhetorical techniques used in public utterance; it should offer an opportunity to examine the function of speech in the development and maintenance of those social and individual values which have derived from our public and private institutions. It should further make an effort to orient the student in a wholesome point of view toward that function. Freedom of speech, with all its social, psychological, and educational implications, can exist only in a form of society essentially democratic in its philosophy; conversely, such a form of society is the only one that can exist where freedom of speech, with all its accompaniments, prevails.

The study of speech, of public speaking, therefore becomes in large part a study of public relations at their highest level and of the place of speech in the rational solution of the manifold problems that arise in those relations.

A textbook written from such a point of view will inevitably consist of something more than a manual of instruction. Such a book must go back of the rhetorical and the psychological and inquire into some of the principles that enable human beings to live and work together for their common good. It must perforce be prescriptive at times; but in the present text an effort is constantly made to base this prescription on the social and the ethical as well as on the rhetorical and the psychological. Aiming at more than immediate utility, it looks to the lifelong effectiveness of the speaker on the basis of personal integrity, the importance of which was recognized a hundred or more years before Aristotle.

The point of view held consistently throughout the text is that no treatment of rhetorical theory can be complete or adequate unless it takes into consideration the relation of that body of theory to human society and the impact of both theory and practice on human welfare and human aspirations. It holds that no principles of public speaking can be sound, even on a purely theoretical basis, which ignore a solid foundation of fact—and truth, so far as it can be identified with facts, is on the side of ethics. Unethical speaking, therefore, is untruthful speaking, which cannot be sound on any basis.

This, then, is the credo to which the authors were and are committed in the presentation of *Public Speaking: Principles and Practice.*

But the speaker's full acquiescence to, or acceptance of, the formulation of fundamental belief enunciated in the preceding paragraphs is hardly enough; the belief must be implemented, put into action. Therefore we submit that more than honest thinking and speaking is needed today—as much as if not more than ever before. What would seem to be demanded is *courageous* speaking as well as ethical speaking in our social, political, economic, educational and perhaps even religious areas of thought and endeavor.

May we therefore supplement the credo that we offered eleven years ago with a codicil, so to speak? May we urge upon all teachers as well as students of public speaking, first, a recognition of the need for speakers of ability who will have the courage of honesty, and second, a willingness, even an eagerness, to take the opportunities that come to them to voice their honest and well-considered convictions with clarity and forcefulness?

As before, it is quite evident that full acknowledgement of our indebtedness to all who have influenced our thinking in the codification of the present text and its writing is quite impossible. Our colleagues, both in our own department and in other institutions, have been generous in their comments; they have given us valuable guidance in the rewriting. Material drawn from specific sources has been recognized in footnotes on the appropriate pages; for all such material we are profoundly indebted. However, we particularly wish to thank Lorraine Boss Allen for the illustrations that will be found in this book.

Perhaps we might emulate the example of the ancient Athenians who, the Apostle found, had erected a statue to "the unknown God," to insure that no deity had been omitted in their eagerness to propitiate them all. We offer, in a similar pattern, an informal dedication to "the unknown contributors" who, both through the current years and through many past years, have contributed much, much more to our thinking in general and to this text in particular than either they or we know.

Giles Wilkeson Gray
Waldo W. Braden

July, 1962

PART I

MAKING
A
START

1

Why Study
Public Speaking?

You are now beginning the study of a branch of learning, both theoretical and applied, known as *public speaking*. There are a number of reasons why each of you has made this start. Some of you undoubtedly are genuinely interested in developing your abilities in vocal utterance and discovering the reasons for some of the things you will learn to do. Others of you may have acquired the idea somewhere that a number of "tricks of the trade" are all you will need to know in order to become an effective speaker, and that a course in the subject is just the place to find out what they are.

Still others of you are looking forward to entering a vocation, such as the legal profession, politics, the ministry, or possibly the diplomatic service, in which the need for public speaking ability is more or less obvious. And who can deny that the football coach, especially the successful one, is in constant demand as a speaker?

Most educators today are convinced that there is a definite place in the academic program for speech in its various aspects, and that such courses as public speaking fill a definite need in the educational process. In most colleges and universities, and in an increasing number of secondary schools, speech in one or more forms is now taught, with public speaking high on the list of courses offered. Even in the elementary schools, programs in speech improvement and speech therapy are being organized all over the country.

But student enrollments are constantly changing; a new "generation" of students enters college, especially at the undergraduate level, every time a class graduates. You are all familiar with the Biblical story of Joseph, who, sold into Egypt as a slave, became the most powerful man in the country, second only to the king himself. But in the course of time, the Pharaoh died. ". . . And Joseph died, and . . . there arose up a new King over Egypt, which knew not Joseph." (Exod. 1:6, 8). The rest of the story, concerned with what happened to the descendants of Israel under the new rulers, is well known. But for us moderns it illustrates the fact that very often things that were well known to a past generation have been forgotten, and that later generations have to be reminded of them all over again.

So it is with the study of public speaking. Entering schools and colleges every year are a large number of students who do not know that this subject, anciently known as rhetoric, was for many years at the very heart of the educational program. Unless it has been emphasized in the lower school levels, these students have not had impressed upon them the importance of speech training in general or the study of public speaking in particular. It becomes necessary for them to learn what students before them, over many generations, have learned: that there are indeed as many values, both tangible and intangible, consequent upon acquiring an understanding of and proficiency in that particular mode of communication called public speaking as there are in learning the various other methods of social adaptation, integration, and cooperation.

WHAT CONSTITUTES PUBLIC SPEAKING?

As we all know, there are many situations in which people communicate orally. We engage in everyday informal *conversation*, and occasionally in conversations of a more formal order; within groups of people problems arise, generating *discussions*, which may take a number of different forms. Frequently we have occasion to *read*, from either a manuscript or a printed page, material often of a literary nature that others have written previously or we have written ourselves.

Many of us enjoy participation in dramatic activities, where we are *actors* for a short time. Then, too, if we are active members of a club or society of one kind or another, we may engage in the *debates* that arise whenever an action is proposed on which there are divergent opinions. And finally, there are occasions when we find it necessary or highly important to stand before or within a group and say the things we feel should be said. It is this last type of activity that we think of as *public speaking*.

This course and this text are primarily concerned with this type of oral discourse. No suggestion is offered that public speaking is in any way superior to any of the other forms of communication; all have their function in a communicating world. During your lifetime you may at one time or another participate in every one of them; you will want to do all of them well. But in this course we are interested in that specific type of speaking activity in which one person—you—will have some demanding occasion to stand before a group, small or large, and say those things which you feel cannot be left unsaid or which you cannot leave to others.

The Speaking Situation

You will find yourself in a situation consisting of four elementary factors. First, there will be an *occasion* which makes the speaking necessary or important. Second, there will be an *audience*, consisting of the listeners, the people you want to think, feel, or act the ways you want them to. Third, you will have a *subject*, a *speech*, in which you will be talking about something. And finally, there will be yourself, the *speaker*, whose specific task on that particular *occasion* is to discuss your chosen or assigned *subject* with that specific *audience*.

These elementary factors and their interrelations constitute the province of the subject which we are to study in the course you are now beginning. All of these elements, together with other aspects of public speaking growing out of them, will be developed at length in later chapters.

REASONS FOR STUDYING PUBLIC SPEAKING

As has been said, the public speaking situation is only one of many situations in which we speak. It is nevertheless a very important one. There are a number of reasons why it should be studied, which we shall briefly discuss.

Public Speaking Is an Asset

You will all enter into the life of your community, state, or country in greater or lesser degrees of activity. Our whole society is based on the principles of freedom to exchange ideas, opinions, and experiences; freedom of utterance is one of our most jealously guarded rights. But it is more than a right; it is a responsibility. The effectiveness of a democratic society is determined by the effectiveness with which its individual members participate in all its activities. The greatest threat to its institutions comes not so much from definitely subversive elements as from indifferent or ineffective participation, or total lack of participation, on the part of the members themselves.

The courses of action taken by a democratic society such as our own tries to be are the outgrowth of the free exchange of information, attitudes, opinions, and wisdom, much of which takes place in public speaking situations. The tendency at times to sit back silently and let those opposing our views or those who are more aggressive present all the argument, whether valid or invalid, even to doing all the rousing of emotional attitudes, makes us at those times completely useless as members of such a society.

Admiral Rickover, the noted scientist and engineer who has made a significant contribution to his profession and to the national welfare, recently argued that " 'verbal' men are on the way out," and that "The man of the future on whom we shall depend is the technical expert."[1] If this scientist has in mind the merely loquacious, whose only stock in trade is a copious flow of language and a loose tongue, many of us would encourage him to speed the day. No one will dispute the pressing need for more and more technical experts. But there are now, and will be during the lifetime of your grandchildren, men and women who can enlighten the uninitiated, convince the skeptical, persuade the reluctant, and arouse to still greater fervor those who already believe.

A large number of people have something significant to say and are interested in improving their ability to say it. As their ability to express their ideas increases, so also will their capacity to have ideas and their willingness to urge them upon their listeners.

The simple truth is that there is just as much need for speaking in public today as there ever was and perhaps even more, partly because there are more conflicting ideologies to be analyzed, discussed, and acted upon. When the human race ceases to speak in either public or private, it will no longer be human; it will consist of an aggregate of robots.

Mass Media Use Much Public Speaking

The increasing use of mass media gives greater opportunities for speaking to large numbers than our forebears had, though some authorities believe that such inventions have "weakened the habit of more direct and intimate forms of interpersonal communication."[2] Whatever their shortcomings and limitations, these media will stay with us for a long time. Many of our problems will center about the question of using them most effectively for the common good. This is an age of confusion, of attacks upon our basic beliefs, our political, economic, social, and religious philosophies and heritages. Ideas and ideologies are being urged vigorously—not all from beyond our own borders—and just as strongly opposed. In the struggle for the minds of men and women, even of children, mass media play an important role. There is need for men and women who have capacities for ideas and the ability and the compulsion to advance, through all the techniques and materials of communication available, those ideas that are concerned with the betterment of mankind.

[1] H. C. Rickover, *Education and Freedom*, Dutton, 1959, p. 19.
[2] Joseph Bram, *Language and Society*, Doubleday, 1955, p. 19.

There is no reason to anticipate that the world will see within our lifetime, if indeed it ever sees, developments—one cannot necessarily call them advancements—that will render needless or impotent the man of words.

Public Speaking Must Be Learned

Freedom of speech has been called a right or privilege. Your privilege or right to use this freedom, however, is of little practical value to you or to anyone else unless you possess also the *ability* to exercise it. Your own effectiveness as a citizen is essentially a matter of direct, individual participation, usually in a face-to-face situation, in the affairs of your community, large or small. That participation, in turn, is largely dependent on two things: having ideas that will contribute to the objectives of your group, and having the ability to present those ideas clearly, forcibly, and convincingly. As Thomas Mann says in his *Joseph in Egypt,* "Who knows how to set his words well and hath a gift of expression, upon him gods and men nod with applause, and he findeth inclined ears."[3] Two hundred years ago James Burgh, writing on *The Art of Speaking,* raised the pointed query, "And what avails a weapon without skill to wield it?"[4]

Perhaps the simplest answer to the question of why the study of public speaking, or any other speaking activity, is necessary if one wants to be proficient is that there is no other way by which we can develop our ability to the maximum. If we are going to acquire an effective skill in any of the arts of speech, we have to study the principles pertaining to that art, and then consciously apply them until they become habitual.

There is no speech instinct. There is no instinct for speech, any more than there is for playing golf or riding a horse or flying an airplane. On the contrary, speech, like these other activities, is a learned skill. There is some question whether even the singing of birds is entirely instinctive or "innate," since it is said that young birds reared by members of species different from but related to their own will often acquire the song of their foster parents: "A specialist from Cornell has recently reported that a young bluebird will never be able

[3] Thomas Mann, *Joseph in Egypt,* Knopf, 1938, Vol. I, p. 148.
[4] 1st ed., 1761, p. 39.

to sing the typical melody of its species unless it hears other blue-birds in full song before it is a year old."[5] And Wesley E. Lanyon, of the American Museum of Natural History, New York, points out that although "Most birds, except those that normally mimic others, show a preferential receptivity to the sounds of their own species," at the same time "We know that certain song birds that have been reared from the egg in sound proof rooms are capable of developing original song motifs, but these are only suggestive of the song of their respective species. . . . This important role of learning in the normal development leads to distinct geographical dialects of bird song."[6]

The child acquires in two or three years what it took the race countless millennia to learn. Whereas primitive man, in learning his language from the beginning, had nothing to go on but elemental cries and vocalizations expressive of his feelings and emotions, the child comes into an environment in which the patterns of the language have already been established. He learns to speak mainly by imitating those patterns as used by the people around him. At first the parents provide the models for imitation; later the child's playmates and teachers become his models. How the child learns to speak depends primarily on those it must imitate in its early formative years. Regardless of the language of its ancestors, it will learn the language and the mode of utterance in which it has been reared.

Native aptitudes alone are insufficient. Many people seem to have a "knack" for one type of speech activity or another. But such a native aptitude is unlikely to give a secure foundation upon which to build a solid structure of understanding and proficiency if it is the sole foundation. Some years ago our dramatic director was casting for a major production. For the leading role the choice narrowed down to two. When the final selection was made the director was asked why he had selected that particular girl, who did not have the dramatic background of the other one. "Peggy read her lines in the tryouts better than Betty," he replied. "But Peggy is as good now as she will ever be; Betty will grow into the role, and by the time of the production will be much the better of the two."

[5] "Science Marches On," *New York Times Magazine*, March 12, 1961, p. 49.
[6] "The Ontogeny of Vocalizations in Birds," in W. E. Lanyon and W. N. Tavolga, eds., *Animal Sounds and Communication*, Pub. No. 7, American Institute of Biological Sciences, 1960, Washington, D.C.

Maximum improvement in speaking, then, demands study and practice; it is not derived from any instinct to speak, even though there may be native impulses to vocalize, to utter sounds for one primitive purpose or another. But uncultured vocalizations are not even speech, much less speech at its best.

Having Ideas Comes Largely from Being Able To Express Them

For still another reason study and practice are essential. There is an old story of the man who would not write or speak until he had developed his ideas fully, all ready to be broadcast to the world. When he finally felt that he was ready, he learned to his dismay that he had lost even the capacity to have ideas. Study and practice in the expression of ideas, then, whether in writing or in speaking, is the best possible means of developing the capacity to have ideas to express.

"Orator fit, non nascitur."   The Romans had the saying, with respect to the training of a speaker, *"Orator fit, non nascitur,"* meaning, "The orator is made, not born." It is not expected that everyone will become a Demosthenes, a Cicero, a Roosevelt, or a Churchill. There are natural aptitudes in speaking, as in every other activity that must be learned. Only a relatively few athletes each season become superlatively proficient in golf, in baseball, and in football, in track. For more than three decades batters have been trying to break Babe Ruth's home run record, and the record for the 100-yard dash held for some decades. Not everyone, regardless of the time and effort expended, can become an Isaac Stern, an Eleanor Farrell, a Toscanini, or a Leonard Bernstein. Individual differences, plus a prodigious amount of work, account for the Websters, the Einsteins, the Wieners, the Whiteheads, and the Hemingways.

However, though few if any in a given speech class will reach the heights of oratorical eminence, all of you can, by judicious study and practice, learn to speak more effectively than you can now. Few of you are likely to find yourselves in situations calling for the type of exalted speaking that commonly goes by the name of oratory; yet none of you will escape entirely the opportunity, even the responsibility, of saying simply, clearly, and with some forcefulness the things that will need to be said if you are to participate actively in the affairs of the various groups in which you are to live.

It is toward this type of speaking that the present course is directed. Later, if you want to pursue your study and practice further, you may go as far as your ambitions, your individual ability, and your persistence can take you. You will not become an orator or even a good speaker overnight. But for the present remember that any one of you who is willing to spend a reasonable amount of time and effort on the necessary work will make a significant improvement in his ability to speak before a group of listeners.

Practice does not always make perfect.   Some of the specific directions that that improvement is to take will appear in the succeeding chapters. The old saying that "practice makes perfect" is not altogether true; it may even be entirely misleading. Practice only fixes habits, good or otherwise, making them that much harder to change whenever change is necessary to develop more efficient modes of activity. But *intelligent* practice, based on an understanding of what you are trying to do and why you are doing it and on conscious (and conscientious) effort to apply the principles of good speaking, will certainly bring about an improvement. How much is a matter for you alone to decide.

Training in Speaking Is Also Training in Evaluation

We are bombarded almost constantly with public speech, either directly or by way of the media of mass communication, such as radio and television. It is a daily, at times almost an hourly occurrence, difficult often to escape. It seems on occasion as ubiquitous as the radio and television commercial, and often, even, as annoying.

It is not always easy to sift out what is worth listening to, to differentiate between truth and half-truth, to exercise rational judgments regarding what constitutes sound reasoning, objective reporting, and valid interpretations of events and what are rather appeals to emotion, prejudice, and personal and group biases. We need to be able to detect pernicious propaganda (not all propaganda is pernicious), and excessive use of clichés, slogans, and stereotypes intended to throw a smoke screen over meaningless or misleading utterance.

In reading advertisements or listening to radio or television commercials, avoid glowing descriptions of various products which do not describe at all, because the terms used in the "descriptions" bear no relation to anything you have ever experienced. Terms are used which sound impressive but actually mean nothing simply because they are meaningless; they are intended to arouse attitudes instead of giving factual information about the products being advertised.

The speeches you listen to as well as the speeches you make should be so developed that they will meet a similar challenge. The story is told that after one of the Lincoln-Douglas debates back in the middle of the last century, a group of rustics were discussing the two speakers. Finally one of the men summed up his impressions: "Y'know, that tall skinny guy up there made sense."

Training in Public Speaking Is Training in Democratic Living

The essence of a democratic order lies in the free and open participation of its members in the affairs of the society: ". . . the effectiveness of the group process is a function of participation by all the members of the society."[7] In the exchange of information, opinion, attitudes, and the accompanying arguments, both the group as a whole and the individual members stand to profit. To the extent that such participation does not exist, whether through lethargy among the members or because of pressures to prevent such free interchange among them, to that extent the society falls short of being a genuinely democratic society.

Training and experience in public speaking will enable the student to choose his speech subjects in relation to himself, his listeners, and the occasion; it will teach him to select materials for his speeches that will be interesting, informative, appropriate, and convincing, as the occasion may demand. It will show him how to organize those materials so that they will be logically arranged and easily followed, understood, and retained; it will give him instruction in choosing language that will contribute to understanding, stimulate appropriate imagery, and arouse or intensify desired attitudes. Finally, it will

[7] Alex Bavelas, "Communication Patterns in Task-Oriented Groups," *Journal of the Acoustical Society of America*, 1950, **22**: 725–730.

reveal to him the importance of an effective presentation—the suitable use of voice and visible body action that will reinforce and make specific the language and the ideas which that language seeks to present.

All these are important in the training for the most effective and ethical participation in a democratic society. So vital is such participation that without it such a society itself cannot exist.

ADVANTAGES OF CLASSROOM STUDY

Self-instruction is often helpful in improving oneself in various ways. But for many things, speech among them, it is more economical and efficient to study in the classroom situation. This is the only method in which you have the advantage of *directed* study, careful analysis and evaluation of your efforts, and authoritative guidance in your improvement. Furthermore, you have the sympathetic hearing of other students whose problems are parallel to your own. Your fellow students will also give helpful suggestions to you and to each other on what may be done in the program of general improvement in public speaking. You have the opportunity to listen to these same fellow students and to learn from what they do or do not do what makes them effective or ineffective speakers. Finally, the discussions of the principles involved, in which all members of the class may participate, are usually of great help in clarifying points of theory that might otherwise be hazy and uncertain.

"Random" habits, those developed or acquired with no conscious attention to the details of technique, are rarely as effective as those which are the result of careful, directed study. In learning speech it is unsafe, as has been indicated, to depend wholly on your own native ability, just as it is in any activity based on understanding and skill. You may be a fairly fast runner, but if you want to break records, you have to train; there is such a thing, even in running, as form. The individual who "never had a lesson" may be a nuisance when he sits down at the piano.

Both effective speech and *good* speech—ethical speech—are based on a solid body of theory that has been developing over a period of two-and-a-half thousand years. As such it is not to be picked up in "ten easy lessons," or by no lessons at all, or even by the "shot-in-the-arm" type of confidence building so prevalent today. It takes more than mere confidence, which itself is most potent when it has the background of understanding and careful, persistent, intelligently directed training.

QUESTIONS AND TOPICS FOR STUDY AND REVIEW

1. List some points of view opposing the study of speech or public speaking that you have heard, or that you have expressed yourself.
2. What led you into a course in public speaking?
3. What values do you hope or expect to derive from such a course?
4. Show by diagram and by explanation the relationships among the four basic factors in the speaking situation.
5. In what ways will ability in public speaking be an asset in the vocation you expect to enter?
6. What might be some justification for suggesting that there is no further use or need for the "verbal man" or the "man of words"?
7. Comment on the statement, "There is no speech instinct."
8. Develop the point that "The capacity to have ideas is largely a function of the ability to express them."
9. What evidence exists of any relation between the size of one's vocabulary and vocational success?
10. Identify the people named on page 10.
11. Cite an example from your own experience, in speaking or in some other activity, in which you learned "the hard way" that practice does not make perfect.
12. In what way or ways is training in speech also training in evaluation?
13. What has been the significance, in the development of our democratic society, of Article I in the Bill of Rights?

PROJECTS

1. *Opening Speech of Introduction.* In a two- to four-minute speech introduce yourself to the class. Give your name, your home town, your college or curriculum, your major field of interest, and some interesting biographical facts that will aid your classmates in knowing you.
2. Give a talk in which you tell about your previous speech experiences: talks you have given, either directly to audiences or over the air, meetings or clubs over which you have presided, dramatic performances in which you have acted, different speaking contests in which you have participated, groups in which you have served as counselor or instructor, courses you have taken. What texts have you studied, and who were your instructors?

3. Tell about the probable opportunities for speaking you will have in your chosen vocation. What speaking do you anticipate in your civic and community activities?
4. Tell why you agree or disagree with Admiral Rickover's statement that " 'verbal' men are on the way out," and that "The man of the future on whom we shall depend is the technical expert." To what extent, if at all, can the technical man dispense with the need for speaking? Are the two incompatible?
5. Tell in a short talk of three or four minutes how you can know whether you have succeeded in establishing a favorable attitude on the part of your listeners.

SUPPLEMENTARY READINGS

Baird, A. Craig, and Franklin H. Knower, *General Speech: An Introduction,* 2nd ed., McGraw-Hill, 1957, chap. 1, "Essentials of Effective Speech."

Braden, Waldo W., and Mary Louise Gehring, *Speech Practices: A Resource Book for the Student of Public Speaking,* Harper, 1958, chap. 1, "The Study of Speeches and Speakers."

Brigance, William Norwood, *Speech: Its Techniques and Disciplines in a Free Society,* Appleton-Century-Crofts, 2nd ed., 1961, chap. 24, "Dynamic Persuasion in an Industrial Democracy."

Bryant, Donald C., "Rhetoric: Its Function and Its Scope," *Quarterly Journal of Speech,* December, 1953, 39: 401–424.

Bryant, Donald C., and Karl R. Wallace, *Fundamentals of Public Speaking,* 3rd ed., Appleton-Century-Crofts, 1960, chap. 1, "The Study of Public Speaking," pp. 3–15; chap. 2, "Definition and Scope of Public Speaking."

Clark, Robert D., "These Truths We Hold Self-Evident," *Quarterly Journal of Speech,* December, 1948, 34: 445–450.

Hudson, Hoyt H., "The Field of Rhetoric," *Quarterly Journal of Speech,* April, 1923, 9: 167–180.

Lillywhite, Harold, "A Re-Evaluation of Speech Objectives," *Quarterly Journal of Speech,* December, 1947, 33: 505–508.

Quintilian, *Institutes of Oratory,* bk. II, chap. 15–22.

Sarrett, Lew, William Trufant Foster, and Alma Johnson Sarett, *Basic Principles of Speech,* 3rd ed., Houghton Mifflin, 1958, chap. 1, "You and Your Three Worlds"; chap. 2, "Seven Basic Principles."

Scanlan, Ross, "Freedom, Knowledge, and Public Speaking," *Quarterly Journal of Speech,* October, 1949, 35: 310–315.

Thonssen, Lester, and A. Craig Baird, *Speech Criticism,* Ronald, 1948, chap. 18, "Toward a Philosophy of Rhetoric."

Wallace, Karl R., "The Field of Speech, 1953: An Overview," *Quarterly Journal of Speech,* April, 1954, **40**: 117–129.

Winans, James A., *Speech-Making,* Appleton-Century-Crofts, 1938, chap. 1, "Introduction."

NOTE: Most of the references cited in this as well as in all the other chapters of this text offer a number of further resources for supplementary readings. We would like to recommend that some of these resources be explored for additional understanding of the principles involved in the several chapters in order that the student furnish himself with the broad knowledge which we believe is one of the minimum essentials to good speaking.

2

Planning Your First Speeches

In planning assignments for your class in public speaking, your teacher faces a dilemma: which should come first—principles or practice? If you are required to give talks before you have had an opportunity to study the text, you may develop undesirable habits and waste much time and effort in searching for methods. On the other hand, if you wait to present your first talk until after you have thoroughly studied the text, you will undoubtedly be denied many opportunities to practice and to perfect your skills. But like many a dilemma, this one is not really a dilemma, for it permits more than two possibilities. There is a third alternative: during our early preview of certain of the basic principles of public speaking we shall be able to mingle principles and practice and have you talking to the group from the beginning of the course. The objective of this chapter is to give you some of the first principles needed.

When you later study the various principles in more detail, you will become increasingly aware of their complexities, and you will consequently be in a better position to refine your techniques. For the present these refinements can be delayed. In keeping with the foregoing explanation, the assignments throughout this course are planned with two purposes in mind: first, to provide for you as many and as varied speaking assignments as possible, and second, to stress one principle at a time until you have built up a substantial body of information about speaking in public.

YOUR APPROACH TO EARLY SPEECHES

Some of you will notice little difference between your opening assignments and numerous other speaking activities in which you have engaged for many years—at Scout meetings, at Sunday School, before your clubs, and of course in your numerous school activities. As a result, you may look upon these assignments as experiences similar to those of the past, and probably will not waste your energy worrying about yourself or your progress. But although these assignments are very similar to your previous experiences in speaking, do not make the mistake of thinking they can be carried out successfully without preparation. You will learn quite as much about public speaking from the planning as you will from the presentation.

Others of you may react quite differently. Some of you will magnify some aspect of your past experience in speaking, or of the present situation, beyond its proper importance and as a result may indulge in unnecessary anxiety and needless worry. Alarm may arise because of your inexperience, fear of your classmates, a feeling of inadequacy, an awareness that you are to be graded, a dislike of personal criticism, a belief that the speech class will approximate some past unhappy experience, or a failure to understand the nature of what is called stage fright.

You certainly are not alone in such attitudes. Many of these negative reactions are typical responses to a new speaking situation and, if not allowed to persist, are not serious. Many of them should disappear after a few speeches to the class. However, you must work consciously to eliminate these negative or fear reactions and attempt to substitute positive or favorable ones in their stead.

Study carefully the two lists of student reactions given below. Notice that those on the left resist and make improvement difficult, while those in the other column look toward the effective use of oral communication. If you react negatively to speechmaking, begin at once to substitute attitudes similar to those on the right, below.

Negative Reactions	Positive Reactions
1. "I know that I shall make a fool of myself when I get up to speak."	1. "I am eager to learn to speak effectively in public."
2. "Public speaking will be of no value to me in my future profession."	2. "Public speaking will be an asset to me in the future."
3. "I have nothing interesting or worthwhile to talk about."	3. "Each time I speak I shall attempt to improve."
4. "My personality (or my voice) is a great handicap to me."	4. "I hope that my teacher will give constructive criticism in order that I may improve my performance."
5. "I am not capable of delivering a speech in public."	5. "I am going to observe carefully the performances of my classmates in order that I may avoid their mistakes."
6. "I am unfortunate because my classmates are all superior to me."	6. "I like to talk to my classmates."
7. "I know that I am going to flunk this course."	7. "I shall strive to get as much out of this class as possible."

Sound advice to the beginning speaker is, stop feeling sorry for yourself. Think about your subject; develop an eagerness to talk about it to other people.

SELECTING A SUBJECT

First, select a subject that will enable you to draw heavily on your private stock of unique experiences and personal convictions.

As a starting point, ask yourself this question, "What do I know most about?" Perhaps you have a specialty, a hobby, a preference, or an unusual background. Is there any one of these upon which you can speak with authority? Consider the activities with which you have spent the most time or about which you have an unusual opportunity to get first-hand information.

Speakers are as a rule most fluent, most dynamic, and most persuasive about those subjects with which they are thoroughly familiar and in which they believe intensely. Even the untrained speaker, when forced to defend what he regards as sacred or important, often forgets himself and becomes vigorous and forceful, with the result that what he says is effective, impressive, compelling, and even eloquent. You will probably do better with subjects you are eager to share with your listeners.

Second, select a subject in which your listeners are interested or in which you can interest them.

Your class presents you with a realistic speaking challenge; your classmates constitute an audience to be interested, informed, challenged, and moved. Already you have had some opportunity to get acquainted with them as they introduced themselves. Through their opening speeches they have given you much valuable information about their training, insights, occupations, interests, and wants. You may be sure that those pursuits and activities which make their lives easier, promise them security, increase their incomes, or promote the welfare of their loved ones are usually the most important and interesting to them. Furthermore, they dislike the commonplace and the routine; consequently, if you are wise, you will attempt to use a fresh approach without seeming to be peculiar.

Third, select a topic that is specific in nature, limited in scope, and well within the listeners' experiences.

Avoid the philosophical, the subjective, and the theoretical. For your first talks discuss familiar objects that can be seen or activities that can be personally performed by the listener. The two lists given below illustrate the difference between concrete and abstract subjects:

Abstract Subjects	Specific Subjects
The struggle for freedom	How to operate a voting machine
The meaning of democracy	How to bind a book

The hope for peace
The value of patriotism
My philosophy of life
The improvement of personality
The importance of agriculture
Engineering as a profession

Planning a pep rally
How to use a hammer
The two-cycle gasoline motor
Building a birdhouse
Life in a beehive
The refining of sugar

PLANNING THE SPEECH

Frame a Central Thought or Proposition

As a starting point in the preparation of the informative talk, you will want first to frame, in a single sentence, a central thought around which to build your talk. The only requirement is that you make clear to the listener your particular approach to the subject. The sentence may take any one of the following forms:

1. It may be stated as a question to be answered by the speech.
2. It may consist of a brief definition of the subject.
3. It may evaluate the subject.
4. It may state your intentions in giving the speech.
5. It may partition the subject.

When the central thought is in question form you pose a question and then answer it in your development. You may ask how, when, why, what, or where. Or you may develop your talk around a question like the following: What are the qualities of an effective speech? How can one improve his personality? How can the scientist keep the public informed about the latest developments?

When the central thought constitutes a brief definition of the subject, it answers the question, "What is it?" The speech is devoted to expansion of the definition by the use of facts, illustrations, diagrams, comparisons, or whatever is necessary to make the listeners understand. Frequently the speech describing a process, a procedure, or an operation employs this type of central thought. Below are some examples of this type:

Speech is an overlaid function.
Rhetorical criticism involves a process, a method, and a declaration of judgment.

Poi is a simple Hawaiian food.
The life of a football player is not "the life of Riley."

The central thought may also evaluate the subject, answering the question, "What is its value?" This type of central thought is used in the presentation of oral criticism. For example, you may build a talk around the following sentence: Macbeth is a true tragedy. The development of your speech will show in one-two-three order why you hold this opinion concerning the play. Listen to your instructor give an evaluation of the performance of your colleagues. In each instance he may build his presentation around a central thought, such as, "Your indirectness is a serious handicap to your effectiveness" or "Your organization was confused."

Other examples of the central thought which evaluates are the following:

Carelessness causes many forest fires.
Group insurance operates on sound business principles.
Adequate nutrition is essential to happy living.
The Frasch process of extracting sulfur is a simple one.

Again, sometimes the central thought may simply reveal the plan or parts of the speech. In other words, you may say that there are two, three, or four steps in the procedure or process. You actually tell the listeners what to expect. In your speech class you will hear speeches developed around central thoughts like these:

Three major speech dialects exist in the United States.
The effective speech possesses nine essentials.
The refining of sugar is a four-step process.

The speech may also be built around a central thought that reveals what the speaker intends to do in the speech. In such a declaration you say, "I wish to describe the latest Paris fashions," or "Let me tell you events of my recent trip to Denver," or "I want to explain how sulfur is mined in Sicily."

Select and Arrange Main Points

A second step in preparing a speech is to determine how many supporting points to put into the development proper. In making this decision you should consider such aspects as the complexity of the subject, the time available, the type of listeners to be present, opportunities for note taking, and any handicaps inherent in the speaking situation.

You may decide to give a single-point speech with a single illustration, similar to the parables in the Bible. Or you may partition your subject into several main points. Whatever you decide, keep the organization as simple as possible. The inclusion of more than four or five points probably will complicate your presentation considerably. Many speakers favor no more than two or three points.

If you find that you have too many points, you can frequently combine similar ones, subordinate minor points, and delete others.

For your first speech, select three or four points that will expand the central thought into a speech. If possible, word these points also in simple declarative sentences. You should now have an outline like one of the following:

Central thought: Bees have a complicated social organization.
  I. The queen lays the eggs.
 II. The females are the workers.
III. The males are the drones.

Central thought: The mighty Mississippi is a real antagonist.
  I. Its floods are constant threats to life and property.
 II. Its channels are constantly shifting.
III. Its currents carry away millions of tons of rich soil.

Central thought: The muskrat lives an interesting life.
  I. He is an ardent homemaker.
 II. He is blessed with many children.
III. He is a ward of the state.

Use a Deductive Development

The overall organization of the development proper is largely determined by how and where in the speech the speaker presents the central thought or proposition. Should he include it near the opening of his speech, or should he wait until later for the presentation? The answers to these questions may suggest the basic organization of the speech.

For the informative speech, the location of the central thought is determined on the basis of how much the audience knows about the subject. Since there is little to be gained by concealing the central thought, the speaker is wise to give it early in his development. As a general rule, the real advantage in this procedure is that the listener knows what to look for in the development. As a result, understanding is facilitated. Following these suggestions, the speech is developed as follows:

Introduction

1. Gain attention and arouse interest.
2. State and clarify the central thought.

Development

3. Develop the central thought.
   a. Point I.
   b. Point II.
   c. Point III.

Conclusion

4. Restatement of central thought and summary of points.

Ordering the Points

Another phase of speech organization concerns the arrangement of the supporting points. Maximum effectiveness demands that your scheme of arrangement meet the following tests:

1. Does it hold attention and interest?
2. Does it fit the peculiar requirements of the subject?
3. Is it designed to facilitate understanding and retention?
4. Does it keep the speech marching toward your goal?

The point may be arranged according to anyone of several orders. Some of these are the following:

1. Chronological or time order
2. Operational order
3. Developmental or procedural order
4. Spatial or geographical order

DRAFTING A SPEECH OUTLINE

The third phase of speech organization is to make a complete outline of what you wish to say. It will help if you use complete sentences in your plan; try to word the points the way you intend to develop them in your presentation.

Use the following skeleton outlines as a guide.

Skeleton Outline

I. How I intend to get an attentive hearing.
II. How I intend to relate subject to interests and wants (motives) of listeners.

Central thought: _____

Point I: _____
  A. _____
  B. _____
Point II: _____
  A. _____
  B. _____
Point III: _____
  A. _____
  B. _____

Summary:
  I. _____
  II. _____
  III. _____

Model Outline

How To Use a Paint Brush

Introduction

I. The do-it-yourself fad has become a necessity in these days of high wages.
II. One of the first tasks you will probably encounter as a householder is redecorating.
III. Let me acquaint you with how to use a paint brush effectively.
CENTRAL THOUGHT: There are three steps to remember in using a paint brush.

Development

I. The first step is dipping the brush into the paint.
  A. Dip halfway the length of the bristle.
  B. Lightly slap off excess paint on side of container.
II. The second step is the proper approach.
  A. Grip only handle and metal ferrule.
  B. Apply paint only with end of bristles.

III. The third step is the application of the paint on the surface.
  A. Lay the paint on the surface with light, short, slightly curved strokes.
  B. Lift the brush gradually at the end of the stroke. This precaution saves leaving a thick edge of paint.

Conclusion

Remember these three simple steps:
  I. The dip—half way the length of bristle.
  II. The approach—with the tip.
  III. The application—a light, short, slightly curved stroke.

PUTTING THE SPEECH TOGETHER

Formula for Putting a Speech Together

The informative talk may be epitomized in the following four steps:

1. Gain attention and relate the subject to the wants (motives) of the listeners.
2. Preview what you intend to say by listing the main points.
3. Develop each point around the following pattern:
   a. State the point.
   b. Give the evidence.
   c. Restate the point.
4. Summarize: repeat the main points.

If the speaker includes a preview, signposts, and a summary, he actually has stated each point four times. First, he previews the points he intends to develop; second, he states each point as he takes it up; third, he restates each point when it is developed; and fourth, he repeats his points again in the summary.

Plan an Interest-Getting Introduction

Your opening sentences make a first impression for you and your speech and may determine the success of your entire effort. Therefore they must be carefully planned. Strive to accomplish three objectives in opening: (1) gain a hearing, (2) establish your right to speak, and (3) clarify the subject.

he attention of the audience may be attracted by one of the
wing methods:

> Arousing their curiosity.
> Making a startling statement.
> Relating an exciting incident.
> 4. Telling an amusing story.

Clarifying the topic means announcing the subject and explaining
any confusing terms. Occasionally you may wish to trace the development of the subject or to show that the subject itself is timely.

Speakers ordinarily find that a *preview* of the main points of the
speech helps in achieving unity and clarity.

A *preview* is an enumeration of all the points early in the speech.
In other words, the speaker says in effect to the listener, "Let me first
list my points so that you may know what to look for during my discussion."

If you feel that your effectiveness may be hampered somewhat by
feelings of nervousness, you can avoid inarticulateness in the opening
moments by writing out and memorizing the first few sentences.

Develop Each Point

The basic unit of the speech is the single point which sometimes
is referred to as an argument, a subdivision, or a cell. It should be
carefully organized and developed. Here is a simple formula for its
presentation:

1. State your point in a single sentence.
2. Give your supporting material.
3. Restate the point.

Let us translate this formula into other terms:

1. Tell them what you intend to say.
2. Tell them how, when, why, or where.
3. Tell them what to remember.

Use Signposts

The signpost or point indicator consists of labeling or numbering
the points in order that they may be recognized. In other words, you

may simply say, "My first point is. . . ." "My second point is. . . ."
"My third point is. . . ."

As the name implies, a signpost in a speech, like a road marker,
serves as a guide. It tells the listener where the speaker is and how
far he has gone. If the listener's attention strays during the first point,
at least you give him an opportunity to orient himself upon hearing
the announcement of the second point. In his speech "Which Knew
Not Joseph," Bruce Barton introduced his main points in the following manner: "So the first very simple thing I would say . . . is. . . .
Now the second very simple thing which I might say to you is. . . .
The third very simple thing and last that I suggest is this. . . ."[1]

Signposts need not be numerical in nature. The speaker may de-
vise other means of calling attention to his main points. Thomas
DeWitt Talmage devised a novel set in his lyceum lecture, "Big
Blunders."

Blunder the first:	Multiplicity of occupations . . .
Blunder the next:	Indulgence in bad temper . . .
Blunder the next:	Excessive amusement . . .
Blunder the next:	The formation of unwise domestic relations . . .
Blunder the next:	Attempting life without a spirit of enthusiasm and enterprise.[2]

In each of the foregoing cases, the speaker also has relied upon
another technique to make his main points obvious: he has worded
the key sentences in parallel form. Note how effective this repetition
is.

Gather Your Supporting Material

An outline is not a speech; it is only a beginning, a series of related
thoughts, a skeleton which probably will have little if any effect on
your listeners. If you intend to hold interest and accomplish your
goal, you must put meat on those bones, clothe them in an attractive
outfit, and generally glamorize the result.

One of the best ways to make a speech impelling is to pack into
it many examples and extended illustrations. Audiences like specific

---

[1] Bruce Barton, "Which Knew Not Joseph," in William Norwood Brigance,
ed., *Classified Speech Models*, Crofts, 1928, pp. 24–30.

[2] Thomas DeWitt Talmadge, "Big Blunders," in James Milton O'Neill, ed.,
Classified Models of Speech Composition, Century, 1921, pp. 828–844.

instances, and they like stories. Here you can learn a lesson from Abraham Lincoln. When an important premise was involved or when the atmosphere was tense, Lincoln in his simple but subtle way made his point by telling a story. In so doing, he was using a form of proof that ordinarily is effective for most speakers. You need not go far afield to find this type of supporting material, for your own experience should offer an unlimited supply. But if you are not satisfied with what you find at home, look to your daily reading, to the biographies of famous men, to history, and to literature.

If you feel the need of additional support, there are many other types as the following list will suggest:

1. Statistics
2. Competent statement from authority
3. Comparisons and contrasts
4. Explanation
5. Descriptions

In a later chapter each of these will be discussed at length.

QUESTIONS AND TOPICS FOR STUDY AND REVIEW

1. After studying the positive and negative reactions found on page 19, list the negative attitudes with which you have difficulty. You are quite likely to have some problems not noted there. What in your background contributed to these problems? Discuss your list with a fellow classmate. Does he have other negative attitudes? Prepare a set of positive attitudes to be substituted for the negative ones. At the end of the semester, check yourself to see how well you have done.
2. Make a list of twenty-five topics that seem to meet the requirements listed on pages 19–21. Revise these topics, making them suitable for presentation to your speech class.
3. Evaluate the following topics as possible subjects for five-minute speeches to your classmates:
   a. The development of the atomic bomb
   b. Trade with Communist China
   c. Building the Golden Gate bridge
   d. Planning a home talent show
   e. Learning a dance step
4. Write ten central thoughts for speeches to be delivered in your class.
5. What problems have you encountered in preparing your first speech? Be sure to ask your instructor for suggestions about problems not discussed in this chapter.

PROJECTS

1. *Speaking Assignment.* Explain the correct as opposed to the incorrect way of doing something such as (a) a golf stroke, (b) playing tennis, (c) washing dishes, (d) diving, (e) a dance step, (f) casting, (g) playing a musical instrument.
2. *Speech Analysis.* The speech given below can be delivered in less than a minute and a half, and yet it demonstrates many of the principles that have been discusssed in this chapter. What principles does it illustrate? What are its strong points? How could the speech be improved?

The Camel That Broke the Man's Back

Remember the old story about the merchant and the camel? It was a cold night, and the camel begged to warm his nose—only his nose—in the tent. Then what happened? Little by little, the camel inched in his shoulders, his front legs—until he took over the whole tent. And the merchant was out in the cold.

That's how government agencies are inching their way into the electric business. First, public funds were set aside to build dams—*for flood control and navigation.* Then it was argued that the water behind the dams could be used to make electricity.

That led to the building of power lines, and then to more dams, more lines, and so on. Now these same agencies want more millions of dollars to build fuel-burning power plants—*which have nothing to do with floods or navigation at all.*

Yes, the camel of State Socialism is creeping further and further into the tent of the electric business. What it is doing here it can do in other industries. For when a government can enter *one* business in unfair competition with its own citizens, it is but a short step to entering *all* businesses—and eventually taking over *all business.*

Like the camel and the tent. What business are *you* in? This can affect you, too. Write your Congressman about it.[3]

SUPPLEMENTARY READINGS

Braden, Waldo W., and Mary Louise Gehring, *Speech Practices: A Resource Book for the Student of Public Speaking,* Harper, 1958, chap. 2, "How Speakers Prepare Their Speeches"; chap. 3, "How Speakers Or-

---

[3] From a full-page advertisement of the Electric Light and Power Companies which appeared in *Time,* May 23, 1949, p. 103. Used by special permission of N. W. Ayer and Son, Inc.

ganize Their Speeches." These chapters give insight into how prominent speakers assemble their speech materials. Actual speakers' notes are reproduced on pp. 35–38. Also see model of informative speech on pp. 28–30.

Brigance, William Norwood, *Speech: Its Techniques and Disciplines in a Free Society,* 2nd ed., Appleton-Century-Crofts, 1961, chap. 3, "First Steps in Managing Ideas."

Bryant, Donald C., and Karl R. Wallace, *Fundamentals of Public Speaking,* 3rd ed., Appleton-Century-Crofts, 1960, chap. 4, "The First Speech."

Reid, Loren, *First Principles of Public Speaking,* Artcraft, 1960, chap. 6, "How To Make a Short Speech."

Weaver, Andrew Thomas, and Ordean Gerhard Ness, *An Introduction to Public Speaking,* Odyssey, 1961, chap. 3, "Preparing Speaking Assignments."

3

Delivering Your
First Speeches

PRACTICING YOUR SPEECH

Though it is often helpful to write out and memorize the opening sentences of a speech, do not attempt to commit the entire speech to memory. For the beginner especially, memorizing a speech has two hazards: first, during delivery the speaker is haunted by the fear of forgetting, and sometimes the failure to recall a single word may upset his whole presentation; second, he is likely to sound artificial and mechanical in his delivery, losing that spontaneity which accompanies the presentation of a thought for the first time. Often, if not usually, memorization results in concentration upon remembering rather than on the communication of ideas.

Oral Practice

In rehearsing your speech, use what is called the *extemporaneous* method. After you have prepared your outline and collected your supporting material, practice your speech by "talking" it out, that is, by discussing aloud the ideas you wish to present until you can crystallize your thinking and your language.

As a first step, memorize your central thought and your main points. It is desirable to keep the wording of these the same throughout the speech in order to aid the listeners in following your development. As we said before, you will probably repeat the main points three or four times during the speech: when you *preview* the points in your introduction, when you *present* each point individually, and when you *summarize* the speech. As the old-time preacher said in describing his method of building a sermon, "Fust I tells 'em what I'se gwine to tell 'em; then I tells 'em; and finally, I tells 'em what I'se done tole 'em!"

Do not be discouraged if your first oral attempts are hesitant and awkward. With continuing practice your fluency and confidence will increase; but you must work for them. Two or three short periods of rehearsal well spaced are superior to a single extended period.

Use of Notes

In your first speeches you may find that the use of a few notes will relieve you of anxiety about forgetting, keep you from rambling, and serve to remind you of the main points. Your notes should be brief enough to be placed on a small card (a three-by-five-inch index card should be large enough) which can be easily held, will not attract attention, and can be disposed of at any time. Above all, do not try to conceal your notes; you will succeed only in making them more conspicuous.

The following outline suggests what you might include in your notes:

Muskrats

Important to Louisiana
    I. One hundred thousand persons employed
    II. Eight to ten million trapped
    III. Ten-million-dollar income

The muskrat lives an interesting life
I. Homemaking
   A. Swamp or bayou
   B. Dome-shaped mound
II. Many children
   A. Four to twelve in litter
   B. Five litters a year
III. Ward of state
   A. Protected nine or ten months
   B. Trapping regulated
   C. Penalties for mistreatment

Summary

Mental Preparation

The word *worry* comes from the Anglo-Saxon *wyrgan,* meaning "to strangle"! Truly, worry about a speech can strangle a speaker and render him inarticulate. In the interim between the time of preparing your speech and delivering it, constant anxiety about your success, abnormal dissatisfaction with yourself, belittling of your ability, and the anticipation of dire consequences will serve only to increase your tenseness and your inarticulateness. These are the very things you want to avoid. Do not let worry be your master. Do not let yourself be strangled.

By mental discipline it is possible to avoid thinking about unpleasant aspects of the speaking situation. As suggested earlier, the easiest way to accomplish this is to substitute wholesome attitudes for the negative ones. Think about how to make your presentation more compelling; develop an eagerness to speak on your subject, an "urge to communicate."

DELIVERY OF THE SPEECH

Your Approach

When your turn comes to speak, walk to the front of the room with quiet dignity, and stop at about the center of the platform or stage. If you are speaking from a platform, keep away from the edge; if in a classroom, do not crowd the front row of chairs. In an effort to appear informal, students will occasionally half sit on the edge of the table, lean on the lectern or reading stand, or even put one foot on the rung or seat of a front-row chair. Learn to stand on your own two feet without support from the furniture. Informality can be overdone even in an informal situation. Take your position, and pause two or three seconds before speaking in order to give your listeners an opportunity to prepare themselves to listen. Do not start your speech while you are still walking.

Posture and Bodily Activity

As a general rule, and for the time being, if your physical activity does not call attention to itself, it is probably satisfactory.

The excellent speaker shows his alertness by his posture; he stands up straight but not stiff, with his feet not too far apart, his hands at his sides, his head erect. He does not hide behind or lean on a lectern or table.

If you are nervous and ill at ease, you may want to put a hand in your pocket or behind you. So long as such devices do not interfere with your ability to communicate, they are not to be condemned.

Face your listeners and make them feel that you are speaking to them, that you expect them to listen, and that you have something important and interesting to say. Borden suggests the following:

> Look at your listeners.
> Look at your listeners all the time.
> Look at all your listeners.
> Actually see your listeners.[1]

Voice

Longfellow once said, "The soul of man is audible, not visible." There can be no doubt that your auditors will base many of their impressions of you on how you sound. If you have a voice like the one William Jennings Bryan had, you will be able to thrill people by the richness of your tones. But few people are so gifted. No mat-

[1] Richard C. Borden, *Public Speaking as Listeners Like It,* Harper, 1935, pp. 93–96.

ter how good or how bad your vocal equipment may be, there are certain minimum essentials which probably are entirely within your capacity.

1. *You can be heard if you are willing to put forth sufficient effort.* You can also be understood if you will give careful attention to your articulation. At all times strive for distinctness and for audibility. There are very few inviolable rules in public speaking; two of them are quite simple: you *must* be heard, and you *must* be understood!

2. *You can be conversational in your tone and manner.* You need not preach or "orate," thereby making yourself ridiculous and giving the impression of insincerity. You must, of course, amplify your conversational style sufficiently to put over your meaning. But at the same time, strive to give the impression that you are sincerely conversing with each member of the audience.

3. *You can attempt to make your voice fit the occasion and the subject.* The humorous talk may demand gaiety and joviality, while the sales talk demands a businesslike approach. You need not drone along in a monotone.

4. *You can talk at a rate commensurate with distinctness and with your listeners' rate of easy comprehension.* If you speak too slowly, you put them to sleep; if you speak too rapidly, you wear them out with trying to keep up with you.

5. *You can avoid unpleasant and distracting "and-a," "uh," and other meaningless vocalizations.* Normally these are simple matters of habit which can be eliminated if you try.

The five requirements named here are minimum essentials. If you cannot meet these elementary standards, you probably need the special guidance of a speech clinic. On the other hand, if you can meet them at the beginning of your course of study, you can hope confidently to make steady improvement in the use of your voice.

Mannerisms

You will reveal your nervousness and other interfering attitudes by your individual mannerisms. Work to eliminate those which prevent your freest and easiest communication with your audience or which may even make you seem peculiar and ridiculous. Here are some common annoying habits:

1. Wringing hands
2. Folding and unfolding notes
3. Jingling money or keys
4. Buttoning and unbuttoning coat
5. Pulling ear or nose
6. Fumbling with pencil
7. Putting thumbs under belt
8. Standing with arms akimbo (hands on hips)
9. Scratching
10. Fussing with ring, watch, or beads
11. Fixing tie or pin
12. Clutching or straightening skirt
13. Cracking knuckles
14. Constantly looking at ceiling or out the window
15. Shifting eyes from place to place without letting them come to rest definitely
16. Looking constantly at the floor
17. Folding arms
18. Giving nervous or silly laugh
19. Standing with feet wide apart or too close together
20. Rocking backward and forward from heels to toes
21. Standing cross-legged
22. Pacing excessively
23. Shifting sideways from one foot to the other
24. Placing foot on chair or table
25. Leaning heavily on lectern or reading stand
26. Wetting lips too frequently
27. Repeatedly smoothing hair or replacing stray wisps

YOUR ATTITUDE TOWARD CRITICISM

One of the essential phases of a public speaking course is criticism. Admittedly you can learn much by studying speech principles and by striving to put them into practice, but your progress will be greatly facilitated if you have someone to evaluate your performance, to ascertain your weaknesses, and to suggest ways in which you can improve. Points in which you are already strong will also be noted, so that you will know where to put the emphasis in the matter of improvement.

Making such evaluations and giving criticism is one of the chief responsibilities of the speech instructor. At the mere thought of having a speech criticized many students assume that the criticism will be adverse and hence unpleasant. But criticism is not necessarily destructive. Good criticism is an evaluation in which the critic observes favorable as well as unfavorable characteristics of your performance. Its objectives are (1) to strengthen good points, (2) to correct weak points, and (3) to eliminate errors.

No matter how observing, how tactful, and how skillful your instructor may be in explaining how you can go about improving your speech, you will derive no benefit whatever if you turn a deaf ear to his comments, reject his evaluation, or refuse to follow his suggestions. To get the greatest value from the discussion of your presentations, follow these suggestions:

1. *It is important that you understand the criticism itself.* Criticism must be definite and intelligible so that you can understand it. Your instructor has the responsibility of making it clear, and if he does not, that is likely to be his fault. But you too have a duty. If you do not understand his comments, seek additional information; if you do not, that is *your* fault. If you feel embarrassed about asking questions in class, make an appointment for a personal conference.

2. *You need to develop, if you do not already have it, a wholesome attitude toward criticism.* Instead of fearing or dreading or even resenting what your teacher may say about your speaking, you should look forward eagerly to his suggestions. Insist that he tell you how you can improve.

3. *Avoid emotionalized self-defense and rationalization when a fault is pointed out.* Many students fail to improve because they are continually excusing themselves for their failures. They rationalize with such excuses as these:

1. I didn't have time to prepare.
2. The teacher picks on me.
3. The teacher (or the class) dislikes me.
4. I can't be expected to do as well as the others in the class.
5. If I really wanted to, I could improve.
6. I am much better than some of those the teacher compliments.
7. The teacher does not know a good speech when he hears one.
8. It isn't worth the effort anyway.

View yourself as objectively as possible; this means that you must see yourself as others see you. The instructor is really interested in your improvement; that is his purpose in being in the class. Remember that criticism is given you to make you more effective in your speaking.

4. *Avoid developing a feeling of hopelessness or futility.* Many students apparently believe that after attending classes for two or three weeks, they will have learned all there is to know about speaking; and when they discover that they are not yet fluent and polished in their performances, they give it up as hopeless. They do not appreciate the fact that the preparing, the practicing, and the presentation of speeches is not something they can learn immediately. When they discover, therefore, that learning to speak in public requires effort, they become discouraged. Each time the instructor offers another suggestion, they become even more disheartened and finally drop out altogether.

Development in public speaking is usually slow; years of study go into the making of a truly great orator. Your improvement in the present course will depend on several factors, among which are your native ability, your eagerness to improve, your willingness to work, and your receptivity to criticism. The individual who cannot make some improvement probably should not be in college at all.

QUESTIONS AND TOPICS FOR STUDY AND REVIEW

1. Report on the delivery of some speakers (politicians, ministers, professors, etc.) whom you have personally observed. Study carefully their unique qualities. In what do they conform and in what do they deviate from the suggestions made in this chapter?
2. By what standard should a critic judge the bodily action (posture, facial expression, gestures, and movement) of a speaker?
3. Should the beginning speaker attempt to imitate the voice and bodily action of his favorite speaker? What problems may he encounter?
4. What mannerisms did your fellow students exhibit in their first speeches? Did you have any mannerisms? If the teacher failed to comment on your bodily activity in your first speech, ask him for some frank criticism. If you are afraid to ask, what negative attitudes are dominating you?
5. What is meant by the word *criticism?* Is criticism the same as fault-finding? What definitions of criticism can you find in a dictionary?
6. What is good criticism? What elements would be considered in evalu-

ating a speech? How can you get the most out of the criticism of your speeches? Do you really want to have your speeches evaluated orally before the class? Why? Or why not?

7. What is rationalization? Do you rationalize about your speaking? Why?

8. What do you hope to accomplish in this course? What handicaps do you have? Does the course seem to be designed to help you? How much do you think you can achieve? Why? How do you think you compare in ability with your fellow students?

PROJECTS

1. *Speaking Assignment.* Give a talk of two to four minutes (from three hundred to six hundred words) on a subject with which you have had direct personal experience. You may wish to speak on a subject similar to one of the following:
   a. The author or poet of the year
   b. How to select a good movie
   c. How to spend your leisure time
   d. A "pet peeve"
   e. An embarrassing moment
   f. Finding and holding a job
   g. How to be the "life of the party"
   h. A vacation I shall never forget
   i. A business experience
   j. My experiences on the farm (in the shop, behind the counter, as a door-to-door salesman, etc.)

2. *Speaking Assignment.* Deliver a five-minute informative talk in which you develop three or four points. Follow this procedure: after a brief introduction, give a preview of your points; as you present each point, write it on the blackboard; in your conclusion, review the points developed by pointing to them as you repeat them orally.

3. *Written Assignment.* Prepare a written analysis of the most effective speaker you know. Prepare a list of his speaking qualities. What are his unusual characteristics?

4. *Speech Practices.* Carefully read Chapter 1 in *Speech Practices: A Resource Book for the Student of Public Speaking* by Waldo W. Braden and Mary Louise Gehring (Harper, 1958).[2] This chapter discusses the elements which a critic should consider in evaluating a

---

[2] Throughout this textbook we have included many projects based upon the resource book *Speech Practices*, which will hereafter be referred to by the shortened title in these exercises. The models found in the book are planned to help the beginning speaker think more objectively about speechmaking.

speech. Using these elements, evaluate in not more than 500 words a speech which you heard recently. Be as specific as possible.
5. Make three to five copies of the criticism form found on page 42. (Your teacher may mimeograph this form for you.) Using these forms, evaluate some of the speeches of your classmates. Ask some of your friends to evaluate your speech and give you their comments.

SUPPLEMENTARY READINGS

Brigance, William Norwood, *Speech: Its Techniques and Disciplines in a Free Society*, 2nd ed., Appleton-Century-Crofts, 1961, chap. 4, "First Steps in Managing Yourself."

Capp, Glenn R., *How To Communicate Orally*, Prentice-Hall, 1961, chap. 2, "How To Judge What Constitutes a Good Speech."

Crocker, Lionel, *Public Speaking for College Students*, 3rd ed., American Book, 1956, chap. 2, "Self Confidence and Directness."

White, Eugene, *Practical Speech Fundamentals*, Macmillan, 1960, chap. 2, "A Positive Approach to Speaking."

Speech-Criticism Blank
(For Beginners)

	Poor	Below average	Average	Excellent	Superior
1. Did the speaker choose an interesting subject?	1	2	3	4	5
2. Did the speaker supply the audience with any new information?					
3. Did the material presented seem to be from the speaker's own experience?					
4. Did the speaker look at his audience?					
5. Did the speaker talk to his audience?					
6. Did the speaker show his enthusiasm and interest in the subject?					
7. Did the speaker assume a pleasing posture?					
8. Did the speaker manifest a sufficient amount of physical activity?					
9. Did the speaker reflect a wholesome attitude toward the speaking situation?					
10. Did the speaker seem to notice and respond to the reactions of the audience?					

Additional remarks:

Grade........

PART II  THE SPEAKER

4

Minimum Essentials
for Good Speaking

If you want to learn to speak well in public, you will need to consider a few essentials, mainly concerned with attitudes involved in the study and practice of speaking. You will, of course, learn how to do some things that are necessary from a more or less technical point of view to make a good speech. But you will also need to examine some of the basic points of view toward speech and its functions which good speaking in a democratic society of today requires. In other words, you should give some thought to why public speaking is vital in a society such as ours, as well as to your own place in that society, once you have acquired something of an ability to influence the thinking, feelings, and actions of others.

GOOD SPEAKING REQUIRES AN EXTENSIVE STUDY OF PRINCIPLES

It was emphasized in a preceding chapter that speech is a learned activity, and that the development of a high order of proficiency requires a great deal of study. True, there have been "natural" speakers who could hold and sway audiences without knowing how they did it or without knowing anything about the principles of public speaking; but they have been extremely rare. Some of these who later learned something about these principles were probably like the industrial foreman who for some weeks attended an extension course in public speaking. After class one evening he stopped to speak to the instructor. "These techniques you have been giving us," he said, "I have been using for several years; but this is the first time I ever understood why."

In this chapter we shall discuss briefly some of the specific aspects of speech and the study of speech that need such close attention.

The "Four Phases of Speech" Make a Good Starting Point

Several years ago one of our leading theorists and teachers of speech analyzed the subject into four basic "phases," all closely interrelated and all integrated into the common phenomenon we know as speech. These four are, in order of importance, *thought, language, voice,* and *action.*

In value [he said] these four rank in the order shown. The best is to have meaning, next is to master words, third is to control voice, and last is to govern the outer manner. None is often perfect; manner can be deceitful, voice can tell what is not so, words can hide thought, while meaning can be devious and vile. Yet meaning is the inner reality.

As revealed to men, meaning can thus be withheld from the listener by three bars, and these bars are met in the reverse order from their value. A man speaking is first seen, then heard, then understood, then known for what he is. If he looks what he is not, a bar stands in the way of voice, words, and meaning; if, while looking what he is, he still is not what his voice speaks, a bar is yet seen in the way of language and meaning;

finally, if he looks and speaks aright he may yet use words at fault, and a bar will lie across the path to meaning. First men see, then hear, then understand.[1]

The study of speech, of public speaking, is directed at a mastery of all four of these phases. The only basis on which listeners can evaluate a speaker and his speech is what they hear and see him say and do. Contributory to that evaluation, further, is what they know from indirect sources concerning what he has been seen and heard doing under circumstances other than the particular speech they happen to be listening to at the moment.

Woolbert's statement, which in general provides the basis for much of the teaching of speech today, should then be broadened to include, besides the impressions of the speaker gained in the present situation, further knowledge of the consistency with which the four phases of speech have been utilized in his other speeches, as well as in his behavior in other kinds of situation in which public speech may not have been involved at all.

The point being made here, of course, is that a given speech is more than an event of the moment; it is the resultant of forces and influences that have molded the character and wisdom and personality of the speaker during his entire lifetime. The effect of the speech on the audience depends, of course, in great degree on the extent to which these influences have been made known to the listeners. Some of them, if known, may entirely negate the entire speech.

In your study of public speaking, therefore, you will need to work toward the development of those visible aspects of physical bearing, of general bodily activity, that will arouse favorable responses in your listeners. Part of the impression you create depends on your clothing and grooming. If your hearers have come to the meeting direct from their work, that does not mean that you have to "dress down" for the occasion and wear work clothes like theirs.

Try to develop those aspects of voice, including phrasing and inflection patterns, that will make language more meaningful than if you speak in a lifeless monotone. Within the language background of many of us are some pronunciations that are definitely substandard. Learn to use the *acceptable* pronunciations rather than holding

---

[1] Charles Henry Woolbert, *The Fundamentals of Speech*, Harper, 1920, pp. 3–10; 2nd ed., 1927, pp. 5–10; 3rd ed., with Joseph F. Smith, 1934, pp. 7–12.

to substandardisms. These acceptable forms will rarely attract attention or arouse unfavorable attitudes among your listeners; even the unlettered are coming more and more to accept forms of speech other than their own. But do not try to adopt forms characteristic of other dialectal areas; most people recognize that differences do exist, and are not likely to be greatly disturbed by those that you use. On the other hand, it is often distressing to hear people in fairly high positions use a manner of speech that can be best characterized as *ignorant*. A candidate in a recent election was heard to say over the radio that under existing conditions a certain outcome was "in-e-*vite*-a-ble" [m i 'vaɪt a bļ]. Apparently he had never before read the speech which someone had written for him. But it is doubtful if such locutions are geographically concentrated.

Much more will be said on this point in Chapter 28, "Vocal Aspects of Delivery."

Your articulation, it is hardly necessary to point out, should be sufficiently distinct that immediate intelligibility is possible. It is not enough that you make it possible for your listeners to understand you; you should make it impossible for them to misunderstand you. At the same time, avoid the exaggerated articulations that make speech sound pedantic or stilted.

Your vocabulary, which should be growing all your life as you broaden your study and meet new concepts which require new terminology, should express as wide a range of meanings as you might need for any speech you ever have occasion to give. It should enable you to express the finer shades of meaning that will give your speech precision and specificity. At the same time, it should be adaptable to the vocabulary of your audiences, at their highest level of understanding. Do not hesitate to explain your terms if there is any likelihood that you are using them in a sense different from the common usage of your audience. The problem of meanings themselves will be discussed briefly in the next section of this chapter, as well as more fully in a later chapter.

GOOD SPEAKING REQUIRES BROAD KNOWLEDGE

In the early days of the study of public speaking, in ancient Athens, the orator was expected to master the whole world of knowledge. Hippias, for example, one of the famous teachers of that time and a man of prodigious memory, boasted that he could give a speech on any subject at a moment's notice. With the present accumulation of the world's store of knowledge, however, such an achievement would obviously be impossible, and no such boast would be taken seriously. At the same time, it is essential in the development of your own maximum effectiveness in speech that you secure as broad an understanding as possible. The person who knows only one field, even though he may know that one thoroughly, is certain to be limited in his ability to speak to general audiences even on that one field, because he cannot relate it to anything else.

Your chosen field of specialization, whatever it may be, will not stand alone, you may rest assured. It will be closely related to and interdependent with many other subjects. To be thoroughly grounded in your own field of knowledge you should be able to orient it with these other subjects; you should be able to appreciate those interdependencies themselves.

Literary history, for example, is unintelligible without social history; physics cannot be understood without a knowledge of mathematics. Orthodontists, in addition to performing necessary oral operations, are increasingly interested in the effect of those operations on the formation of speech sounds, as well as the resulting outward appearance of the patient to himself and others. An engineer who builds a bridge across the Mississippi River should see that structure as both an engineering achievement and a means to further social communication and integration. The road builder may understand his technical job, but he can also appreciate the effect of highways on the breaking down of social and economic isolation.

Similarly, the speaker who addresses an audience of farmers may want to show how they can increase their crops; he should also have some understanding of what increased crops will mean to his listeners in terms of economic and social advantages.

Literary and Biblical allusions are often effective, but to use them you must know your literature, both secular and sacred, and the application to the point at issue of the particular passage you use.

Recounting the course of events leading up to some final conclusion may require a knowledge of history. Instances are recorded in which a lawyer's knowledge of chemistry or medicine was a vital factor in winning a case. Lincoln once "broke" a trial by showing that on the night in question an alleged identification by moonlight would have been impossible because on that night, and at the significant hour, the moon had not yet risen.

Preparation for Speaking Is of Two Sorts

There are in general two types of preparation for speaking. The first involves the acquisition of broad knowledge and experience we have been describing. The other type takes place when you prepare for a specific speech to a specific audience on a specific occasion.

You are always making general preparation. Everything you read, every new place you visit, every different thing you do may provide, sometimes unexpectedly, valuable material for your speeches. You are constantly making this sort of general preparation, because you are constantly acquiring new experiences, new information, and new ideas.

This is not the preparation that goes into any single speech; it is the kind of preparation you will be making all your life for speaking in general, for just living. When Webster was asked how long it had taken him to prepare his "Reply to Hayne," mentioned above, he answered, "I have been preparing for that speech all my life." Great speakers have always been great readers; they have always been eager to learn new things, to become acquainted with more people from whom they could get new ideas.

It is in the acquisition of broad understanding that you make your general preparation for speaking, which is not to be confused with planning *a speech*. The broader and deeper the foundation of that understanding, the more solid will be the preparation you will be able to make for your specific speeches. "Besides the art of words," said a sixteenth-century educator, ". . . [the student] must be stuffed with a store of matter."[2]

For still another reason a broad education is essential for the good speaker. Someone has recently said, "Ignorant eloquence is as subversive as heresy." We should not need to say that the speaker should be sincere in his utterance. But important as sincerity is, it alone is not enough; what is required is, as will be developed later in this

---

[2] Laurence Humphrey, *The Nobles; or, the Nobilitye: the Original Nature, Dutyes, Right and Christian Institution Thereof Thres Bookes . . .* , T. Marshe, 1565; quoted in Foster Watson, *The English Grammar Schools to 1660*, Cambridge University Press, 1908, p. 87.

chapter, *enlightened sincerity.* Twenty-four centuries ago the great philosopher Plato wrote, "A solid art of speaking without a grip on truth, there is not nor will be hereafter, ever." Only the broadly educated person is truly educated, for only he may come close to gaining that "grip on truth" of which Plato wrote. But Plato also said, "Mere knowledge of the truth will not give you the art of persuasion."[3] "A merely well informed man," says Whitehead, "is the most useless bore on God's earth."[4] And wisdom without eloquence, according to Cicero, is of no benefit to the State, whereas eloquence without wisdom is a great danger.[5]

Leonard Lyons recently recalled in his column "The Lyons Den" various episodes in the life of the late Ernest Hemingway: "There was the dinner at his home in Havana, where my eldest son asked Hemingway, 'How do you write a novel? Do you make it up?' 'Yes,' said Hemingway, 'you make it up, out of everything you've ever known, out of everything you've ever seen, out of everything you've ever felt. Then you write it down, simply, as if you're telling the story to yourself or a child.' "[6]

If you would achieve your maximum proficiency as a speaker, then, you must acquire as broad a background as possible. Probably you will never have occasion to use some of your material; but you should have a ready store of knowledge upon which to draw as the occasion and the nature and the knowledge of the audience may permit or necessitate.

Specific speeches require specific preparation. The other sort of preparation you will need for speaking takes place when you are getting ready for a specific speech to a specific audience on a specific occasion. It is then that you will make your special preparation, which will be different in its details from that made for any other speech you may have given or will give. These differences will not necessarily be major changes in material or organization; they may consist only of changes in your approach, depending on differences in audiences, as you will see later when we discuss audience adaptation.

[3] Both quotations from the *Phaedrus.*
[4] Quoted by George D. Stoddard in a panel discussion, "Are We Educating for the Needs of the Modern Man?" in A. Craig Baird, ed., *Representative American Speeches, 1948–1949,* H. W. Wilson, 1949, p. 188.
[5] *De Inventione.*
[6] Baton Rouge *Morning Advocate,* July 8, 1961

In your specific preparation you will assemble all the pertinent material available, selecting what will contribute most to the accomplishment of your purpose on that particular occasion and for that particular audience. You will organize your material and work out in some detail exactly what you plan to say. In this specific preparation you will draw on the experiences and knowledge you have been accumulating through your years of general preparation, taking an item from this field, another from a second, still another from a third, and so on, bearing always in mind the audience and the occasion, what will appeal to your hearers under the existing circumstances, what will maintain interest, and what will be most likely to motivate your listeners to accept what you have to say.

GOOD SPEAKING REQUIRES THE URGE TO COMMUNICATE

It may be said with some justification that in any speaking situation there are two basic factors: what is being said and the people to whom it is being said. The immediate purpose of the speaker is to get across to his listeners a specific idea. The broad results of successfully joining these two factors constitute what have been called the "general ends" of speech. As an immediate or a remote consequence of getting the speaker's idea or his purpose, the listeners may (1) acquire new information, new experiences; (2) have their already accepted beliefs, attitudes, and courses of action strengthened and revitalized; (3) have these beliefs and attitudes changed, even reversed, without actually having been urged to do anything about making a change in their overt behavior; (4) decide upon a new and altered course of action, different from that which they have hitherto been following or even directly opposed to it; or (5) simply derive amusement, entertainment, and diversion as a result of an idea that the speaker has evoked or stimulated.

The communicative situation arises whenever one individual with an idea and the urge to share it finds one or more persons who are willing or can be persuaded (or motivated) to listen to him. The types of occasions giving rise to such situations are obviously many and varied, no two being exactly alike. The speaker himself is the medium through which idea and listener are brought together. As we have already pointed out, acquiring the means to realize this objective demands considerable thought and study.

Not only are there various types of occasions giving rise to a speech situation; there are also various reasons for speaking. As a young speaker eager to gain further experience in addressing groups, you may justifiably seize upon every reasonable opportunity to speak in public. Bear in mind, however, the long-established principle that though the privilege of speaking cannot be denied under orderly procedures, no speaker can *demand* that his potential audience listen to him. The right to be heard—rather to be listened to —must be earned.

If you are really interested in improving your own ability, never refuse an opportunity to speak so long as you have a worthwhile contribution to make to the discussion and so long as you stop well short of making a nuisance of yourself. You may merely feel the need of adding an item of information in a discussion of some subject of interest or importance. You may advocate the acceptance or rejection of some proposal which has come before your group for decision. Young people's groups—social, religious, preprofessional, and so on—offer frequent opportunities for speaking. If such opportunities do not present themselves, you can follow the example of former Senator Ashurst of Arizona who, it was said, used to declaim to the mountains and to his cattle as he rode the range in his own state. As you gain in experience and knowledge, in confidence and poise, you will find plenty of occasions for speaking, and you will come actually to enjoy such experiences.

One of the most popular and effective speakers before the American public since near the close of World War I has been Lowell Thomas. He has much to say about the value of the speaking experience itself: "To repeat what doesn't seem to be common knowledge, practice in speaking before live audiences does magic things. . . . So sure I am of this, that if I were in charge of the schools of the world, I would put practice in speaking first, followed by the three R's. On your feet before an audience, more than at any other time, you are on your own, Brother."[7]

[7] Theodore R. McKeldin and John C. Kantz, *The Art of Eloquence*, Williams and Wilkins, 1952, p. vi. It might be of interest that Mr. McKeldin has been both mayor of Baltimore and governor of Maryland and Dr. Kantz is a professor of pharmacology in the University of Maryland School of Medicine. Both have had wide speaking experience.

Whatever the speaker's motivation may be in speaking, whatever the situation in which effective speaking is important, he must feel the urge to communicate. He must, in other words, feel that the idea in his mind is one that should be in the possession of his hearers and that he is the medium by which this audience and this idea are to be brought together. There is no effective speaking that does not arise from the urge to communicate.

GOOD SPEAKING REQUIRES HONEST THINKING

Broad knowledge is of great importance to the speaker, as we have seen; but to be of greatest value it must be interpreted by honest thinking. The true scientist understands what is meant by intellectual honesty, and his studies, at least in his own field, are characterized by that type of thinking. He examines the facts as they come to him through his investigations, interprets those facts in the light of what is already known, and by means of logical inferences arrives at his conclusions on the basis of those interpretations. He sees what is there rather than what he is looking for.

In his *Introduction to Research in Speech*, Auer emphasized the importance of formulating "hypotheses," which he defined as "a proposition (stated categorically or in question form) providing a tentative answer to a question about the nature of the possible relationship between two or more variables." The research itself consists of testing these hypotheses to determine their validity, that is, whether they hold true or not. Sometimes the researcher discovers that what he sees is quite different from what he anticipated; but unless he is willing to accept his interpretations and to base his conclusions on the facts as he discovers them, he is no true scientist. He is under a profound moral compulsion in his search for the truth of the scientist; this compulsion he is totally unable to escape, nor, if he is a scientist, does he want to.[8]

One of our students some years ago was assured by authorities in Southern history that there was no information available on the theater in the South between 1861 and 1865 for the simple reason that during those years there were no theatrical activities. She re-

---

[8] J. Jeffery Auer, *An Introduction to Research in Speech*, Harper, 1959, pp. 72–76, 185–187.

fused to accept the hypothesis as final, and as a result wrote a very good dissertation which showed that the theater was in fact very active in the Confederate States during that period.

For generations after Magellan's little fleet completed its voyage around the world, people refused to discard the idea that the phrase "the four corners of the world"—or "the three corners of the world," as Shakespeare had it[9]—was to be taken literally. French Academicians persisted in their rejection of Pasteur's findings until the sheer weight of evidence forced them to recognize the validity of his conclusions. The atomic submarine was finally built despite the opposition of presumed authorities who persistently refused to believe that it was either possible or feasible.

In your thinking, then, you should follow those procedures which contribute to intellectual honesty and avoid those that violate the principles of sound thinking. In arriving at your judgments you will encounter favorable as well as unfavorable facts, that is, some details that agree and others that disagree with your present beliefs and attitudes. Most of our beliefs are little more than hypotheses, anyway. Do not permit your emotional biases to outweigh your reason in evaluating these apparently contradictory data. Do not ignore the unfavorable in arriving at your final judgments. Recognizing that there are unfavorable aspects may help your judgments to be all the more sound when you do make them.

If your judgments are formed only after you have accumulated sufficient knowledge of the problem, they will then be more easily defended because they have a sounder basis in fact and logical inference; even then, be ready to accept new information as it comes to you and modify your judgments accordingly.

In your speaking make it your aim to clarify rather than to confuse the thinking of your listeners. Avoid half-truths; in being only half-truth, they are likely also to be half-falsehood. Falsification through omission is no less misleading than through commission. Misrepresentation, distortion, and concealment of facts for your own purposes are to be condemned. As we shall point out in a succeeding chapter, you will inevitably appeal to motives, which are closely related to the emotions. But when you do, put those appeals on a rational basis. Back up your emotional appeals by sound reasoning.

[9] *King John*, V, vii, 116

GOOD SPEAKING REQUIRES A REALIZATION
OF SOCIAL RESPONSIBILITY

From what has been said, it seems obvious that in such a form of social organization as our own the ability to speak effectively is highly important. Yet that ability alone is not enough, any more than sincerity alone is enough; the need, as we pointed out earlier in this chapter, is for *enlightened sincerity*. The rabble rouser may be sincere, though this is sometimes doubtful; but if he is actually ignorant, if his emotional fervor is misdirected, he can be just as dangerous to society as one who deliberately sets out on a program of subversion. He can mislead the misinformed as easily as can the fully informed speaker who tries to maintain integrity in his leadership.

If we are to preserve our present social structure or to make the changes that seem advisable from time to time, it is vital that the members of the social organization be able to express their ideas and opinions clearly and forcibly; it is equally important that they know when to use that ability and for what social ends.

Consider, for example, the medical profession. Students in medical colleges learn not only the arts of disease prevention and healing but also the rigid code of ethics that governs the practice of medicine. The "Oath of Hippocrates" is for the physician a statement of the ethical principles by which he governs his professional conduct, although arguments are occasionally heard that it is outmoded and needs to be brought up to date.

The speaker, like the physician, also has a social responsibility. In his developed ability to affect the thinking, feelings, and actions of those who come under his influence, he has the opportunity to contribute to either the welfare or the detriment of the social order and of individual members of that order.

As students of speech, therefore, your concern should be not only with the improvement of your capabilities for public utterance but also with the uses to which you intend to put that ability.

As a people we are committed to the maintenance of what is called the democratic way of life. The term has meant many things to many people. Essentially it refers to willingness to grant others the same privileges we ask for ourselves; insistence on as much freedom in our actions as will not interfere with like freedom for others; insistence on determining without coercion or hindrance our own course of conduct, and conceding to our neighbor the same right; the right to discuss freely and openly the problems that arise from time to time, and to exchange as freely and openly with our associates our ideas, information, opinion, experiences; the formation of decisions on group action only after full, open, and free discussion participated in by all concerned and the acceptance of the expressed decision of the majority; and unrestricted selection of those who are to lead us in our group activities and removal of any who do not perform the group will.

Whether one uses his ability in speaking for the good or ill of society is essentially a matter of the speaker's own sense of ethical and social values, of his own motives in speaking, of the honesty of his own thinking, and of the genuineness of his concern for human welfare. There is not today, nor has there ever been, any great speaking which was directed toward the debasement of humanity, the enslavement of people, or the denial or destruction of human freedoms. There has never been a truly great speaker whose efforts were directed toward such end results. As Emerson once said, "There is no true eloquence unless there is a man behind the speech."

In recent years we have heard much about the potentialities of nuclear energy. Its terrific destructive force has been demonstrated; we are assured that it has equally great possibilities for constructive work. What may not be so clearly realized is that, tremendous as that energy is, it is still relatively insignificant in its possibilities for good or ill as compared with the power of the spoken word. The atom bomb at Hiroshima snuffed out the lives of scores of thousands of victims in a single blinding, searing instant; the hydrogen bomb, with its megatons of capacity for devastation, can make the power of the atom bomb seem by comparison like no more than a Fourth of July firecracker. And there are more than hints of a still more powerful nuclear bomb which will make the others pale into insignificance.

It was the fiery harangues of Hitler and Mussolini and their carefully trained speakers that brought on World War II which cost the lives of millions of people and the destruction of untold billions in property. Today the machinations of Khrushchev and his followers, together with the complete refusal of others of his political and social persuasion to consider even the possibility of peaceful coexistence except on their own terms, threaten to make the holocaust of World War II merely a preliminary skirmish.

Even more tragically, through the passionate speech of the dictators the minds of whole nations of people, adults and children, have been and are still being warped almost beyond recovery. Throughout the world a relentless war of words is being waged for the minds of men. In this war one of the chief weapons being used by those charged with the responsibility for the spread of ideologies subversive to democratic thought and destructive of human freedoms consists of skill in the techniques of speech.

The processes of group manipulation, of parliamentary procedure, are also used for purposes of deception and confusion. The workers have received intensive training and know all the tricks. The one thing they cannot and will not survive is the full, free, open discussion of the issues at stake under conditions in which everyone who wishes may enter into the discussion with no fear of reprisals for the views he may hold and advocate. "Tyranny cannot flourish," says Thonssen and Baird, "where responsible men have the right to say responsible things."[10] If the fundamental purposes of a democracy are to be achieved and tyranny prevented or overthrown, this right becomes an obligation. What is needed is a dedication comparable to that of Jefferson when he said, "I have sworn hostility against every form of tyranny over the mind of man."

Because of the power of effective speech to influence others to think, feel, and act very much as the speaker wants them to, it is not difficult to understand that the speaker himself assumes, as his speech becomes more and more effective, so grave a responsibility. He needs, then, to examine closely his own ethical standards, his motives in speaking, and the possible effect of his utterances on the welfare of those affected—not just a segment of his audiences, both direct and indirect, but all of those who may come under the influence of his voice. "The magic of the tongue is the most dangerous of all spells."[11]

It has often been said that science and the scientist are or should

---

[10] Lester Thonssen and A. Craig Baird, *Speech Criticism,* Ronald, 1948, p. 468.
[11] *Eugene Aram* (Edward Bulwer Lytton—Lord Lytton), Harper, 1832, bk. I, ch. 7.

be strictly neutral; that science itself is amoral—not concerned with such things as social values; and that scientists themselves are not, as such, interested in the social implications of "pure science."

In 1960 the Committee on Science in the Promotion of Human Welfare of the American Association for the Advancement of Science reported the results of its inquiry into the responsibilities of scientists in relation to public affairs. "For nearly two decades," the report opened, "scientists have viewed with growing concern the troublesome events that have been evoked by the interaction between scientific progress and public affairs." The report recognized that since World War II "there has been a considerable growth in scientists' participation in political affairs," but also that that "growth has been intermittent, and based on a variety of views of the scientists' relation to social problems." The conclusions take the form of three statements which are especially relevant in any consideration of the social responsibility of scientists themselves, and of the need among scientists for the ability to express themselves clearly and unequivocally, in both speech and writing.

First, says this group of scholars, "if we regard participation in the resolution of public issues related to science as a part of the scientists' professional responsibilities, we must conclude that the scientific community has not yet developed a consistent, widely supported way of meeting this obligation."

Second, "in the matter of providing citizens with the knowledge required to make informal decisions on science-related public issues, the scientist and his organizations have both a unique competence and a special responsibility. As the producer and custodian of scientific knowledge, the scientific community has the obligation to impart such knowledge to the public."

Third, "In sum, we conclude that the scientific community should, on its own initiative, assume an obligation to call to public attention those issues of public policy which relate to science, and to provide for the general public the facts and estimates of the effects of alternative policies which the citizen must have if he is to participate intelligently in the solution of these problems. A citizenry thus informed is, we believe, the chief assurance that science will be devoted to the promotion of human welfare."[12]

A well-known speech teacher put it this way: "Skillful utterance

[12] "Science in Human Welfare," *Science*, July 8, 1960, **132**: no. 3419, 68–73.

can be totally destructive unless it is motivated by honest thinking, a feeling for justice, and a genuine concern for the well-being of humanity."[13] Nineteen centuries ago Quintilian wrote in his famous *Institutes of Oratory,*

> When Nature, that indulgent Mother, endowed man with Speech, to distinguish him from other creatures, she would have acted the Part not of a Parent, but a Tyrant, had she intended that Eloquence should herd with Wickedness, oppose Innocence and destroy Truth. It had been more kind in her, to have ordered Man to be born mute, nay, devoid of all reason, rather than that he should employ the gifts of Providence to the Destruction of his Neighbor.
> . . . should a wicked man be eloquent, then Eloquence herself becomes Wickedness: because she furnishes that Man with the Means of being more wicked; and a bad Man will be sure to use them.[14]

About the same time these lines were being written in Rome, another man in the East, who also claimed Roman citizenship but whose basic philosophy was quite different from Quintilian's enlightened paganism, was writing to his friends in Corinth a parallel sentiment which is equally valid today: "Though I speak with the tongues of men and of angels, and have not love, I am become as sounding brass, or a tinkling cymbal."[15]

QUESTIONS AND TOPICS FOR STUDY AND REVIEW

1. Assuming that you are studying to be a lawyer, what are some things besides the law itself you might be called on to know? Show that in different legal careers the "side" subjects may vary widely.
2. In what way or ways may the use of propaganda violate the principle of honest thinking? Give some examples of the worthy use of propaganda.
3. How much credence can you give to a dentifrice whose manufacturers advertise that you need use it only once a day? Make some inquiry among dentists to find your answer.
4. On the basis of your own general preparation up to now, on what subject or subjects would you be prepared to speak with a half-hour's notice? Set down an outline of a speech that you would give.

[13] Joseph F. Smith, from an address at the Association Dinner of the National Association of Teachers of Speech, Chicago, December 29, 1944.

[14] William Guthrie, T. Walker, 1756, vol. 2, bk. XII, chap. 1, pp. 495, 503.

[15] I. Cor. 13:1.

5. To what extent do you verify or have you verified the statements you make as *fact*? Set down ten statements that you can vouch for as based on actual fact.

6. What are some peculiarities in your own language background that you have become aware of? Have they been such that you have tried to change your mode of speaking appreciably?

7. What "side" areas of interest has your study in your major field led you into, even slightly? Have you found that this "side interest" has affected your main subject of interest?

8. What is the difference between the right to speak and the right to be listened to? What burden does that right put on the speaker?

9. In the study of your own field of interest what emphasis if any is placed on the question of social responsibility? To what extent is such a question of importance?

10. What is the significance of the first word in the concept of "enlightened sincerity"?

11. Construct a code of ethics for speakers that is intended to implement the principle of social responsibility.

12. What evidence is there to support the hypothesis that an international language such as Esperanto would contribute materially to the eradication of international conflicts and misunderstandings?

13. Comment on the comparable problems of the speaker and the scientist with respect to social responsibility.

PROJECTS

1. Write a speech biography in which you analyze your own assets and liabilities as a speaker. Consider such questions as the following, insofar as they apply:
   a. Why I enrolled in a public speaking course. (If it is required, state the probable reasons why it is required in your curriculum.)
   b. What I hope to accomplish as a result of taking the course.
   c. The kind of speaker I should like to be.
   d. The social and professional uses to which I may put my ability in speaking.
   e. Any pleasant or unpleasant experiences I may have had as a speaker.
   f. My present recognized faults in speaking.
   g. Difficulties in speaking that I hope to overcome.

2. Be prepared to discuss in a symposium the following questions:
   a. Why is training in public speaking essential in a democratic society?
   b. What is the function of speech in what is called the "American way of life"?

    c. What are the relations between speech and "personality"?

    d. Is there a correlation between proficiency in speech and success in the rest of your school work? What is the probable effect of your speech grade on your general average?

    e. Why, in case of armed invasion, are the communication centers (telephone exchanges, radio and television stations, etc.) among the first points to be attacked and captured?

3. Read one of the speeches in the magazine *Vital Speeches of the Day*, and try to determine what different fields of knowledge contributed to the speaker's general and specific preparation. Discuss the results of your inquiry before the class.

4. Give a talk in which you show how, in order to discuss some topic you want to speak about, you must draw on a number of different areas of knowledge.

5. Describe a specific occasion, one that actually occurred, in which speech was the only method of communication that would have been effective, and why no other would have sufficed.

6. Illustrate a number of "nonverbal" methods of communication, and discuss their peculiar values in the areas in which they are used.

7. Develop in a speech the principle quoted in the chapter that "There is a built-in moral component right in the core of the scientific activity itself."

SUPPLEMENTARY READINGS

Baird, A. Craig, and Franklin H. Knower, *General Speech: An Introduction*, 2nd ed., McGraw-Hill, 1957, chap. 13, "The Speaker's Personality."

Beardsley, Monroe, *Thinking Straight*, Harper, 1956.

Benne, Kenneth D., *et al.*, "Participation and Democracy," *Adult Leadership*, May, 1952, 1: 25–27.

Bois, J. Samuel, *Explorations in Awareness*, Harper, 1957.

Brigance, William Norwood, *Speech: Its Techniques and Disciplines in a Free Society*, 2nd ed., Appleton-Century-Crofts, 1961, pp. 208–209; chap. 19, "Ethical Persuasion."

Chase, Stuart, *Guides to Straight Thinking*, Harper, 1956.

Lippmann, Walter, *The Public Philosophy*, Little, Brown, 1955.

Oliver, Robert T., *The Psychology of Persuasive Speech*, 2nd ed., Longmans, Green, 1957, chap. 2, "The Ethics of Persuasion."

Sarett, Lew, William Trufant Foster, and Alma Johnson Sarett, *Basic Principles of Speech*, 3rd ed., Houghton Mifflin, 1958, chap. 2, "Seven Basic Principles."

Schrier, William, "The Ethics of Persuasion," *Quarterly Journal of Speech,* November, 1930, **16:** 476–486.

Thonssen, Lester, and A. Craig Baird, *Speech Criticism,* Ronald, 1948, chap. 13, "The Character of the Speaker"; chap. 18, "Toward a Philosophy of Rhetoric."

Winans, James A., *Speech-Making,* Appleton-Century-Crofts, 1938, chap. 19, "The Speaker Himself."

5

Stage Fright and
What To Do About It

If you are like most beginning students of speech you may be
seized, whenever you contemplate appearing before an audience,
with a sort of nervous apprehension which attacks in various forms
and degrees of severity. Even if you have had some experience in
speaking, you may still experience such feelings. Sometimes they
continue for a while even after you have sat down; now and then
they disappear soon after you begin speaking. They are quite common among all speakers.

The milder attacks seldom result in more than a momentary uneasiness, which soon fades away when the speaker gets under way. Usually, not much attention is paid to them, because they do not seem to interfere greatly with the speaking, and do not last long anyway. But the more severe experiences, which may even force one to give up the whole idea of speaking, may be and probably are more serious. It is these attacks to which the term *stage fright* is commonly applied.

Not only do they appear when the student approaches the "moment of truth," when he is called on to come before the class and say what he has planned to say; they are known to attack an individual when he even considers taking a course in public speaking. Some students are so afflicted that they leave the campus without ever finding out what, if anything, they might have done about it. Another result is that they postpone taking the course until the final term or semester, often to discover before the course is over that speaking can actually be a pleasant experience and that all the worries were needless.

APPROACHES TO THE PROBLEM

There are various approaches to the problem of stage fright in public speaking or other courses in speech in which actual performance is required. Each of these approaches has its adherents and its rationale and each can be justified on the basis of psychological and pedagogical principles. Usually, whatever the particular approach followed, the net result is that at the end of the course the student is able to come before his audience with much greater ease and poise than he could at the beginning—which is about as much as one can hope to achieve in such a short time.

Ignoring Stage Fright

Some teachers attempt to deal with the problem by minimizing its importance and refusing to take the initiative in discussing it before their classes, thinking that attention will thereby be directed away from it and into more positive channels. They may talk about it briefly if it comes up in the classroom or they may discuss it in personal conferences. Such an approach means that the subject does not come to the sharp attention of many who probably need no more than a suggestion to imagine all sorts of dire and unpleasant experiences.

The "Personality" Viewpoint

Others think of stage fright as evidence of a disturbed or maladjusted "personality," sometimes caused by lack of poise. "When there is a lack of poise the entire speech personality is disturbed and made less efficient in its adjustments. This lack of poise is known as stage fright in the larger audience situations." But "Poise," he says, "is a state of inner calm, serenity, and well-being."[1] Once the personality disturbance or maladjustment is corrected or adequate poise is achieved, stage fright is supposed to disappear.

The "Emergency" Approach

In still other instances discussion of the problem in the classroom is withheld unless or until it is brought sharply to the attention when some student seems to be incapable of fulfilling the speaking assignment. This may also be thought of as the "positive" approach, in which the matter is treated as one of developing confidence rather than of eliminating the unpleasant and negativistic indications of lack of self-confidence.

The "Free and Open Discussion" Approach

Another method of treating the topic is to bring it out into the open, to discuss it freely as a common phenomenon among both students of speech, and experienced speakers who have been accustomed for years to appearing before audiences of all kinds. The idea here is that once we understand the nature of the experience and its symptoms, as they appear both to the student himself and to his listeners, and learn to live with it, at least we have some knowledge of what it is all about, and can go ahead with the business of speaking. We may even accept the fact that we may never conquer it entirely. Possibly it is not even desirable for us to get rid of it entirely.

It is probably significant that of eleven current texts on public

[1] Elwood Murray, *The Speech Personality*, Lippincott, 1939, p. 91.

speaking, only two ignore entirely the subject of stage fright; the other nine discuss it freely and openly, describing its symptoms, its prevalence, its causes, and its treatment. Some of them analyze it in terms of building confidence, but most of them treat it in terms of fears, fright, nervousness, and similar concepts. Most of them, moreover, introduce the topic quite early in the text.

This last approach is the one followed in this text. It is the considered belief of the present authors that stage fright or some facsimile is in fact one of the familiar, important, and normal phenomena associated with speaking in public, and should be recognized as such by both teachers and students. Like other phenomena in this particular mode of communication, it deserves a frank discussion. Partly through such discussion and partly through as many speaking experiences as can be acquired during the course, the so-called ravages of stage fright are alleviated, especially in situations comparable to those encountered in the classroom.

Moreover, this relief from embarrassment is usually carried over into the unfamiliar and unusual situations which anyone, as soon as he acquires some status as a speaker, may find himself involved in. We do not know all about it yet. But perhaps, if we make use of what we do know, we know enough so that stage fright need not prevent our doing what we set out to do.

TERMINOLOGY AND GENERAL CHARACTERISTICS
OF STAGE FRIGHT

The phenomenon itself is referred to under various names: "negative reactions to the speech situation"; "nervousness"; plain "fear"; "maladjusted personality"; "excessive tensions," and so on.

Whatever the specific terminology, it usually refers to those emotional and physiological states characterized by excessive muscular tensions, heavy perspiration, thickness of the tongue, and trembling of the hands, knees, and so on. A higher pulse rate as well as higher blood pressure have been observed under experimental conditions. But just going into a doctor's office will have the same effect on many people. Under such conditions neither thoughts nor words flow with conversational ease; and memory is often unreliable. One writer lists some seventeen symptoms reported by students questioned, of which the most important seem to be the following:

1. Inability to finish speaking.
2. Weak voice.
3. Inability to look at audience.
4. Tremor of knees, hands, etc.
5. Feeling that audience is disapproving.
6. Inability to produce voice.
7. Excessive perspiration.[2]

To these might be added the inability to move one's lower limbs enough to get up from one's seat and stand before the classroom audience! It appears from Greenleaf's study that the more severe the attack, the more of these symptoms are noted.

Classification of Symptoms

Again according to the study just cited, the symptoms of stage fright seem to fall into three general classifications: "evaluational, such as 'feeling that the audience is disapproving of you'; physiological, such as 'stomach upset'; and avoidance tendencies, such as 'desire to escape from the situation'."[3] Four groups of students were studied and classified according to their own admissions of experiencing of stage fright as *none, mild, moderate,* and *severe.* Within three of the groups the order of frequency of appearance of the seventeen symptoms mentioned was essentially the same. But any speaker, beginning or experienced, will easily recognize many of these symptoms, and probably add a few of his own that are not even listed.

PREVALENCE OF STAGE FRIGHT

Speech Students Are Not Alone

Students in speech courses should take some comfort in the knowledge that they are by no means the only people who are troubled by symptoms of stage fright. It is common among actors, athletes, and musicians, among others. After a brilliant performance by a noted concert violinist a short time ago, a group of fellow musicians,

---

[2] Floyd I. Greenleaf, "An Exploratory Study of Stage Fright," *Quarterly Journal of Speech*, October, 1952, **38**: 326–330.
[3] *Ibid.*

themselves somewhat more than merely competent artists, were asked the question, "Do you suppose the violinist was at all nervous just before he came on the stage?" The reply was, "If he is human, he was."

A recent All-American halfback enrolled in a course in public speaking. He was questioned about his feelings at the beginning of a crucial game, when he was lined up under the goalposts waiting for the opening kickoff. "Butterflies," he replied without hesitation. An Olympic hurdler, when asked about his feelings while he was waiting for the starter's command, "On your marks!" replied frankly, "Pretty nervous."

Possibly athletes and musicians compare with speakers in the respect that, as Cicero pointed out two thousand years ago, "The better the orator, the more profoundly he is frightened of the difficulty of speaking, and of the doubtful fate of a speech, and of the anticipations of an audience."[4]

Of himself Cicero said, ". . . just as I generally perceive it to happen to yourselves, so I very often prove it in my own experience, that I turn pale at the outset of a speech, and quake in every limb and in all my soul; in fact, as a very young man, I once so utterly lost heart in opening an indictment, that I had to thank Quintus Maximus for doing me the supreme service of promptly adjourning the hearing, the moment he saw that I was broken-down and unnerved by fear."[5]

It is said that the first time Demosthenes attempted to speak in the Athenian Assembly, he was laughed down because of his very evident fear and consequent ineptitude in speaking.

Stage Fright Is Common to Most Modern Speakers

There is ample testimony from famous modern speakers that they too have felt those nervous tremblings which Cicero confessed. As for students, among the 789 whom Greenleaf studied at the State University of Iowa, 89 percent reported that they had experienced some degree of stage fright, 57 percent had moderate or severe fright, and 11 percent experienced none at all. But only 10 percent reported that they had felt severe fright.[6]

[4] Cicero, *De Oratore,* Loeb ed., bk. I, chap. XXVI, p. 85.
[5] *Ibid.*
[6] Greenleaf, *op. cit.*

It can safely be said, therefore, that the great majority of people, students and experienced speakers alike as well as others who have occasion to appear before audiences, experience some degree of what may be called stage fright in connection with the contemplated or the actual appearance.

EVALUATION

Effective Speaking Demands Some Tension

There is fairly general agreement among authorities that some tension, beyond the tonus necessary for adequate alertness and animation in the speaker, is necessary for the best speaking. Cicero felt that the speaker who had no such feelings at all deserved more than reprimand; he deserved punishment for even appearing before an audience![7]

A modern critic, writing on the subject of the tensions and feelings of nervousness that assail the speaker, insisted that "when a speaker takes the platform, he assumes an obligation, an obligation not to be indifferent to those before him, not to waste their time or to disappoint the attention with which they greet his appearance. . . . The speaker who feels no fear in such a situation is in no better position than the tramp who demonstrated that he was not afraid of work by lying down and going to sleep beside any job offered him." He goes on to say, "On the day when a public speaker in this republic is roundly hissed, and that not because he dwells upon the frail humanity of one of our founding fathers, or utters other offending sentiments, but because he functions so damnably as a speaker and disregards the rights of his hearers as an audience, on that day the craft of speech among us will begin to look up."[8]

The Effects Can Be Overcome

Of course, if nothing at all is done about stage fright, if one makes no effort at overcoming its effects, the nervous and muscular tensions and all the other symptoms will probably not only persist but even grow more intense, so that one finally gives up altogether and

[7] Cicero, op. cit.
[8] Hoyt H. Hudson, "The Knees of Demosthenes," American Speech, May, 1927, 2: 337–340.

refuses to try to speak in public at all. We are not here discussing those entirely normal heightened tensions, that hypertonicity, that one feels on various kinds of occasions and which rarely if ever prevent one from doing what he sets out to do.

Now and then some highly proficient musician has had perhaps a single experience, especially at the beginning of his career as a musician, in which he was unable to complete his performance. As a result he has henceforth rejected all invitations to play even before his friends. Such an outcome is unfortunate in that it deprives not only the musician himself but his friends as well of the privilege of enjoying the fine performances he is really capable of giving.

Similarly, when a speaker refuses or neglects to take advantage of the knowledge and the opportunity which may enable him to become an effective speaker, he is denying himself the chance for high-level participation in the affairs of his community and the community itself the benefit of his knowledge, experience, and wisdom.

It is not necessary, it is not even desirable, for all heightened tonicity to be reduced to a condition of complete relaxation. It is, as a great number of widely experienced speakers have said, an essential and stimulating aspect of the speaking experience itself, if one is genuinely concerned about the success of one's efforts.

THE CAUSES OF STAGE FRIGHT

To most beginners in public speaking this nervousness is a matter of deepest concern. Often, one of the first questions raised in speech classes is, "Why do I get so nervous when I try to speak?" or "How can I get rid of my nervousness?" So deep is this concern, in fact, that many have apparently developed a belief that such feelings are an indication of some pathological condition, that if they were entirely normal they would be completely at ease before an audience.

Some Nervousness Is Practically Universal

As already suggested, the truth is that nervousness before an audience and especially prior to facing an audience is a very common experience; one might say that it is practically universal. It is likely, as has also been indicated, that practically every speaker since the time of Pericles, who antedated Demosthenes by a century, has experienced the same symptoms if he has been anything of a speaker at all. So common is it, in fact, that one might almost say, as Cicero intimated many centuries ago, that its presence rather than its absence is an indication of normalcy.

Fear of Loss of Status May Be a Cause

Stage fright may arise in part from a type of apprehension, not of physical danger or harm, but rather of loss of status with the audience. The good opinion of others, psychologists recognize, is a powerful incentive in behavior, and the prospect of losing that good opinion fills us with dismay. When you appear before a group of listeners as a speaker, you stand to lose that regard unless you are effective in your speech—in its content, its organization, its language, its presentation. The mere possibility of forgetting what you planned to say often gives rise to apprehension.

Any doubt or apprehension regarding your ability to measure up to the demands of the occasion will usually engender some nervousness. For the beginner, then, stage fright may be due to a lack of self-confidence.

Being an Object of Scrutiny May Cause Self-Consciousness

Many people, even with extensive speaking experience, become self-conscious as soon as they become aware of the fact that they are being observed, especially if that observation is in any way critical. They begin to worry about making mistakes. They too develop all the symptoms of stage fright and make the very errors they are afraid of making.

The feeling is not limited to beginners by any means. A competent secretary will sometimes become extremely self-conscious when she is aware of someone looking over her shoulder and watching her fingers on the typewriter keyboard. In such a case fear hardly enters into the feeling; it may be no more than an increased tension arising from the self-consciousness itself which, by directing her own attention to what she is doing *and how she is doing it,* leads to errors. It may resemble the well-known myth about the centipede which, when it began to consider which leg it moved first, found that it could not walk at all.

The Causes of Stage Fright Are Not Wholly Understood

The underlying causes of stage fright are still the subject of much inquiry. It is highly probable that there are many factors in the social situation as yet even unidentified, factors which stem from the speaker's feeling of responsibility (for the irresponsible speaker is much less likely to be affected); apprehensions arising from feelings of possible inadequacy, on one basis or another; the sharp awareness of being in the focus of attention of one's audience. Any or all of these may contribute to those feelings of nervousness which *can* be, but which seldom are, almost totally incapacitating. The whole phenomenon appears to be highly complicated and worthy of intensive study.

THE SIGNIFICANCE OF BODILY CHANGES

What is felt, what comes into consciousness, in experiencing stage fright is partly if not wholly the awareness of extensive physiological changes taking place in the body. These changes are similar if not identical to those that take place when one suddenly encounters a dangerous situation; they have been discussed in some detail by Lomas. Generally, they consist of a greatly increased supply of adrenalin and sometimes of thyroxin in the blood, together with the presence of "some object or situation to which the emotion is directed and around which the emotion is intellectually organized." It might be said that some suddenly threatening situation sets off a reaction, part of which is the increased glandular flow, giving rise to feelings which, because of their similarity to the fear reaction, are themselves interpreted as identical with fear, or in other words as fear itself. Some of these situations quite probably contain none of the elements which might normally be expected to cause a genuine fear reaction; but since the reactions they do stimulate are difficult if not impossible to differentiate from actual fear, no such distinction is made or even attempted. To all practical purposes, they *are* fear responses.[9]

Brigance has described the symptoms caused by the excess glandular flow, but he points out that all these changes take place in

[9] Charles W. Lomas, "The Psychology of Stage Fright," *Quarterly Journal of Speech*, February, 1937, **23**: 35–44.

extreme stage fright: "In mild stage fright, the body undergoes the same changes in lesser degree, and we feel faintly seasick, have faint disagreeable sensations, or are simply keyed up and tense."[10]

The bodily changes that are set up in varying degrees of severity are glandular, visceral, and muscular. The glandular changes are probably in large part responsible for visceral and muscular.

Types of Bodily Change in Stage Fright

Among the visceral effects of stage fright are changes in heart rate and blood pressure; sometimes the surface capillaries distend and the face flushes, and at other times the blood vessels contract and the skin becomes pale. Respiration often quickens and becomes more shallow; at other times it may become inhibited. Digestion is affected—one of the effects which cause what is popularly known as "butterflies." The salivary glands in the mouth cease functioning normally and the tongue and roof of the mouth become dry. Nerve impulses move downward from the great vagus nerve and up into the larynx and other mechanisms of voice and articulation, causing them to tighten up; the result is usually a high, tense voice and thick, indistinct utterance.

As these changes take place, the glandular secretions are also going to the skeletal muscles, those responsible for bodily movement, making them stiff and rigid.

Now, all these changes, plus a few others, internal and external, may take place in extreme stage fright; they are probably the worst that can happen. Some of them are present to some slight degree in mild attacks, and can usually be ignored. They are also what give the speaker the needed extra energy which help to make his speech animated, alert, and lively.

REMEDIAL MEASURES

You are of course interested in knowing what all this has to do with speaking, particularly with the delivery of your speech, which is right where it strikes—it is much less likely to affect seriously the preparation itself. You are also interested in knowing what if

---

[10] William Norwood Brigance, *Speech: Its Techniques and Disciplines in a Free Society,* 2nd ed., Appleton-Century-Crofts, 1961, pp. 68–69.

anything you can do about it, or perhaps what your instructor can do about it. It should be quite obvious, as many of you will testify from your own experiences, that nervousness does have a definitely inhibiting effect on the presentation of a speech. Only when you are at ease are you able to speak with maximum effectiveness. Remedial measures should follow two definite lines, both essential and both dependent on your own efforts entirely. Your instructor can discuss these with you and give you suggestions for applying them; but what is actually done you will have to do for yourself.

1. Cultivate a Positive Attitude

In the first place, you must develop a different attitude toward the phenomenon of nervousness and hypertension from the one you no doubt hold at present. Attempt to change your habitual way of looking at stage fright. You will find it possible to make such a change if you consider these three aspects of the problem.

Nervousness is important when it interferes with your speaking. Nervousness itself may or may not be important. What is important is the degree to which you permit it to prevent your doing what you set out to do. The story is told of General Grant—and probably has been told of many others—that when he was a young lieutenant in the Mexican War he observed just before one of the battles that his knees were shaking and knocking together. Looking down at them he said grimly, "Go on and shake! You'd shake more than that if you knew where I am going to take you!" Most men who have seen active service in the armed forces will readily admit to experiencing the same feelings just before going into combat. If every flight student had chosen to stay on the ground the first time his instructor said "Take 'er up!" there would be no Air Force today.

Once one becomes engrossed in what one is doing the nervousness tends to disappear. Don't give way to it. The violinist mentioned earlier gave a brilliant performance despite his nervousness before going on the stage; the All-American halfback still made his touchdowns; and the Olympic hurdler went ahead to win his races.

Nervousness is not pathological. Realize that nervousness at the prospect of making any public appearance is no evidence of a pathological personality. On the contrary, it is a perfectly normal reaction. Almost without exception, the world's greatest speakers—those who have been in the vanguard of the world's most significant movements—have felt exactly as you and your fellow students do, and most of them, for all their experience, have never been able completely to dispel their trepidation as they looked forward to facing their audiences. They simply refused to allow themselves to be overcome. In your experience you are in the company of the oratorical immortals!

If you had come up from the first grade accustomed to making regular public appearances as a part of the day's work to be taken largely for granted, you probably would not be troubled today. Unfortunately, except for a few of the especially "talented" or in some of the progressive schools today, public appearances are the exception throughout the school system. The result is that for most of you it is a relatively new experience, and its very newness leads to uncertainty and nervousness. You will find, however, that each speech will reduce your perturbation. By the time you have finished the course you should be able to stand before most audiences with considerable poise and equanimity.

You will probably find, too, that if you have been speaking repeatedly to the same group, as in the speech class program, you will lose or be largely unaware of all tensions in approaching the class hour. But if you change to another audience or a different type of situation the nervousness is quite likely to recur for a time, though less strongly than at the beginning of your speaking "career."

Developing the urge to communicate.   The urge to communicate will go far toward creating a wholesome attitude about the function and processes of speaking. It will further serve to direct your attention away from yourself and to the thing you set out to do. When the football player gets into the play, he has little time to think about himself. There is no place for "grandstanding"; his interest is in fulfilling the specific assignment the play calls for. Your assignment when you are making a speech is to bring an idea to a group of listeners. The attitude that you have a message and that you are the one to deliver that message will enable you to concentrate on what you are actually trying to do so that you will not have a great deal of time to devote to yourself; the time for that is in your preparation.

As Woolbert has said, "A speaker ought to be reaching out to meet his hearers, eager to get in touch with them, even to mingle with them; but the shaking, stammering novitiate on the platform giving one of his earliest public addresses has little inclination to get in touch with anybody; what he wants is to get away from people; he would much rather run. In fact, that is just what half of him is trying to do when he quakes and shakes."[11]

2. Adopt Specific Procedures

While cultivating wholesome attitudes toward nervousness as it affects you individually is essential, adopting a few simple procedures will serve to implement these attitudes. While they may not entirely rid you of your tensions, they should help you to overcome their effects.

Be sure you have made adequate preparation. Stage fright arises, as has been indicated, partly from a lack of self-confidence, a feeling of inadequacy, or at least a feeling that the audience may not think you are well prepared. Probably nothing else you can do will increase your confidence in yourself, your sense of adequacy, quite so much as knowing that you are fully prepared for what you have to do.

Know your subject thoroughly, the sequence of ideas, your supporting materials; have your facts and their interpretations well in mind, and take whatever steps may be necessary to recall them when you need them. A few notes may help you in your early speeches. You should even do some serious thinking about the specific language you will use to phrase your ideas, provided you do not try to memorize the speech as a whole.

Thorough preparation involves also some consideration of the manner in which you are going to present your materials. It involves practicing your speech aloud; no skill or art was ever learned to any degree of proficiency without much practice and then more practice.

It will help if you know beforehand the nature of the occasion, the

[11] Charles Henry Woolbert, *The Fundamentals of Speech*, 2nd ed., Harper, 1927, p. 75.

audience, and the physical surroundings, even to the acoustics of the room. How formal or informal is the occasion? What is to precede or follow? *Just* how much time will you have? These considerations are discussed fully in a later chapter, but knowing about them is part of your preparation.

Complete preparation, including practice, will give you, as nothing else can, increased self-confidence, which in turn is conducive to ease in speaking. Self-confidence makes you feel that you will be able to meet any emergency that may arise. If your feelings of inadequacy are reduced or indeed prevented from rising at all, your nervousness and stage fright themselves will tend to fade out and finally to disappear altogether. Floyd Patterson, after his third bout with Ingemar Johannsen, is reported as saying, "When you don't have the skill, you get scared."

Bryant and Wallace list four specific "psychological aids" that are the result of thorough preparation: "(1) a speaker knows that he is ready to meet the situation; (2) he knows that he is better equipped to cope with any last-minute adjustments to his audience than if he were not well prepared; (3) he knows that good preparation means less chance of forgetting; and (4) he gains confidence."[12]

Do not try to conceal your nervousness.   Consciously trying to conceal your nervousness means that you are trying to hide from your audience the peripheral evidences of stage fright, which consist mainly of trembling arms, hands, and legs and knocking knees. But in trying to hold your limbs still, you will succeed only in tightening up these muscles all the more and bringing still other muscles into play, all of which merely adds to the total effect of nervous tension and makes it more obvious to the audience.

Relaxation, not more tension, is the key to relief. When the situation is quite informal, some speakers actually make some jocular reference to their feelings at the moment; but if you use this device, you should take care not to dwell on the matter and thus fix your own attention on your nervousness. The effort should be rather to direct your attention away from yourself and to the subject and development of your speech.

[12] Donald C. Bryant and Karl R. Wallace, *Fundamentals of Public Speaking.* 3rd ed., Appleton-Century-Crofts, 1960, p. 217.

Move about before the audience. A muscle in smooth action is not nearly so likely to stiffen up as one you are trying to hold rigid. In any fear reaction, as we have seen, an excess of adrenalin and thyroxin is poured into the blood stream. If this excess is not used up it creates a hypertension. But movement designed to use up this surplus energy must itself be moderate; if too vigorous it will serve to increase rather than diminish that excess. It is neither necessary nor desirable to dispel all of it; but a moderate amount of movement will help to use up the *surplus* energy and decrease the tendency to tighten up.

Avoid pacing to and fro like a caged lion; avoid playing with a pencil, a button on your coat, a piece of chalk, or any other article. Walk to the blackboard and draw a chart, so long as it is in broad lines and contains a minimum of detail; use a pointer to indicate some particular feature of a visual aid you are exhibiting; use a pencil somewhat as a pointer or a wand, so to speak; move freely from one side of the platform, lectern, or reading stand, so long as you do not move in a rhythmical pattern. Turn from one side of the audience to the other, making sure that all parts are given attention during the speaking.

Use your hands, arms, facial expression, whole body to give added meaning to what you are saying, as well as to give you relief from the excessive tensions that interfere with your speaking.

Take a speech course. Reid insists that your present enrollment in a speech course is the best way of learning what to do about stage fright.[13] Such a course provides for the student the two most helpful aids in overcoming nervousness in speaking. It gives him "actual speaking experiences" (much more, it might be added, than could be obtained under any other procedure), and it gives him "perceptive and sympathetic suggestions for improvement." This suggestion presents another good reason for the study of speech in an organized program of speech training (see also pp. 13–14).

Select subjects in which you are keenly interested. Some years ago a coed in one of our classes chose to talk on some aspect of geology. After she sat down she was asked about her particular interest in

[13] Loren Reid, *First Principles of Public Speaking*, Artcraft, 1960, p. 11.

geology. It turned out that she had selected the topic only because, as she admitted, she "had to talk about something." Another student, also a girl, gave a talk one day on "Inside Baseball," giving as her reason that she has been interested in baseball all her life. "Yes, but how do you happen to know these details about 'inside baseball'?" "Well," she said, "my father was a professional baseball player, and my brother is now." It was only then that her home town and her last name were associated with a famous big-league pitcher; of course she knew what she was talking about. She had lived with it all her life.

Familiarity with your subject is very important in giving you confidence, especially if you know significantly more about it than your listeners do. In such a case, you stand in a position of some superiority—you have "status." It almost goes without saying that you will be much more interested in subjects you are familiar with than in those you know little or nothing about.

Now and then you will become especially interested in some subject which you have just begun to study. You don't know much about it yet, but you do know enough to give a good, interesting talk to your fellow students who know still less than you do. You might even center your talk about your own curiosity and the things about the subject that have aroused your interest. But there is no inspiration in giving information about a subject on which your listeners have as much information as you have, and possibly more.

There may be a subject you are so familiar with that you do not realize it would be suitable for a good talk or even a series of talks. One student, another coed, incidentally, complained that she could not think of things to talk about. After making several suggestions, the instructor finally said, "If you can't think of anything else, talk about your home town. There is usually something about everyone's home town that is enough different from others to make it good for at least one talk. By the way, what is your home town?" "Natchez," was the unexpected reply. "How long have you lived there?" "All my life; I was born there." "Do you mean to say that you have lived in Natchez all your life and still can't find anything to talk about?"

Another student discovered that, after a series of talks on insects —"bugs"—that were damaging to farm crops, the class was "fed up" on bugs, and he wanted to talk about something else. Athletes sometimes want to center all their speeches on athletic subjects, just as students in other activities want to talk about their special interests. Such individual programs do little to implement the insistence that "broad knowledge" is important to the speaker if he would be fully effective in his own specialty.

We tend, however, to take for granted so many things with which we are familiar that we do not realize that those very things would be highly interesting, even fascinating, to others who are entirely unfamiliar with them. Some flowers, for example, which are found in every back yard in one section of the country may be presented in another part of the country as a token of esteem.

By selecting a subject which is very familiar to you and in which you are also deeply interested, you will have a good beginning toward making that subject interesting to your listeners: moreover, and more importantly, from your present point of view, you will so much enjoy talking about it that you may forget all about excessive tensions, "butterflies" in your stomach, and most if not all of the other symptoms of stage fright.

SUMMARY

By adopting attitudes toward the phenomenon of stage fright like the ones suggested and by following the procedures outlined, you should be able to overcome the effects of any excessive nervousness you may feel at the outset of your speaking experiences. Other procedures may help. Whatever will enable you to put your muscles into moderate action and at the same time contribute to the total impression you are trying to make and to the idea you are trying to bring to the audience should be of some value in helping you to develop ease and poise.

Do not expect to be able to prevent the onset of some nervousness when you approach your hearers; do not even try to get rid of it entirely. If you could succeed in looking upon the task of speaking, of saying worthwhile things to serious audiences or even nonsensical things to audiences that are anticipating mainly pleasant experiences, with no qualms whatever regarding the responsibility you have assumed, you would probably become careless, indifferent, and even dull and uninspiring, and your appearance before your listeners would be no compliment to them.

But if you remain alert, fully aware of your responsibility as a speaker, of the significance of the occasion on which you have been asked to speak, and of the things you speak about, you may find yourself among those elect of whom it will be said, "And the people heard him gladly."

QUESTIONS AND TOPICS FOR STUDY AND REVIEW

1. What seems to be the actual extent of your hypertensions, if any, in relation to speaking or to other public performances? Do these feelings ever appear when there is no "public" to observe your performance?

2. Which of the approaches to the subject discussed in the text seems best to meet your individual problem? To what extent does some understanding of the phenomenon of stage fright help to overcome its effects?

3. What other symptoms than those mentioned in the text have you yourself experienced?

4. A psychiatrist recently said that if one did not have some feelings of nervousness just before speaking, he probably had no business trying to speak at all. What would be your comment on such a statement?

5. Comment on the second statement of Hudson (p. 70) regarding the speaker who disregards the rights of his hearers as an audience.

6. To what specific factor or factors, if any, do you attribute the origin of your own hypertensions?

7. How can you differentiate, if at all, between "nonfear" hypertensions and genuine stage fright? Do both types of bodily reaction yield to similar remedial procedures?

8. Under what conditions may hypertensions be of considerable concern, either for the speaker or for other kinds of public performers?

9. Under what conditions other than public performance do similar excess tensions occur?

10. How can you differentiate between self-confidence and overconfidence?

11. Which is preferable in your own case and why: to recognize your apprehensions freely, or to attempt to minimize them by insisting that they do not exist? Can one be argued out of one's nervousness?

12. To what extent may "inferiority complexes" contribute to stage fright?

13. To what extent do speaking experiences (or other types of public performance) help to lessen the effects of nervousness? Can you answer this question from personal experience?

PROJECTS

1. Write a full description of your emotional and bodily phenomena when contemplating or approaching a speaking occasion and during the speaking itself. What were your feelings upon entering this course?
2. Give a talk citing specific examples of people in public activities other than speaking who have experienced such hypertensions. To what extent could you observe the outward indications of excessive tensions? What was the apparent effect on the performance?
3. Give a talk based on your own experience (which need not have been a speaking experience) in which your nervousness or hypertensions were not intense enough to be designated as stage *fright*.
4. Write out an account of your own actual experiences with stage fright in connection with either speaking or other types of public performance. What symptoms have been especially predominant, and to what extent have they been overcome? What factors contributed most definitely to overcoming or counteracting the excessive nervousness itself?

SUPPLEMENTARY READINGS

Baird, A. Craig, and Franklin H. Knower, *General Speech: An Introduction,* 2nd ed., McGraw-Hill, 1957, chap. 8, "Developing Confidence."

Brigance, William Norwood, *Speech: Its Techniques and Disciplines in a Free Society,* 2nd ed., Appleton-Century-Crofts, 1961, chap. 4, "First Steps in Managing Yourself," especially pp. 67–73.

Brown, Charles T., *Introduction to Speech,* Houghton Mifflin, 1955, chap. 19, "Fear and Confidence."

Bryant, Donald C., and Karl R. Wallace, *Fundamentals of Public Speaking,* 3rd ed., Appleton-Century-Crofts, 1960, chap. 13, "Emotional Problems of the Speaker."

Cicero, Marcus Tullius, *De Oratore,* bk I, chap. XXVI.

Greenleaf, Floyd I., "An Exploratory Study of Stage Fright," *Quarterly Journal of Speech,* October, 1952, **38**: 325–330.

Henrikson, Ernest H., "Some Effects on Stage Fright of a Course in Speech," *Quarterly Journal of Speech,* December, 1943, **29**: 490–498.

Hudson, Hoyt H., "The Knees of Demosthenes," *American Speech,* May, 1927, **2**: 337–340.

Lomas, Charles W., "The Psychology of Stage Fright," *Quarterly Journal of Speech,* February, 1937, **23**: 35–44.

Oliver, Robert T., *New Training for Effective Speech*, 2nd ed., Dryden, 1951, chap. 3, "The Personality of the Speaker."

Reid, Loren, *First Principles of Public Speaking*, Artcraft, 1960, pp. 4–10.

Weaver, Andrew Thomas, and Ordean Gerhard Ness, *The Fundamentals and Forms of Speech,* Odyssey, 1957, chap. 4, "What To Do About Stage Fright."

Winans, James A., *Speech-Making,* Appleton-Century-Crofts, 1938, pp. 40–41.

Woolbert, Charles Henry, *The Fundamentals of Speech*, 2nd ed., Harper, 1927, pp. 74–75, 86, 110; 3rd ed. with Joseph F. Smith, 1934, pp. 97–99.

6

General Principles
of Delivery

Much of the early theory of public speaking centered about the five "arts" which the speaker must master if he would win the highest success: (1) he must have something to say (a requirement that is much more involved than one is likely to think); (2) he must organize his material on that subject into some orderly pattern; (3) he must frame his speech in language that will be clear, vivid, and elegant; (4) he must devise or follow some method by which he can retain in his mind what he has to say until he finishes speaking; and (5) he must deliver his speech to an audience in such a way that what he says will have the maximum effectiveness.

A BRIEF REVIEW

In this body of theory the delivery of the speech was recognized as just as important as any of the other "arts," for it was through his delivery that the speaker brought his ideas to his listeners with the maximum impact. The success of the whole enterprise depended very largely upon how the speech was presented. It was not even a speech until it was delivered to an audience.

DELIVERY AND MEANING

The delivery of a speech, or of speech generally, is important specifically because the meanings, the ideas you want to present to your listeners, are determined as much by the way you use your voice, your body, your hands, your fingers, your facial expression as they are by your choice of words and the way you put them together. By changing your manner of utterance you can completely alter the sense of almost anything you want to say. You can call your best friends by the most scurrilous names if, as Owen Wister's Virginian insisted, you "smile when you say that." Women not infrequently address their bitterest social enemies in the most endearing terms.

When Macbeth and Lady Macbeth argue as to whether they shall proceed with the murder of Duncan, Macbeth raises the question, "If we should fail?" to which Lady Macbeth replies, "We fail! / But screw your courage to the sticking point, / And we'll not fail." Now, there have been many discussions of the specific manner in which Lady Macbeth would say, "We fail!" If spoken one way it means one thing, and the succeeding line will be given one pattern; spoken another way, it means something else, and the pattern of the next sentence will also be different. The whole sense will be altered. Again to quote Burgh, "What we mean, does not so much depend upon the words we speak, as on our manner of speaking them. . . ."[1]

Delivery and Your Meaning

When you speak to an audience, be it large or small, you have in mind certain ideas you want to impart to your listeners. If you were to write these ideas down on paper, you would be limited in

[1] James Burgh, *The Art of Speaking*, 1795 ed., p. 17.

your expression to words alone, plus an occasional underlining for emphasis. True, a great deal can be expressed solely through words and the way they are put together—evidenced by the great mass of literature that has accumulated through the centuries among all literate peoples. But people who read some of that literature aloud often differ sharply on just what the author was trying to say, and different readers give different interpretations—different meanings—to that literature by the different ways in which they read it.

When you write, no reader can possibly know the particular inflections of your voice, the stresses you put on the words, the exact phrasing of the sentences; for if you write meaningfully, you probably write with a great deal of subvocal expression, and perhaps with certain facial expressions as well. If the ideas contain a strong emotional content you may lean a little more heavily on your pen or strike the keys of your typewriter a little more vigorously. All these are lost to the reader, especially if what you wrote is printed, or even if you use an electrical typewriter, for then even the possible effect of your own typewriting touch is gone. Your penmanship, we are told, reveals quite a bit about your personality; but an electric typewriter is quite impersonal, and even the most competent and sympathetic of secretaries can hardly be expected to transfer to the typed page all the shading of meaning you expressed in your dictation.

In other words, your delivery is not a matter of adding something to your language just for the sake of making a good appearance, or of avoiding seeming dull and uninterested in what you are saying. Delivery is an integral part of oral communication. It is your manner of speaking that makes your words fully intelligible; and if you are not at least intelligible your listeners will not know whether you are even intelligent, and what you know will not do so much good. Through delivery you give emphasis to the words and phrases that are especially important in your sentences; through delivery you give your sentences themselves the phrasing that will enable your listeners to follow your development more easily.

Delivery in Relation to Clarity, Vividness, and Impressiveness

Delivery helps to make language clearer by making meanings more complete and specific. It contributes to vividness by helping to arouse more vivid imagery, and it aids impressiveness by revealing the speaker's attitudes and feelings about the matter under discussion.[2]

Two Aspects of Delivery

Speech in its completeness consists of a dual system of symbols, those which we hear and those which we see. The former may, on superficial consideration, be the more obvious, but, as Woolbert said, a speaker "is a thing to be seen, shown to the sight, a being of action to be noted and read through the eye."[3]

The audible system or code—the first of the two aspects of delivery just mentioned—includes both the words we use and their manner of utterance. These are the subject matter of more extended development in later chapters.

The visible system or code of symbols consists of all that we see the speaker doing that in any way contributes to or detracts from the communication of the ideas he is trying to convey to us. This visible code is important, too, and we shall give it much attention. The entire final chapter of this text is devoted to its discussion.

Delivery in Speech Is Inescapable

In speech, meanings are conveyed (so long as we understand what we mean by that expression) not by language *and* delivery, but by *delivered language*. By reinforcing meanings and making them more specific, delivery is as much a part of the total language pattern as are the words themselves. Do not be misled into thinking that if you do nothing—as you think—by way of visible action, you thereby eliminate the factor of delivery entirely, for even making no observable movements at all is in itself a mode of delivery; furthermore, you cannot avoid the effects produced by your voice, for although you speak in a monotone, you are still using a definite manner of vocal utterance—in this case one that is particularly ineffective. If, moreover, you make no attempt to empha-

[2] See Giles Wilkeson Gray, "Problems in the Teaching of Gesture," *Quarterly Journal of Speech*, June, 1924, **10**: 238–252.

[3] Charles Henry Woolbert, *The Fundamentals of Speech*, 2nd ed., Harper, 1927, p. 5.

size significant words or phrases, your delivery will stand in the way of your saying what you intend to say. If you rush on without pausing or logical phrasing, your delivery will be a bar to your listeners' getting even the sense of your speech.

If you speak at all, then, you cannot avoid the element of delivery. The question remains one of the degree to which your manner of presentation contributes to or detracts from your intended meanings—that is, reinforces or negates the ideas which you intend your words to convey. Delivery in itself has little or no significance in the public speaking situation, though we can and often do arouse meanings by our actions and by our more or less inarticulate vocalizations. Occasionally, too, one may need to use some pantomime for some special effect. The principal if not the only function of delivery is to contribute to the processes of bringing the idea, thought, or content from the speaker to the listener. It is in relation to that function that it is to be studied here.

DELIVERY IS CHARACTERIZED BY A
FEW BASIC ATTRIBUTES

Effective Delivery Helps Establish Rapport
Between Speaker and Audience

To be fully effective you must establish with your listeners what has been termed *rapport*. Oliver has explained the concept as follows:

There must be a bond of sympathy uniting a great speaker and his audience. There ought to be a current of warm and cordial understanding which flows both ways. For a genuine communication, the speaker and his auditors should become almost one unit. They may not always agree with him, but they should be stirred by his feelings, and he should respond quickly and accurately to theirs. This, I take it, is the general meaning of the term *rapport*. A speaker without *rapport* may be clear, fluent, intellectual—even convincing—but he cannot be great. To arouse his auditors, a bond of strong feeling must unite the speaker with them.[4]

[4] Robert T. Oliver, "Wilson's *Rapport* with His Audience," *Quarterly Journal of Speech*, February, 1941, 27: 79–90. Oliver's description recalls somewhat Woolbert's analysis of "polarization," written in 1916 (Charles Henry Woolbert, "The Audience," *Psychological Monographs*, 1916, 21: 37–54).

This *rapport* with the audience, this "bond of sympathy," this "current of warm and cordial understanding," is largely the result of an effective delivery, which in turn is based, first, on the speaker's own (initial) attitude toward the audience, and second, on the "urge to communicate" with them. Unless such a speaker-listener relationship is established—and the speaker's manner of delivery will have much to do with it—one might with justification insist that he will never quite reach the highest level of effectiveness with his audience.

This "bond of sympathy," this *rapport*, is indeed one of the primary factors in the difference between speaking and writing as modes of communication, namely, that *because* spoken language is delivered in a face-to-face situation, it is possible to create that strong bond of sympathy between speaker and audience. It is the factor of delivery that makes the difference.

Effective Delivery Does Not Attract Attention to Itself

As we have said, the primary if not the whole objective in a speaking situation is to bring an idea and an audience together. Whatever in the process distracts the listeners' attention away from the idea makes the basic process of speaking that much less effective. Only in rare instances is good speech exhibitory; seldom should one want to impress his hearers with the excellence of his speaking technique.

The good speaker with an idea to communicate and the urge to impart that idea has no desire to place himself on exhibition. Exhibitionism and communicativeness are mutually antagonistic. If you want to put on a show—and this effort may be entirely legitimate—don't try at the same time to say anything worth while. If you want to communicate an idea, don't do anything to direct attention to any phase of your delivery, for this will erect a barrier which will interfere with the process. What your audience sees, no less than what it hears, must contribute to the meanings you are trying to arouse.

At the same time, bear in mind that delivery includes what the audience may hear as well as see. Your use of language and voice must therefore also be limited to what they can contribute to those meanings. However, this requirement puts little restriction on your use of the voice. It merely means that you should not use such elements as flexibility, with its rises and falls of pitch, or accents, stresses, and emphases primarily to show that you have a flexible voice of especially good quality.

Ancient Greek audiences, we are told, were accustomed to applaud an exceptionally clever turn of phrase, a particularly apt figure of speech, or an unusually well-worded passage of praise or invective. So much were these bits of rhetorical adornment praised that many of them were used over and over. Such repetition was not uncommon within relatively recent times. For example, a well-known senator from one of the Midwestern states rarely gave a public speech, especially of a ceremonial nature, without including somewhere in it his famous description of a sunset. People would come repeatedly to listen to him, not because he had anything of great importance to say, but hoping that they would get to hear again his description of the sunset. And Henry W. Grady used identical passages from his "Homes of the People" on more than one occasion, with different subjects.

Repetition may be acceptable for ceremonial speaking, but it is hardly in place in either the informative or the persuasive kind of public utterance. On the other hand, as will be shown in Chapter 27, repetition can be used very effectively in achieving impressiveness.

Effective Delivery Is Consistent with the Total Speaking Situation

The speaking situation includes the occasion, the audience, the physical surroundings, the subject, and the speaker himself, together with such further factors as events of the immediate past. Some situations permit a strong, vigorous, even vehement delivery; others demand a restrained, quiet, reserved manner. A gentle, well-loved member of the community died a few years ago, and a large number of his friends came to the funeral to pay their last respects. The funeral sermon was delivered in such a vehement manner that one would have thought the minister was calling upon those present to recant their transgressions lest they be cast into outer darkness—as, indeed, he was!

Some subjects do not lend themselves to vigorous tones and strong gestures. People generally accustomed to making fine distinctions, to sedentary occupations and intellectual pursuits, do not ordinarily like to be stirred too deeply by overdynamic speaking. Learn to gauge your situation; determine as many aspects as you can, and let your delivery be governed by those factors.

Effective Delivery Makes Full Use of the Principle of Variety

No one likes to hear a speaker who within a few sentences is shouting at the top of his voice and who maintains that loudness throughout his speech; he soon loses his effectiveness. For the same reason listeners do not like to see a speaker use the same gestures over and over, trace and retrace the same path in his movements about the platform, or follow any other persistent pattern in his manner of presentation.

In practicing delivery, then, work for variety for two reasons: first, it makes you much less tiresome to listen to and to look at; second, just as the ideas themselves and the words you use to express those ideas change from moment to moment, so also should the delivery vary in keeping with the changing thought. In other words, maintain your constant pattern of delivery *only* if you keep repeating the same idea in the same language over and over again. And that is likely in a very short time to become extremely monotonous.

Effective Delivery Is Animated and Alert

Effective speaking is characterized by an alertness and an animation that grow out of the speaker's attitude toward the total situation. They are revealed in the general tonus of the body, alert bearing, flexible voice, expressive face and eyes, clear and distinct utterance, and variety in total delivery pattern that add significantly to the content of the speech itself.

Such animation develops out of the speaker's attitude, which should be one of liveliness or keen interest in both the subject matter of his speech and his own talking about it. Closely related to this attitude is what has been referred to repeatedly as the "urge to communicate," which is in itself an emotional attitude.

To the audience, animation as a rule denotes sincerity and honesty of purpose, though many a speaker has attempted to compensate by an excess of animation for shallow content or questionable ethics.

The story is told of a minister who was in the habit of making nota-
tions in the margins of the notebook in which he wrote out his sermons, describing the appropriate manner of delivery. At various
points he would write, "Rising inflection here," "Emphasize strongly,"
"Pause here for the effect," and so on. But on one page he penned in
the margin, "Weak point; yell like blazes!" (This story, we might add
goes back to the sixteenth century.)

It is possible, of course, to overdo the matter of liveliness, but the
beginning speaker is much more likely to underdo, to use far too
little activity, rather than too much. Whether you use much or little,
your delivery must be purposeful, not random; communicative, not
exhibitory. More important, it must be in keeping with the total
speaking situation, as has been explained.

Effective Delivery Is Simple, Unaffected, "Natural"

The belief is held by many that all the speaker has to do to ensure
an effective delivery is to "be natural," and that the delivery will
somehow take care of itself. This is much the same as the idea that
if one has his thought well in mind he is sure to have an effective
presentation.

As a measure of delivery, however, *naturalness* is a misleading concept. What is often called *natural* is likely to be nothing more than
what is *habitual*. You are so accustomed to doing a certain thing a
certain way—tying your shoe, for example—that that way feels perfectly natural and any other way is awkward. Any habit feels natural,
because it is performed almost automatically, outside the focus of
consciousness. But any new habit which is built up to replace an old
one comes to feel just as natural as the old when it too can be performed.

Whenever you want to relearn any activity which you have been
performing for some time in order to perform more skillfully and
effectively, you must replace a number of old, ineffective habits by a
number of new, more effective ones. Anyone who has ever attempted
to learn to play golf under a good instructor, after having played for
a number of years, will attest to the validity of that statement.

To say, then, that you should "be natural" is usually to say no more
than "do the thing as you habitually do it." The "natural" in speech
may or may not be effective, depending on how effective your early

habits of speech have been. You acquired those habits slowly and over a considerable period of time; most of them you learned years ago by imitating models which in many instances were none too good. This is one case in which practice has not made perfect; all it has done has been to fix habits, many of them bad. As a result, your "natural" mode of speaking is in all probability characterized by many ineffective habits.

What needs to be done is obviously, as has been said, to replace as many of these habits as possible with more effective modes of speaking, and to practice on the new modes until they in turn become habits and hence are just as "natural" as the ones they replace.

There is one sense, however, in which "naturalness" can be recommended. This more usable interpretation of the term is analyzed by Woolbert as follows:

1. Be unaffected; use a minimum of display; show off only enough to reveal power; make the exhibitory factors of speaking thoroughly secondary.
2. Be normally vigorous; speak as you do when you are in earnest anywhere, earnest enough to convince people that you mean what you say.
3. Seem to be at home; speak as you speak freely among those you know and trust. Be unconstrained and as free from nervousness as among your own people.
4. Be at your best; eliminate awkwardness, dullness, and inefficiency. Be what you believe your most interesting self to be.
5. Be free from stiffness, equally tight or loose all over; not stiff in the neck and limp in the knees or stiff in the knees and limp in the neck.
6. Be simple; beware of undue exaggeration. Don't be highflown, pompous, puffed up.
7. Be forthright; connect straightaway with your hearers. Count yourself one of them.
8. Be communicative; cultivate what has been called "a lively sense of communication."[5]

Effective Delivery Is Free from Excessive Tensions

As we have said, a certain degree of what is called tonus is essential to lively, interested speaking, as it is to all life itself. No one enjoys listening to a speaker who lounges over the lectern or reading

[5] Woolbert, *The Fundamentals of Speech*, p. 23.

stand or slouches on the corner of the desk. Neither do we like to listen to speech that is carelessly uttered or mumbled so badly that it is indistinct or even unintelligible. Such speech is generally the product of a general lassitude, an overrelaxation that neither indicates interest on the part of the speaker nor arouses interest on the part of the listeners.

At the opposite extreme, neither do we like to watch or listen to a speaker whose whole manner is characterized by extreme tensions. Because we tend to follow, to imitate unconsciously the behavior of those we are observing, such a speaker becomes very wearisome to his audience. This phenomenon of excessive tensions, as described here, is not identical with stage fright, which was discussed at some length in the preceding chapter. It arises not from fear of adverse criticism or apprehension with respect to one's own capabilities, but from an eagerness to say what one has to say, from the normal excitement resulting from the occasion itself, which goes beyond the customary tonus necessary in any effective behavior. It resembles stage fright only slightly, "as the mist resembles the rain."

Such tensions are not peculiar to public speaking or acting or interpretative reading. Musicians and music teachers assure us that it occurs in musical performances, even when the conditions which might cause stage fright are not present. Golfers recognize a difference between the feelings of nervousness that occur just before teeing off in an important match and those which accompany a practice drive, when there is no gallery present and nothing is at stake in the game. The excess tensions that occur on such occasions are often designated as "pressing."

Baseball players, in their eagerness to make a quick play or to hit the ball out of the park for a home run; football players, anxious to catch that pitchout for a long run and a touchdown or to drive into the line to check an opposing ball carrier; trackmen, eager to get off the starting blocks with the crack of the pistol—all these at one time or another may be affected by excess tensions to such a degree that they pop to the infield or strike out, or jump offside, or are penalized for jumping the gun.

Automobile drivers may occasionally be seen going down the highway at the terrific speed of thirty miles an hour while they fiercely grip the steering wheel as if they expected it to tear itself out of their hands. To such hypertensions as these tranquilizers are no solution.

When such hypertensions are experienced by the speaker, they operate against the maximum ease and flexibility of thought, voice, and action. They tend to produce stiffness, awkwardness, tightness in the throat, and inability to move about or to use bodily action that contributes to the total communicative process. What is needed is just enough muscular tonus to give you animation, alertness, the appearance of interest in your subject and in telling your listeners about it. The graceful speaker, according to Woolbert, is one who combines economy of motion—using just enough to produce the desired effect —with an adequate display of strength.[6] Tranquilizers in such cases may not only reduce the hypertensions, but even prevent the needed tonus for effective speaking.

Concentration on what you have to say, on the audience to whom you are saying it, and on your own mission in bringing the two factors together will go a long way toward relieving these tensions and achieving an effective balance between tonus and relaxation—that is, between strength and economy of action. Experiences in speaking and continuous efforts at relaxation will tend to dispel them.

SUMMARY

Delivery, then, is highly important in speaking because it helps arouse the desired meanings in the minds of the audience. It is characterized by a few basic attributes:

1. Effective delivery aids in establishing *rapport* between the speaker and his audience.
2. Effective delivery does not attract attention to itself.
3. Effective delivery is consistent with the total speaking situation.
4. Effective delivery makes full use of the principle of variety.
5. Effective delivery is animated and alert.
6. Effective delivery is simple, unaffected, "natural."
7. Effective delivery is free from excessive tensions.

QUESTIONS AND TOPICS FOR STUDY AND REVIEW

1. It has been said that one's delivery is an aspect of one's speaking "style," in much the same way as is his use of language. Comment on this statement.

[6] *Ibid.*, pp. 79 ff.

2. Explain how and why the delivery of one's speeches will vary with the subject, the occasion, and the audience.
3. George Bernard Shaw once said, "There are fifty ways of saying Yes, and five hundred of saying No, but only one way of writing them down." Illustrate vocally some of the different ways of saying each of these two words.
4. What are some of the attributes of the voice that affect the meanings of the words we speak?
5. It has long been argued that the diaphragmatic or abdominal type of breathing is the most effective type for voice production in speech and singing. What is the evidence for or against such a theory?
6. Can there be any value to practicing such techniques as voice flexibility—various inflectional patterns, stress patterns, and the like—apart from ideational content? Might such practice be comparable in any way with "shadow boxing"?
7. If it is true that effective delivery does not attract attention to itself, then why is delivery important at all? Does one's *language* usually call attention to itself?
8. Point out some essential differences between speaking and writing as media of communication.
9. What skills have you had to relearn after you had practiced them for some time? To what degree have the new ways of doing those things come to feel "natural"?
10. Read aloud two selections of verse, expressive of widely differing emotions. Study to make your voice expressive of the emotion suggested by the words of each selection.
11. Years ago a writer on language made the statement that "Language implies identities to which nature conforms not. . . Language unites under one name, as identities, what is only partially identical."[7] What is the writer trying to say, and how can the resulting confusion be at least partially resolved?

[7] A. B. Johnson, *A Treatise on Language; or the Relation Which Words Bear to Things,* Harper, 1836, p. 66.

PROJECTS

1. Describe by *pantomime only* some event or process: tell a story, play one hole of a golf game, shine your shoes, make a cake, get breakfast (as in the play "Our Town"), etc.
2. Characterize some type of person by your walk, your posture, your voice, or other verbal and nonverbal characterization (other than simple language).
3. Give the statement, "I'll get you for that," in the following ways:

    a. Playfully, as to someone who has played a light joke on you.

    b. Mildly reprimandingly, as to a teasing child.

    c. Threateningly, as to someone who has done you an irreparable injury.

4. Give a talk on some subject that touches the everyday affairs of your listeners. Get as close to the front row as you conveniently can, and try to get a direct reaction from the audience. You may address specific questions to individual members, asking for additional information, for verification, for opinion, etc. Establish as high a degree of *rapport* through your manner of presentation as you can.

5. In as near studio conditions as possible, give a talk into the microphone and record it. Make sure you have no audience. Do not listen to it. Later, give the same speech in class and at the same time record it again. Now listen to both presentations. What differences do you observe? To what may these differences be ascribed?

6. Compare the speaking of two members of your class, with particular reference to manner of delivery.

7. After one of your speeches write a description of the reactions of different members of your audience. What evidence did you have that you had maintained their interest and attention? Be specific in your descriptions; what did your hearers actually *do* that led you to think that you had (or did not have) their attention, or had (or had not) aroused their interest?

8. What principles of delivery might be applied to the reactions of the audience?

9. Write out a speech of about 750 words. Revise, refine, rewrite, and polish the language as much as you can. Lay the manuscript aside and do not look at it again for the time being. Later in the course you will give the same speech extemporaneously, without referring to your manuscript, but recording the speech. At that time you are to listen to the recorded speech, with the manuscript in your hands, following the latter as you listen to the former, and make notes on the differences you perceive.

SUPPLEMENTARY READINGS

Bryant, Donald C., and Karl R. Wallace, *Fundamentals of Public Speaking*, 3rd ed., Appleton-Century-Crofts, 1960, chap. 11, "Intellectual and Communicative Aspects of Delivery"; chap. 12, "Delivery: Methods of Development."

Gray, Giles Wilkeson, "Problems in the Teaching of Gesture," *Quarterly Journal of Speech*, June, 1924, **10:** 238–252.

Monroe, Alan H., *Principles and Types of Speech*, 4th ed., Scott, Foresman, 1955, Part 2. "Basic Principles of Delivery." Contains four chapters on different aspects of delivery.

Oliver, Robert T., Dallas C. Dickey, and Harold P. Zelko, *Communicative Speech*, rev. ed., Dryden, 1955, pp. 41–62.

Parrish, W. M., "The Concept of 'Naturalness,'" *Quarterly Journal of Speech*, December, 1951, **37**: 448–454.

Quintilian, *Institutes of Oratory*, bk. XI, chap. 3, "Concerning the Best Manner of Delivering a Pleading or Discourse."

Thonssen, Lester, and A. Craig Baird, *Speech Criticism*, Ronald, 1948, chap. 16, "The Delivery of a Speech."

White, Eugene E., and Clair R. Henderlider, *Practical Public Speaking*, Macmillan, 1954, chap. 9, "An Introduction to Delivery."

Winans, James A., *Speech-Making*, Appleton-Century-Crofts, 1938, chap. 2, "Conversing with an Audience"; chap. 20, "Further Study of Delivery."

7

Listening

Throughout this text most of the discussion is concerned with the speaker's problems. From the emphasis on these problems one might easily infer that the sole responsibility for the success of the speaking performance rests on his shoulders, and that any breakdowns in the process of communicating his ideas to his audiences arise from his own ineptitude.

Obviously the speaker does bear a heavy responsibility when he attempts to influence the thoughts, the feelings, or the actions of his listeners, for he is the initiator of the communication. If he himself is entirely unskilled, or indifferent, or seemingly antagonistic toward his hearers, his speaking is not likely to have much effect on them; at least it will not have the effect he appears to desire. Or if he raises any other barriers to the free flow of ideas or makes those ideas unpalatable to a high degree, he can hardly blame his audience for their failure either to hear him willingly or to accept what he has to say. Undoubtedly the speaker does have a responsibility that he cannot throw off on anyone else.

On the other hand, it is too much to ask the speaker to carry the whole burden for the success of the communicative process, just as the writer is not wholly at fault if some of his readers do not understand or believe what he has written. For communication, including speaking, and particularly public speaking—for that is what we are now interested in—is a two-way process in which the listening is no less important than the speaking itself. No matter how effective the speaker or how favorable the speaking conditions, a great deal of the effectiveness of the total communication must depend on the responses of the receiver, the listening audience—on their receptivity to the stimuli that are reaching them from the speaker. No speaker can possibly influence as he desires a group of listeners who cannot or will not listen to him.

Research has shown that of the four basic skills involved in interpersonal communication—reading, writing, speaking, and listening—we spend more time in the last, listening, than in any of the other three. According to Rankin, adults spend 70 percent of their waking hours in some sort of verbal communication. Of this time, 9 percent is spent in writing, 16 percent in reading, 30 percent in speaking, and 45 percent in listening.[1] That is, we spend three times as much time in listening as we do in reading, and five times as much as we do in writing. We devote 50 percent more time to listening than we do to speaking. It is possible, of course, that the growth of television has increased the percentage of time spent in listening—and viewing. Unfortunately, however, much less attention is paid in our educational program to listening than to any of the other aspects of verbal communication.

One result is that people of all ages experience difficulties of one kind or another in listening. Wiksell reported some time ago that "Thirty percent of 1335 college graduates, 39 percent of 703 high

---

[1] Paul Tory Rankin, "The Measurement of the Ability To Understand Spoken Language," doctoral dissertation, University of Michigan, 1926, University Microfilms, 1952, Pub. No. 4352; cited by Ralph G. Nichols and Leonard A. Stevens, *Are You Listening?* McGraw-Hill, 1957, p. 6.

school graduates, and 34 percent of 577 grammar school graduates reported difficulties in listening in interviews and conferences." Twenty-four percent of the college graduates were reported as also having difficulties in listening to addresses.[2]

Nichols and Stevens report one man who discovered that his employer "was paying him 35 to 40 percent of his salary for listening on the telephone, to say nothing about listening in other situations."[3] They also cite a study made by the Survey Research Center of the University of Michigan in which it was found that only 27 percent of political information in the 1952 elections was derived from newspapers and magazines, while 58 percent, or more than twice as much, came from radio and television.[4]

It seems obvious, then, that first, we spend much more of our time in listening than we are likely to realize, and second, a large number of people, judging from their own reported difficulties, do not seem to be very proficient listeners.

THE OBJECTIVES IN LISTENING

The reasons for attending speaking occasions—occasions on which some form of speaking is a significant aspect of the situation—are many and varied. A group of persons does not congregate or remain assembled as a rule by mere chance or accident. Now and then someone will drift into a meeting for no other reason than that a group is assembled, and he is interested both in just being a member of the crowd, however tenuous the association may be, and because he is curious to know what is going on and what is being talked about.

But the essential characteristic of an audience is, as the term itself implies, that it is composed of people who have come to *listen*, and possibly to participate. "The motives which may lead people to assemble are essentially the same as those which impel to any other type of behavior."[5] But in order to satisfy those motives they must listen to what is being said.

[2] Wesley Wiksell, "The Problem of Listening," *Quarterly Journal of Speech*, December, 1946, **32**: 505–508.

[3] Nichols and Stevens, *op. cit.*, p. 7.

[4] *Ibid.*, p. 8.

[5] Giles Wilkeson Gray and Claude Merton Wise, *The Bases of Speech*, 3rd ed., Harper, 1959, p. 395.

Information

One of the basic reasons for listening in a speaking situation is to acquire information or understanding. Whether the occasion is a lecture, a discussion of one type or another, or a debate on some controversial subject, we attend in order to be informed, to have facts presented and interpreted by a speaker (or group of speakers) who has made a study of the problem and presents those facts with his own inferences in a condensed, organized, intelligible manner. To assemble and analyze all that information ourselves would be a monumental task that would leave no time for anything else.[6] We are motivated to listen, then, by either simple curiosity or the need for information that will enable us to chart our own course more intelligently. The knowledge itself satisfies our desire to know, whether or not we intend or expect to use it in any practical way.

Listening to obtain information applies as well in conversation as in lectures and discussions. My day lilies, for example, have what looks like a type of petal blight. I want to find out whether petal blight is actually there and what I can do about it, if anything. Therefore I go to my friend the plant pathologist to get information on the subject, and we engage in a rather extended conversation about the causes, symptoms, and remedy for petal blight on day lilies, or whatever it is that is affecting them, and try to arrive at some determination of the actual malady and the remedy therefor. But in order for the conversation to do me or the plants any good, *I have to listen.*

Participation in Group Activities

A second objective of listening is to enable us to engage more intelligently in the speaking activities of the various groups in which we may be active. In a society like ours such participation is an obligation as well as a privilege if we are to have any practical value as members. Effective social organization demands that every member have the opportunity of exercising that privilege *and* that obligation. Exchange of opinion and information is essential, but no exchange can take place unless each member is willing to listen to

[6] Nichols and Stevens, *op. cit.,* p. 19.

what other members have to say. There can be no effective pooling of experience, wisdom, and attitudes among the members of a society unless and until all those who have something to contribute have had a chance to be heard—until they have been listened to, in other words. You cannot know what the other person is thinking if you will not listen to what he has to say. Nor can you make your own argument on a given proposition effective if you do not know what arguments have been put forth on the other side. You cannot fit your own ideas and opinions and information into the total corpus of idea, opinion, and information that is already before the group unless and until you have heard that information and those ideas and opinions expressed; and to hear you must listen.

In short, you cannot be a good participant in group speaking activities if you are not a good listener.

Appraisal

The study of public speaking, with its emphasis on principles as well as practice, should give one a basis for evaluating the speeches he hears. There is a vast amount of speaking now going on in every medium of transmission, most if not all of which is available to the speaker—and to the listener. This ranges from the radio and television commercial to scholarly lectures and well-developed analyses of current happenings. Some of it is presented by authorities in their respective fields, and some of it by ill-trained announcers who are simply given the script of a radio or television commercial to read. One hears some pretty horrendous reading!

Whether they are commercials or supposed newscasts, some of these renditions are so manifestly absurd that we listen to them mainly to laugh. Others are blatant propaganda so obvious that few intelligent people would be taken in by them, or so one would think. Still others are sound analyses or authoritative, careful reporting that will stand the tests of objectivity.

In order to be able to sift these out so the chaff can be discarded and the solid grain retained, we need to be able to listen carefully. Much that is misleading, confusing, and even pernicious can be so dressed up that the fallacies, the half-truths, even the egregious untruths are difficult to recognize unless we are listening critically.

It is here, as well as in the preparation of one's own speeches, that the broad knowledge discussed in Chapter 4 finds one of its most important values; for one of the best ways of detecting these gross though often subtle fallacies is to have a good command of the facts involved and of the principles of sound reasoning.

Faulty reasoning can be very cleverly concealed, so-called facts easily distorted, and unsound premises advanced, either deliberately or through ignorance, so that one who listens only casually or by just catching a phrase now and then cannot get the full import of the argument presented.

We form our judgments and opinions from the evaluations we make of what we read and what we listen to. In order that these judgments and opinions be valid and defensible, we must listen objectively and critically to the information we hear and be attentive to the inferences we draw and that are drawn for us.

Beighley suggests that "A people trained to listen with comprehension will not, perhaps, be misled by the specious promises of a demagogue."[7]

Another possible value emanating from the evaluation of the speeches we hear is that our own shortcomings may be and often are pointed up to us. When we become keenly aware of the errors that others make, we may be just a little more inclined to listen to ourselves to see whether we might be making the same or even worse mistakes. Listening to ourselves is just as important as listening to others.

Stimulation

All of us need now and then a renewal of faith, a revival of attitudes, an inspiration to intensify and accelerate our well-doing. We attend the services of the church of our choice, participate in the congregational singing of the hymns, engage in the responses in the liturgy, and listen to the sermons. We don't listen in order to gain information, although sometimes we do learn something new. We do not seek to have our beliefs or courses of action changed or reversed; we are already in agreement with the minister's point of view and

[7] K. C. Beighley, "An Experimental Study of the Effect of Four Speech Variables on Listener Comprehension," *Speech Monographs,* November, 1952, **19:** 249–258.

what he is trying to do. We listen to be stimulated, to have our attitudes verified and revivified.

We go to lectures on current topics of the day, often for the same purpose. We agree with the lecturer's political or economic or social point of view; but we listen, again, to have our own beliefs supported, strengthened, and verified.

Whether we want to agree or not, the fact is that ritual plays an important part in fixing attitudes and beliefs. Lodge members will go through the same formulas night after night and year after year, listening attentively to the same rites over and over; we rise to our feet when the flag passes before us, and salute when the national anthem is played.

These things we listen to for their value in stimulating attitudes which we generally agree are rather more wholesome than otherwise. They reinforce something of a sense of dedication which is one of the cementing factors in society itself.

Appreciation

Closely allied to stimulation and perhaps identical with it to some extent is the element of appreciation. Now, the art of reading aloud is millennia old. It was engaged in by the ancient rhapsodists, the medieval minstrels and bards, actors in the Miracle and Morality plays, and such famous modern readers as Charles Dickens, Fanny Kemble, Ruth Draper, Cornelia Otis Skinner, Charles Laughton, and Emlyn Williams. People went to hear them in earlier days; they still go to hear them in modern times. They go partly for entertainment, but partly also to gain an appreciation of language set down in beautiful form, as well as of the literature in all its values—for much if not most of literature appeals to the ear even more than to the eye. It was said of S. H. Clark, one of the most admired readers in the late nineteenth and early twentieth centuries, that "he made a significant contribution to the restoration of interpretation as an artistic performance. . . . [He] acted as an example of what sincerity and simplicity of presentation can do to make spoken literature a thing of beauty and pleasure."[8]

[8] Lucile May Current, "A Study of Solomon Henry Clark as a Teacher of Interpretation," unpublished master's thesis, Northwestern University, 1938, p. 112.

Good reading is not the only thing that people will listen to primarily for appreciation; they will also listen to good music, good drama, to many things that have aesthetic value. The sale of recorded readings of good literature by accomplished readers is presently very much on the increase. One record publishing house was reported as early as 1957 to have sold 125,000 copies of Dylan Thomas's recordings. Libraries have found that oral storytelling, particularly to children, develops an interest in the literature itself among the listeners, so that they want to read the stories for themselves. "When children hear stories, their literary appetites are whetted and they return to read."[9]

THE LISTENER AND THE SPEAKER

People do not as a rule attend an occasion of speaking because of the effect their presence will have on the speaker, although it is true that we do now and then attend in order to give encouragement, especially to a young, inexperienced speaker. We go also to an amateur play or other performance so that the young actors or artists will know there are a few friendly and sympathetic listeners in the audience.

But speaking is a two-way process; the listeners are influencing the speaker quite as much and as truly as the speaker is influencing them. Any speaker, just as any musician or actor, likes a good responsive audience. Agreement or acquiescence is not necessarily a factor, but one likes to realize that one is being listened to. Actors are generally very sensitive to differences in audiences and their responses at different performances. They invariably give a better performance when they sense that the people beyond the footlights are keenly appreciative of what is taking place on the stage.

Unfavorable Types of Audience Reaction

Members of the audience sometimes do various things that may be highly disconcerting to the speaker. For one thing, they can withhold attention and divert it quite obviously to other things. Students in speech classes often use the time when their fellow students are speaking before the class to prepare for the next hour's assignment.

[9] Nichols and Stevens, *op. cit.*, pp. 24 ff.

They read texts for other courses, work mathematics problems, write on assigned papers—sometimes they even write personal letters or read the student newspaper. Of course, the instructor may be largely at fault in such instances for permitting these distracting activities to go on at all. Even the practice of "doodling" is likely to disturb the speaker.

Members of the audience sometimes show by the expressions on their faces that they are totally uninterested in the subject of the presentation. They give every indication that their thoughts are far away, that they are scarcely aware that the speaker is talking at all. Their eyes are directed out the window, at something that has been left on the blackboard, or at the ceiling or floor, and they seldom if ever glance at the speaker.

Shuffling feet often indicates an impatience to be up and away; wiggling suggests restlessness, and slouching in one's chair usually exhibits complete lack of responsiveness.

In short, the potential listener does nothing to indicate to the speaker that he is listening, or even that he is enough interested to give the appearance of trying to listen. It might be better if he were permitted simply to get up and remove himself from the situation. At least he would not then be interfering with those who are trying to hear what is being said.

Favorable Types of Audience Reaction

A number of things that you as a listener can do will not only be a stimulation and an encouragement to the speaker, enabling him to derive the maximum benefits from your responses, but at the same time will permit you yourself to benefit greatly by effective listening.

For one thing, you can look at the speaker. It is hardly necessary, though, to fix your gaze on him and hold it there throughout, with no deviation or relaxation. It should not be distracting for you to give evidence occasionally that some point has struck home and you want to take a moment or two to consider it; so you turn your eyes away from the speaker for that time in order that your own thoughts will not be disturbed. Generally, however, you will profit most by keeping your eyes on the speaker, and the speaker in turn will know that he is being heard.

Another thing you can do is to come to the meeting on time, so that your arriving and finding a seat will not be distracting and bothersome to either the speaker or the listeners already there. Plan to sit well down in front, where interruptions from others coming in will not be so great, and where you will feel in closer *rapport* with the speaker. If the opportunity is offered, be prepared to ask intelligent questions.

Facial expressions, other than the direction of your gaze, can also inform the speaker that he is being both heard and understood. They can similarly suggest that the point just made might bear clarification, further justification, support with examples, or other amplification for fuller understanding.

Positive avoidance of things which are distracting or even discouraging to the speaker will help him give his full attention and effort to the process of communicating what he has to say to you and the rest of the audience who are there for the serious purpose of listening.

Listening is an active process. We do not merely sit back and let the waves of sound and light from the speaker wash over us and the other presumed listeners so that the energy is absorbed and somehow transformed into meaningful content. It is something we do rather than something we permit to happen to us. The ability to listen effectively is not innate; we have to learn to listen just as much as we have to learn to speak, although our earliest meaningful experiences in verbal communication are in the capacity of listener.[10]

FACTORS IN LISTENING COMPREHENSION

It may be assumed that a basic purpose in listening is comprehension of the material heard. Other objectives are important, but for the most part they are dependent, to some degree at least, on initial understanding. Nichols investigated the factors in listening comprehension, and concluded that

. . . the following factors influenced the listening comprehension of the students who served as subjects in the study:

  Intelligence
  Reading comprehension
  Recognition of correct English usage
  Size of the listener's vocabulary

[10] See Gray and Wise, *op. cit.*, pp. 476 f.

Ability to make inferences

Ability to structuralize a speech

(That is, to see the organizational plan and the connection of the main points.)

Listening to main ideas as opposed to specific facts

Use of special techniques while listening to improve concentration

Real interest in the subject discussed

Emotional adjustment to the speaker's thesis

Ability to see significance in the subject discussed

Curiosity about the subject discussed

Physical fatigue of the listener

Audibility of the speaker.[11]

Other factors possibly having some influence on listening comprehension included speaker effectiveness, admiration for the speaker, susceptibility to distraction, parental occupation, room ventilation and temperature, high-school scholastic achievement, high-school speech training, and experience in listening to difficult expository material.

Few if any of these factors relate specifically to the listening process itself, but rather to the conditions that may be more or less conducive to effective listening. Though many of these conditions are obviously entirely external to the listener himself, they probably do influence the effectiveness of the listening process.

But any improvement in conditions which are conducive to good listening may be worth the undertaking. Some of them indicate specific directions in which listening itself may be improved, or in which improved conditions may contribute to better listening.

IMPROVEMENT IN LISTENING COMPREHENSION

Improvement in listening ability will be found to involve much more than simply saying to yourself, lo, from now on I will listen more carefully and effectively than I have been doing. The whole process of listening has not yet been adequately analyzed or defined; it is thought to consist of a number of skills rather than a single skill, but just what these specific skills are we do not yet know. The fourteen factors Nichols found to influence listening comprehension

[11] Ralph G. Nichols, "Factors in Listening Comprehension," *Speech Monographs*, 1948, **15**: 154–163.

have already been listed. The ten "components of effective listening" are somewhat different. These components are as follows:

1. Previous experience with difficult material
2. Interest in the topic at hand
3. Adjustment to the speaker
4. Energy expenditure of the speaker
5. Adjustment to the abnormal speaking situation
6. Adjustment to emotion-laden words
7. Adjustment to emotion-rousing points
8. Recognition of central ideas
9. Utilization of notes
10. Reconciliation of thought speed and speech speed[12]

Perhaps from these lists we may suggest some of the directions which improvement in listening might take, and what you yourself may be able to do to improve your own listening habits. Some of these you can start on right away, and you might notice some improvement in a relatively short time. Others will require extended work over a considerable time. The question of whether listening can be taught is perhaps less important than the question of whether it can be learned.

Develop Broad Interests in Many Areas of Thought

Whether you are going to use information from many subjects or not, some of them are worth knowing about by anyone whose education is well-rounded. They are a part of that general preparation which was discussed at some length in Chapter 4. For example, although he is not an astronomer, the writer of this section was tremendously interested in Dr. Shapley's discussion of "The Expanding Universe"; and he found an account of one of the expeditions to the South Pole, led by Admiral Byrd, nothing short of fascinating.

Make up your mind, whenever you are planning to attend a lecture, that you are going to find in the discussion much that will be interesting, that has some relation to what you are interested in, that even though you do not at first see any immediate relation to your vital interests it does offer some ideas you may not have thought of,

[12] Ralph G. Nichols, "Ten Components of Effective Listening," *Education*, 1955, **75**: 292–302.

some information you do not already possess, or a point of view you have not considered. Incidentally, you might just discover that you have passed from the stage of secondary or voluntary attention to that of the derived primary, or interested, attention.

Develop an Attitude of Expectation or Anticipation

A number of factors are involved here. First, make sure you are seated in a good place where you can see and hear; that is, put yourself in a receptive position, where your interest may become active. Being unable to *watch* the speaker or being so far away that you cannot hear and see easily is one of the best ways of losing whatever interest you may have had or developed. Avoid seats near entrances or exits, or where people coming in or going out will cut off your vision or hearing, or will necessitate your rising to give them access to their seats; such disturbances are distracting in the extreme, and tend to break down any attitudes of expectation or anticipation.

Though many listening situations provide comfortable divans, chairs for lounging, and the like, such arrangements are not conducive to alertness or active expectancy; in fact, they often lead to sleepiness so that listening itself suffers from too much comfort. You will find yourself able to concentrate more consistently on the speaker and what he is saying if, in fact, you are just a little less than entirely comfortable. Your attitude of anticipation will remain active.

This attitude of anticipation or expectation grows in part out of the interest mentioned in the preceding section. However, primary attention, which is to be discussed in Chapter 12, may actually be the result of such anticipation; and you may find your interest aroused to the point that the effort required for voluntary attention has been greatly reduced and that listening itself no longer requires the effort.

Do Not Fake Interest or Attention

Most writers on the subject of listening caution against making attempts to simulate an attention or interest that does not exist. Such simulation is quite different from a consciously assumed attitude of anticipation. In the latter you are intentionally and deliberately taking on an attitude because you want to get something out of the presentation; in the former you are not interested in doing more than making the speaker and those around you *think* you are honestly trying to listen.

Discard Bias and Prejudice

Most of us, when we contemplate attending a lecture or other speaking occasion, tend to carry with us certain attitudes, favorable or unfavorable, toward the subject under discussion and sometimes toward the speaker himself. These attitudes may be the result of careful, long-continued study of the question, out of which a point of view, a belief, or an attitude has developed through sound reasoning based on a careful balancing of evidence. All too frequently, however, they are the product of snap judgments, inadequate information, or biases and prejudices which have long been held without any solid foundation at all.

None of us can possibly have had the opportunity to examine all the evidence on any controversial question or area of information: there is always something more to be said about it, and it may happen that something is just enough to lead us to question at least the finality of our particular point of view.

In any event, we need to be willing to listen to whatever may be said on either side of the question so long as it is said honestly and with a background of knowledge and understanding, and whether or not all that is presented agrees with our beliefs. Such a demand does not presuppose that our attitudes are necessarily going to be changed; but if we can listen with open minds—hear contrary evidence objectively—we may be more ready to recognize that there are honest differences of opinion, and that others are just as much entitled to their viewpoints as we are to ours.

Listen Continuously Rather than Intermittently

We shall assume that the speaker has made the special preparation that was discussed in Chapter 4 for this particular occasion. He has therefore carefully thought out his development of the ideas he wants to bring to you so that the divisions and subdivisions, the supporting materials, the illustrations, and so on fall into their right places to make the whole speech a unit. Any lapses of attention, any "wool-gathering" or mind-wandering on your part, is going to interfere with your ability to follow this development. Once you permit a gap in your comprehension you cannot go back, pick it up, and fill in, as you can in reading. One might paraphrase Omar the Tentmaker thus:

> The Moving Tongue speaks out; and having spoke
> Moves on; nor all your Piety nor Wit
> Shall lure it back to rehear any Sound,
> Nor all your Tears recall a Word of it.

Perhaps you think you can attend to something else and listen to the speaker at the same time. But you cannot focus your attention on two things or two events at the same time.[13] One or the other, and probably both, will suffer, so that comprehension is lost. You have to listen throughout. A possible exception may be during some phase of the speaker's development in which he is digressing from the main argument, so to speak, or when he is bringing in illustrative material to exemplify his point, or when he is amplifying a point already made. But even in such cases you must be ready to get back to his development as soon as he picks it up again.

Remember, you cannot take a backward look and pick up a point you did not get the first time. In listening to a speech there can be no backward look, no filling in of gaps in essential material.

Look for the Main Argument Rather than the Supporting Material

If the speech is well organized it will almost always center about a single central thought. The speaker is trying to bring one idea to his listeners, and the speech itself is the development of that idea. When we begin to study the organization of speeches you will realize how definitely the central thought stands out. Occasionally it is merely implied, but so specifically that there is no difficulty in recognizing it. In his well-known Funeral Oration for Caesar, Mark Antony never once tells his listeners what he wants them to do. But

---

[13] Recent news dispatches report that monkeys in the California Institute of Technology have been trained to perform two distinct tasks at the same time. But it was necessary to cut the nerve fibers that linked the two hemispheres of the brain. The operation is not recommended for human beings.

there is no doubt in their minds, when he is finished, of just what he has been driving at.

Get the central idea. The central idea may not always be formulated at or even near the beginning of the speech; it may not come until the end or near the end. But you must know what it is. The speaker may state it; if he does not arrive at a specific statement, you must formulate it for yourself. You know the familiar story of the inexhaustible orator who never did say what he was talking about. Speakers worth listening to are not like that.

Recognize the main points. The central idea will always be developed by a number of main points. Learn to identify these and to recognize their function in the development of the central idea. You may be able to remember some of the facts brought out in support of the main points; but it is more important to recognize and remember the main points themselves.

Summarize as you go along; try at intervals to see how far you have come along the road the speaker has laid out for you to follow.

Look Beyond the Speaker's Shortcomings

The perfect speaker has not yet been heard. Every speaker has some shortcoming, some fault. He may be awkward; his voice may not have great flexibility; he may mispronounce a word now and then or be guilty of some minor lapse in grammar. Within each of the various modes of speech heard in different areas of the country are certain dialects, such as the so-called Cajun dialect of Louisiana, the dialects of the Ozarks and the Great Smoky Mountain regions, the Scandinavian influence in the north central states, and so on. But nowhere in the world can one travel so far and speak with so many people and be so easily understood, or so easily understand those one encounters.

When a speaker does have peculiarities that make his speech different from what we are accustomed to, *listen to what he says.* His imperfections (from our point of view) will seldom actually interfere seriously with his communicativeness or with the significance of what he is saying.

Listen Evaluatively

Follow closely the speaker's line of reasoning; is it sound and logical and based on valid information? Observe the validity of his illustrative material. Weigh his emotional biases where evident, and try to estimate the weight of those biases in his objectivity. To what extent is he using deliberate half-truths and refusing to recognize any side of the problem other than his own? Is there a patent or a covert attempt to propagandize? Does he seem to have an "ax to grind"?

Do not allow yourself to be persuaded to "sign on the dotted line" before you have taken time to evaluate the "sales pitch." People can be swindled out of their votes as well as out of their savings— and the ultimate cost can be even greater.[14]

The suggestions presented here may in some instances assist in making the process of listening itself more effective, whatever may be involved in that process. They should in any event make the listening somewhat more productive than otherwise, both in comprehension of what is heard and in retention of what is significant, so that it may not be said of you, as it is said of the listening public at large, that you never remember more than 25 percent of what you hear.

QUESTIONS AND TOPICS FOR STUDY AND REVIEW

1. How would you weigh the comparative responsibility of speaker and listener for the success of a speaking occasion?
2. List some of the conditions in the physical surroundings that may be conducive to or interfere with effective listening.
3. What specific difficulties do you yourself have in effective listening?
4. Can you think of objectives in listening other than those discussed in the chapter?
5. Comment on the suggestion of Beighley that "A people trained to listen with comprehension will not, perhaps, be misled by the specious promises of a demagogue." What does the word *specious* mean?
6. Attend a public reading of some good literature. What factors kept

[14] Some of these suggestions have been adapted loosely from Wilhelmina G. Hedde and William Norwood Brigance, *American Speech*, 4th ed., Lippincott, 1955, pp. 159–160.

your interest sufficiently to induce you to listen throughout, or caused you to lose interest so that you listened to only a part of the program or perhaps none at all?

7. What radio or television programs do you listen to or like to watch? Do you like to listen to radio or television *talks?* Listen to one of perhaps a half-hour in duration, and after it is over, set down the central thought and the main points.

8. "Types" of listening have been described by some writers. What types can you differentiate? On what basis can such differentiations be made?

9. Identify in your own listening behavior various favorable and unfavorable types of reaction to a speaker.

10. What would you suggest for the speakers in your class that would stimulate more effective listening?

11. Comment on the statement in the text that listening is an active process.

12. What is meant by the direction to discard bias and prejudice as a means of improving listening ability?

13. Devise a score sheet that will enable you to check your own listening proficiency from time to time.

14. Much is being said nowadays about overcoming "barriers to communication." Discuss in a class speech some of the listening barriers you have experienced or observed.

15. It has been said that often we hear what we want to hear. To what extent have you found this to be true, and to what degree and in what ways does it affect your listening habits?

PROJECTS

1. Listen to a classroom speech and attempt to evaluate the statements of *fact* that were presented. Note down what tests of the validity of the facts you applied or could apply to the statements.

2. Evaluate the reasoning by which a classroom speaker arrived at his conclusions in a persuasive speech.

3. Listen to a radio or a television speech and evaluate the arguments that were presented. What was the speaker trying to accomplish? What use did he make of motive appeals? Could you identify them?

4. Listen to instructions telling you how to get from where you are to where you want to go (within a limited area). After the instructions are finished, draw a rough map of the route you are to take.

5. Using a large area road map, tell the class how to go by highway to some distant point, stopping off at a number of places on the way. Tell also how to return. Then have some member of your class repeat

those directions to see if he has heard your instructions and can repeat them.

6. Give to the class a report on a speech you have heard. Make clear the speaker's central thought and his main points, with such supporting material as time will permit.

7. Hand in an evaluation of the class speakers on a day when you are not to speak. Include the principal facts and arguments, with the most important supporting materials.

8. Ask someone to tell you *once* how to perform some relatively simple task with which you are unfamiliar, such as making a particular kind of uncomplicated drawing, or how to multiply or divide on a slide rule. Then without further instruction follow the directions to see if you are able to perform the act.

SUPPLEMENTARY READINGS

Babcock, C. Merton, *The Harper Book of Communication Skills*, Harper, 1957, chap. 12, "Acquire Proficiency in Listening."

Baird, A. Craig, and Franklin H. Knower, *General Speech: An Introduction*, 2nd ed., McGraw-Hill, 1957, chap. 14, "Informational and Critical Listening."

Brown, Charles T., *Introduction to Speech*, Houghton Mifflin, 1955, chap. 10, "Listening."

Brown, James I., "The Objective Measurement of Listening Ability," *Journal of Communication*, 1951, 1: 44–48.

Education, 1951, 75: no. 5, "Listening Number," is given over to articles on the subject of listening.

Gilman, Wilbur E., Bower Aly, and Loren Reid, *The Fundamentals of Speaking*, Macmillan, 1951, chap. 22, "Listening to Speeches."

Gray, Giles Wilkeson, and Claude Merton Wise, *The Bases of Speech*, 3rd ed., Harper, 1959, pp. 60–65.

Hedde, Wilhelmina, and William Norwood Brigance, *American Speech*, 4th ed., Lippincott, 1955, chap. 9.

Johnson, Wendell, *Your Most Enchanted Listener*, Harper, 1956.

McBurney, James H., and Ernest J. Wrage, *Guide to Good Speech*, 2nd ed., Prentice-Hall, 1960, chap. 9, "Listening to Speech."

Nichols, Ralph G., "Factors in Listening Comprehension," *Speech Monographs*, 1948, 15: 154–163.

Nichols, Ralph G., "Listening: Questions and Problems," *Quarterly Journal of Speech*, February, 1947, 33: 83–86.

Nichols, Ralph G., and Thomas R. Lewis, *Listening and Speaking*, Brown, 1954, chaps. 1–6.

Oliver, Robert T., *New Training for Effective Speech,* 2nd ed., Dryden, 1951, chap. 4, "The Role of the Listener."

Reid, Loren, *First Principles of Public Speaking,* Artcraft, 1960, chap. 19, "How To Be a Better Listener."

Sarett, Lew, William Trufant Foster, and Alma Johnson Sarett, *Basic Principles of Speech,* 3rd ed., Houghton Mifflin, 1958. Different aspects of listening are discussed throughout the text; see the Index for specific references.

Thonssen, Lester, and A. Craig Baird, *Speech Criticism,* Ronald, 1948, pp. 197–198.

Weaver, Andrew Thomas, and Ordean Gerhard Ness, *The Fundamentals and Forms of Speech,* Odyssey, 1957, chap. 5, "How To Listen Effectively."

Wiksell, Wesley, "The Problem of Listening," *Quarterly Journal of Speech,* December, 1946, **32:** 505–508.

PART III  THE SPEECH SITUA-TION

8

Analyzing the Time
and Place of the Speech

Your success in public speaking will many times rest upon your ability to understand the speech situation and your shrewdness in adapting your materials to its peculiar requirements. An effective speech must be timely and appropriate for the occasion. In addition, it must appeal to the listeners and promise to satisfy their desires, their moods, their biases, and their preferences.

Study of the occasion and the audience is therefore a necessary early step in planning a speech. In most instances it is the first step. It is on the basis of what you learn about your audience and the occasion that you will determine your goals, frame the thesis or central thought, select the pattern of development, weigh the supporting material, and choose the language.

THE SPEECH SITUATION

Actually the speech situation involves four important interacting forces: (1) the speaker, (2) the listener, (3) the occasion, and (4) the speech. The successful speaker understands how each element influences and is influenced by each of the others and how to integrate the four. The following diagram suggests several of these interactions.

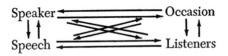

A little thought about the diagram will suggest that effective communication cannot take place when one of these lines either is not established or is broken. Remember that talking to listeners is not a one-way but truly a two-way process. You will have no difficulty in understanding the arrows which indicate how the speaker reaches his listeners through the speech and the occasion.

But why two sets of arrows—arrows going in opposite directions? The answer is in the two-way nature of communication, or what is sometimes referred to as feedback.[1] The arrows from the listeners to the speaker suggest the cues or signals which the speaker receives from his listeners and his surroundings. Suppose the speaker observes that many of his listeners seem to be drowsy, uninterested, and unresponsive. He therefore postpones a long presentation of statistics in favor of a funny story. What happens may be diagramed as follows:

Listeners ——————→ Speaker ————→ Speech ————→ Listeners
(Unresponsive) (Reacts: speech (Omits statistics (Become more
               is not going   in favor of anec- responsive)
               over)   dote)

---

[1] In electronics the term *feedback* refers to the return of a part of the output of electric oscillation into the input at proper phase in order to amplify or decrease the strength of the signal. The analogy to communication should be obvious. If, for example, a listener gives off a signal of dissatisfaction, the speaker modifies his output to meet it. See David Berlo, *The Process of Communication*, Holt, Rinehart & Winston, 1960, pp. 102–103 and chap. 5.

In terms of our first diagram the feedback process has operated as follows:

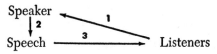

The speaker could react in a different way. Upon observing drowsiness, he might look to the physical setting for a cause and decide that the problem is high humidity and lack of ventilation. He immediately asks to have a window opened and a fan turned on; he may also request his listeners to stand for a moment. This feedback may be diagramed as follows.

Place ⟶ Listeners ⟶ Speaker ⟶ Place ⟶ Listeners
(Stuffy)   (Drowsy)   (Reacts: speech   (Opens   (More alert)
                       is not going   window)
                       over)

This situation illustrates the other side of the original diagram.

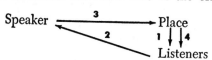

Of course, we have oversimplified to make our point; these reactions and many others occur almost simultaneously because the four elements of the speaking situation are so interrelated.

THE OCCASION

The times and places men speak are legion. Talks are made on the slightest provocation. Inaugurations, farewells, political rallies, meetings of service clubs, banquets, community forums, barbecues, funerals, prayer meetings, and worship services are all occasions for speeches. Each event requires a different approach, different subject matter, and different delivery. In choosing your strategy for a given speech, weigh the following elements of the occasion: the time of the meeting, the assembly place, the prevailing customs of the locality, and the purpose of the gathering.

The Time of the Meeting

The time of your appearance—sometimes even the hour of the day—may make a considerable difference in your success. What immediately precedes and follows your speech should also be weighed thoughtfully. But your analysis may not stop here; it may also consider the broad historical trends which have given rise to the assembly. For this reason a knowledge of history may be of great advantage to you. Some of our greatest speakers have been thorough students of history, sometimes spending months or even years in acquiring insight into the background of an occasion. For example, when he delivered his address at Plymouth, Massachusetts on December 22, 1820, Webster was well aware of the significance of commemorating the landing of the Pilgrims. With carefully selected evidence, a magnificent manner, and elevated language, he inspired his fellow citizens also to take pride in that two-hundredth anniversary.

Speaking at Cooper Union in New York on February 27, 1860, Abraham Lincoln was conscious of the historical forces at work, particularly in the North. He realized that the opportunity for a Western lawyer to address influential New Yorkers did not come often. Contrary to his practice in some of his earlier speeches, he now marshaled many facts with which to persuade his educated Eastern listeners. His speech was successful because he adapted it to that occasion.

In studying the time, consider such questions as these:

1. What are the broad historical antecedents of the speech?
   a. Political?
   b. Economic?
   c. Religious?
2. What immediate past events give rise to the meeting?
   a. Are these known to the audience?
   b. Has the program committee or chairman been aware of these in calling the meeting?
3. How does the time of the meeting affect the speaker and the audience?
   a. Is it a convenient time?
   b. How does the time affect the speaker?
   c. How does it affect the auditors? Are they
      (1) Alert?
      (2) Sleepy?
      (3) Tired?

(4) Bored?

(5) Neutral or passive?

The Place of the Meeting

The importance of giving careful thought to the place in which you are to speak cannot be overstressed. The physical surroundings may be either an asset or a liability. One place may require restraint and awe, while a second may call for frivolity and gaiety. A church, a historical landmark, a cemetery, or a lodge room often inspires contemplative silence. On the other hand, a stadium, an opera house, or a gymnasium-auditorium may stimulate incessant chatter and laughter. Poor ventilation may contribute to drowsiness and inattentiveness. The speaker should study carefully the size of the place, its acoustical properties, and the comfort of the audience.

Consider for a moment how the physical surroundings affected Lincoln when he spoke at Gettysburg, Pennsylvania, on November 19, 1863. On the credit side of the ledger he talked to an audience who deeply revered the setting. On that site Confederate and Union armies had engaged in a fierce battle and had buried there thousands of their finest young men. Those present had come to dedicate a national cemetery. During the four minutes he spoke, Lincoln made three references to the place, referring to it as "a great battlefield of that war," "a portion of that field," and "this ground." He closely associated his remarks with "this ground" in order to heighten the emotional effect of his speech.

But what difficulties did the surroundings provide? Lincoln spoke outdoors to a crowd of 15,000 to 30,000, most of whom were standing and many of whom could not push close enough to the speakers' stand to hear or even to see the President. The nature of the gathering and the surroundings meant that persons could wander away from the area without embarrassment. In addition to these difficulties, no doubt many already were weary of listening to Edward Everett, who, preceding Lincoln, had talked for over two hours. It goes without saying that these were challenging circumstances, some of which, incidentally, Lincoln could not overcome.

As a speaker, you must decide what the place of the meeting requires of you. In a small room, you must exercise restraint and finesse, keeping your voice conversational and quiet, your gestures few in number, and your movements subdued. On the other hand, since there are probably fewer distracting influences in a small room than elsewhere, you can present your material more concisely. To be effective in a large room or outdoors, you must be more vigorous and energetic, especially if no public address system is available. You must use more movement, broader gestures, and an amplified conversational tone. Your rate of speaking must necessarily be slower. Difficult speaking situations will also require more thought breaks. They may require greater use of humor, and more illustrations and examples.

Study carefully *where* your speech is to be delivered. Take an inventory of the items suggested below.

1. Where is the speech to be delivered?
   a. Is the speech to be delivered indoors or outdoors?
   b. Is the meeting place famous (or infamous)?
      (1) Have important events occurred there?
      (2) What important speakers have spoken there?
      (3) How familiar is the audience with this place?
   c. In what kind of community is the meeting place located:
      (1) Rural or urban?
      (2) Industrial or residential?
      (3) Cottages or mansions?
      (4) Business district or suburb?
   d. What are the taboos of the place?
   e. Is it a hired hall, a permanent meeting place, or a community center?
2. What will be the comfort of the auditors?
   a. Will they sit, stand, or both?
   b. Will they be crowded or scattered?
   c. Will they be confined to a small area?
   d. Will there be adequate ventilation?
      (1) Air conditioning?
      (2) Fans?
   e. How will the surroundings influence the auditors?
      (1) Are there distractions with which to compete?
      (2) Are the surroundings pleasant or unpleasant?
      (3) Will all listeners see the speaker with ease?
3. What are the lighting facilities?
   a. Will the speaker be able to see the facial reactions of the listeners?
   b. Will the room be darkened?
   c. Will natural or artificial lighting be used?
   d. Will footlights or a spotlight be used on the speaker?

4. What are the acoustical problems facing the speaker?
   a. Will a public address system be available?
   b. Will the speech be broadcast or recorded as it is being presented?
   c. Is the place acoustically treated?
   d. Will there be disturbing reverberations?
5. What are the comforts of the speaker?
   a. Is there to be a lectern?
   b. Is the speaker to be above or below the auditors?
   c. Are the listeners directly in front or on all sides of the speaker?

Prevailing Customs

The prevailing customs the speaker should be aware of are those which dictate what he may or may not do as a public speaker. Think for a moment about the wide difference in the conduct of various religious groups. In some church buildings the men wear hats; in others the practice is very much out of place. Clergymen of one faith prefer to be called Father, others insist on Reverend, while the Quakers ask that their leaders be addressed simply as Mister. Some congregations would be shocked if their pastor did not speak from the pulpit in a subdued, mystical manner; others expect much pounding and shouting. Equally wide differences can be found in the practices of secular groups. These habit patterns may be dictated by the community as a whole, by the nature of the occasion, or by the place of assembly. Good advice is, "When in Rome, do as the Romans do."

Of value in discovering "what the Romans do" are the following questions.

1. What is considered appropriate public speaking practice
   a. With reference to dress?
   b. With reference to delivery?
   c. With reference to language and diction?
2. What is the audience etiquette?[2]
3. What is the custom with reference to admission and honorarium?
   a. Is an admission to be charged?
   b. Will the speaker receive an honorarium? Is this the usual or a greater amount?

[2] Audience etiquette refers to customs, forms, and manners which dictate what is appropriate behavior for the listeners. It may relate to responsiveness, applauding, appropriate dress, time of arrival, intermissions, seating, curtain calls, etc.

4. Is the group regulated by parliamentary laws?
   a. Robert's Rules of Order?
   b. Individual bylaws?
   c. Informal rules?
   d. No rules?
   e. Mob rule?

The Purpose of the Meeting

The purpose for which the meeting is called may place additional restrictions upon a speaker. If you speak to a businessmen's luncheon club, you will probably find fellowship, fun, and good food prevailing. The members of a trade union may assemble in an angry mood to discuss a violation of contract, strike strategy, or grievances against a foreman.

Contrast the difference in purpose of a Sunday-morning worship service and a social meeting of a church brotherhood. In the former, speaker and audience are required to follow a ritual. In the latter, though the same auditors may meet in the same building (in a different room), they feel none of the restraints of the former meeting.

In your analysis of the purpose of the meeting, consider the questions given below. Many of these will overlap queries concerning audience analysis, considered in the following chapter.

1. Is it a regular or called meeting?
   a. Is the purpose of the meeting well known to the auditors?
   b. Is there general agreement on the advisability of the goal?
2. Who formulated the goal of the meeting:
   a. The whole group?
   b. A select group?
   c. Some outside source?
   d. You yourself?
3. Is instruction or training a goal of the meeting?
   a. Is instruction to be administered to all or some?
   b. Has instruction been a previous goal?
   c. Is the speaker to help in giving instruction?
4. Is entertainment of the auditors a goal?
   a. Is it to be the broad, slapstick type?
   b. Do they expect restraint and dignity?
5. Does the meeting commemorate or celebrate an important event?
   a. Is the event related to the history of the group?

     (1) To other similar groups?

     (2) Only to this group?

   b. Did the listeners participate in the event commemorated?

   c. What are their sources of information about the event?

6. Is the purpose of the meeting associated with persuasion?

   a. What kind of change is expected:

     (1) Covert?

     (2) Overt?

   b. Does the audience expect to profit from the meeting?

   c. How is the purpose related to betterment?

QUESTIONS AND TOPICS FOR STUDY AND REVIEW

1. What happens when the speaker assumes that speaking is a one-way process? Give examples of several speakers who have made this mistake. Have you observed this tendency among college professors?

2. What is meant by the term *feedback*? What does it mean when used in connection with a public address system? Is this meaning analogous to what is referred to on page 124? Can you think of other examples of feedback in other areas?

3. How would you diagram (see p. 124) the following speech situations?
   a. The speaker who has stage fright
   b. The speaker who uses language unfamiliar to the listeners
   c. The speech which is ruined by failure of the public address system
   d. The audience who refuse to pay attention to what the speaker is saying

4. How does the place where the speech is to be delivered influence the speech? The size of the hall? The lighting? The location? Illustrate your answers with speeches you have heard personally.

5. What sources of information about the occasion are open to the speaker? Where and from whom can he get pertinent information about the time and the place of the meeting?

6. Can you think of other aspects of the occasion, not mentioned in this textbook, which should be considered?

7. Can you illustrate how failure to consider an aspect of the occasion caused a speaker to fail? Or the reverse, how careful adjustment to an unexpected occurrence resulted in success for a speaker?

PROJECTS

1. *Speaking Assignment.* Deliver a short speech in which you analyze how a speaker's analysis of the occasion contributed to his success or

failure in a given situation. If possible, report on a speech situation which you have actually observed.

2. *Speaking Assignment.* Deliver a short speech in which you show how the adjustment of a speaker to an unexpected occurrence or problem arising from the time or place of the speech resulted in a successful outcome or in failure.

3. Report to the class on the occasion of a famous American or British speech. Consider the elements suggested in this chapter. You might wish to investigate one of the following speeches or a similar one:

a. Wendell Phillips's "The Murder of Love Joy," December 8, 1837.

b. Henry W. Grady's "The New South," December 22, 1886.

c. George W. Curtis's "The Puritan Principle—Liberty Under the Law," December 22, 1876.

d. Booker T. Washington's "Atlanta Exposition Speech," September 18, 1895.

e. Douglas MacArthur's "Address to Congress," April 19, 1951.

f. Richard M. Nixon's "My Side of the Story," September 23, 1952.

SUPPLEMENTARY READINGS

Arnold, Carroll C., Douglas Ehninger, and John C. Gerber, eds., *The Speaker's Resource Book*, Scott, Foresman, 1961.

Baird, A. Craig, ed., *American Public Addresses, 1740–1952*, McGraw-Hill, 1956.

Black, Edwin, and Harry P. Kerr, eds., *American Issues: A Sourcebook for Speech Topics*, Harcourt, Brace & World, 1961.

Braden, Waldo W., and Mary Louise Gehring, *Speech Practices: A Resource Book for the Student of Public Speaking*, Harper, 1958.

Brandt, Carl G., and Edward M. Shafter, Jr., eds., *Selected American Speeches on Basic Issues (1850–1950)*, Houghton Mifflin, 1960.

Brigance, William Norwood, ed., *Classified Speech Models*, Appleton-Century-Crofts, 1928.

O'Neill, James Milton, ed., *Classified Models of Speech Composition*, Century, 1921.

Parrish, Wayland, and Marie Hochmuth, eds., *American Speeches*, Longmans, Green, 1954.

Thonssen, Lester, and William L. Finkel, eds., *Ideas That Matter: A Sourcebook for Speakers*, Ronald, 1961.

Thonssen, Lester, ed., *Representative American Speeches* H. W. Wilson, published annually. From 1938 through 1959, the series was edited by A. Craig Baird. In the twenty-two numbers issued under his editorship are more than 400 addresses from 300 orators.

Thorndike, Ashley, ed., *Modern Eloquence,* Modern Eloquence Corp., 1923, (or Collier, 1936), 15 vols.

Vital Speeches of the Day, bimonthly magazine devoted entirely to speeches.

Wrage, Ernest J., and Barnet Baskerville, eds., *American Forum: Speeches on Historic Issues, 1788–1900,* Harper, 1960.

Wrage, Ernest J., and Barnet Baskerville, eds., *Contemporary Forum: American Speeches on Twentieth-Century Issues,* Harper, 1962.

NOTE: The publications listed here contain speeches and excerpts which will prove challenging to you in your study of public speaking. In later chapters, certain model speeches are cited for specific study, and the collections where they can be found will be referred to by shortened titles.

9

Analyzing the Audience

"The first simple rule in all good speaking in any situation," advises Overstreet, "is: think of your audience."[1] What to say and how to say it are related to where, when, and to whom. In their famous debates for the Illinois senatorship in 1858, Lincoln and Douglas were adroit in altering their arguments as they moved from antislave northern to proslave southern Illinois and back again. The state of Louisiana offers a real challenge to the stump speaker, because northern Louisiana differs markedly from the southern French parishes. Furthermore, to employ the same arguments and techniques in the hill country beyond the Red River and in cosmopolitan New Orleans is to invite failure.

[1] H. A. Overstreet, *Influencing Human Behavior,* Norton, 1925, pp. 72–73.

The audience, of course, refers to those persons who constitute your listeners. In the face-to-face situation you have a visible audience, those within the natural or amplified range of your voice. In the classroom your auditors are your fellow students. On other occasions you may have for a visible audience a Rotary Club, a jury, a community forum, the Ladies' Aid, or a trade union council.

The printing press, the motion picture, the radio, and television have made possible what may be called a *greater audience* or an absent audience, consisting of those persons who hear the speech by radio or television or who read it. Describing this group, Hollingworth points out, "There is of course no aggregation or congregation of people involved, and hence the group phenomena which an assembled audience may display will be missing."[2] On many occasions today this greater audience dwarfs the immediate audience in importance and size. On the evening of May 27, 1941, President Franklin Roosevelt spoke to an immediate, select audience of 300 persons assembled at the White House. Before him were Western Hemisphere diplomats and their families, but out on the airways an estimated 65 million tuned in to listen. Later the same speech was broadcast by short wave in fourteen languages to additional millions abroad.[3]

On September 26, 1960, John F. Kennedy and Richard M. Nixon met in a Chicago television studio to participate in their first face-to-face debate in the 1960 presidential campaign. In the studio were only a small number of people, but seventy million are reported to have viewed and heard the debate via radio and television. Never before had presidential campaigners had such an opportunity to reach so many in a single appearance. Kennedy and Nixon spoke to a thousand times more listeners in a single telecast than Lincoln and Douglas did a hundred years before in their seven debates in Illinois.

The following day, many newspapers printed the speeches in part or in full. The audience was thus further increased. Radio and television audiences may be augmented by millions who gain their impressions by what they read in newspapers and magazines. Unfor-

---

[2] Harry L. Hollingworth, *The Psychology of the Audience,* American Book, 1935, p. 26.
[3] Franklin Delano Roosevelt, "A State of Emergency Exists," in A. Craig Baird ed., *Representative American Speeches: 1940–1941,* H. W. Wilson, 1941, pp. 57–74.

tunately, many of these readers never see a full text of the speaker's remarks; consequently, they may read only garbled statements of whatever censors permit to slip through. Quotation marks frequently are omitted. A reporter or an editor may do a thorough "rewrite."[4] Nevertheless, this reading audience is of great significance to many speakers.

Some speakers actually project their audiences into the future by addressing their remarks to posterity. What historians will say becomes important to many, particularly those who imagine that "the halo of greatness" is descending upon them. For this reason some congressmen take particular care to revise what appears in the *Congressional Record.*[5] A senator or representative may frankly admit in opening that he intends his remarks "for the record," meaning that he wants a printed statement upon which to be judged at a later date—perhaps at the next election or even by generations yet unborn.

To summarize, your audience may include both those persons in the immediate assembly and those reached through the press, radio, or television. Just as it cannot be limited in place, neither can the audience be limited in time; the speaker may even address his remarks to the reader of the future.

TYPES OF AUDIENCES[6]

As a rule, no group of persons congregates or remains assembled by mere chance or accident. Some motivating force in the speaking situation pulls them together and unites them into what we commonly refer to by the collective term *audience.*

Many persons attend a speech merely to satisfy their curiosity about the speaker. Public figures often command large lecture fees not because they speak so effectively but because at the moment they have attracted public attention. On other occasions listeners may assemble because they are loyal or obligated to an organization such as Rotary, Young Democrats, or Junior Chamber of Commerce. A student body group may meet because it is commanded to be present.

[4] See Walter Lippman, *Public Opinion,* Harcourt, Brace, 1922, chap. 5.

[5] Zon Robinson, "The Accuracy With Which Speeches Are Reported in the Congressional Record," in Harold F. Harding, ed., *Eastern Public Speaking Conference, 1940,* H. W. Wilson, 1940, pp. 290–300.

[6] This material was adapted from Hollingworth, *op. cit.,* pp. 19–32.

To be successful, you as a speaker must consider carefully the cohesive forces, the degree of organization that has taken place, and the group anticipations. You must decide why the auditors have come to the meeting and why they should remain.

The Spontaneous Group

The spontaneous group possesses the lowest degree of cohesiveness, integration, and organization, for the members possess few common ties. They assemble by chance. The street-corner gathering, window shoppers passing a display, commuters waiting in a station, and people huddled together in the same bomb shelter are all spontaneous groups. To transform such a group into an audience is a real challenge to a speaker, for he has no outside aids to unify them. He must gain a hearing and develop interest in the subject before he can hope to present his main thoughts.

The Discussion Group

The discussion or conversation group cannot be considered an audience in the usual sense of the word, for each member looks upon himself as a participant or speaker with an equal right to speak whenever he wishes. When he is not speaking, he is, of course, a listener; but he is hesitant to let anyone speak too long. Any attempt to monopolize is regarded as a breach of etiquette. To transform a discussion group into an audience, the speaker must gain the consent of the other members.

The Inactive Audience

Unlike the first two types of audiences just described, the inactive audience is bound together by the willingness of its members to recognize and give attention to something—whether it be a speaker, a singer, a juggling act, or a play. Members regard themselves as onlookers and listeners, not speakers or participants. Ordinarily they come with the intention of being spectators, of remaining inactive, sometimes even inert. The dinner club, the theater crowd, and some classes are inactive groups. After they come and pay whatever admission is charged, they expect to be entertained.

With an inactive group, the speaker is at least assured of an initial hearing; consequently, holding attention and directing interest are less of a problem than with the spontaneous group. If he expects more, he must work for it. Something about the speaker, the occasion, or the subject has attracted the auditors to the meeting place and made them ready to listen. Discovery of this something is the key to reaching this type of group. Either their anticipation must be satisfied, or something more urgent must be substituted.

The Selected Audience

The selected audience possesses greater unity and organization than the inactive audience, because there is a common basis for membership in the group. The PTA, a lodge, a patriotic society, or an alumni group are typical examples. Selectivity and membership requirements result in greater homogeneity, thus simplifying somewhat the speaker's problem. Group objectives further unite the members and offer the speaker a common ground upon which to reach them. If you ally yourself and your cause with their common ideals, symbols, and taboos, you are assured of interest and attention.

The Disciplined Audience

The disciplined group is usually characterized by previous training, complete orientation, and regimentation. The athletic team, the military unit, and the airplane crew are examples. An order from the leader is sufficient to secure action without question or hesitation. Since there is no freedom of choice, this type ordinarily falls beyond the realm of persuasion. A speaker in authority merely has to issue an order to get action.

SOURCES OF INFORMATION ABOUT THE AUDIENCE

Never before our time has the speaker had available so much information, so many techniques, or so much help. The social psychologist, the sociologist, and the geographer, with their extensive studies of group conduct, population trends, attitudes, and prejudices, make valuable allies. The public opinion poll and consumer's research yield much information that you can often utilize.

Although you may not have the resources or the time to conduct elaborate studies or hire the services of professional pollsters, you can learn much from them. Public-opinion polls published in newspapers and magazines give many hints concerning trends in popular thinking on a wide variety of subjects.

For political units as small as townships or wards, state and federal census reports give detailed population statistics relative to age, sex, education, occupation, racial background, religious affiliation, school attendance, literacy, and many other topics. When political issues are to be analyzed, election returns often serve as a valuable source of information. In addition, the *Statistical Abstract,* the *World Almanac,* and *Information Please Almanac* may be helpful.

In some cases local newspapers or magazines give information valuable in audience analysis. Before you formulate opinions from them, however, ascertain the political bias of the editor as well as the unique features of the publication, and remember that newspapers mold as well as reflect local attitudes. Editorial pages contain many clues concerning the nature and policy of a paper. One newspaper should be checked against other papers and against additional sources and observers.

In every community there are key persons whose judgment regarding the community mores and local attitudes is astute and trustworthy. On many occasions such persons will be your principal source of information about what is expected of you and about what is appropriate. Ordinarily, the program chairman, the outstanding citizen, a speaker who has previously addressed the group, the committee in charge, or the officers will make valuable informants. The more individuals you consult, the more likely you are to make an accurate judgment about your audience.

The discussion above no doubt gives the impression that audience analysis is a tedious task. If so, your conclusion is correct. Naturally, for a five-minute class performance or a brief appearance before a luncheon club, a detailed study is probably unwarranted. Some speaking situations will necessitate consulting many sources, while others may be handled successfully if you talk with a few persons in the community. But the resourceful speaker is constantly alert to signs indicating shifts in opinion. Flexibility and adaptability are important qualities of the effective speaker.

IMPORTANT QUESTIONS FOR ANALYSIS
OF THE AUDIENCE

In What Ways Are Your Listeners Homogeneous?

Many persons speak of audience adjustment as if the speaker's task were simply to adapt his materials to the group as a whole. But, as Hollingworth puts it, "the audience is an unreal abstraction."[7] Certainly a number of persons meeting together do not lose their identity and fuse into a single entity with an oversoul or superpersonality. They may keep their individuality, or, more likely, they may group themselves around certain conditioners of opinion. Adjustment to each individual would be highly desirable, but it is obviously impossible if the gathering is large. Usually you must adapt your materials and appeal to certain groupings or segments of those present. The accomplishment of this task depends upon your success in learning in what respect your listeners are homogeneous. Polling agencies provide us with a convenient list of topics around which they believe people group themselves. They insist that the important conditioners of opinion are occupational groups, sex, age, place of residence, education, income level, race, religion, and political preference.[8] You will therefore do well to find the answers to the following questions.

1. What are the predominant characteristics of the majority of the prospective audience?
    a. Is the audience to be composed of men, women, or both?
    b. What are their age characteristics—juvenile, young adults, middle-aged people, old, mixed?
    c. Where do the majority of the members of the audience live— large city, suburban area, village, rural area, mixed?
    d. What is their average income—wealthy, average, poor, on relief, mixed?
    e. What are their racial characteristics—foreign-born, or first-generation Americans, colored, white, minority group, mixed?
    f. What are their religious characteristics—if Protestants, Fundamentalist or Modernist? Catholic? Non-Christian?

[7] *Ibid.*, p. 27.
[8] George Gallup, *A Guide to Public Opinion Polls,* Princeton University Press, 1948, pp. 31–33.

g. What are their political affiliations—Northern or Southern Democrats, Republicans, liberals or conservatives, third-party groups, independents, mixed?
2. What other characteristics might be significant in influencing opinions?
   a. Secret societies?
   b. Fraternal affiliations?

What Do Your Listeners Know About You?

If you are to be effective, you must also attempt to ascertain what your reputation is with your listeners and how they arrived at their conclusions. On the basis of what you learn, you must determine the kind, amount, and type of personal or ethical appeal essential for the success of your speech.

When he arose to deliver his Bunker Hill oration,[9] Daniel Webster found little need to establish himself with his listeners, for he knew that those present held him in such high esteem that extensive personal appeals would have been most inappropriate. In direct contrast, William L. Yancey, ardent states' righter and secessionist, found it necessary to pack much personal appeal into his speeches before Northern audiences during the presidential campaign of 1860. His political foe, Stephen A. Douglas, the senator from Illinois, came to a similar conclusion when he spoke to Southerners. Both Yancey and Douglas, experienced speakers, strove to disarm their listeners before attempting serious presentations of their own ideas.

In evaluating the attitudes of the audience toward yourself, be as objective as possible. If possible, determine what the real attitudes are, no matter how much some of them may irritate or disturb you. Put the following questions to yourself.

1. What are the attitudes of the majority of the audience toward me as a speaker?
   a. How familiar are they with my background and reputation?
      (1) What are their sources of information?

[9] Delivered June 17, 1825, at the laying of the cornerstone of the Bunker Hill Monument at Charlestown, Massachusetts.

(a) Are these sources reliable?
(b) Are they biased?
(2) Is ethical appeal necessary?
2. What are the similarities and differences between my background and that of the majority of the auditors?
   a. Are these known to the audience?
   b. Do they constitute a basis upon which to establish a "common ground"?
3. What do the majority of the listeners expect from me?
   a. Did they come to hear me?
   b. Do they have selfish motives in coming?

What Do Your Listeners Know About Your Subject?

To cover ground familiar to the audience and not be aware that it is familiar is to waste valuable time and to risk putting your listeners to sleep. But to assume that they are better informed than they actually are is equally disastrous. The purposeful speaker starts with the auditors where they are and moves them toward his desired goal. What your audience knows then becomes an important consideration.

In these days of rapid communication and extensive news coverage, it is not unusual for an audience to have a résumé or even the complete text of a talk before it is delivered. In this event, the speaker must take special pains to adapt his presentation carefully to the local situation.

What the audience knows about your subject will be an important determinant in your strategy. You will do well, therefore, to investigate the following questions.

1. What is the attitude of the majority of the listeners toward the speech?
   a. Has the title aroused curiosity?
      (1) Is it misleading?
      (2) Does it need clarification?
   b. What advance publicity has the speech received?
      (1) Amount?
      (2) Type?
      (3) By whom?
      (4) Purpose?

   c. How much does the majority know about the subject?
     (1) Source of information:
       (a) Careful study?
       (b) Hearsay?
       (c) Habitual association?
     (2) Has the audience had the opportunity to read the speech
       or a résumé?
2. Will the text be available afterward?

What Attitudes and Opinions of Your Listeners Are Favorable to Your Position?

Assuming now that you have ascertained what general information your listeners have concerning your speech as a whole, you will need more specific information about their opinions and attitudes with reference to the position you take and the arguments you expect to advance. G. W. Allport defines an attitude as "a mental and neural state of readiness, organized through experience, exerting a directive or dynamic influence upon the individual's response to all objects and situations with which it is related."[10] Opinions and beliefs are usually considered the expression or verbalization of attitudes. Experience, environment, and conditioning cause persons to develop inclinations, predispositions, and states of readiness to act toward issues, institutions, activities, groups, and processes.[11]

When you are aware of and can capitalize on a state of readiness to act, you are more likely to win your point and then to achieve your goal. For example, if you are seeking donations for a cancer society, you are likely to encounter greatest responsiveness from those who have had cancer or whose relatives have. Because they are well aware of the threat of the disease, these persons are in a state of readiness to act, and your appeal will trigger the desired response.

Your task as a speaker is to decide how, by making use of existing favorable attitudes and opinions, you can move your listeners

[10] Gordon W. Allport, "Attitudes," in Carl Murchison, ed., *A Handbook of Social Psychology*, Clark University Press, 1935, p. 810.
[11] For detailed discussion of attitudes, see Eugene L. Hartley and Ruth E. Hartley, *Fundamentals of Social Psychology*, Knopf, 1958, chaps. 20–22.

closer to your position. If you wish to persuade them that the United States should prohibit further exportations of gold, you may find it to your advantage to stress first the theme that the good citizen should be willing to make sacrifices for the good of his country, or in President Kennedy's words, "Ask not what your country can do for you—ask what you can do for your country."[12]

Generally the speaker selects his propositions for a stimulating speech from favorable attitudes and opinions. This subject is developed more fully in Chapter 21.

What Attitudes and Opinions of Your Listeners are Unfavorable to Your Position?

In the light of what has just been said, an extensive development of how to deal with unfavorable attitudes and opinions of your listeners is unnecessary. As a speaker, it is as important that you know what attitudes and opinions stand in the way of winning your point as it is to know those which favor your position. If you are advocating prohibiting the export of gold, you are likely to find that some auditors resist your arguments because they object to the government's interfering with any individual initiative. This negative predisposition must be overcome before you can develop your main theme.

Many convincing and actuating speeches are built around the elimination of attitudes and beliefs unfavorable to the speaker's proposition.

Is a Significant Percentage of Your Listeners Hostile, Neutral, or Partisan?

Norman Thomas, veteran political campaigner, observes, "On controversial issues in any sizeable audience, the speaker should count on three general groups: some confirmed opponents who may have come out of curiosity or to collect information for further criticism; some who are curious and undecided; and finally positive sympathizers."[13] In other words this veteran of several presidential cam-

---

[12] From "Inaugural Address," delivered January 20, 1961, in *Vital Speeches of the Day*, February 1, 1961, 27: 226–227.

[13] Norman Thomas, *Mr. Chairman, Ladies and Gentlemen*, Hermitage House, 1955, p. 114.

paigns and many speaking tours discovered through practical experience what social scientists have verified through extensive testing and experimentation and what directors of debate have employed in the so-called shift-of-opinion ballot. Attitudes may be said to differ in degree or direction and may be represented on a scale like the following:

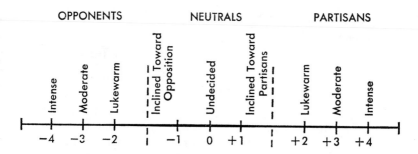

On any proposition or issue, listeners may be concentrated anywhere along the scale from intense partisanship to intense opposition ($+4$ to -4), with some individuals scattered throughout the continuum. We have arbitrarily divided the scale above into equal thirds, but with an actual audience you may speak on an issue on which 95 percent stand at the -4 position. Or a large percentage may be neutrals who do not care one way or the other or who do not have enough information to have an opinion. At another time you may have a rowdy group of partisans ($+4$).

In making an audience analysis, you must find the answer to the important question: what degree of commitment or conviction exists among my listeners? Or how are they distributed along the attitude scale? Of course, your greatest concern should be with the group which holds the balance of power or controls the audience.

An experience the noted preacher Henry Ward Beecher had in England and a century ago provides a good example of astute audience analysis. In 1863 he faced a difficult speaking assignment in the cotton mill city of Manchester. At that time thousands of Englishmen who worked in cotton mills had been made idle by the Northern blockade of the Confederacy. Beecher later explained what happened as follows: "I took the measure of the audience and said to myself, 'About one fourth of this audience are opposed to me, and about one fourth will be rather in sympathy, and my business now is not to appeal to that portion that is opposed to me nor to those that are already on my side, but to bring over the middle section.' How to do this was a problem."[14] Notice that Beecher decided to concentrate upon "the middle section" or the neutrals, who had not formed an opinion on the issues of the Civil War.

How Intense Are the Attitudes and Opinions of Your Listeners on Your Proposition?

Rough classification of listeners on the basis of the direction of attitudes—that is, into opponents, neutrals, and partisans—omits important dimensions involving intensity or degree of commitment or conviction. Generally, as listeners move toward the extremes or away from the neutral position, their attitudes and opinions are likely to be more firmly set, held with greater tenacity. Persons in the extreme positions resist change and are not likely to be moved by ordinary persuasion. The group we referred to on page 138 as a disciplined audience, often falls into this category (-4 or $+4$). Discussion groups are in between—neutrals or undecided ($+1$, 0, -1). Figure 1 on page 147 illustrates this point.

In studying the chart, notice that as you move in either direction away from the neutral position (0) the lines of the graph indicate that the attitudes become more intense. The chart suggests that persons who are at the extreme positions (-4 and $+4$) have the most intense attitudes—that is, they hold to their positions more firmly and are consequently more difficult to change.

What Will Be the Target Group?

Your purpose in doing a careful study of your listeners is to help you plan your presentation intelligently. In the light of what you learn, you must (1) limit your subject if that seems desirable, (2) decide upon your immediate and ultimate goals, (3) frame your proposition, and (4) choose your main points and supporting materials. In order to make these decisions you must select a target

---

[14] Lyman Abbott, *Henry Ward Beecher: A Sketch of His Career*, American Publishing, 1887, pp. 171–172.

group, that is, a group upon which you intend to concentrate your efforts in order to achieve your purposes.

If your listeners are much alike in their attitudes and opinions— that is, they are concentrated at a given point on the attitude scale— you may decide that the entire audience is your target. If your auditors are all intense partisans (+4), you will know that your purpose must be to reinforce their existing attitudes. If your group is composed largely of opponents, (−3, −4), then your approach must be very different.

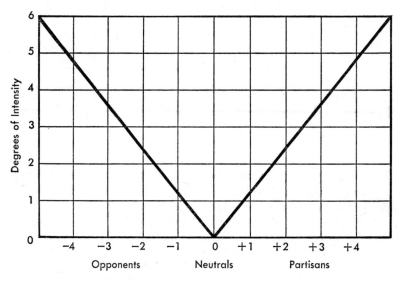

FIG. 1.   Classification of Listeners on the Basis of Attitudes

Adapted from Hadley Cantril, "The Intensity of an Attitude," *Journal of Abnormal and Social Psychology,* 1946, 41: 129–135.

What should your approach be when you find your listeners widely scattered? Should you attempt to select the entire audience as a target or should you concentrate upon a segment? This involves the problem of whether a speaker adjusts to an audience or to listeners. Of course much depends upon the nature of the assembly. When the group operates under parliamentary procedure, you need to know what percentage of votes controls the assembly. This number is usually 51 percent, but may be as much as two-thirds, or even unanimity in the case of a jury. As a rule, you will be wise to select as your target group those listeners who are nearest to your position. Let us illustrate this principle:

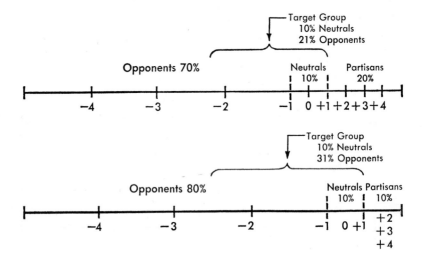

In all cases your goal should be to move as many of your listeners as you can as far as possible in the direction of your position and to prevent any regression toward the opposite pole.

In brief, you must attempt to achieve four tasks: (1) convert the undecided, (2) keep your supporters enthusiastic, (3) move wavering opponents into the undecided group, and (4) avoid offending opponents in order not to drive them into the opposite direction.

QUESTIONS AND TOPICS FOR STUDY AND REVIEW

1. What are the differences between a face-to-face audience and the greater audience? What is meant by the sentence, "Some speakers . . . project their audiences into the future . . ."?
2. In this chapter we have described five types of audiences. Give five examples of each type found on your campus or in the local community.
3. In addition to those given on pages 138–139, what other sources of information are available?
4. Explain the statement, "You must speak in terms of people's wants." What is meant by "wants"? Give some other names for "wants."

5. How can the radio or television speaker overcome the absence of feedback?
6. Why is it not possible on most occasions to adapt a speech to an entire audience? Under what circumstances could you accomplish this feat? What would be the characteristics of such a group?
7. On page 140 we mention several "conditions of opinion." What others operate in your home community or on the campus?
8. Analyze the problems you have in speaking to your classmates. What do they know about you which can be used to your advantage when you speak?
9. How would you go about attempting to change intense attitudes on the part of the audience (a) toward you as a speaker, (b) toward the subject, (c) toward the purpose of the speech?
10. What is meant by a target group? Why is it important to the speaker?
11. What would be your target group in each of the following cases:
   a. 95 percent partisan and 5 percent neutral?
   b. 40 percent partisan, 25 percent neutral, and 35 percent opponents?
   c. 20 percent partisan, 2 percent neutral, and 78 percent opponents?

PROJECTS

1. *Speaking Assignment.* Deliver a short talk on analyzing the audience. Analyze for your classmates how a speaker you have heard personally succeeded or failed because of good or poor adjustment. Here are some suggested topics:
   a. How a poor audience analysis caused a speaker to fail
   b. How on-the-spot adjustment to the speaking situation saved the day
   c. How an unforeseen incident wrecked a speech
   d. How an inappropriate subject embarrassed a speaker
   e. How a speaker's appearance or platform deportment contributed to ineffectiveness
   f. How a speaker made a difficult subject meaningful
   g. A difficult subject that caused a speaker trouble
   h. How courage scattered a mob
   i. How a famous speaker coped with a difficult speaking situation
   j. My "pet peeves" about speakers
2. *Speech Practices Discussion.* Carefully read Chapter IV, "The Speaker Meets the Audience," in *Speech Practices* by Braden and Gehring. Carefully analyze how each speaker meets the unique problems presented by each speech situation. Try to answer the questions at the close of each section. Your instructor may ask you to write out your answers to at least one set of questions.

3. *Research Assignment.* Prepare a written analysis of a typical visible audience in your home community.
4. *Research Assignment.* Prepare a written analysis of a typical radio audience which listens to a radio station in your home town or one nearby.

SUPPLEMENTARY READINGS

Berlo, David K., *The Process of Communication,* Holt, Rinehart & Winston, 1960, chap. 6, "Social Systems."

Brembeck, Winston Lamont, and William Smiley Howell, *Persuasion: A Means of Social Control,* Prentice-Hall, 1952, chap. 7, "Attitudes, Sentiments, and Stereotypes in Persuasion."

Bryant, Donald C., and Karl R. Wallace, *Fundamentals of Public Speaking,* 3rd ed., Appleton-Century-Crofts, 1960, chap. 19, "The Audience: Partisan, Neutrals, Opponents."

Capp, Glenn R., *How To Communicate Orally,* Prentice-Hall, 1961, chap. 4, "How To Analyze the Audience and Speaking Occasion."

Oliver, Robert T., *The Psychology of Persuasive Speech,* 2nd ed. Longmans, Green, 1957, chap. 4, "The Speaker and His Audience."

Thonssen, Lester, and A. Craig Baird, *Speech Criticism,* Ronald, 1948, chap. 10, "Reconstructing the Social Setting."

10

Using Motive Appeals

All of your speaking will be for the purpose of securing from your auditors some kind of response. This response may be simple enjoyment, understanding of a hitherto unknown set of facts, intensification of already held beliefs and attitudes, acceptance of new beliefs, or adoption of a course of action. All these types of reactions may be made by members of your audiences. In order to make your efforts successful, therefore, you should know something of the background of human behavior—the reasons why people do the things they do, the impulsions behind the choices of action they make from time to time. Without some understanding of these bases, you will be likely to flounder aimlessly or to select an appeal to which your listeners will not respond at all.[1]

[1] The term *appeal,* which will be used here frequently, does not refer necessarily to perfervid exhortations or supplications but rather to any procedure

Why did you come to college? If you enrolled voluntarily for this course, what was back of your deciding to take public speaking? Why did you choose the particular vocation for which you are studying, or, for that matter, why are you studying at all? Why do we surround ourselves with objects of beauty—music, pictures, flowers, literature, well-kept lawns? Why do we contribute to the Red Cross, the United Givers' Fund, or other worthy charities, or to the church? Why do we take measures to protect our health, to ensure a reasonably long life? Why do we seek the approval of others or at least try to avoid their disapproval? Why do we work to improve our economic status, or run for office on the campus, in the community, or in the state or nation? Why do we reject the philosophy of communism and adhere to those principles of democracy which we have taken the trouble to understand? In short, why do we do the things we do?

TYPES OF MOTIVE APPEAL

Psychologists and others have found motives and motivation difficult to explain. Perhaps the concepts may be clarified somewhat by suggesting a few fairly specific "motive appeals" the speaker can make use of in order to induce his listeners to listen more willingly, to believe his arguments, and perhaps even to do the things he is advocating. We have no intention of attempting a complete catalogue of such appeals; there are many such lists and no two writers or teachers agree entirely on any one of them. But you will find the few we discuss here and others readily adaptable to your purposes in speaking. Studying and applying them may make the whole idea of motives and motivation somewhat more intelligible.

Security

The desire for security is strong in most of us. It may be directed into many different channels: avoidance of physical danger, provision for support in old age, assurance of happiness in this world and

---

which will bring about some response, whether it be to impel the listeners to think, to feel, or to act. The "appeal" is usually directed toward some factor in the human constitution which contributes to the tendency to respond in certain desired ways.

afterwards, and so on. We like to feel secure in our vocations, in our social relations, in our reputations. We do many things to avoid social ostracism.

Speeches built around such central ideas as the following would be likely to make their appeal to the desire for security as it is revealed in various ways.

1. Our government should adopt a positive policy against subversive activities at home and abroad, if we would preserve our national integrity.
2. Fluoridation of our public water systems will provide the greatest protection against tooth decay among our children, and thus contribute to their continuing health.
3. The campaign for highway safety is a never-ending one; it needs constant vigilance by all of us.
4. The increase of chain stores in almost all aspects of merchandizing is one of our greatest threats to individual enterprise.
5. Since war has become an all-out struggle, the provision of bomb shelters is a public responsibility.
6. Your best protection against unemployment is thorough preparation for your job.

In his "Gettysburg Address," Lincoln made a powerful appeal to the motive of security in calling for a renewed dedication to the "great task remaining before us" and for a new resolution that, among other things, "government of the people, by the people, for the people, shall not perish from the earth."

Social Approval

Many psychologists consider the desire for the good opinion of others, for social acceptance, the strongest of all motives. There is probably no more devastating experience for a youth—or even an oldster—than the feeling of being shut out, of not being wanted, of always being left on the fringes, so to speak, and never being completely accepted into the inner circle of one's group. This can be one of the greatest tragedies confronting the retiree: having once been an influential member of the group, he is often made to feel that neither his counsel nor his experience has any further value.

This desire for the approval of others extends beyond the motivations of individuals. Groups of all sorts, both large and small, seek the good will of other groups of their own kind. Nations send representatives to other countries to establish and maintain that good will; business firms advertise extensively to build up public good will toward themselves as well as toward their products.

Appeals to the desire for social approval may be based on such typical central ideas as these:

1. Our school cannot maintain its present standing if the proposed budget is seriously curtailed.
2. Let's make this university one that our athletic teams will be proud to represent.
3. Acceptable use of the mother tongue is one of the marks of an educated person. Don't be satisfied with substandard speaking or writing.
4. Our treatment of visitors who come to us from abroad has a tremendous impact on the opinions of us they carry back home.
5. Business executives are constantly looking for young men and women who can express themselves effectively in both speech and writing.
6. If you would achieve stature in your profession, remember that there is no more direct approach than sound and thorough scholarship.

It takes but little thought to recognize that many of the actions of people of all ages have status as their primary objective. Students gain the favorable opinion of their fellow students by engaging in various campus activities, such as going out for athletic teams, joining societies of various kinds, and seeking student government offices. Now and then one seeks approval by maintaining high scholastic standards—partly because he may as a result be "tapped" for some honor society. And professors likewise gain public approval, especially in their own fields, by giving interesting lectures in their courses, writing fair examinations, publishing books and articles, conducting research, participating in the activities of their professional organizations, and also by engaging in community enterprises.

On the other hand, most of us avoid doing many things that would create unfavorable opinions among others. The fear of being put in jail with its attendant stigma, for instance, is undoubtedly a powerful deterrent to doing many things we might like to do. It follows, of course, that the weight of that social approval in influencing your actions or the actions of the people you are trying to influence depends largely upon the significance of those whose approval you are seeking, either for yourself or for your audience. Are the favorable attitudes of such people worth cultivating? Right now you probably would not urge your listeners to take a certain course of action primarily because it would please Nikita Khrushchev or a group of people bent upon evading every law they might come up against. As a professional man or woman, certainly you would want the approval of your professional associates. If you live in a community of beautiful, well-kept homes, you will or should want to maintain your home so that it will meet the approval of your neighbors. If you belong to a certain social group, you will probably avoid the kind of behavior in their gatherings that will evoke frowns of disapproval. If you write a textbook, you normally hope that it will not only be useful as a text in the teaching of a certain course but that it will draw favorable reviews and also will be adopted by your fellow teachers.

As a motivating influence, then, social approval is not as a rule a broad, all-over effect, but rather more or less particularized among those whose approval is significant in some fairly specific area.

Ownership or Possession

In the little one-act play, *Joint Owners in Spain*, by Alice Brown, one of the characters, an old woman living in the poorhouse, is made to say, "I don't want much, but I want it mine." People take great satisfaction in acquiring and saving, that is, in becoming owners and in preserving what they have. People collect many different things, strange things, not for their intrinsic value but to satisfy the desire for ownership.

Such possession not only provides satisfactions in itself; it also has a number of side values—"fringe benefits," so to speak—which satisfy additional motives. Thus, a savings account gives the satisfaction of possession; it provides additional security from want, from the economic disaster of prolonged illness, and so on. It provides a measure of certainty that we will be able to give our children an adequate or better education. It may also enable us to have still other things we want from time to time, including a certain degree of social approval. To be able to speak casually of the stocks and bonds one may happen to possess can ensure a certain status.

Many people, though it is not always apparent, are still interested in economical buying. Fancy chrome costs more on an automobile; hence it is eschewed by many purchasers. The car that will give more miles per gallon of gas consumed has attractions from a financial point of view. A suit that will wear well offers economic advantage over one that is good only for a single season.

Typical central ideas that appeal to the desire for ownership, possession, and economy are the following:

1. The college graduate can normally expect to earn an average of $200,000 more in his lifetime than he would without such an education.
2. Top business and professional people are all extensive readers.
3. A program of regular exercise will keep your doctor's bills down.
4. You cannot afford not to take an occasional vacation.
5. Our public welfare costs are far higher than they should be.
6. The prices for the drugs we require today are exorbitant.

If you study your listeners' particular types of acquisitiveness, you have a powerful leverage to persuasion. But do not urge satisfaction of this motive to the disadvantage or damaging loss of others. Whenever possible, tie in personally oriented with socially oriented motives—maintaining your own property will uphold the attractiveness of your whole neighborhood. These will be discussed later in this chapter.

Exploration

As soon as the infant learns to crawl he begins to explore. About the house are dozens of fascinating places to examine, things to handle, steps to climb, cabinets to open. He wants to go to places he hasn't been, see things he hasn't seen, do things he hasn't done. Many people retain much of that urge to explore as they grow older so that it becomes a strong motive for discovery. The satisfaction of curiosity is an incentive to investigation in many different possible directions.

Millions of people every year take trips to foreign places, or tour our own country from coast to coast, from the Gulf of Mexico to the Great Lakes. Others delve into the mysteries of science; still others investigate the works of the world's great thinkers. There is no limit to the opportunities for exploration and discovery, and there are always many people who will make use of those opportunities.

Read the advertisements that appear in our newspapers and magazines, especially the sections dealing with travel, and see for yourself how extensively this motive of exploration is appealed to in one way or another. Here are a few central ideas that may suggest others that you can use in your own appeals to the motive of exploration:

1. Travel by jet; you can visit more places in the time you have.
2. This encyclopedia will open up to you the world of knowledge.
3. The possibility of space flight offers unlimited opportunity for exploration beyond all our present horizons.
4. What we do not know in the many branches of science is yet much more than what we do know; the field for research is unlimited.
5. How did language begin? What were the origins of speech?
6. Visit the Evangeline Country; you will find it beautiful and interesting.

The curiosity of the listeners can sometimes be aroused by proposing to give them information they do not already have. "Do you know . . ." is often an attention-getting beginning. One speaker began his talk on the soft treatment of criminals with the startling statement, phrased in the form of a rhetorical question, "Do you know that there are more murderers at large in America today than there are members of all the polices forces of this country?"

Freedom from Restraint

When personal freedoms are threatened, people are likely to swing into action. Groups resent any attempt by outside forces to limit their autonomy, to curtail their authority to determine their own course of conduct. You can make powerful appeals if you can show how this freedom can be made more secure, or how it can be expanded still further.

While freedom may be very abstract in a general sense, it is very specific in its application. Freedom to do what? The things that we are free to do are limited, first, to what is possible, and second, to what others around us are also free to do. There is no point in urging someone to take wing and fly under his own power so long as it remains a physical impossibility. It would likewise be futile to prompt some beginning student in a public speaking course, who has not yet learned to overcome his nervousness, to appear before some highly important group of people and urge action on them in elevated oratory. When Hamlet urges his friend Guilden-stern to take the flute and "discourse sweet music" thereon, his friend replies, "But I have not the skill."

The motive of freedom to do the things we want to do often con-flicts with other motives, such as that for security. Maximum security is incompatible with maximum freedom; we have to decide which we prefer in larger degree, as well as how we are to maintain a desired degree of each. Do not hold out to your listeners the hope of attaining goals which are mutually incompatible, or deliberately conceal from them unfavorable implications of their choice of goals.

You can use many approaches in appealing to this powerful motive of freedom from external restraint. Remember, though, that because many forces and influences can operate to limit and restrict our freedoms, the specific appeals that can be employed should be varied accordingly. Following are some examples of topic sentences that illustrate a few of these approaches:

1. Creeping communism is a direct threat to the liberties we have always prized so highly.
2. "Is life so dear, or peace so sweet, as to be purchased at the price of chains and slavery?"
3. Federal aid to education will (will not) deprive the states of their freedom to operate their own education systems.
4. Modern methods of communication have expanded the "neighbor-hood" and extended man's horizons.
5. Bridging the Mississippi has increased immeasurably our freedom to travel between East and West.
6. Develop your ability to speak, and thus make freedom of speech more nearly a reality for you.

Aesthetic Enjoyment

Most of us enjoy things that are aesthetically pleasing, and go to some lengths to satisfy our desire for such things. We tend to look askance at people who dress oddly or who are careless of their own appearance. We enjoy visiting homes that are neat and at-tractive.

We visit art galleries, stand in contemplation and awe before architectural masterpieces, attend symphony concerts, and pur-chase symphonic records so that we can have them whenever we want them. We clothe ourselves neatly and attractively; we adorn our homes with furnishings that are pleasing to the eye and comfortable to the body. The old Ford, which, it was said, "made riding an ordeal and walking a pleasure," has given way to cars with "built-in" comfort and pleasing external lines and internal upholstering. We like things that give us aesthetic pleasure, and will, as we just said, go to great lengths to provide them. The desire for such things is for most people a strong motive for action.

Here are a few central ideas or topic sentences that may suggest how you can appeal to this motive:

1. Billboard and other advertising should be banned from the field of vision along the new interestate highways now being built.
2. City planners should be prevented from destroying historic shrines to make way for modern architectural eyesores.
3. The "play-it-yourself" musical instruments now being marketed reduce the impulsion to learn how really to play.
4. For lasting beauty in your home, nothing takes the place of wood.
5. Appreciation in the area of tastes and smells and the other senses should be taught, just as is appreciation of art or music.
6. To get the greatest enjoyment from your camera, learn some of the basic principles of art.

Different things are aesthetically pleasing to different people; some prefer camellias, others azaleas. In another part of the country, many grow lilacs and roses. Whereas some enjoy the older masterpieces of music, others fill their record cabinets with Copland and Hindemith. You can hardly hope to convince an addict of modern popular jazz that Mozart and Grieg are preferable. Modernistic furniture will probably not be aesthetically satisfying to one whose tastes run to early American or sixteenth-century French.

Benefits and Satisfactions to Others

Certainly not all behavior is based on anticipated benefits and satisfactions to the individual himself. Much of what we do is done for others' pleasure, present or remote, or the relief of possible or actual distress. While it is true that we derive much personal satisfaction from generous actions, it is also true that our own feelings of self-gratification are usually in the background and are probably not the principal factor. This type of motivation can be seen in the many instances of immediate and generous aid in times of disaster, even when the tragedy occurs thousands of miles from us and to people with whom we have no acquaintance. When the eastern seacoast was hit by a terrific hurricane some years ago that brought destruction as far north as New England, supplies, food, clothing, medicines, money, and personnel were rushed from all parts of the country.

Similarly, when southwestern Louisiana was devastated a few years ago, the same types of assistance were made immediately available by people hundreds of miles away for hundreds of sufferers totally unknown to the givers. These donors were not taking credit to themselves for giving; they simply recognized that the people in those areas were in desperate need of help.

Shortly after the close of World War II a large signboard beside the street leading from a university campus into the city carried for several weeks this simple appeal:

Children in Europe Are Hungry. Send a CARE Package.

". . . altruism," says Bois, "is not a matter of choice; it belongs to the nature of man."[2]

In addition to the relief of distress, most people enjoy giving to others because it affords the recipients pleasure. Who has not seen a child's face light up when someone brought him some small present? The old Biblical saying that "It is more blessed to give than to receive" is as true today as it was when originally uttered.

The speaker is confronted with many opportunities to appeal to this particular motive. In fact, when he attempts to persuade his listeners to perform some act that will bring certain benefits to them, he may himself be acting on the basis of a socially oriented motive, in that their action can bring him no appreciable benefits or satisfactions beyond the incidental one that some pleasure or value has been given to someone who will appreciate it.

Topic sentences that illustrate an appeal to socially oriented motives might be such as the following:

1. To many children in our own country Christmas means nothing. You can give it meaning for them.

[2] J. Samuel Bois, *Exploration in Awareness*, Harper, 1957, p. 195.

2. Join the Peace Corps and share your "know-how" with those who don't know how.
3. The teaching profession (or the ministry or medicine) will give you great opportunities for service to mankind.
4. "Adopt" a child in Korea (or Hong Kong, Vietnam, Laos).
5. Contribute to the United Givers' Fund.
6. This section of our city is in desperate need of adequate park facilities for its children. Let's start a move to establish one.

It would be possible to enumerate and illustrate many more of the motives that underlie human behavior, and how the speaker can appeal to them in order to elicit responses. But those discussed above will be sufficient to exemplify the principle that, if you want to influence your listeners, you must stimulate the internal impulsions and drives that lead human beings to do the things they do.

CHARACTERISTICS OF MOTIVES

Motives Are Basic to Behavior

It has long been recognized that within each organism are strong internal forces which direct it toward certain goals[3] and without which there would be no directed activity—only a random, futile sort of behavior for its own sake. But even that would still be the result of some inherent impulsion. When properly stimulated, these forces may set off a chain reaction of behavior which does not entirely subside until the goal toward which the activity is directed is reached. The strivings toward these goals or end results are generally referred to as *motives*, though some of the lower-level impulsions, such as purely physiological ones like hunger and thirst, may be known as *needs, drives,* or by some similar term. Many of these impulsions to which the term *motive* is commonly applied are either biosocial or almost entirely social.

Social approval, for instance, is hardly a basic necessity for continued existence, but it is vital in maintaining our personal integrity as members of human society. Much of our existence is spent in satisfying these motives; they are in fact the impelling force for all or almost all we do.

[3] Floyd M. Ruch, *Psychology and Life,* new ed., Scott, Foresman, 1941, pp. 65 ff.

Thus most of us go to great lengths to conserve our health and prolong our lives. We join certain organizations partly to gain a measure of social approval and partly in quest of congenial companionship. We keep our houses painted to add to their appearance and to keep what we have longer. We contribute to the United Givers' Fund, the Red Cross, and the church in order to satisfy the normal human desire to be helpful where help is needed. We react vigorously against attempts to place rigid restrictions on our freedom of action; we resent coercion.

As we said earlier, these desires are not basically matters of reason, although once we recognize certain goals we can and should resort to reason to discover how these end results can best be achieved. Motives have been called "mainsprings of action": they are what give us drive. They are the impelling forces which form the basis for practically all of our behavior. They are among the most important aspects of human existence. So far as it is related to speaking, *motivating* is the process by which the speaker arouses or stimulates these motives or internal compulsions in the listeners to render them more favorably inclined to respond as he intends they should.

Motives Are Difficult To Classify

Many attempts have been made by psychologists as well as by teachers of speech to classify motives, to reduce their apparently large numbers, and in many cases to attribute all of them to a very small group of fundamental biological needs. It would be difficult to find two lists of motives that agree entirely. ". . . motives are as numerous," says Dewey, "as are original impulsive activities multiplied by the diversified consequences they produce as they operate under diverse conditions."[4] Says Ruch, "Any classification of human motives would be merely for convenience in talking about them."[5] It has recently been said that "every act has its own intrinsic motive."[6]

There is no standard guide to motivation, says Cofer, but " 'everyone' has some idea as to what the term refers to." Usually, he continues, the subject is "picked up" in connection with some other

---

[4] John Dewey, *Human Nature and Conduct,* Holt, 1922, p. 122.
[5] Ruch, *op. cit.,* p. 86.
[6] Cited in Charles N. Cofer, "Motivation," in Paul R. Farnsworth and Quinn McNemar, eds., *Annual Review of Psychology,* Annual Reviews, Inc., 1959, pp. 173–202.

topic such as "personality, and by social, abnormal, clinical, and counseling psychology." As a distinct concept, Cofer suggests, "motivation might well disappear." However, as a concept in influencing human behavior, it has a very useful place in public speaking. The commonly presented "classifications" of motives are hardly more than listings of familiar motive appeals that may be used to influence human behavior. Any classification should, it would seem, be somewhat more basic.

Motives May Be Personally or Socially Oriented

For purposes of convenience, then, let us roughly classify these impelling motives into two general types, which, for some reason, have been called the "lower" and the "higher" motives. These designations are not satisfactory, mainly because they suggest evaluative attitudes that are inaccurate and basically unfair. The lower motives direct our actions toward goals which bring satisfactions directly or indirectly to *ourselves*, either individually or in groups. They have also been called the "selfish" motives. The higher motives, which are here designated as the socially oriented, are concerned with forms of behavior engaged in primarily because of the benefits or advantages which may be brought to *others*. They may also be thought of as "altruistic."

This distinction or the labels which have been attached to the two general types carries no implication that the "lower" or "selfish" goals are in themselves necessarily reprehensible or that the "higher" or "altruistic" motives are always justifiable. There certainly is nothing blameworthy in maintaining one's own good health; on the other hand, one may request favors for other people who do not deserve them at all.

But because of the unfortunate connotations in the terms commonly used, it may help clarify the distinction and the basis for differentiation between the two broad classes to think of them as being "personally oriented" and "socially oriented."

Motives Rarely Occur Singly

These various motives, or impulsions to action, rarely stand alone; a given act seldom arises from a single motive. Usually a number of them are active simultaneously. One selects a new car, for example, for several reasons: economy, safety, comfort, attractiveness, and so on, each of these representing some motive appeal.

Often, too, the "personally oriented" and the "socially oriented" are found side by side, so to speak, both giving impulsion to the same activity or action. The seventy-five-yard off-tackle smash in the last three minutes of the game that scored the only touchdown was an outstanding triumph for the halfback; but it also won the game for the team and for the school. The man who donates a tract of land for an open park has made a distinct contribution to his community; but his name will be seen over the entrance gate for many generations, and at the same time the donation will permit a substantial deduction for income tax purposes.

Turning back the Communist threat on our very doorstep would certainly let the people of America rest a little easier; it would also free the people of a neighboring country from a tyranny that has already become oppressive to them. It is becoming increasingly evident that the welfare and prosperity of any one part of the country or of the world depend in the long run on the welfare and prosperity of every other part. These are all examples of what has been called "enlightened self-interest."

Conflicts often arise between and among motives. Sometimes two or more motives that arise together can be so coordinated that the outcome, the end result, satisfies both. But different motives can also be directed simultaneously to mutually incompatible end results. That is, we often want two or more different things and, in the normal situation, realize that we can have only one. We may have to decide whether to take one position that will pay a better salary, or stay where we are where the working and other conditions are more agreeable and the chances for advancement greater. We may even have difficulty in deciding what line of work follow. We are constantly having to make such decisions.

Communities and groups of all sorts, even legislatures and decision-making bodies at still higher levels, are faced with the same necessity as are individuals of making decisions affecting the welfare of their groups. If there were no competing, conflicting motives, these problems might not arise—but then, if problems of decision-making are never to arise, the question of making choices is also nonexistent. And usually, as we said, what people want is not in itself a matter of reasoning things out; one doesn't as a rule decide on the basis of rational thinking, just what he does want, even though he does have to decide on which of his wants are going to be satisfied. Our wants are likely to have an emotional basis, not one of intelligent deliberation. We may even decide on what we want, and then try to find the reasons for the decision. That is, we often make our choices before applying intelligent consideration; by that time, if we adhere to these decisions, there is no room left for such intelligent weighing of the different motivations. Such rationalization is the opposite of rational decision-making.

Motives Vary in Strength

The same motives do not seem to be equally strong among all people, nor are all motives equally strong in the same person. Furthermore, any motive may be dormant for a time; that is, in any one person a motive may vary in strength from time to time, so that as far as awareness is concerned it may be entirely quiescent during a given period. Too, various motives may on occasion come into conflict. When these conflicts arise, decisions may have to be made on the basis of which particular motive is strongest at the time. Thus, in time of financial distress, a factory owner may relinquish his profits in order to ensure that his workers will not be laid off and lose their own living. Parents give up things they have long wanted in order to send their children to college.

Universality of Motives Must Be Qualified

It has sometimes been thought that there is a universality to motives, that all peoples everywhere, regardless of culture level, have by nature the same basic impulses, or even the same impulsions which in their very nature are at least partially socialized or the product of acculturation.

It is probable that certain biological drives and needs are inherent; whether the motives presumably arising from such drives are *therefore* universal is another matter.

As the individual develops in the social environment, however, motives [these original biological drives] must become socialized, modified in such ways that the motivations of others will have equal room for play; otherwise the conflicting wants and desires of the various members of the group would lead to disorder and anarchy. In the process of enculturation, moreover, additional motives are acquired which have a direct bearing on one's relations with one's associates. The result is that long before adulthood such a structure of motive has been erected that the original drives with which one started are recognized with difficulty, if at all.[7]

McClelland accounts for the so-called universality of motives thus: ". . . the probability of certain common motives developing in all people is very high. . . . Socialization occurs in all cultures for all individuals and it involves certain common problems in all cultures. . . . some associations . . . are laid down in all individuals in all cultures, at all times, simply because with very few exceptions everybody is faced at one time or another with achievement problems."[8]

Motives, then, may be thought of as "universal" to the extent to which they are based on either (1) common physiological needs or drives among people generally, or (2) common elements in all the cultures in which people generally have been reared. For motives may be quite as much the product of acculturation, or socialization and maturation, or even of habit as they are of innate physiological traits.

The speaker's problem is to discover which motives are dominant at the time among the listeners to whom he is to speak, or what dormant motives he may be able to arouse which will impel his hearers toward the end results he is seeking. The members of most of the audiences to whom you yourselves will speak will probably have sufficiently similar *basic* cultural backgrounds for you to think of them as essentially homogeneous in this respect.

COORDINATED MOTIVES AND REASON

Although motives themselves are seldom if ever the product of rational deliberation, they can and should be coordinated with reason if rational behavior is to result. Two problems arise in arriving

---

[7] Giles Wilkeson Gray and Claude Merton Wise, *The Bases of Speech,* 3rd ed., Harper, 1959, p. 390.

[8] "Notes for a Revised Theory of Motivation," in David C. McClelland, ed., *Studies in Motivation,* Appleton-Century-Crofts, 1955, pp. 226–234.

at intelligent decisions regarding what course of action is to be taken, what beliefs are to be accepted, or even what set of data is to be understood as representing the facts in a given situation: what motive to choose and how to satisfy it.

The Motive To Be Satisfied Must Be Intelligently Chosen

In the first place, in attempting to win the responses you want from your audiences, you must in your speaking stimulate, arouse, or strengthen the motives which are present to some degree in nearly everyone. The selection of the particular motive to which you will appeal will usually depend on (1) the present situation, (2) the events of the immediate as well as the remote past, and (3) the habitual attitudes and modes of thought of the people to whom you are talking. Often, however, you may find it more to your purpose to awaken dormant motives, that is, to stimulate those which for one reason or another have been allowed to lapse into quiescence. Many people, for example, do not recognize the threat to our own national safety by the strengthening of the Communist foothold close to our own borders.

The inhabitants of one choice residential street may be indifferent to the deplorable slums in the next block unless the dormant motive that all decent people possess to relieve distress is awakened or unless they are made to realize that their own welfare is in jeopardy; perhaps they suddenly become aware of the threat to their own property values. Minority groups are permitted to live in social and economic squalor unless the members of majority groups are stimulated to provide better living, working, and recreation conditions. We may fail to recognize that "minority groups" may become dissatisfied with their subordinate status *as* minority groups, or we may seek by various means to remove the disqualifications that adhere to such a status.

Your first task as a speaker, then, may be to aid in resolving the conflicts that may have arisen between or among competing motivations, or to help select the particular motive to be satisfied. Your group, let us say, has the choice of air-conditioning their own church and making themselves more comfortable, or of using the money to support a mission church in an outlying district that cannot as yet support itself. Here is an obvious conflict of motives among the members of the group. On what rational basis, if any, is a choice to be made between such opposing motives? Or is there any way that a compromise can be reached that may satisfy, to some extent at least, both desires? It would seem that any choice must make some kind of rational sense.

The problem usually centers about which motive is strongest at the time, or whether immediate satisfactions provided by pursuing one are more desirable than the more permanent satisfactions provided by the other.

It is thus that democratic decisions are made. Obviously, effective persuasion is of maximum importance in such deliberations, and the persuasive speaker is often the key man in the group's coming to a rational decision.

Methods Must Be Found to Satisfy the Chosen Motive

The second way in which reason must be applied to motive if rational decisions are to be made is in determining how that motive is to be satisfied. Inability to find such methods often leads to severe frustrations unless some other motive can be accepted which will bring approximately equal satisfactions.

Do the nations of the world actually want to establish peaceful relations among themselves? Then someone must show how this may be done in a way that will be acceptable to all the nations concerned. Do you, as students, want to get the best education for your chosen vocation? Then you will need to discover how and where you can acquire that training. Furthermore, you must be motivated actually to put that procedure into operation. If you are interested in beautifying your residential property or want to rid your lawn of destructive insects, you will have to find out what method you should use to bring about the wanted end results.

We all want, or think we do, the best school system our funds will provide, so that our children will receive a good education; but merely wanting it will not establish such a system. We have to know what we must do in order to set one up and maintain it, and we have to want such a system more than we want the results of failure to establish some systematic program. Farmers have traditionally insisted on their "independence"; they also, with justice, expect a fair return for their investment and labor. Are these necessarily incompatible? How can both be provided satisfactorily? We all want increasing services from our national, state, and local governments; is it possible to provide these services without increasing our taxes? How, in other words, can we get these increased benefits?

It is not unusual for two or more motives to be incompatible at one time or under one set of circumstances and actually complementary or even interdependent under another set. In such instances, compromises again have to be arrived at. Freedom and security need not be incompatible; but while one may have the maximum security in prison, one has little freedom.

The problem of the speaker here is one of clarification, or weighing the possible advantages of one choice as against the other, and then, probably, some advocacy in order to guide the listeners into choices that will give the most lasting satisfactions to the greatest number.

Know your audiences. Study their interests, their habitual attitudes and modes of thinking, the particular motives that seem uppermost at the time or that can be aroused if dormant, and if at all possible base your appeal on those characteristics. Frequently your proposal will touch no motive that is especially active at the moment; but a quiescent motive may often be associated with one that is already active.

GENERAL PRINCIPLES GOVERNING THE USE OF MOTIVE APPEALS

In your use of the motive appeals there are a few general principles which you should follow.[9]

The Motive Itself Must Be Worthy of the Deed

Most people do not like to admit that they are selfish, inconsiderate, or uninterested in human welfare; they can often be aroused by an appeal which is socially acceptable even when they tend to deny any particular altruism on their own part. In fact, those whose actions are most often directed toward some social benefit are frequently the very ones to be modest with regard to

[9] The first four of these are adapted from Gray and Wise, *op. cit.*, pp. 366–388.

their own "public spirit." As an investment, a slum-clearance project might not appeal; if to the expectation of a modest return on one's investment is added a reference to the social value of decent living quarters for low-income groups, the motive appeal would thereby be elevated to the point where it would become "worthy of the deed," as Winans expresses the idea.[10]

At the same time, the deed proposed must be worthy of the motive. As Winans suggests, " 'Don't use a sledgehammer to kill a fly.' If the plain and sufficient reason for voting for John Smith for dog-catcher is that the town needs a good dog-catcher, don't tell me that to vote for Smith is a patriotic duty, even though in essence it may be."[11]

The End Result Must Be Worthy of the Effort

If a group of college or high-school students can be shown that the study of public speaking will repay them handsomely, they are more likely to work just a little harder on the course.

Is the gain achieved by a long-drawn-out strike worth the lost income from the resulting unemployment? Is the securing of America and of the entire Western world worth the expenditures it is costing the American people? Is our freedom of action of such value as to warrant a defense of that freedom at all costs? Was Patrick Henry's appeal a valid one when, as we have already quoted, he challenged the Virginia Convention: "Is life so dear, or peace so sweet, as to be purchased at the price of chains and slavery?"

The Action Suggested Should Lead to the Desired Result

If you did not feel that your education would actually enable you to obtain the results you want, you might be very reluctant to spend these years in college. Will a certain treatment effectually have a good chance of curing a head cold, or arthritis, or a cancerous growth? Will the adoption of a proposed agricultural program contribute to the solution of the present problem of surpluses with their high costs of maintenance?

[10] See James A. Winans, *Speech-Making*, Appleton-Century-Crofts, 1938, p. 313.
[11] *Ibid.*, p. 311.

At the same time, one may feel that the course being advocated has such an element of "rightness" to it that one is willing to urge its adoption even though recognizing that there is little if any chance of success. A generation or so ago General "Billy" Mitchell, who advocated a strong air force, struggled in vain for years, and was court-martialed for his efforts before such a military branch was actually established. He never lived to see the fulfillment of his objectives. Admiral Rickover was faced with the same opposition in urging the building of nuclear submarines, but he was more successful than General Mitchell—the submarines are fully operative.

The Appeal Should Be Made to the Highest Possible Motives

If an appeal to motives of self-interest is necessary, attempt to associate them with motives having to do with the welfare or happiness of others. That is to say, try to link personally oriented with socially oriented motives.[12]

An automobile driver may respond to a safety campaign for the sake of his own life; but it can also be shown that his life is of some value to others, and furthermore that reckless driving endangers others as well as himself.

One might not be drawn into the teaching profession solely by the promise of monetary rewards; but one might be if one were convinced that such a profession would provide a comfortable living and would at the same time contribute a much needed service to the youth of the community. A recent appeal for donations to the United Givers' Fund was concluded with the amazing suggestion, "Wear your little badge to show what a good guy you are!" Fortunately for this campaign, this particular motive appeal was not continued very long.

Appeal Should Generally Be Made to More than One Motive

Remember that motives are of different strengths at a given time for different people and at different times for the same people. One motive appeal might influence one person or group of persons, whereas another motive appeal would influence others. Actually,

[12] George Pierce Baker and Henry Barrett Huntington, *The Principles of Argument*, rev. ed., Ginn, 1905, p. 321.

a number of good reasons or motives can usually be found for most actions, and if more than one of these are presented there is more likelihood of your getting the desired response.

It Is Often Best to Omit All Mention of Specific Motives

The desirability of the end result may be so obvious or may be presented so effectively that nothing more is needed. People generally do not like to be appealed to on the basis of purely selfish motives, and are sometimes embarrassed by appeals to altruism, especially in small groups or when such appeals are too obvious. They may even refuse to admit any influence of the socially oriented motives.

Motives Should Not Be Dictated

You cannot tell people what they ought to feel. They are likely to resent being "shamed" into any kind of action. You cannot insist that they should be under the impulsion of certain motives. The best you can do is to discover those motives which are already operative or which can be aroused indirectly, and make use of them.

You may have to reveal to your listeners that certain motives are actually present but are dormant for the time being. Listeners are often surprised when a speaker comes out with an idea that strikes a responsive note, and they react with some such comment as, "That's just what I've been thinking for a long time."

Motives Should Not Be Overworked

Most people are willing to do their "duty," but will resent the persistent repetition of the appeal. They would much rather determine for themselves where their duty lies. After all, it is often a rather delicate matter to insist that someone is insensitive to his obligations to society, and that another person must remind him.

Generosity can usually be appealed to successfully, but it can easily be overworked. Before such combined efforts to obtain donations for worthy causes as the United Givers' Fund or the Community Chest were established, many people would be thoroughly tired of repeated appeals for the separate causes. With the united campaigns, they will probably give more than they would to all the individual appeals.

Vary your appeals. You will probably find that you will not have occasion to use the same ones very often, anyway.

QUESTIONS AND TOPICS FOR STUDY AND REVIEW

1. "Motives provide the basis upon which must rest any appeal the speaker can make." Explain and illustrate this statement.
2. What is meant by the term *motive*? What are some other terms for motives?
3. Explain the concept of "higher" or socially oriented and "lower" or personally oriented motives. Show how they may be combined in urging a given response to a speech.
4. Give specific instances, other than those in the text, in which it may be necessary to arouse dormant motives.
5. Give examples of common, everyday conflicts of motives. On what basis are these conflicts resolved? Name some forms of unwholesome solutions of conflicts.
6. What is meant by "ulterior" motives? To what degree are the motives of the speaker in his own speaking subject to examination by his hearers?
7. Differentiate between biological, biosocial, and social impulsions to behavior. Give examples of each.
8. Can it be said with justification that any of these three general types of impulsion is necessarily "universal"? What is the basis of the concept of "universal" motives? What does the term itself mean?
9. Discuss the question of whether people are ever impelled by motives other than those of personal gratification.
10. How would you use the element of motivation in an informative speech?
11. Describe the two aspects of motivation in which reason must be combined with motive to elicit rational behavior.
12. In democratic action it is obvious that not everyone is able to satisfy all his own motives. What happens to those motives which must be rejected for the sake of group agreement on action to be taken?
13. It is said that the purpose of group discussion is in general agreement. What is the difference, if any, between such agreement and what is often referred to as conformity? What happens to motives in such cases?
14. Give an example of motives that are in conflict under one set of conditions and entirely compatible under another set.

PROJECTS

1. Analyze your own motives in (a) seeking an education, (b) choosing your particular vocation. Exactly what part does the acquiring of ability in public speaking contribute to the satisfaction of these motives?
2. Present an account of an instance in your own experience of a conflict of motives. What were the deciding factors in the final resolution of the conflict?
3. Bring to class a half-dozen or more full-page advertisements from magazines, posters, and the like, and make a talk with these as visual aids, showing how advertisers appeal to certain motives in attempting to sell their merchandise.
4. Read a persuasive speech, and analyze the motives to which the speaker is appealing. What does he offer in his speech by way of satisfaction of those motives?
5. Give a talk in which you make a definite link between one of the "selfish" and one of the "unselfish" motives. Make use of the idea of "enlightened self-interest." In your preparation, analyze your own motives in urging the course of action you propose for your listeners to follow. What is your particular interest in the matter?
6. Present a talk in which you appeal primarily to one of the motives discussed in the chapter. Observe carefully the general principles, and *show* that the end result is worthy and attainable. Do not specifically mention the particular motive to which you are appealing.
7. Select some individual who has recently been before the public eye largely through his speaking. On the basis of his public utterances correlated with his public actions, what would you say of his probable motives in (a) requesting support at the polls, (b) urging the adoption of certain policies, (c) urging support of another candidate for office?

SUPPLEMENTARY READINGS

Baird, A. Craig, *Argumentation, Discussion, and Debate*, McGraw-Hill, 1950, chap. 18, "Persuasion: Techniques of Motivation."

Bryant, Donald C., and Karl R. Wallace, *Fundamentals of Public Speaking*, 3rd ed., Appleton-Century-Crofts, 1960, chap. 18, "The Audience: Motives and Basic Lines of Thought."

Gray, Giles Wilkeson, and Claude Merton Wise, *The Bases of Speech*, 3rd ed., Harper, 1959, pp. 388–414. See footnotes to this discussion.

Monroe, Alan H., *Principles and Types of Speech*, 5th ed., Scott, Foresman, 1962, chap. 10, "Selecting the Basic Appeal."

Oliver, Robert T., *The Psychology of Persuasive Speech*, 2nd ed., Longmans, Green, 1957, chap. 3, "Human Motivation," and pp. 391–393. The whole of Part I of this text is concerned with "Motivation in Human Affairs."

Reid, Loren, *First Principles of Public Speaking*, Artcraft, 1960, chap. 15, "Persuading Through Emotions, Attitudes."

Sarett, Lew, William Trufant Foster, and Alma Johnson Sarett, *Basic Principles of Speech*, 3rd ed., Houghton Mifflin, 1958, pp. 408–414, 439–444.

Winans, James A., *Speech-Making*, Appleton-Century-Crofts, 1938, chap. 15.

11

Attention and Interest

THE FUNCTION OF ATTENTION

Closely related to the problem of motivation in speaking is the dual problem of attention and interest. So closely related are these problems, in fact, that though they can be thought of and discussed more or less separately, at the same time they can hardly be thought of as separable. For in general people pay attention to and are interested in the things that promise some satisfaction of their wants, needs, and desires—in other words, of their motives. As Brigance pointed out many years ago, "Effective arguments must appeal to human wants."[1] We might add that effective expository or informa-

[1] William Norwood Brigance, *The Spoken Word: A Textbook of Speech Composition*, Appleton-Century-Crofts, 1927, p. 174.

176

tive talks and even entertaining speeches must make their appeal to some aspect of human nature that will get and hold attention; they must influence the listeners at least to want to listen.

Obviously, unless you can get your audience to listen to you there is no point in speaking at all: you actually have no audience. It was pointed out many years ago that everyone may have the right to speak, but no one can compel his audience to listen to him. However, audiences generally listen when the speaker has something to say worth listening to.[2]

One of your primary problems, therefore, is to secure and hold the attention and interest of your listeners. This statement applies regardless of the type of speaking situation—whether it be conversation, a classroom lecture or demonstration, a discussion, the reading aloud of a piece of literature, the presentation of a play, or the delivery of a speech.

Attention Defined

Attention may be defined from two points of view. In the first place, it may be thought of as a physiological phenomenon, a bodily "set" in which the responsive apparatus is made more sensitive to certain stimuli while it is less sensitive to others which are momentarily less significant. Thus, in a crowd we often pick out the face of someone we know while all others fade, so to speak, into the background. From the highly complex sounds emanating from an orchestra we can often isolate a single violin or other instrument. From a babel of conversation we can often select a single voice. These selections are made through a process of sharpening our acuteness for some particular stimulus which may have a peculiar significance at the moment. It is a sensory-neuromuscular act.

Attention may also be defined as a psychological phenomenon, that is, an element of consciousness. From this second point of view, attention is a process by which our awareness of a given stimulus or type of stimulus is heightened, the particular stimulus thereby entering more directly into what the psychologist James called the "focus of consciousness," while all other stimuli are relegated to the "fringe" or "margin" of awareness.

[2] John Hatsell, *Precedents of Proceedings in the House of Commons,* 2nd ed., 1781, II, 77–78.

Actually, we cannot make a distinction between the physiological and the psychological aspects of attention; any possible differentiation is essentially a matter of how one looks at the phenomenon. Both aspects are present in every act involving attention.

Your problem as a speaker, then, is to bring your subject into the "focus of consciousness" of your listeners, while other matters are permitted to fade or even forced into the background or "fringe" of awareness. If you can maintain the attention and interest of your audience for the problem at hand, preventing their being diverted to other subjects or to conflicting ideas, your success is more nearly assured.[3] Woodrow Wilson once said that the first job of any book is to get itself read. Similarly, the first job of any speech is to get itself listened to. Your hearers may not accept your ideas, but at least they will have listened to you. Sometimes that will be as much as you can expect.

Adaptation

No one can attend strictly to any stimulus for more than a few seconds at a time. We become so accustomed to many of the sounds, sights, and other sensations about us that we are hardly aware of them at all. The myriad stimuli of all kinds impinging upon our sense organs have by their very constancy lost their attention-holding value. We have become *adapted* to them. So complete is this adaptation that whatever response they may arouse remains itself far in the margin of consciousness or even beyond.

This same phenomenon of adaptation can and often does take place in both public speaking and private conversation. We do not listen very long to a speaker who is telling us things that we have known for a long time; and while he is droning on we are scarcely aware even of the fact that he is speaking at all, and we have no idea of what he is saying. The very monotony of utterance of some speakers, without a spark of life or liveliness in either the development of thought or the manner of presentation, can easily result in

[3] A theory of persuasion was once based wholly on the principle that if you could keep your listeners from letting any contrary ideas come into their minds, holding their attention without wavering on the point you were making, they could not avoid carrying out your proposals. It was a pernicious theory, which fortunately is seldom used today except in the process of persuasion known as brainwashing.

the loss of both attention and interest on the part of the listeners. They are no longer listeners, in fact; they have become so adapted to those particular stimuli that they are no longer responding, so that while the physiological stimuli are maintained, one can say that the psychological stimuli have ceased to exist.

Once you have lost the attention of your audience it is extremely difficult to regain it with any degree of effectiveness. For one thing, the continuity of your thought has been broken, and it will not be easy for your listeners to pick up in the middle of an explanation or an argument. Then, too, they will have formed a judgment of you and your ideas which you have trouble dislodging or reversing.

The Relation Between Attention and Interest

As we noted at the beginning of this chapter, attention and interest are usually thought of together and often identified with one another. However, it is probably best to think of them as more or less distinct, though closely related, phenomena. Attention is a definite though not always voluntary act by which stimuli are brought into sharper focus. Interest is likely to be of longer duration, and may be thought of as an attitude arising out of the motives through the force of which we obtain our satisfactions.

Each act of attending is a separate act, but one's interest in a given subject may persist through any number of such acts. One may be continuously interested in civic improvement, for example, even though he may be giving his attention during business hours to his own commercial enterprises. A statesman may for relaxation enjoy mystery stories, giving them his undivided attention while reading them; but that does not argue that he is no longer interested, even for the time being, in the national welfare. His interest is simply temporarily quiescent.

We attend more readily to things in which we are interested; but just as our active interest fluctuates from time to time, so also does our attention. We may be interested in many things and maintain this interest over a period of years. As various occasions arise, we give our attention now to one, now to another of those interests. The speaker's problem, therefore, is one of selecting those interests which may at the time have the greatest attention value and involve the most pressing problems.

TYPES OF ATTENTION

In varying degrees, attention may take one of three general forms, all of which may be useful, to some extent at least, to the speaker: involuntary or primary, voluntary or secondary, and interested or derived.

Involuntary or Primary Attention

Frequently certain aspects of the stimulus or within the listener's organism—the impulse to sneeze, for example—may arouse immediate attention without any effort on the part of the hearer. Sudden or great changes in the stimulus pattern have strong attention value: loud noises, like a crack of thunder during a storm; sudden flashes of bright light, like a nearby flash of lightning; the stopping of the clock in a quiet room; a sharp emphasis by the speaker who has been going along at an even or monotonous tone—these all have potential attention-arousing value. Since ordinarily we are unable to avoid these sudden and strong stimuli, the attention thus aroused is designated as primary or involuntary.

Within ourselves as listeners are also certain factors which lend effectiveness to this sort of stimulus. Among these are one's own habits of attention, one's own emotional state at the moment, one's own prevailing interest. An orchestra conductor, for example, has so trained his listening habits that he can detect, out of all the sounds emanating from the instruments in his ensemble, a single false note by a single instrument; and he can usually spot the specific instrument itself. We become so "keyed up" emotionally sometimes that we are ultrasensitive to stimuli to which ordinarily we are entirely adapted. A mother may have been quite oblivious during the day to the noises made by her children, but by the end of the day she has become thoroughly sensitized to their voices and their behavior. If we are in the market for a new car we are likely to be drawn involuntarily to a show window in which stands the very car we would like to buy. You see and listen to what you are interested in.

While the speaker may be limited in his use of the external aspects of stimulus patterns which may excite involuntary attention, his use of factors which reside within the organism, such as those suggested in the preceding paragraph, is well-nigh unlimited. The attentive habits of his hearers, their present emotional states, and their interests of the moment all provide avenues for immediate appeals to attention. Through these avenues he can direct the attention of his audience to the subject he is discussing or intends to discuss.

Voluntary or Secondary Attention

When the individual forces his attention on some object or activity, usually with some effort or strain, he is making use of *voluntary* or *secondary* attention. You settle down for an evening of study and attack a subject which has not as yet aroused your keen interest. However, recognizing that the work has to be done if you want to pass the course, you force yourself to get to work and give your attention to the text. So long as the attention is given by direct and conscious application, it remains voluntary, and the sense of effort will persist. It tires you to have to attend to such tasks for any length of time, because attention itself involves muscular activity, and forced attention involves muscular strain. If you attend a lecture not because you are interested but because you feel you should, and you force yourself to listen carefully to everything that is said, at the end of the lecture you will be worn out.

Some speakers make it difficult to listen to them without effort. They speak indistinctly or in such low voices, or both, that they are neither easily audible nor readily intelligible. Their discussion itself may be dry, unrelieved by any kind of animation. The language is obscure, the ideas abstract. They wear us out trying to listen to them. Many people simply will not expend the effort necessary to follow the speaker who depends entirely on voluntary or forced attention on the part of his hearers. Some college and university professors never get beyond this kind of attention in their lectures.

Interested or Derived Primary Attention

Sometimes after you have directed your attention for a time by sheer effort to a given activity, subject, or phenomenon, you find that your interests are awakened, and your attention is held thence-forth without effort. This type of attention partakes somewhat of the nature of the primary or involuntary in that it requires little or no conscious effort; since it is derived from the primary or voluntary type, it is designated as *derived primary*. Since it is based on interest, whatever its origins, it is sometimes termed *interested* attention.

The lesson you started to study through the exercise of determination or through conscious effort may contain information that stimulates your interest so that attention is no longer a strain. As you go further into the subject it becomes more and more interesting, and you read on, unaware of the passage of time. Attention, which began by being consciously directed, requires no effort, and you have no feeling of weariness from the energy expended. The attention itself becomes more or less habitual with respect to that particular subject. Sometimes the interest is present to begin with, so that no transition is necessary.

You have all enrolled in courses for no other reason than that they were required in your curriculum. For the first few weeks you undoubtedly needed considerable effort to apply yourselves to preparing the assignments. As time progressed, however, you probably found yourselves becoming more and more interested, until it required no heroic act of will at all to continue your study. By that time your attention had passed into the third stage where it was almost if not entirely effortless.

Stagner and Karwoski, who describe involuntary and habitual attention as dominated by external conditions, consider voluntary attention and a different type, *anticipatory* attention, to be dominated by internal conditions.[4] For example, we may plan to attend a speaking occasion because we want to know what is to be said about the subject, and we therefore go with an attitude of keen anticipation; the attention we give to the speaker arises out of our expectation, our hoping to learn what we can from the speaker.

APPLICATIONS TO THE SPEAKER'S PROBLEM

You cannot maintain the involuntary attention of your listeners very long. You need variety in your speaking—in your use of language as well as in your delivery. But variety itself can become

[4] Ross Stagner and T. F. Karwoski, *Psychology*, McGraw-Hill, 1952, pp. 197 ff.

monotonous; if you continue to use the same patterns over and over, they lead to adaptation and hence loss of attention. Avoid overdoing your habitual patterns of variety—the inflections, pauses, changes in emphasis, and so on—because they themselves can become very monotonous. They may also tend to divert the attention of the listeners away from what you are trying to say, especially when they seem to be used primarily for their own sake and do not contribute to the meaning of what you are saying.

Similarly, the extensive use of such external devices as irrelevant visual aids or bizarre platform behavior is likely to draw attention away from the subject. The writer once observed a speaker who used the element of movement about the platform very definitely. He would stand on one side of the lectern for a time, and then move smoothly across, with three steps, to the other side. After a while he would move just as smoothly, again with three steps, back to where he had started. His movements were so regular that his crossings to and fro were timed by the second hand of a watch. It was found that they actually occurred *every twenty-eight seconds*—and he kept it up for the better part of a half-hour! What he said has long since been forgotten.

Avoid, then, the use of those external devices or patterns of delivery that will draw attention to themselves or become monotonous. Sometimes, however, they can and should be made a part of the communicative process; if they will contribute to the meanings you are trying to stimulate, they may be used freely. However, no attention-getting device or procedure should ever be used which violates the atmosphere of the occasion. Visual supports, which come within the classification of external devices, are discussed at some length in a following chapter.

You *may* have to arouse involuntary attention at the outset by the use of heightened stimulation; you may have to ask your listeners to give you their voluntary attention for a time, though you should not put it in just that way. But the sooner you can pass from the stage of either involuntary or voluntary to the derived primary or *interested* attention, the easier your task will be. And the longer you can maintain your hearers' interest, the longer you can hold their attention. On those relatively rare occasions when you cannot assume that your audience is already interested either in you or in what you say—that is, when there is no basis for the presence of the anticipatory type of attention—your problem is one of striking immediately at their interests and maintaining a high level of that interest throughout your speech.

As a rule subjects in themselves are neither interesting or uninteresting. Almost any audience can be interested in almost any subject if that subject is approached by connecting it to one in which they are already interested. It is related of Woodrow Wilson that when he was a professor at Princeton University, he told his student audience one day that Gladstone could make even a four-hour talk on the budget interesting. "Young men," he said, "it is not the subject that is dry; it is you that are dry."[5]

One of the writers once introduced the presumably dull subject of spelling to a group of parents with the query, "How did little Johnny or Mary know which one of the 42,000 ways of spelling the word *circus* the teacher wanted?" A student opened a talk on forest fires with the question, "Do you know that the house you hoped to build next summer has already burned down this fall?" Another student opened his talk on the amazing variety of uses to which petroleum and petroleum products are used today by posing the query, "Did you ever stop to wonder why most people disapproved of cosmetics when grandma was a girl? It wasn't due," he went on to say, "to our Puritan heritage, as most people think—the Gay Nineties lived up to their name. No, it was because most store-bought cosmetics in grandma's day smelled bad—I should say, smelled like sin."[6] Bruce Barton's famous speech on labor-saving devices in the home has the intriguing title, "How Long Should a Wife Live?" Somewhat in a similar pattern, a talk on the importance of people's working together and having definite rules to guide their cooperation began, "Has it ever occurred to you that physically, pound for pound, man is one of the weakest creatures on earth?"

Holding Attention

Gaining the initial attention of the audience and holding it throughout the speech are two different things. The fact that you may have undivided attention at the outset is no guarantee that you

---

[5] See pp. 185–194 for examples of the application of this principle.

[6] Joe Sanchez, "Our Daily Oil," in Waldo W. Braden and Mary Louise Gehring, *Speech Practices: A Resource Book for the Student of Public Speaking*, Harper, 1958, pp. 102–103.

will be able to hold it until you are through. In the usual situation, your listeners have given you that attention because they are interested in what *you* have to say, whatever the topic, or because they want to hear what you or anyone else has to say about a subject that vitally concerns them; either way, they have come in a state of anticipatory attention. Perhaps they are expecting to have their beliefs, their faith, strengthened or renewed; or they may have come simply because they have heard that someone is going to talk about something, and their curiosity is aroused as to just what is going on. Or perhaps they see that a crowd has assembled, and they linger to find out what is going to happen. At any rate, you have, let us say, their initial attention. Your problem then is not so much one of getting it as holding it. And this is where the interest factor becomes especially operative.

Audiences Are Not Passive

Audiences may be relaxed and inactive so far as can be observed, *but they are not passive.* Because they have assembled for some purpose, usually fairly definite, even though externally they may reveal no intense eagerness, they have assumed a mental or bodily "set" which has the effect of directing their attention to the speaker as soon as he appears. The anticipatory attention has now become active. If through his own ineptitude the speaker loses that attention, if he fails to satisfy that anticipation, it is likely to be his own fault. If the listeners were not interested to begin with, they would stay away. Sometimes, though, external circumstances entirely beyond the control of either the speaker or the audience may break into the situation and destroy all chance of any *rapport* between them.

Occasionally, however, a situation occurs in which such initial attention cannot be taken for granted—the after-dinner speaking program, for example. The people there have come primarily to enjoy the fellowship engendered by simply eating together. They may know that there is to be at least one speech; if the speaker or the subject is of sufficient importance, that may be one of the reasons they are there. But their immediate interest and hence their attention are directed to the usually genial conversation among the group within a small circle, and they are paying no attention at all to the head table. They are in no hurry to break up the existing atmosphere, and it is often necessary to divert their attention from the immediate group and direct it toward the program.

This redirection is usually the task of the toastmaster or whoever is in charge of the program. Sometimes all he needs to do is rise and stand there quietly. A change in the stimulus pattern is thus made, one of the basic factors of attention. A greater change would be effected by rapping on the speaking stand or the table or tapping the edge of a water glass, thereby adding an auditory stimulus change to the visual.

Now and then a speaker will need to have some change made in the arrangements—a projection screen to be set up, some apparatus to be put together. This activity will also provide a change in the stimulus pattern and thus serve as a factor of attention.

Such a change in the stimulus pattern must be of sufficient magnitude to intrude itself into the awareness of the listeners. Furthermore, the change should be fairly abrupt, so that the new element in the stimulus pattern will break sharply into the configuration that has been established. We are less likely to have our attention drawn by changes that are so weak or so slow that they are hardly stimuli at all.

Such devices as these, as well as others, can be used on occasions when it is necessary to draw the attention of the audience specifically toward the business at hand. Audiences generally, however, are usually quite willing to listen to speakers when they know that the occasion itself involves some kind of speaking program. As a rule, therefore, such proceedings are unnecessary, and may even draw the attention of the audience to the devices themselves rather than to the speaker and what he has to say.

APPEALS TO ATTENTION AND INTEREST

How can you apply the principles of attention and interest in the construction and delivery of your speeches? In part, at least, by using certain specific appeals which are calculated to stimulate the interests of your listeners. Always bear in mind that people will listen to discussions of those subjects or types of subjects in which they are interested.

Somewhat as in the case of motives, no final and rigid classification of these appeals is possible. There are about as many lists as there are people making them. In any such classification, moreover, the various categories are not mutually exclusive; you can make use of two or three appeals at the same time. But again for purposes of convenience the following list is suggested:

1. The *vital*, the satisfaction of basic motives
2. The *new and old*, when carefully taken together
3. The *concrete*, as opposed to abstractions
4. *Activity*, rather than the static
5. *Suspense*, rather than premature revelation of the outcome
6. *Struggle*, with reasonably balanced sides
7. *Humor*, partly for its own sake, and partly for relief from too much seriousness

Passages illustrating these appeals will be found in the speeches listed in project 10 at the end of the chapter.

The Vital

Whatever affects life itself, freedom of action, comfort, possessions, security—satisfaction of the basic motives, in other words—is of immediate concern to most of us. Such things are vital to human existence, to physical and mental welfare, or to the welfare of those for whom our affection, our sympathy, or our pity has been aroused. Because they are of such importance in the business of living, any discussion of topics related to them is likely to be listened to attentively. Find out, therefore, what the active motives of your listeners are at the time, and relate your subject to them whenever such a reference can be made.

Occasionally you will talk on some subject on which your audience has no particular feelings at present, and which at the outset has no apparent relation to their current active motives. In such a case you may find it necessary to arouse dormant motives.

Special devices may sometimes be used to direct what may be thought of as involuntary attention to a subject generally considered to be of little interest. When a speaker said to his classmates, "I don't know which one of you it is going to be, but one of you will spend some time as a patient in a mental hospital," he got immediate attention. From that opening he led his listeners through a statement of the amazing prevalence of mental illness, and then to a consideration of the treatment of mental patients in many state as well as private institutions. Still another created interest in a rather humorous description of the divergent timepieces on the campus by beginning, "You were late to class this morning because the clock in the tower lied to you; in fact, it told four lies at the same time, because no two faces on that clock were together, and no one of them was correct."

The New and Old

People are interested in familiar scenes, familiar faces, accustomed activities; they are also interested in new scenes, making new acquaintances, and doing different things. But they tend frequently to make comparisons and contrasts between the new and the old. They like to hear old ideas, many of which will bear repeating; but they also want a new one now and then. Entirely new ideas which have no relation to what is already known, however, are likely to have little appeal. Neither the new nor the old by itself is interesting.[7] A generally accepted principle in educational theory, to proceed from the known to the unknown, is equally applicable in public speaking. You will want to present new ideas, but they will be more readily listened to if they are associated with already accepted and understood ideas.

Old ideas can often be put together in new ways so that they can be made to seem like new ideas; the new synthesis may in fact be highly original. Bruce Barton, for example, used the Biblical story of Joseph in Egypt to illustrate the importance of continuous advertising. He pointed out that with all the success, position, and wealth accumulated by Joseph under the Pharaoh, in the course of time Joseph died, and "Now there arose up a new king over Egypt, which knew not Joseph" (Exod. 1:8). And there was no one to tell the people of that country what a great man he had been. Similarly, there are constantly growing up in this country children who do not know, for instance, that "Ivory soap floats."

You will on occasion reiterate old, familiar thoughts, as in commemorative addresses. In such cases you will often create more

[7] William James, *Talks to Teachers on Psychology, and to Students on Some of Life's Ideals*, Holt, 1907, p. 108.

interest if you can give the old ideas a novel slant, a different approach, a new emphasis. For example, on December 4, 1958, while he was Secretary of State, John Foster Dulles spoke to the California Chamber of Commerce on "Policy for the Far East." He opened his address with a reference to the Preamble to the Constitution: "I always consider that United States foreign policy is designed to serve one of the basic purposes of our Constitution, to 'secure the Blessings of Liberty to ourselves and our Posterity.' There was a time when foreign policy played a minor role in that great task. Today its role is major."[8]

In any case, your audience is your starting point. You cannot take the attitude of the rustic who was asked by a bewildered traveler how to get to a distant city. The native pondered for some time. Finally he replied, "Stranger, if I wanted to go to that place, I wouldn't start from here." You must start from where your listeners are, whether in knowledge, in understanding, or in interests and attitudes.

If your hearers already know something of the subject or if they have some interest in it or in a related subject, start from there, with perhaps a brief summary of what is known or the degree to which their interests tie in with your subject; but go on from that knowledge or those interests to introduce new material.

Since new material based on the old has attention value, illustrative material drawn from instances that are close in both time and space is likely to be especially effective. The report of a traffic accident occurring today in your own locality and involving people you know will have a far greater effect than a report of one occurring a year ago in some distant part of the country and involving no one either you or your listeners ever heard about. A Louisiana student talking about forest fires to an audience in that state will do well at least to mention the fact that such fires do occur in Louisiana, not merely on the Pacific Coast, and that they create great economic losses.

A speaker discussing soil conservation should present information on what has happened recently or is happening in the area in which he is talking. A student speaker on juvenile delinquency, although treating the topic as a widespread problem, made her

[8] In A. Craig Baird, ed., *Representative American Speeches: 1958–1959*, H. W. Wilson, 1959, p. 36.

speech more effective by gathering much of her material from the social welfare and police agencies of the city in which the university is located.

The Concrete

Concrete terms generally arouse greater interest than abstract terms because they come closer to actual experience and thus arouse more specific meanings.[9] For example, *dwelling* is more specific than *building;* if you want to make the concept still more concrete, use *cottage, mansion, palace, cabin, shanty, hovel,* and so on. But remember that to one who has never seen even a picture of a palace the term would mean very little. Similarly, there are scores of words concerned with moving from one place to another under one's own power: *walk, dash, stroll, stagger, stalk, plod* ("The ploughman homeward *plods* his weary way"), *march, run, gallop, trot,* to say nothing of the more picturesque and colloquial *hightail, highball,* and *hotfoot.* Such terms relate more closely to the peculiar quality of our actual experiences than the more inclusive and general terms *dwelling* and *go,* and call up a more specific and descriptive imagery.

Abstract terms cannot be entirely avoided. In a sense, as will be discussed in Chapter 25, pp. 459–463, all words are abstract, just as all concepts are abstract. We all speak of democracy, laissez-faire, integration (as a sociological or pedagogical theory), Americanism, "the American Way of Life," and so on, as if we understood what they mean. In August, 1914, the German armies overran Belgium in their march toward Paris. For two years Cardinal Mercier and the German governor-general kept up a bloodless duel. On July 21, 1916, in the Cathedral of Brussels, the Cardinal preached on the theme, "Today the hymn of joy dies on our lips." Comparing the Belgians under the occupation with the ancient Hebrews in their Babylonian captivity, he said, "Today the hymn of joy dies on our lips. The Jewish people in captivity at Babylon, sitting in tears on the banks of the Euphrates, watched the waters of the river flow by. Their dumb harps were hung on the willows by the bank. Who among them would have the courage to sing the song of Jehovah in a strange land? 'O Jerusalem,' cried the Psalmist, 'if ever I forget thee, let my

[9] See Chapter 26 for a brief statement of the difference between concretes and abstracts.

right arm wither; let my tongue cleave to the roof of my mouth if
I do not remember thee; if thou art no longer the beginnings of my
joys.' "[10]

The passage from Roosevelt's radio speech to the American people
on December 9, 1941 (found on p. 512), in which he recounted the
collaborated invasions by Germany, Italy, and Japan over the preceding decade, is a further illustration of the effectiveness of the
concrete as opposed to the abstract.

Every field of thought that departs from the objectivity of material science (and scientists are realizing more and more how very
subjective science is) makes use of expressions intended to be concrete; yet even such terms as *force, energy,* and *inertia,* though they
are used with specific meanings, are still highly abstract to laymen.
But so long as they are used by everyone working in that particular
field and mean approximately the same to speakers and listeners
alike, no confusion is likely to arise.

So far as possible, put your own understanding of the language
you use in terms of concrete reality and specific imagery which correspond closely with similar experiences, imagery, and realities of
your listeners. In so doing you will be better able to form intelligent
concepts and attitudes yourself toward the things represented by
your words; you will also be able better to arouse intelligent concepts and attitudes toward these same things in your listeners when
they are suggested by your language.

Activity

Anything stationary soon loses its interest, and hence its attention
value, for most of us. People are interested in events, in things happening. Narrative is therefore more effective, as a rule, in presenting a principle than any amount of explanation. Lincoln's stories
made his points far better than lengthy argument could have done.
Bruce Barton, in impressing his listeners with the importance of
continuous advertising even though the merchant and his goods
are well known, told the simple story of the rural church which
everyone knew had been on the same spot for many years; yet the
church bell was rung every Sunday morning.

[10] From Houston Peterson, ed., *A Treasury of the World's Great Speeches,*
Simon & Schuster, 1954, p. 703.

Your examples and illustrations can be factual, fictional, or hypothetical. Factual examples are specific instances of actual occurrences, conditions as they actually exist or have existed, or
procedures which have actually taken or are taking place. Use every
means of making such descriptions or narratives alive, as Mark Antony did in addressing the mob in the Roman Forum:

> You all did see that on the Lupercal
> I thrice presented him a kingly crown,
> Which he did thrice refuse: . . .
> (*Julius Caesar,* III, ii, 100–102)

Examples of the fictional illustration are the short anecdote, the
fable, the parable, the allegory, or even the concise, pithy utterance
attributed to some fictitious person. Karl T. Compton, then President of the Massachusetts Institute of Technology, opened a talk
on "The State of Science" by comparing his inadequacy for the task
to that of the sprinter who, when congratulated on his running
the 100-yard dash in 9½ seconds, replied, "I could run that race
in 9 seconds if it wasn't for the longness of the distance and the
shortness of the time."[11] While John Bunyan could write a book-
length allegory in *Pilgrim's Progress,* it is much better to limit yourself to a short narrative or illustration in which you come quickly
to the point, make it, and then move on.

It is doubtful, though, if the fictitious item or incident has as
much impact as the factual, though it can be made very effective,
since you can construct your story to fit the specific point you are
trying to make. It is often difficult to find factual narratives that are
wholly appropriate for your argument. Introduce fictitious names if
necessary, but avoid such designations as "Mr. X" or, as frequently
seen in the Victorian novel, "Mr. S———." The central character of
your fictitious narrative might well be called "A friend of mine. . . ."

The hypothetical example is usually introduced by some such
expression as "Suppose . . . ," or "It is as if . . . ," or "Imagine this
situation," or the like. The suppositious instance, either narrative or
descriptive, might have happened, but so far as you actually know
never did, except in your imagination. The talk mentioned earlier
in this chapter, "Our Daily Oil" (p. 184), is based almost entirely on

---

[11] In Harding *op. cit.,* p. 294.

suppositious conditions. The speaker says, "Just for the fun of it, let's run through a day in the life of one of you ladies to see what it would be like to be without these many contributions [of the oil industry]. Let's make believe it's Sunday morning, and we'll boycott all products made from or powered by petroleum."

The speaker then makes much use of factual detail, and is undoubtedly effective in establishing or "proving" his point. But generally the hypothetical example can be used mainly for clarification —perhaps more effectively in many cases than a factual example, in that you can fill in the details to fit the necessities of the situation, somewhat as in the fictional narrative. At the same time, your hypothetical account must be plausible; the instance could have taken place just as you describe it, unless for some specific effect you deliberately exaggerate, in which case you should so inform your audience.

Activity in relation to delivery.   Activity applies also to the speaker's own behavior before the audience. People get tired of listening to the same tone of voice for any length of time. Therefore develop vocal flexibility, partly just for the sake of variety itself and partly because the flexible voice can actually say more than the monotonous voice, and say it more precisely.

Your behavior on the platform should be active, alert, animated. Show yourself to be alive. Move about freely but purposefully. Don't just move, however, without making your movements meaningful. Use your head, your arms, your hands to contribute to communication. Keep your listeners' attention and interest by exhibiting your own interest in the subject and in talking about it. Your "urge to communicate," if genuine and sincere, will in itself give you a foundation on which to build an effective manner of speaking. It is highly probable that no lackadaisical speaker ever aroused a high interest either in himself or in what he was saying.

Your ideas should progress in such a way that your audience will be able to follow you easily. Keep your development moving and carry your hearers along with you. Once a point is taken up, finish with it before going on to the next; then you will not have to retrace, which can be very confusing to your hearers.

But avoid remaining on one point so long that it becomes overworked and your audience loses interest in it. When you make the point and advance to the next, be sure to let your hearers know that you are moving. The progression should be orderly. Aimless, disorganized shifting from one idea to another and back again gives the effect of incoherent rambling. *Never* offer to your audiences "a few scattered thoughts"; it will be an insult to their intelligence and an affront to their courtesy in coming to listen to what you have to say.

Suspense

During the run of one of the early motion picture mysteries a cartoon appeared in one of the metropolitan newspapers showing a small boy being led out of the theater by his mother. The boy is shouting at the top of his voice, to the consternation of the crowd waiting at the ticket window, "The butler done it!"

The popularity of the mystery story and the crime novel is due in part to the high degree of suspense the author succeeds in creating. Uncertainty as to the outcome of some event is almost sure to arouse great interest. Highly publicized courtroom trials receive columns of space, sometimes for many weeks, before interest dies down. The popularity of the so-called comic strips arises from the manner in which their creators keep their readers on edge while one episode after another is unraveled.

You are surely familiar with the element of suspense in the various types of athletic contests, particularly when the contestants are evenly matched. The winning basket in the last few seconds, the eagle putt on the twentieth hole, the horse that forges up to a photo-finish in the final furlong, the home run in the bottom of the last inning that won the World's Series in 1960—people do not leave the stands under such suspenseful situations.

In a speech suspense may be created in various ways. For one thing, you may present in the beginning only a broad, initial outline of the points you intend to bring out. These points should be of such significance as to stimulate a desire on the part of the listeners to hear them discussed or supported, and a willingness to wait until they are developed. Again, in your discussion you can mention in passing, so to speak, a point which you may or may not bring out in detail later on. Mark Antony's mention of Caesar's will is an example of such suspense. The relevance of the point must be shown, however, when you do mention it.

Another way of introducing suspense is to trace a chain of events, withholding the inciting incident until the chain has been firmly forged, and then presenting the initial episode that led to the chain in the first place. Wilder used this technique in developing the story of *The Bridge of San Luis Rey*.

In any case, hold back the most significant points, which may be either the cause, or the final outcome, or the key element in a description, until a strategic moment, building the suspense higher and higher, the listeners' interest and attention rising correspondingly.

Struggle

As a factor of interest and attention, struggle is closely allied to suspense. Most people enjoy games of one kind or another, either as participants or as spectators. Usually the closer the game, the harder the struggle, and the more uncertain the outcome, the greater is the enjoyment and the keener the interest and the attention. Although struggle is often closely associated with suspense, not all suspense involves struggle. The young employee hoping for a promotion may suffer keen suspense, though he may not be in competition with another for the advancement. Any young instructor in a college or university department, hoping for a promotion or a raise, can testify to the existence of such suspense.

Many people enjoy argument because of the opposition of ideas and opinions it provides. These "debates" involve competition or struggle. A public discussion is much more interesting when there is a clash of opinion. Speeches on controversial issues are almost certain to draw interest; attacks on entrenched political figures, on waste in government, on negligence or malfeasance in public office, and on economic, juridical, or social indignities provide good opportunities for making the maximum appeal to public interest in conflict, in struggle, in competition.

Humor

It certainly cannot be said that every speech should have some humor injected into it. However, some element of humor is often helpful in disarming an unfriendly audience and in illustrating a point to even a favorable audience. David E. Lilienthal tells of his egg man who quit work at Oak Ridge, where highly secret work was under way on the first atom bomb during World War II. When asked why he quit, he replied that he couldn't find out a thing about what the government was making, but he decided that whatever it was, it would be cheaper just to go out and buy it!

To have the best effect humor should have certain characteristics:

1. It should be appropriate to the occasion.
2. It should contribute to the point you are making.
3. It should, as a rule, be genial.
4. It should be brief.
5. It should always be in good taste.
6. It should be spontaneous.
7. It demands a delicate perception of the incongruous.
8. It should not be used so continuously as to give the speaker a reputation as a humorist, unless that is the reputation he wants to create.

Humor in its place can serve to lighten up an otherwise deadly serious situation. Shakespeare introduced comedy scenes into some of his deepest tragedies to provide relief for pent-up emotions. Unless it is your deliberate intention to establish yourself as a humorist, employ it sparingly. Then when you do use it, the effect will be all the more telling.

The stimulation and maintenance of attention and interest are as a rule the means to an end rather than the end in itself. The speaker almost never stops when he has secured the attention of his audience, or even when he has aroused their intense interest. The basic purpose of these devices and methods is to get the audience to listen to him in order that he may more effectively accomplish his real purpose, which is to elicit the desired response. The one exception is perhaps the purely entertaining speech in which the sole objective is to maintain audience interest and provide enjoyment for the occasion. In all other types of public address, attention and interest are aroused for objectives over and above themselves.

QUESTIONS AND TOPICS FOR STUDY AND REVIEW

1. One psychologist has said that "only those [stimuli] which fit the needs of the moment are reacted to." Illustrate this principle from your own experience.

2. Describe the sounds that have been going on around you while you were reading this chapter. When do such peripheral stimuli become distracting?

3. No effort is made in the text to include all the qualities of stimuli that draw your attention. What are some others?

4. To what extent and in what ways does constancy of attention have economic implications? What are some characteristics of peripheral stimuli that often cause distractions?

5. Have you had any experience in extrasensory perception? If you have, can you identify the elements of attention that make the perception possible?

6. Discuss the problem of the reliability of reporting what one has seen or heard, in relation to the phenomenon of attention.

7. In what different ways may one's interests in a given area of thought or activity which have never been active, be stimulated?

8. Is the interest of the writer or researcher on a given subject—say, history—of the same "quality" as that of the reader of or listener to discussions on that same subject? How would you evaluate the two?

9. Much has been said of arousing and maintaining the interest of listeners in the subject being discussed by a speaker. What are some of the evidences of the speaker's own interest in both the subject itself and in his talking about it?

10. Under what types of situations may the speaker *not* assume that the audience is interested either in him or in the subject he has planned to present? Cite a specific—factual or hypothetical—instance, and indicate how the speaker solved the problem.

PROJECTS

1. Describe instances in which two or more persons, though in the same situation, "saw" different things because of their differences in interests.

2. Present a speech in which you make an appeal to two or more of the factors listed on page 187. You do not need to indicate these factors by name; your appeal may be more effective if you do not. They should be readily identifiable, however.

3. Give a speech on some subject in which your listeners are not particularly interested; in fact, one they have not even been thinking about so far as you know. Show how it is related to one or more of the factors listed on page 187, and attempt through those avenues to arouse interest. In your presentation give ample evidence of your own interest.

4. Give a talk on a generally serious subject, enlivening the discussion by the injection of occasional bits of humor. Be sure that your humor meets the requirements discussed in the text.

5. Analyze the factors of interest in one of the speeches in a recent issue of *Vital Speeches of the Day*.

6. Give a five-minute speech in which you concentrate on making specific application of two or three of the factors of attention and interest. At the close of your speech your classmates will be asked to identify the factors you have used and to evaluate your effectiveness in using them.

7. Give a five- to ten-minute speech in which you stimulate interest at the opening by exhibiting a picture or an object of unusual nature. Be sure that your display has a direct bearing on the subject; show how it is of significance to your listeners.

8. Present an oral analysis of some interesting speech you have recently heard. Point out those aspects of the content of the speech which first drew your attention and then held your interest. Differentiate, if possible, between the factors of attention and those of interest, and then note what aspects of the speaker's presentation attracted your attention and interest. To what extent, would you estimate, did the manner of presentation add to or detract from your interest? Would the speech be as interesting if you were to read it to yourself as it was when you heard it? Try to analyze the reasons for your answer.

9. Discussion questions for class symposiums:
   a. How does magazine, radio, and television advertising utilize the factors of attention and interest? To what extent are its techniques not available to the speaker? Discuss instances you have observed of the use of these techniques in ways that may have been misleading or otherwise unethical.
   b. What techniques of gaining attention and interest can the speaker use that are not available to the magazine, radio, or television advertiser?
   c. Are there significant differences in the speaker's and the radio or television advertiser's use of attention- and interest-gaining techniques when appearing directly before the audience?
   d. Discuss in symposium the methods of stimulating interest in a subject which is ordinarily thought to be dull and uninteresting.
   e. What part can the listeners play in arousing interest in a speech?

10. The Lyceum and Chautauqua lectures of several years ago revealed great skill on the part of the speakers in gaining and holding the interest of their listeners. A speaker might present the same address to from fifty to a hundred audiences. Study one of the following

named speeches (or a similar talk) and make a written analysis of the factors of attention and interest used. Remember that these talks were prepared for audiences of several years ago, but many of them contain ideas that are still worth consideration:

William Jennings Bryan, "The Prince of Peace," in *Modern Eloquence*,[12] Vol. VIII, pp. 68–88.

Robert Jones Burdette, "The Rise and Fall of the Moustache," in *Modern Eloquence*, Vol. VIII, pp. 102–130.

Mark Twain, "The Sandwich Islands," in *Modern Eloquence*, Vol. VIII, pp. 131–168.

Russell H. Conwell, "Acres of Diamonds," in *Modern Eloquence*, Vol. VIII, pp. 138–168. This speech is found in many other collections.

Thomas H. Huxley, "On a Piece of Chalk," in *Modern Eloquence*, Vol. VIII, pp. 215–236.

Wendell Phillips, "The Lost Arts," in *Modern Eloquence*, Vol. VIII, pp. 276–290. This address is found in many other collections.

Roe Fulkerson, "Inheritance Tax," in *Classified Speech Models*, pp. 407–413.

Thomas DeWitt Talmage, "Big Blunders," in *Classified Models of Speech Composition*, pp. 828–844.

11. Attention and interest can be evaluated only in terms of the audience. Any appeals to interest, any attempts to stimulate attention, must consider the listeners in relation to the total situation. Study the situations as they are described in connection with the speeches listed in some current collection, such as *Representative American Speeches*[13] or *Vital Speeches of the Day*. Determine the basic interests of the listeners on those occasions and the extent to which the speaker made use of those interests. Were dormant interests stimulated, or were the appeals to already active interests? What specific techniques were employed by the speaker in stimulating attention and arousing interest or in maintaining it?

SUPPLEMENTARY READINGS

Brigance, William Norwood, *Speech: Its Techniques and Disciplines in a Free Society*, 2nd ed., Appleton-Century-Crofts, 1961, pp. 143–165.

Bryant, Donald C., and Karl R. Wallace, *Fundamentals of Public Speak-*

[12] For full references to this and the following sources, see Supplementary Readings, pp. 132–133. Your library may have a different edition of *Modern Eloquence;* check the volume on "Famous Lectures."

[13] Edited by Lester Thonssen. A Craig Baird was the editor from 1938 through 1959.

ing, 3rd ed., Appleton-Century-Crofts, 1960, chap. 3, "The Psychological Basis of Oral Communication," and pp. 126–128, 174–180, 267–270.

Gilman, Wilbur E., Bower Aly, and Loren Reid, *The Fundamentals of Speaking*, Macmillan, 1951, chap. 20, "Holding the Attention of an Audience."

Gray, Giles Wilkeson, and Claude Merton Wise, *The Bases of Speech*, 3rd ed., Harper, 1959, pp. 414–421.

Hollingworth, Harry L., *The Psychology of the Audience*, American Book, 1935, pp. 1–18, 41–62.

Monroe, Alan H., *Principles and Types of Speech*, 5th ed., Scott, Foresman, 1962, chap. 13, "Choosing Material That Will Hold Attention."

Oliver, Robert T., *New Training for Effective Speech*, 2nd ed., Dryden, 1951, pp. 222–228.

Oliver, Robert T., *The Psychology of Persuasive Speech*, 2nd ed., Longmans, Green, 1957, chap. 6, "Attention," and pp. 179–191.

Overstreet, H. A., *Influencing Human Behavior*, Norton, 1925, chap. 1, "The Key Problem: Capturing the Attention"; chap. 6, "Crossing the Interest Deadline."

Weaver, Andrew Thomas, and Ordean Gerhard Ness, *The Fundamentals and Forms of Speech*, Odyssey, 1957, chap. 10, "The Principles of Attention."

White, Eugene E., and Clair R. Henderlider, *Practical Public Speaking*, Macmillan, 1954, pp. 151–163.

Winans, James A., *Speech-Making*, Appleton-Century-Crofts, 1938, chap. 1, "Interest"; chap. 8, "Methods of Interesting."

PART IV  SPEECH
COMPO-
SITION

12

Finding Subjects
and Materials

"The grass is always greener on the other side of the fence." Far-off places, the events of long ago, and the lives of strange tribes always seem to possess more charm and enchantment than life close to home. His own experience ordinarily seems commonplace to the beginning speaker. Frequent complaints are "Nothing exciting has ever happened to me"; "My home town is just like other small towns"; "I have not lived long enough to have had any exciting experiences." So it goes. As a result, the beginner may choose from a magazine digest a subject such as "Life in the Arctic," "Giant Ants of the Amazon," or "Tribal Customs of the Senegalese."

When these topics fail to turn into successful speeches, the beginner feels frustrated and discouraged. Was the topic not unusual? Was it not exciting? Did he not read a whole magazine article in gathering his material? Did he not almost memorize what the author had written? Why, after all this preparation, did he not sound convincing?

We must admit that this student did partially fulfill the requirements of *specific preparation*. But since he was reporting the experience of another, he was limited by the number of details the author had presented. Unfortunately, nothing in his own experience or background could be used to enrich his presentation. As a result what he said did not ring true, it was not convincing, it was not a part of him. He probably failed to put over his ideas because he was concentrating upon *remembering* ideas instead of *presenting* ideas.

Speaking technique cannot cover up shallow thinking, trite commonplaces, and ill-digested facts. Nor can it give a speaker the assurance, poise, and persuasiveness that come with rich experience, being generally well read, and being specifically well-informed upon a given subject.

In brief, the wise speaker is one who selects a subject which will enable him to draw extensively upon his own general background.

GENERAL BACKGROUND

In Chapter 4 we stressed the importance of a broad background for effective speaking. Through direct experience, conversation with friends, listening to radio and television, seeing movies, and reading current magazines and newspapers as well as serious books, you can increase your reservoir and your effectiveness as a speaker.

Students of public address have long recognized that serious reflection, systematic thought, and extensive reading are primary requisites of excellence in public speaking. In this sense Cicero was an extremist when he observed, ". . . no man could ever excel and reach eminence in eloquence, without learning, not only the art of oratory, but every branch of useful knowledge." By eloquence Cicero refers to the ideal toward which most speakers strive.

A study of great speakers substantiates the importance of having an extensive background. Edmund Burke, remembered as a writer and political philosopher as well as a parliamentary orator, committed large portions of Vergil, Horace, and Lucretius to memory. Bacon, Milton, and Shakespeare were among his favorites. His companions in conversation included some of the leading intellectuals of his day.

Trained as a lawyer, Daniel Webster numbered Pope, Addison, Shakespeare, and Milton among his favorite English writers. He mastered Latin literature and frequently quoted it in his speeches. He kept Caesar, Vergil, and Livy on his desk. In addition, he was a careful student of history and law.

Calhoun, Webster's great rival, was at home with the classics of both England and the ancient world. Theodore Parker, a great preacher of the last century, accumulated a library of 20,000 volumes in thirty languages and in such diverse fields as history, literature, theology, philosophy, logic, mathematics, zoology, chemistry, physics, law, and biography. The evidence is that he used most of these.

Theodore Roosevelt wrote an imposing historical series, *Winning of the West*. Long before he attracted public attention, Woodrow Wilson was a recognized authority on congressional government and had written an impressive list of books and articles. Ordinarily thought of as a lawyer and congressional debater, William E. Borah read and reread the writings of Shakespeare and Milton, memorized masterpieces of American and British oratory, and knew his Bible thoroughly. Much of his leisure reading was devoted to a study of history and the rise of constitutional government. Among his acquaintances he had the reputation of being "a great bookworm" and "an omnivorous reader"—not a bad reputation to have but one not too common among senators.

Expansion of the list above seems unnecessary, for the implication is clear. Many orators of the past were more than masters of technique; they were profound students and thinkers. Because of the richness of their backgrounds, they brought to the platform a persuasiveness that transcended the glibness of many of their contemporaries. Men were attentive to these speakers because they had something significant to say, messages too important not to be heard.

A broad cultural background cannot be acquired in a day, a semester, or even a year. If the would-be speaker has a narrow outlook, if his attitudes are warped, or if his perceptive powers are dull, he probably will have difficulty in achieving eloquence. His intellectual sterility will be a factor in his ineffectiveness.

What are the signs of intellectual sterility? The student who is constantly complaining that he has nothing worth while to say is troubled with this difficulty. He probably does not know how to utilize his previous experience. He ought to do some serious thinking about the needs of his community and the needs of his auditors. What does he have personally to say that is important? His difficulty may, of course, be that he is unaware of or insensitive to the cultural, political, social, and economic problems that exist all around him; or perhaps the sphere in which he lives is so limited that he possesses insufficient confidence to express himself outside his little circle. Again, overspecialization may have made him a hermit.

The person who suspects that he needs to broaden his outlook— and that includes most of us—should set himself a definite program of reading. At the top of his list he should place "the great books,"[1] the Harvard Classics, or some other set of distinguished volumes. He needs to do what Emerson referred to as "creative reading"— reading with inquiring alertness and constant questioning. "One must be an inventor to read well," said Emerson. "As the proverb says, 'He that would bring home the wealth of the Indies, must carry out the wealth of the Indies.' There is then creative reading as well as creative writing. When the mind is braced by labor and invention, the page of whatever book we read becomes luminous with manifold allusions. Every sentence is doubly significant, and the sense of our author is as broad as the world."[2] Certainly the speaker needs to be "as broad as the world," forgetting his provincialism.

But the student faced with the prospect of meeting a speech class two or three times weekly demands to know what he can do immediately to get additional ideas for his speeches. Some excellent sources of speech material are your own experience, the radio and TV, and current newspapers and magazines. The adoption of the following program is a step in the right direction:

1. Read at least one newspaper daily. Don't limit your reading to the comics and don't overlook the editorials.

---

[1] For an excellent list, see Mortimer J. Adler, *How To Read a Book*, Simon & Schuster, 1940, pp. 377–389.

[2] Ralph Waldo Emerson, "The American Scholar," oration delivered before the Phi Beta Kappa Society, Cambridge, August 31, 1837.

2. Listen to at least thirty minutes of radio or TV news daily.
3. Read weekly a news magazine such as *Newsweek, Time, The Reporter, United States News and World Report,* or *New Republic.*
4. Read each month a literary magazine: *Harper's, Atlantic Monthly,* or *Yale Review.*
5. Read at least one nonfiction book for every novel you read.
6. When a good speech topic occurs to you, write it down for future reference.

THE SPEAKER'S NOTEBOOK

To digest and remember all that is significant in your reading is, of course, impossible. The most you can expect to remember is the general theme, a pertinent thought, or perhaps a quotation. Therefore the necessity of jotting down pregnant ideas and interesting information is quite evident. Ralph Waldo Emerson daily recorded his meditations in his *Journal,* which he called his "savings bank." This store house served him well when he prepared a lecture or an essay.

William E. Borah filed pertinent material away in large manila envelopes properly labeled. Into these repositories went clippings, letters, petitions, pamphlets, magazine articles, personal reflections, and outlines. Choice sentences were underlined and marginal comments made. He directed his stenographer to copy quotations that he particularly liked. For a given subject this collecting process might continue for several months or even years. But when the occasion to speak arose, Borah had an extensive accumulation from which to draw.[3]

You too will probably find it profitable to keep a speaker's notebook in which to accumulate speech materials.

1. One section should be devoted to speech topics. When a likely subject is suggested by reading, meditation, or a speech, record it immediately. In this manner you can soon collect a long list of excellent topics.
2. Another section should be devoted to quotations, anecdotes,

[3] Waldo W. Braden, "The Bases of William E. Borah's Speech Preparation," *Quarterly Journal of Speech,* February, 1947, **33**: 28–30.

jokes, and unique illustrations. Clippings may be pasted in for future reference.

3. It will probably be profitable for you to retain written speech criticisms, speech outlines, and other material prepared for class speeches.

IMMEDIATE PREPARATION

Frequently students inquire, "How much time should I devote to preparing a speech?" This is a hard question to answer. Some say that little immediate preparation is necessary; the clever student, they argue, can make a good five-minute speech by just "shooting the breeze"—meaning, of course, that the clever student needs to give little actual thought to a speech before facing his fellow students. Preparing a speech for any audience is often an arduous task which should be spread out over a considerable period. As in other learning situations, work at spaced intervals will probably yield greater results than continuous concentration for a long period.

There has been considerable speculation on how much time Abraham Lincoln devoted to the preparation of the "Gettysburg Address," which he delivered in less than five minutes. Modern Lincoln scholars now assure us that this gem of American eloquence was far more than an overnight production; it represented the thought of a man who had devoted his lifetime to the study of government and politics, a man whose sympathies had been mellowed by three years of awful war, a man keenly aware of the import of the occasion. The manuscript that Lincoln carried to Gettysburg was the product of much reflection. The night before the ceremony the Illinoisan felt compelled to rewrite his speech once more. The version we revere thus went through additional revision before it reached its present form.[4]

Daniel Webster frequently spent from two weeks to two months preparing his speeches.[5] After diligent research to collect material, Theodore Roosevelt sometimes revised his speeches five or six times.[6]

[4] For an interesting discussion, see James G. Randall, *Lincoln, the President,* Dodd, Mead, 1945, II, 303–320.

[5] Glen Mills, "Misconceptions Concerning Daniel Webster," *Quarterly Journal of Speech,* December, 1943, **29:** 423–428.

[6] William A. Behl, "Theodore Roosevelt's Principles of Speech Preparation and Delivery," *Speech Monographs,* 1945, **12:** 112–122.

His cousin, Franklin D. Roosevelt, likewise prepared his major addresses with great care. With the aid of a talented staff, he did extensive research and carefully checked his facts. He put his speeches through sometimes as many as eight or ten revisions.[7]

In other words, there is no simple answer to the question of how much time it takes to prepare a good speech. These matters cannot and must not be judged in terms of time. The amount of time spent depends upon how eager you are to succeed, how much you already know about the subject, the availability of materials, the enthusiasm with which you work, and the standards you impose upon yourself.

The preparation for a speech may be divided into eight steps:

1. Finding a subject
2. Taking an inventory of what you already know about the subject
3. Acquiring additional general background on the subject
4. Crystallizing, rewording, and narrowing the subject
5. Formulating an appropriate thesis
6. Locating additional material; preparing a bibliography
7. Selecting material to be covered
8. Reading, synthesis, and note taking

FINDING A SUBJECT

Selecting a speech topic is, indeed, an individual matter, depending upon many variable factors. Therefore it seems futile to list a large number of specific subjects which might catch the fancy of the student. A complete list, of course, would be as broad as life itself, for speeches are made about all phases of human conduct.

Taking a suggestion from the ancient rhetoricians, we list the following areas or realms of activity to stimulate your thinking. The topics are by no means mutually exclusive; there is much overlapping. Hundreds or thousands of subjects may be developed from each area. What the student makes out of the following suggestions will depend largely upon his creative inventiveness.

The resourceful speaker should be constantly on the alert for good subjects. Creative thinking may be stimulated by creative

[7] For a detailed account of how the Roosevelt speech staff worked, see Waldo W. Braden and Mary Louise Gehring, *Speech Practices: A Resource Book for the Student of Public Speaking*, Harper, 1958, pp. 17–20.

Sources of Speech Subjects

Speeches to Inform	Speeches to Entertain	Speeches to Stimulate	Speeches to Convince and to Actuate

1. Criticism
  a. Movies
  b. Plays
  c. Speeches
  d. Literature
2. Current events
3. Definitions
4. Descriptions
5. Explanations and demonstrations
  a. Apparatus
  b. Machines
  c. Tools
  d. Processes
  e. Procedures
6. Reviews
  a. Books
  b. Plays
  c. Movies
7. Interpretations
  a. Social customs and mores
  b. Religion
  c. Political affairs
  d. Government
  e. History
8. Travelogues
	1. True stories
	  a. About yourself
	  b. About others
	2. Travel accounts
	3. Character studies
	4. Fantastic or believable tales
	5. Reports
	  a. Books
	  b. Plays
	  c. Movies
	6. Humorous situations
	7. The trivial but spectacular mishap
	8. Exaggeration
	9. Paradox
	10. Parody-travesty
	11. Satire
		1. Acts of courage and bravery
		2. Heroes and great characters
		3. Memorable and revered events
		4. Significant institutions and organizations
		5. Patriotic themes
		6. Religious themes
			1. Political problems
			  a. International
			  b. Regional
			  c. National
			  d. Sectional
			  e. State
			  f. County
			  g. Local
			  h. Personal
			2. Agricultural problems
			3. Industrial problems
			4. Business problems
			5. Labor problems
			6. Educational problems
			7. Family problems
			8. Religious problems
			9. Philosophical and ethical problems
			10. Social problems
			11. Scientific problems
			12. Personal affairs

reading of challenging editorials, magazine articles, and thought-provoking books and by listening to news commentators and significant speakers. In this respect the beginning speaker may find help in listening to a daily news broadcast or telecast like "Meet the Press," "Face the Nation," and similar programs or in reading *Vital Speeches of the Day*, the *Congressional Digest*, and the best weekly news magazines. Excellent collections of speeches are Chauncey Goodrich's *Select British Eloquence* (Harper, 1852), *Modern Eloquence*, edited by Ashley Thorndike (Modern Eloquence Corp., 1923, or Collier, 1936), and the annual *Representative American Speeches*, edited by A. Craig Baird through 1959, and currently by Lester Thonssen (H. W. Wilson).

The inspiration for the speech topic should grow out of the speech situation, that is, the speaker, the audience, or the occasion. Some important considerations are the following:

1. What "leads" has the program chairman or committee-in-charge given?
2. What do your motives in delivering the speech suggest?
3. What subjects are you most capable of presenting under the given conditions?
4. What is considered appropriate and inappropriate for the occasion?
5. What would the audience like to hear discussed?
6. What topics are in the public eye?

TESTING THE SUBJECT

In an earlier chapter we made several suggestions to the beginner concerning choosing a topic. Our emphasis in each case was upon simplifying his task. Now let us broaden our treatment to consider criteria that can be used in testing the suitability of any speech topic. Necessarily, some of these tests will be only a further development of what was said earlier.

Test 1. Do I Have a Reserve of Information About the Subject?

Or phrase the question another way: am I qualified to discuss it? Have I had personal, direct experience with the subject? This test is an outgrowth of a suggestion made in Chapter 2 and needs little elaboration beyond what was said earlier. Conservation of time demands that you concentrate on those areas about which you know the most. To go far afield in search of a speech topic is to invite certain failure.

Test 2. Am I Enthusiastic About the Subject?

Do I have an urge to communicate this subject to an audience? Do I look forward to delivering a speech on this topic? This test is further development of a point discussed in Chapter 2. The old adage, "Enthusiasm is contagious," explains the importance of this test. Your eagerness and enthusiasm are reflected in your preparation, your manner, and your voice. In turn, sensing your interest the listeners are swept along toward the goal which you hope to achieve.

After a lifetime of speaking and of observing and studying other great speakers, Senator Albert J. Beveridge wrote, ". . . speak only when you have something to say. Be sure that you have a message to deliver. . . . This means, of course, utter sincerity. Never under any circumstances or for any reward tell an audience what you, yourself, do not believe or are even indifferent about." [8]

Test 3. Are Other Sources of Information Readily Available?

Can additional materials be found in the local library? Are there local persons who through interviews might give me information?

Personal experience, invaluable as it is, seldom is sufficient for the complete development of a speech. Embarrassing gaps ordinarily exist in your information. If you are to study the subject from many angles, you must have abundant reserves close at hand.

Test 4. Can the Subject Be Made To Interest the Audience?

What aspects of the subject will be interesting to the listeners? Can the subject be adapted to fit their wants? As we pointed out earlier, Russell Conwell, famous American lecturer, presented his talk "Acres of Diamonds" over 6000 times in a period of fifty years.

[8] Albert J. Beveridge, *The Art of Public Speaking*, Houghton Mifflin, 1924, pp. 19–20.

Yet Conwell's speech seemed never to grow old to his generation; he built it around an appeal which peculiarly touched Americans of that time. Keenly aware of the social, political, and economic forces at work, he emphasized that opportunity and riches were actually close at hand for the man who would but look for them. His appeal to the fundamental wants of security and well-being was one that few Americans could resist.[9]

Since subjects related to the auditor's wants are likely to stimulate greater responsiveness, they require less effort for successful presentation. It is a wise speaker who keeps this fact in mind in selecting a subject.

Test 5. Is the Subject as Stated Well Within the Listeners' Understanding?

It is not difficult to see that the general level of intellectual ability of an audience is another important determinant in choosing a speech topic. Some groups might have some difficulty comprehending certain aspects of the fourth dimension, general semantics, relativity, atomic research, radar, and calculus. But if they are sufficiently limited and clearly presented, any of these topics might fall within their comprehension. If you have a topic which appears to be above the intellectual capacity of a group, either limit it to a phase well within their intellectual attainment or select another subject.

Test 6. Is Oral Presentation of the Topic Possible Under the Circumstances?

Physical surroundings and available equipment must also be considered in deciding on a subject. Motion picture projectors, film strip projectors, chart, chart racks, and blackboards may make considerable difference in the final outcome of your speech.

If, for an expository talk, you choose to discuss the operation of a jet airliner, you need certain equipment. Since it is hardly possible to bring an airplane to class or to take the class to the airport, you

[9] Mary Louise Gehring, "The Invention of Russell H. Conwell in His Lecture, 'Acres of Diamonds,'" unpublished master's thesis, Louisiana State University, 1949.

should have charts, pictures, and models available or at least a blackboard. If none of these is available, your talk is probably doomed to failure.

Test 7.   Is the Subject Timely? Is This an Opportune Time to Discuss It?

Has the subject received favorable attention recently? Dueling was timely during the first half of the nineteenth century, but it is no longer of general interest. For the same reason, trial by jury, popular election of senators, a six-year term for the president, and military occupation of Haiti hold less interest for us today than they once did.

Carefully weigh what advantages will accrue from a presentation of the subject at a given moment. Subjects which have received attention in the press and over radio and television will be familiar to your auditors. Your success on many occasions may depend upon how skillfully you read the signs of the times and take advantage of current interest.

Test 8.   Is the Subject Appropriate for the Occasion?

Will a discussion of it be considered in harmony with the spirit of the assembly? Is it important that you do not give the impression of being inconsiderate and thoughtless about community customs. To violate the spirit of an occasion reflects upon your good judgment and good character.

Such thoughtlessness could have had a serious consequence when Lincoln spoke at Gettysburg. When the news was released that he had accepted an invitation to appear, the story was circulated that Lincoln would deliver a political stump speech. Recognizing that such a choice was inappropriate for the dedication of a national cemetery, he naturally chose to do otherwise. After reading the advance copy of Edward Everett's two-and-a-half-hour address, he planned a short, five-minute inspirational talk, which proved to be most "fitting and proper" for that occasion. You too should always make sure that your subject will be "fitting and proper" for the meeting.

Test 9. Is the Subject Sufficiently Limited in Scope for Adequate Development Within the Time Limit?

As a general rule, a topic should be as specific as possible. Broad philosophical and theoretical questions are difficult to treat, especially within a short period. Limit your subject sufficiently to ensure complete development. Instead of attempting to speak upon the general subject of world government in a ten-minute speech, you will probably be more successful if you discuss a limited phase such as "United Nations Efforts To Institute Atomic Control," "How the Individual Citizen Can Contribute to the United Nations," or "What the United Nations Accomplished in Indonesia." The student who decides to speak upon the topic of "Industrialization of the South" in a five-minute speech has failed to consider this test. His talk will be improved if he narrows his subject to the industrialization of one city or one county. If he does not narrow it, his treatment will be superficial and hurried, his assertions sweeping, and his evidence scant.

In light of the extensive discussion of this test in the chapter on "Planning Your First Speeches," further discussion does not seem necessary.

COLLECTING EVIDENCE

Once a bibliography is completed, you are ready to collect additional arguments and evidence. As early as possible the subject should be narrowed to fit the time limit, and a thesis should be formulated. Of course, as you pursue your study, you may recast your main thought several times. The argument and type of supporting material you select to substantiate your position depend upon your own familiarity with the subject, the length of the speech, and the time available for study.

As you read, you should keep before you such queries as the following:

1. Is the material primary or secondary?
2. What are the reputation and professional standing of the author and publisher?

3. Does the date of publication affect the validity of the material?
4. What was the author's purpose in presenting the material?
5. Are the materials and conclusions based upon careful and thorough research?
6. Is the author consistent?
7. Has the author explained his method of research sufficiently that his findings can be checked?
8. Are his conclusions verified by other authorities in the field?

TAKING NOTES

The most frequently recommended method of note-taking involves recording materials on index cards or small slips of paper easily filed. If slips of paper are used, they should probably conform to standard sizes of filing boxes—3 by 5 and 4 by 6 inches.

Some uniform system of labeling should be adopted. As soon as possible a standard set of topics should be drafted under which to file information. The subject should be placed in the upper left corner with the source immediately following the quotation.

```
Requisites of good speaking

    "The art of speaking depends on great
labor, constant study, varied exercise,
repeated trials, the deepest sagacity, and
the readiest judgment."

Quintilian, Institutes of Oratory, John S.
    Watson, translator, Henry G. Bohn, 1856,
    vol. 1, pp. 136-137.
```

Care should be taken that the bibliographic reference is complete. The following suggestions should be observed:

1. Label clearly and uniformly.
2. Write clearly, and do not crowd material.
3. Place one subject on a card.
4. Do not distort meaning by lifting material out of context.
5. If you copy verbatim, enclose in quotation marks. For a quotation within a quotation, use single quotes.
6. Delete unnecessary portions and indicate by using three dots (. . .) for deletion within a sentence and four dots (. . . .) for deletions at end of sentence.
7. Quote exactly. If the material seems in error, if words are omitted, or if words are misspelled, place [sic] immediately following the discrepancy to indicate that the mistake or deletion has been noted.
8. To indicate interpolation within a quotation, place remark within brackets, not parentheses.
9. Indicate italicized words by underlining.
10. After copying material, check it against original before proceeding.

QUESTIONS AND TOPICS FOR STUDY AND REVIEW

1. What is involved in the general background necessary for great oratory? How is this related to the broad knowledge described in Chapter 4? What are the sources of general preparation?
2. What are the dangers for the speaker of overspecialization? Illustrate.
3. Make a list of general sources of speech subjects which apply particularly to you. Classify your subjects under the same headings used on the chart on page 210.
4. In addition to the eight steps suggested on page 209, are further steps necessary? Some of these steps may grow out of your preferences.
5. Emerson said, "Books are the best things, well used; abused, amongst the worst. . . . They are for nothing but to inspire" ("The American Scholar"). Do you agree or disagree with this statement? Support your position with evidence.
6. How do famous speakers make immediate preparation for their speeches? (See Braden and Gehring, *Speech Practices*, Chapter 2.)
7. Many students argue that they have nothing worthwhile to discuss. Make several suggestions to help such students find some interesting speech subjects.
8. How well do your fellow students conform to the nine tests of a

speech subject? With which one or ones do they seem to have the greatest difficulty?

PROJECTS

1. *Speaking Assignment.* Deliver a three- to five-minute speech in which you explain the operation of some apparatus. If possible, actually bring the apparatus to class for demonstration. Divide your explanation into three or four steps or points.

2. *Speaking Assignment.* Report orally to the class on the steps you followed in finding the answer to one of the problems given below. Tell why you know that your answer is correct. (Review section on collecting evidence.) If you are unable to find what you consider a satisfactory answer, discuss with the class the steps you followed, and analyze why you failed. The answers are not as simple as they may appear.

   Questions for research:

   a. What was the speaking rate of Franklin D. Roosevelt?
   b. How many speeches did Harry Truman deliver in the campaign of 1948?
   c. Why did Napoleon sell Louisiana?
   d. Who won the Lincoln-Douglas debates?
   e. What was the physical appearance of Lincoln in March, 1860?
   f. Did George Washington write his "Farewell Address"?
   g. Who wrote Shakespeare's plays?
   h. How many official versions are there of the "Gettysburg Address"?
   i. Can you verify the handwriting of Franklin D. Roosevelt?
   j. In 1860 how many persons in Alabama owned more than 300 slaves each?
   k. How many horses were there in Knox County, Tennessee, in 1860?
   l. Who won the World Series in 1948?
   m. What color clothes did the Pilgrims wear?
   n. Did the Pilgrims land on Plymouth Rock?
   o. Did Patrick Henry utter the phrase "Give me liberty or give me death"?

3. *Speaking Assignment.* Read carefully one of the following speeches or a similar one from another source. Prepare a four-minute oral summary or criticism of the speech as a whole or of some pertinent idea found in the speech. Notice also the sources indicated by your speaker.

   Ralph Eubanks, "Know Thy Worth," in *Vital Speeches of the Day,* July 15, 1961, **27**: 604–606.

Hobart F. Heller, "The Climate of Learning," in *Vital Speeches of the Day*, November 15, 1961, **28**: 87–91.

Lester Markel, "The Future of the Printed Word," in *Vital Speeches of the Day*, April 1, 1956, **22**: 381–384. Also portion quoted in *Speech Practices*,[10] pp. 143–145.

Richard Lardner Tobin, "A Little Learning," in *Vital Speeches of the Day*, April 15, 1956, **22**: 414–416.

G. Meredith Wilson, "Patterns of Leadership," in *Vital Speeches of the Day*, October 1, 1961, **27**: 760–762.

4. *Written Assignment.* In the light of what you already know about your classmates, prepare a list of fifty topics which would be appropriate for five-minute speeches. Make your topics as specific as possible. List them under these headings: speeches to stimulate, speeches to entertain, speeches to inform, and speeches to persuade.

5. *Research and Speaking Assignment.* Investigate how some famous speaker prepared his speeches. On the basis of your findings, deliver a five-minute oral report to your classmates. For interesting material on the speech preparation of famous speakers, see the following:

William A. Behl, "Theodore Roosevelt's Principles of Speech Preparation and Delivery," *Speech Monographs*, 1945, **12**: 112–122.

Waldo W. Braden, "The Bases of William E. Borah's Speech Preparation," *Quarterly Journal of Speech*, February, 1947, **33**: 28–30.

Earnest Brandenburg, "The Preparation of Franklin D. Roosevelt's Speeches," *Quarterly Journal of Speech*, April, 1949, **35**: 214–221.

Dayton D. McKean, "Notes on Woodrow Wilson's Speeches," *Quarterly Journal of Speech*, April, 1930, **16**: 176–184.

Glen Mills, "Misconceptions Concerning Daniel Webster," *Quarterly Journal of Speech*, December, 1943, **29**: 423–428.

Loren Reid, "Did Charles Fox Prepare His Speeches?" *Quarterly Journal of Speech*, February, 1938, **24**: 17–26.

Charles Ross, "How Truman Did It," *Collier's*, December 25, 1948, pp. 13, 87–88.

Eugene E. White and Clair R. Henderlider, "What Harry S. Truman Told Us About His Speaking," *Quarterly Journal of Speech*, February, 1954, **40**: 37–42.

Eugene E. White and Clair R. Henderlider, "What Norman Vincent Peale Told Us About His Speaking," *Quarterly Journal of Speech*, December, 1954, **40**: 407–416.

Russell Windes, Jr., "Adlai E. Stevenson's Speech Staff in the 1956 Campaign," *Quarterly Journal of Speech*, February, 1960, **46**: 32–43.

[10] For full reference, see p. 15.

SUPPLEMENTARY READINGS

Adler, Mortimer J., *How To Read a Book*, Simon & Schuster, 1940.
Aldrich, Ella V., *Using Books and Libraries*, 4th ed., Prentice-Hall, 1960.
Excellent brief guide to how to find books and materials in a library.
Auer, J. Jeffery, *An Introduction to Research in Speech*, Harper, 1959, chap. 4, "Bibliographical Resources."
Baird, A. Craig, and Franklin H. Knower, *General Speech: An Introduction*, 2nd ed., McGraw-Hill, 1957, chap. 4, "Finding Material."
Braden, Waldo W., and Earnest Brandenburg, *Oral Decision-Making*, Harper, 1955, chap. 4, "Finding Facts."
Bryant, Donald C., and Karl R. Wallace, *Fundamentals of Public Speaking*, 3rd ed., Appleton-Century-Crofts, 1960, chap. 6, "Collecting and Handling Information."

13

Selecting a
Speech Goal

In the light of what you know of the audience and the occasion, it is important to consider carefully your speech purpose. To ensure purposeful activity, you must know what response you want in order to select materials and to make plans that enable you to achieve it. Keep your speech moving toward your objective.

The general goal of speaking is *response* or, in more technical language, a neuromuscular or neuroglandular activity of one kind or another. When at dinner you say in a quiet voice, "Please pass the sugar," you expect your neighbor to satisfy your request. If your car mires in the mud, you call anxiously for help, hoping for a response—a push or a pull. Before you drive the golf ball down the fairway, you shout a healthy "Fore!" with the intention of clearing the line of flight. In each case your objective is a *response*. Likewise, in a public speech you have a similar goal—some kind of response.

Your goal must meet at least two requisites. First, you must have a definite idea of what response you want. Second, you must select a response which you have a reasonable expectation of eliciting. In other words, the goal must be one which you can achieve by your speech. It must neither theoretical nor ideal. You must select it on the basis of careful study of the attitudes, biases, preferences, and beliefs of your listeners and a thorough analysis of the occasion. There is nothing haphazard or accidental about an effective speech; it is the result of careful thought and thorough planning.

AUDIENCE RESPONSE

If the advice above is to be your guiding philosophy, early in your preparation you must answer four questions.

1. What kind of response do I want?
2. When do I want my listeners to respond?
3. How long do I want them to respond?
4. Do I want my listeners to respond as individuals or as a group?

Let us consider each of these queries briefly.

What Kind of Response Do I Want?

Is the response to be *covert*, entirely within the auditor? Or is it to be *overt*, openly manifested? In the first, you may ask the listener to do no more than to think, recall, evaluate, associate, be amused, or feel excited. When you unfold a new procedure to your colleagues, you work for understanding. The droll story usually has as its objective quiet though perhaps unobservable delight. Many patriotic speeches attempt to do no more than stimulate additional pride in country. The goal in each of these cases is a covert response.

On the other hand, you may work for a response that you can see, an overt response; that is, your hearers may applaud loudly, shed tears, buy a vacuum cleaner, or cheer the home team.

The foregoing discussion is not meant to imply that overt and covert responses are opposites; rather, they should be viewed as parts of the same process, differing only in degree. Indeed, it is often difficult to say where one stops and the other begins.

When Do I Want My Listeners to Respond?

Is the reaction to be immediate or delayed? When you explain a simple gadget, you expect almost immediate understanding, but if you are discussing a complicated machine, you may have to give considerable explanation before you can hope for understanding from your auditors. In the latter case you are working for a delayed reaction. If you ask for a show of hands, a contribution, or a signature on a petition, the reaction you want is immediate, that is, it occurs during or immediately after the speech. If, however, the goal involves getting the listeners to write to their congressmen, read the newspapers, or boycott a merchant, the reaction is delayed. Here you must generate enough urgency to motivate your listeners to act some time after the speech has been concluded.

How Long Do I Want the Audience to Respond?

Is the response to be momentary or sustained? How long is it to continue? Understanding a fact may be momentary, but retention of that fact is a sustained response. To applaud the coach for an inspirational pep talk may be momentary, but to play sixty minutes of "heads-up" football requires continued effort. A show of hands or a signature is momentary, and you succeed if you can bring sufficient pressure to bear at the right instant. In "converting a sinner," the minister hopes to do far more than get the person to signify his intention to join the congregation; he wants the man to change his way of living. The insurance salesman has a particularly difficult task in this regard, for the signature on the original application is immediate and momentary, but payment of the premium should be continued fifteen or twenty years or even a lifetime. It is evident that arousing a momentary response is much simpler than arousing a reaction which is to be sustained.

Do I Want Individual or Group Response?

If an individual response is your goal, you attempt to inform, to stimulate, or to influence members of the audience individually. No set number of conversions is required for success. The teacher, of course, works on the basis of individual response, for learning is an individual response. Another excellent example of this phenomenon is the revival meeting in which the minister asks his converts to come forward when they "feel the call."

In the case of group response, you seek a favorable vote of the group, a show of hands, or some other indication that the gathering affirms your stand and will follow your directions. You seek to commit the group to your program. As indicated in an earlier chapter, if many ties bind the listeners together, the task of securing a group response is easier. In fact, with the regimented audience such as an airplane crew or a military unit, the social integration has been sufficient to ensure that a mere command will result in action. In less indoctrinated groups the significant question is, what percentage of the listeners can obligate or compel the whole group to act?

METHODS OF OBTAINING GOALS

In addition to knowing where you want to go with your speech, you should know what *route* you wish to travel in order to reach your destination. In general, five routes are available: entertaining, informing, stimulating, convincing, and actuating. Of course, two or more of these may be brought into play in the development of a single subject. An informative talk might include entertaining material for interest purposes. In an attempt to persuade or to actuate you might resort to humor, to information, and to stimulating material.

Entertaining

A speech to entertain is self-defining. Since its nature is obvious, let us direct our attention to its purposes or goals. In seeking to amuse your listeners, you may want either a covert or an overt response; that is, you may be satisfied if your auditors quietly attend to your speech, or you may strive to elicit from them perceptible evidences of amusement ranging from faint smiles to boisterous laughter. Ordinarily the reaction desired is immediate and momentary, but if the development is subtle or the listeners are slow to see the point of the humor, you may have to be content with silence or delayed laughter, neither of which is fully gratifying to the speaker. Little more than attention and interest, however, are required for the success of this type of speech.

From the auditor's point of view, this type of speech is solely a means of passing the time, forgetting cares and troubles, and relaxing. Once the speech is completed, he feels free to go his own way with no further responsibilities or obligations.

Informing

The informative speech may include description, narration, definition, interpretation, analysis, synthesis, explanation, demonstration, criticism, or any combination of these. It demands, in addition to attention and interest, that the audience understand, retain, and perhaps recall what is said. Their reaction may be immediate or delayed, sustained, covert or overt. Sometimes the sign of success is performance or demonstration by the auditors.

What should the listener expect from an informative speech? Since a premium is placed upon understanding and retention, he demands above all else that the speech be clear and specific. Ordinarily he prefers plenty of illustrations and, if possible, demonstration. He resists attempts to present material too rapidly. He is pleased with thought breaks, short sentences, and entertaining material. In many cases he fears being questioned and hopes to depart without being tested.

Stimulating

The stimulating speech strives to strengthen the listeners' attitudes, opinions, or beliefs already present but ineffective or inactive. As a speaker you hope to rekindle or heighten appreciation for a principle, a person, a group of persons, or an institution. In this type of speech you seek mainly covert response, either immediate or delayed. Probably you desire a sustained reaction. Classical rhetoricians called this a ceremonial speech or one of "praise or blame." Eulogies, pep talks, some sermons, reunion addresses, speeches of courtesy, patriotic orations, and dedicatory talks are stimulating talks.

Since the stimulating speech is based upon revitalizing latent wants, the auditors usually find little in it to resist. If the talk is based upon pleasant emotions (pride, reverence, patriotism), the listener finds the presentation pleasant. On the other hand, if the motivation utilizes unpleasant or negative emotions (fear, horror, shame), he may find it unpleasant or even embarrassing.

Convincing

Persuasive speeches seek to change attitudes and beliefs and in some cases strive to move the auditors to action. Herein they differ from stimulating speeches, which seek to strengthen and re-vitalize attitudes which are present but dormant. A basic requirement of the persuasive speech then is that you as a speaker hold a position which differs from that held by a significant number of your listeners.

In the convincing speech you seek either an immediate or a de-layed reaction. It may be momentary, but more frequently it is a sustained reaction. The distinguishing characteristic here, however, is that the goal is a covert response. For example, you may speak on such propositions as these: "Polio is still a threat"; "The social drinker is a menace on the highways"; "The gasoline tax is unfair." In any of these cases you ask for no more than mental agreement. Your speech may be preparatory to another in which you urge action, but so far as the present occasion is concerned, you are satisfied with mental acceptance.

Actuating

Like the speech to convince, the so-called actuating speech is also classified as persuasive. The latter goes a step further than the convincing talk in that it urges the listener to pursue a course of action, or, in other words, to give an overt response. The proposi-tions cited earlier could be adapted to this type by changing the wording to read as follows: "Donate to the National Foundation"; "You should oppose social drinking in your fraternity"; "Ask your congressman to oppose the high gas tax."

The two types of persuasive speeches are, of course, comple-mentary. The first can ordinarily be transformed into the second by adding a section proposing a solution to the problem and including additional and more powerful motive appeals. Obviously the demand for overt response requires greater effort than the demand for a covert response. Of the various types, persuasive talks are the most difficult, for they aim at changes of attitudes and beliefs. Departures from the *status quo* are often frustrating to the listener, because he senses a threat to his security, dislikes the thought of deserting tested modes of behavior, and objects to having his past thinking challenged. He may feel that to accede to your demands constitutes a blow to his prestige.

Summary Chart

Methods of Obtaining Goals	General Ends	Kind of Response	When?	How Long?
Entertaining	Enjoyment Diversion	Covert or overt	Immediate	Momentary
Informing	Understanding	Covert or overt	Immediate or delayed	Sustained
Stimulating	Appreciation	Covert or overt	Immediate or delayed	Sustained
Convincing	Mental agreement	Covert	Immediate or delayed	Sustained
Actuating	Action	Overt	Immediate or delayed	Momentary or sustained

KINDS OF GOALS

Immediate and Remote Goals

In the previous section we discussed the speaker's methods of obtaining goals and the general end to which each leads, namely diversion, information, appreciation, mental agreement, and action. But for any given speech, these general ends must be phrased in terms of the specific immediate goals or responses that you intend to elicit. This matter is discussed and illustrated in the final section of this chapter. When you are determining the goal of a speech you should realistically ask yourself: What is the most that I can hope to achieve with this audience? The wise solicitor seeks a donation well within his patron's capacity to pay. The effective teacher weighs the intellectual capacity of a class before making an assignment.

Since objectives selected in the light of prevailing attitudes and intellectual capacities may fall far short of what you really hope to accomplish, you may, for a given speech, also select an *ultimate* or *remote* goal, a distant objective. The time when this remote objective is achieved will be determined by the number and size of the obstacles to be overcome and the skill with which you move your listeners step by step toward overcoming them. Some objectives might require a dozen speeches, supplemented by other techniques such as advertising, group pressure, or dramatization. A college president speaking on school spirit may have in mind the day when he intends to ask you to contribute to the college endowment; strong loyalties now may mean donations later when you have a substantial income. The politician gives to charity now with an eye on the future; admiration today means votes tomorrow, he hopes.

Certainly the purposeful speaker must often have in mind his remote goal as well as his immediate one.

Announced and Concealed Goals

Ordinarily, the immediate goal, whether stated or implied, is evident to the audience by the close of the speech. Remote goals must often be obscured or concealed, because the speaker realizes that for the moment his auditors are not ready for the final plunge. Premature revealing of future objectives may make listeners more difficult to manage.

Is it ethical to have a goal which you cannot announce? Are you not thereby deceiving your listeners? The answers to these questions depend upon whether your goals are consistent with the best interests of the group. If they are, you need feel no chagrin at not announcing your ultimate objectives. But if your ends are selfish and injurious to the welfare of the group, you should indeed be censured. (See Chapter 4, "Minimum Essentials of Good Speaking," for further discussion of ethics.)

SELECTING A GOAL

Though we normally assume that the speaker is a free agent in selecting the goal he wishes to achieve, this is seldom entirely true. Many times the goal grows out of demands of the listeners or requirements of the occasion. Much depends upon why the group assembles.

If the meeting has been called for the specific purpose of giving you an opportunity to speak, you may certainly determine your own method and objective. But if the audience assembles because of some aspect of the occasion—a patriotic celebration, a presentation ceremony, a dedication service—then you must be guided by the requirements of the occasion. The humorous talk is frequently associated with the after-dinner occasion. The persuasive talk is often associated with the pulpit. In some churches the preacher is always expected to conclude his message with invitations for converts. The informative talk is often associated with the classroom. You must, therefore, always ask yourself, does my proposed goal fit the requirements of the occasion?

Sometimes the audience invites you through a program chairman to speak on a certain subject. The representative may say, "We should like to hear an entertaining talk on your recent trip to Hawaii." Or you may be asked to tell the local service club "How To Make a Successful Speech," "How To Solicit Funds," or "What Is Democracy?" You must honor such a request, else you may disappoint or even offend the group. In such cases, what is important is that you align your own purposes with those of the audience.

In the matter of determining goals it is important to consider how the audience is divided upon your topic. Ordinarily a group can be divided into three large categories: opposition, neutrals, and partisans. Usually these terms apply to persuasive speeches, but they may also be adapted to the other types of speeches, as the chart on page 230 shows.

WORDING THE SPECIFIC PURPOSE

The wording of the specific purpose for a given speech must relate the speaker's goal to the audience and the occasion. The importance of the specific purpose becomes more apparent when it is realized

Attitudes Listeners May Hold with Reference to Your Subject

Type of Speech	Opposition	Neutral	Partisan
Speech to entertain	Bored	Passive	Attentive
Speech to inform	Uninformed (ignorant)	Indifferent	Informed
Speech to stimulate	Lethargic	Uninterested	Enthusiastic
Argumentative:			
To convince	Antagonistic	Undecided	Mental agreement
To actuate	Antagonistic	Undecided	Ready to act

that the remainder of the analysis must stem from it. For an entertaining speech, a speaker might word his specific purpose as follows:

> To amuse my fraternity by ridiculing our rival fraternity
> To entertain the members of the speech class by discussing Christmas shopping
> To entertain the Kiwanis Club by relating the events of my recent trip to Mexico

The specific purpose of an informative speech may read:

> To tell the speech class about my survey in sociology
> To relate to the members of the debate squad the history of Pi Kappa Delta
> To demonstrate to the first-aid class how to apply a tourniquet
> To discuss before the community forum the city-manager plan

If it is to be a stimulating talk, you might word the specific purpose in this manner:

> To praise the OHS football team in the presence of the Down Town Kiwanis Club
> To stir up the hatred of my social club for the Communists
> To stimulate the student body to appreciate Coach Smith
> To heighten the appreciation of the Ramblers for Shakespearean plays

The convincing speech may involve such specific purposes as the following:

> To convince the members of the PTA that Highland School needs a gymnasium
> To convince the speech class that improper dieting endangers health
> To convince parents of school children that many television programs are harmful to children
> To convince the freshmen that cramming does not pay

The specific purpose of an actuating speech may be worded as follows:

> To solicit gifts from the American Legion for local orphanages
> To "sell" bankers on the need for advertising
> To persuade Cub Scouts that they should study the Manual
> To persuade Professor Jones that my grade should be raised

Notice that each of these specific purposes mentions the following elements: (1) the method (to tell, to stimulate, to convince, to persuade), (2) the audience, and (3) the specific subject.

QUESTIONS AND TOPICS FOR STUDY AND REVIEW

1. This chapter makes use of the term *response* many times. What are some synonyms for this word as used in context?
2. This chapter states, "The general goal of speaking is response." Is there any type of speech which does not have response as a goal?
3. Are covert and overt responses mutually exclusive? Consult a psychology textbook on this question. After you have formulated your answer, find several examples.
4. Why is it difficult for a listener to differentiate between speeches to stimulate, to convince, and to actuate? Give some reasons why two persons hearing the same speech might disagree on its goal. When listeners disagree about the goal of a speech, what problem does the speaker have?
5. Decide whether the speaker wants an immediate or delayed response in the following situations and justify your answer.
   a. Selling Christmas seals
   b. Asking the listeners to use a new type of face soap
   c. Telling a horror story
   d. Asking the voters to go to the polls and vote

e. Asking the Dad's Club to sponsor a Little League baseball team

f. Evaluating a movie

g. Demonstrating a new washing machine

6. Now, analyze the cases given in the problems above from the point of view of whether the speaker wanted a momentary or sustained response, and justify your answer.

7. David Berlo says, "A response that is covert to a layman may be overt to a physician, the clinical psychologist, the bio-chemist" (*The Process of Communication*, Holt, Rinehart & Winston, 1960, p. 76). How do you explain this observation? Find some specific examples to support your answer.

8. State the basic differences between the argumentative and the stimulative situation (that giving rise to argument and that giving rise to stimulation).

9. What goals would you select in each of the following situations?

a. Opponents 85 percent; neutrals 10 percent; partisans 5 percent.

b. Opponents 30 percent; neutrals 40 percent; partisans 30 percent.

c. Opponents 20 percent; neutrals 10 percent; partisans 70 percent.

10. When you face a strong opposition, what methods could you use to break it down?

PROJECTS

1. *Speaking Assignment.* Deliver an oral analysis of the goals of three advertisers as shown in full-page newspaper or magazine advertisements.

a. Determine what were the immediate, the remote, and the concealed goals.

b. Explain fully how you reached your conclusions.

c. Determine whether you think the advertiser is ethical in his objectives.

d. Carefully organize and rehearse your speech before you come to class.

2. *Discussion Questions for Class Symposiums.*

a. Is it possible for a speech to have two goals? More than two?

b. Is it always necessary to determine the specific goal of a speech?

c. What were the speech goals of the various candidates in the last presidential election? How did these goals affect their speaking?

d. As a listener, how can you determine a speaker's goals? Why is it important for you to ascertain his goal as soon as possible?

e. If you discover that a speaker has an undesirable goal, what should be your course of action?

SUPPLEMENTARY READINGS

Brembeck, Winston Lamont, and William Smiley Howell, *Persuasion: A Means of Social Control*, Prentice-Hall, 1952, chap. 16, "The Purposes of Persuasive Speeches."

Brigance, William Norwood, *Speech Composition*, rev. ed., Appleton-Century-Crofts, 1953, chap. 3, "The Speech Purpose."

Crocker, Lionel, *Public Speaking for College Students*, 3rd ed., American Book, 1956, chap. 11, "The Purposes of Speaking."

Oliver, Robert T., and Rupert L. Cortright, *Effective Speech*, 4th ed., Holt, Rinehart & Winston, 1961, chap. 8, "Setting the Goal."

14

Outlining and Planning

AN OVERVIEW OF SPEECH PREPARATION

1. Locate a subject.

2. Narrow the subject.

3. Study the occasion and audience.

4. Select a desired response.

1. China.

2. U.S. support of Nationalist China.

3. To be delivered before Speech 51, a class composed of twenty-two men: eleven from the College of Agriculture, eleven from Engineering.

4. To gain (a) immediate (b) mental agreement (c) which continues to dominate thinking.

5. Word the specific purpose.

6. Phrase the proposition.

7. Determine the type of proposition: recommending or assertive.

8. Choose the pattern of partition: (a) chronological, (b) spatial, (c) causal, (d) parties involved, (e) fields of endeavor, (f) another order.

9. Word the main points in sentence form.

10. Check the logical structure of the speech outline.

5. To convince (a) the class (b) that Nationalist China should have (c) our support.

6. Nationalist China is worth saving.

7. Assertive proposition.

8. Fields of endeavor that are (a) political, (b) economic (c) military.

9. Nationalist China is worth saving, for
   a. It is a valuable political ally in United Nations.
   b. It is a good customer.
   c. It provides a strategic military base in the Far East.

Steps 1 through 5 have been covered in earlier chapters. The present chapter considers the remaining steps.

THE PROPOSITION

Definition

A pertinent question to ask of the speaker is, what is the central point you are trying to develop? Throughout his speech the speaker must make the answer to this question apparent to the largest possible percentage of his listeners. If at any moment he loses sight of his central thought, he is wasting your time. As we have noted before, the speaker may choose to withhold an exact statement of his central thought until he considers that it will receive a favorable reception. Even then, whatever he says and does should be directed toward making his listeners understand, think, feel, believe, or do what he says.

This key or central idea around which the speech is built is called the proposition. It is the epitome or very heart of what the speaker says. To describe it in another way, if the speaker were suddenly to learn that his extended remarks have to be limited to a single sentence, that sentence will undoubtedly be a statement of his *proposition*, for its acceptance means the accomplishment of his goal. It is easy to see that, if a unified impression is to be made, the proposition must be worded in a single meaningful sentence. If the listeners fail to hear or to understand this proposition, they are sure to be confused. If they try to decide what they "think you are driving at," they may develop a dozen different interpretations of your line of thought or the course of action you propose. Under such conditions of uncertainty, unity of thought, feeling, or action is impossible.

Kinds of Propositions

The *assertive* proposition (often referred to as a proposition of fact or value) affirms or denies the existence of a fact, a truth, a condition, an influence, a quality, or a relationship. It demands of the listener no more than a covert response, a mental agreement. Naturally stated or implied in this type of statement is some form of the verb *to be*. Note the following propositions: (1) "There is a communistic influence in our state." To develop a speech around this statement, the speaker must prove that a communistic influence does exist, but recognition of the threat is all he seeks. (2) "Our church needs (is in need of) a new organ." Again, the speaker asks no more than recognition of a need or a condition. You might deliver a stimulating talk around the statement, "Eisenhower was a great President." In such a talk you would seek to stir admiration and pride.

Here are other examples of assertive propositions:

1. Baton Rouge provides many business opportunities.
2. Democracy is superior to communism.
3. Washington was a greater military strategist than Cornwallis.
4. The South is America's new frontier.
5. Labor unions are undemocratic.
6. Labor has a right to use the sit-down strike.
7. Passive resistance is the best policy.
8. Latin America is a great potential market for consumer goods.
9. There is no Santa Claus.
10. Our taxes are too high.

The *recommending* proposition (sometimes referred to as one of policy) goes one step further than that of assertion: in addition to telling the listener what to believe, it proposes what he should do, thus demanding an overt response. In other words, it argues the expediency or advisability of following a certain course of action. Perhaps it rightly should be called a "should" or "ought" proposition, for one of these words, either stated or implied, is usually combined with a transitive verb such as *build, demand, join, buy, sell, support, give, adopt,* or *vote.*

The following are examples of this type:

1. You should vote for home rule.
2. You should support the Community Chest.
3. Traffic laws should be enforced.
4. You should contribute to the National Foundation.
5. You should buy U.S. Savings Bonds.
6. You should tithe for your church.
7. Our teachers should receive higher pay.
8. We should enlarge our stadium.
9. Buy a health-insurance policy.
10. Buy a Mayfield washer today.

Framing the Proposition

Framing the proposition means crystallizing a speech topic into a single meaningful thought. The process is sometimes a slow one. It may be much easier to express the key idea of a speech in two or three sentences or in a paragraph than in a single sentence. Consequently, the temptation is to say, "Oh, well, I am sure that they get the general idea anyway." But this rationalization should be countered with the question, how can a speaker communicate an idea so nebulous that he cannot phrase it concisely?

There are at least two ways to arrive at a wording of a proposition.

You may wait until inspiration strikes. The objection to this is that inspiration seldom comes when it is most needed. On the other hand, you may work deliberately and systematically. The method of exploration has to be an individual matter, each person following the system best adapted to himself. We cannot hope to give a complete explanation of this process because it involves the whole question of how to think, which indeed is beyond the scope of this book. However, the following suggestions may prove helpful in framing a proposition.

1. Prepare a list of speech topics that seem appropriate for the speaking situation. At this stage expand the list as much as possible.
2. Study the list carefully. Strike out duplicates, combine those which overlap, and eliminate doubtful choices.
3. From the remaining list select the topic that seems most appropriate.
4. Expand the topic into a written paragraph or two which summarizes your view of the subject. It may help to "talk the subject out," that is, present it orally as you would to an audience. In writing down an idea, do it as rapidly as possible without regard to style, word choice, or sentence structure.
5. Give the paragraph the "rest" treatment by laying it aside until you have had time to relax and forget it. Then check to see if it still seems to express the general idea. If not, improve the paragraph or discard it and start over.
6. By careful scrutiny of your paragraph you may find a sentence which with some rewording and alteration can be made into a proposition. If you see several possibilities, write them all down for further study. Take plenty of time to weigh the various possibilities.
7. Select one thought and reword it into a meaningful, simple, declarative sentence.

In many cases it may not prove necessary to go through all seven steps. Naturally you should make the process as short and efficient as possible. As a rule, some such orderly process as this, designed to crystallize your thoughts, will prove superior to waiting passively for an inspiration.

Wording the Proposition

Future analysis and acceptance of the speech by your listeners will depend upon how well the proposition is worded. The following principles make helpful guides in the wording process.

The proposition should be worded in a complete declarative sentence. A topic or a phrase may announce a title, but it does not express a point of view. A question is also neutral. A declarative sentence by its very nature is a complete thought; it cannot be neutral. If a speaker announces that he is going to speak upon intercollegiate football, he has revealed nothing concerning his point of view. As a result the listener does not know whether the speech is to be one to inform, to stimulate, to convince, or to actuate. But when the speaker says, "I shall explain to you the system of scouting which our football coaching staff uses," he sets his course for the listener and for himself.

On the other hand, if the speaker says, "Intercollegiate football is a financial burden to Blank University," or "University College should discontinue football next year," he has told the listener to expect an argumentative or persuasive speech, and has taken a stand. A declarative sentence gives the listeners a clear understanding of what the speaker hopes to achieve.

Putting the central thought or proposition in a single declarative sentence also helps the speaker in making his preparation and selecting his supporting points. When he decides to speak upon the topic of scouting as stated above, the speaker must pursue a narrative form or give the steps which the coaches follow. But when he chooses to contend that University College should discontinue football, he must find reasons to support his contention—meaning that he has moved into the field of argument and persuasion.

The proposition should be a simple sentence—limited to one thought. Avoid compound, complex, or compound-complex sentences, because they express two or more thoughts. When the proposition is a single thought the unity of the speech is easier to maintain. Furthermore, the fewer words the proposition contains, the simpler it will be for the listener to remember. Although no iron-clad rule can be formulated, the chances of retention are much higher if the proposition is short.

The proposition should be stated in language instantly intelligible. Ambiguous or unfamiliar terms result in a multiplicity of impressions. The language of a proposition should require as little definition as possible. Figures of speech should be used sparingly. The proposition "Democracy needs us to take up for it" is vague because of the phrase "to take up for it." An improved wording might be "You should defend the American form of government," or "The army needs you to protect overseas bases," or "We should teach more history in our schools." Each represents an attempt to put the phrase "to take up for it" or its equivalent into concrete, meaningful language that is instantly intelligible.

The proposition should be worded in the language of the listeners. Each listener ought to feel that the speaker is talking directly to him. A common fault of speakers is making their propositions impersonal. In the statement "The United States should adopt national health insurance," the individual listener is completely ignored. Worded in terms of the audience, it might read, "Urge your senator to vote for national health insurance." The use of collective words—*people, persons, citizens, voters, the American public, men, ladies, everyone,* as well as the third-person pronouns *he, she, they*—also contributes to indirectness. The proposition "Every home should own a pressure cooker" can be made more impelling when reworded to read, "You should buy a pressure cooker." Let there be no doubt about the listeners to whom the speaker is directing his remarks.

The verb in the proposition should be in the active voice. The passive voice is indirect. Note the weakness in the proposition "A new suit should be bought by you." Such a statement may be made more direct by wording it "You should buy a new suit."

The proposition should be easy to remember. Since it embraces the very essence of the speech, the proposition must stand out. In this respect the problem of wording is much the same as that of the slogan maker; the wording and the title should be unique.

The proposition must be adapted to the audience and the occasion. Care must be taken not to alienate the listener. For example, for many groups south of the Mason-Dixon line, the proposition "Segregation should be ended" would not be given a hearing, because once the word *segregation* is mentioned, the audience would become emotional and refuse to listen. The mere mention of segregation is a stimulus sufficient to arouse an unfavorable response.

A dignified formal occasion demands a formally stated proposition elevated in its general implications. For this reason, a speaker finds a marked advantage with church groups in using a quotation from Scripture as a thesis. On the other hand, "Beat 'Bama for Bernie" would be appropriate and extremely effective at a pep meeting.

The proposition should be sufficiently short to fit the time limit and to ensure adequate development. The person who insists upon exceeding his time limit is extremely discourteous to his audience, to other speakers on the program, and to the chairman. His thoughtless enthusiasm or his inability to come to the point may make his speech ineffective. His audience may become tired and restless, or his treatment may be hurried and superficial.

In summary, therefore, a proposition should be a complete, declarative, simple sentence, stated in language instantly intelligible, and worded in the audience's terms. It should be stated in the active voice, and it should be easy to remember, appropriate to the speaking situation, and sufficiently limited for development within the time limit.

PARTITIONING

Recommending Proposition

The question here is, how can a recommending proposition be divided logically into its parts? By its very nature, this type of proposition contains two elements: a problem and a recommended solution. These two are discernible in the sentence "You should contribute five dollars to the Community Chest." The problem probably is that in the community there are many worthy charities and philanthropic causes, such as the YMCA, Boy Scouts, Salvation Army, and Red Cross, all needing financial support. The solution is "You should contribute five dollars." The word *should* implies that you "ought" to do it because it is highly desirable or expedient for you to do your part.

Immediately it becomes apparent that certain key questions can be devised which may be utilized in the study of most propositions of policy. The stock or key questions may be worded as follows:

1. What is the problem or what conditions make a change necessary?
   a. What are the causes of the problem?

    b. Does the problem arise from a structural or inherent weakness of the system?

    c. Do the weaknesses seriously impair the operation of the system?

2. Is the proposal or solution desirable?

    a. How is it an improvement over the *status quo?*

    b. How will it benefit the parties involved?

    c. Is it legally and morally justifiable?

    d. Will the proposal correct the difficulties without introducing new difficulties?

3. Is the proposal feasible?

    a. When would it be put into operation?

    b. Who would administer it?

    c. What would be the cost of such a plan?

    d. How would the change from old to new be made?

The list of "stock" questions above must be altered and adapted to fit a given proposition. The subquestions are not mutually exclusive and are not intended to be, nor can all the questions be applied to every problem. They are suggestive of queries that may be raised. The amount of time devoted to each will be determined by the speaker's interests, the occasion, and the audience.

Partition of an Assertive Proposition

Many assertive propositions are in reality a part of larger recommending propositions. The relationship is evident in the following outline:

Proposition: You should join the Hospital Insurance Plan, for

  I. Hospital bills are difficult to pay.

 II. Hospital insurance provides a cooperative way of sharing costs.

III. Payments are easily made in monthly installments.

The proposition is clearly a recommending one, because it advocates that "you" follow a course of action. However, notice that the subpoints have the characteristics of assertive propositions. They seek to prove three premises involving what is: "bills are . . . ," "insurance provides . . . ," and "payments are. . . ." Taken alone, each premise demands only mental agreement, but each one is designed to move the listener a step nearer complete acceptance of the main proposition.

The same is true of the following outline:

Proposition: The state of Louisiana should launch an extensive program of advertising, for
  I. Persons outside the state are unaware of the potentialities within the state.
 II. Such a program would result in many benefits to the state.

The course of action proposed is "an extensive program of advertising," but the subpoints supporting the proposition possess the characteristics of the assertive proposition.

In the analysis of the assertive proposition, two steps are therefore necessary.

1. Determine whether the statement is a part of a larger recommending proposition. In other words, it is futile to consider the statement "A communistic threat exists in the United States" without thinking in terms of the ultimate goal. If the speaker is purposeful, he has in mind a larger thesis which might be worded as follows: "The United States should outlaw the Communist party," or "The United States should declare war on any foreign power responsible for fostering subversive activities in this country."

2. Divide the proposition into subpoints. Obviously, the assertive proposition does not lend itself to the use of the key questions applied to recommending propositions. Each statement of this type must be approached on the basis of its individual merit. In this respect the following patterns of partition may prove useful:

According to chronological development: past, present, and future or the reverse order. In a speech the first point might be worded in terms of what has happened, the second in terms of what is happening, and the third in terms of the future.

According to the parties involved: for instance, students, faculty, and alumni; Democrats, Republicans, and Progressives; Protestants, Catholics, and atheists; or French, Germans, and Italians. In this type a point is directed at each party.

According to spatial arrangement or the physical layout: this basis of division ordinarily is most commonly associated with description, but a speech can be planned on the basis of geographical location.

Such an approach might involve the South, the West, and the North or the state, the nation, and the world.

According to a causal pattern: normally such a development involves two points: cause and result. The order is not important.

According to the order used by the opposition: the refutative order is used when a speaker is answering points advanced by an opponent.

According to fields of endeavor: this basis is probably employed more frequently than any of the others. Fields might be political, social, and economic; the home, the school, and the church, and like divisions.

To illustrate some of these methods of partitioning or division as it is sometimes called, let us apply several of the patterns to the statement "Beacon is a thriving city."

Chronological	Parties Involved	Spatial	Fields of Endeavor
1. Beacon has a rich tradition.	1. Beacon is good for the business and professional man.	1. Beacon has a prosperous business district.	1. Beacon has excellent business opportunities.
2. Beacon has an enviable present.	2. Beacon is good for the civil servant.	2. Beacon has a beautiful residential area.	2. Beacon has excellent schools.
3. Beacon has a promising future.	3. Beacon is good for the average citizen.	3. Beacon has a progressive suburban development.	3. Beacon has excellent recreation facilities.

From the discussion above, it becomes evident that in a proposition of policy both schemes of analysis will be utilized. To determine the large main points, the speaker will use the stock issues, but to subdivide the resulting contentions, he will probably employ one of the methods of partition described above.

OUTLINING THE SPEECH

First, let us anticipate a typical student's reaction to outlining. He may ask, why not prepare the speech and then prepare the outline, or for that matter, why prepare an outline at all? This attitude probably indicates that he does not understand the principles of analysis and partitioning. Actually, outlining should make speech preparation easier and provide a method for systematically breaking a subject into its parts, arranging the parts, and checking the speech structure.

Why outline? To ensure precise, orderly thinking.

A speech outline will make it easier for your potential listeners also, for the outline will make your presentation more systematic and more orderly. It will help you see your subject as a whole and make clear to your listeners how you propose to develop it. Furthermore, during your speech you will be able to show where you are in the development and when you have reached your destination.

Again, why outline? To ensure precise, orderly presentation of your ideas.

Kinds of Outlines

Ordinarily there are two kinds of speech outlines which may be used in the preparation of a talk: the topical outline, and the sentence outline.

The type of outline you select for a given speech will depend upon two factors: first, the nature and scope of the subject, and second, the use to which you wish to put the outline.

The topical outline is often cryptic and therefore meaningful only to the person who prepares it. The following is a specimen topical outline.

Keep Money Green

I. Discussion of Multicolored bills
by Treasury Department
II. Multicolored bills—unsatisfactory
A. Cause confusion
B. Change—expensive
C. Aid counterfeiters
III. Restatement and appeal

This abbreviated type of outline requires the same thoughtful analysis and partitioning that the sentence outline involves and may be all that is necessary for short talks and simple subjects. It is quite adequate for a speaker's notes or his own outline.

Ordinarily we recommend, however, that you prepare a sentence outline for your class assignments and for more serious efforts. Putting your thoughts into sentences will give you a greater opportunity to crystallize the key ideas of your speech and to make sure that you have ordered your materials wisely. Follow a form similar to that given below.

Model Skeleton Outline

TITLE: _____

SPECIFIC PURPOSE: _____

Introduction

I. _____

II. _____

PROPOSITION: _____

Development

I. _____
   A. _____
      1. _____
         a. _____
            (1)_____
            (2)_____
         b. _____
      2. _____
   B. _____
      1. _____
      2. _____
II. _____
   A. _____
   B. _____
III. _____

Conclusion

I. _____

II. _____

Following are three specimen outlines conforming to the skeleton outline above.

Outline for Informative Speech

TITLE: The Four C's of Sugar Refining
SPECIFIC PURPOSE: To tell the speech class about the refining of raw sugar

Introduction
I. During the depression, we all heard about the C.C.C. or the three C's.
II. Today I want to discuss the four C's of sugar refining.

PROPOSITION: The refining of raw sugar involves four C's.

Development
I. The first C stands for crushing.
   A. The cane is placed on a conveyor belt.
   B. It is carried through two sets of knives.
   C. The finely chopped cane is passed through crushers.
   D. The juice is carried into the next step.
   E. The bagasse is sent to the furnace room or the storage area.
II. The second C stands for clarification.
   A. The juice contains many impurities such as mud and particles of fiber.
   B. Lime is added to accomplish the following:
      1. To neutralize the natural acidity.
      2. To remove suspended impurities.
      3. To precipitate dissolved nonsugar.
      4. To decolorize the juice.
   C. Lime is permitted to settle.
III. The third C represents concentration.
   A. Juice is sent through a series of multiple-effect evaporators.
   B. Excess water is evaporated.
IV. The fourth C stands for crystallization.
   A. Concentrated juice is passed through vacuum pans which facilitate the formation of crystals.
   B. By centrifugal action crystals are separated from molten liquor.

Conclusion
Remember the four C's of sugar refining:
I. Crushing
II. Clarification
III. Concentration
IV. Crystallization

Outline for Convincing Speech[1]

TITLE: That Green Stuff

SPECIFIC PURPOSE: To convince the speech class that multicolored currency is undesirable

Introduction

I. Is there anyone here who does not know what I mean by "green stuff" or "lettuce"?
II. The Treasury of the United States has proposed that we change our bills—go modern; put them in bright new dresses.

PROPOSITION: Multicolored currency is undesirable.

Development

I. Multicolored bills would result in confusion, for
    A. We are accustomed to green bills.
    B. Old and new bills would be circulating at the same time.
II. Reissuance of currency would be expensive, for
    A. Development of new inks and dyes and new plates would require much work and experimentation.
    B. Recovery of all currency in circulation would take many years.
III. Multicolored currency would aid counterfeiters, for
    A. Users would not scrutinize multicolored bills as carefully as they do present bills.
    B. Counterfeiters might copy the new shades.

Conclusion

I. Why change the color of our "green stuff" when thus far it has been so satisfactory?
II. Remember the following:
    A. It would be confusing.
    B. It would be expensive.
    C. It would aid counterfeiters.

Outline for Actuating Speech

TITLE: Buying a Saucepan Pressure Cooker

SPECIFIC PURPOSE: To persuade the ladies of the Circle that they should buy a saucepan pressure cooker

Introduction

I. Everybody wants to save.

[1] Prepared by Sue Scarbrough for an assignment in Speech 51-H, at Louisiana State University.

II. In your kitchen of today or the future you will probably want to save time, money, and food value.

III. There is one kitchen utensil that is invaluable in the kitchen as a saving device.

PROPOSITION: You should buy a saucepan pressure cooker.

Development

I. It saves time, for
   A. It cooks food in the shortest possible time.
   B. A whole meal can be prepared at once.
   C. It is simple to use.
II. It saves money, for
   A. It uses less fuel than ordinary cooking methods.
   B. Less expensive cuts of meat and types of food can be used more readily.
III. It saves food value, for
   A. It uses a small amount of water.
   B. It creates a near vacuum.

Conclusion

You should buy a saucepan pressure cooker, for it saves time, it saves money, and it saves food value.

PSYCHOLOGICAL ORGANIZATION

The schemes of partitioning we have been discussing may be referred to as logical means. A study of the chart on page 244 will indicate that each method illustrated there develops out of a careful study of the proposition and its nature. But throughout this book we have continually stressed that the successful speech is audience-centered, meaning that it is planned with the listener in mind. What would be the basis of division when you attempt what may be referred to as psychological organization?

In such cases you may wish to let the interests, attitudes, and information of the listeners guide you in planning your speech order. You would therefore want to consider the factors of

1. Importance
2. Interestingness
3. Complexity
4. Acceptability

Importance. Using the factor of importance you would arrange your points in the order of their relative importance in accomplishing your goal, that is, with reference to their potency to satisfy the listeners. The order of arrangement would be from most important to least important or the reverse.

Interestingness. Using interestingness, proceed from more interesting to less interesting or vice versa. In this approach you would arrange your presentation in the order which seemingly coincides with the factors of interest. Audience preferences become the determining factor.

Complexity. With complexity as the factor, proceed from known to unknown or from simple to intricate. For this approach you would start with what the auditors understand or what seems simple and moves in the direction of what they do not know. The experience and knowledge of the listeners are the controlling elements.

Acceptability. When acceptability is the factor, proceed from less controversial to more controversial or vice versa, from areas of agreement and acceptance to those which are more controversial.

These approaches are not mutually exclusive; in fact, they overlap in many cases. What is most important may be most interesting and most acceptable. The complex is probably not interesting, but it may be very important. It behooves you to order your points according to the scheme which will produce the best effect on your listeners.

RÉSUMÉ OF THE PRINCIPLES OF OUTLINING

A significant part of your speech preparation is outlining. It is not an easy or simple task, but requires concentration and effort. If it is carefully done, it provides you with another opportunity to test your materials and the ordering of your points and to check the unity and coherence of your thinking. It will increase your mastery of the subject.

Study carefully the model outlines. Notice the following points:

1. Speech outlines contain six parts: title, specific purpose, introduction, central thought or proposition, development, and conclusion.

2. Standard outlining symbols are used, with subpoints indented to indicate an inferior position:

I.
  A.
    1.
      a.
       (1)
         (a)

3. Only complete sentences are used.
4. Points are worded in the language which the speaker intends to utter in his speech.
5. Subpoints explain main points.

CHECKING THE LOGICAL STRUCTURE OF A SPEECH OUTLINE

The logical structure of a speech outline may be checked by asking a series of questions.

Is the outline divided on the basis of one principle only? This test can best be explained by an analogy. To sort apples by using the divisions of large, small, and red would be foolish because some red apples are large and others are small. In other words, the division was based upon two principles—size and color. Similarly, in planning a speech you must be consistent, using only one basis of division.

Is there overlapping in the outline? All points should be exclusive of each other, that is, no two points should cover the same material. The principle would be violated if a student attempted to treat his speech from the point of view of fraternity men, independents, and members of the YMCA. The first two are mutually exclusive, but the third is not; a member of the YMCA would be either a fraternity member or an independent.

Are parallel points of equal value? A fault of this nature occurs when a speaker makes a major point and a subpoint equal in value. Such is the case in the following partition:

Milford should build a larger stadium, for
  A. The present bowl cannot accommodate the crowds.
  B. The showers are inadequate for the visiting teams.

Probably B is a subpoint of a larger unstated premise which is of more equal value to A.

Are any subpoints equal to main points?   Partition, of course, implies dividing a proposition into its parts. If a subpoint equals a main point, no partition has taken place. This fault ordinarily occurs when the student merely restates a point, believing that he has divided it. The fault is apparent in the following:

The Utah legislature should appropriate money to build a new stadium, for
  A. The old stadium is inadequate.
  B. A new stadium should be built.

This second point is not a reason for building the new stadium but a restatement of the main statement.

QUESTIONS AND TOPICS FOR STUDY AND REVIEW

1. How does the proposition or central thought of an informative talk differ from that for a persuasive talk?
2. Study the relationship of the supporting points to the proposition. How does this relationship for the informative talk differ from that of the argumentative or persuasive talk? (This point is an important one.)
3. Many students confess that they prepare their speeches before they make their outlines. What is the weakness of this approach to speech preparation?
4. Study the patterns of partitioning suggested in this chapter. Prepare a list of other patterns and illustrate each.
5. What is the difference between the proposition that aims at action on the part of the listeners and the one that attempts to establish the principle that something should be done?
6. Students are told not to partition a point unless there are at least two subpoints. What is the reasoning back of this recommendation? Does this principle apply equally to outlines for persuasive and for informative speeches?
7. Students sometimes complain that standard outlining symbols are unimportant. In what ways are they useful and important?
8. Find an example of an outline which violates the checks given on pages 251–252. Identify the error and redivide the proposition correcting the error.

9. "No one has ever thought something out thoroughly and precisely until he has translated his ideas from the fluidity of thinking into the solidity of vocal or written expression—preferably to an audience outside himself" (editorial, *Christian Science Monitor*, November 7, 1959). What support can you find for this statement?

10. "Dignity and power come from full knowledge, deep thought, and sure faith as well as from personality" (Albert J. Beveridge, *The Art of Public Speaking*, Houghton Mifflin, 1924, p. 59). How does this statement apply to the beginning speaker?

PROJECTS

1. *Written Assignment.* Prepare five propositions on each of the following topics:

   Conservation
   Ownership of the Mississippi barge lines
   High- and low-cost housing
   Our local schools
   Our local church
   Improving participation in government

2. *Written Assignment.* Write a detailed evaluation of the following student outline. Consider its strong and its weak points, and revise the outline into one that you consider logical and effective.

TITLE: Erosion
SPECIFIC PURPOSE: To familiarize the audience with soil erosion

Introduction
I. Erosion may be caused by two agents.
   A. Erosion may be caused by water.
   B. Erosion may be caused by wind.

PROPOSITION: Erosion should be controlled.

Development
I. Erosion can be controlled by contour farming.
   A. Contour farming conserves some of the water.
   B. Contour farming hinders the flow of water toward the base of the slope.
II. Erosion should be controlled by terracing.
   A. Terracing checks the flow of water.
   B. All the water is conserved.
III. Reforestation controls erosion.
   A. Trees effectively check wind erosion.
   B. Trees effectively check water erosion.

Conclusion

I. To maintain our health, progress, happiness, and prosperity, we must control erosion by good management, contour farming, terracing, and reforestation.

II. The soil is the foundation of our health, happiness, progress, and prosperity.

3. *Written Assignment.* Prepare a detailed sentence outline of a speech that you have read in *Vital Speeches, Representative American Speeches, Modern Eloquence,* or some other collection.

SUPPLEMENTARY READINGS

Brigance, William Norwood, *Speech: Its Techniques and Disciplines in a Free Society,* 2nd ed., Appleton-Century-Crofts, 1961, chap. 11, "Organizing the Speech."

Bryant, Donald C., and Karl R. Wallace, *Fundamentals of Public Speaking,* 3rd ed., Appleton-Century-Crofts, 1960, chap. 9, "Outlining the Informative Speech."

Lomas, Charles W., and Ralph Richardson, *Speech: Idea and Delivery,* Houghton Mifflin, 1956, chap. 5, "Organizing Speeches."

Monroe, Alan H., *Principles and Types of Speech,* 5th ed., Scott Foresman, 1962, chap. 16, "Adapting Speech Organization to the Audience: The Motivated Sequence"; chap. 17, "Outlining a Complete Speech Using the Motivated Sequence." This book is recognized for its presentation of the five-step motivated sequence involving attention, need, satisfaction, visualization and action.

White. Eugene E., and Clair R. Henderlider, *Practical Public Speaking,* Macmillan, 1954, chap. 4, "Making the Outline"; chap. 5, "Organizing the Discussion."

15

Introducing the Speech

Upon meeting someone for the first time, you often, if not usually, make a quick estimate of him. If you know nothing of him, you decide that you like or dislike him entirely on the basis of what you see and hear. Given sufficient time, you may change your opinion, but if your acquaintanceship is brief, that first impulse becomes your permanent impression. Frequently a speaker is judged also on the basis of the first impression he makes in his opening sentences. Winston Churchill learned this lesson through years of experience. It is reliably reported that England's great orator was seldom satisfied with an introduction to one of his speeches until he had dictated a dozen versions. Churchill knew that those crucial beginning words probably mean success or failure.[1]

[1] Raymond Daniell, "Churchillisms," *New York Times Magazine*, September 12, 1943, p. 9.

The opening moments of your speech are your chance to win your way into the good graces of your listeners. Your introduction must be planned to gain you a favorable hearing in which your listeners are in a state of readiness to give serious consideration to the main part of your speech.

What is a favorable hearing? It involves three aspects:

1. An attentive hearing
2. A friendly hearing
3. An intelligent hearing

An attentive hearing implies sustained attention and directed interest. A friendly hearing means that the listeners respect the character and authority of the speaker and are willing to listen to him discuss the subject. An intelligent hearing implies that the auditors understand the subject and are desirous of further information.

SECURING AN ATTENTIVE HEARING

When a door-to-door salesman rings your doorbell, he faces much the same problem that you do at the beginning of a speech. When you answer the doorbell, the salesman momentarily has your attention, but unless he acts immediately you are likely to dismiss him. His problem is to hold your attention and direct your interest toward his product. Somehow he must persuade you to unhook the screen door and invite him inside to present his sales talk. A successful canvasser knows how to play upon the factors of attention and interest and how to appeal to your wants. The magazine salesman, to surmount initial obstacles, works on your sympathy by posing as a struggling college student attempting to earn his way through college. The Fuller Brush man, if permitted to enter, promises you a free vegetable brush. The encyclopedia salesman flatters you by suggesting that you are one of a select group for a special introductory offer. The insurance man volunteers to advise you without cost or obligation on how to reinvest your money. Each has his way, sometimes not too commendable, of opening the door.

A speaker in his opening sentences must also be adept at "opening the door." As we said earlier, few audiences are inactive, at least when you rise to speak. For a moment they will attend, but the problem is to hold their attention and direct their interest toward your subject. To be successful you must understand the psychology of attention and motivation.

In securing an attentive hearing you may find one or more of the following methods useful:

1. Use an animated delivery.
2. Relate the subject to the vital interest of the listeners.
3. Stir curiosity.
4. Make use of humor.
5. Establish a common ground of understanding.
6. Strive to be different.
7. Keep within the framework of the familiar.
8. Hurl a challenge.
9. Be specific.

Use an Animated Delivery

Probably the first way to make an audience want to hear you is to approach your subject with zest and enthusiasm. Give your listeners the impression that you sincerely believe what you say and that you believe it to be important for them to listen and accept your ideas. Animation seems easier to achieve if you possess some or all of the following characteristics:

1. An intense belief in your subject.
2. Confidence in your ability to present your subject.
3. Eagerness to address the particular audience.
4. Knowledge of opening sentences (memorize them).
5. A fervent desire to aid your listeners.
6. Abundant information on the subject.

In addition to your mental attitude, your platform behavior gives the audience many important cues: how you sit, how you await your turn to speak, how you respond to the remarks of preceding speakers, how you approach the platform. The following suggestions should help you give the impression of animation.

1. Listen carefully and intently to what the preceding speakers say.
2. Walk to the platform with restrained vigor.
3. Stand erect and alert.

4. Pause until the audience is quiet, giving the impression of poise and confidence.
5. Look directly at your listeners.
6. Give the impression that what is to follow will be worthy of attention.

Relate the Subject to the Vital Interests of the Listeners

Ordinarily when you rise to speak the listener has foremost in his mind such questions as the following: "Why should I listen to this person?" "What has this speaker to say that is important to me?" "Will he say anything worth while?" Satisfy these queries as soon as possible by suggesting how your subject is related to his welfare and self-interest, those vital wants which are powerful incentives. Furthermore, it will be to your advantage to make additional application of the principles of motivation discussed in Chapter 10. Directly or indirectly, you might weave into your remarks a theme like one of the following:

1. Your life or your property is in danger.
2. The safety of your loved ones may be involved in this matter.
3. Your material prosperity is dependent upon my subject.
4. This scheme will save you work and worry.
5. My plan will make you money.
6. Following my advice will make you famous.
7. The God-fearing man believes in this cause.
8. By this means you can become important and respected.
9. Patriotism demands that you listen.

In his inaugural address as the forty-ninth governor of New York, Nelson A. Rockefeller demonstrated how to utilize the vital concerns of his listeners in his opening sentences. He said:

As this sixth decade of our twentieth century nears its end, we are nearing, too, what could be the fatal testing time for free men—and freedom itself—everywhere.

Over the span of many a century, many a generation thinks its own age is a moment of historic decision. We know it.

We know it because we have witnessed—for more than twenty-five years now—the tragic ordeal of freedom. We have seen the tyrant—first Fascist, then Communist—strike down free nations, shackle free peoples, and dare free men everywhere to prove they can survive.

We know this to be such a time of historic decision, because we see the world divided, the weapons of war perfected to deadly extremes, and humanity seeming, at times, about to turn and prey upon itself.

And we know something else: we know how and why this world is divided and imperiled.[2]

Stir Curiosity

As we have said before, people like the unpredictable, the puzzling, the mysterious. Remembering man's exploratory tendencies, his eagerness to participate in the chase, publishers sell magazines by featuring continued stories; movie and TV serials run for many years. Soap operas kept millions of American women close to their radios. This inquisitiveness, which always seeks to learn "what happened next," can be put to good use in your introduction. If you can keep your listeners guessing, if you can provoke and encourage them to speculate on what is going to happen next, you are assured of continued attention and directed interest.

Methods of arousing curiosity are so numerous that the following list can be only suggestive.

1. The speech may be given a unique title.
2. The speaker may create doubts as to his real position.
3. The speaker may tell an exciting story.
4. He may ask a dramatic question or series of questions.
5. By his manner he may give the impression that he is going to reveal a secret or confidential matter.

Bruce Barton made use of curiosity in a speech by saying: "My Friends: My subject today is 'How Long Should a Wife Live?' "[3] The title was unique—it stirred his listeners.

Make Use of Humor

Few persons can resist a witty story or a clever turn of language. Therefore on many occasions a humorous illustration or anecdote makes an excellent introduction. The ability to tell a witty story well

[2] A. Craig Baird, ed., *Representative American Speeches: 1958–1959*, H. W. Wilson, 1959, pp. 110–115.

[3] Bruce Barton, "How Long Should a Wife Live?" in J. M. O'Neill and Floyd K. Riley, eds., *Contemporary Speeches*, Century, 1930, p. 255.

puts a speaker in a favorable light, breaks down resistance, elicits initially a favorable group response, and creates an air of expectancy.

Many amateurs have the impression that humor is so important that the relevancy or length of the story is unimportant. Anything for a laugh is their motto. Such persons may hold attention momentarily, but since they fail to direct interest toward the key idea of the speech, when the laugh is over the audience is no nearer the main consideration than before. An irrelevant story may even give the listeners a false cue and thus direct their attention elsewhere. The speaker should always try to make his humor grow out of the situation at hand and to point it toward the main idea of the speech.

Edward G. Olsen used humor to open his speech before an audience of school administrators and teachers of Fort Wayne, Indiana, September 6, 1960.

In tackling this subject with you today—Building Cities Glorious—I think of little Willie and his definition of gender. The teacher said, "Willie, define gender." "Yes'm," said Willie. "Gender is divided into masculine and feminine—masculine is temperate and intemperate, and feminine is frigid and torrid." Now I will try to be temperate in my remarks this morning if you will not be frigid in your discussion of them!

I take it that my job here today is to provide something of an overview upon the responsibility of modern education to improve human relationships: to indicate some of the things teachers and administrators and citizens can do, *practically*, about the pressing civic need to use education as a process—consciously, deliberately planned—to build better racial, religious, nationality-background and social-class understanding in our schools and communities. Well, if that's my job, perhaps you have a job, too, and maybe yours is to take what I say very personally and professionally. Will you examine these ideas critically, imaginatively, and decide for yourselves what you think your responsibility and opportunities are in this new school year, just beginning here today.

Maybe you and I both might keep in mind the story told about the Sunday School teacher. It seems that she was having the little boys and girls draw pictures in Sunday School as one of their projects, and as she looked at what Jimmy had drawn she said, "Oh my goodness, Jimmy, it looks like you've drawn a picture of a cowboy walking into a saloon." "It is," said the boy. "But don't worry, Miss Jason, he isn't going to drink anything, he's just going to shoot a man." So I think of the minister's prayer who said, "Oh Lord, forgive us for being so sensitive about the things that don't matter very much, so insensitive to the things that do."

So today, and in this new school year, let's try to be more sensitive about the things that matter so very, very much—foremost among them being the problem we face in Fort Wayne, Indiana, in the Mid-West, in America, in the World: building better human relationships.[4]

Establish a Common Ground of Understanding

Finding a common ground of understanding implies the discovery of those areas and activities about which there is no disagreement. Although Yankees and Southerners may quarrel vigorously over states' rights, they can always find a common ground in their love for the United States. You may disapprove of a man's religion but admire his golf game tremendously. A Democrat will take criticism from a fellow Democrat that he would bitterly resent from a Republican. To remind your listeners of the common grounds that exist between you and them is an excellent way to open a speech; for listeners to learn that the speaker believes as they do ordinarily results in closer attention and quicker conversion.

Being schooled in the techniques of stirring up hysteria and violence the agitator and demagogue, systematically using this technique, concentrate upon blind spots, biases, and prejudices. They may center their vitriolic attacks upon a scapegoat, for example, a minority—Negroes, Mexicans, or Catholics; or an institution—the Supreme Court, Wall Street, international bankers, or even the church. This is reprehensible and to be condemned, no matter where or when it occurs. It violates all that we have said about recognition of social responsibility in Chapter 4.

On the other hand the speaker may identify with the aspirations and sentiments of his listeners in a perfectly ethical way. In pursuit of this goal he may express admiration of cherished heroes, reverence for a historical event, love of country, or respect for democratic procedures.

Stress also common goals and objectives that you share with the audience. It will tend to minimize differences that may arise over method if you show your listeners you are in agreement on the end desired. Frequently a Republican remembers this method when the majority of his listeners are Democrats. During the war President

[4] Edward G. Olsen, "Why Build These Cities Glorious," in *Vital Speeches of the Day*, November 15, 1960, **18**: 76–81.

Roosevelt attempted to play down political differences and sought to emphasize instead the goal of winning the war.

Strive To Be Different

An audience welcomes a change from the usual and the common-place. The speaker who can introduce a tired old subject in a novel way is assured of continued attention from the first. David Lilienthal must have held the attention of an audience of editors when he opened an address in this way:

This black object that I hold in my hand is a cylinder of pure uranium. The amount I hold here is small as you can see. It is harmless. Five years ago no man had ever seen even this much pure uranium. Not that it was rare, but it was simply of little importance. Tonight this black metal, this inanimate substance is the central figure in the councils of the peoples of the world.

Why this should be so is not difficult to understand. Look at this small cylinder for a moment. It weighs about 2½ pounds. That much coal or oil, burned under the boilers of industry, would provide a trifling amount of useful energy. Compare the technical opportunities of the controlled release of nuclear forces. The energy resulting from the fission of the 3 million billion billion atoms in this small cylinder, converted into electricity, would equal about the total daily use of electricity in the city of Washington, which now requires about 2600 tons of coal.[5]

Roe Fulkerson employed novelty in the following introduction: "Dearly Beloved: The sermon today will be on the topic of dollar chasing. The text is taken from the first verse of the first chapter of the Gospel of Common Sense, which reads as follows: 'What does it profit a man if he gain the whole world and leave a rich widow?' "[6]

Keep Within the Framework of the Familiar

As valuable as novelty in an introduction is the familiar as a means of promoting interest and attention. Many times we enjoy hearing an old story retold; we like to meet old friends; we treasure our

[5] David E. Lilienthal, "Atomic Energy," *Congressional Record*, April 22, 1947, 93: A 1923–1924.

[6] Roe Fulkerson, "Dollar Chasing," in Homer D. Lindgren, ed., *Modern Speeches*, Crofts, 1926, pp. 359–366.

memories; we appreciate the speaker who conforms to our ideas of proper behavior. The Fourth of July orator, for example, can well begin by mentioning revered events held in pleasant memory by those present. Two cautions are in order. First, do not confuse the familiar with the commonplace or the trite. Avoid stereotyped introductions which open with sentences like the following:

> "Unaccustomed as I am to public speaking. . . ."
> "It is a great pleasure to be here."
> "I have a few remarks which I want to make."
> "I am sure that someone else is more capable of saying this, but I . . ."

Second, maintain a nice balance between the novel and the familiar. Eisenson explains, "We generally . . . strive for a state of equilibrium, one between the two extremes in which neither too little of the novel, or too much of the familiar is present."[7]

Says Overstreet, "The wise proponent of a new idea will make sure that the new is sufficiently tied to the old to be at least interesting as well as acceptable."[8] As long as the new remains within the framework of what is considered decent and normal, the novelty will not shock or embarrass. But if the listeners draw the conclusion that the speaker is peculiar, that he is ridiculous, or that he is exercising poor judgment, then the speaker has stepped outside what is considered familiar.

Harvey C. Jacobs made use of the novel and the familiar in the opening sentences of a speech before a high-school audience at Warren Central High School, April 20, 1956. The quotation of Sir William Berkeley shocked his listeners; although the second statement may have been new to them, the listeners were probably well acquainted with Thomas Jefferson and the events mentioned. Notice how adroitly these quotations lead into the speaker's subject.

Come with me, if you will, to the year 1671—to the colony of Virginia, where a hard-boiled British Colonel wrote to his superior officer in England: "Thank God there are no free schools and printing, and I hope there will be none these hundred years, for learning has brought dis-

---

[7] Jon Eisenson, *The Psychology of Speech*, Appleton-Century-Crofts, 1938, pp. 233–240.

[8] H. A. Overstreet, *Influencing Human Behavior*, Norton, 1925, p. 24.

obedience, heresy and sects into the world, and printing has divulged them and other libels against the best governments. God keep us free from both."

From these words of Sir William Berkeley let us pass quickly over an eventful century and read what another Virginian, Thomas Jefferson, had engraved on his tombstone: "Here lies buried Thomas Jefferson, author of the Declaration of Independence, the Statute of Virginia for Religious Freedom, and Founder of the University of Virginia."

The drama in the lives and in the points of view of these two men illustrates the historic and continuing struggle of mankind to possess the *freedom to know.*[9]

Hurl a Challenge

In planning your opening remarks, remember that almost everyone enjoys a good fight, as evidenced by attendance at football games, horse races, boxing matches—or a common fist fight. If you as the speaker enlist your listeners on your side against a common foe, or if you put up a good fight against a real or even an imaginary enemy, you are assured of continued attention.

John Foster Dulles, Secretary of State in the Eisenhower Administration, used the challenge approach in a speech to the Kiwanis International, June 21, 1956. In the light of Communist aggression, he included these sentences in his opening:

The forces of despotism are more highly organized than ever before. Already they control one third of the entire human race, and they openly proclaim their ambition to extend their system throughout the world.

So far, their gains have come through the use of violence, or the threat of violence. During the Stalin era, fifteen nations, in whole or in large part, were forcibly subjected to Soviet Communist dominion. But the free nations became aroused to the danger. They built up their deterrent power and joined in measures of collective defense. It was no longer possible for Soviet communism to pick up nations one by one.

So the Soviet rulers now say that they will renounce the use of violence. But they say that they still expect their system to win its way in the world because, they say, it is so good that all will want it.[10]

Occasionally audience inattention demands a bolder approach, that is, a direct challenge to them to listen. Under these circum-

---

[9] In *Vital Speeches of the Day,* July 15, 1956, **22:** 590–593.
[10] In A. Craig Baird, ed., *Representative American Speeches: 1956-1957,* H. W. Wilson, 1957, pp. 25–35.

stances the speaker may question a favorite belief, a sacred custom, or a cherished tradition. Josh Lee, a former speech teacher who became a congressman, relates how an evangelist used this method: "He walked directly to the front of the platform while his eyes searched the audience. He stood for a moment and then announced his text in a low-pitched voice, vibrant with meaning—'The fool hath said in his heart, there is no God.' "[11]

The more dramatic and sensational the method, the more adroit the speaker must be to avoid stirring up antagonisms which cannot be overcome later. Says Overstreet, "Challenge, therefore, must be fair. It must show good sportsmanship. It must give even the opponent his due. But above all, it is most powerful when it enlists others in the fight. Not 'Come, see me wipe up the earth with this false prophet,' but rather, 'Come, let's join in the fight.' "[12]

Be Specific

In the chapters on language we discuss at length how abstract words, indefinite references, and trite phraseology will kill interest and attention. Trite supporting material has the same effect. Inclusion of names, dates, and places lends reality to an opening. Material taken from the lives of the persons addressed is familiar but also specific. Putting an introduction into the first or second person likewise contributes to directness as Russell Conwell demonstrated in his "Acres of Diamonds" speech.

SECURING A FRIENDLY HEARING

We listen more attentively to those we like or admire than to those we distrust or dislike. Early in your speech you need to work your way into the good graces of your hearers and establish your right to speak on the subject.

Cicero explains that this process involves the speaker's personality, the personalities of the judges, and those of his opponents:

. . . the first steps to secure good will are achieved by extolling our own merits or worth or virtue of some kind, particularly generosity, sense

[11] Josh Lee, *How To Hold an Audience Without a Rope*, Ziff-Davis, 1947, p. 121.
[12] Overstreet, *op. cit.*, p. 23.

of duty, justice and good faith, and by assigning the opposite qualities to our opponents, and by indicating some reason for or expectation of agreement with the persons deciding the case; and by removing or diminishing any odium or the popularity that has been directed against ourselves either by doing away with it or diminishing it or by diluting it or by weakening it, or by selling something against it or by making an apology.[13]

Obtaining a friendly hearing involves at least three factors: reputation, appearance, and ethical appeal during the speech.

Reputation

Reputation, or "the antecedent impression," embraces what the listeners know about the speaker's past. If at the outset you are held in high regard, you do not need to establish your right to speak on the given subject. The President of the United States receives close attention whenever he makes an official pronouncement; because of the dignity and importance of his office he is assured of a friendly hearing. But when he speaks as a party leader his partisanship is challenged, and some may even accuse him of taking unfair advantage of his official position. In this case he must win a friendly hearing before he can be effective.

Otto H. Kahn, well-known financier, once said about reputation: "Remember that the most serviceable of all assets is reputation. When you once have it, and as long as you hold it, it works for you automatically, and it works twenty-four hours a day. Unlike money, reputation cannot be bequeathed. It is always personal. It must be acquired. Brains alone, however brilliant, cannot win it. The most indispensable requisite is character."[14]

The skillful speaker must know when to rely upon reputation and when to pack into the opening sentences some effort to establish his right to speak on the subject.

Appearance

"Actions speak louder than words," advises the authority on good manners. "Pretty is as pretty does," says the anxious mother to her teen-age daughter. "Clothes make the man," insists the clothing

---

[13] *De Partitione Oratoria*, VIII:28, found in Cicero, *De Oratore*, Harvard University Press, 1948, III, 333.

[14] Otto H. Kahn, "A Talk to Young Business Men," November 13, 1924, in Ashley Thorndike, ed., *Modern Eloquence*, Collier, 1936, V, 55–61.

salesman. These clichés, overworked and oversimplified as they are, nevertheless reflect the importance our society places on appearance. Consciously and unconsciously the speaker's appearance and his platform deportment have a marked influence upon us. If we like what we see, we are more likely to give continued attention, to show greater interest, and to believe what we hear. If we dislike or question what we see, we reserve judgment and become more difficult to persuade.

In the opening moments of the speech, the audience forms many lasting opinions of the speaker, based upon his physique, his clothing, and his manner. A friendly countenance and genuine manner arouse enthusiasm; austerity and grimness inspire frigidity. Will Rogers, the humorist, won his way into the hearts of millions of Americans by his simple and unaffected manner. The smile and friendliness of Franklin Roosevelt were significant factors in his great popularity. Abraham Lincoln realized the value of being a humble man. In each case, these men won friendly hearings.

Even the bodily build of a speaker may influence an audience. Large men are often regarded as more commanding in appearance than men of slight build. For this reason the large man must not attempt to hide his size by slouching. It likewise behooves the smaller person to take special precautions to appear dignified and impressive.

Even this late in the twentieth century there lingers occasional prejudice against women on the platform. Such attitudes are carry-overs from the past, when some felt that woman's only place was in the home. Some regard women's voices as not forceful enough for public speaking. Women like Eleanor Roosevelt, Margaret Chase Smith, and Maurine Neuberger provide proof that these attitudes are unfounded; nevertheless, a woman speaker needs to take cognizance of them when she decides to speak.

The speaker's attire must be appropriate for the occasion. Being overdressed or being slovenly is damaging to your cause. A dress suit may be a "must" for some banquets, but at other times it is inappropriate. A cigarette holder, pince-nez, or even a loud tie can give a wrong impression. Flashy clothes or overdressing may be a factor in creating an unfriendly hearing. The woman who dares to speak in a startling hat, trimmed with a dangling flower or a waving feather, may direct attention to her hat at the expense of her speech.

A good rule concerning appearance is: the speaker should strive to be what his listeners expect him to be; he should mirror what they consider acceptable appearance.

Ethical Appeal

The third factor in obtaining a friendly hearing in the introduction has been called ethical appeal or *ethos*. It may be defined as the speaker's attempt during his speech to give the right impression of himself and by his appearance and manner to give evidence of his own merits, worth, and virtues. Certainly he should make every effort to avoid giving an impression of cockiness or overconfidence, but at the same time he should establish that he has a right to speak on the subject, that he is interested in the welfare of his listeners, and that he is a person to be trusted. As Aristotle puts it, he must present himself as a man of (1) good character, (2) good will, and (3) intelligence.[15]

Good character.   The "good man" is persuasive because his listeners accept what he says without question and because his authority is so impelling that other persuasive devices are unnecessary. As Aristotle said, ". . . we trust men of probity more, and more quickly about things in general, while on points outside the realm of exact knowledge where opinion is divided we trust them absolutely."[16] The speaker who gives the impression of having good character must demonstrate that he possesses some of the virtues: justice, courage, temperance, magnificence, magnanimity, liberality, gentleness, prudence, and wisdom.[17]

Good will.   Good will and friendly disposition involve the speaker's attitude toward the listener. Does the speaker have the interests of his listeners at heart? Lincoln once said, "If you would win a man to your cause, first convince him that you are his sincere friend. Therein is a drop of honey that catches his heart, which, say what he will, is the great highroad to his reason, and which when once gained, you will find but little trouble in convincing his judgment

---

[15] Lane Cooper, *The Rhetoric of Aristotle*, Appleton-Century-Crofts, 1932, pp. 90–92.
[16] *Ibid.*, p. 8.
[17] *Ibid.*, pp. 46–55.

of the justice of your cause if indeed that cause really be a just one."[18]

In this way the "high-pressure" salesman or the spellbinder fails, for somehow, in his eagerness to sell his product, he unconsciously gives the impression that he is more interested in making the sale for selfish reasons than for the benefit of the customer. Consequently the client immediately reacts negatively.

Intelligence. The third aspect of *ethos* is intelligence. Early in the speech, you must establish that (1) you are well informed on the immediate subject, (2) your experiences qualify you to speak, and (3) in general you possess sound judgment. A speaker may be sincere and virtuous, but if the audience is in doubt concerning his information, his cause is lost.

Auguste S. Gerard, foreign expert on the Congo, took a direct approach to establish that he had a right to speak upon his subject. Notice how he emphasized that he had personal experience which enabled him to make first-hand observations.

It seems appropriate, ladies and gentlemen, that I should begin by offering you my credentials. First, I have devoted a good deal of my life to the Congo, principally in the sector of private enterprise. I first went to the Congo in 1926, and stayed four years. I have spent nine of the last twelve months in the Congo. I was there in April of this year and shall be returning next month.

I hope, therefore, that I can contribute some first-hand observations, that will be of interest to you for I suspect that the role of private enterprise in the Congo is incompletely known on this side of the Atlantic.

My other reason for appearing before you is that we share a good deal in common, notably the belief that private enterprise working through incentives, competition, and the pressures of the marketplace is a splendid system for improving the lot of mankind—in fact, the best yet devised.[19]

[18] From an address before the Springfield Washingtonian Temperance Society, February 22, 1842, found in John G. Nicolay and John Hay, eds., *Complete Works of Abraham Lincoln,* Lincoln Memorial University, 1894, I, 193–209.

[19] "Private Enterprise in the Congo," delivered to a press conference for business and financial editors and writers, University Club, New York City, June 13, 1961; found in *Vital Speeches of the Day,* July 15, 1961, **27:** 592–595. The speaker was the director of the Compagnie du Congo pour le Commerce et l'Industrie and director of the Federation des Associations Provinciales des Entreprises du Congo.

SECURING AN INTELLIGENT HEARING

The third objective of the introduction is to clarify the subject sufficiently to secure an intelligent hearing for the remainder of the speech. The audience must understand what the subject is, what it means, and what the speaker proposes to do with it. The subject may be clarified by such means as these:

1. State the nature of the subject to be developed.
2. Reveal the thesis or the proposition.
3. Give the cause for discussion: why is the topic timely?
4. Define unfamiliar terms.
5. Give the history of the case (narration).
6. Summarize the plan of development (division).

Not all these means are applicable to every speech; the nature of the occasion and the audience will determine whether any or all are necessary.

Notice how Andrew T. Weaver, distinguished speech educator of the University of Wisconsin, set his listeners straight on his subject in his introduction to an address delivered at the Convention Luncheon of the Speech Association of America, December 29, 1960:

Today I shall not discuss the "sales-talk" uses of speech. I shall not concern myself with the clever arguments of candidates competing for the prize of public office. I shall not be thinking of such mighty rhetoric as that which Cicero hurled against Catiline. What we have thought and taught about the power speech gives us over others is not now the object of my consideration. For the few moments you lend me, I am asking that we focus our attention upon a nobler and more basic role of speech in the lives of men. I suggest that we raise our sights above the lowlands where speech serves self-interest to the higher plateau where it brings the satisfactions of companionship and mutual understanding. All too often, I think, we have emphasized the objective of manipulating and controlling our fellow man to satisfy our egoistic drives, and have neglected the loftier goals of cooperation and understanding.[20]

After telling what he was not going to talk about, he stressed that he would consider "the loftier goals of cooperation and understanding."

[20] "Toward Understanding Through Speech," in *Vital Speeches of the Day,* February 1, 1961, **27:** 244–247.

Cardinal Cushing demonstrated his forthrightness in the opening sentences of his address at Boston College, October 13, 1960, leaving no doubt as to what he intended to talk about when he opened as follows:

The controversy over the recognition of Red China has lasted for 10 years and attained greatest publicity, and indeed, success at recent meetings of the United Nations. The question is, Should other nations and especially the United States diplomatically recognize the present regime on the mainland of China? If we do, Red China would be in a good position to occupy the Chinese seat in the United Nations and to adjust her international relations with the free nations. If that ever happens, we might be forced to withdraw entirely from the U.N. But despite the fact that the margin of victory for the American position was smaller this year in the U.N. than it had ever been before, I do not believe that we are fighting for a lost cause.[21]

ADAPTING THE INTRODUCTION TO THE
SPEAKING SITUATION

We have stressed constantly in this book that above all else the audience must remain paramount in your thinking. At each step in your preparation you must re-evaluate the question, what means and methods will produce the greatest audience response? The preparation of the introduction, of course, is no exception. Your opening remarks must grow out of the demands of the speaking situation. In planning your opening strategy, put these questions to yourself:

1. Do I need to strive for interest and attention, or will the audience naturally be curious as to what I shall say?
2. Is it necessary to sell myself to the audience? What do they know about me? Is it favorable or unfavorable?
3. Does the subject need clarification? Is there confusion about the terms?
4. Should the foregoing three elements have equal stress?

Once you have determined where you need to concentrate your fire—on interest and attention, yourself, your subject, or all three—

[21] "The Recognition of Red China," in Vital Speeches of the Day, February 1, 1961, 27: 242–244.

then you must decide on the kind and amount of ammunition needed. The best introductions are developed out of the speaking situation: they involve the speaker or his experience, the audience and its interests, implications of time and place of the speech, the nature of the subject. In other words, the speaker should in some way make reference to himself, the audience, the occasion, or the subject.

The following outline is suggestive of some of the possibilities open to the speaker.

1. Reference to the speaker:
   a. Relate a personal experience that qualifies you to speak on the subject.
   b. Relate a personal experience that you have had in common with the listeners.
   c. Tell a joke on yourself.
   d. Mention your interest in and an analysis of the subject.
   e. Explain or allude to your desire to help the audience.
   f. Indirectly stress your good character.
   g. Give the impression that the chairman has flattered you.
2. Reference to the audience:
   a. Connect the subject with the vital interests of the audience.
   b. Allude to a common experience or goal that you share with the audience.
   c. Praise the accomplishment or aspirations of the group.
   d. Eulogize a hero of the group or a respected member, such as the president.
   e. Hurl a challenge.
   f. Relate the subject to a hero or patriot.
   g. Ask the audience a series of personal or challenging questions.
3. Reference to the occasion:
   a. Relate the subject or yourself to a revered day or event (a great battle, a holiday, or historic moment).
   b. Show why the occasion is important.
   c. Mention in connection with the subject a current event foremost in the minds of the listeners.
   d. Eulogize the history of the group.
   e. Recall other speakers who have spoken in the given meeting place.
   f. Contrast or compare your own views with those of a previous speaker.
   g. Tell a joke on the chairman or a previous speaker.

4. Reference to the subject:
   a. Ask a series of questions which lead listeners to think about the subject.
   b. Give a startling statement which focuses attention on the meaning of the subject.
   c. Relate an anecdote or story containing the central point of the speech.
   d. Plunge into the development of a significant point.

QUESTIONS AND TOPICS FOR STUDY AND REVIEW

1. In what ways are the beginning of a speech and a speech of introduction similar?
2. What are some vital interests of your classmates which you could use in opening a speech?
3. How is the problem of securing a favorable hearing related to the factor of motivation?
4. How is *ethos* or ethical appeal related to ethics?
5. Is there a necessity for a *good* person to include ethical appeal in a speech? Explain.
6. Make a list of the common grounds which you could emphasize with the following persons:
   a. A citizen of Panama
   b. A bricklayer
   c. A member of a rival fraternity
   d. A labor-union member
   e. A member of the Daughters of the American Revolution
7. Some speakers attempt to gain attention in their introductions by sensational means. What problems arise from such techniques? If possible, report on an actual case which supports your argument.
8. Analyze the soundness of the advice: "Always open your speech with a funny story." In what situations would humor be considered out of place?
9. What is the significance of the statement, "The best introductions are developed out of the speaking situation"?

PROJECTS

1. Below are two introductions for study and discussion. Analyze how each speaker attempted to win (1) an attentive hearing, (2) a friendly hearing, and (3) an intelligent hearing.

When I was invited by the National Foreign Trade Council to address The Americas luncheon today, I accepted with a deep sense of pride and humility. I owe much to Latin America. I owe much to the friends I have made there. For the past twelve years, I have traveled and I have lived amongst these wise and ancient people. I as well as members of this audience have respect and deep affection for their culture and for their proud tradition. All of us have learned to understand and sincerely sympathize with their hopes and with their aspirations for a better and fuller life. We have all seen enlightened leaders of government and industry in Latin America work unceasingly for the realization of these hopes and aspirations. During these years abroad, I have met many of the men that represent business firms from the United States. I am aware of the enormous contributions they have made and are making to the development of Latin America. They should be encouraged to continue.

It is obvious to anyone that is informed on Latin American affairs that the Alliance for Progress is doomed to failure if governments participating in this important program do not work hand and hand with private enterprise, which can provide experience, know-how, and capital. What I mean, and I make this statement without reservation, is that no government, no alliance of governments, can hope to supply all the capital and know-how needed to accomplish this far-reaching ideal, the Alliance for Progress, without the active particiation of private enterprise.[22]

As I contemplated the title of this talk, I wrote it originally— "What Will Make America Strong in the Sixties?" But as I developed my thoughts, I realized that I had to change it to—"What Could Make America Strong in the Sixties?"

"Could" instead of "Will" because as of the moment there is uncertainty in my mind as to whether in the Sixties the American people will elect to become a free and independent people, or to become more and more dependent on government, at all levels, for actions and decisions which heretofore have been regarded as the yardsticks by which the freedom of man can be measured.

Such an introduction would point to this as a political speech, and perhaps it is, although I shall make no plea for either political party. My plea will be for a strengthening of our political system, a strengthening without which I wonder whether our children will

[22] Robert C. Hill, former U.S. Ambassador to Mexico, speech to the Forty-Eighth National Foreign Trade Convention, New York City, October 30, 1961; in *Vital Speeches of the Day*, December 1, 1961, **28**: 104–106.

live in the kind of America we have loved and fought for; under the freedom we have enjoyed, but have taken so much for granted that we could lose it without realizing we were doing so.

It seems appropriate, therefore, in this national election year, for us to examine whether we might strengthen our political system; whether we think such strengthening would lead to a truly stronger America; and, most important, how this strengthening could be accomplished.[23]

2. Decide which one of the introductions in project 1 is the best. Write your opinion in not more than 200 words. You may wish to read the complete speeches in the magazine *Vital Speeches.*

3. Make a study of how a contemporary American speaker adapts his introductions to his listeners. You may find it interesting to follow a given speaker through a political campaign (consult *The New York Times* for speeches). Choose someone like the following: F. D. Roosevelt, Harry S. Truman, Richard Nixon, Adlai Stevenson, John F. Kennedy, Estes Kefauver.

SUPPLEMENTARY READINGS

Braden, Waldo W., and Mary Louise Gehring, *Speech Practices: A Resource Book for the Student of Public Speaking*, Harper, 1958, chap. 4, "The Speaker Meets the Audience." You will find here some excellent introductions for analysis and study.

Monroe, Alan H., *Principles and Types of Speech*, 5th ed., Scott, Foresman, 1962, chap. 15, "Beginning and Ending a Speech."

Reid, Loren, *First Principles of Public Speaking*, Artcraft, 1960, chap. 7, "How To Begin and End the Speech."

White, Eugene E., and Clair R. Henderlider, *Practical Public Speaking*, Macmillan, 1954, chap. 7, "Developing the Introduction."

[23] Fred C. Foy, president of Koppers Company, Inc., speech to the Economic Club of Detroit, September 19, 1960; in *Vital Speeches of the Day*, November 15, 1960, **27**: 66–71.

16

Concluding the Speech

The conclusion must pull the speech together into a unified whole. The entire development must be blended into a single impelling impression designed to accomplish your specific purpose. The audience must feel the impact of the speech in its entirety, must appreciate its significance, and must respond to your suggestions. An effective conclusion demands careful and thoughtful preparation. The inspiration of the moment cannot be trusted. Richard Whately, who wrote a significant book on rhetoric early in the last century, has the following to say about rambling and fumbling: "It may be worthwhile here to remark that it is a common fault of an extemporary speaker, to be tempted, by finding himself listened to with attention and approbation, to go on adding another and another sentence after he had intended, and announced his intention, to bring his discourse to a close; till at length the audience becoming manifestly weary and impatient, he is forced to conclude in a feeble and spiritless manner, like a half-extinguished candle going out in smoke."[1]

In order to avoid ending "like a half-extinguished candle," you must prepare your final remarks with great care, and only on rare occasions will you let anything alter your plans. Continue making the speech march toward its goal.

Long ago Aristotle suggested that the conclusion—or epilogue, as he called it—may involve four elements or parts:

1. You may attempt to render the audience well disposed or favorable toward yourself or your cause.
2. You may amplify what is important and minimize what is unimportant in your speech.
3. You may summarize your speech.
4. You may strive to excite the emotions of your listeners.[2]

Whether you concentrate on one or on all of these elements will depend upon the nature of your subject, your specific objective, and other aspects of the speaking situation. The informative speech, for example, may require no more than a simple restatement of your central thought or a summary. The conclusion of a persuasive talk sometimes includes all four elements.

PERSONAL ELEMENT IN THE CONCLUSION

In some situations, it may seem desirable to conclude with a reference to yourself or to your own feeling about the subject. During the development of the speech you may sense that in some way your personal appeal has been weakened and that a defense of your character or your line of attack is necessary. The criminal lawyer frequently uses a personal reference in his conclusion. A personal reference may be advisable in such situations as the following:

1. You may feel that you need to justify the length of your remarks.

[1] Richard Whately, *Elements of Rhetoric*, James Monroe & Company, 1858, pp. 207–208.
[2] Lane Cooper, *The Rhetoric of Aristotle*, Appleton-Century-Crofts, 1932, pp. 240–241.

2. You may wish to emphasize that your interests in the subject are not selfish.
3. You may desire to express your appreciation for the attention which the audience has given you.
4. You may want to express your pleasure in receiving the invitation to attend the meeting and address the group.

Clarence Darrow, famous criminal lawyer, gave a personal justification in the final sentences of his defense of Loeb and Leopold, the youthful murderers of Bobby Franks, stressing his high motives in making his defense.

I feel that I should apologize for the length of time I have taken. This case may not be as important as I think it is, and I am sure I do not need to tell this court, or to tell my friends that I would fight just as hard for the poor as for the rich. If I should succeed in saving these boys' lives and do nothing for the progress of the law, I should feel sad, indeed. If I can succeed, my greatest reward and my greatest hope will be that I have done something for the tens of thousands of other boys, for the countless unfortunates who must tread the same road in blind childhood that these poor boys have trod,—that I have done something to help human understanding, to temper justice with mercy, to overcome hate with love.[3]

Used effectively, your good character and your genuine interest in your hearers are powerful persuasive forces. Quietly but surely they may exert persistent pressure in behalf of your cause. Therefore, let nothing in the speaking situation weaken your hearers' good opinion of you.

RESTATEMENT

When Aristotle suggested that a speaker may find need to amplify what he has said, he probably had in mind a forceful restatement of the central thought or proposition of the speech or the reemphasizing of an important idea. Restatement in the conclusion may take any of the following forms:

[3] Clarence Darrow, "Defense of Richard Loeb and Nathan Leopold, Jr.," in William Norwood Brigance, ed., *Classified Speech Models*, Crofts, 1928, pp. 136–205.

1. In the simplest form you may merely repeat or rephrase your proposition or central thought. For example, you may say, "Let me suggest once more that you urge your congressman to support the recommendations of the Hoover Commission."
2. You may use an apt quotation or illustration which embraces the central philosophy of your speech. Naturally, such a quotation adds dignity and authority to what has been said, and the novelty may be a source of renewed interest or awareness.

In one of his Fireside Chats, delivered during the darkest days of World War II, President Roosevelt relied on the words of another to restate in his conclusion the theme of his speech.

Never before have we been called upon for such a prodigious effort. Never before have we had so little time in which to do so much.

"These are the times that try men's souls."

Tom Paine wrote those words on a drum-head by the light of a camp-fire. That was when Washington's little army of ragged, rugged men was retreating across New Jersey, having tasted nothing but defeat.

And General Washington ordered that these great words written by Tom Paine, be read to the men of every regiment in the Continental Army, and this was the assurance given to the first American Armed Forces:

"The summer soldier and the sunshine patriot will, in this crisis, shrink from the service of their country; but he that stands it now, deserves the love and thanks of man and woman. Tyranny, like hell, is not easily conquered; yet we have this consolation with us, that the harder the sacrifice, the more glorious the triumph."

So spoke Americans in the year 1776.

So speak Americans today![4]

Note how the familiar words of Tom Paine heightened the dramatic appeal of the speech.

SUMMARY

Probably the most common type of conclusion is the summary. The oral process demands that the speaker repeat his ideas if he

[4] Franklin Delano Roosevelt, "Fireside Chat on the Progress of the War," February 23, 1942; in B. D. Zevin, ed., *Nothing to Fear*, Houghton Mifflin, 1946, pp. 312–322.

wants them to be remembered; consequently, a terse repetition of your main points in one-two-three order is an excellent way to hammer home your ideas. In some cases, it may be to your advantage to repeat the same language used when stating your points the first time. You may say, "In this speech I have made three points. First I pointed out . . . . Second I said . . . . My final point was . . . ."

Some intercollegiate debaters conclude their argument by saying:

Since there are children in this country that are denied adequate education,

Since the states are unable to provide adequate education for these pupils,

Since these states contain the greatest percentage of our children,

And since education is the responsibility of the entire electorate,

Therefore we urge the adoption of federal aid to education.

W. Norwood Brigance, well-known speech teacher and able speaker, used a summary conclusion in his stirring address "The Backwash of War":

These, then, are the especial problems that face us in this backwash of war: First, the problem of the returning soldier adjusting himself to civilian life; second, the danger of transferring our hatred of the Japanese and Germans to other groups; third, the danger that in fighting against militarism, we ourselves shall become militaristic; and finally, the danger of permitting too much of a moral holiday now that we are relieved from the Spartan discipline of war.

We do not face these problems with fear. We do not face them with hesitation. To the timid and faint-hearted who long for security and repose, we quote the answer of Mr. Justice Oliver Wendell Holmes "Security is an illusion, and repose is not the destiny of man." We shall meet these problems as a people who are conscious of their destiny.[5]

Notice his one-two-three summary, his equally effective challenge, and his restatement in the words of Mr. Justice Holmes.

APPEAL

Aristotle's fourth element of the conclusion refers to what he called putting the audience into the right state of emotion or the appeal for acceptance or action. Facts and inference alone probably will not

---

[5] William Norwood Brigance, "The Backwash of War," in A. Craig Baird, ed., *Representative American Speeches: 1945–1946,* H. W. Wilson, 1946, pp. 75–84.

be enough to achieve your purpose; you will need to appeal to your listeners on the basis of their motives—show how the proposal will bring benefits, pleasures, and satisfactions. Such appeals may be to selfish motives as well as to altruistic ones.

Newton N. Minow demonstrates how to put a stirring appeal for action. In the closing paragraphs of his widely heralded speech at the Thirty-Ninth Annual Convention of the National Association of Broadcasters, May 9, 1961, he said:

> In his stirring inaugural address our President said, "And so, my fellow Americans: ask not what your country can do for you—ask what you can do for your country."
>
> Ladies and gentlemen, ask not what broadcasting can do for you. Ask what you can do for broadcasting.
>
> I urge to you to put the people's airwaves to the service of the people and the cause of freedom. You must help prepare a generation for great decisions. You must help a great Nation fulfill its future.
>
> Do this, and I pledge you our help.[6]

Notice how Minow appealed to his listeners' patriotic motives and emphasized the importance of the broadcasters' role in helping "prepare a generation for great decisions." He demonstrated herein how to use higher motives.

In its simpler forms, an appeal merely stresses how the listener will benefit from the adoption or acceptance of the speaker's ideas. You may want to dress up your final remarks, add a bit of grandeur to the tone of your speech.

Challenge

It will usually be to your advantage if you can make the audience feel that they are a part of a struggle against some common foe. Such an approach says in substance, "Let us unite," "Let us put down our enemy," "Let us even this battle." Most persons are flattered to think that they are part of a good cause.

Former President Franklin Roosevelt frequently packed powerful motivation into his closing sentences. The conclusion to his "Victory Dinner Address," delivered March 4, 1937, challenged the Democratic party to follow his lead in dealing with the pressing problems of the nation.

[6] *Congressional Record*, May 11, 1961, **107**: A3302–A3304.

It will take courage to let our minds be bold and find the ways to meet the needs of the nation. But for our party, now as always, the counsel of courage is the counsel of wisdom.

If we do not have the courage to lead the American people where they want to go, some one else will.

Here is one-third of a nation ill-nourished, ill-clad, ill-housed—now!

Here are thousands upon thousands of farmers wondering whether next year's prices will meet their mortgage interest—now!

Here are thousands upon thousands of men and women laboring for long hours in factories for inadequate pay—now!

Here are thousands upon thousands of children who should be at school, working in mines and mills—now!

Here are strikes more far-reaching than we have ever known, costing millions of dollars—now!

Here are spring floods threatening to roll again down our river valleys —now!

Here is the dust bowl beginning to blow again—now!

If we would keep faith with those who had faith in us, if we would make democracy succeed, I say we must act—now![7]

Notice how the effect of these closing words is intensified by effective use of repetition and parallel structure.

Woodrow Wilson closed the speech in which he submitted the Peace Treaty to the Senate with a challenge: "The stage is set, the destiny closed. It has come about by no plan of our conceiving, but by the hand of God who led us into this way. We cannot turn back. We can only go forward, with lifted eyes and freshened spirit, to follow the vision. It was of this that we dreamed at our birth. America shall in truth show the way. The light streams upon the path ahead, and nowhere else."[8]

ADAPTING THE CONCLUSION TO THE SPEAKING SITUATION

There is no formula to help the speaker select what elements of the conclusion he will use under given conditions. As we noted at

---

[7] Franklin Delano Roosevelt, "Victory Dinner Address," in A. Craig Baird, ed., *Representative American Speeches, 1937–1938*, H. W. Wilson, 1938, pp. 101–110.

[8] Woodrow Wilson, "Submitting the Peace Treaty to the Senate," in Brigance, *Classified Speech Models*, pp. 208–221.

the beginning of this chapter, some speeches may require only one, while others need all four. The speech goal gives some aid in selecting the elements to be used. The informative speech may demand a summary or a restatement or both. Indeed, it would be difficult to generalize about the speech to inform. The persuasive speech ordinarily requires some type of appeal.

Actually, two or three or all the elements are frequently combined into a conclusion. Bruce Barton, in "How Long Should a Wife Live?" used both summary and restatement. Brigance (see p. 280), utilized three elements: summary, restatement, and appeal.

QUESTIONS AND TOPICS FOR STUDY AND REVIEW

1. How is the type of conclusion related to the speech purpose? Determine what elements would occur in the conclusions of each of the following types: (1) the informative speech, (2) the stimulating speech, (3) the actuating speech.
2. Under what circumstances would a speaker find it necessary to include a personal reference in his conclusion? Can you think of an actual speech situation in which you have heard this type demonstrated?
3. How are the different types of conclusions related to different types of speeches? For example, what type of conclusion would you use in a good-will speech? A eulogy? An after-dinner speech? An exposition?
4. Josh Lee, former speech teacher and later senator from Oklahoma, has said: "The two most important parts of a speech are the beginning and ending. . . ." Do you agree or disagree? Give evidence to support your point of view.
5. Monroe divides a speech into five steps: attention, need, satisfaction, visualization, and action. It is obvious that the action step is another name for the conclusion. To what type of conclusion does he refer? (Consult Alan H. Monroe, *Principles and Types of Speech*, 5th ed., Scott, Foresman, 1962, Chapter 16.)
6. List some common faults of speakers in concluding their speeches.
7. What determines the length of a conclusion?

PROJECTS

1. Using the present chapter as a guide, prepare a written analysis of the conclusions of the speeches found in one issue of *Vital Speeches*.

Classify according to the following: personal element, restatement, summary, and appeal.

2. Investigate what classical writers on public speaking have to say about development of a conclusion. Consult the following:

   a. Aristotle's *Rhetoric*

   b. Cicero's *De Oratore*

   c. Quintilian's *Institutes of Oratory*

3. Analyze the two conclusions quoted below. Determine the elements (see p. 277) used in each one. Pay particular attention to the use of motive appeals. Also make a judgment as to their effectiveness.

America has always been both realistic and idealistic. As we go forward into the future let us, as individuals, preserve this vital blending. Humanics and economics are very natural and necessary partners.

Freedom to fail is really nothing but the spirit of adventure which built our nation, and our gravest hour will come when, if ever, we lose that spirit. Security is a natural desire, but we must bear in mind that it is only a short step from security to complacency, and complacency is the most insecure footing of all.

It is vital to our future and to our way of life that we never limit our freedom to fail. We should concentrate on opportunity, not security. We must never become content with just a little success. That is the sure path to mediocrity.

I want to wish all of you great individual success. In doing so, I am really wishing a great future for America because the collective achievements of you and your counterparts all over our country will largely determine what America will be.[9]

As Americans, you are faced with the greatest challenge that history has ever hurled at you. As Americans, you have always been mortal enemies of tyranny and despotism; of mass executions and mass imprisonment; of the concentration camp and the torture chamber; of viciousness and cruelty and oppression. Time and again you have fought against these things; and now you must fight against them once more.

Yesterday, you called these things nazism and you fought and won. Today these same things are called communism; and again you might fight and win. For if you do not face the issue squarely, you will go down to inevitable defeat, and the entire world will become prey to the forces of evil.

[9] Ray R. Eppert, president of Burroughs Corporation, commencement speech at Detroit Institute of Technology, June 21, 1961; in *Vital Speeches of the Day*, September 1, 1961, 27: 694.

Your forefathers never wavered, never hesitated, never counted the risks, never considered the odds . . . and they won. You, their descendants, cannot allow this precious heritage to be destroyed.

The fate of the entire world is at stake. You hold too much of the future of mankind to allow it to slip so heartrendingly from your hands.[10]

SUPPLEMENTARY READINGS

Brigance, William Norwood, *Speech: Its Techniques and Disciplines in a Free Society*, 2nd ed., Appleton-Century-Crofts, 1961, chap. 12, "Beginning and Ending the Speech."

Lee, Josh, *How To Hold an Audience Without a Rope*, Ziff-Davis, 1947, chap. 10, "A Strong Finish Leaves Them Applauding."

Monroe, Alan H., *Principles and Types of Speech*, 5th ed., Scott, Foresman, 1962, chap. 15, "Beginning and Ending a Speech."

White, Eugene E., and Clair R. Henderlider, *Practical Public Speaking*, Macmillan, 1954, chap. 8, "Developing the Conclusion."

[10] Carlos Todd, former political editor of the *Times* (Havana), speech to the Kiwanis Club, Miami, Florida, August 11, 1961; in *Vital Speeches of the Day*, October 1, 1961, **27**: 754–755.

17

Weighing Facts
and Arguments

Everyone has probably followed at some time the construction of a large building; excavating for the basement, driving the piling, laying the foundation, and maneuvering the structural steel into place are fascinating and exciting to watch. But even when the last girder has been bolted down, there is yet little to suggest what the final structure will be. It may turn out to be a factory, a car storage garage, an office building, or even a fashionable apartment house. Bricks, finishing materials, hardware, interior design, and decoration finally transform the pile of steel into a building.

In many ways the same is true of a speech. The research, the study of the audience and the occasion, and the outline are necessary forerunners; but no matter how thoroughly done, they do not finish the speech. They are as necessary as excavations, foundations, and structural steel, but they need supporting material to constitute a speech.

The supporting materials for a speech may serve any one of three purposes: (1) to clarify, (2) to prove, and (3) to amplify. Their extent and kind are suggested by the following outline.

  I. Oral materials
    A. To clarify
      1. Explanation
      2. Description
      3. Narration
    B. To prove
      1. Facts
        a. Testimony
        b. Examples
        c. Statistics
      2. Inference—inferred facts
        a. Argument from specific instances
        b. Circumstantial detail
        c. Causal inference
        d. Analogy
    C. To amplify
      1. Restatement, summary
      2. Adage, maxim
      3. Rhetorical question
 II. Visual supports

SUPPORTING MATERIALS TO CLARIFY

Sometimes explanation, description, and narration are considered types of informative speeches (see Chapter 19), but they may also serve as supporting materials within other types, namely, entertaining, stimulating, and persuasive speeches. It is in this sense that we discuss these types in the present section.

Explanation and Exposition

Explanation and exposition are frequently included in a speech as supporting materials. The word *explain* comes from the Latin *ex-*

planare, which means to spread out. In other words, explanation implies the spreading out of an object, process, or procedure in order that it may be understood; it defines or relates how and why something operates or evaluates something. *Exposition* comes from the Latin *exponere*, to place. Exposition, then, is a working equivalent of explanation. Genung says, "By exposition people generally understand setting forth the meaning of things; and this we may regard as its fundamental office. It is not concerned primarily with establishing the truth or falsity of a thing; it seeks rather what the thing is—what is its real nature, its scope, its relation."[1]

The speaker may also clarify his subject by a careful definition of important terms or concepts before he argues for the adoption of a proposition. With well-informed listeners whose only reason for not acting may be merely failure to understand a solution, the speaker may limit his presentation almost entirely to exposition.

The following excerpt illustrates how explanation may be used as supporting material. David Rockefeller, president of the Chase Manhattan Bank of New York, employed exposition to support a point.

The international monetary mechanism as it now stands is clearly inadequate. It places too heavy a burden on the dollar and the pound, and it restricts action on the domestic scene, often at the expense of American and British citizens.

More and more this fact is gaining recognition among economists, bankers and government officials. A number of proposals have now been put forward to rectify it. Perhaps the most far-reaching of these is the so-called Triffin Plan, developed by Professor Robert Triffin of Yale University. Many of you will recall that Prof. Triffin would transform the present International Monetary Fund into what, in effect, would be a super-central bank. He would set up procedures to lead member countries eventually to transfer most of their official dollar, pound and other foreign currency balances into the Fund. In addition, they could make a further transfer of gold. For all of this, they would receive deposits in the Fund. Most nations would then hold the bulk of their official foreign exchange reserves in the form of deposits with the Monetary Fund, and the Fund would hold as assets both gold and liquid claims on other nations. In the case of the dollar, for example, the Fund might eventually take over most of the $12 billion of Treasury bills, time deposits and other liquid assets now held by foreign central banks. The Fund would earn interest

---

[1] John F. Genung, *The Practical Elements of Rhetoric*, Ginn, 1899, p. 383.

on such assets, but it also would pay out interest to the central banks on their deposits with it.

A unique feature of the Triffin Plan would be the ability of the Monetary Fund to "create deposits," if necessary, under certain strict rules and procedures. In doing this, the Fund would provide added foreign exchange to countries needing it—exchange in a form acceptable to most other nations. Thus, the fund would become in the international field a "lender of last-resort," just as the Federal Reserve System is in the United States today.[2]

Description

Frequently description also is helpful in clarifying a topic. If you can make the listeners visualize what is being said, you can enhance attention and perception. The clever real-estate salesman sells a lot by vividly describing a ranch-type house for that location. The more vivid he makes the description, the easier it is for him to weaken the client's sales resistance. The travel agency sells you a ticket to a faraway place by describing warm sun, romantic nights, sandy beaches, and friendly natives. Have you ever selected your clothes on the basis of an advertiser's description?

William E. Borah, master orator, concluded one of his important addresses with a passage that contains many descriptive details. Notice how each sentence summons up a picture.

A few evenings ago, in calling upon a friend, I passed by that monument to Abraham Lincoln which stands in Lincoln Park, the monument representing Lincoln with the kneeling slaves and their broken shackles.

I thought again over the life of Abraham Lincoln and tried to comprehend its greatness. I saw the awkward country boy in his cabin home in the forests of Kentucky. I saw him as he covered his mother's new grave with autumn's withered leaves and went back to his humble home to enter the race for fame. I saw him as he walked near the auction block in the slave market of New Orleans and heard him utter his curse upon the institution of slavery. I saw him in after years when, as one of the greatest rulers upon the earth, he walked with patience and compassion the paths of power. I heard men denounce him as a tyrant and a usurper. I listened for the answer, but he quietly submitted to it all.

[2] David Rockefeller, "Gold, the Dollar, and the Free World," delivered March 7, 1961, before the Economic Club, New York City; in *Vital Speeches of the Day*, May 1, 1961, 27: 438–441.

I saw him in storm of civil strife as he steered the ship of state into the Union Harbor. At last the storm began to clear, the light break through the rifted clouds, and I saw Abraham Lincoln walking in the morning of a new day with four million human beings unloosed of their fetters striving to walk by his side.[3]

Narration

The illustration, which ordinarily is a brief narrative, serves also to clarify difficult points. The speaker may either give an actual illustration or invent a hypothetical one.

Lester Thonssen, successful and well-known speech teacher, demonstrated in a commencement address how to use a story to drive home a point.

Some years ago, a Texas cowboy took a job in Arizona. His first order from the new boss was to ride out on the range and find some cattle that had strayed from the herd. Suddenly and quite unexpectedly, he found himself on the south rim of the Grand Canyon. No one had told him there was a canyon, and he had never heard of it. Wide-eyed and almost horror-stricken, he looked into this fantastic abyss, wiped his forehead, and said: "Good heavens! Something has happened here."

Something has also happened *here* during your stay at the college. Profound changes have taken place in you: in your beliefs, your attitudes, your point of view, your ways of meeting problems in private and public life.[4]

Mrs. Maurine Neuberger, senator from Oregon, emphasized a point by reporting an actual incident about her husband, who before his death had preceded her in the Senate.

When my husband was a Member of this body he sat in the back row by a very distinguished colleague, the late Senator Alben Barkley. One day my husband was commenting with reference to another Senator, in effect, "Oh, I don't think he knows what he is talking about." Former Senator Barkley said to him, "young fella"—he always called Dick "Young

[3] William E. Borah, "Constitutional Government," September, 1937; published in pamphlet form by J. H. Bordeaux Company, West Springfield, Massachusetts.
[4] Lester Thonssen, "The Unrecorded Legacy," commencement address at Huron College, May 26, 1958; in A. Craig Baird, ed., *Representative American Speeches: 1958–1959*, H. W. Wilson, 1959, pp. 133–146.

fella"—"I should like to to remind you of something. Many people have
tried to come to the Senate of the United States and many have fallen
by the wayside. Any Senator who achieves the prize of a seat in the U.S.
Senate has certainly demonstrated to the people of his State his integrity,
his ability, and his right to serve those people. You must remember that
he is an outstanding citizen, whether he agrees with you or not."

I felt I should say this today, because we have welcomed a new
Senator. Whether we agree or disagree as to the amendment, I am sure
we all express the belief that we have a right to agree or to disagree.[5]

SUPPORTING MATERIALS FOR PROOF

Facts

When there is disbelief or disagreement over the acceptance of a
line of thought or the desirability of a course of action, the speaker
must resort to *proof*, which involves supporting his conclusions or
generalizations with *facts* and *inference* (reasoning).

What are facts? Larrabee says:

What we usually think of as a fact is something known to us directly
in experience. It is what is appealed to as the ground for some human
assertion or judgment. It is the stuff of evidence; it is the foundation of
primary datum upon which a claim to knowledge rests. When we use
such expressions as: "To get down to the facts . . . ," "Now the fact
of the matter is . . . ," we call attention to some lower or more fundamental stratum upon which our assertions rest. To talk about "true facts,"
as people often do, is redundant: facts just *are*. They cannot be false.
To demand the facts is to signify our intention to find out what it is
that we are obliged to take account of—that is, to move away from the
sphere of the merely possible: guesses, conjectures, and fancies, toward
actuality—"the world as it really is."[6]

Facts for a speech normally come in three forms: testimony, statistics, and examples.

Testimony. Much of what we know necessarily comes from the
observations and experience of others. "Seeing is believing," goes
the old adage, but our lives are so short and our spheres so limited

---

[5] *Congressional Record*, June 15, 1961, **107**: 9802.

[6] Harold A. Larrabee, *Reliable Knowledge*, Houghton Mifflin, 1945, p. 128.

that we are forced to depend on others for information. Assertions or judgments coming from other persons are referred to as *testimony*.

Also included in testimony are written statements of opinion, catalogues of facts, and statistical tables, as well as oral reports in various forms. Testimony likewise embraces what you get from books, in the classroom, out of newspapers and magazines, over the radio and television, by way of the grapevine, and even in chance conversations.

Checking Sources of Testimony

When you rely on others for information, you must check your source carefully and frequently for accuracy and fair reporting.

Below are six suggestions which should help you in testing what you hear and read.

1. *Is the statement from a primary or a secondary source?* This test has to do with whether you receive a direct report from an eye-witness (a participant) or whether you receive the information from a person who is reporting what someone else told him. Primary sources include oral reports, direct quotations, manuscripts, letters, legal documents, memoirs, and autobiographies. As a principle, the closer you can get to the event the more likely you are to receive an accurate and fair view.

2. *Is the statement a recent one?* Recent events or findings are often more applicable as speech materials than those which occurred sometime ago because conditions change and intervening events may completely alter the significance of facts. For example, mortality rates of 1925 have little bearing on mortality rates today because of the intervening improvements in medical techniques, the discovery of new drugs, the increase in hospitals, and better training for doctors. You should also always question the accuracy of information in which the reporter's memory has played a part. When time elapses between an event and its reporting, inaccuracies are likely to creep into the final account.

3. *Is the statement the result of careful and thorough investigation?* The test conditions and the reputation of the observer and reporter are important considerations in testing what you accept and reject. How did the reporter find his facts? Was he an eyewitness? Under what conditions did he make his observations? Is he considered a skilled observer? Did he use some well-established technique

or procedure? These and similar questions may give you important indications of whether you wish to rely on a set of facts.

4. *Is the statement specific and internally consistent?* Generalities, inconsistencies, and shifts of position within a statement are signs of shallow or crooked thinking. When you decide to use a quotation in a speech, make sure that it is definite and to the point. Generalities and abstractions may be open to a variety of interpretations and hence lead to confusion. A political speaker, knowing this tendency, may intentionally state his case in vague or sweeping generalities in hopes of insulting no one and pleasing everyone. For this reason party platforms are general and noncommittal—the planks are planned to mean whatever the reader wants them to mean.

5. *Is the statement reported accurately and fairly?* Observations and reporting are two processes. The skillful observer who cannot use language meaningfully is likely to give an incomplete or misleading report. The good reporter is objective and as free of bias as possible. He guards against slanting, misrepresentation, and lifting material out of context. The self-interest test—inquiring into how the reporter may profit by having his statement accepted—is a good way to identify bias. If his sponsor or employer stands to gain by your acceptance, be wary of the statement. For example, when a professor urges you to major in his subject, is he interested in your welfare or in increasing his own prestige among his colleagues? He is, of course, an interested party.

In reading a newspaper give attention to how the story is presented. The page location, the position on a given page, the size and nature of the caption, accompanying pictures, and type of language are all important signs.

Radio and television listeners should distinguish between straight news reporting and news commentaries. How does the sponsor influence the presentation? Production devices may add interest, but in no way do they increase the dimension or significance of a story.

6. *Is the statement supported by other sources?* Is the reporter or writer recognized by other authorities who are trained and qualified to judge? Check his training and experience, his reputation for reliability, and his standing in his field. Statements which seem to run contrary to what others have reported should be viewed with special care.

Statistics. Statistics permit the speaker to make a large collection of data meaningful, usable, and understandable. Douglas Dillon, Secretary of the Treasury of the United States, carefully made his point to the American Society of Newspaper Editors by using a few well-chosen statistics:

> The recession from which we are now beginning to emerge has been relatively mild. For example, in terms of constant dollars which allow for inflation, gross national product is now only 2.2 percent below last year's peak, compared with a decline of 4.7 percent in the 1958 recession. Personal income and industrial production have also fallen less than in previous postwar recessions.
>
> However, before we take too much satisfaction from these figures, let us remember that they are relative. The absolute figures tell a far different story. Current unemployment, with 6.9 percent of our labor force out of work, approaches the worst days of the 1958 setback. A record number of our cities are classified as areas of substantial unemployment.[7]

Notice how Dillon stressed the difference between *relative* and *absolute* figures.

In using statistics, guard against oversimplification or dependence upon too few instances. On the other hand, statistics must be presented in as simple form as possible in order not to confuse the listener. Some engineers and scientists, ignoring this principle, present statistics to their listeners in table form, forgetting their span of attention. As a result, they soon lose their listeners.

Finding and interpreting statistical data is a serious and difficult problem for a speaker. One writer suggests that speakers consider such questions as the following: "How carefully did you check that statistic you used . . . ? Did you pick it up from a speech you heard or read, or from a magazine article, and then repeat it as the gospel truth? Did you go back to the source and get it straight, in unadulterated form? More important, did you accept it at face value or did you dig into all of its ramifications and limitations and get a perspective of its real meaning?"[8]

[7] Douglas Dillon, speech delivered April 21, 1961, at the Statler-Hilton Hotel, Washington D.C.; in the *Congressional Record*, April 24, 1961, **107**: A2766–A2767.

[8] T. M. Stinnett, "Check That Statistic," *Educational Record*, April, 1957, **38**: 83–84.

Testing Statistics

Statistical methods have become so complex and so highly technical that the average person must often turn to a specialist for interpretations and applications. However, the four following questions should help in selecting statistical data to include in speeches.

1. *Who is responsible for the statistics?* The agencies of the U.S. government and the great independent private research foundations can usually be depended upon for accuracy and validity. Pressure groups, special interest pleaders, and sales organizations are likely to give biased reports.

2. *Are the statistics based upon accurate and tested methods of observation reporting and/or experimentation?* Under this heading, you will want to consider the following subquestions: (a) Who gathered the data? (b) How were the data gathered? (c) Was the investigation of sufficient scope? (d) How were the data treated? (e) How were the data interpreted? The person not trained in handling statistical data should consult an expert to help him answer many of these questions.

3. *Can the results be verified?* In other words, has the reporter provided an adequate description of his method and sufficient data so that another investigator can verify his findings or repeat his experiment? Be suspicious of reports which are incomplete or which contain no explanation of how the facts were collected and the conclusions drawn.

4. *Are the statistics supported by other findings and other sources?* We again return to tests similar to those we use in checking an authority. What do other experts say about the findings and the interpretations?

Increasing the Effectiveness of Statistics

The following simple rules may increase the effectiveness of statistics.

1. *Reduce statistics to round numbers.* Instead of telling your listeners that the population of your state is 9,543,676, simply say, "nine and a half million." Many times percentages are more effective than the raw data. Notice how J. Edgar Hoover makes his point by using percentages: "Our country is recording an alarming new crime rate and society's lack of progress in reducing this scourge has been indeed disheartening. During the first six months of 1960, serious

crimes increased 9% over the same period in 1959. In 1959, 79% of those arrested for auto theft were under 21 and 64% were less than 18 years of age."[9]

2. *Present statistics in a form familiar to your listeners.* To Europeans and to scientists the metric system is entirely clear, but to the average American audience metric measures are certainly confusing. You will be more likely to communicate your message if you stay with the familiar measures of tons, yards, miles, gallons, and so on. Centigrade temperatures are meaningful to the technically trained but meaningless to Iowa farmers and those of us who have always talked in terms of Fahrenheit measurements.

3. *Use as many visual aids as possible.* Since statistics are a compact representation of numerous facts, it is often desirable to present them in visual form. As we will discuss in the next chapter, charts, diagrams, and graphs skillfully presented clarify points and reduce misunderstanding.

4. *Avoid presenting too many statistics at a given time.* Because of their abstract nature, statistics require greater concentration than some other types of support. Long lists should be avoided. Thought breaks, illustrations, and humor should ensure attention and interest.

5. *Dramatize your statistics.* In other words, suggest to your listeners what is back of a given number. If you are discussing the thousands of automobile accidents, describe a wreck or two so that the listener will realize the full implication of your remarks. Notice how in the following quotation the speaker put over his point with a striking comparison: "One of today's basic scientific tools is the electron microscope. It is essential in producing polio vaccine, and is furnishing clues which may some day lead to the conquest of cancer. While the ordinary light microscope enlarges a specimen to about 2,000 times life-size, the electron microscope can blow it up more than 300,000 times. At this degree of magnification, an ant would become a colossus able to stand astride the St. Lawrence River."[10]

Magnification of 300,000 times is difficult to conceive, but the

[9] J. Edgar Hoover, "America—Freedom's Champion," in *Vital Speeches of the Day*, January 15, 1961, **27**: 197–200.

[10] John L. Burns, "The Endless Frontier," in *Vital Speeches of the Day*, October 15, 1960, **27**: 21–24.

thought of an ant astride the St. Lawrence dramatizes the point.

6. *Strive to present statistics fairly and meaningfully.* In spite of what we have just said about putting statistics in a palatable form, a word of warning about misusing them is in order. You have probably all heard such oft-quoted statements as "Figures never lie, but liars figure," or "You can prove anything by statistics." This point is clearly illustrated in the following comment:

Now, let us take one of those glamorous catchall statements that again causes the educational writers, editors, and speakers to jump apprehensively through verbal hoops. The statement asserts "that to supply our need for elementary and secondary school teachers in the next decade will require one-half or more of all of our college graduates. And of course this is impossible." To our best knowledge, this statement was first made by an official of one of the wealthy foundations. It was published in the Fund for the Advancement of Education's excellent booklet *Teachers for Tomorrow* and, based on the assumptions set forth in the text, a good case is made for its soundness. This statement has been widely publicized and has been repeated in thousands of speeches. It goes on and on like the poetic brook. At first this statistic seems unassailable. But is it? Let us examine it for a moment.

Currently the schools are consuming anywhere from 150,000 to 175,000, maybe more, new teachers each year, whereas college graduating classes were down to 285,000 in 1955 and to an estimated 325,000 in 1956. These data alone would support the statement. But let's dig in a little. If it could be assumed that all teachers who take jobs each fall must come from the previous college graduating class, the statement would be conservative. Actually, however, thousands of college graduates from former years who had prepared for teaching but who went on to graduate schools, or went into the armed services, or into industry, or even into marriage return each fall to teaching. In what numbers these people enter teaching each year is not known. We do know that some states are recruiting as high as one-half of their new teachers each fall from these sources. Moreover, if all states now required, or should require in the near future, college graduation as a prerequisite to certification and teaching, the statement would be more nearly valid. The fact is, or was at the time the statement was made, that some twenty-one states and territories still are certificating beginning elementary teachers below the degree level. But, of course, these teachers cannot be counted in the estimate as having to come from the college graduating class.[11]

[11] Stinnett, *op. cit.*

Example or specific instance. From the point of view of interest and attention, the example is the most effective form of proof. Since he may not have time to review innumerable instances, the speaker may present one or two instances which he considers typical and sufficient to establish his point. The proud farmer hands his friend an ear of corn, commenting, "That is the kind of corn I grow on my farm." The validity of such a generalization depends upon whether the farmer selected a representative ear of corn.

Edward R. Murrow, director of the United States Information Service, stressed his point by using several specific instances:

In Africa we attract a significant response to teaching English. In Somalia, one-third of the national Legislature is studying English with USIS. When we started up in Togo this summer 40 out of the country's 51 members of Parliament were in the first class. In another country we number half a dozen cabinet members, and the President of still another country has urged us to teach English in his capital and has promised to be the first to enroll.

Or take our libraries. When we opened a new one in Blantyre, Nyasaland, 400 people were lined up on the street waiting for entry. Within 3 hours 600 of the library's 750 books were borrowed and gone; the shelves were soon bare. In Marrakech the response to our opening was so overwhelming that membership cards had to be limited to attendance one day a week, with a different color for each day.[12]

The two tests you should apply, either as speaker or as listener, in evaluating examples as supporting material are the following:

1. Are the examples representative of their class? If a generalization is to be drawn upon a limited number of cases, those instances must be typical; they must be the rule, not the exception.
2. Has a sufficient number of examples been presented to constitute a fair sample? The more cases presented, the more the likelihood that the conclusion will be valid.

Since it is almost always difficult to present numerous examples in a limited time, the ethical speaker should take great care that the instances presented are representative. If challenged, he should be able to give additional statistical support to his conclusions.

[12] Edward R. Murrow, address to the Public Relations Society of America, found in the *Christian Science Monitor*, December 5, 1961.

Inference

Woodrow Wilson once said, "There are whole worlds of fact waiting to be discovered by inference." What did he mean? Just this: facts in isolation are meaningless and neutral, but the industry and resourcefulness of the individual can make them "diadems or fagots." In other words, through analysis and synthesis, the thinker must seek out their implications and draw conclusions from them. Baird has aptly described the mental process of inference as "an intellectual leap in the dark, a voyage from the known to the unknown."[13] The thought process is similar to a manufacturing process in which the raw materials are facts, the manufacturing process is inference by which facts are put together in various combinations, and the finished product is a conclusion.

The Reflective Thought Process

Raw Materials	*Processing*	*Finished Products*
Facts	Inference	Conclusions

Four types of inference are discussed here: (1) argument from specific instances, (2) argument from circumstantial details, (3) causal reasoning, and (4) analogy.

Argument from specific instances. Argument from specific instances involves drawing generalizations from statistics, specific cases and examples, or the extended illustration. It may be represented as follows:

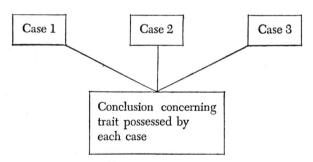

[13] A. Craig Baird, *Discussion: Principles and Types,* McGraw-Hill, 1943, p. 147.

When the judge polls the jury for its verdict, he utilizes this type of inductive process. After hearing each response, he generalizes concerning the opinions given and thus determines the guilt or innocence of the accused.

If nine out of ten members of Speech 51 make low grades on a snap quiz, the teacher might well conclude that many of the students are not studying enough. What other generalizations might explain these results? Obviously, the more cases considered, the more likely it is that the conclusion can be relied upon. Of course, absolute certainty is possible only in *perfect induction,* which involves finding a common trait in *all* members of a class. Since this possibility only occurs when small groups are concerned, the conclusions reached are ordinarily probabilities, that is, likely to be true.

Common Types of Fallacies

Many fallacies may occur in this type of inference. Four of the most common types are described below.

1. *Unsupported generalizations.* When sweeping assertions are made without any basis or proof, the statements must rest entirely on the authority of speaker or writer. For example, a speaker may insist that Louisiana State University has a better football team than the University of Alabama, or that college graduation insures a young man of a $15,000-a-year job, or that members of a given fraternity are more intelligent than men of other social groups. Each statement is an assertion until concrete facts are offered to back it up. If you have great respect for the person, you may accept the pronouncements as trustworthy, but generally you want to question an assertion.

2. *Careless use of* all, every, no, none *in generalizations.* Sometimes the speaker may claim too much for a generalization; he may suggest that his conclusion includes or excludes an entire class. If the class is small—for example, the children of a family or the members of an advance seminar—he may have engaged in perfect induction, but he will have difficulty finding conclusions which apply to such large classes as poor whites, Italian Americans, Louisianians, or football players. Question seriously sweeping assertions which use words that are all-inclusive or all-exclusive.

In the excerpt quoted below both speakers in one brief interchange use sweeping generalizations. Notice Wickard's phrase "every time" and Capehart's "haven't gained one soul, one inch."

MR. WICKARD: I don't know who brought up this question of one party being for war or peace. I never knew that peace was a controversial or partisan subject with the American people. What I am trying to say is, you opened up this question of whether we are getting into the affairs of the world and apparently we are.

Now what we are gaining by it is a moot question, but we are in them and every time we work out a compromise the Communists gain just a little bit more.

SENATOR CAPEHART: There never was a more unfactual statement than that. The Communists haven't gained one soul, one inch of land since President Eisenhower has been President. Furthermore, we settled the Korean matter, the Formosa matter, the Indochina War has been settled, Austria has her peace treaty, Germany has her sovereignty.[14]

3. *Generalizations based upon too few instances.* When he knows that the instances he has cited are typical, the speaker has a right to talk with confidence. However, when he draws inferences from a few cases, he may have no way of knowing whether they are typical or exceptional. For example, if you meet three members of a given society who make straight A's you could conclude that the group is made up of honor students, but when you interview additional members you would probably discover that your first generalization was hasty. When a so-called authority has examined only a small number of cases, accept his conclusion with reservation.

4. *Generalizations based upon selected or nontypical instances.* Have you ever bought a box of strawberries because of the large ripe berries on top? In all probability you later discovered that the large ones on top hid the small berries in the bottom of the box. You have had an unhappy demonstration of the type of misleading thinking we are considering here. When the investigator takes his examples from limited areas or presents only those cases which support his conclusion, he is engaging in untrustworthy thinking.

[14] Discussion entitled "The Battle for the Senate," broadcast over NBC, September 23, 1956, on "The American Forum"; in the pamphlet *The American Forum* (published by Ransdell, Inc., Washington, D.C.), vol. 19, no. 36. Participants were Homer Capehart, senator from Indiana, and Claude Wickard, senatorial candidate from Indiana and former Secretary of Agriculture under President Roosevelt.

Notice how Senator Homer Capehart supported the generalization that "the wealth in the Senate is on the Democratic side" with non-typical instances: "Now, let me say this: You talk about the millionaires. Well, my goodness, Harriman is a one hundred million dollar millionaire. Mr. Lehman in the Senate is one of our richest men in the United States. Mr. Murray, a Senator, is one of the richest. In fact, the wealth in the Senate is on the Democratic side, Claude. You just haven't been reading your record. You haven't been reading Dun and Bradstreet."[15]

Argument from circumstantial details.   Argument from circumstantial details is another type of argument involving generalization. Instead of reasoning from a number of cases from the same class, the reasoner fits together a series of incidents, related details, or clues. The suggested relationship or sequence which emerges leads the reasoner to infer a conclusion. The historian, detective, or archaeologist frequently pursues this approach in his work.

Let us analyze the process. Upon finding the first clue, the reasoner formulates one or more hypotheses or guesses which he surmises may explain the occurrence. We say he has deduced a conclusion or engaged in deduction. As he uncovers each additional clue, the reasoner strengthens his confidence in his first hypothesis, modifies it to fit new circumstances, or selects what seems to be a more tenable one.

The men who search for the Abominable Snowman high in the Himalayas have reasoned from circumstantial detail. The legend among the natives, reports of large tracks, and hearsay reports are the clues. Those who have looked into the mystery have developed the following hypotheses:

1. It is a huge ape.
2. It is a wild man.
3. It is an evil spirit.
4. It is a figment of imagination.

The last hypothesis seems to be best—until another report lures the adventurers back for additional searching.

[15] *Ibid.*

Testing this type of reasoning may involve tests like the following:

1. The reasoner should attempt to establish a causal link between the sign and his hypothesis.
2. The reasoner must test the hypothesis by what occurred in similar instances.
3. The reasoner must keep firmly in mind that he is dealing with probability and that conclusions must always be tentative until positive identification is made.

Causal reasoning. A student at Louisiana State University became so irritated by true-false examinations that he wrote a letter to the campus paper arguing that he had failed a certain course because the professor had used this type of test. Whether he knew it or not, this young man indulged in some causal reasoning. His failure to pass the examination, he thought, was the *effect* of the true-false test—the *cause*.

This type of inference is usually divided into three types: (1) cause-to-effect (a priori), (2) effect-to-cause (a posteriori), and (3) effect-to-effect (sometimes called argument from sign).

Cause-to-effect (a priori) sequence moves toward the future. If two related events in the past are considered, the one which occurred first is the *cause* and the second is the *effect*. Causal reasoning enables the reasoner to guess about the future. The small child is admonished, "If you get too close to the stove [cause], you may get burned [effect]."

The following passage contains several causal inferences. Notice that a further increase in exports (cause) is to solve our balance of payments (effects) and that "to press beyond" (cause) will result in several things, according to David Rockefeller.

I wish that we could rely completely on a further increase in exports to solve our balance of payments problem. Unfortunately, this would be unrealistic. Our trade balance already is large, and though we can and should stretch it further, there is a logical limit. To try to press beyond this would undoubtedly call forth vigorous counter-reaction by competitors in world markets. Of course there are several additional steps that can be taken. For example, the expansion of tourism in our own country, and the removal of foreign restrictions on the flow of capital into the United States. And yet—in the final analysis—I doubt whether all of these together will be enough to bring our international payments into balance.[16]

Some time ago the police of a Southern city arrested twenty-one hoboes who had drifted into the town. When a reporter asked the oldest one, "What do you think makes men go on the bum?" he received the following causal analysis: "That's easy, it's liquor. Liquor and women. Oh, well, some of them just got the wanderlust. But mostly it's liquor. A man gets to drinking. He loses his job. His wife leaves him. He goes on. Gets arrested. Told to get out of town, and then there he is. He's sunk."

In this example, the speaker gave numerous causes explaining why there are hoboes. Interestingly, each *result* (effect) becomes a *cause* for the next event. Usually causality is exceedingly complex, and is consequently difficult to untangle.

Effect-to-cause sequence moves toward the past. A given event becomes an effect with a cause somewhere in the past to be located. A man's car is ruined by fire during the night. When he investigates, he finds the dashboard melted and the wiring still smoking. He concludes therefore that the cause was defective wiring.

E. J. Haney used the following effect-to-cause reasoning in analyzing the problems in international trade: "Our balance of payments in foreign exchange deficits are the result of many transactions that can be summarized as follows: we must pay for imported goods and services, for military aid we give to foreign countries, for economic support we give to our friends and to underdeveloped nations, for capital investment in foreign countries by American business or by government, and support for all our personnel in foreign bases throughout the world in support of our Cold War defense objectives."[17]

Effect-to-effect inference attempts to relate two events by locating a common cause. Persons who make high scores on IQ tests seem to be able to perform intellectual feats more readily than those who make low scores. The test score, seemingly, is the result of the same factor which accounts for performance in intellectual feats. William

---

[16] Rockefeller, *op. cit.*

[17] E. J. Haney, "Let's Stop Exporting Jobs," delivered before the "Management Problems for Executives Group," University of Pittsburgh, October 14, 1960; in *Vital Speeches of the Day*, December 15, 1960, **27**: 153–157.

Trufant Foster, a prominent authority on public speaking, made significant use of this type of reasoning in his speech "Should Students Study?" Below is a part of that speech:

Is it a fact that good students in high schools are more likely than others to become good students in college? Professor Walter F. Dearborn . . . compared the records of hundreds of students at the University of Wisconsin with their records in various high schools. He found that above 80 per cent of those who were in the first quarter of their high-school classes were in the upper half of their college classes throughout the four years, and that above 80 per cent of those who were in the lowest quarter in their high-school classes failed in college to rise above mediocre scholarship. The parallelism is striking. Except in scattering cases, promise in high school becomes performance in college. Indeed, only one student out of five hundred in this investigation who fell among the lowest quarter in the high school attained the highest rank in the university. . . .[18]

Causal inference is full of hazards. Certainly the speaker who employs this type of thought needs constantly to guard against over-simplification. A given event may and probably does have many causes. For example, let us analyze the case of the young man who thought he failed the course because the instructor gave true-false examinations. Any of the following causes could have accounted for his failure:

1. Too little study
2. Poor eyesight
3. Defective hearing
4. Malnutrition
5. Purchase of wrong textbook
6. Mirror reading
7. Limited vocabulary
8. Too little sleep
9. Too much social life
10. Lack of confidence in his own ability

Causal reasoning may be checked by the following tests.

1. *Are the alleged facts true?* Before attempting to ascertain

[18] William Trufant Foster, "Should Students Study?" in Lew Sarett and William Trufant Foster, eds., *Modern Speeches on Basic Issues*, Houghton Mifflin, 1939, pp. 64–75.

whether a causal relation exists, the actual occurrence of the events must be verified. In a murder trial, the lawyer must prove first that the murder did take place before he can attempt to establish a motive.

2. *Is there a genuine connection between the events under consideration?* The causal reasoner must distinguish between the coincidental sequence and the causal sequence. In other words, Spanish moss on a dead tree does not necessarily indicate that the moss killed the tree.

Here are some questions that may aid you in determining whether a connection is genuine.

a. Does the alleged cause ever occur without the effect?
b. Does the effect ever occur without the alleged cause?

3. *Is the cause of sufficient magnitude to produce the alleged effect, and vice versa?* The likelihood of a single mole moving a mountain is indeed remote. How shall we evaluate the long series of tragic events that supposedly accompanied ownership of the famous Hope Diamond? Does the fact that Marie Antoinette wore this notorious gem explain why she was beheaded? Did possession of it account for the fact that Sultan Abdul Hamid lost the Turkish throne? Or did this 44½-carat stone cause the deaths in the family of the late Evelyn Walsh McLean, Washington society leader, who recently owned it? In spite of the chain of events, we have to conclude that the diamond had nothing to do with the tragedies because it is too limited in its power to produce the alleged effects.

4. *Are other causes operating which may explain the effect?* Let us repeat, causality is indeed complex; a single effect seldom has a single cause. Remote as well as immediate causes may have operated. Return for a moment to the example of the Hope Diamond. When jeweler Harry Winston received the famous jewel, he scoffed at the legend of tragedy. He then engaged in some causal analysis, saying: "It is childish to suppose that diamonds themselves exert any influence for good or evil. It's not the diamonds themselves that cause misfortune but the people who handle them." Mr. Winston, an expert in his field, concluded that other forces were operating which caused the tragic events.

Analogy or comparison. Analogy is that form of inference by which it is reasoned that, if two objects or events are alike in certain respects, they resemble one another in other respects. The reasoner, knowing the characteristics of one, can ascertain the unknown characteristics of the other. Many times we select our reading matter by analogy. If we find John Smith's short story about the Caribbean exciting, we are likely to conclude that other stories by him with a similar locale will be equally good reading. Our reasoning may be diagramed as follows:

First Case	Second Case
1. By John Smith	1. By John Smith
2. A short story	2. A short story
3. About the Caribbean	3. About the Caribbean
4. In *The Atlantic Monthly*	4. In *The Atlantic Monthly*
5. Was exciting	5. Must be exciting, since first one was

Ordinarily, analogies are either *literal* or *figurative*. The literal analogy compares objects or events in the same class. For example, World War I is compared with World War II, or the White Sox baseball team is compared with the New York Yankees. On the other hand, the figurative analogy links objects in widely different fields, such as the federal government and a three-legged stool.

Note how L. L. Colbert employs a literal analogy in the following paragraphs.

Competition is a potent force for safety. Let one company come out with a good safety feature—let it be well-received by the motoring public—and other companies are sure to come out with the same feature, often an improved version.

We might take a brief look at what a dynamic combination of public enthusiasm and competition can do for highway safety. The horseless carriage of 1895 had no top, no doors, and no windshield. The body—what little there was of it—was flimsily constructed of wood. The drivers steered with a tiller. And the vehicle crept along at only a few miles per hour—when it moved at all.

Compare that old horseless carriage—wonderful in its own time—with the car you are driving today. You are protected all around by a steel body and safety glass. You steer with ease and comfort. And at a light touch, you have all the power you need to get you safely across a city intersection or around another car on the highway. Add such features as power brakes, power steering, automatic transmission, padded sun-visors and instrument panel, flasher-lights, and all the other safety equipment available by option on the modern automobile—and you begin to understand the full significance of what I said a few minutes ago about added protection.[19]

Contrast the Colbert argument with the following figurative analogy which William E. Borah used for exposition and vividness: "You might just as well say, 'I will stop midway after I start over Niagara Falls' as to say, "I will advocate a super state, but I will not accept internationalism.' "[20]

John S. Gleason, Jr., made excellent use of a figurative analogy by comparing the firing of fine china to the trial by suffering of the handicapped.

Fine china does not come about from placing clay in the sun to dry. To become china, clay must go through the white heat of the kiln. In the intense heat of firing . . . a few pieces may be broken . . . but those that come through are no longer clay . . . but the beautiful substance we call porcelain.

And so it is, my friends, with those who have come through the fire and the intensity of human suffering . . . of deprivation of one or more of their faculties.

Those who pass along the links of the chain of rehabilitation . . . are the men and women with spirits of porcelain . . . hard, and beautiful, and above all, *useful*.[21]

Tests of Analogy.

1. *Do the points of likeness outweigh the points of difference?* If valid conclusions are to be reached, it is evident that the two objects compared must be alike in essential particulars or in those which have a direct bearing on the point under consideration. The first step in checking an analogy is to make a rough tabulation of the points of similarity and those of dissimilarity.

2. *Are the characteristics considered of major importance?* Once

---

[19] L. L. Colbert, "Highway Safety," delivered at the Safety Luncheon of the Sixty-Ninth International Convention, General Federation of Women's Clubs, Washington, D.C., June 13, 1960; in *Vital Speeches of the Day,* September 15, 1960, **26:** 732–735.

[20] William E. Borah, speech before the Senate, February 4, 1919; in the *Congressional Record,* **57:** pt. 3, 2656.

[21] John S. Gleason, Jr., Administrator of Veterans Affairs, speech at the Governors' Conference on Employment of the Handicapped, Wilmington, Delaware, October 3, 1961; in *Vital Speeches of the Day,* November 15, 1961, **28:** 95–96.

you have determined the points of likeness, you need to decide whether these characteristics are essential to your consideration. If you are comparing literacy in Denmark with that in the United States, you must show that the two nations are similar in essential characteristics. The fact that one has a sparse population and the other a dense population may be significant, but the size of the two may not be important.

3. *Are the facts upon which the analogy is based accurate?* Valid conclusions cannot be based upon assertions or what seems to be true. A comparison of public ownership of utilities in Australia with that in the United States must be based upon verified facts.

4. *Is the analogy supported by other forms of reasoning?* Comparisons may give us a hint about a relationship; they should be checked by argument from specific instances, by causality, and by deduction. What are the opinions of experts on the subject?

SUPPORTING MATERIALS TO AMPLIFY

Have you heard a stern parent say, "I tell my child just once and then . . ."? This type of person does not believe in amplification. Unfortunately, in most associations with others you cannot act with the assurance of the stern parent; you may have to tell your listener your thought in two or three different forms to "get through" or before it "soaks in." In this case you use amplification—that is, you repeat, elaborate, enlarge, review, expand, and even exaggerate and dramatize.

The successful speaker highlights his important ideas and devotes sufficient time to each one to ensure immediate understanding. As Winans put it, ". . . often single ideas need to be dwelt upon. It is evident that for clearness and for conviction, information and evidence must be introduced; but there are other reasons for amplification. Some ideas are too difficult for a hearer when put into condensed statement. Moreover, if you succeed in setting your hearer to thinking he needs time to consider and assimilate. . . ."[22]

An idea may be dwelt upon in a variety of ways. In fact, any type of supporting material—testimony, examples, statistics—serves to amplify a thought expressed. If you prove an assertion by an extended illustration two or three minutes long, you have dwelled

[22] James A. Winans, *Speech-Making*, Appleton-Century-Crofts, 1938, p. 191.

upon the thought long enough so that your listener should more readily comprehend it.

Some stylistic devices, however, serve little purpose except amplification. For example, you may recast your thought in different words in order to enhance the auditors' appreciation. Or you may restate the sentence in your own words. Winston Churchill did so in the following:

In the first half of the twentieth century, fanned by the crimson wings of war, the conquest of the air affected profoundly human affairs. It made the globe seem much bigger to the mind and much smaller to the body. The human biped was able to travel about far more quickly. This greatly reduced the size of his estate, while at the same time creating an even keener sense of its exploitable value. In the nineteenth century Jules Verne wrote "Round the World in Eighty Days." It seemed a prodigy. Now you can get round it in four; but you do not see much of it on your way. The whole prospect and outlook of mankind grew immeasurably larger, and the multiplication of ideas also proceeded at an incredible rate. This vast expansion was unhappily not accompanied by any noticeable advance in the stature of man, either in his mental faculties, or his moral character. His brain got no better, but it buzzed more. The scale of events around him assumed gigantic proportions while he remained about the same size.

By comparison therefore he actually became much smaller. We no longer had great men directing manageable affairs. Our need was to discipline an array of gigantic and turbulent facts. To this task we have certainly so far proved unequal. Science bestowed immense new powers on man and at the same time created conditions which were largely beyond his comprehension and still more beyond his control. While he nursed the illusion of growing mastery and exulted in his new trappings, he became the sport and presently the victim of tides and currents, of whirlpools and tornadoes amid which he was far more helpless than he had been for a long time.[23]

In this statement, Churchill did little more than reword his second sentence, "it [air travel] made the globe seem much bigger to the mind and much smaller to the body."

At first glance the sentence which reads "This vast expansion

[23] Winston Churchill, "United We Stand Secure," delivered March 31, 1949, at the Mid-Century Convocation of Massachusetts Institute of Technology; in A. Craig Baird, ed., *Representative American Speeches: 1948–1949*, H. W. Wilson, 1949, pp. 35–50.

was unhappily not accompanied by any noticeable advance in the stature of man, either in his mental faculties, or his moral character" will seem to be another thought, but in reality Churchill is clarifying what he means by "seem much bigger to the mind."

If you wish to be more subtle, find a quotation or epigram which rephrases your thought. In addition to amplifying your idea, you may also impress your listeners with your learning. Such is the case in the following quotation. Paul Hoffman uses a quotation effectively in the conclusion of a speech; Pearson's words emphasize and give dignity to his final thoughts.

> If we are going to get out from under these terrific costs we must move toward peace. And that is what the $2 billion per year will do for us. Why? Because out of the yearnings of the hundreds of millions of people for a better life will come, if those yearnings are ignored, one explosion after another in this troubled world. But if heed is given to these yearnings, if we can give the assistance we should, then there can come a better world than we have ever dared dream of.
>
> In closing, may I recall some words used by the Honorable Lester Pearson of Canada: "The grim fact is that we prepare for war like precocious giants and for peace like retarded pigmies."
>
> It is time we began acting like giants in waging peace.[24]

The rhetorical question can also be used as a form of amplification. In effect such questions stimulate the listener to rethink the thought being amplified. Senator Fulbright of Arkansas uses the rhetorical question skillfully in the following passage.

> Can anyone here deny that the distinguishing feature of American society during much of the decade of the 1950's was its weakness for the easy way? Can anyone deny that in this period, we were the opposite of what our Founding Fathers had in mind for the new America?
>
> The Founding Fathers said—and here I quote from the first paragraph of the *Federalist* papers—they said:
>
>> It seems to have been reserved to the people of this country, by their conduct and example, to decide the important question, whether societies of men are really capable of establishing good gov-

[24] Paul Hoffman, "The Expanding World Economy—An Essential Goal," delivered to the Chicago Council of Foreign Relations, March 30, 1961; in the *Congressional Record*, May 22, 1961, 107: A3636–A3638.

ernment from reflection and choice, or whether they are forever destined to depend for their constitutions on accident and force.

But I ask you now: What show of "reflection and choice" was there in much of the decade of the 1950's when the word "egghead" became a word of abuse; when education was neglected; when intellectual excellence became a cause for suspicion; when the man in public life, or the writer, or the teacher, who dared articulate an original thought risked being accused of subversion. [*sic*] What show of "reflection and choice" was there in this period when the man of distinction was the man who had a station wagon, a second car plated with chrome, a swimming pool, a tax-free expense account, and a twenty-one-inch color television set with the thirty-six-inch star on its screen?[25]

In summary, therefore, amplification may be accomplished by three means: (1) recasting the thought in different words, (2) giving a quotation which restates it, and (3) using rhetorical questions.

QUESTIONS AND TOPICS FOR STUDY AND REVIEW

1. What are some other names for supporting material? What are three ways in which supporting material may be used? What are the various subtypes of each one?
2. How are exposition, narration, and description interrelated? How are they different?
3. How is the narration or description used in an entertaining speech different from that used in an informative speech?
4. What is the strongest type of proof? In other words, in what type of proof can you place the most confidence?
5. We sometimes hear someone say that he has "proved conclusively that" or "this is a fact." These statements suggest certainty or complete proof. What must be done to achieve absolute certainty?
6. Why should a speaker use with care terms like *all, every, none, no one, everyone, never, always?*
7. Under what circumstances could a speaker use these terms? When would it not be advisable?
8. Inference has been referred to as "an intellectual leap in the dark." Explain the meaning of this sentence.
9. Discuss the implications of the sentence, "Causal inference is full of hazards." What are the hazards?

[25] Sen. J. William Fulbright, speech delivered in the United States Senate, August 21, 1958; in Baird, *op. cit.* (1959), pp. 126–132.

10. What are the differences between truth and theory? Between theory and opinion?
11. Distinguish between certainty and probability.

PROJECTS

1. *Speaking Assignment.* Deliver a five-minute argumentative speech in which you develop your proposition by an extended illustration. (Christ used this method in the parables.)
2. *Speaking Assignment.* Deliver a five-minute talk in which you develop your speech by using only one or two types of supporting material.
3. Make an analysis of the forms of support used by one of your classmates in a speech. After the speech, check with the speaker to see if you have found the ones he thought he used.
4. Bring to class five examples of inference that you have found in your local newspaper (look on the editorial page). Be able to present an oral analysis of these for your classmates.
5. Make a list of ten valid "either-or" situations. Remember that the choice must be mutually exclusive, and there must be only two possibilities.
6. Make a list of ten situations in which you can have perfect induction.
7. Bring to class several unsupported popular generalizations you have heard recently.
8. Bring to class several generalizations that have been proved by exceptional instances.
9. Identify the type of inference used in the examples given below. If the inference is not valid, explain where the error lies.
   a. Mississippi is poor because it has few material resources.
   b. Dr. Earl Jones, professor of speech at Warren University, says, "My book *Argumentation* is a good textbook."
   c. Students who make high grades in high school are likely to make high grades in college.
   d. Bill Smith makes good grades because he studies.
   e. Dr. A. M. Smith, professor of speech at the State University, says "Jones's *Argumentation* is a good textbook."
   f. The YMCA, the YWCA, the Methodist Youth Center, the Baptist Youth Center, Tau Kappa Alpha, and Kappa Kappa Gamma did not contribute to World Student Service Fund. Therefore, it is probable that the campus organizations did not support the World Student Service Fund.
   g. John Brown belongs to a fraternity and he is popular.

h. Since all members of class Speech 51 got high grades last semester, I am enrolling in Speech 51 this semester.

i. Each year more persons are killed or injured by automobiles than were killed in World War I.

j. From my experience with the Iroquois Indians I have decided that you cannot trust Indians.

k. A man who makes a million dollars is a success. It seems evident, therefore, that John D. Rockefeller was successful.

l. Since several students failed to return last semester, it is evident that MSU is not pleasing its students.

m. Louisiana is a great state because it is located upon the Mississippi River.

n. The richest man in my home town has a fourth-grade education. It seems to me that proves that schooling is not important.

10. Identify the type of inference and supporting materials used in each of the following quotations.

Some years ago the FBI conducted an intensive study of traffiic accidents, and concluded that in at least 85 per cent of accidents there was no deliberate violation of the law. Instead, it found that the great majority of accidents are the result of lapses in attention or errors in judgment by well-meaning and normally law-abiding drivers.

The National Safety Council confirms these findings. The Council reports that 85 per cent of all accidents occur at speeds below 40 miles an hour. Even in fatal accidents, according to their records, seven out of ten drivers were not exceeding legal speed limits.[26]

Another factor in the alarming crime picture can be observed by tuning in to almost any television channel. The private citizen can see for himself what dangers he faces today at the hands of the criminally inclined. The continuous diet of mayhem, murder and violence served daily to our television audiences constitutes a monumental insult to the genius that developed this medium of mass communication.

The students of a California college reported findings of a study made early this year of television programs in their area. In one week, 3,696 acts of violence were recorded, including 1,261 agonizing deaths through shootings, beatings, stabbings and other violence.

The explosive danger to society from excessive television violence is obvious. Many seriously concerned authorities feel that brutality and violence are becoming accepted as normal behavior by young impressionable minds. Correction of this problem can begin with

[26] Colbert, *op. cit.*

each citizen informing his local television station of his displeasure over flagrant incidents of bad taste. Sponsors and advertisers, who are also acutely sensitive to the good will of the public, will likewise act promptly to curtail the repetition of offensive programs when contacted by the public.[27]

SUPPLEMENTARY READINGS

Beardsley, Monroe C., *Thinking Straight*, Prentice-Hall, 1950.

Black, Max, *Critical Thinking*, Prentice-Hall, 1952, chap. 13, "The Grounds of Belief." The author discusses evaluation of authority.

Braden, Waldo W., and Earnest Brandenburg, *Oral Decision-Making*, Harper, 1955, chap. 5, "Evaluating Facts"; chap. 6, "Evaluating Argument."

Braden, Waldo W., and Mary Louise Gehring, *Speech Practices: A Resource Book for the Student of Public Speaking*, Harper, 1958, chap. 5, "The Speaker Supports His Proposition." Examples of various types of proof are included.

Brembeck, Winston Lamont, and William Smiley Howell, *Persuasion: A Means of Social Control*, Prentice-Hall, 1952, chap. 11, "The Logical Technique of Persuasion: Argument from Statistics, Circumstantial Detail, Comparison and Analogy"; chap. 12, "The Logical Technique of Persuasion: Argument by Generalization, Authority, Condition, Alteration and Category."

Chase, Stuart, *Guides to Straight Thinking*, Harper, 1956.

Ewbank, Henry Lee, and J. Jeffery Auer, *Discussion and Debate*, 2nd ed., Appleton-Century-Crofts, 1951, chap. 7, "Exploring the Problem: Evidence."

[27] Hoover, *op. cit.*

18

Visual Supports

In the preceding chapter we discussed at length the various types of verbal supporting materials. Although these are normally the principal substance of a speech, many times they are not enough to accomplish the speaker's goal. Because of the abstract nature of language, oral materials sometimes fall short of holding interest, of making the subject clear, or of giving a speech the necessary persuasive quality. Just as it is not wise to put all your eggs in one basket, so it is often unsatisfactory to depend upon your voice alone to move your listeners. Authorities on visual education emphasize that the number of sensory stimuli and the strength of the stimulation are directly related to learning: appeals to two senses are more effective than appeals to only one; two appeals to the same sense or a sustained appeal will produce greater results than a single momentary effort. A speaker can therefore improve his speech by working for multisensory appeals.

Immediately it is obvious that you can hardly avoid appealing to more than one sense in the face-to-face situation. Listeners judge a speech by what they see as well as by what they hear. A listless manner, a blank expression, and awkward gestures will create an unfavorable impression. Your facial expression, gestures, posture, and movement can be made to support your ideas. When you explain or describe, you may use gestures to indicate size, shape, location, and direction. If you choose, you may reflect horror, disgust, disinterest, or approval through your facial expression. You may suggest a mood or an attitude by your movement or posture. In each of these cases, you reinforce your spoken words by visual imagery.

A speaker can also increase his multisensory appeals by including in his speech what are commonly referred to as visual aids. Among those ordinarily most available are the following:

Graphic and Pictorial Materials

1. Charts
2. Diagrams
3. Graphs
4. Sketches and drawings
5. Cartoons
6. Posters
7. Maps
8. Globes
9. Pictures
10. Photographs

Practical Devices

1. Models
2. Specimens
3. Full-scale objects

Projected Pictures

1. Motion pictures (films)
2. Film strips (slide films)
3. Slides

THE PURPOSES OF VISUAL AIDS

Under various circumstances visual aids are used in a variety of ways, and hence accomplish different ends. Some are not speech materials in any sense of the word. Let us investigate briefly their relationship to speech composition.

Visual aids such as motion pictures may be complete in themselves and require no additional explanation. The moviemaker weaves into his production all the necessary materials to accomplish his predetermined objective. If he wishes to solicit funds for the National Foundation, he includes powerful persuasive appeals designed to make the audience deposit dimes in a box in the lobby. In this event the visual aid is a complete unit and not a type of speech material. In this form it is a subject for courses in cinematography or visual education, but not for a speech class.

On the other hand, visual aids may be used as supporting materials in the accomplishment of a speech goal. They may serve the same functions as the verbal forms of support, namely, to attract attention, to hold interest, to clarify meanings, to amplify, and to prove arguments. The title of this chapter, "Visual Supports," was chosen advisedly to suggest this aspect of visual aids, which does fall within the province of a course in public speaking.

To Gain Attention and Interest

Often the speaker finds occasion to include some form of visual support in a speech to attract attention and direct interest. The principles involved are the same as those considered at length in Chapter 11 and therefore need little further development. Many visual aids are especially effective because they are concrete and novel. We like pictures, charts, and diagrams because they are definite. They provide us as listeners with something upon which to focus our attention. Furthermore, because they ordinarily necessitate movement in presentation, they provide a welcome change from a straight oral presentation.

A colorful poster, a vivid picture, an appealing chart, or a carefully selected film strip often adds novelty and keeps interest from lagging. Curiosity can be heightened by a series of drawings or pictures or by a strip chart. In the latter case each point is covered by an easily removable strip of paper. When the point fits with the speech, the speaker dramatically uncovers it.

To Clarify

Visual aids can assist in clarifying what otherwise might seem abstract. They often approach or suggest the real thing which the speaker is attempting to describe or to explain. They illustrate or suggest graphically subjects that are difficult to describe orally. In fact, it is impossible to present some subjects clearly without visual aids. Things that are too complex, too big, too small, too fast, too slow, too inaudible, too inaccessible, or too untimely for first-hand experience must be presented in a manner to assist normal perception. If first-hand experience is hazardous or unpleasant such aids are even more desirable. Certainly most auditors prefer to learn about such subjects as malaria, leprosy, poison gas, snakes, and atomic explosions from afar. Diagrams, graphs, flow charts, enlarged photographs, microphotographs, slides, and motion pictures simplify the treatment of these difficult subjects. For example, on the screen the audience may see pictures of the real thing: the landing on a distant beachhead, the storming of a pillbox, the eruption of a volcano, the results of a hurricane. He may thus become a party to many experiences that otherwise would be denied him.

To Amplify

Amplification makes a subject more vivid and more impressive. Certainly visual aids are excellent ways of dwelling upon a subject in order to make it more real and stimulating. The presentation of a chart, specimen, or film ordinarily permits the speaker to spend more time in developing the point. The multisensory appeal requires additional orientation; the listener thinks of the subject in a new light. Hence the shift in medium increases the vividness and impressiveness of the subject. Perhaps this explains the old Chinese proverb that a picture is worth a thousand words.

To Prove

Many listeners who refuse to believe a speaker otherwise may be convinced by a demonstration or exhibit. "Seeing is believing," states the old adage. Frequently a prosecuting attorney moves a jury not by words but by *real* evidence. He startles his listeners by displaying the knife with which the accused supposedly stabbed the murdered man. He points to the bloodstained coat. "Here is where the knife entered," he says. The jurors, shocked and horrified by these gory details, are moved to vote for conviction.

The scientist exhibits a slide, a photograph, or perhaps the real object to support his hypothesis. The salesman skillfully pares a potato in order to sell the housewife the peeler. Demonstration and performance make the presentation believable.

SELECTION OF VISUAL SUPPORT

There is no magic in visual aids; including them in a speech does not necessarily mean a short cut to success. Since on most occasions they supplement verbal materials, they must be selected with great care; they must be carefully fitted into the speech; and they must be skillfully presented. Like other materials they must be adapted to the speaking situation in such a way that they keep the speech moving toward the speaker's goal. In selecting a visual aid, ask yourself six questions.

1. *Is sufficient equipment available for the presentation?* Materials and apparatus available will determine largely what you can use. Anything as simple as a blackboard sketch requires chalk, an eraser, and a board solid enough for sketching and large enough to be seen. Without a projector, a screen, and a darkened room, motion pictures are out of the question. Checking essential equipment is the first step in selecting visual supporting materials.

2. *Does the visual aid support the point under consideration?* Like any other supporting material, visual support must accomplish its objective—to prove, to amplify, or to clarify. Many of the materials must be adapted or altered to fit into your plan. If they do not support the point or cannot be made to support it, omit them.

3. *Is the visual aid appropriate for the audience?* The intellectual capacity and the experience of the listeners will have much to do with the type of visual aid you decide to include. Elaborate charts or long statistical tables prepared for careful reading may prove highly unsatisfactory for oral presentation because they demand greater concentration than listeners can give. Some types of flow charts, graphs, maps, and diagrams may be too technical for the average audience but very effective for engineers or specialists. These aspects must be considered.

4. *Is the visual aid appropriate for the speaker?* Each of these methods requires some special skill for presentation. If you plan to use a blackboard, you must be able to write or print legibly. Projected pictures require a trained projectionist who understands how

the slides or pictures are to be presented. You certainly would be foolish to select a visual aid with which you are clumsy and not thoroughly acquainted.

5. *Can the visual aid be presented in the time available?* By nature these visual means are great time consumers. Their introduction and presentation may require more time than you can wisely devote to that phase of your talk. You will need to make a careful timing of your presentation to determine whether you have the time available. Guard against the temptation of becoming so engrossed in the operation of a gadget or projector that you slight or neglect the oral part of your presentation. The visual aids must be kept supplementary to your development because they are not ends in themselves but another type of supporting material.

6. *Can the visual aid be made an integral part of the speech?* Like any other supporting material, visual aids must be blended into the development in such a way that they do not destroy unity and coherence. A film or slide may be entertaining, but the vital question is, does it stress the point that the speaker wishes to make? The specimen may be novel, but does it support the lecturer's point? These and similar questions should constantly be kept in mind by the speaker who wishes to supplement his oral proofs with visual aids.

PRESENTING VISUAL AIDS

Chalkboard Presentations

The chalkboard—which many of us still refer to as a blackboard, regardless of its color—can be of great help to a speaker attempting to make his message clear. It is usually readily available and relatively simple to use. A speaker who senses that his listeners are not comprehending can often reinforce what he is saying with a quick sketch or diagram, or simply by writing unfamiliar terms on the board. An impromptu sketch may be altered or redrawn if you feel that someone has misunderstood. The chalkboard is especially useful in presenting a step-by-step procedure or a flow diagram which depicts successive phases in a process.

The chalkboard is best suited to simple lists and schematic drawings which can be made as the talk progresses. Time is usually too precious and the listeners' attention span too short to permit elaborate drawing while the audience sits by and watches.

The following suggestions will help you improve your effectiveness in using the chalkboard.

1. Keep the chalkboard clean.
2. Make the drawings large enough so that every listener can see them with ease.
3. Write or label clearly and legibly.
4. Keep labels short and simple.
5. Do not try to put too much on the chalkboard.
6. Place drawings in a logical order, moving from left to right. Number steps if necessary.
7. Suggest main features without attempting exact reproductions. Use schematic drawings.
8. Strive for novelty and variety in drawing.
9. Intersperse drawing and oral presentation. Don't keep the audience waiting while you make elaborate drawings.
10. Leave material on the board until the audience has had time to see it.
11. Be prepared to draw or sketch with ease and surety; avoid crude drawing, frequent misstarts, and slow presentation.
12. Use colored chalk whenever possible for contrast.

The Flannel Board

On many occasions the speaker will find the flannel board a convenient way to make his message more impelling. Now in wide use in education and industrial training, this type of board comes in various sizes and is covered with a fuzzy or wooly textile such as flannel or duvetyn. The picture or label to be displayed has a similar material glued to the back. When it is pressed against the board it adheres readily but can be plucked off,

Fig. 2. Flannel Board

moved about, or even put aside after a point is made. A similar arrangement can be achieved with screen wire; small magnets are glued to the visuals in this case to make them adhere.

Since this type of illustration is unusual, it is likely to hold atten-

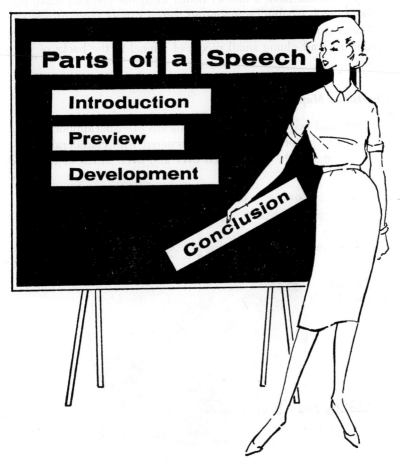

Fig. 3. Flannel Board Technique

tion. The flannel-board technique is well suited to the presentation of processes involving several steps or figures or machines with interrelated parts. When you wish to introduce a new aspect you merely press the visual in its proper place, thus indicating clearly direction and spatial relationships. If you are speaking of the Philippine Islands, for example, you can mount each island separately, showing it in its relative size and appropriate location. Lists may be displayed in the same manner.

If you do not have a flannel board available you can make one without much trouble by mounting cotton flannel (sold at any department store) on a piece of plywood, wall board, or even heavy cardboard, and gluing small pieces of flannel to the backs of your cutouts.

Charts and Maps

Charts and maps provide another means of visual support. These graphic and pictorial materials, if prepared with considerable care prior to the speech, can be used over and over. Much of what we

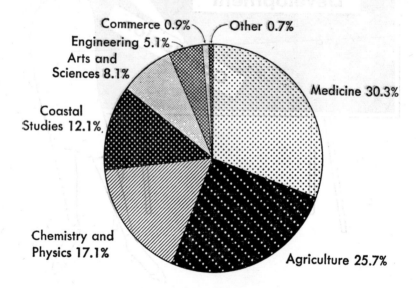

TOTAL: $819,224.58

Fig. 4.   Pie Diagram—Distribution of Gifts and Grants for Research at Louisiana State University, 1955–1956

From Louisiana State University *Graduate Report,* April, 1957, p. 2.

have said about drawing, labeling, and exhibiting on the chalkboard applies to charts and maps as well. You may use any of the graphic means of presenting data: the pie diagram, organizational chart, cutaway, bar graph, line graph, or picture graph.

Two special types of charts, the strip chart and the flow chart, call for some comment. The strip chart is one in which the parts or labels are covered by masking paper, usually fastened by scotch tape or some other adhesive. When the speaker wishes to reveal an item to the audience he simply pulls off the strip.

The flow chart is used usually in presenting steps in process. The speaker arranges his items in the order in which the process unfolds.

Many times the speaker can achieve a better effect by using several small charts in preference to one large one, devoting a small chart to a single phase, aspect, or step. The presentation of each additional chart focuses attention on the point under consideration.

Posters are eyecatching and easy to read.

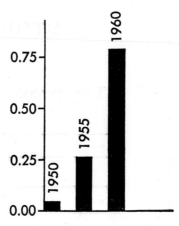

FIG. 5. Organizational Chart—Louisiana State University Medical School Research Grants (in Millions of Dollars)

From Louisiana State University *Graduate Report*, July, 1961, p. 4.

Whether the presentation is achieved by a chalkboard, a flannel board, or a skillfully prepared chart, the objective in each case is to present the material at the moment that it reinforces or amplifies the point under consideration. The following suggestions should improve your effectiveness in using visual aids.

1. Select a visual aid large enough to be seen by all auditors; page-size material can best be presented by using an opaque projector.
2. Avoid aids containing unnecessary details not pertaining to subject.
3. Select aids using color wherever possible.
4. Mount the aid in a place where all can see it.

5. Mount or display aids in a secure position.
6. Label parts with simple printing large enough to be read with ease.
7. Focus attention on important points by using a pointer.

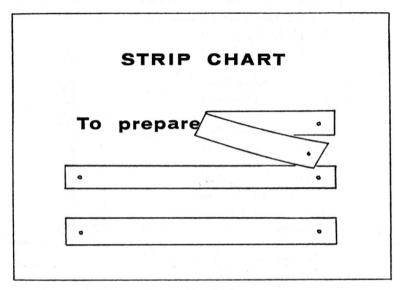

Fig. 6.

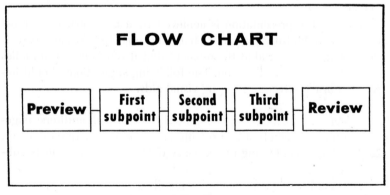

Fig. 7.

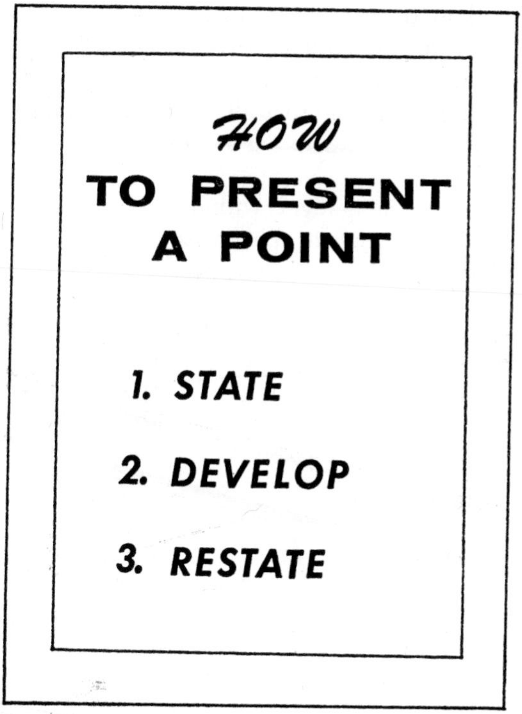

HOW

TO PRESENT
A POINT

1. STATE

2. DEVELOP

3. RESTATE

Fig. 8.

Practical Devices: Actual Objects, Specimens, and Models

Actual objects are the things themselves; they may be anything about which a speaker might talk: a golf club, a potato peeler, even a tractor. A specimen is a small part or sample of the real object. A model is a replica, smaller or larger than the object.

Since these visual supports come nearer reality than any of the other types discussed, their use is to be encouraged whenever possible. If the speaker wishes to discuss how to hit a golf ball he will do well to have golf clubs at hand.

General rules concerning effective presentation of such devices are difficult to formulate because each offers unique problems. The following suggestions will probably be helpful, at least in the use of models and specimens.

1. Select only those that are large enough to be seen.
2. If a model is three-dimensional, give the audience an opportunity to view it from different angles.
3. Display it long enough so that all may see; avoid giving the impression that you are attempting to conceal or hurry over difficult points.
4. Be able to manipulate gadgets with ease and confidence.
5. Cover or conceal models or specimens when not in use; don't let them steal attention from other points.

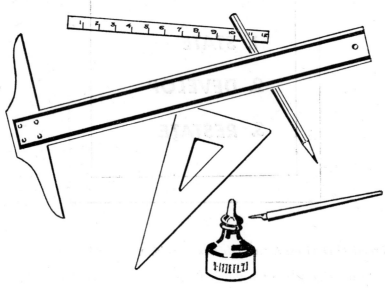

Fig. 9

Projected Pictures

Projected pictures require expensive and technical equipment—a motion picture projector, strip film projector, or opaque projector, as well as some kind of screen. A darkened room is a must. Furthermore, effective showing requires that an operator be employed.

If not shown with great skill, these materials may amount to little more than entertainment. Ordinarily, the sound motion picture must be completed as a unit. In this time the audience may slip away from the speaker because the darkened room may serve as welcome concealment for the inattentive and the disinterested. Introductions, summaries, and efforts to fit the film or picture into the speech are especially important.

In addition, the following hints may increase the speaker's effectiveness in using these materials.

Fig. 10.

1. Check carefully in advance the physical surroundings, electrical outlets and switches, lighting, seating, and ventilation.
2. Check in advance the time required to present a film or picture.
3. Plan the presentation so that no note-taking is necessary during the showing.
4. Rehearse the presentation and plan the cues with the operator.
5. Set up equipment and focus the image on the screen beforehand.
6. Reshow the film for emphasis if the subject is highly technical or difficult.

DISPLAYING VISUAL AIDS

Visual aids may be adapted to a speech in many ways. One of the first problems in this respect concerns the display of your materials. Two methods are possible: (1) to present the visual aid from the front of the room, or (2) actually to place it in the hands of the listeners.

Display from the front of the room can be effective if the visual support is suggestive in nature and intricate details are not important. Of course the drawing or object must be large enough to be seen and must be placed where the listeners can see with ease. Obviously, most graphic and pictorial materials, practical devices, and projected pictures may be presented from the front of the room. If the visual aid is in the front of the room, the speaker has the advantage of directing attention to those aspects which emphasize his point. Except in the case of projected pictures, he also has the advantages of face-to-face delivery, direct eye contact, and careful observation of audience reaction.

The speaker may also place visual aids in the hands of the listeners. Small models or specimens, outlines, summaries, page-size charts and maps, and detailed drawings can be presented only in this manner. Under these conditions more intricate details may be examined.

When you distribute visual materials to your audience, keep in mind four requirements.

1. Each listener should have a copy. The distribution of too few encourages inattentiveness because some listeners must examine the visual material while the presentation advances.

2. The parts should be carefully labeled and numbered. If the listener is to notice details, he must be constantly aware of what part of the visual aid is under discussion. By including numbers and labels the speaker can reorient the listeners frequently.

3. The speaker must be able to persuade the listener to lay aside the visual aid when he is through discussing it. If the listener becomes too engrossed in the material that he has in hand he may fail to follow the development, with the result that he misses the main points. The speaker must be adept at saying to his listeners, "Please listen to what I have to say," "Now I should like to have you observe the visual aid which I have given you," and "Will you please lay

aside the visual aid while I consider another point." This feat is indeed most difficult.

4. The method of distribution must be carefully planned. The speaker may distribute his material before he starts speaking, during his speech, or at the close of his presentation. The first possibility is usually the most satisfactory, for it avoids prolonged breaks in the actual presentation. The practice of distributing materials during a speech can result in confusion, a waste of precious time, and an interest lag. However, if you have several assistants who have been carefully instructed, you may be able to effect a distribution without serious consequences. In this event you can, of course, direct attention more specifically to the point by withholding materials until they fit into your development.

Distribution following a speech is satisfactory only if you expect the audience to do further study. In your speech you give the highlights and rely on printed material to provide more complete and more detailed information.

FITTING VISUAL AIDS INTO A SPEECH

Visual supporting material may be incorporated into a speech in two ways: it may be interspersed throughout the talk, or it may be presented as a unit before or after some explanation. It is ordinarily desirable to present blackboard sketches, charts, models, and film strips as they apply, using them to reinforce a point.

You should have your material so organized that you can move along without hesitation and long periods of silence. Delays while you make elaborate drawings or set up equipment are likely to kill interest and also to destroy the unity of your talk. If possible cut time-consuming operations to a minimum by careful preparation.

Motion pictures are usually presented in the second way, that is, as a unit. Starting and stopping the projector can seriously interfere with the thought contained in the picture. Occasionally, after a continuous run, a rerun of the film may be interrupted, but ordinarily such a procedure defeats the entire purpose of *motion* pictures. Introductory and summary remarks must be skillfully planned to point up what you want the auditor to remember.

Regardless of the type of visual aid, four steps are necessary for the effective use of visual support in a speech.

1. Introduce the visual aid, stressing its importance to the speech. Prepare the listeners for what to anticipate and what to observe.
2. Present the visual aid. Make sure that it is clearly visible and that the important points are emphasized.
3. Upon completion of the presentation, review the main points to be remembered.
4. Relate the point stressed by the visual aid to the line of thought it supports.

QUESTIONS AND TOPICS FOR STUDY AND REVIEW

1. What contribution do visual supports make to the effectiveness of communication?
2. What types of visual supports does the speaker have within himself?
3. What types of external visual supports are available to the speaker?
4. What four purposes do visual supports accomplish?
5. What factors should be considered in selecting visual supports?
6. What methods can you use to display your visual supports?
7. How do the following types of persons make use of visual supports in their speaking: (a) clergyman, (b) physics teacher, (c) gym teacher, (d) football coach, (e) auctioneer, (f) automobile salesman, (g) Fuller Brush man, (h) home demonstrator?
8. How do persons fail in the use of visual supports? Use illustrations from your own observation.
9. What visual supports are available to you as speech students?

PROJECTS

1. Deliver a speech in which you use a chart or map you have constructed.
2. Deliver a speech in which you make use of colored chalk and chalkboard illustrations.
3. Deliver a speech in which you use a model or specimen.
4. *Research Assignment.* Check available film strips or motion pictures on the following subjects.

Arranging furniture	Conservation	Rockets
Atom bombs	County fairs	Rural life
Better health	Gardening	Space flights
Calendars	Human relations	Soil erosion
Telephoning	United Nations	Weather

For each subject locate a film title, the place it is available, and the rental, and give the source of your information.

SUPPLEMENTARY READINGS

Dale, Edgar, *Audio-Visual Methods in Teaching*, rev. ed., Holt, Rinehart & Winston, 1957.

Educational Film Guide, H. W. Wilson, published annually, with monthly supplements.

Educators' Guide to Free Films, 21st ed., Educator Progress Service, 1961.

Educators' Guide to Free Filmstrips, 13th ed., Educator Progress Service, 1961.

Falconer, Vera M., *Filmstrips: A Descriptive Index and Users' Guide*, McGraw-Hill, 1948.

Filmstrip Guide, 3rd ed., H. W. Wilson, 1954, with annual supplements thereafter.

Loney, Glenn M., *Briefing and Conference Techniques*, McGraw-Hill, 1959, sec. 2, "Audio-Visual Aids for Speakers."

Reid, Loren, *First Principles of Public Speaking*, Artcraft, 1960, chap. 9, "How To Use Visual Aids."

Wiksell, Wesley, "Making Effective Use of Audio-Visual Aids in Teaching Speech," chap. 18 in Waldo W. Braden, ed., *Speech Methods and Resources*, Harper, 1961. The chapter discusses how to make effective use of all types of visual aids, and gives the addresses of many firms which provide them.

Wittich, Walter A., and Charles Francis Schuller, *Audio-Visual Materials, Their Nature and Use*, 2nd ed., Harper, 1957.

PART V 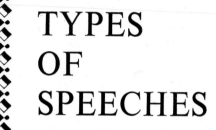 TYPES OF SPEECHES

19

The Informative Speech

In our society the informative talk is probably delivered more frequently than any other type of speech. It prevails wherever instruction is in order—in the classroom, laboratory, machine shop, Army camp, trade school, factory, boys' and girls' camps, lodge conclave, study club, Farm Bureau meeting, Sunday School, and many other situations. The informative speaker is known by a number of names: instructor, leader, coach, teacher, critic, guide, tutor, counselor, director, or lecturer.

Regardless of its form, the informative talk is always directed toward the accomplishment of a twofold objective: to elicit understanding and to encourage retention. The first objective, understanding, may involve correcting misinformation, increasing insight, presenting new facts, or sharpening the critical powers of observation and discrimination. It may also be broadened to include what might be called training—breaking old habits, developing new skills, or teaching how to manipulate a machine or a gadget.

Retention, the second objective of the informative talk, is the power to remember or to hold in mind for a period of time what the speaker has said. It is hardly worth while to make something understandable if immediately thereafter the listener or student forgets what has been said. The informative speaker, therefore, must not only make his subject clear and meaningful, but must also make it vivid and impressive.

In contrast to the argumentative speech, the informative talk is not concerned with changing attitudes or beliefs or with producing action. The use the listener makes of the knowledge or skill you impart is not your concern; that choice remains with him. If he understands and remembers the information presented, your task as a speaker is accomplished.

INSTRUCTIONS AND SIMPLE EXPLANATIONS

The simplest and probably the most usual type of informative talk is the one which gives instructions or directions to a listener. For example, if a passer-by asks the way to the nearest town, you might point in the right direction and say, "Go five miles north, turn left at the schoolhouse, and follow the blacktop for two miles." This obviously does not constitute a "talk" in the formal sense, but in an expanded form it represents a typical informative situation.

Of the same nature but longer and more detailed in development is the how-to-do-it speech. This type includes the presentation in which the speaker demonstrates and teaches the listener to perform a skill or operate an apparatus—how to improve your golf, bake a cake, repair a light switch, sew in a zipper. Visual aids, demonstration, supervised performance, and the critique are often a part of this type of presentation.

Below is an excellent example of a how-to-do-it speech. Notice in this excerpt how Dr. Arthur H. Steinhaus teaches a group of Detroit businessmen a simple exercise.

How can you shut the doors, close the windows, and turn out the lights to reduce stimuli that activate the all important "eyes and ears" of the muscles, the proprioceptors as they are called? This requires a special kind of training. . . . Would you in the next two minutes, take a little exercise with me—one that you can do at your desk in just the time it takes us to do it here. . . . Just follow me then. Contract your arm muscle. Contract it tightly. Do you feel that? That is tension. Now let go. Contract it and feel it—that's tension. Let it go. Now tighten muscles in the other arm. Feel that tension? Let it go. Next take the leg muscles—flexors, extensors of lower leg, of upper legs, in turn every muscle of the body, starting with the arms and legs, then chest, back, abdomen, and finally the face. The face is the hardest thing to let go, and the eyelids the hardest of all in the face. But with training one can learn to recognize tension and then let go. Try this when you want to fall asleep.[1]

Keep in mind three suggestions for talks of this type:

1. Keep the talk brief and simple.
2. Carefully enumerate the steps to be followed.
3. Give the listener ample opportunity to ask questions concerning anything that is not clear.

INFORMATIVE DESCRIPTION

A second common type of informative speech is description. Engineers, teachers, foremen, sales managers, supervisors, department heads, and others may be called on to describe to their protégés a new model, a layout, a display, a new building, a geological formation, an attitude, or even a quality. You will often be asked to give oral informative descriptions.

Description is the portrayal of a scene, person, object, quality, or emotion by means of language. This definition contains three items worthy of further comment. First, the word *portrayal* implies more than merely an enumeration or cataloguing of details. It suggests that discussion of the object, as a whole and in its parts, will create a unified and consistent picture for the listener. With vivid, specific, and concrete words, you use imagery to move your auditors to envision or sense the object under consideration. For example, the phrase "bright red hat" should give your listeners a vivid picture. If your language is clear, specific, and well chosen, your words will

[1] Dr. Arthur H. Steinhaus, "How Much and What Kind of Physical Exercise Should a Business Man Take?" February 13, 1956, Economic Club of Detroit, Michigan; in *Vital Speeches of the Day*, April 15, 1956, **22**: 408–411.

be translated into shape, color, light, sound, odor, taste, and movement.

Second, description deals with an individual object, not a class. Genung explains, "The aim of description . . . is to give the qualities wherein one object is individualized, unlike other objects; and has nothing to do with the class except in so far as referring it to a class may serve to localize it."[2]

The third implication of the definition is that you may describe qualities, attitudes, mental states, or characteristics as well as material objects such as automobiles, salt domes, or diamond rings. When the doctor asks, "How do you feel?" he wants you to describe one of these intangibles. Often in the courtroom a lawyer describes an intense emotion which somehow helps to explain an act of the accused. At a patriotic gathering it is not unusual to hear talks on loyalty, patriotism, courage, fortitude, or the like. The play director may stop a rehearsal in order to describe how he thinks Shylock must have felt about Christians. In each of these cases, the speaker gives an informative description of what may be referred to as an immaterial thing.

The preparation of an informative description involves the following steps:

1. Analysis of the whole and its parts
2. Selection of details
3. Arrangement of details

As a starting point in preparation, study the structure or make-up of the object to be described. If it is a concrete object, consider its class, its shape, its size, its position, its location, and its dominant sensory appeals. Investigate how it is put together and how it may be utilized in presenting the details to the listener.

For intangible or immaterial things you will be interested in predominant qualities, characteristics, and traits. The description of a man's character, for example, will necessitate an attempt to assess the traits he possesses. The portrayal of a fear will involve its characteristics.

After you are thoroughly familiar with the object and its parts or divisions, you are ready for the second step. Put to yourself two questions: which particulars shall I choose, and how many details will I need to make the subject clear? If you are to succeed in your

---

[2] John F. Genung, *The Practical Elements of Rhetoric*, Ginn, 1899, p. 327.

description, you must select particulars which will give a fair representation of the whole and result in accurate insight and lasting retention. Selecting exceptional or unimportant details, of course, will result in distortion and misunderstanding.

The particulars must be sufficient in number to give a clear picture of the whole but sufficiently limited for presentation within the time limit. The story of the blind men's description of an elephant exemplifies the points made above: asked to describe an elephant, they described what they could feel. Hence the one that touched the animal's side reported that the elephant was like a wall. His colleague who grasped the tail thought that it was like a rope. Each blind man failed in his description because he knew only an isolated characteristic which was neither representative nor of sufficient magnitude to give an adequate picture of the whole elephant.

Once you have selected the details for presentation you probably have already reached some conclusion about arrangement, the third step.

In ordering your points, you must obey two voices: that of the subject and that of the audience. The subject may suggest an arrangement, but this arrangement must be planned also to facilitate the understanding and retention of the audience.

In describing a tangible object you probably will discover that *contiguity*, or what lies next in space, serves as a basis for arranging your points. The description of a drainage project may follow the flow of the stream. If you are describing the Empire State Building, for example, you may choose to move from bottom to top, or vice versa. The play director, in describing a stage setting to his cast, may move from left to right or from upstage to downstage. Below are some possible orders that you may pursue.

1. From far to near or near to far
2. From top to bottom or bottom to top
3. From front to rear or rear to front
4. From right to left or left to right
5. From corner to corner
6. From outside to inside or inside to outside

In describing an immaterial thing you probably need to arrange the details according to a natural sequence, such as similarity and contrast or cause and effect. Since such qualities are abstract and subjective in meaning, you need to compare or contrast them with qualities or feelings which have meaning in common for you and your listeners. For instance, you may describe the insecurity that the speaker feels (stage fright) by comparing it with "buck fever" or the parachute jumper's fear.

Here are a few hints for making the informative description more effective.

1. Orient the listener so that he will understand his physical position with reference to the object. In other words, is he supposed to assume that he is looking at the side, the top, or the bottom of the object?

2. Make your starting point clear. Where does the sequence of details start? At the northwest corner? At the extreme right? At the bottom? At downstage left?

3. At the beginning announce the order you intend to follow, the direction in which you are moving in presenting your descriptive details.

4. Frequently reorient your listeners as to their position, your position, the direction you are traveling, and how far you have progressed.

INFORMATIVE NARRATIVE

Storytelling has been a favorite pastime from the beginning of time and thus has been associated with entertainment. But the relating of a true story may likewise constitute a way to enlighten and to inform. The primary concern of the informative narrative is accurate reporting of the actual sequence of events, with little effort to develop characterization or suspense. The participants, complicating forces, and setting are presented as impersonally and objectively as possible. Make every effort to avoid emotional coloring and loaded words which may distort meanings. These may be used in storytelling for entertainment but not here. The final test in informational narrative is, does the listener know what happened?

The recounting of a process or procedure is usually in narrative form, following the natural sequence of events as they occur. Since each phase, step, or period in the development may actually involve a minute description, some writers place informative description in that category. Ordinarily it falls under one of two headings: an operational pattern or a developmental pattern.

An operational pattern involves a step-by-step presentation of a process from beginning to end. The speaker may for example trace a product from the receiving of the raw material to the finished item. When sugar refining is the subject, the speaker carries the listener along from the unloading of raw cane to producing white sugar (see outline on p. 247). When the baking process is under consideration, the speaker tells what happens from receiving the flour at the bakery to the packaging of the loaves.

A developmental pattern relates the sequence of events which have taken place in creating of an organization. For instance, someone tells the story of how a company has grown from a one-room establishment to a skyscraper. Obviously the two types are closely related.

Other types of informative narrative are (1) simple narrative, (2) autobiography, (3) biographical sketch, (4) travelogue, and (5) historical account.

The *simple narrative* recounts a short incident. Examples are on-the-spot reporting of a search or rescue, a radio or TV broadcast of a fire, or an account of events leading up to an accident. Many radio newscasters and news analysts and sports commentators give little more than simple narrative in broadcasting information. Alan Shepard, the first American astronaut, told a television audience about his successful flight into space in simple narrative form.

Autobiography and *biography* recount information about human beings. Employers frequently ask prospective employees for an autobiographical sketch. The refugee or displaced person detailing his past life in his homeland is giving autobiographical information. Reverend Harold W. Rigney used this form when he told an audience of Chicago businessmen about the months he had spent in a Communist Chinese prison. He opened by saying, "Let me say that what I talk to you about now, about brainwashing, are things, facts and events which I myself have observed or undergone."[3]

A *travelogue* is an account of a trip, expedition, or exploration. During World War II American flyers gave this type of talk each

[3] Rev. Harold W. Rigney, former Rector of Fu Jen University, Peiping, China, speech to the Executive Club of Chicago, Illinois, April 6, 1956; in *Vital Speeches of the Day*, June 1, 1956, 22: 504–509.

time they returned from a mission over Germany or Japan and reported the raid as accurately and completely as possible to intelligence officers. After a visit to Latin America, Adlai Stevenson, United States Ambassador to the United Nations, used the travelogue form to give the National Press Club in Washington, D.C., a running account of his trip and his observations of conditions in many of the South American nations.[4] Upon his return from conferences in Europe, President John F. Kennedy reported to the nation via radio and television, setting the tone of his speech with this opening: "I returned this morning from a week-long trip to Europe and I want to report to you on that trip in full. It was in every sense an unforgettable experience. The people of Paris, of Vienna, of London were generous in their greeting."[5]

A *historical account*—a history lecture in the classroom, for example—is concerned with events of the past: the battle of Gettysburg, the fall of Hungary, the struggle to climb Mount Everest, the development of Standard Oil. Incorporated in such accounts may be autobiographical or biographical sketches and travelogues, for various types of narrative obviously overlap; frequently one type is subordinated to another, or two or more are combined to make a more complete presentation.

Edward R. Murrow, director of the United States Information Service, used the historical approach in a speech before the Public Relations Society of America, devoting his time to giving a narrative of what his agency was doing to meet the Russian threat in Berlin.

It was August 13 when Khrushchev's vicious vivisection began. I arrived in Berlin that Saturday night four hours before it all commenced. I was "privileged," if that be the right word, to witness the barbarous brutality of a way of life that clanged shut its Iron Curtain on its own people. It was a moving story.

This is how we told it.

Films, radio, television and newsreels, press and periodicals, exhibits, pamphlets, libraries and lecture programs—all turned their immediate collective efforts to the Berlin theme. We spread the news of what occurred. The theme was a simple one. We told the truth.

The Voice of America, now on the air over 100 hours every day in 36

[4] See Adlai Stevenson, "Cooperation Between North and South America," June 26, 1961; *Vital Speeches of the Day*, August 1, 1961, 27: 632–637.

[5] John F. Kennedy, speech delivered from Washington, D.C., June 6, 1961; in *Vital Speeches of the Day*, July 1, 1961, 27: 546–549.

languages, concentrated on Berlin news coverage, commentaries and features. We did a one-hour documentary, "Berlin, 1961," a three-part series, "The Manufactured Crisis," and another seven-part series, "The Berlin Story." These were placed world-wide on local stations.

President Kennedy's July 25 Berlin speech and his September 25 United Nations address went round the world live in English, and were re-broadcast at peak listening times in 35 other languages. Total estimated audience for each broadcast—over 20 million.

In motion pictures, we filmed the President's two addresses, and today upwards of 900 prints of each of them are circulating in 95 countries.[6]

You will do well to make your speech follow the chronological sequence of the events. In other words, if your subject is oil refining, you may well trace the process from the crude-oil stage to the refined product of gasoline and the various by-products. If you wish to trace the growth of your home town you will describe it from its founding to the present.

In presenting an informative narrative, these suggestions will help you to be effective.

1. Divide your procedure into two to five steps.
2. Give your listeners a preview of the steps early in the speech.
3. Tell your listeners frequently how far you have progressed in your development.
4. Use visual supports such as diagrams, flow charts, and slides where they are relevant.

ESSENTIALS IN PREPARING THE INFORMATIVE SPEECH

Know Your Subject Thoroughly

If you are to inform listeners, you must first master your subject matter. Understanding comes through objectivity, accuracy, and thoroughness.

Objectivity. First, you must be objective in your investigation of the subject. In your study and analysis, you must attempt to see details and relationships as they really are, not the way you would like to have them. Your point of view should be detached and imper-

---

[6] In the *Christian Science Monitor*, December 5, 1961.

sonal. You must bypass preferences and biases in an effort to get the picture—the true picture and the whole picture.

Accuracy.   You must be accurate in recording and reporting details. This requirement should need little elaboration. If you accept the responsibility of presenting information to an audience, you must report the facts—the embarrassing ones as well as those that seem to favor or to be consistent with your "pet" theory.

Thoroughness.   Your goal in studying and analyzing a subject should be to accumulate ample reserves upon which to draw. Then you will have no difficulty with the unexpected question, and your supply of information will give you additional confidence and poise.

Limit Your Subject to the Time Available

How many words can you present in five minutes? You probably speak at a rate of from 100 to 200 words per minute; in other words, you can deliver between 500 and 1000 words in five minutes. If you read at a comparatively rapid rate, you may cover as many as three pages of this book in five minutes. But your speaking rate for an informative speech will be much slower than your reading rate, particularly when you include visual aids or movement about the platform. Other activities may further reduce the number of words you can present. You might aim at speaking at about 150 words per minute.

An informative talk must be presented so that the listener can think through the new material and not feel that he is being pushed. What demand does this requirement put on you as a speaker? For one thing, you must simplify your presentation in order to facilitate understanding; at the same time you must present enough details to give a clear picture. Obviously you must limit the subject sufficiently to present it in the time available. When you are tempted to exceed your allotted time, remember how you feel when your instructors fail to stop at the end of the class period.

Use Simple and Clear Organization

In the informative speech make sure the listener understands at all times what you are doing and how what you are saying relates to the subject. Try to develop insight through presenting cogent details and making clear their relationships to the main subject. To do this it is essential to keep the structure of the speech obvious, simple, and easy to follow. You can achieve these objectives by four techniques.

1. Use a deductive arrangement in which the central point and the purpose are clearly presented in the introduction and the main points follow in the development proper.
2. Arrange the main points of the development proper in a consistent pattern, and check to see that points have been selected by one principle only. The informative talk is usually organized around time, space, topical, or functional patterns (see pp. 243–244).
3. Word main points in simple declarative sentences. Complex or compound sentences complicate the thought and are more difficult to comprehend. The short, simple sentence is easy to understand and to remember.
4. Limit your main points to no more than five.

Include as Many Listener Cues and Aids as Possible

Here we are concerned with the actual delivery of the speech. During your presentation you should give your listeners as many *listener cues* and *aids* as possible. What is a listener cue? It is a word or signal or hint to the listener that he should be alert for what is about to occur. It is a way to make him aware of a new point, a transition, or an important piece of evidence. Previews, signposts, obvious transitions, restatements, and final summaries are frequently used in this manner. (See Chapter 2.)

As cues you may number your points, saying, "My first point . . . . My second point . . . . My third point . . . ." Or you may use such obvious devices as "Now, this point is important," "Carefully watch this step," or "You must understand this phase in order to understand what is to come," or "Remember this point."

You need to emphasize the structure and interrelation of your points. See how the preview of points in the speech introduction given on page 270 prepares the listeners for what is to come. You can also reinforce your presentation by writing your main points on the chalkboard or displaying them on a chart or flannel board.

A concise summary in the conclusion further emphasizes the main points and gives the listener a last opportunity to make sure that he understands the points.

Relate Your Subject to the Interests and Motives of Your Listeners

Motivation and the factors of attention and interest are almost as important in the informative speech as they are in the persuasive talk. You should therefore make clear how the listeners can profit from your presentation. To this end, utilize the principles of motivation and of attention and interest discussed in Chapters 10 and 11. An illustration will show why these principles are important. In speech classes occasionally a young lady will demonstrate a new type of hair curler or a young man will demonstrate a new type of wrench or tool. At such moments the opposite sex is usually little concerned with the presentation, since subjects are too far removed from their interests, wants, and needs. The effective communicator shows the listener that he has something to gain through attending to the talk. He keeps his presentation moving; he arouses curiosity; he inserts humor; he emphasizes the satisfaction which comes with knowing about the subject.

Approach the Speaking Situation with Enthusiasm

Students at the University of Missouri, commenting upon their instructors, said, "Some instructors seem to live in their courses, while others seem to regard their teaching as drudgery. A good instructor is enthusiastic about his subject. Students appreciate an instructor's efforts to make his material interesting."[7]

Interest and attention are much easier to maintain when the speaker demonstrates that he has an urge to communicate and that he is sincerely concerned with the listener. Enthusiasm is contagious. Your listeners will pick up your eagerness and return it to you by showing themselves eager to learn and to receive the information you are trying to impart.

The good speaker, following careful preparation, approaches his subject with a positive, optimistic attitude, determined to present his subject effectively. He never apologizes for his inexperience or

[7] Elmer Ellis, ed., "Toward Better Teaching in College," *University of Missouri Bulletin,* May 1, 1954. 55: 43.

for his inability to cover intricate details. Nor does he bluff or attempt to laugh off mistakes. When he encounters a question which he cannot answer, he says frankly, "I don't know."

Select Appropriate Materials for Your Listeners

It is particularly important that you plan your presentation and select your supporting materials to fit the levels of comprehension of your listeners, their capacity for absorbing new ideas and new techniques, and the time available for your speech.

To underestimate the maturity and ability of your listeners is likely to result in wasting time and may even turn them against you. Listeners appreciate being treated like mature human beings. They resent being talked down to, and they quickly lose interest in material which is unrelievedly familiar or which seems unimportant.

To overestimate listeners' capacity is equally bad, for the result is likely to be confusion and disinterest. Beware of losing yourself in your subject. When you are intensely interested in a topic you can easily forget your listeners and pursue some theoretical or remote aspect which you enjoy discussing, but which is not really significant in the development of your topic. College professors frequently offend in this way by shooting over the heads of their students. College students know the results of this type of folly.

Select Supporting Materials Which Give a Clear Picture

Since he cannot transfer to the listener the picture he himself perceives, the speaker through his words must try to stir up within the listener the desired image. Words are sometimes fragile carriers of meaning. The simple word *home* for example will suggest one picture to the speaker and an entirely different one to the listener. A speaker may think that he has in mind a clear picture of what he thinks a *democracy* is, while his listener has no picture at all when he hears the word in a speech. The speaker may announce that he is going to discuss the aardvark, a mammal of the genus *Orycteropus*. Although they may be curious about what he is going to describe, most listeners will have no picture of what is to come. Actually the speaker will be more likely to communicate if he has a photograph of the "earth pig" or African anteater.

The speaker must be definite and concrete in all of his language and supporting development. The principal supporting materials of an informative speech are definitions, illustrations, examples, comparison, statistics, and visual supports.

The best informative talks are packed full of concrete examples and apt comparisons. Abstract and unfamiliar language becomes meaningful when the speaker is able to illustrate with an incident or example.

Professor Loren Reid of the University of Missouri, who is a superior speech teacher and a most interesting lecturer, made a study of what students liked and disliked about the teaching methods of their professors. His conclusion about the use of examples expresses well the point of this section.

Illustrations, anecdotes, specific instances, and practical applications all add to the effectiveness of a lecture. One student mentioned a professor of philosophy who had a large fund of examples to illustrate faults of reasoning and types of propaganda. Another mentioned a professor of history who frequently exemplified his points by parallel incidents from other centuries or countries. Another described a freshman English instructor with a ready supply of unusual ways of beginning themes, developing paragraphs, and ending themes. Another told of a scientist and his stock of interesting intellectual curiosities. Another related how a professor of sociology chose illustrations from many different trades and industries. . . . Although students appreciate the generalizations, they are particularly intrigued by the specific examples. The margin of knowledge between the student and their teachers is very often great. Largely through the examples do they learn to appreciate the generalizations.[8]

Make Use of Visual Supports

The effective speaker attempts to utilize as many channels of communication as possible in a speech. These avenues through which the speaker must reach the listeners are the human senses: seeing, hearing, smelling, tasting, and touching. The straight lecture, of course, relies primarily upon the channel of hearing, but to a limited extent sight is also involved, since the listener reacts to the movements and often the physical attributes of the speaker. When

[8] Loren Reid, "How To Improve Classroom Lectures Fifty Percent," *University of Missouri Bulletin*, May 1, 1954, **55**: 20–21.

the speaker uses visual aids, he makes a more direct and important use of the channel of seeing. A cooking school teacher is likely to utilize all five senses.

Generally the speaker will be assured of greater insight, more comprehension, and longer retention when multisensory appeals are utilized. Therefore you improve your informative talk by making use of charts, diagrams, maps, photographs, flannel boards, chalkboards, slides, film strips, and films. See the discussion of visual aids in Chapter 18.

Supplement Oral Presentations by Demonstration

Often teachers do too much telling and too little showing. The straight lecture may become a one-way street—from speaker to listener—with nothing happening at the listening end. You can improve receptivity by showing, for example, how a machine or tool operates. In fact, many subjects which almost defy explanation are relatively simple to demonstrate. The formula for successful training by informative speaking is as follows:

Explain ⟶ Demonstrate ⟶ Performance by trainee ⟶ Critique

Following demonstration, you should if at all possible, of course, let the trainee perform the operation under your supervision. Then you can determine what additional instruction is necessary.

Seek Questions from the Listeners

In the informative speech strive to keep two-way communication operating. One of the best ways to judge whether listeners are understanding you is by the questions they ask. By this means you will

Speaker ⇌ Listener

know what they misunderstand and whether your rate of presentation has been too fast.

The number of questions asked after a speech or even during it often depends upon whether you make it clear that you welcome them. In the introduction the speaker might say, "Please ask questions when you fail to understand." When a listener puts a question, the speaker must demonstrate tact and courtesy by what he says and how he acts. If he gives an unsatisfactory answer, ridicules the questioner, or seems to be bothered at having his flow of words disturbed, he will probably shut off further queries. You must be prepared to understand and answer the poorly phrased question, the confused question, and the searching question. When queries come, you must be able to give your answer within the framework of your development. Some questions should be ignored, some delayed, and some answered.

Use Language Which Is Definite and Exact

The language of the informative talk should measure up to the standards of clarity presented in Chapter 26. Ideally the informative speaker should confine his remarks to language which carries meaning but which is nondirective. However, it is almost impossible to avoid directive language and probably it is not entirely desirable to do so, since report language is dull in large doses. The important caution to observe is to speak in language which is immediately understood—and that means the language of the listener. On many occasions you must forego the use of technical jargon and the display of your extensive vocabulary. In contrast to the high-powered persuader who attempts to short-circuit thought, the informative speaker does everything possible to stir the listener to reflect and to analyze.

QUESTIONS AND TOPICS FOR STUDY AND REVIEW

1. Sometimes a narrative in its various forms is considered a type of entertaining speech. When its purpose is to give information how does it differ from the entertaining type?
2. Distinguish between the informative talk and the argumentative talk. Consider the following: analysis, central thought, organization, and supporting materials.
3. In this book we have discussed criticism as a type of informative speech. What justification is there for considering it a type of argumentative speech?
4. What were the teaching methods of your most effective teacher? Which if any of these methods can be applied to the delivery of an informative talk?

5. What were the teaching methods of your most ineffective teacher? Can you profit by his or her mistakes?
6. As a rule, how much should you expect listeners to remember of what you say in an informative speech?
7. How can you as an informative speaker improve the retention of your hearers?
8. What are several ways to stimulate listeners to ask questions?
9. Should the speaker ever refuse to answer questions? When? How?
10. To what group should the informative speaker adapt his material in the informative speech—the slowest group, the average, the most intelligent?
11. Consider carefully historical writing. Is it straight narrative? Criticism? What justification is there for stating that it is a type of argument? (Ask your history teacher.)

PROJECTS

1. *Speaking Assignment.* Deliver a five-minute informative talk in which you tell the class how to construct a map locating your home. Ask members of the class to draw the map as you give instructions. When you have finished your speech, collect the maps, and see how effective you were in giving simple instructions. Write a brief estimate of your effectiveness.
2. *Speaking Assignment.* Deliver a five-minute informative talk in which you use one of the following types:
   a. An informative description of a building in your home town
   b. An informative narrative of a trip you have taken
   c. A historical narrative
3. *Speaking Assignment.* Deliver a five-minute explanation in which you explain a plan of organization, a procedure, or an operation.
4. *Speaking Assignment.* Deliver a five-minute talk in which you attempt to make the audience appreciate (a) a great distance, (b) a great value, or (c) a great size.
5. *Speaking Assignment.* Deliver a five-minute informative talk in which you attempt to stimulate questions from the floor. (See Alan H. Monroe, *Principles and Types of Speech,* 5th ed., Scott, Foresman, 1962, Chapter 23.) You will be graded partially on the questions you stimulate and the manner in which you answer them.
6. *Speech Practices.* Carefully read the excerpts of speeches found on pages 120–131 of *Speech Practices.* Analyze carefully the following: (1) organization, (2) forms of support and (3) stylistic devices. Do any of these selections suggest that the speaker might have had a purpose other than giving information?

SUPPLEMENTARY READINGS

Baird, A. Craig, and Franklin H. Knower, *General Speech: An Introduction*, 2nd ed., McGraw-Hill, 1957, chap. 15, "Informative Speaking."

Monroe, Alan H., *Principles and Types of Speech*, 5th ed., Scott, Foresman, 1962, chap. 20, "The Speech To Inform."

Oliver, Robert T., and Rupert L. Cortright, *Effective Speech*, 4th ed., Holt, Rinehart & Winston, 1961, chap. 18, "The Speech To Inform."

Sarett, Lew, William Trufant Foster, and Alma Johnson Sarett, *Basic Principles of Speech*, 3rd ed., Houghton Mifflin, 1958, chap. 15, "Instructing Through Speech."

Weaver, Andrew Thomas, and Ordean Gerhard Ness, *An Introduction to Public Speaking*, Odyssey, 1961, chap. 5, "Informing an Audience."

Winans, James A., *Speech-Making*, Appleton-Century-Crofts, 1938, chap 11, "The Expository Speech."

20

The Persuasive Speech

A chemical engineer who spends much of his time in research recently said, "We are all persuaders, whether we admit it or not." In his laboratory he had discovered that on many occasions he was asked for more than a straight, factual presentation: he was asked to justify his procedure, to present arguments for or against a procedure or project; sometimes management wanted to be sold on a new development. Although he supposedly dealt with facts and careful experimentation, he discovered that he also worked with human beings who required persuasion.

In the present context we are thinking of persuasion in its broadest sense, that is, implying that the speaker consciously attempts to change opinions and beliefs and/or move his listeners to action. This definition suggests at least four aspects:

1. The speaker has a predetermined goal which he wants to achieve with his listeners.
2. To achieve this goal, he consciously selects and organizes his materials and arguments.
3. Through his appeals, his voice, and bodily activity, he attempts to redirect, neutralize, or change attitudes and opinions.
4. Generally speaking, he has as an ultimate goal a response involving acceptance, which may involve covert or overt response.

Contrary to popular belief, a speaker need not be unethical or underhanded in this process—he need not attempt to deceive, mislead, trick, or brainwash. Instead, he will attempt to combine logical argument and facts with motive appeals.

The persuasive talk becomes the order of the day when a speaker is dissatisfied with existing conditions in a certain area or with the attitudes or conduct of his listeners. He is confident that he has a valuable insight into the problem and also that he has a solution which satisfies his own motives and those of his listeners. He may discover that some of his listeners are unaware of, uninterested in, or lethargic about his problem. Others range in their attitudes from mild to violent opposition. He will find his task easier, of course, when there are several partisans present.

THE CONVINCING SPEECH

The first type of persuasive speech we shall discuss, the speech to convince, seeks a covert response or mental agreement. The speaker asks the listener to accept, believe, affirm, approve, admit, or recognize. A convincing speech may be built around an assertive proposition (sometimes referred to as a proposition of fact or value) like the following:

1. The State University faculty is underpaid.
2. State University is understaffed.
3. Castro is a threat to the United States.
4. U.S. policy with reference to Latin America has failed.
5. U.S. foreign policy is short-sighted.
6. Communism is our greatest threat.

On the other hand, a convincing talk may also be planned around a recommending proposition (proposition of policy) which is worded to demand a general or undirected response, one about which the immediate audience can do little directly. Many of the propositions used by high-school and college debaters are of this type. Here are some examples:

1. The English-speaking nations should form a strong federation.
2. NATO should be abolished.
3. The federal government should institute a national sales tax.
4. Germany should be united.
5. The federal government should establish compulsory health insurance.

In upholding any of these sentences the speaker advocates a course of action with which his immediate listeners can agree but upon which they cannot act and, in fact, have little direct influence on the outcome. What can the citizens of Des Moines, Iowa, or Salt Lake City, Utah, or Water Proof, Louisiana, do about reuniting Germany or instituting a national sales tax? They can, of course, declare their agreement with the speaker's analysis, but they are so far removed from where these problems are to be settled that any overt action is improbable.

In summary, propositions like the two types discussed are so constructed as to demand no more than mental assent. The speaker is satisfied when his listeners declare at the end of his presentation, "I agree with what you say," "It is obvious that you are correct in your analysis," or "You have changed my opinion on the subject." With a convincing speech you move your listeners in the direction of your position. Whether you follow up your gains later with a speech making a specific request for action will depend upon your purpose and reason for speaking.

THE ACTUATING SPEECH

The actuating speech seeks an overt or action response, one which is observable. Its goal is one step beyond that of a convincing talk in that it argues that a specific course of action should be followed. In addition to the commitment sought by the convincing speech, the actuating speech seeks to influence the listeners to move from the ranks of opponents and neutrals into those of active partisans. This type of speech is the medium of the salesman, the politician, the labor organizer, the revivalist, the courtroom lawyer—men who want action. Since the proposition is directive, it is constructed around the words *should, ought,* or *must* together with verbs like *act, build, contribute, give, donate, move, join,* and *march.* Below are some examples.

1. You should give a pint of blood to the blood bank.
2. You should build a birdhouse.
3. You should join the American Association of University Women.
4. You should urge your congressman to vote against compulsory health insurance.
5. The League of Women Voters must play an active part in the coming election.

If you contrast these propositions with those listed on page 356, you will immediately observe that each of these propositions directs the listeners present to do something. "You should give . . ."; "You should build . . ."; "You should urge . . . ." A proposition of a convincing speech can usually be reworded to make it a proposition for an actuating speech. Thus "The federal government should institute a sales tax" can be made into a proposition for an actuating talk by rewording it to read, "You should write your congressman to support a federal sales tax," or "You should organize a local committee to promote a federal sales tax."

THE RELATIONSHIP BETWEEN THE CONVINCING AND THE ACTUATING SPEECH

The purposeful speaker may seek an immediate goal of mental agreement in anticipation of achieving an ultimate goal involving an overt or action response. In following this sequence, the speaker acts upon the following premises:

1. Covert and overt responses differ not in kind but in degree of commitment.
2. Covert responses are easier to arouse than overt responses.
3. When a covert response has been activated, an overt response is easier to procure.
4. It is preferable to select a lesser goal for a given speech than to risk failure by asking for an unattainable goal.

Under what circumstances should the speaker choose to deliver a convincing talk—the lesser goal? When he feels that the controlling segment or target group (see pp. 146–147) cannot be moved to action, he may be content with a lesser immediate response, one which is nearer his position and which he has a reasonable expectation of achieving. With each speaking effort he hopes to move his listeners in that direction.

We can illustrate this principle with a hypothetical audience in which 75 percent oppose the proposition, 20 percent are neutral, and only 5 percent agree with the speaker.

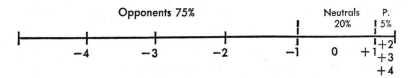

With an audience like this one in which many are opposed, he is likely to have considerable difficulty winning a favorable majority or stirring any significant overt response; consequently he would be wise to try for a limited response in anticipation of achieving his ultimate goal involving action at some later time. If he concentrates upon the 26 percent mildly opposed (−3, −2), he will perhaps be wise to seek mental agreement on a subproposition of an assertive nature, realizing that conversion may require several persuasive efforts.

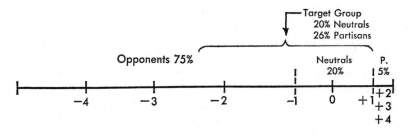

The guiding principle involved here may be stated as follows: when the degree of audience commitment (division of opinion) or the intensity of their attitudes suggest that he may have great difficulty in gaining a significant immediate overt response, the speaker would be wise to give a convincing talk which demands only mental agreement, preparatory to an actuating speech later.

Now consider a second hypothetical audience in which the degree of commitment is as follows: 40 percent for the proposition, 20 percent undecided, and 40 percent in the opposition. Now the controlling segment or target group is in the neutral position (−1, 0,

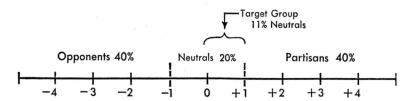

+1), with the most significant part probably those nearest the *for* position (at least 11 percent). Given this audience the speaker can deliver with some optimism an actuating speech demanding an immediate overt response.

To summarize, the actuating talk is in order when the degree of commitment and the intensity of attitudes suggest that the speaker can move sufficient members into the *for* position to gain control of the assembly or at least to satisfy his purpose.

THE RELATIONSHIP BETWEEN THE STIMULATING SPEECH AND THE PERSUASIVE SPEECH

As we have seen in an earlier chapter, the stimulating speech attempts to reinforce existing attitudes and to activate dormant ones. It aims at greater enthusiasm, strengthened loyalties, and greater effort. How does this differ from the persuasive talk? The persuasive talk seeks to change attitudes, opinions, and behavior, to move neutral or opposing listeners into the ranks of the supporters. In short, the two words *reinforce* and *change* characterize the difference in degree between the stimulating speech and the persuasive speech. The two are neither discrete types nor opposites; they may be part of the same process. In a speaking campaign, they can be presented in the following two sequences:

1. Stimulating speech→Convincing speech→Actuating speech
2. Convincing speech→Actuating speech →Stimulating speech

In the first instance (1) the speaker delivers a stimulating speech in order to reinforce favorable attitudes, hoping that he will thereby weaken unfavorable ones. For example, if he has as an ultimate goal to discourage social drinking, he might prepare his listeners by first speaking upon a related proposition: "Safety is important on the highways." By reinforcing the attitudes on safety he prepares the way for presenting the convincing proposition: "Driving and drinking don't mix."

In the second case (2) the speaker may use a stimulating speech at the other end of the sequence with a partisan group which is slow to execute a plan. In this case he follows an action-demanding speech with one designed to intensify attitudes.

On page 358 are listed four premises upon which convincing and actuating speeches are based. Now let us add to these two premises that summarize what has been presented in this section:

5. Intensification of favorable attitudes may weaken closely related unfavorable attitudes.
6. Intensification of favorable attitudes may move partisans more firmly into your position (+4).

ORGANIZING THE PERSUASIVE TALK

Problem-Solution

How can you partition logically an argumentative proposition of the recommending type? A very old system proposes that you ask yourself three stock questions:

1. Is there need for a change in the present system?
2. Is there a feasible solution to the need?
3. What benefits are likely to result from the proposal?

The stock questions will give you a start on almost any *should* proposition, for you will generally find yourself planning in terms of (1) the problem, (2) the solution, and (3) the benefits.

These stock questions or issues provide an effective overall speech arrangement, with the speech divided into the following five steps:

1. Gaining attention
2. Analysis of the problem

3. Presentation of a solution
4. Demonstration of the benefits
5. Appeal for action

The first step includes the traditional introduction and involves getting the listeners to attend to the presentation. The speaker attracts attention, relates the subject to motives of the listeners, and demonstrates his right to speak.

The *problem step* involves citing the unsatisfactory conditions and usually presenting the causes of these conditions.

The *solution step* tells what you propose to do about the problem. Actually your proposition may state the course of action you advocate: "Give a pint of blood," "Build a bird house," "Join the AAUW," or "Vote against compulsory health insurance."

In the *benefit step* you attempt to show what will result from your proposal. You may list concrete advantages or paint a picture of the new day under your proposal.

The *action step* is the final appeal in which you pull together all of your arguments and relate them to the motives of your listeners.

Deductive Order

The overall organization of a persuasive speech is often determined by how and where in the speech the speaker decides to present the proposition. Should he put it near the opening of his speech, or should he wait until later for the presentation? His answers to these questions may give him three choices in the basic organization of the speech: (1) deductive order, or moving from the general (the proposition) to the specific (the points), (2) inductive order, or moving from the specific to the general, or (3) presentation by implication.

As in the case of the informative speech, the proposition may come early in the speech, before any of the main points are presented. This type of developmental order is generally best suited to the convincing speech. It is exemplified below:

PROPOSITION: Baton Rouge offers many advantages to the businessman, for

I. The city is located in the heart of a rich agricultural area.
II. The river provides cheap transportation.

III. The state capitol attracts thousands of tourists.
IV. The many industries have large payrolls.

Stating the proposition early in the speech offers both advantages and disadvantages. Its chief advantage is that it enables the speaker to clarify his topic early, to keep reminding his listeners of his proposition, and to stress the logical relationships that exist between the proposition and the supporting points and between the supporting points themselves.

The principal disadvantage arises when an audience contains many opponents. In this event, revealing the proposition may serve to crystallize the opposition before you have had an opportunity to present the speech.

Inductive Order

With a hostile audience it is often wise to reverse the order—to present the proposition after the main points or in an inductive order. This order serves well for the actuating speech. The inductive approach—which moves from the specific to the general, that is, to the conclusion—gives the speaker the opportunity to advance from the least controversial points toward the points of greatest disagreement. In other words, you build a sound foundation before you risk a direct statement of your proposition. A slight variation is to give the proposition after one strong point has been developed in order to win a friendly hearing, bolster up the wavering, or perhaps quiet a militant minority.

A speech following an inductive approach might be developed as follows:

I. At present the danger of nuclear attack on this country is greater than ever before.
II. A nuclear war is likely to be an attack on the civilian population.
III. Personal survival depends upon knowing what to do in case of attack.

PROPOSITION: You should immediately study carefully the materials made available by Civil Defense.

Inductive development may also take a form similar to a special type of refutation called the method of *residues*, in which all possibilities are eliminated but the one you support. In the 1960 presi-

dential primary race, a Kennedy supporter might have argued as
follows:

I. Don't vote for Adlai Stevenson.
II. Don't vote for Lyndon Johnson.
III. Don't vote for Stuart Symington.
IV. Vote for John F. Kennedy.

Presenting the Proposition by Implication

The speaking situation may demand that you lead up to your
proposition indirectly. One excellent method is to make the development so pointed that the audience frames the proposition without
being told specifically what it is. This strategy demands that the listener be kept active and alert. Then, if he puts the pieces together
correctly and reaches the intended conclusion by himself, he may
experience such self-satisfaction that he will be more easily converted to your way of thinking.

Shakespeare demonstrated this method superbly in *Julius Caesar*
in the famous speech of Mark Antony. Remember how he opened
by calling Brutus an "honorable man" and declaring that he had
come "to bury Caesar, not to praise him." As the speech unfolds,
Antony skillfully reviews the good deeds of Caesar and thus gradually turns the mob against Brutus and Cassius. Without ever stating his proposition, he produces the action he desires. In the end
he is able to say:

> Now let it work. Mischief, thou are afoot,
> Take thou what course thou wilt!

Obviously, presenting the proposition by implication requires careful planning, great skill, and forceful delivery. For the mature
speaker it can be highly effective, but for the novice it should be
undertaken cautiously.

SOME BASIC PRINCIPLES OF PERSUASION

Size Up the Speaking Situation

As we have remarked repeatedly, a successful speech is audience-
centered; that is, it is planned for a specific group meeting on a

specific occasion. All of the principles discussed in Chapters 8 and 9 are important to the speaker, but audience analysis is the crux of the matter, for the success of the persuasive speech depends upon the speaker's deciding who is to be the target group. In other words, the successful persuader plans to win that segment of his listeners who can carry the day for him. Once he decides where to concentrate his effort, he must weigh carefully the intensity of the attitudes and opinions and the points of common ground he may have with his target group. His planning must also include secondary goals to keep partisans enthusiastic and opponents quiet.

Select an Attainable, Immediate Goal

We have likewise stressed the fact that the goal of all purposeful speaking is response involving covert or overt action. There is little point in changing opinions and beliefs if no attention is given to where the listeners are to go or what they are to do if they decide to carry through. You may ask, why shouldn't the persuasive speaker demand an overt response on every speaking occasion? But such a procedure would consider only what the speaker wants, overlooking the extent of listener commitment and the intensity of their attitudes. Why ask for more than you can expect? To try for an overt response of too great a magnitude and fail might only reinforce existing opinions and attitudes or even drive persons away from the position of the speaker.

Remember that conversion in many instances may come only after several persuasive efforts. In the beginning it may be wise to concentrate on building up common ground or to work for mental agreement which will involve only intensification or modification of existing attitudes and opinions. Therefore select an immediate goal, limited in extent, hoping for conversion or action at a later time.

Let us illustrate how the achievement of a lesser goal may lead to an ultimate goal of great magnitude.

Ultimate (unannounced) goal: To persuade the voters to authorize a five-million-dollar bond issue to build a new school in Beacon.

Lesser ultimate goal: To gain mental agreement that an expanded education program is desirable for Beacon.

Lesser immediate goal: To gain mental agreement that Beacon High School should institute a program of vocational agriculture.

Lesser immediate goal: To gain mental agreement that every American child has a right to vocational training.

The goal with which the speaker starts will depend upon the degree of commitment among the listeners. In a township where there is violent opposition to higher taxes and additional bond issues, a speaker might at first attempt to achieve no more than the goal which involves only modification of attitudes and opinions (the fourth goal above), but which moves the listeners toward the speaker's position.

Step I	Step II	Step III	Step IV
Agree that all children have a right to vocational training	Agree that Beacon H.S. should institute a program of vocational training	Agree that expansion of the entire educational program is desirable	Vote for $5,000,000 bond issue

These four steps are not the only possible ones; many intermediate ones might require development with some groups. Furthermore, a speaker might accomplish two, three, or all of these steps in a single speech.

Frame the Proposal in a Single Short, Meaningful Proposition

Once the speaker has determined his target group and his speech goal, he is ready to frame his proposition (see Chapter 14).

For the convincing talk seeking a covert response he will use an assertive or recommending proposition which asks for a generalized response. For the actuating speech he will use a recommending proposition which states a specific course of action.

The speaker must know what he wants before he begins to speak; before he finishes he must make sure that his listeners, too, know what he wants. The novice speaker may insist that he cannot possibly express his demand in less than a paragraph or without some careful qualification. He should be made to understand that he is likely to leave his listeners confused and bewildered unless he succeeds in phrasing his proposition in a single concise sentence. Grove Patterson, editor-in-chief of the *Toledo Blade* and veteran speaker, advises: "Write down exactly what you want to say in one sentence. Make up your mind: This is it; this is the idea I want to sell."[1]

Select an Overall Plan Which Fits the Speaking Situation

The plan you select will depend upon your goal and your audience. You will word your proposition and plan your presentation in terms of these two factors. As a rule, with the audience in which there are many neutrals or uncommitted persons who do not hold intense attitudes, you will use the deductive order, stating the proposition early in the speech.

With the actuating speech, particularly when the attitudes are intense, habitual, and emotionalized, you would be well advised to use the inductive order, developing your main points before you reveal your proposition. It will often be to your advantage to structure your speech in the five steps suggested at the beginning of this chapter: gaining attention, analyzing the problem, presenting a solution, demonstrating benefits, and making an appeal for action.

Establish Your Right To Speak on Your Subject

Aristotle observed that listeners trust the wise, the honest, and the credible "more fully and more readily than others."[2] He even contended that this type of appeal, which he referred to as *ethos*, was the most effective one available to the speaker. The same quality was upheld by Phillips Brooks, the eminent preacher, in speaking of preaching: "The truth must come through the personality, not merely over . . . [the speaker's] lips, not merely into his understanding and out through his pen. It must come through his character, his affection, his whole intellectual and moral being."[3] You will discover that persuading listeners is easier when they believe in you—your ability, your good character, and your sincere interest in them. If there

[1] Grove Patterson, "How to Make a Speech," *Limelight*, Vol. I No. 3.
[2] W. Rhys Roberts, tr, *Aristotle's Rhetoric and Poetic*, Modern Library. Random House, 1954. *Rhetoric*. Bk. I, Chap. 2, p. 25, 1356a.
[3] Phillips Brooks, *Lectures on Preaching*, Dutton, 1898, p. 8.

is any doubt about you as a person or your right to speak on your subject, you may need to make some reference to your experience. In speaking at a convention of investment bankers Charles H. Percy established his qualification to speak by mentioning his long experience: "Certainly from my own experience of 22 years' association with Bell and Howell, I can testify that we rely heavily on our friends and associates in the investment banking field for advice and counsel."[4] Senator Margaret Chase Smith, speaking to the Overseas Press Club, remarked that her observations were based upon "two overseas trips . . . to twenty-three countries covering fifty thousand miles,"[5] thus telling her listeners that she was speaking from first-hand experience, not hearsay.

Following this Aristotelian advice, you will likewise do well to establish your good character and good will when you are not well known to your audience. Let us hope that when you come to the platform you bring a reputation for honesty and fair-mindedness. But in case there is any doubt about these matters you must deal with the problem directly, as in the examples just cited. For further discussion of this subject, see Chapter 15.

Have Your Supporting Facts and Arguments Ready

Contrary to what some believe, facts and sound arguments are highly important in changing opinions and moving persons to action. Many listeners, particularly those who are well educated, will immediately suspect either your intelligence or your motives, or both, if you do not back up your assertions with adequate support. As a result, they will dismiss you without a hearing. And they will be wise to do so. The skilled speaker strives to reinforce his motive appeals with logical support, and he will have difficulty separating the two.

Likewise the speaker who is motivated by honest thinking and a "realization of social responsibility" will be eager to base his presentation on careful research and thorough analysis.

[4] Charles H. Percy, "The Challenge We Face," delivered to the Investment Bankers Association of America, November 30, 1960; in *Vital Speeches of the Day*, January 15, 1961, **27**: 222–224.

[5] See Waldo W. Braden and Mary Louise Gehring, *Speech Practices: A Resource Book for the Student of Public Speaking*, Harper, 1958, p. 55.

Fill Your Talk with Specific Examples and Illustrations

One of the ways to make what you say vivid and impressive is to pack your talk full of specific material. To succeed, the persuader must capture your attention and hold it until he has carried you through his various steps to his appeal for action. Bruce Barton demonstrated the importance of illustrations in his speech "How Long Shall a Wife Live?" (see pp. 393–395). Russell Conwell used this principle in his famous lecture "Acres of Diamonds," which he delivered to more than 6000 audiences, and which we have referred to several times. As he moved from community to community, he picked his illustrations from the lives of those to whom he spoke. Many groups invited him to return to deliver the same speech year after year because they knew that what he said would be interesting, and appealing.

Make your proposal live in the imagination of your listeners. Instead of complicated chains of reason, emphasize your conclusion by illustrations. Give the listeners something they will remember.

Move From Areas of Agreement to Areas of Disagreement

Effective persuasion generally depends upon holding listeners' attention until the very final appeal. In discussing the effects of mass media, Joseph T. Klapper remarked that when listeners encounter persuasive communications they are likely to indulge in "self-protective exercises" of selective exposure, selective perception, and selective retention. When they encounter what they consider "unsympathetic material, they often seem not to perceive it, or to recast and interpret it to fit their existing views or to forget it more readily than they forget sympathetic material."[6] The persuasive speaker must always start in a conciliatory mood, building common ground and common understanding as he proceeds. In contrast to the informative speech, which is organized around a deductive pattern (see p. 362), in the persuasive speech it is often advantageous to follow an inductive order, in which the proposition is not revealed until near the end of the speech. The inductive order in a persuasive speech was discussed on pages 363–364.

[6] Joseph T. Klapper, *The Effects of Mass Communication*, Free Press, 1960, p. 19.

The foregoing principle is well illustrated in Patrick Henry's famous "liberty or death" oration, delivered in 1775. On the day of that much-quoted speech the Virginian faced many hostile colleagues; the vote promised to be exceedingly close. Consequently he started in a conciliatory tone: "No man thinks more highly than I do of the patriotism as well as abilities of the very worthy gentlemen who have just addressed the House. But different men often see the same subject in different lights; and therefore I hope that it will not be thought disrespectful to those gentlemen, if, entertaining as I do opinions of a character very opposite to theirs, I shall speak for my sentiments freely and without reserve." He then systematically showed that the American colonies had exhausted all remedies short of armed rebellion. He summarized his feelings thus: "Sir, we have done everything that could be done to avert the storm which is now coming on. We have petitioned, we have remonstrated, we have supplicated, we have prostrated ourselves before the throne. And have implored its interposition to arrest the tyrannical hands of the ministry and parliament."[7]

After moving step by step toward his solution, Patrick Henry declared his proposition in three short words near the end of his presentation: "We must fight." If he had reversed the order he probably would have been shouted down or at least would have lost the opportunity to present his entire argument.

We can illustrate this principle another way by using the subject of donating to the Red Cross, using the following four propositions which are arranged inductively:

1. Great disasters often leave thousands of persons in dire need of minimum essentials of food and clothing.
2. Anyone may encounter great disaster at some time in his life. [Almost no one would disagree with this argument.]
3. The Red Cross has a proved record of aiding persons in disaster areas efficiently and effectively.
4. Contribute five dollars to the Red Cross.

Each of these propositions prepares the way for the next one. Notice that the Red Cross is not mentioned until the speaker has established his need argument.

[7] Found in Wayland Maxfield Parrish, and Marie Hochmuth, *American Speeches*, Longmans, Green and Co., 1954, pp. 91–94.

Make Acceptance Easy for Your Listeners

A salesman will tell you that the most difficult and the most important step in a sales presentation is the final conversion of the listener—that is, getting him to sign the application or to reach in his pocket and pull out a five-dollar bill.

Have you noticed how magazines use the mails to attempt to persuade you to subscribe? The printed matter you receive is usually inviting and attractive, well-printed and richly illustrated. Little effort is needed to read the large print and look at the attractive pictures. Notice the attempt made to appeal to your motives—prestige, adventure, material possessions, and so on. But most important is the convenient card enclosed, stamped and ready to mail. All that is required of you is to sign your name and drop it in a mail box. In a few days the magazines start coming, but the bill arrives only after you have received an issue or two. The promoter has made it very simple and very easy for you to comply with his request.

Here is an example in which a student demonstrated this principle in a speech asking his classmates to contribute to CARE. He said:

What can we do? Let me tell you about CARE, C-A-R-E, Cooperative for American Remittances to Europe. CARE will deliver forty-nine pounds of foods to any designated person in most of the countries of Europe. This parcel contains 40,000 calories. Forty thousand calories, another number, but this time a large one. Food for twenty days of life, twenty days of life with a human diet. To these people, food as luxurious as an American Thanksgiving Dinner. CARE, this forty-nine pounds of food an immeasurable good will cost you only $10.

You may designate the individual you wish to receive the food, or the overseas official of CARE will see that it is received by a worthy person. This person will sign a receipt acknowledging the food, which is returned to you. In most cases the receipt is accompanied by a grateful letter.

For further information, write CARE, 50 Broad Street, New York 4, New York.

In conclusion, let me summarize briefly. There is little chance that France can successfully recover without outside aid. Shall this aid come from us, or from Communist Russia?

Second, when we consider the past, the bonds of friendship that unite, not just our governments, but more important, the people of our countries, it is clear that we must help those who are now at the great crossroads of history. Are the deeds of the French in our American Revolution and the symbol of the Statue of Liberty to be forgotten?

CARE offers us an easy way to repay our debts, and more, to show what is really in our hearts. Each package is a breath of freedom, and a bit of appreciation, a part of the Statue of Liberty going back across the ocean.

Write CARE, 50 Broad Street, New York 4, New York.[8]

Notice the ways in which the speaker made acceptance convenient for the listeners:

1. He made sure by mentioning the word CARE eight times that it was firmly fixed in the minds of his listeners.
2. He gave the listeners the specific address, repeating it twice to enable them to see if they had it correctly.
3. He did not request a large amount (ten dollars).
4. He reviewed his motive appeals by pulling them together in a summary.

EXTRINSIC MEANS OF PERSUASION

The means of persuasion considered thus far in this chapter may be thought of as *intrinsic* means, or means within the inventive power of the speaker. For their effectiveness they depend upon speaking skill and rhetorical insight. Now let us turn to the *extrinsic* means of persuasion which may aid in getting responses but which are outside the province of the speaker's art. Many of these devices are obviously of highly questionable ethical nature and are therefore to be censured. Alert citizens need to be able to recognize them and be constantly on guard against them.

Providing Surroundings Conducive to Persuasion

Listeners are more likely to remain attentive and interested when they are comfortable. Good seats, adequate ventilation and lighting, satisfactory acoustics, and a well-regulated public address system are real boons to the speaker. Equally important is minimizing dis-

---

[8] Charles Fellers, "A Citizens' Marshall Plan," delivered in a public speaking class at Louisiana State University in 1948.

tracting influences: unpleasant noises, a glaring spotlight, a crying baby, and inclement weather. The listener is not likely to discommode himself to listen to you, but he will listen if you make it worth his time and it does not require too much exertion on his part.

Physical Aids to Focusing Attention

The seating arrangements in lecture rooms or auditoriums are designed to focus attention on the speaker, to make it easy for the listener to look in his direction. However, there are many additional ways to direct attention to the speaker. He may wear a special uniform or robe which sets him apart from the others. A spotlight focused on the podium also helps. The soapbox street-corner orator is well aware of some of these means, and he climbs on a box in order to stand above his listeners. Mussolini had a fondness for appearing on balconies or high platforms from which he could look down on his cheering followers. Frequently a speaker surrounds himself with revered symbols: flags, crosses, flowers, or a picture of a saint or departed leader. Almost invariably you see a great picture of Lenin at Communist meetings.

Prearranged Seating or Grouping of Partisans

The carnival barker or street-corner peddler insists on listeners coming in close, urging them to crowd near in order to see and hear better. He knows that this strategy brings the sucker into a position where it is difficult for him to escape. The most susceptible, brought into close proximity, will soon respond and thereby influence others standing nearby.

In an auditorium the supporters may for the same reason be seated near the speaker in order to support what he says with cheers and applause. This enthusiasm may be sufficient to start a chain reaction among other listeners.

Using the Common Response Technique

In mass meetings and political rallies we have all observed the use of common response techniques—saluting, marching, cheering, handclapping, singing, praying, group reading, and the like. The persuader knows the advantage of stimulating these modes of conduct until he can get a signal response whenever he needs it. Actually he may train some of his listeners to respond to a sign—a gesture, a symbol, or some other device. The college cheerleader, too, capitalizes on such techniques.

During World War II Winston Churchill held up two fingers to signify V for victory. At mass meetings this signal always brought a cheer and surge of patriotic feelings. Hitler and Mussolini had their own unique salutes, and now De Gaulle and Castro have theirs.

An evangelist may train his listeners to say "amen" at vital moments in the sermon. When he senses a lack of responsiveness he simply calls, "Let's have another amen." Under the right conditions he may work his listeners to near-hysteria by keeping the common response going.

Such devices as these have served parties and cliques as means of spotting outsiders and unresponsive persons.

Using a Claque or Canned Applause

A persuader sometimes uses a claque and canned applause as a means of heightening the band-wagon effect or giving the impression that he is supported by large numbers. Radio, film, and television permit the utilization of these devices to great advantage because the listener or viewer has no way of checking on the honesty of the presentation. The persuader in such a situation can give emphasis to any idea he wishes by merely signaling for a demonstration or outburst of applause. Frequently at national nominating conventions on radio and television we witness staged demonstrations, which may include a band as well as sign-carrying marchers. Seemingly each candidate tries to have his demonstration be noisier and last longer than that of his opponent.

Associating the Persuader or His Cause with Prestige Personalities and Institutions

A speaker will sometimes attempt to increase his *ethos* by having prominent celebrities introduce him or appear with him on the platform. Often a politician will load the platform with prominent local personalities; local office seekers like to be seen in the company of a

United States senator or a governor. Politicians sometimes persuade a military hero or a sport star to travel with them on campaign trips. A Louisiana politician once employed Jack Dempsey to speak at his rallies. A prominent charity persuaded the Vice President of the United States to appear at its meetings. Automobile manufacturers would like to have the public associate their latest models with great football heroes or baseball stars. Many big TV shows are planned on this principle.

Keeping the Opposition Quiet and Submissive

The overzealous persuader never likes competition or debate, preferring to transmit his carefully planned message to his listeners without interruption, interference, or alteration. He therefore usually attempts to avoid questions, speeches from the floor, impromptu remarks, hisses, boos, and mass departures. He is likely to meet hecklers with ridicule, sarcasm, humor, and even character assassination. He attempts to maintain rigid discipline over his followers. Any one of them who dares question his authority may be reduced in rank, excommunicated, publically censured, ostracized, or even physically mutilated. Hitler, Stalin, and Franco applied these techniques. In fact anyone who dared challenge them was immediately pounced upon and pulled forcefully from their meetings.

QUESTIONS AND TOPICS FOR STUDY AND REVIEW

1. Differentiate among the following terms: argumentation, persuasion, conviction, propaganda, brainwashing.
2. Some authorities have argued that all persuasive speeches have action as a goal. What justification is there for this point of view?
3. Some authorities have argued that no distinction should be made between the informative and the persuasive speech. What justification is there for this point of view?
4. Under what circumstances is it possible to change opinion by means of the informative speech?
5. Under what circumstances is it possible to give understanding by means of a persuasive speech?
6. Many persons believe that persuasion and propaganda are unethical. Under what circumstances would they be unethical? Under what circumstances are they necessary?

7. Under what circumstances could a speaker, moved by a full realization of his social responsibility, use extreme methods of persuasion which might be considered unethical at another time?

8. What personality traits do you associate with the successful persuader?

9. What does the problem-solution organization have in common with Monroe's motivated sequence? (See Alan H. Monroe, *Principles and Types of Speech*, 5th ed., Scott, Foresman, 1962, chap. 16.)

10. What is meant by extrinsic means of persuasion? Can you think of other methods which should be listed in this section?

PROJECTS

1. *Impromptu Speaking Assignment.*   Your instructor will draw up a list of speaking topics from recent issues of a local newspaper or news magazine. He will prepare as many topic slips as there are students in the class and place them face down on a table. When your turn to speak comes, you are to go to the table, pick up three topics, select one, and replace the other two. You then are to discuss the topic you have drawn.

2. *Extemporaneous Impromptu Speaking Assignment.*
   a. *Selecting a subject for the unit.*   As a class select a general proposition similar to the intercollegiate debate question or some other broad subject such as capital punishment, national health insurance, or relations with the European Common Market. The topic should be worded in the form of a proposition and partitioned carefully.
   b. *Extemporaneous speaking phase.*   The class will be divided into groups of five or six; each group will be assigned a phase of the proposition and on an assigned day will conduct a symposium, with each member delivering a five-minute speech on some limited aspect. Following the formal speeches, the discussion will be opened to questions from the floor.
   c. *Impromptu speaking phase.*   After each group has presented its phase, the instructor (or a class committee) will prepare a list of topics for impromptu speaking. When your turn comes, your instructor will give you a topic to discuss. At the close of your speech you will be expected to answer questions from the floor.
   d. *Group evaluation.*   After each member of the class has delivered an impromptu speech, each will be asked to rank his classmates, listing them in order from the most effective to the least effective student in the two assignments. Ranks can be averaged by a class committee to determine final rating.

3. *Speaking Assignment.* Prepare an actuating speech. Plan your speech so that your classmates can give an overt response. Be sure to make acceptance easy for the listeners.
4. *Speech Practices.* Study carefully the advertisement found in *Speech Practices* (p. 142). Analyze the organization. Try to divide it into five steps: introduction, problem, solution, benefits and appeal. Study the slanted language. What kinds of words are associated with refugee problems?
5. *Speech Practices.* Analyze President Franklin D. Roosevelt's "War Message to Congress" (p. 146) in terms of introduction, problem, solution, benefits, and appeal. Which gets most attention? Why?

SPEECH MODELS FOR STUDY

Beveridge, Albert J., "The Star of Empire," in *Selected American Speeches,*[9] pp. 218–239.

Bryan, William Jennings, "The Cross of Gold," in *Selected American Speeches,* pp. 178–189.

Curtis, George William, "The Puritan Principle—Liberty Under the Law," in *American Speeches,* pp. 359–364.

Dinwoodie, S. David, "The Inner City—Our Shame" (student speech), in *The Speaker's Resource Book,* pp. 246–248.

Eaton, Lewis H., Jr., "Help Today for Health Tomorrow" (student speech), in *Speech Practices,* pp. 33–35.

Henry, Patrick, "Liberty or Death," in *American Public Addresses,* pp. 29–31, and in *American Speeches,* pp. 91–94.

Lincoln, Abraham, "The Cooper Union Address," in *Selected American Speeches,* pp. 137–155, and in *American Speeches,* pp. 284–304.

Lincoln, Abraham, "A House Divided," in *American Forum,* pp. 180–187.

MacArthur, Douglas, "Address to Congress," in *The Speaker's Resource Book,* pp. 273–280; excerpt included in *Speech Practices,* pp. 60–63.

Myers, Nancy Jeanne, "Moppet Manipulation" (student speech), in *The Speaker's Resource Book,* pp. 113–116.

Phillips, Wendell, "Toussaint L'Ouverture," in *American Speeches,* pp. 311–332.

Roosevelt, Franklin D., "A Plea For Neutrality," in *Selected American Speeches,* pp. 405–409.

Roosevelt, Franklin D., "War Message to Congress," in *Speech Practices,* pp. 146–147, in *American Speeches,* pp. 507–509, and in *American Public Addresses,* pp. 265–267.

[9] For full references to this and the following sources, see Supplementary Readings, pp. 132–133.

Washington, Booker T., "Atlanta Exposition Address," in *American Public Addresses*, pp. 189–192.

Wilson, Woodrow, "War Message," in *Selected American Speeches*, pp. 301–310, and in *American Speeches*, pp. 472–481.

Zimmermann, Ralph, "Mingled Blood" (student speech), in *The Speaker's Resource Book*, pp. 99–101.

SUPPLEMENTARY READINGS

Braden, Waldo W., and Earnest Brandenburg, *Oral Decision-Making*, Harper, 1955, chap. 23, "The Means of Persuasion."

Brembeck, Winston Lamont, and William Smiley Howell, *Persuasion: A Means of Social Control*, Prentice-Hall, 1952.

Brigance, William Norwood, *Speech: Its Techniques and Disciplines in a Free Society*, 2nd ed., Appleton-Century-Crofts, 1961, chap. 7, "The Architecture of Persuasion."

Bryant, Donald C., and Karl R. Wallace, *Fundamentals of Public Speaking*, 3rd ed., Appleton-Century-Crofts, 1960, part VI, "The Persuasive Speech." This section is composed of seven excellent chapters dealing with audience analysis, suggestion, analysis, and planning.

Gray, Giles Wilkeson, and Claude Merton Wise, *The Bases of Speech*, 3rd ed., Harper, 1959, chap. 1, "The Social Basis of Speech."

Thonssen, Lester, and A. Craig Baird, *Speech Criticism*, Ronald, 1948, chap. 11, "The Integrity of Ideas"; chap. 12, "Emotion in Speech"; chap. 13, "The Character of the Speaker."

21

The Stimulating Speech

The classical writers on public speaking divided public address into three types: deliberative speaking for the assembly, forensic speaking for the court, and ceremonial speaking for the festival, funeral, and display. For speeches of the third type the Greeks sought men who could deliver noble and elevated thoughts which would both honor and uplift. For example, in 431 B.C. the Athenians invited Pericles, a respected leader who was known as the "first of the Athenians," to speak at a ceremony in honor of those who had fallen in battle. On this occasion the great Greek whose name is applied to his age said among other things: "For the whole earth is the sepulcher of illustrious men; nor is it the inscription on the columns in their native land alone that shows their merit, but the memorial of them, better than all inscriptions, in every foreign nation, reposited more durably in universal remembrance than on their tombs."[1] This sentiment honored those who had passed on, provided a noble example for those present, and inspired those who were to come. The power of his address lay perhaps in the broad dimension he suggested for the deeds of those he memorialized. He stirred deep feelings of pride and respect in those who came to hear him, and they must have gone away with a deeper appreciation of Athenian ideals.

In their discussion of Daniel Webster and his great ceremonial speeches Howell and Hudson present an excellent analysis of the nature of stimulating or epideictic speaking:

> The persuasive end of such oratory, according to Aristotle, is to establish honor or shame; that is, the epideictic speaker persuades an audience that some man or action or institution is to be praised to be reviled. Yet such an orator as a rule has no heavy task of changing people's minds. Most American listeners already believe that the American Revolutionists deserve honor. The orator's task is rather to objectify those deserts and that honor (just as the deliberative orator objectifies the expediency of a proposed action), making them have palpable reality and weight. He is working for the most part with intangibles, and his success depends upon the truth and force of his imagination. He will draw word pictures; he will dramatize; he will elevate, enlarge, and dignify. Above all he will stir and create emotions, knowing that imaginations are released by emotional disturbance and then act to heighten the very emotion that has set them free.[2]

In our own day there are many occasions for speeches of praise or blame, or what we refer to in this chapter as speeches to stimulate: commencements, inaugurations, anniversaries, memorials, academy meetings. Contrary to what the speech of Pericles and this list suggest, the occasion for this type of speech need not always be lofty and grand. It may be a pep rally, a safety meeting, a Sunday morning church service—even a meeting of a class before an examination.

THE NATURE OF THE STIMULATING SPEECH

Many students asked to deliver a stimulating speech assume that they are expected to give a highly interesting or exciting speech—

[1] Ashley Thorndike, ed., *Modern Eloquence,* Modern Eloquence Corp., 1923, IX, 2–9.

[2] Wilbur Samuel Howell and Hoyt Hopewell Hudson, "Daniel Webster," in William Norwood Brigance, ed., *A History and Criticism of American Public Address,* McGraw-Hill, 1943, II, 665–733.

perhaps a *stimulating* informative or *stimulating* persuasive speech. As we have suggested earlier (see Chapter 13), we think of a stimulating speech as a specific type in which the speaker attempts to strengthen or intensify existing attitudes or opinions; he seeks to cement loyalties and to develop appreciation for a person, a group or society, an ideal, an institution, or an event. Brembeck and Howell suggest that this type of speech "has to do with ideals, appreciation, duties, sentiments, aspirations, desires, affections, moods, courage, endurance, faith, loyalty, and other values that make for the enduring satisfactions of life."[3]

The audience for the stimulating speech is largely a partisan one; that is, the speaker and listeners are in general agreement on the proposition.

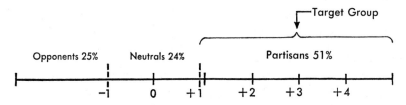

Why does the speaker decide to deliver this kind of speech? He or those in charge of the occasion may find four situations which would seem to make it appropriate.

1. The listeners may not have sufficient view of the subject to appreciate it.
2. The listeners may not demonstrate their support with sufficient overt manifestation.
3. The listeners may not realize the full meaning and significance of the occasion.
4. The listeners may not be completing a project with sufficient vigor.

The speaker may seek either a covert or an overt response. On the one hand he may want only reverence, devotion, faith, respect, loyalty, or admiration. On the other he may seek to stir cheering, shouting, applauding, praying, or even marching or ceremonial dancing.

[3] Winston Lamont Brembeck and William Smiley Howell, *Persuasion: A Means of Social Control*, Prentice-Hall, 1952, p. 297.

Let us illustrate. On Sunday morning the minister may preach on the proposition "God is good," knowing full well that no faithful parishioner disagrees. He merely hopes to re-emphasize a basic tenet in the creed and to stimulate piety and worshipfulness.

A factory foreman develops the proposition "Safety pays" at a meeting of his section. Why? Clearly, no workman will deliberately risk a maiming accident. But the foreman may fear that his men are taking safety precautions as a matter of routine and hopes to stir them to think about their procedures and to become more sensitive about carelessness.

Theodore Roosevelt once spoke to a Republican club on "The Strenuous Life." What did he seek to do? In his own words, "I wish to preach not the doctrine of ignoble ease but the doctrine of the strenuous life; the life of toil and effort; of labor and strife; to preach that highest form of success which comes not to the man who desires mere easy peace but to the man who does not shrink from danger, from hardship, or from bitter toil, and who out of these wins the splendid ultimate triumph."[4]

Notice how Roosevelt contrasts "ignoble ease" (the condition he finds) with "the strenuous life" (what he wants) and "the man who desires mere easy peace" with "the man who does not shrink from danger, from hardship, or from bitter toil." In other words, he suggests an intensification of effort in order to win "the splendid ultimate triumph" (the goal).

The central thought of a stimulating speech is often an assertive or recommending proposition. Below are some sentences which could be developed into excellent talks of this kind.

1. George Washington deserves to be called "the father of his country."
2. Theodore Roosevelt was a rugged individualist in the highest sense.
3. Al Smith was justly called "the happy warrior."
4. The landing of the Pilgrims was a significant event in world history.
5. Woodrow Wilson merits emulation as a great American.
6. We must rededicate our lives to the achievement of our objectives.
7. The erection of this monument is a fitting tribute to our war dead.
8. The history class is deeply indebted to Professor Jones.
9. My father stood for high ideals.

[4] Theodore Roosevelt, "The Strenuous Life," delivered at Appomattox Day Celebration of the Hamilton Club, Chicago, Illinois, April 10, 1899; in Thorndike, *op. cit.*, VII, 334.

10. The spirit of the pioneer must be preserved.
11. LSU must win tomorrow.
12. Let us "highly resolve that these dead shall not have died in vain."
13. Serious study pays off.
14. Teaching is a noble profession.
15. Esso Refinery must exceed its 1962 safety record.

The proposition which expresses thought on which the speaker and listeners agree is often worded in figurative language and in many cases has an epigrammatic quality. For example, Kenneth I. Brown built a speech around the sentence "Be men and women with antennae,"* meaning that one should be sensitive to the needs of others.[5] Likewise Charles L. Anspach captured the imagination of a college audience with the proposition, "Do not walk too long alone."[6] Bishop G. Bromley Oxnam stirred an international audience of church leaders with the proposition "We intend to stay together,"[7] which he repeated ten times in his short speech.

SPEECHES OF PRAISE

The Eulogy

A eulogy is a speech commending the character and actions of a deceased person, a hero, or some famous person of another age or another country. It may be long or short, depending on the occasion. Funeral orations usually fall under the classification of a eulogy.

Aristotle said, "The eulogist draws his materials from the noble deeds, actual or reputed, of the man he is praising."[8] The speaker must show that his subject, by his character and actions, demonstrated that he possessed the virtues esteemed by the society of which the audience is a part. He draws his evidence from such sources as (1) traits of character, (2) aspirations and goals, (3)

[5] Kenneth I. Brown, "Men and Women with Antennae," in Waldo W. Braden and Mary Louise Gehring, *Speech Practices: A Resource Book for the Student of Public Speaking,* Harper, 1958, pp. 132–135.

[6] Charles L. Anspach, "He Walked Too Long Alone," delivered at the "Annual Senior Swingout," Central Michigan University, May 23, 1956; in *Vital Speeches of the Day,* July 15, 1956, **22:** 599–601.

[7] In A. Craig Baird, ed., *Representative American Speeches, 1954–1955,* H. W. Wilson, 1955, pp. 145–152.

[8] Lane Cooper, *The Rhetoric of Aristotle,* Appleton-Century-Crofts, 1932, p. 156.

outstanding accomplishments, and (4) influences on men and the times.

The speech of praise cannot be merely a biographical summary or an enumeration of dates, events, and places. Indeed a prolonged recitation of dates, number of children, years of schooling, and membership in professional societies is likely to put almost any audience to sleep. A eulogy which consists entirely of a chronological account of a man's life is in fact no eulogy at all. Too often such a speech is no more than a factual report, and falls far short of being a speech of praise. The eulogist should strive to make his subject unique in character and stature.

The inexperienced speaker should find the following suggestions helpful in preparing a eulogy.

Ordinarily, since the speaker wishes to praise his subject, he will use a central thought similar to either of the following: "——— was worthy of praise," or "——— was a great man, worthy of emulation." These topic sentences may be expressed in countless different ways and in more polished language, but essentially they express the theme of most eulogies.

The subpoints used to develop the central theme will be statements about the subject's traits, virtues, or accomplishments. They may be worded somewhat as follows:

1. He was brave.
2. He was kind.
3. He was sincere.
4. He was generous.

Or, if the speaker wishes to use comparisons to develop his central thought, the subpoints might read:

1. He was more intelligent than ———.
2. He was more generous than ———.
3. He was more daring than ———.

For supporting material the speaker searches his subject's life for episodes that illustrate the subpoints. In other words, the eulogy will be composed of a central theme or thought, statements concerning the man's traits, and illustrations to support each statement. Below is a skeleton outline of a eulogy.

Theodore Roosevelt was a great man, for

I. He was a brave soldier.

II. He was an excellent scholar.

III. He was a great statesman.

The Commendation

The commendation is a speech that strives to show the affection, the admiration, or the respect of a group for a living person. Such speeches grow out of situations like these: a worker achieves a new production record; a businessman is recognized for his work in civic improvement; a local citizen demonstrates great valor; the high-school football coach has a winning team. Ordinarily the speaker reviews in some detail the accomplishments and achievements of the recipient of the honor in the presence of many of his colleagues. The preparation is much the same as for the eulogy. The commendation is somewhat like the speech of presentation, which is discussed in the next chapter.

The Commemorative Speech

The speech of commemoration is a stimulating speech which celebrates an important or significant day or event. Centennials, bicentennials, the Fourth of July, Labor Day, Armistice Day, Memorial Day, and the like frequently call for commemorative speaking. The laying of a cornerstone, the completion of a building, or the erection of a monument may also inspire this type of speech. At both the laying of the cornerstone of the Bunker Hill Monument and its dedication Daniel Webster gave commemorative speeches.

The speech of commemoration is similar in method and substance to other types of inspirational talk.

1. The central theme ordinarily stresses the importance of the day or the event.

2. The speaker works to arouse feelings of loyalty, pride, and patriotism. Webster, in his "Plymouth Oration," expressed the purpose of his speech in these words:

We have come to this Rock [Plymouth], to record here our homage for our Pilgrim Fathers; our sympathy in their suffering; our gratitude for their labors; our admiration of their virtues; our veneration for their piety;

and our attachment to those principles of civil and religious liberty, for
which they encountered the dangers of the ocean, the storms of heaven
. . . to enjoy and to establish.

His key words here—homage, sympathy, gratitude, admiration,
veneration, and attachment—are the sentiments which most talks of
this type attempt to arouse.

3. The supporting materials may be of various types, but the historical example and the analogy or comparison find frequent use.
In the "Plymouth Oration," for example, Webster developed the
importance of the New England colonies by comparing them with
the colonies of Greece and Rome and those in Asia and the West
Indies. Naturally he stressed how the Pilgrims were far superior
to other colonists.

SPEECHES OF GOOD WILL

Each year large corporations spend millions of dollars in quest of
an intangible something in the public attitude which is called good
will. Keeping their names and trademarks before the public in a
favorable light and maintaining happy relations with actual and
potential customers are significant phases of this campaign. Great
efforts are made to give the public information that casts a favorable
light on the company's activities. High-powered public relations
experts are employed to devise new ways to build up good will.
Complaints are answered promptly. "The customer is always right."

In arousing good will the company builds its reputation, that is,
the favorable attitude of the friends it already has; it seeks further
to create a similar attitude among as many others as possible. Many
advertisements do not even suggest that the reader buy the product
described or become a customer of the company. This is what is
called "institutional" advertising. The speech of good will, as an
aspect of such a campaign, has for its purpose therefore to *win
friends*—nothing more, at least in organization and apparent objective.

In the speech of good will the speaker attempts to make friends
for a movement, an organization, a business firm, or even a person.
Every year thousands of talks are presented in behalf of the Boy
Scouts, the Girl Scouts, the YMCA, the YWCA, the Red Cross, the

Salvation Army, the National Foundation, the Community Chest, the Cancer Fund, blood banks, and savings bonds. These talks are usually delivered in the form of informative talks, and from one point of view that is just what they are: the immediate goal of the speaker is to elicit understanding, to add to the knowledge of the listeners. But the ultimate goal, which is closely connected with persuasion, remains unexpressed. Such speeches are related to persuasion in the sense that, by giving information and establishing attitudes, their ultimate aim is overt response.

So long as the information presented is true to fact and the ultimate purpose is neither to conceal nor to mislead, nothing in this type of speech is inherently unethical.

The formula of the good-will speech is something like this: information concerning worthy activities or worthwhile products makes friends; these friends will make other friends; as a result of acquiring strong friendships, contributions of effort and money may be expected in the future, or all these friends will buy the things they need when the need arises from the organization that has created the good will for itself.

The plan of the good-will talk is often developed around the following pattern:

1. The introduction relates the organization or cause to the audience.
2. The background of the organization or campaign is traced.
3. The present needs are mentioned.
4. The results of the organization's efforts or of the campaign are related to the self-interest of the audience or to their interest in the well-being of others.
5. An appeal is made for sympathy and understanding.

ESSENTIAL STEPS IN THE STIMULATING SPEECH

Study Carefully the Occasion and the Listeners

The occasion is a most significant aspect of the stimulating speech. Inaugurations, commencements, conventions, funerals, holidays, and religious festivals have unique requirements to which the speaker is obliged to conform. In the traditions, customs, precedents, and rituals involved as well as the inspiring event or person to be celebrated, the speaker can usually discover excellent sources of material and common grounds and sentiments to be developed. The planning committee for a given event may structure the occasion to make the speech the culmination of the entire celebration. In this case the speaker must live up to the expectations of the program planners and prepare to meet the listeners in a spirit consistent with the other events on the agenda.

He must of course be sensitive to how the time and place affect his listeners. Oftentimes he can be assured of attention, even if passive, because the listeners find the reason for their presence in the nature of the celebration. They may even regard him as their representative, their voice, and they want him to say eloquently what they would like to say if they had the oral ability. They participate vicariously in the act of speaking, feeling pride in the elevated remarks of the speaker.

The speaker will do well to study the ways in which his listeners are homogeneous (see pp. 140–141), how well informed they are about the cause or event to be memorialized, and the extent to which they regard him as their representative. He will usually find that his task centers around the intensification of favorable attitudes.

Frame a Proposition on Which There Is General Agreement

The framing of the proposition of the stimulating speech is much the same as that for the convincing or actuating speech (see pp. 356–358), though the speaker may of course attempt a wording which gives distinction to his central thought. He sometimes chooses figurative language or an epigram or maxim, both of which are stimulating in nature, developed around a verse of Scripture—for example, "Love . . . believes all things."[9]

Blend the Outline into the Development

In the informative talk, as we have seen, speech outlines are indicated by the use of previews, signposts, and obvious transitions. Almost the opposite is true of the stimulating speech, where the

---

[9] See Eugene Carson Blake, "Good Faith," sermon, in A. Craig Baird, ed., *Representative American Speeches, 1957–1958,* H. W. Wilson, 1958, pp. 168–183.

speaker usually attempts to unfold his development with finesse and subtlety. In his preparation he works out a careful outline, but in the development of his speech he keeps it well concealed, moving toward his goal without stressing logical sequences or interrelations of premises and subpoints. He hopes for an emotional response rather than an intellectual one.

Keep the Dominant Theme Clearly Before the Listeners

In delivering a stimulating speech the speaker depends to a large measure upon the emergence of his proposition or theme, that key thought he wishes to reinforce and energize. Restatement of the theme will usually accomplish this purpose. As James Winans observed, "Wise restatement is not 'idle repetition.' "[10] The speaker can give variety to this device by phrasing his central thought in different ways. For example, he can use figurative language or even a quotation to express it. Kenneth I. Brown used this technique in his speech "Men and Women with Antennae." He did not state bluntly his proposition that one should be sensitive to the needs of others, but worded this thought indirectly: "Be men and women with antennae." When he wanted to restate it he quoted John Donne, "No man is an island, neither can he live within an all-inclusive government of one," and repeated the idea in two other forms: "Love is giving of self to another's need," and "There is a surging demand today for nations to be nations with antennae."[11] Restating the idea in new forms gives it added importance.

Select Supporting Materials Which Amplify Your Proposition

Because the speaker and listeners are in essential agreement on the proposition, proof is unnecessary. What is important is to find means to magnify the thoughts or, as Aristotle put it, "to invest them with magnitude and beauty."[12] We discussed this subject of amplification in Chapter 17. These principles apply also to the stimulating talk. Speakers make use of epigrams, proverbs, maxims, vivid examples, figurative analogies, and quotations from revered authorities.

[10] James A. Winans, *Speech-Making*, Appleton-Century-Crofts, 1938, p. 192.
[11] See Braden and Gehring, *op. cit.*, pp. 132–135.
[12] Cooper, *op. cit.*, p. 54.

Many of these principles are illustrated in the passage quoted here from Wendell Phillips's famous eulogy of Toussaint L'Ouverture, the Negro general of Haiti. Phillips elevated, enlarged, and dignified his character by comparing him with Cromwell, Napoleon, and Washington. The following paragraph is typical of his treatment.

You remember Macaulay says, comparing Cromwell with Napoleon, that Cromwell showed the greater military genius, if we consider that he never saw an army till he was forty; . . . Napoleon at the age of twenty-seven was placed at the head of the best troops Europe ever saw. They were both successful; but, says Macaulay, with such disadvantages, the Englishman showed the greater genius. Whether you allow the inference or not, you will at least grant that it is a fair mode of measurement. Apply it to Toussaint. Cromwell never saw an army till he was forty; this man never saw a soldier till he was fifty. Cromwell manufactured his own army—out of what? Englishmen—the best blood in Europe. Out of the middle class of Englishmen,—the best blood of the island. And with it he conquered what? Englishmen,—their equals. This man manufactured his army out of what? Out of what you call the despicable race of negroes, debased, demoralized by two hundred years of slavery, one hundred thousand of them imported into the island within four years, unable to speak a dialect intelligible even to each other. Yet out of this mixed, and, as you say, despicable mass, he forged a thunderbolt and hurled it at what? At the proudest blood in Europe, the Spaniard, and sent him home conquered [cheers]; at the most warlike blood in Europe, the French, and put them under his feet; at the pluckiest blood in Europe, the English, and they skulked home to Jamaica. [Applause] Now if Cromwell was a general, at least this man was a soldier. I know it was a small territory; it was not as large as that Attica, which, with Athens for a capital, has filled the earth with its fame for two thousand years. We measure genius by quality, not by quantity.[13]

Strive for an Emotional Response

As we have already noted, the stimulating speech is emotional and not intellectual in nature. The very occasion is one which stirs loyalty, patriotism, reverence, respect, admiration, and devotion. The listeners come because they want and expect to have their

[13] Wendell Phillips, *Speeches, Lectures and Letters,* Lee and Shepard, 1863, pp. 468–494.

deeper feelings stirred. They may even want to have the opportunity to shed tears and express themselves in other overt ways. In a sense they delight in such an emotional experience.

In order to achieve these objectives, the speaker must take advantage of the old and the new. Obviously he wants to utilize the old: old customs, old stereotypes, old heroes, old loyalties, cherished memories. He gives due recognition to revered symbols: flags, crosses, tokens, and emblems. But he must also utilize the new; that is, he must express his ideas in a fresh form, he must give new interpretations to the old and represent its influence in new relationships. The listeners must be made to think of the old in a new way.

Polish the Language

Stimulating speeches are often more literary and more polished than other types of public address. The speaker may have in mind to reach far beyond his immediate audience, to those who will later read his speech. In such cases he has the same goal as a writer—permanance and beauty. Therefore, he devotes much of his effort to the rhetorical canons of style. He seeks to be vivid and impressive (see Chapters 26 and 27). He carefully constructs his sentences and paragraphs to achieve a pleasant, harmonious flow, sometimes rhythmical and even poetical. He uses parallel structure and repetition of thought patterns frequently. He makes his language directive, highly figurative, and of course emotionally loaded. The style should be "exact and finished, capable of minute and delicate touches, expressive of all the finer shades of feeling."[14]

Deliver the Speech with Dignity and Restraint

Beautiful language means little in a speech if the delivery is not appropriate. Often a good stimulating speech becomes dull because the speaker reads it, with little attempt to establish *rapport* or speak directly to his listeners. With head down and eyes glued to his manuscript he drones away—and his listeners drift away and even sleep.

The stimulating speaker must make sure that his mien and manner fit the ceremonial requirements of the day. In dress and ap-

[14] J. W. H. Atkins, *Literary Criticism in Antiquity*, Smith, 1961, I, 148.

proach he must be consistent with the character of the occasion, and he must speak eloquently and impressively.

QUESTIONS AND TOPICS FOR STUDY AND REVIEW

1. Prepare a list of some specific occasions at which stimulating speeches were delivered in your home community.
2. Under what circumstances might a stimulating talk become a convincing or actuating talk?
3. "A eulogy which consists entirely of a chronological account of a man's life is in fact no eulogy at all." Consider this statement carefully and support or refute it. As evidence you may wish to cite several speeches.
4. How do the eulogy and commendation differ from other types of stimulating speeches?
5. What is a good-will speech? On what kinds of occasions would it be delivered? In what ways is it like an informative speech? What distinguishing characteristic makes it diffeernt from the informative speech?
6. The outline of a stimulating speech is often concealed. Why is this advisable?
7. Name some famous stimulating speeches and give the occasions at which they were delivered. Consult an anthology such as *Modern Eloquence*.
8. "Fourth of July oratory" is now a derogatory phrase. To what characteristics does this phrase refer? Why have negative attitudes developed with reference to speaking on the Fourth of July?
9. The style of many ceremonial speeches is often more polished than that of other types. How do you explain this?

PROJECTS

1. *Speaking Assignment.* Prepare a stimulating speech. If possible, speak upon a subject of current interest to the class.
2. *Speaking Assignment.* Deliver a eulogy on some great American, using a topical arrangement. In other words, do not just repeat the events of the man's life in chronological order, but attempt to discuss his great traits of character.
3. *Speaking Assignment.* Deliver a brief eulogy on some person you have known personally.
4. *Speaking Assignment.* Deliver a short commemorative speech that

would befit the celebration of some national holiday or an anniversary important in the life of your university or local community.

5. *Speech Practices.* Analyze "Men and Women with Antennae," found in *Speech Practices*, pp. 132–135. To what extent does the speaker make use of the steps suggested on pages 387–392?

6. *Research Assignment.* Make a comparative study of several eulogies of the same man. Consider structure, content, and language. Your best source will probably be the *Congressional Record*. Check the index of the session under such headings as "Eulogies," "Memorial Services," or the name of the deceased congressman or other person. You will find numerous eulogies of Lincoln in the various collections of speeches.

7. *Speech Analysis.* Bring to class six or eight display advertisements from popular magazines which are designed solely to create good will. Make a talk showing how the copywriter has adapted the principles of the good-will speech to the writing of the advertisements.

8. *Speech Analysis.* In the following speech, analyze Bruce Barton's attempts to reinforce the attitudes of his listeners. Remember that he was speaking to an audience made up of persons who were already well sold on their jobs, hoping to make them even more enthusiastic.

How Long Should a Wife Live?

My Friends: My subject today is, "How Long Should a Wife Live?" My remarks will be brief and informal, and before I reach the end I will refer to the title and answer the question which it raises.

I am emboldened to refer to the ladies because I have been given the privilege of knowing, in advance, something of the wonderful message which Mrs. Sherman, President of the General Federation of Women's Clubs, is to deliver to you tomorrow regarding a nation-wide survey of home conditions. What a vision is spread out before us by the plan which she will outline! If *every* home in the United States were as well equipped with household conveniences as the *best* home, what a difference it would make in the lives of American women! What a difference in their children's lives!

Some years ago there was a celebration in Boston in honor of the landing of the Pilgrim Fathers. After several very laudatory speeches had been made by men a bright and vivacious woman was called on. Said she:

"I am tired of hearing so many praises of the Pilgrim Fathers. I want to say a word about the Pilgrim Mothers. They had to endure all that the Pilgrim Fathers endured, and they had to endure the Pilgrim Fathers besides."

Do you know what happened to the Pilgrim Mothers, my friends? I will tell you. They died. They died young. It took two or three of them to bring up one family. The fathers were tough and lived long, but work and hardship made short work of the wives. Listen a minute:

Of the men who graduated from Yale between 1701 and 1745, 418 became husbands. What happened to their wives?

> 33 wives died before they were 25 years old
> 55 died before they were 35 years old
> 59 died before they were 45 years old

Those 418 husbands lost 147 wives before full middle age.

Harvard wives fared no better. Take the Harvard class of 1671 as typical. It had eleven graduates, of whom one died a bachelor at the age of twenty-four. Of the remaining ten

> 4 were married twice
> 2 were married three times

For ten husbands, therefore, there were eighteen wives.

It has been truly said that you can measure the height of any civilization by the plane upon which its women live. Measured by that standard, we have made great progress in the United States, but we have not made enough. An electric motor which runs a washing machine or a vacuum cleaner works for three or five cents an hour. There are still millions of women doing this work which motors can do; selling their lives at *coolie* wages of three cents an hour, having to neglect the highest work entrusted to human beings, the work of motherhood.

Some day you gentlemen expect to have every home in the United States electrified. My friends, why should you wait until *some day*? Why don't you do it immediately, next year, within the next twelve months? Does that seem impossible? I tell you that I believe it would be possible, by the right sort of concerted advertising, to arouse such a sentiment in the minds of the women of this country that *every* woman would realize that it is beneath the dignity of human life for her to work for three cents an hour.

The time in the life of a child when a mother can exert her influence is terribly brief. "Give me a child until he is seven years old," a great philosopher said, "and I care not who has him afterwards." Seven years in which to mold character; seven short, fleeting years! What a tragedy that a single moment of these years should be wasted in work which an electric machine can do.

It is a thrilling subject. It opens a whole new world of opportunity to us; it gives us a new interest, a new enthusiasm. Every day that we lose in this business of electrifying homes costs the nation in its richest wealth—the training of children, the lives and happiness of mothers. The title of this speech is, "How Long Should a Wife Live?" The answer, in the old days, was "Not very long." The homes of those days had two or three mothers and no motors. The home of the future will lay all of its tiresome, routine burdens on the shoulders of electrical machines, freeing mothers for their real work, which is motherhood. The mothers of the future will live to a good old age and keep their youth and good looks to the end.[15]

SPEECH MODELS FOR STUDY

Brown, Kenneth I., "Men and Women with Antennae," in *Speech Practices*,[16] pp. 132–135.

Carleton, William C., "Effective Speech in a Democracy," in *The Speaker's Resource Book*, pp. 5–12.

Churchill, Winston, "To the French People," in *Speech Practices*, pp. 65–66.

Ingersoll, Robert G., "At a Child's Grave," in *American Speeches*, pp. 447–448.

Ingersoll, Robert G., "At His Brother's Grave," in *American Public Addresses*, pp. 177–179.

Kennedy, John F., "Inaugural Address," in *The Speaker's Resource Book*, pp. 256–259.

Lincoln, Abraham, "Gettysburg Address," in *American Public Addresses*, pp. 114–115, and in *American Speeches*, pp. 306–307. See copy of manuscript in *Speech Practices*, pp. 44–45.

Lincoln, Abraham, "First Inaugural Address," in *American Public Addresses*, pp. 107–113.

Lincoln, Abraham, "Second Inaugural Address," in *American Speeches*, pp. 308–310, and in *American Public Addresses*, pp. 116–117.

Pericles, "Funeral Oration," in *The Speaker's Resource Book*, pp. 216–220.

Roosevelt, Franklin D., "First Inaugural Address," in *American Speeches*, pp. 501–506, and in *American Public Address*, pp. 260–264.

Stevenson, Adlai, "The City—A Cause for Statesmanship," in *The Speaker's Resource Book*, pp. 250–255.

[15] Bruce Barton, "How Long Should a Wife Live?" delivered at the Forty-Eighth Convention of the National Electric Light Association, San Francisco, June 18, 1925; James M. O'Neill and Floyd K. Riley, eds., *Contemporary Speeches*, Century, 1930, pp. 255–257.

[16] For full references to this and the following sources, see Supplementary Readings, pp. 132–133.

SUPPLEMENTARY READINGS

McBurney, James H., and Ernest J. Wrage, *The Art of Good Speaking,* Prentice-Hall, 1953, chap. 16, "The Methods of Evocation."

Monroe, Alan H., *Principles and Types of Speech,* 5th ed., Scott, Foresman, 1962, chap. 21, "The Speech To Stimulate."

Oliver, Robert T., *The Psychology of Persuasive Speech,* 2nd ed., Longmans, Green, 1957, chap. 20, "The Speech To Stimulate."

Oliver, Robert T., and Rupert L. Cortright, *Effective Speech,* 4th ed., Holt, Rinehart & Winston, 1961, chap. 21, "The Speech To Inspire."

22

Other Types of Speeches

A few years ago a prominent surgeon made a hurried call upon a speech teacher friend with an urgent request for some assistance. As head surgeon at a local Catholic hospital he had been asked by a group of his colleagues to present a gift to the Mother Superior. Although he had the knowledge, skill, and control to perform several delicate and difficult operations daily, even before a number of interns, he was terrified at the thought of standing before a group of listeners and making a five-minute talk. "How do you make a speech of presentation?" he asked. To tell him just to utter "what was in his heart" was not enough. He wanted to be told exactly what was appropriate for such an occasion and how to go about preparing a suitable speech.

397

Another well-known physician would not even go that far. He had been asked to make a short talk to a class of graduating nurses, but would not trust himself to speak at all without a carefully prepared manuscript—and he had someone else write the speech for him!

Actually, the occasional speech is simple; it does not require great oratory, though the special situation may at times bring forth speaking of a high degree of eloquence. Like any other speech, however, it can present difficulties for those who are not familiar with it. This chapter is dedicated to those physicians and surgeons who allowed a simple speech to worry them, and to the many other people who, like them, find themselves selected to represent special groups on special occasions or who are thrust into situations calling for the simple expression of a genuine sentiment.

You too will need now and then to know what is appropriate for speeches like the ones the physician and the surgeon were asked to give. You will probably have the opportunity to present talks which find their cause for being in some aspect of the occasion: a situation arises which demands a speech of a special type—in other words, an occasional speech.

The extent of this type of speaking is suggested by the following outline, which is by no means exhaustive:

1. Speeches of courtesy
   a. Introductions
   b. Welcomes
   c. Responses
   d. Presentations
   e. Acceptances
   f. Farewells
2. Speeches of entertainment

SPEECHES OF COURTESY

Ceremonial occasions usually call for speeches of courtesy. You may be asked to introduce a speaker or guest, to extend a welcome to newcomers, or to present a gift or an award to someone. On the other hand, if you are the recipient of an award or honor, you will usually be expected to reply with similar acts of courtesy: a speech of welcome usually calls for a response, and the receipt of an honor or a gift may necessitate in turn a speech of acceptance. If you are leaving a group, you may be moved by a desire to express your regrets in a speech of farewell. On some of these occasions you may act as a spokesman for a group, or you may act for yourself. When you represent a group you will utter those sentiments which express the common feelings of the members of the organization. When you speak for yourself you will express the sentiments and emotions which you feel most deeply at the time.

In general, speeches of courtesy have in common five character-istics.

1. They are usually short. Verboseness in speeches of this type is a sign of insincerity and vain display. Seldom should these speeches take more than five minutes to deliver.

2. They are streamlined and have their own patterns of organiza-tion. Attention and interest are rarely a problem. In the development, subpoints are blended together and may be difficult to identify. The summary-appeal conclusion is both unnecessary and inappropriate. Every effort should be made to fuse the speech into a unified whole, expressive of some deep and fitting sentiment.

3. These speeches usually have one of three goals: to entertain, to inform, or to stimulate. They rarely if ever attempt to convince or actuate.

4. They are sincere and genuine in tone. Language and delivery should give the impression of modesty and genuineness. High-flown language and a grand manner which attract attention to themselves and distract attention from the occasion are highly inappropriate, as in all other types of public address.

5. They are normally pleasant in mood. They need not be sober or solemn; in fact, well-chosen humor is often considered quite re-freshing and fitting, especially if it creates an atmosphere of good cheer and good fellowship.

The Speech of Introduction

Of all the speeches of courtesy the speech of introduction is prob-ably the most common; it is also probably the one that is most often poorly done. One authority epitomizes the perfect introduction in a single clause: ". . . one that puts the audience in an expectant state of mind."[1] That is, the introduction must make the audience expectant with reference to the speaker being introduced and to his speech. By his few remarks the introducer should make the audience receptive, establish why the speaker is qualified to speak on the subject, focus attention on the subject, and impress the audience with the importance of paying close attention. He seeks, in other words, to secure for the speaker a favorable hearing.

In preparing the introductory speech, remember four simple rules.

1. *Subordinate your own speech to the main speech.* Like the best man or the maid of honor at a wedding, you must help make the occasion a success. In no way should you compete with the speaker. The chairman, or whoever does the introducing, should be seen, but should be heard no more than is absolutely necessary.

2. *Prepare your introduction carefully.* Before you start your preparation gather such information as the following: the nature of the meeting, the duties expected of you, and as much significant data on the speaker as possible. Your remarks should be thought out carefully and rehearsed. However, if at all possible, speak extemporaneously, without notes. The memorized introduction usually sounds stilted and mechanical.

3. *Be brief.* Most authorities agree that one minute, or 100 to 150 words, is enough for any speech of introduction. When you exceed such limits you are on precarious ground, since it is easily possible to ramble on indefinitely. Probably the most famous of all speeches of introduction is that in which Dean Shailer Mathews, of the University of Chicago Divinity School, introduced Woodrow Wilson:

LADIES AND GENTLEMEN: THE PRESIDENT.[2]

4. *Order your introduction as follows:*

a. Greet your audience.

b. Give whatever biographical data is necessary to identify the speaker and to make him interesting as a person. These data may include his place of residence, educational and professional background, present business or profession, and his connection with the present group or with the subject of his talk.

c. Hold any mention of the speaker's name or subject until the end in order that you may present it as a climax.

---

[1] G. Lynn Sumner, *We Have With Us Tonight*, Harper, 1941, p. 56.
[2] In James Milton O'Neill, ed., *Classified Models of Speech Composition*, Century, 1921, p. 671.

If the audience is already familiar with many of these data, there is no need to use up the time of the speaker in reviewing them. In the speech just cited, nothing that Dean Mathews could have said would have added to the audience's knowledge of President Wilson.

The introductions given below are excellent examples of this type of speech. In the first, Sam Rayburn, who during his long service as Speaker of the House had occasion to introduce many famous personages, presented Charles de Gaulle:

> Members of the Congress, this for us, the representatives of the people of the United States of America, is a proud and historic occasion. We welcome into this Chamber today the representative of a great, a proud, and a free people, and a people who will remain free as long as they have the leadership of this great man.
>
> Consequently, I deem it a proud privilege and distinguished honor to be able to present to you the President of the Republic of France.[3]

Notice that in paying eloquent tribute to France as well as to De Gaulle, Rayburn uttered less than 100 words and used language free of "honey-dripping superlatives."

Lewis W. Douglas, former Ambassador to Great Britain and president of the Academy of Political Science, introduced Mr. Abba Eban, Ambassador from Israel, to a scholarly group:

> Our next guest is a very distinguished man indeed. He first saw the light of day in Cape Town, where the sun rises and sets not as it does north of the Equator. He is a graduate of Cambridge University. He was a member of the staff at Queens College, at Cambridge University.
>
> All of you have perhaps seen "My Fair Lady." If you have not, I commend it to you. I am not giving an advertisement for this particular musical comedy, but there is a line that Rex Harrison recites, "O, why can't the English learn how to speak?" Well, our next guest is a great example of how the English language should be spoken. He speaks it fluently. He has been a distinguished servant of his country. He has served the world well, and we, the members of the Academy, are most grateful to you, Your Excellency, Ambassador Eban, for appearing tonight and for your willingness to address us and to talk with us about the elements of peace in the Middle East.[4]

The chairman or person who introduces a speaker may find that he has other duties and responsibilities. Whenever you are called on

---

[3] *Congressional Record*, April 25, 1960, **106**: 8643.
[4] *Proceedings of the Academy of Political Science*, May 26, 1957, **26**: 304.

to serve in such a capacity, consult with the program chairman to make sure that you understand fully what is expected of you. As host you may have the responsibility of recognizing distinguished guests, checking the public address system if there is one, quieting hilarious and possibly impolite members, keeping the program moving on schedule, making the speaker aware of his time limits, and conducting the question period if one is to follow the main speech.

In summary, then, here are several important final hints that should be observed in making speeches of introduction.

1. An introduction should be carefully prepared; don't try to do it impromptu.
2. An introduction should be spontaneous and natural; never read an introduction.
3. When presenting an introduction look at the audience; don't talk to the person being introduced.
4. Don't speak at length on the speaker's subject.
5. Play a supporting role; don't try to steal the show or embarrass the speaker with profuse compliments.
6. Avoid insincere flattery, and rarely if ever use glamour words or superlatives like *greatest, famous, darling, unique, wonderful,* and so on.
7. Avoid hackneyed sentences like "Our speaker needs no introduction."
8. Avoid anything that might give offense or might otherwise be considered to be in poor taste.

Speeches of Welcome and Response

When newcomers are in our midst, we often feel a desire and obligation to extend to them a few well-chosen words of welcome. Mayors and secretaries of chambers of commerce, as representatives of their organizations, make frequent speeches of welcome to distinguished guests, to conventions, and to other visiting groups. A speech of welcome often greets a new member of a club or extends a welcome to visitors. In speeches of this type the speaker attempts to make the newcomer feel at home, to utter appropriate pleasantries, and to express appreciation of the opportunity to enjoy the presence of the visitors.

In preparing one of these speeches ask yourself these questions, insofar as they apply to the specific occasion:

1. Who is the person to whom you are extending the welcome?
2. What is the nature of the organization you are greeting? What is its purpose, its history, its program?
3. Why has the person or the organization come to your community?
4. What common bonds exist between you and the newcomer or newcomers?
5. What can the newcomer be expected to contribute to your organization or community?
6. What can your organization or community offer to the newcomer?

Like the speech of introduction, the speech of welcome should be kept genuine, direct, and short. Good humor and graciousness must prevail.

Senator William Fulbright of Arkansas, chairman of the Committee on Foreign Relations of the Senate, gave a speech of welcome to Clement Attlee, former Prime Minister of Great Britain, when he visited the Senate of the United States, May 17, 1961. Senator Fulbright said:

Mr. President, we have the honor today to welcome, both in the Foreign Relations Committee and here on the floor, a former Prime Minister of Great Britain, the Earl Attlee, for many years a leading figure in the House of Commons, and now a Member of the House of Lords. I know all of us are acquainted with his great contribution to the leadership of our ally, Great Britain. He is now engaged in a very important work, traveling about this country and other countries.

I think it is a great privilege for us to have the opportunity to greet him. I hope all Members of the Senate will take this opportunity to shake hands with Lord Attlee.[5]

Ordinarily, upon receiving a welcome some representative of the group or the person himself who is so honored gives an impromptu reply, referred to as a speech of response. The materials for this type of talk must come directly out of the immediate speaking situation, particularly from the remarks made in the welcome. The theme of all such responses is, "We are glad to be here. Thank you for your hospitality."

[5] *Congressional Record*, May 17, 1961, **107**: 7651.

Speeches of Presentation and Acceptance

The presentation of a gift or the awarding of a prize often requires some representative of the donors to make a speech of presentation. A club may wish to present a gift to a retiring officer; a philanthropist may give a building to a college; a coach may present letters to members of the football squad.

This type of speech attempts to put into words the feeling of the group for the recipient. In other words, the speaker must transmit the admiration, the respect, and even the affection of a group to the person being honored. Therefore the speech ordinarily attempts to include the following.

1. It must tell why the presentation is being made.
2. It must summarize the sentiments of the group.
3. It must make the recipient aware of the esteem in which he is held.

In accomplishing these objectives the speaker must keep in mind two important don'ts. First, he must avoid overpraise which sounds insincere or which will embarrass the recipient. Second, he must not overstress the gift or its value. Emphasis should be placed upon why the presentation is being made, and sometimes upon how the gift is to be used.

Thomas R. Marshall, Vice-President from 1913 to 1921, was extremely popular as a presiding officer of the Senate. His fairness won him many friends on both sides of the Chamber. Upon his retirement in 1921, the senators presented him with a silver vase in appreciation of his service. Henry Cabot Lodge spoke in behalf of the Republicans as follows:

Mr. President, the Sixty-sixth Congress is drawing to its close. For eight years, sir, you have presided over the deliberations of the Senate. By the passage of time and the process of election you will leave on the 4th of March.

It is the desire of the Senate to manifest in something more than a formal resolution the personal regret which all of us feel at the fact that we are about to separate. Separation in the brief life allotted to us here always has an element of sadness. But I desire—and I am sure I am speaking in behalf of all Senators—to express to you the affection that we feel for you, our sense of your unvarying kindness to each one of us, the thoroughly human way in which you have always dealt with us individually, and we wish that you should take with you a symbol of our feelings. We know that you are not going to forget us, any more than we shall forget you and all our many pleasant relations over a period of great strain and great events; but we have felt that some gift, an inanimate object, might serve from time to time, when your eye rested upon it, to remind you of the feeling that we all have and the regret that we all feel personally that the hour of parting is so close at hand.

On behalf of the Senate—and I know that the leader on the other side will express the same feeling—we all desire to give you every good wish in the future, and that you should know that you take with you our affection, our hopes for your happiness and prosperity, and although I need not express a hope on this that you will not forget the many days we have spent together in the service of our common and beloved country.[6]

Mr. Lodge made his speech genuine and sincere. The spirit expressed can be more fully appreciated when we remembered that in the year prior to the date of this speech the Senate had been deadlocked in bitter debate over the question of whether the United States should participate in the League of Nations, and whether the Senate should ratify the treaty of peace. The speaker accomplished three objectives: (1) he mentioned the occasion for the presentation; (2) he expressed the affection that the members of the Senate felt for retiring Vice-President Marshall; and (3) he wished for the Vice-President a pleasant future. Noteworthy are his choice of simple words and the suppressed emotion reflected by the speech.

Speeches of presentation are made on a great variety of occasions, as we have indicated. On December 29, 1954, Karl R. Wallace, professor of speech and chairman of that department at the University of Illinois, presented the Speech Association of America with a volume of *History of Speech Education in America: Background Studies* (Appleton-Century-Crofts, 1954), the work of a project committee of the Association. In his presentation at the annual luncheon of the Association, Professor Wallace said:

At this time I have the special privilege of presenting to the Speech Association of America a volume of studies which I trust is not only symbolic of the long and honorable history of our subject in centuries

---

[6] Sen. Henry Cabot Lodge, Speech before the Senate, February 28, 1921; in the *Congressional Record*, **60**: pt. 4, 4021.

past but signalizes the maturity of our subject today and prophesies our scholarship in the decades to come. The volume bears the title *History of Speech Education in America*. It is the immediate product of thirty-six scholars in the fields of Speech and the educational theatre who have labored for six years to present some of the fundamental facts of the development of their subjects in the public school and college. It is the ultimate fruit of the energy and wisdom of those mentors whose faith in our work and its history led the Association to undertake the project officially. Hence these studies represent more than the time and labors of the Editorial Board and of the contributors; they are a monument to the original Committee on the History of Speech Education. . . .

In presenting this volume to the Association on behalf of the Editorial Board, I wish to acknowledge particularly the fine co-operation of our contributors and of our publishers. Many of the contributors are recognized as authorities in their lines of study; they were asked to take a fresh look at their materials, to extend their research, and to prepare new studies; this they gladly did. A few of the authors were asked to undertake what to them were new lines of investigation. They, too, responded superbly. Although it is still too early to know how others will judge their work, we believe that their contributions are worth the close observation and critical analysis which both mature scholars and graduate students in Speech can exercise. We are, of course, particularly grateful to our publishers . . . because their faith in this venture has been as great as ours.

Mr. Secretary, if this volume should stimulate in the next ten years new and better studies in the history of our subject, our work will have been well rewarded. The seed may be essential, but it's the harvest which not only multiplies but tests the stock.[7]

The speech of acceptance is much like the speech of response. Normally it is impromptu and grows out of the occasion, and its subject matter is suggested by the preceding speech of presentation. If it is prepared it must be made to seem spontaneous and heartfelt. The recipient must remain modest, and above all he must make his listeners feel his gratitude for the gift or award as well as for the sentiment behind it. This type of speech should normally be extremely short.

Upon his retirement as Secretary of Defense, Mr. James V. Forrestal was presented a remembrance by the Committee on Armed

---

[7] Karl R. Wallace; speech found in *The Quarterly Journal of Speech*, February, 1955, **41**: 62–63.

Services of the House of Representatives. In reply to Mr. Overton Brooks's speech of presentation, Mr. Forrestal said:

> Mr. Chairman, I am too much overcome by what I consider to be a very gracious and a very moving testimonial of your friendship and of those deeper feelings that come from the heart.
>
> I should like to say for the record, however, without venturing to contradict the rhetoric of the chairman, that that tribute which he gave should properly be directed to himself and to the members of this committee because it was the unfailing zeal, the high intelligence, and the continuing zest for work which really built the American Navy and which under the chairmanship of Mr. Vinson will also build the defense forces under the unification which I know will be ably guided by Colonel Johnson, my successor.
>
> I am much too moved to go into a longer appreciation of this most generous and exceptional act. I thank you deeply.[8]

Each paragraph of this speech accomplished a purpose: the first expressed appreciation for the gift, the second paid tribute to the committee making the presentation, and the third concluded the speech by thanking the group. Wisely the speaker devoted more than half of his time to talking about the committee.

Speeches of Farewell

Like other occasional addresses the speech of farewell is primarily a stimulating speech. When a person leaves an organization to accept a position in another firm or to move to another city, he may feel an urge to express his regret over breaking up a pleasant association. Such speeches may express the following points:

1. Regrets over leaving
2. Appreciation for the group
3. Reminiscence of happy times and memories
4. Indebtedness or obligations to the group
5. Closing words of farewell

Perhaps the best-known speech of farewell, which embodies in a few lines all the essential characteristics of such a speech, is the

[8] James V. Forrestal, speech delivered March 29, 1949; in the *Congressional Record*, March 30, 1949, **95:** A1878–1879.

one Lincoln delivered on the occasion of his leaving his home in Springfield, Illinois, for the White House in Washington:

> My friends, No one not in my situation can appreciate my feeling of sadness at this parting. To this place, and the kindness of these people, I owe everything. Here I have lived a quarter of a century, and have passed from a young to an old man. Here my children have been born, and one is buried. I now leave, not knowing when or whether ever I may return, with a task before me greater than that which rested upon Washington. Without the assistance of that Divine Being who ever attended him, I cannot succeed. With that assistance, I cannot fail. Trusting in Him who can go with me, and remain with you, and be everywhere for good, let us confidently hope that all will yet be well. To His care commending you, as I hope in your prayers you will commend me, I bid you an affectionate farewell.[9]

SPEECHES TO ENTERTAIN

Despite the drawing power of movie thrillers, television shows, and sports events, the speech continues to rank as a significant type of diversion, and the speaker who can talk entertainingly is in great demand. In fact, lecture bureaus thrive on supplying speakers to hundreds of organizations seeking this type of entertainment. These booking agencies direct the efforts of thousands of lecturers who go forth to address millions of Americans. But the professional speaker by no means dominates the lecture platform or comes near supplying the requests for entertaining speakers. Toastmaster clubs, service groups, women's organizations, and directors of school assemblies search the community diligently for program material for their weekly meetings, and local citizens are frequently drafted into service. As any program chairman will tell you, there are far too few persons in any given community who can give a really clever, entertaining speech.

Immediately one common misconception concerning the nature of the entertaining talk should be clarified. An entertaining speech need not be funny, sidesplitting, or even laugh-provoking. We have all encountered the so-called speech composed largely or solely of

---

[9] Delivered in Springfield, February 11, 1861; in T. Harry Williams, ed., *Abraham Lincoln, Selected Speeches, Messages, and Letters,* Rinehart, 1957, pp. 135–136.

unrelated jokes. These efforts are frequently not deserving of the name of speeches, and they are often not even entertaining. The entertaining speech has just one basic requirement: it must hold attention and interest in itself. The response sought may be either covert or overt. Though a well-told story, serious and dramatic in detail, may not elicit laughter, it can provide the listener with pleasant diversion and make him forget his problems. There are five characteristics which most entertaining speeches possess.

1. An entertaining speech is well organized and unified. Like other good speeches it is built around a central theme and developed in planned sequence. It is the product of careful preparation.

2. An entertaining speech is ordinarily brief. As a rule entertainers strive to leave their audiences not quite satisfied, in the frame of mind of wanting more. It is better to have your hearers want you to continue than want you to stop.

3. The entertaining speech strives for an immediate, momentary response, either covert or overt. The speaker seldom hopes to control his audiences beyond the limits of his talk, although, it is true, he may give them worthwhile information they will remember for a long time.

4. In the entertaining talk emphasis is on the utilization of the factors of attention and interest. Novelty and suspense are frequently employed. Examples and episodes are often included as supporting material. Delivery may be more animated, even sensational, but it must always remain within the bounds of good taste.

5. In most of its forms, the entertaining speech is usually delivered extemporaneously. Certainly it must sound spontaneous and natural. Giving the "illusion of the first time" is extremely important in maintaining interest.

QUESTIONS AND TOPICS FOR STUDY AND REVIEW

1. Why is it that speeches of introduction are never given when the President of the United States talks to the nation by radio and television? Is the same true for any other personages? Why?

2. Under what circumstances would a speech of introduction for the President be desirable?

3. Make a list of the most common faults of speeches of introduction which you have personally observed. Be prepared to recount an incident to the class.

4. List several occasions in your community at which the following types of speeches were presented:
   a. Speech of welcome
   b. Speech of presentation
   c. Speech of acceptance
   d. Speech of farewell
5. Compare the "Farewell Address" of Lincoln with that which John F. Kennedy gave to the Massachusetts legislature on January 9, 1961 (*Vital Speeches of the Day*, February 1, 1961, **27**: 227–228). What are the points of likeness and difference?
6. Many believe that an entertaining speech must be humorous. On what occasions have you heard an entertaining speech that had a serious theme?
7. "The after-dinner speech is difficult if not impossible to define." What elements in the situation contribute to the great variety of speeches given on after-dinner occasions?
8. Make a list of the after-dinner speeches included in a single volume of *Vital Speeches of the Day.*

PROJECTS

1. *Speaking Assignment.* Deliver a speech of introduction in which you present one of the following persons to your speech class or any other specific group of college students: the president of a neighboring college or university, a local attorney or doctor, a social worker, a prominent professor, a rabbi, a Negro educator, a labor leader, a woman lecturer.
2. *Speaking Assignment.* Deliver a speech of welcome to one of the following:
   a. A new minister in your church
   b. A new resident in the community
   c. The governor of the state
   d. The football, basketball, or baseball team of a neighboring school
   e. A Boy Scout troop
   f. A similar group of your own choice
3. *Speaking Assignment.* Deliver a brief speech of presentation suitable for one of the following occasions:
   a. Awarding letters to the athletic team
   b. Awarding a prize for establishing a record for safe driving
   c. Awarding a $5000 scholarship for study abroad
   d. Presenting a substantial gift to the college or university
   e. Establishing a foundation for some worthy inquiry in the field of medicine, science, or social welfare

4. *Speech Practices.* On pages 136–137 in *Speech Practices,* you will find four short speeches of congratulations which were delivered at the forty-fourth anniversary of congressional service of the late Speaker Sam Rayburn. Notice that they are really speeches of praise or commendation. After making a careful study of these speeches, select one which seems to you the most appropriate for the occasion. Defend your choice in not more than 300 words. In your analysis you will find it helpful to review the characteristics of the speech of commendation found in Chapter 21. Your instructor may decide to use this assignment for a class discussion.

5. *Speaking Assignment.* Deliver a five-minute oral analysis of an effective or ineffective occasional speech you have personally heard.

6. *Speech Analysis.* On April 21, 1961, a delegation of twenty-four members of the Canadian Parliament visited the Senate of the United States. They were in Washington to attend a meeting of the Canadian-United States interparliamentary group, and Vice-President Richard Nixon, presiding officer of the Senate, gave the speech of welcome below. Analyze its structure, content, language, and appropriateness for the occasion.

The Chair wishes to say it is the custom of the Senate that the Presiding Officer is allowed to speak only when he makes a ruling or breaks a tie vote. In the past 7 years there have been only seven occasions when I have been able to break a tie vote.

One exception to the rule regarding the Presiding Officer speaking is when there are distinguished visitors in the Senate Chamber, as there are today.

I know there is little which can be added to the eloquent statements made on both sides of the aisle, but I should like to say that as we consider the good fortune of our own country during the time of our existence, and as we consider our economic progress and our strength today, all Americans should be reminded from time to time, as your visit reminds us, that this has been to a great extent made possible because we have had throughout our history a friendly neighbor along 3,000 miles of our border. We have often thought what would have been the case had we not had a friendly neighbor. The United States would have had to maintain military forces along our northern border, as would have Canada, of course, with the result that neither country could have reached the economic position we both enjoy today.

This is for us a very historic occasion. It is a historic occasion for the Senate and for me personally to be allowed to speak on an occasion in the Senate.[10]

7. *Speech Analysis.* Study the speech given below, considering its structure, content, language, and appropriateness. It is the remarks by Senator Jennings Randolph, Democrat, of West Virginia, introducing the late Speaker Sam Rayburn at the commencement exercises of Woodward School for Boys in Washington, D.C., on June 7, 1961.

Headmaster Lewis, Dr. Mass, ladies and gentlemen, and graduates and guests of Woodward School, there is perhaps no more overworked cliché in the entire battery of introductory comments than the one which begins, "Your speaker today needs no introduction."

Yet, of none could it be said with more truth than of "Mr. Sam"—especially here in Washington. Though he has not been here quite as long as the Washington Monument, there are some who would maintain that he is made of just as durable material.

Speaker Rayburn has not only seen much of American history, he has helped to make it, and he is history—and a potent force in the history that is yet to be written.

Not only has he served longer than any Members of the present House of Representatives—now in his 25th consecutive term—but he has served longer than any Member in the history of the House—and on June 12, just 5 days hence, he will have doubled the former record of tenure as Speaker which was held by Henry Clay.

I find a particular pleasure in introducing Speaker Rayburn in an educational context, because I am one of his many students in the art of government. Though I am inclined to believe he always feels a slight twinge of remorse for those errant pupils who go to "that other body."

Speaker Rayburn's service in the House of Representatives has spanned the administrations of seven Presidents. Yet even such a statement as this does not indicate the deep impress of his life on American Government—an adequate appraisal of which will require the work of many historians in the years to come.

It is with a genuine sense of privilege that I present a man of great knowledge in the affairs of Government and deep wis-

[10] *Congressional Record*, April 21, 1961, **107**: 8464.

dom in the ways of life—the Honorable Sam Rayburn, Speaker of the House of Representatives.[11]

SPEECH MODELS FOR STUDY

Brigance, William Norwood, *Classified Speech Models*, 2d ed., Crofts, 1953. This book includes speeches of introduction, welcome, response, presentation, acceptance, and farewell as well as many other types.

Conwell, Russell H., "Acres of Diamonds," in *American Forum*,[12] pp. 263–275.

DuPont, Henry B., "The Greatest Invention of Them All," in *The Speaker's Resource Book*, pp. 193–198.

Emerson, Ralph Waldo, "The American Scholar," in *American Public Addresses*, pp. 122–137, in *American Speeches*, pp. 264–283, and in *The Speaker's Resource Book*, pp. 36–46.

Lyle, Guy R., and Kevin Guinagh, eds., *I Am Happy To Present. A Book of Introductions*, H. W. Wilson, 1953, "The Artful Introduction," pp. 15–31.

O'Neill, James Milton, ed., *Modern Short Speeches*, Century, 1925. This book contains ninety-eight complete examples, including speeches of introduction, welcome, farewell, presentation, acceptance, congratulations, and response.

Sanchez, Joe, "Our Daily Oil" (student speech), in *Speech Practices*, pp. 102–103.

Speeches delivered at the forty-fourth anniversary of congressional service of Speaker Sam Rayburn by Mike Mansfield, Albert Gore, and Everett Dirksen, in *Speech Practices*, pp. 136–137.

Stevenson, Adlai, "Acceptance Speech," in *American Public Addresses*, pp. 289–294.

SUPPLEMENTARY READINGS

Baird, A. Craig, and Franklin H. Knower, *General Speech: An Introduction*, 2nd ed., McGraw-Hill, 1957, chap. 21, "Speeches for Special Occasions."

Braden, Waldo W., and Mary Louise Gehring, *Speech Practices: A Resource Book for the Student of Public Speaking*, Harper, 1958, chap. 7, "Types of Speeches."

Brigance, William Norwood, *Speech: Its Techniques and Disciplines in*

[11] *Congressional Record*, June 8, 1961, **107**: A4181.
[12] For full references to this and the following incomplete sources, see Supplementary Readings, pp. 132–133.

a Free Society, 2nd ed., Appleton-Century-Crofts, 1961, chap. 23, "Speeches on Special Occasions."

Capp, Glenn R., *How To Communicate Orally*, Prentice-Hall, 1961, chap. 17, "Speeches for Special Occasions."

Oliver, Robert T., and Rupert L. Cortright, *Effective Speech*, 4th ed., Holt, Rinehart & Winston, 1961, chap. 23, "The Speech for a Special Occasion."

Reid, Loren, *First Principles of Public Speaking*, Artcraft, 1960, chap. 17, "Five Types of Short Speeches."

23

Discussion

In the previous chapters of this section we have considered the speaking situation in which the transmission of a message depends upon the efforts of a single speaker. He decides upon and analyzes the subject, selects the points to be developed, finds supporting material, and finally delivers the speech. In the present chapter we turn our attention to speaking activities in which several communicators must cooperate to achieve their communicative goal. Our subject, group and public discussion, or what we might call exploratory and controversial speaking, is sufficient in scope for book-length treatment, but we hope that the brief presentation here will provide sufficient insights to allow a unit of the subject to be included in a course when it seems desirable.

WHAT IS DISCUSSION?

In many communities and even neighborhoods people gather periodically to talk about and analyze their mutual concerns: child rearing, foreign policy, fallout shelters, improved agricultural methods, community improvement, business practices—in fact almost any subject that involves a group, great or small. Such gatherings may be sponsored by neighborhood mothers, a group of friends, a YMCA, a CYO, a local library, a church, the League of Women Voters, or a PTA. The meeting may be referred to by any of a variety of names, including panel discussion, round table discussion, conference, workshop, or forum. Whatever their name, sponsorship, or assembly place, these meetings generally have one thing in common: the members have come to realize that together rather than individually they can better understand and solve their common problems. Immediately it is apparent that this interchange of thinking and pooling of ideas is the very epitome of democratic living.

A Definition of Discussion

Let us pull these ideas together in a formal definition. In the sense in which we shall be using it, group discussion is a "systematic attempt of a group under responsible leadership to evolve consensus on a recognized problem by means of talk and reflective thinking."[1] It is a means of communication by which well-informed persons, acting together, investigate a problem, develop a mutually satisfactory solution, reach a decision, and take or propose action. In other words,

$$\boxed{\text{Problem}} \longrightarrow \boxed{\text{Exploration}} \longrightarrow \boxed{\text{Solution}} \longrightarrow \boxed{\text{Decision}} \longrightarrow \boxed{\text{Action}}$$

this process involves five important factors: (1) well-informed participants, (2) responsible leadership, (3) a recognized problem, (4) a systematic oral sharing of insights and ideas, and (5) reaching a consensus upon which to act.

This process, which Woodrow Wilson referred to as "the process of common counsel," is based upon the premise that several persons

[1] Waldo W. Braden and Earnest Brandenburg, *Oral Decision-Making*, Harper, 1955, p. 185.

thinking and talking together in a permissive atmosphere will develop solutions that are better and more beneficial to the group than the same persons could working independently. In larger terms, Wilson expressed the concept as follows: "For only as men are brought into counsel, and state their own needs and interests, can the general interests of a great people be compounded into a policy that will be suitable to all."[2]

PRIVATE DISCUSSION

In private discussion, sometimes referred to as informal discussion, all members participate and share equal responsibility for the outcome. The oral interchange is directed and conversational; there are no set speeches, and every discusser is both a speaker and listener, taking his turn in the oral deliberation. The group may or may not set for itself a fixed period of time to be devoted to considering the problem.

Private discussion is more productive when the number is small enough to permit all present to contribute. Six to fifteen is an ideal number. The atmosphere is relaxed, informal, and congenial. The role of the chairman is less well defined than it is in larger groups: in presiding he gives guidance to the group, keeping the participants aware of the discussion outline and attempting to make sure that each person has an opportunity to speak and that no one is permitted to monopolize. He tries to maintain and foster a permissive spirit. At times, particularly in a small group, he may enter into the deliberations and contribute his ideas. This kind of activity works well when the members are seated in a circle or around a table in order that each one see every person and thus facilitate direct interchange.[3]

TYPES OF PUBLIC DISCUSSION

In private discussion there is no audience, only participants; in public discussion there are participants with an audience looking on and sometimes participating. In many ways public discussion is

[2] Woodrow Wilson, *The New Freedom*, Dent, 1916, p. 85.

[3] The authors are indebted to Earnest Brandenburg of Washington University who has developed at length the concepts of private and public discussion in Braden and Brandenburg, *op. cit.*, chap. 9.

a public speaking situation in which speakers talk to listeners who sit more or less quietly by, seeking understanding and information. The public discusser must expand his presentation to include the entire circle of listeners. As a result, he selects his topic and supporting materials in the light of listener attitudes. Each participant must speak so that all can hear what he has to say. Usually a time limit is set in accordance with the attention and interest span of the entire assembly.

Round-Table Discussion

A round-table discussion is much the same as a private informal discussion, with the important difference that a nonparticipating audience overhears the presentation. Many radio and television discussions are of this type, the participants, under the guidance of a chairman, following usual discussion procedures. The presence of listeners makes it necessary for discussers to project their presentation so that all can hear and understand. The chairman may take special care to keep the discussion outline before the group.

Panel Forum

The panel forum operates with a small number of discussers, usually no more than seven or eight, with an audience listening in. In form and atmosphere it is similar to private discussion. Following an initial period of perhaps a half-hour when the panel explores the subject, the audience is usually invited to direct questions to members and to present additional information and new points of view.

The participants must of course, as noted above, speak out in order for the listeners to hear. The chairman must do at least three things for the entire assembly: (1) keep the outline before them, (2) restate important points which might be misunderstood, and (3) summarize frequently.

Symposium

The symposium is more formal than the other types, both in organization and in the manner in which it is conducted. It is generally used with a large audience. The chairman opens the meeting, sketches the background of the problem, and introduces the speakers. The main part of the program consists of prepared speeches by two or three persons more or less expert in the field of discussion. Though complete agreement is not necessary, the speakers work cooperatively to give a fair picture of the total problem. Emphasis is on cooperation, not debate, with each participant developing a selected aspect. For example, if a symposium is considering the question, "How can the United States improve its relations with Latin America?" the various speakers might discuss such topics as removing language barriers, increasing cultural exchange, and improving trade. As with the panel forum, the audience is encouraged to participate in the question period.

Debate Forum

The debate forum is similar to the symposium except that it adopts certain debating procedures in the deliberations. (1) The question is stated in the form of a proposition similar to those used for convincing or actuating speeches (see pp. 356–358). (2) The speakers are divided into those who are *for* the proposition (the affirmative) and those who are *against* it (the negative). (3) Persons on a given side may or may not cooperate in case planning. (4) Each side is given an equal amount of time. (5) The affirmative speaker opens the main speeches and presents a criticism of the status quo. (6) Affirmative and negative speakers alternate in presenting their views. (7) After the so-called constructive speeches are presented, the audience may be invited to ask questions or to make brief speeches. (8) The forum may be closed by having short summary speeches on each side.

CHARACTERISTICS OF DISCUSSION PARTICIPANTS

Ideally, the most effective discussion participant, whether he is chairman or group member, is what Quintilian called the "good man speaking well." He possesses at least four characteristics: (1) he is an effective communicator; (2) he respects and appreciates his associates; (3) he has a broad knowledge of the problem; and (4) he understands discussion techniques.

He Is an Effective Communicator

The effective discusser needs the same abilities and skills that any effective speaker does. He must be intelligent and mentally alert. He must know how to engage in research, how to recognize sound facts and solid reasoning, and how to engage in analysis and synthesis. He can speak clearly, forcefully, and interestingly. He is a good listener. In short, he has the characteristics of the good speaker which we presented in Chapter 4.

He Respects and Appreciates His Associates

The participant should be in tune with democratic tenets which recognize the integrity of the individual, protect the rights of the minority as well as the majority, and respect human intelligence as a means of solving problems. He should be willing and eager to work within the group, to suppress his personal ambitions, to put group achievement above personal recognition, and to accept and abide by group decisions. In interacting with others, he must be sensitive to the forces which motivate his associates and to the dynamics which operate within the group, for "Diplomacy, tact, respect, and good will are fundamental rights to be accorded all those around the conference table."[4]

He Is Broadly Educated and Well Informed

Some persons confuse discussion with casual conversation or the bull session; they seem to think that it is a haphazard affair in which the participants lounge around and exchange pleasantries without any advanced preparation. What results from such an activity is a pooling of ignorance. Walter Lippmann has observed, "When men act on the principle of intelligence, they go out to find the facts and to make their wisdom. When they ignore it, they go inside themselves and find only what is there. They elaborate their prejudice, instead of increasing their knowledge."[5]

Cooperativeness is indeed important, but it is no substitute for hard thinking and thorough research. When you accept an invi-

---

[4] *Ibid.*, p. 259.
[5] Walter Lippmann, *Public Opinion*, Harcourt, Brace, 1922, p. 397.

tation to join a panel or round-table discussion, you take on a moral obligation to carry your full share of the deliberation. This demands being well informed.

He Understands Discussion Principles and Techniques

The good discusser is thoroughly acquainted with group behavior and means of resolving of human problems that develop when persons are striving to reach a consensus. He certainly can distinguish between reflective and emotional thinking. Further, he knows how to plan, promote, and conduct various types of discussion.

ESSENTIAL STEPS IN GROUP DELIBERATION

Selecting a Problem Area

A good discussion problem is timely. The most profitable discussions take place when the participants are vitally concerned with the problem, when they have encountered a serious difficulty, and when they have a real stake in resolving the problem. For example, a group of mothers may show little interest in the question of admitting Red China to the United Nations, but they will talk together fervently about questions of child rearing or problems of the local schools.

The problem should also involve an element of controversy or difference in opinion. In other words, it should not be a problem which can be neatly answered by scientific measurement, but one which involves probability and requires the exercise of judgment. Why spend time discussing how many students are enrolled in the State University? It is better to go to the registrar and get the exact information. On the other hand, the desirability of replacing the quarter system with semester terms may stir an excellent discussion. The more points of view expressed, the more likely you are to see all aspects of the problem and its possible effects on the university.

Framing a Good Discussion Question

You can save the group considerable time and effort if you or a small group word the problem in a meaningful question that brings forth comment and thoughtful interchange. The discussion question differs greatly from the proposition used in a speech. The persuasive speaker attempts to put his thought in the highly directive form of a single declarative sentence like "You should join the boosters club," or "The United States should withdraw its forces from Europe." The discussion is built around a question which is not weighted in any direction. Some examples are as follows:

1. Should the United States actively support the free governments in Southeast Asia?
2. Is medical care in the United States adequate?
3. Should we participate in a voluntary health plan?
4. How can we improve our schools?
5. Should the federal government give aid to private schools?

In planning for a public discussion you should take into consideration the audience factor. You will, of course, attempt to select a problem of wide interest, word it to attract attention and stir curiosity, and limit it sufficiently for development within the time limit.

Important criteria for judging a discussion question are the following:

1. It is worded in an impartial question form.
2. It is limited in scope to fit the time limit, particularly for public discussion.
3. It is specific and meaningful, containing no confusing or vague terms.

Deciding on a Discussion Goal

The problem, the occasion, and the sponsors of a meeting will have much to do with the selection of a goal for a discussion, whether private or public. In planning and conducting a meeting it is important for the chairman and participants to keep their objective clearly before them. They may choose any of four goals.

1. A group may meet for a study project in which the members seek no more than to explore and understand the problem. The Great Book study groups, for example, meet to consider the classics. On a given evening members may direct their consid-

eration to Shakespeare's *Hamlet* or Adam Smith's *The Wealth of Nations*. Their goal is to search out how men have met their problems through the ages.

2. A group may assemble to disseminate information to a forum or a community. The symposium and debate forum as well as radio and television panels have objectives of this type. The participants and sponsors believe that increased understanding comes through multisided presentation.

3. A group may gather in order to build *esprit de corps*. Haven't you heard someone say that he met with his associates in order to "clear the air," "to reach an understanding," or "get better acquainted"? Implied in such statements is the goal of developing unity and friendship through talking openly and frankly.

4. A group may have decision-making as its objective. The members have a common problem which they wish to settle in a democratic atmosphere. They are determined to reach a decision through the processes of reflective thinking and free interchange of ideas. This goal is probably the most important of the four.

Drafting a Discussion Outline

As a preliminary to the main discussion it is often highly advisable for the chairman or a committee to draft an outline or agenda to guide the deliberation. This outline may be changed at any moment during the discussion. However, the outline may prevent unnecessary waste of time in attempting to get started. John Dewey's five-step formula for reflective thought serves as a useful guide:

1. Recognizing a felt difficulty or discrepancy.
2. Defining and locating the difficulty.
3. Discovering the possible solutions (supposition, conjecture, guess, hypothesis, or theory) to the problem.
4. Examining the various solutions.
5. Testing the most feasible solution, or in Dewey's words, "further observation and experiment leading to acceptance or rejection; that is, the conclusion of belief or disbelief." [6]

Let us cast these steps into an outline.

[6] John Dewey, *How We Think*, Heath, 1910, pp. 68–78.

1. Why are we discussing this problem?
   a. Is it timely?
   b. How does it concern us?
2. What terms in the question need definition?
3. By what standard shall we evaluate solutions which we consider?
4. What is the problem?
   a. What symptoms, conditions, or signs do we find of the problem?
   b. What are the causes of the problem?
      1. Are these causes inherent weaknesses?
      2. Do the causes result from some problem in administration?
5. What solutions are available which could eliminate the causes?
6. What solution promises the most benefits for the greatest number?
7. Is the adoption of this solution feasible?

Getting the Discussion Started

The chairman is charged with the responsibility of creating a desirable atmosphere and insuring the physical comfort of the participants. He may actually direct the setting up of the room and the provision of useful materials. He checks the availability of visual aids and makes any other necessary preparations. He opens the meeting, introduces the discussions, and, when necessary, sketches the background of the problem. He may orient the panel members with reference to the purpose of the meeting.

Promoting a Permissive Atmosphere

A permissive atmosphere is one in which members of the group like and respect one another, attempt to understand and appreciate one another's problems and inclinations, participate with ease and confidence, and freely exchange their views.

All members must feel that they belong to the group, are free to speak, are expected to contribute, and will receive a fair hearing at all times. The responsibility of maintaining a permissive atmosphere falls upon all participants. Through a careless or thoughtless remark one discusser may destroy the relaxed atmosphere necessary for a free flow of ideas and interchanges. The chairman often sets the general tone and can do much to keep the atmosphere friendly and to promote cooperativeness.

Maintaining the Questioning Attitude

The participant in a discussion should be a seeker or searcher who asks "why" often. He is constantly attempting to understand the problem more clearly, to define unfamiliar, vague, or confusing terms, to look for causes of the difficulty, and to relate these causes to other aspects of the social and political climate. When a fellow member offers an observation or conclusion which is not clear or which may cause confusion, some participant should attempt to draw him out to get more information and clarify the disputed point. Each discusser must follow each development, attempting to see how new information alters previous hypothesis. The chairman can do much to spark the questioning attitude by drawing out the participants and injecting thought-provoking questions. In his role as leader he can often ask for elaboration or more precise language. He may say, "I think a definition of that term would help all of us," or "What is the meaning of that concept?" or "How do you interpret that idea?" Obviously, he must make his inquiry without seeming to challenge or criticize.

Working for Balanced Participation

The members must make sure that all members have ample opportunity to contribute to the progress of the deliberation. As suggested in the preceding section, the chairman may put forth the pertinent questions to draw out hesitant and reticent members. But all members must share in this leadership function. The noncontributing or shy person must be made to feel that his opinion is needed and wanted. For example, a fellow member may direct the question to a silent member, "How do you feel about this subject?" or "I believe Joe has had some experience with this type of problem."

Balanced participation is destroyed when one member attempts to monopolize the discussion or becomes so eager to contribute that he interrupts others continually. Whenever a member fails to recognize the rights or the integrity of others, the chairman and his associates must somehow let the offender know that others present want and have a right to contribute.

Striving To Find a Consensus

The test of successful discussion is reaching an agreement on the proposal under consideration; that is, the group must attempt to arrive at a consensus, which implies finding a solution satisfactory and acceptable to all. Attempting to satisfy all participants is a rigorous standard which seldom can be met. Certainly it cannot be achieved on the basis of a majority vote which leaves the minority unsatisfied and in some cases disillusioned and unhappy. Neither can it be attained through a compromise in which factions trade and bargain to get as much as they can. Consensus should come from objective exploration of available evidence and from the individuals who put group objectives and welfare above personal ambition and triumph.

QUESTIONS AND TOPICS FOR STUDY AND REVIEW

1. How does discussion differ from debate? From conversation?
2. Under what circumstances could a conversation turn into a private discussion?
3. What are differences between private and public discussion? If you want more information, see Braden and Brandenburg, *Oral Decision-Making*, Chapter 9.
4. Describe the various types of public discussion. What are the unique characteristics of each type?
5. What characteristics would a good discusser have that a good public speaker would not have?
6. List the essential steps in discussion. Which ones are more important in private than in public discussion? Are there other steps that should be added to the list given in this chapter?
7. How is a good discussion question different from a speech proposition?
8. What is meant by a permissive atmosphere? When does it develop? Under what conditions does it not develop? Name some types of groups in which you seldom find a permissive atmosphere.
9. What is meant by the dictum that all members must share in the leadership function? In what types of tasks could the members not share?
10. What is a consensus? Under what conditions could a group arrive

at a consensus? How would you know when a group had reached a consensus? How do a majority vote and a consensus differ?

11. In what types of speech situations would you use discussion as a problem-solving method? When would you not use it?

12. It is possible to have disagreement in a discussion? Argument? Persuasion? Compromise?

PROJECTS

1. Phrase ten questions suitable for class discussions.

2. Select a question and prepare a discussion outline, following the form suggested on page 423.

3. *Discussion Assignment.* Divide the class into groups of five or six members. Have each group select a question and prepare a thirty-minute round-table or panel discussion on it. Each group will be assigned a class period to present its discussion. When a group is performing other members of the audience will write critiques of about 200 words.

4. *Discussion Assignment.* With the same groups used in project 3, plan a symposium or debate forum. After a twenty-minute presentation, open the discussion to questions from the floor. Attempt to keep the questioning attitude.

5. Visit a community forum or discussion group. If there is no group to visit, listen to a radio or television discussion. Write a 200- to 500-word evaluation of the deliberations.

6. *Research Assignment.* Investigate a discussion program like one of the following.
   a. Great Books program
   b. Foreign Policy Association Great Decisions discussion groups
   c. Discussion activities of a University Agricultural Extension Service program
   d. The American Heritage program (inquire at local library)
   e. The Georgetown University Forum (Washington, D.C.)
   f. Any other discussion program

7. Check your library to see whether it has a file of the published discussions of the Chicago University Round Table radio program or the printed reports of the American Town Hall of the Air. If you can locate a file on any of these, read several discussions.

SUPPLEMENTARY READINGS

Auer, J. Jeffery, and Henry Lee Ewbank, *Handbook for Discussion Leaders,* rev. ed., Harper, 1954.

Braden, Waldo W., and Earnest Brandenburg, *Oral Decision-Making,* Harper, 1955.

Bryant, Donald C., and Karl R. Wallace, *Fundamentals of Public Speaking,* 3rd ed., Appleton-Century-Crofts, 1960, chap. 25, "Discussion."

Gulley, Halbert E., *Discussion, Conference, and Group Process,* Holt, 1960.

Howell, William S., and Donald K. Smith, *Discussion,* Macmillan, 1956.

Sattler, William M., and N. Edd Miller, *Discussion and Conference,* Prentice-Hall, 1954.

Wiksell, Wesley, *Do They Understand You? A Guide to Effective Oral Communication,* Macmillan, 1960, chap. 16, "Leading and Participating in Conferences."

PART VI  POLISH-ING THE SPEECH

24

The Manuscript Speech

The manuscript speech is not a special type of speech at all. The term refers simply to a particular manner of preparation and presentation, and the speech itself may be of any type, so far as speeches can be typed. Though it has generally been considered the least effective mode of speaking, there are nevertheless situations that provide ample justification for presenting a speech that has been written out in full and is then read from the manuscript, frankly, openly, and without apology. Speeches have been written and read, even memorized, for a long time, and the practice is increasing. Since this mode of preparation and delivery is so widespread, speakers are learning how better to prepare their speeches to be read, as well as how to read them more effectively.

FACTORS THAT MAKE A MANUSCRIPT
SPEECH SUITABLE

The Factor of Time

Convention programs, professional meetings, etc.   Among the conditions for public address in which a manuscript speech may be not merely permissible but advisable or even mandatory is the element of time. Typical situations in which time is a pressing consideration are professional conventions, at which a large number of papers are presented. The overall program is usually made up of many sectional meetings, each one strictly limited in duration. As many as four to six such meeting periods and often more may be scheduled for a single day, at each of which eight to ten programs may be presented in as many meeting places. Obviously, if the general program it to be completed these separate meetings must be opened and closed *on time*. That in turn means that each paper presented must be limited to fifteen or twenty minutes, depending on the number of papers on that particular program. To permit some speaker whose sense of timing is undeveloped to expand his discussion to cover twenty-five or thirty minutes or even more is to impose an injustice and a discourtesy on the others who are scheduled to appear on the same program, and who are entitled to the same amount of time as the long-winded rambler. Reading manuscript papers gives relative assurance that everyone on the program will have approximately equal time to present his discussion.

Television and radio.   In radio and television programming the schedule must meet rigid time limits to satisfy the not unreasonable demands of sponsors who insist on having all the time they pay for. Unless there is a considerable amount of sustaining time left unsold, programs must not run overtime by even a few seconds. On the other hand programs, including speeches, must be so planned that they utilize all the time allotted to them. The surest way of meeting such demands is simply to write out the speech and rehearse it carefully, with the time factor a major consideration.

Precision in Wording

Another condition often makes the reading of papers advisable: the occasional necessity for the utmost precision in the wording of the speech. When one writes a paper or a speech, one has time to revise, rewrite, rework, refine—in short, to polish his development and language until the material expresses precisely and with the greatest economy what he wants to say so there can be no uncertainty or haziness in the ideas presented.

Some speakers, some situations, and some speeches are of such a nature that precision of language is imperative. Many of these become matters of official record, and textual authenticity is highly important in order to ensure that there will be no question about precisely what is said. It is not enough that some future reader of the printed speech know what *was* said; the speaker himself must know in advance exactly what he is going to say. Patrick Henry's "give me liberty" speech was reconstructed by his biographer years after it was heard by the Virginia Convention from the recollections of those who had heard it.

Presidential State of the Union addresses, speeches on major—and minor—policy, speeches by key personnel in all government echelons and in industry, public utterances of men in positions that require maximum security precautions—for all of these a manuscript is imperative. This necessity arises, first, because the record of what has been said must be accurate to prevent misquoting; and second, in order to have assurance that what has been said cannot be used to the disadvantage or harm of the speaker or the group he represents, whether that group be a nation or an industry whose business secrets are its own.

Through revision and polishing, moreover, a manuscript speech can be given the qualities of a genuinely literary production without detracting in the least from its utilitarian value. Sometimes a speech of dedication or commemoration or a commencement address demands for its maximum impact a refinement that would not be required of what we might term an instrumental speech. Such a polish can be given it more effectively if it is written out and then subjected to rigid revision and refining.

At the same time, a manuscript speech is still a *speech*, and not a literary creation. In subject matter, choice of language, and organization it must meet the criteria of a speech, which is constructed to be heard by a group of listeners, large or small, rather than to be read by a number of individual readers.[1]

[1] See in this connection Richard Murphy, "The Speech as Literary Genre," *Quarterly Journal of Speech*, April, 1958, 44: 117–127.

The Importance of Record

A third factor which makes a manuscript speech advisable is possible publication. Many speeches delivered on many types of occasions find their way into print in the *Proceedings* of conventions, in professional journals, or in collections of speeches and addresses like the biweekly *Vital Speeches of the Day* and the innumerable anthologies of addresses of men and women whose speaking has in large part made them famous. There are similar collections of public utterances on topics of current significance.[2]

Publication of a speech manuscript may take a number of different forms. Your paper may appear, as we said, in a professional journal in the form in which it was read; in fact, you may be asked for the manuscript as soon as your program is over. That was what happened to one of the present writers two or three years ago: the manuscript was turned over to a representative of the editor, and the next we heard of it, it was in page proof. On the other hand, another manuscript was submitted as requested to an emissary of an editor for the organization before which the paper was presented, and it hasn't been heard of since!

Your manuscript may reach the desk of an editor who feels compelled to "edit" severely everything that comes to him, and what you actually said may have disappeared or been materially modified by the time the speech is printed so that you hardly recognize it as your own production.

Your speech may also appear in a newspaper report of the meeting at which you have spoken; in this case passages may have been taken out of context to suit the editorial policy of the news-gathering agency or of the paper in which it appears. The result may be that while the words were in part your own, they misrepresent your own broad point of view.

In any event, it is often advisable to have a record of what you said in definite form, especially in any discussion of a highly controversial subject in which attitudes can easily be affected. For your own protection, always keep a carbon copy of your manuscript, with

[2] As examples of such anthologies see Lew Sarett, and William Trufant Foster, *Modern Speeches on Basic Issues*, Houghton Mifflin, 1939, and Harold F. Harding, ed., *The Age of Danger: Major Speeches on American Problems*, Random House, 1952.

such alterations included as you may have made in the reading itself.

Radio and Television

Radio and television speeches are often if not usually written out and read. One reason is that most station managers like to know what is going over the air from their station before it is broadcast. This policy protects the station, which shares equal responsibility with the writer and speaker himself for the nature of the material he delivers.[3] Time as a factor requiring radio and television speeches to be written has already been discussed.

Most writers on the subject of broadcast speaking either take for granted or insist that talks over the air should be read from a manuscript rather than delivered extemporaneously. The unrehearsed discussion type of program does not come within the scope of the subject of manuscript speeches.

"Ghost Writing"

One more condition, at least, would seem to make written speeches imperative, almost a matter of course. A great deal of "ghost writing" is done today, and it frequently comes under severe criticism. But busy officials—political, industrial, commercial—often feel they do not have the time or the ability to construct a speech suitable to their own position or status or the occasion on which they are expected to speak.[4] Or if he does have a fair idea of what would be appropriate he may well lack the time and the skill to put his ideas into acceptable form.

Professional speech writers are not a modern invention. They have been known from the time of ancient Athens, when Lysias, among others, achieved fame for being able to suit the speeches he wrote to the natures of the men who were to present them. So today the professional speech-writer—the "ghost writer"—provides many an

[3] Charles Frederick Lindsley, *Radio and Television Communication*, McGraw-Hill, 1952, p. 207.

[4] See Waldo W. Braden and Mary Louise Gehring, *Speech Practices, A Resource Book for the Student of Speech*, Harper, 1958, "How a Presidential Speech Was Prepared," pp. 17–20, especially the final paragraph on p. 20 explaining why the President himself did not write the speech.

aspirant to public office with speeches which are then read, and often very badly, to the public. They are read badly primarily because the reader has had too little opportunity or perhaps inclination to study them carefully and rehearse them in order to know just what he is going to say and how he is going to say it. Sometimes it is glaringly apparent that the reader has never even seen the speech that is supposed to offer evidence of his suitability for an elective office he is seeking.

You may sometimes find it necessary to read a speech prepared by a ghost writer or one written by a friend who at the last minute is unable to present it himself. In the first instance you are on your own to present "your" speech in such a way that it will be well received *as* yours; in the latter case, when you agree to read the friend's manuscript you are under an obligation to present it as effectively as possible so that the writer, rather than yourself, will receive the approval of the listeners.

PREPARING THE MANUSCRIPT SPEECH

The delivery of a manuscript speech should seem as extemporaneous as possible; because of its flexibility in both construction and delivery, the extemporaneous speech is generally considered the model type of preparation and presentation. Much of the presentation itself will depend on how you have conceived and prepared the manuscript in the first place.

A Speech Is Not an Essay

Throughout your preparation you must bear in mind that what you are writing is not an essay, a report, or an article for publication, even though what you write may be published subsequently. It often happens that a paper which sounded very good when heard by the audience is not suitable for reading. Remember that you are not writing a paper intended primarily to be read from the printed page in one form or another. You are writing a speech, which will reach its recipients mainly through the ear and the eye as you stand before them and present it to them. What you say will depend, as we have pointed out, not only on the words you use and the way you put them together but upon such vocal attributes as phrasing

and emphasis or stressing; it may depend on how easily your listeners can hear you, on how clearly you pronounce your words. It
will probably depend also on what your audience sees you doing.

Your "public," consisting of those whom you reach orally, will be
under the necessity of following and comprehending you as you go
along; they will have no opportunity to go back over any idea you
have presented and scrutinize it for fuller understanding. They must
be able to get it the first time. Your primary obligation is to the
listeners rather than to the readers. The latter can take all the time
they want to go back and reread as much as they please.

Your presentation of a manuscript speech will have certain factors, indicated above, that would not be present if your listeners
were instead to read the published paper for themselves. You will
many times say to yourself or to others, after reading the published
version of some especially effective speech, "I wish I could have
heard that." The story is told of Aeschines that after the fall of the
Athenian democracy he went to the island of Rhodes and set up a
school of speaking. While there he repeated to his students one day
one of the great speeches of his former Athenian rival, Demosthenes.
After listening to the praises of his listeners he said quietly, "Ah, but
what would you have said if you had heard him give it!"[5]

Your voice and visible bodily movements can give your speech, as
James Burgh said two hundred years age, meanings which the words
themselves often give no indication of. These complementary meanings are not revealed on the printed page to the reader.

You are writing a *speech,* then. If you keep that fact in mind as
you write and rewrite, you will be more likely to sound and look
like a speaker than like a writer reading his own essay aloud.

Direct Your Speech to Your Specific Audience

In an extemporaneous speaking situation you can usually make
many adaptations to the occasion and the audience on the ground,
so to speak. Such on-the-spot modifications are more difficult with a
manuscript speech, however, and it is therefore of special importance that, even before you determine your goals, your specific techniques, and your supporting materials, you learn as much as you can

[5] Another version of this story is found at the end of Chapter 30. The difference lies in the emphasis on whether the speech is heard only or seen as well.

about the nature of the occasion and the people who will be there to hear you.[6] It may be fatal for your objectives to misjudge either the nature of the occasion or the attitudes and level of information of your listeners.

In any speaking situation it is essential that *rapport* be established between speaker and audience. It is never easy to create such a relation between yourself and some "to-whom-it-may-concern" group of listeners. In the normal speaking situation the need for *rapport* refers to the relationship between a *specific* speaker and a *specific* group of people assembled on a *specific* occasion. Those who will be sitting before you are those whom you will want to reach, inform, stimulate, entertain, convince, or actuate. Write the speech, therefore, for that particular group.

Write the Speech for the Listener Rather than for the Reader

A speech is *written* for the ear; it is *delivered* to the eye as well as to the ear. Choose each word, write each clause and each sentence, construct each paragraph according to how it will *sound*. Read aloud what you have written, and listen to the way it sounds to your own ear. Subvocal reading will not give you the same effect, though it has its values, too. You don't need grammatical errors, other barbarisms, and highly colloquial expressions to make the speech sound right; good English in good construction can sound very good indeed. But it has to be written with the sound in mind.

In long and complicated sentence structure much of the sense is often lost. "The problem of making the radio speech understandable to the audience is not entirely a matter of vocabulary. The structure of sentences plays an even greater part in the clearness of the material presented."[7] Unfamiliar terms need to be translated into language your listeners will understand. You can eliminate that necessity by being intelligible to begin with. But choose the best language and put it into the most highly polished form that your audience is capable of understanding.

Try to find someone, preferably someone not especially familiar with your subject, who will listen to you read your speech. But don't

---

[6] See Chapter 9, "Analyzing the Time and Place of the Speech," and Chapter 10, "Analyzing the Audience," for detailed discussion of this aspect of speech preparation.

[7] Waldo Abbot and Richard L. Rider, *Handbook of Broadcasting*, 4th ed., McGraw-Hill, 1957, p. 164.

accept flattery from such listeners; it will give you no basis for improving your writing. Insist on honest, objective comment; you may not agree with or accept some of it, but be willing to evaluate criticisms objectively yourself. They just might have some value.

Above all, listen to yourself while you are writing. You will hear things in your own speech that you like and will want to retain; you will also hear things that you do not like and will want to improve—not, perhaps, because the ideas are unacceptable, but because they can be put into language that will say more precisely what you want to say and will at the same time sound better.

Bear in mind as you write—and as you read and rewrite—that the speech will be successful or not according to the way it sounds to your listeners, not to the way it reads silently to yourself; according to the way you appear to the audience as you deliver your speech rather than the way the manuscript looks on the typed paper or printed page.

Criticize, Rewrite, Revise—and Revise Again

In a way, you are never through writing a speech. Russell H. Conwell never finished revising and improving his famous "Acres of Diamonds" speech, although he gave it many thousands of times over a period of many years.

Start working on your speech as soon as you learn that you are going to make it. Your early work may be in the form of determining in your own mind what you are going to try to do, how you are going to organize the speech, what you are going to put into it, and so on. Since you will probably not want to depend entirely on your present information, you may spend some time reading on your subject. Some of this preliminary work will naturally precede any effort at writing, though you may be making copious notes. Begin to set down on paper what you have fairly early in your preparation; it will be a beginning on which you can build.

Write, revise, and rewrite your speech until it is as good as you can make it, and then, if you have a little time, lay it aside for a while. By staying away from your manuscript for a week or so, you will then often be able to return to it with a fresh point of view, a new perspective; you will see more clearly what needs to be done, or whether, indeed, anything should be done at all by way of revision.

Too many beginning speakers and writers are unwilling to spend time and effort in striving for the maximum effectiveness of either speeches or papers written in the hope of publication. As a matter of fact, the best writers and speakers today have achieved their excellence because they were and still are willing to revise and rewrite over and over again. Readers and listeners who read or hear only the finished product are likely never to realize just how much labor went into the polishing of even a single sentence. If you want to impress your listeners by both the solidity of the content of your speeches and the way that content is expressed, such refinement will be highly profitable to you.

Check Your Speech Organization Closely

The organization of a manuscript speech does not differ significantly from that of any speech of a similar nature prepared for any other kind of presentation.

White and Henderlider recommend the following sequence in developing the manuscript speech: "(1) *develop your outline;* (2) *write the first draft of your manuscript;* (3) *revise the first draft;* and (4) *prepare your final copy.*"[8] Throughout the entire process follow the basic principles of speech construction and language usage, working for clarity, vividness, and impressiveness, as these principles are developed in this text. "In rhetoric," says Hudson, "a study of the audience is fundamental; and the essence of it [rhetoric] is adaptation to the end of influencing hearers."[9] As in any kind of speech preparation, keep constantly in mind that whether in preparation or in presentation of the speech, whether in imagination or in reality, you are addressing your audience, your listeners.

DELIVERY OF THE MANUSCRIPT SPEECH

Preparing the Final Copy

The ease with which you will be able to present your manuscript speech will depend largely on what preparations you make for presenting it. First consideration should be given to preparing the final

[8] Eugene E. White and Clair R. Henderlider, *Practical Public Speaking*, Macmillan, 1954, p. 306. Italics are in the original.
[9] Hoyt H. Hudson, "The Field of Rhetoric," *Quarterly Journal of Speech*, April, 1923, 9: 167–180.

copy itself. And the form of that copy will depend in turn on the conditions under which you will have to read it.

The manuscript itself. If it is at all possible to avoid it, never attempt to read a handwritten script. Have it typed or type it yourself. If you cannot avoid the handwriting, write in large, bold script, easily legible.

Never attempt to read a manuscript in single-spaced typing. Double spacing is much better; triple spacing is still preferable.

Be sure there are no typographical or any other errors. Now and then a whole line gets lost in the copying, and you may have difficulty in supplying the missing material unless you spot it at once.

The typing itself should be done with a fresh ribbon, preferably black, on one side only of a good quality paper. If you are speaking over a microphone, whether in an auditorium or on the radio or TV, avoid using heavy bond or onionskin paper; a soft paper is easier to handle without noise.

The lines on a typescript should be fairly short, with no broken words at the end of the lines or especially at the end of a page. If possible, no sentences should be carried over to the next page, though if you are a skillful reader turning the page in the middle of a sentence need not result in any break in the fluency of the reading.

If you are using a reading stand on which you can lay your script, probably the most convenient size page is the standard 8½ by 11 inches; you will have to change pages less often than with smaller sheets. If, however, you are to hold your script in your hand smaller paper may be more convenient. Some speakers prefer half-size pages, 8½ by 5½—simply the standard size sheets cut in half. Still others like the 5 by 8 cards that can be purchased at any stationery store because they are a convenient size, can be held easily in the hand, and can even be used to gesture with. It is often consoling to the speaker to have something to hold in his hands. On one occasion a speaker had in his hands a small pack of cards at which he would look now and then and with which he gesticulated quite freely. When the cards were examined later they turned out to be totally blank on both sides!

"Editing" the manuscript. As we have pointed out, sentences, clauses, phrases, and even individual words can mean different things according to the ways in which they are spoken. In your speech they mean certain definite things to you, and you want them to mean much the same things to your listeners. As you practice reading the script work on various passages until your manner of utterance makes those passages say just what you want them to say. You may want a particular emphasis here, a rising or falling inflection there, a pause at another place.

If you depend entirely on your memory of just how you worked out a certain sentence in your practice, you may forget when you read it to your audience just which of the different meanings you decided was preferable. It is often useful therefore to mark your manuscript with different indicators that will give you a cue to the manner in which those particular passages or those particular words are to be read to give the exact meanings you intended.

Underlining, for example, may be used to indicate emphasis. If you have trouble remembering which syllable of a word takes the accent or stress, you can put that syllable in capitals, or you may underline it. For example, a *gal*lant man may, in another context, be spoken of as a gal*lant*. You may visit a certain locality *fre*quently, or you may fre*quent* it. *Ref*use is something you throw away as waste; but you would re*fuse* a request you did not want to grant.

Certain manuscript marks have become standard: a line sloping upward from left to right above a word or syllable (∕) indicates a rising inflection, sloping downward (∖) a falling inflection. A slanting line (∕) between words or phrases indicates a pause at that point; two such lines (∕∕) indicate a longer pause.

Practicing the Speech

No system of marking will take the place of practice. You may even acquire such dependence on the markings that you lose the sense of what you are trying to say. You will need much practice reading your speech if it is to *sound* like a speech and you are to *look* like a speaker. Practice will help to fix in your mind, as well as in your vocal and bodily patterns of delivery, the meanings you want your audience to get. If those meanings are firmly enough fixed through study and practice, you probably won't need the markings described in the preceding sections. You should have those meanings so well established that one and only one mode of utterance will express them.

Read your speech as if you were delivering it to an audience. In practicing, take the stance you expect to take in the actual presentation, and people the space before you with your listeners. Then *speak* to them, using your manuscript in place of your memory with respect to the content of the speech.

Practice also to increase your eye span on the typed page. How many words can you take in at a glance? How many eye fixations does it take you to go across the line? How many times do your eyes look back? How long do your eyes rest at a single fixation? These are the determinants of rapid reading: a long eye span, to take in as many words or syllables as possible every time the eyes come to rest; a short fixation, to reduce the amount of time it requires to take in these words or syllables; the absence of backward movements or regressions so that you do not have to go back to pick up what you missed the first time over.

By developing the ability to get from the page the greatest number of words and hence the wider scope of meanings, you will have more time to give to the audience. You will therefore become less dependent on the manuscript, and your speech will look and sound more like an extemporaneous speech. It has been estimated that a skillful reader can give his listeners as much as 80 percent of the total time of presentation. Developing the ability to get the meanings on the printed page faster does not mean that you must give those meanings to the audience faster too. If you keep in mind that you are not *reading* a speech but *talking* it, you will find it easier to speak at your normal rate. Because you have the words before you and do not have to grope in your mind for them is no reason for you to gallop through your speech. Don't talk your speech too fast, in other words.

Delivering the Speech

At the risk of seeming unduly repetitious, we remind you again that a manuscript speech is still a *speech;* it can and should sound just as fresh and spontaneous as an extemporaneous speech. You should be familiar enough with the content, and have practiced aloud sufficiently, that you need not be bound to your paper but are able to keep your audience in your vision as much as you expect to remain in theirs.

A common fault in reading, whether a speech, an essay, or any other printed material, is to set patterns of rate, emphasis, and inflectional movement and maintain those patterns throughout. If you have the meanings thoroughly in mind and have practiced giving them to your imaginary listeners, you will be able to break away from such patterns and give those meanings to your actual audience.

In this connection, remember that meanings are twofold: you must let your hearers know not only what you think about a given subject, but how you feel about it. Do not hesitate, whenever it is at all appropriate, to express your attitudes as well as your ideas. Here your manner of delivery is of the greatest importance. The type of monotony suggested in the preceding paragraph may convey information, but it will certainly not go far in stimulating attitudes toward that information.

If you have placed your manuscript on a reading stand, you will be limited in your movement about the platform by the necessity of keeping your paper constantly in the range of vision. Even then your hands and arms, general bodily balance, facial expression, and so on are free to assist in the full expression of your thought. Do not grasp the edges of the stand as if you were afraid of falling, or use the stand itself as a prop, making a tripod of your own two legs and the stand.

You can of course put your hands on the edges of the stand or anywhere else in order to maintain an attitude of informality where informality is permitted; you will be somewhat more restricted on more formal occasions.

Actually, except for the necessity of maintaining contact with your manuscript—and that, as you have seen, can be reduced greatly —there is little fundamental difference between delivering a written and an extemporaneous speech. The essentials are *rapport* with your audience and meaningful flexibility in your voice and visible bodily activity, keeping in mind that you have an idea to present to a group of listeners. Your manuscript, as we have suggested, simply takes the place of the ancient art of memory, ensuring that what you have planned to say will be readily recalled at the specific moment you need it. But the writing and rewriting, revising and refining will give you the opportunity to put a polish on your speech that can be provided only by years of study and experience in extemporaneous speech.

Never attempt to conceal from your audience the fact that you are using a manuscript. No matter how unobtrusive they are, efforts to hide the script will simply draw attention to it. Even when the manuscript is shielded from the audience, as on a reading stand, you cannot conceal entirely your frequent references to it and your turning of the pages. When you have to look at your paper, *look at it.* Sneak glances will only make you look ridiculous, and will do much greater damage than frankly and openly turning your eyes to the pages before you. With experience, you may actually become so adept in the use of a written speech that it will hardly be noticed that you are using one.

This principle is especially applicable when the manuscript is held in your hands. There it is, in full view of your listeners. There you stand also, equally in full view. The manuscript is clearly there for the express purpose of reminding you of what you had planned to say. It can no more be concealed than a rocket can be concealed when it rises from the launching pad at Canaveral. It is worse than useless to make the attempt.

Avoid setting a regular pace, as if you had to utter just so many words per minute every minute, either few or many, and ploughing through the speech at that pace whatever happens. It takes a great deal of skill either to speak extemporaneously or to read a speech effectively, communicatively, and impressively. Practice in either kind of speaking is an absolute essential for the maximum development of that skill.

RADIO AND TELEVISION SPEAKING

Radio and Television Situations Are Different

Despite the common elements in all manuscript speaking, talking over the air is likely to be a quite different experience, both in preparation and in presentation, from speaking to a live, present, and responsive audience. In some situations on both radio and television you may actually have an audience in the studio; but even there certain obvious differences exist. For our present purposes we shall limit the discussion to studio situations in which no audience is present.

Among many people ". . . there seems to be an assumption that if a person is an experienced speaker he will be a good speaker on radio and television. This is probably the most difficult assumption to combat in the whole business of broadcasting. Speakers may get kind comments from their friends and even a few letters from the audience, and they are misled into believing that their performances have been very good. Occasions when one is told that he isn't good are rare."[10]

This is one attitude. Other authorities, however, insist that the problem of effective speaking before the microphone or the camera is essentially one of adapting ". . . modern principles of effective speech to their use in the particular case of radio. A study of speech principles will reveal the little-realized fact that, aside from a few allowances due to the mechanical limitations of a microphone, the best radio speaker is the one who follows most closely the dictates of a competent textbook on public speaking. The added difficulty that lack of a visible audience presents in broadcasting only increases the necessity of observing speech rules."[11]

A few basic differences between speaking directly to a present, live audience and speaking on radio or television to a large number of widely scattered and unseen people need to be observed in both the writing and the presentation of the broadcast speech.

No "feedback" from the audience.   In neither radio nor television broadcasting does the speaker have the stimulation of an audience which he himself can see and hear. This handicap is overcome somewhat when there are studio audiences; but usually the speech is addressed to an unseen, unresponding, indefinite number of possible listeners. There is no "feedback"; the speaker has no way of knowing who, or how many, or what kinds of people are listening, or whether anyone is tuned in at all.

On the other hand, in a current television series broadcast by a local station in cooperation with a university, the range of culture levels represented in the comments that have come to the station, the participants, and the State University is surprising. Commendatory observations have come from laborers as well as from a justice

---

[10] Sherman P. Lawton, *The Modern Broadcaster: The Station Book,* Harper, 1961, p. 262.
[11] Abbot and Rider, *op. cit.,* p. 80.

of the State Supreme Court. But these comments are received after the broadcasts, when it is too late for them to modify in any way the programs themselves. From those belated observations we have reason to believe that they do have a widespread audience; we just can't see them and hear them during the broadcasts.

No compulsion to listen. Another factor which is of some importance is the awareness that whereas once the program begins the live audience is a more or less captive audience, the radio or television audience is under no social or other obligation to listen; all they have to do is turn the dial of the radio or the television to another program. Few listeners, except those in aisle seats or in the rear of the auditorium, will walk out on a speaker after he starts speaking; people just don't want to make themselves conspicuous. But the speaker over the air has no way of knowing how many have turned to programs with higher "ratings"!

In one sense, there is no radio or television audience. In addressing an audience in an auditorium there is a live, assembled group of people, large or small, which may be called an audience. In speaking over the air there is no such thing as an assemblage of radio or television listeners or viewers, except in the cases of closed-circuit or pay television in large theaters.

Over the air you are speaking to individuals or small family groups, or small groups of friends and neighbors gathered to hear a specific talk on a topic of particular interest to them all. The "mass communications" concept may be quite misleading. All it means is that a speaker has the opportunity of speaking to a great number of people—sometimes millions—at the same time. But this is not a *group* consisting of all his listeners; there is no opportunity for the development of "group cohesion," or any degree of polarization between speaker and audience. They do not, in fact, constitute an "audience," as the term is commonly used.[12] However few or many there may be, they all retain their individual identities; there is never any merging into any kind of social unit that might be termed an audience. The speaker is talking to individuals. Part of his task is to make them feel that he *is* talking to them personally. As Abbot

[12] See in this connection Charles H. Woolbert, "The Audience," *Psychological Monographs*, 1916, **21**: 37–54.

and Rider point out, the speaker has none of the "advantages to be gained from interstimulation, so commonly noticed in crowd psychology."[13]

A Few Procedures That May Be Helpful

Chester and Garrison developed a number of specific procedures that will be helpful, even necessary, in preparing a speech that is to go over the air.[14] These suggestions are somewhat expanded and interpreted here.

Gain attention immediately. "The opening of a radio speech is crucial." It takes the listener only a moment to decide whether he wants to listen to a program or not, especially a radio or television talk. In this connection, review the discussion of appeals to interest and attention in Chapter 11, "Attention and Interest."

Avoid the rococo in style. Do not use an artificial, flowery style or "ornate and literary words" and threadbare stereotypes. Variety may be the spice of life, but one's diet can be too highly seasoned.

Use simple language. This principle is discussed earlier in the present chapter. It is applicable to most public addresses, but it is of particular importance in radio and television speaking, when, as we have seen, immediate comprehension is necessary. Two of the "best and most perfect examples of oratory" in the English language[15] are characterized by the utmost simplicity, without any sacrifice of grandeur of thought. These are Lincoln's "Gettysburg Address" and "Second Inaugural." Obviously these were not radio or television addresses, but the former was at least a manuscript speech, the copy of which Lincoln held in his hand at the ceremony.[16] In any event, these two may be considered models of simplicity which any speaker might try to emulate, whether he is addressing an audience directly or speaking to millions of listeners

---

[13] Abbot and Rider, *op. cit.*, p. 81.

[14] Giraud Chester and Garnet R. Garrison, *Television and Radio: An Introduction,* Appleton-Century-Crofts, 1956, pp. 290–294.

[15] Earl Curzon of Kedleston, *Modern Parliamentary Eloquence,* Macmillan (London), 1914, pp. 72–75.

[16] Cited by Braden and Gehring, *op. cit.*, p. 46.

and viewers by way of the microphone and camera. They achieve a refinement, a polish, a grandeur of style seldom approached. Yet they are characterized throughout by the utmost simplicity of style, a simplicity seldom achieved on such occasions as the ones on which they were delivered.

A good example of simplicity of style in a radio broadcast speech is "The Vanishing Family Farm," given over CBS on February 9, 1956, by Eric Sevareid. His subject was perhaps not so exalted as Lincoln's, but it is one that touches the lives of a great many American families. Here is a typical paragraph: "Beneath the surface of these policy quarrels over stopgap measures [on the farm problem], a profound change is coming over agricultural life in the country. It may be progress, it may just be inevitable, but it does have its tragic aspects, and it is happening with remarkable rapidity. An American way of life as old as our deepest traditions is passing away. The source spring of much of our moral outlook, our conceptions of individualism, our politics, our folklore is drying up. The small family-size farm and farm-family life are vanishing, as fast as the Indian villages vanished a century ago. And America is never going to be quite the same."[17]

Repeat, repeat, repeat! Repetition, as discussed elsewhere in this text, is a highly useful technique in impressiveness.[18] In the form of restatement it is also useful in achieving understanding. Also, as we have seen, use of previews and signposts can help keep your listeners oriented to your development. Listeners over the air are likely to have many distractions that will cause them to lose the train of thought. Frequent repetitions, therefore, are helpful in enabling them to keep track of your development.

Build mental pictures through words and stories. This technique is developed to some extent in Chapter 26 in the discussion of achieving vividness. In television speaking it can easily be supplemented by the use of visual supports, which are illustrated and discussed at some length in Chapter 18.

Talk it out. In other words, as we have emphasized earlier in the

[17] Eric Sevareid, in *ibid.*, pp. 140 f.
[18] See Chapter 27, "Achieving Impressiveness."

present chapter, write your speech for your listeners; read it aloud; seek an informal and conversational style.

"Stick to your own last." That is, don't try to assume a personality different from your own or presume to be someone other than who you are. Avoid mannerisms, artificialities, oddities of language—anything that is markedly different from the gestures and speech you use every day—as well as much of the current gross slang. Be at your best, but don't strain to be studiously better than your best. "Pedantry is worse than blundering," said George Herbert Palmer.[19]

The famous evangelist Billy Sunday, who had once been a major-league baseball player, never forgot that experience. In his evangelistic exhortations he was continually injecting illustrations, terms, and allusions taken from his baseball days. He refused to assume a different background from what his had actually been, but he made rich capital out of that.[20]

Time your speech as you rehearse. Study the rate at which you speak. As you read aloud, mark in the margin of your manuscript either the time you have taken up to a given point or the time remaining to you. Decide whether you need to eliminate material, add more, or alter your rate of speaking. If you attempt to change your habitual rate too greatly, you are likely to lose in expressiveness. Often you can edit your own manuscript by changing the wording slightly to add or delete, or you may need to rewrite whole paragraphs.

But even before writing the first draft find out about how long your manuscript is going to have to be. Determine your approximate reading rate, whether it is 125 or 175 words per minute, and how many words you will put on a single page. Knowing the exact length of the speech, the rate of speaking, and the number of words per page, you can estimate quite accurately the length the manuscript needs to be. Revising and rehearsing it will produce changes, but by the final draft you should know, by indications in the margins, exactly where you should be in the reading at specific periods of time. You will not then have to be watching the director to see whether you need to speed up or slow down.

[19] *Self-Cultivation in English,* Houghton Mifflin, 1909, p. 16 ff.
[20] "Faces from the Past—III," *American Heritage,* August, 1961, **12**: 39.

Studio Behavior

Not even a manuscript that has been approved in every detail and practiced assiduously is going to insure a successful broadcast. Many details of studio behavior in both radio and television need to be understood and observed. For example, where should you stand in relation to the microphone or the camera? If the microphone is suspended by a ribbon around your neck, as is sometimes the case, you won't have to worry about it. As for the camera, the studio personnel will move that about, "shooting" from different angles and distances, so that will be taken care of.

How loudly should you speak? Don't shout. Here again that is usually taken care of in the control room, though you may be asked to speak up a little or to soften your voice.

If you are accustomed to using a microphone and public address system when speaking directly to an audience, you may already have some familiarity with microphone technique. In such a case you have probably learned not to get your lips too close to the microphone, and not to cup it in your hands and thus hold it too close.

If you are accustomed to speaking over the air, you have probably been instructed on how to use the microphone and what to do about the camera which may be poking its eyes, the lenses, into your very face. But if you are going into the studio without previous experience or training, your best course is to be guided by the station personnel, who are in the best position to observe, from the control room, what you should do to make your speaking more effective. They will be just as eager as you for the program to be good enough for people to listen to it and to others like it. Do not be dismayed if you have to go over your speech a number of times; practice at home is essential, but there are still a few things that can be learned only under studio conditions.

If you own a tape recorder or have access to one, a recording may tell you a number of things about your voice; but have someone listen with you who can point out things you may not notice. It is a revealing experience to hear your voice come back to you for the first time—still more so when you can hear and see yourself in action, as you can in modern methods of teletape recording. People have been known to refuse to speak on the air after hearing a recording of themselves. On the other hand, you may have important, responsible things to say, and people will listen to you even if you do not have quite the voice and the assurance of a professional radio or television announcer or actor. The studio management can also tell you many things that will help you become a more effective speaker on the air.

QUESTIONS AND TOPICS FOR STUDY AND REVIEW

1. Does the use of a manuscript in speaking necessarily denote a weakness in speaking extemporaneously?
2. Name several particular influences that may have led to an apparent increase in the use of the manuscript.
3. Why is it important to be able to keep your eyes on your listeners as much of the time as possible? One text suggests as much as 90 percent.
4. What elements are involved in the refinement or polish of the manuscript speech?
5. What has been the extent of actual, usable instruction you have had in your entire school program in the *written* use of English, for example, in grammar and in writing, as of themes and term papers? What has been the nature and extent of the teachers' criticisms of your writing?
6. If composition for speech involves factors different from composition for writing, how can a speech manuscript have literary value?
7. What is your attitude toward the ethics of ghost writing, or of giving a speech as your own that someone else has written? How would such a procedure compare with the ghost writing of theses and dissertations?
8. What is the relation between yourself as the speaker and a "to-whom-it-may-concern" group of listeners?
9. Comment on the statement by Hudson (p. 440) that "In rhetoric a study of the audience is fundamental; and the essence of it is adaptation to the end of influencing hearers." How is that different from writing to influence readers?
10. If you are holding your manuscript in your hands while reading, where should the script be held in relation to the line from your eyes to the audience? Explain your answer.
11. Of what value to the speaker is the stimulation from an audience he can see and hear? Can the absence of such a stimulation while speaking over the air be compensated for in any way?

12. What is meant by this sentence: "In a sense, there is no radio or television audience"? What does it take for people to become an "audience"?
13. Certain major differences are described between speaking directly to an audience and speaking over the air. Just what effects do these differences have on the style or the use of language?
14. It has been said that one does not "read" a manuscript to an audience; one "talks" it. What is the difference, and why is it important?
15. In writing your speech, whether to be delivered directly to the audience or over the air, what are some of the things you can do to make your speech more readily intelligible to the audience?

PROJECTS

1. Establish the minimum time it should take to *get* the meanings from a printed or typed page on the one hand, and on the other, the time it should take, at an average rate of speaking, to *give* those meanings to your audience. What percentage of time should you be able to devote to your listeners?
2. You may have as one of your assignments a manuscript speech. As soon as you learn the nature of it, start working on it. Follow the suggestions given in this chapter and in your other readings. Practice delivering it communicatively, and try to establish and maintain *rapport* with your listeners.
3. Write a report on some inquiry you have made. State your problem, your sources of information, the nature of that information, and the specific material itself. Draw your inferences from your material, and come to at least some tentative conclusions. Read this report to the class. Use whatever visual supports you may need, but coordinate them in your presentation with the use of the manuscript.
4. Practice reading a passage from a speech or an entire short speech, giving your imaginary audience as much of your attention as you can. Go over the speech a number of times, trying to improve on the three basic factors in reading speed and consequently on your ability to speak for longer and longer times between glances at the page. *Read meaningfully.*
5. Report on radio and television talks you have heard, basing your evaluations on the discussions in this chapter and on your supplementary readings.
6. Read for recording a speech you have written as if to go on the air. In the presence of others, your class, for example, play it back and

have your listeners criticize it as if they had heard it over the air. (Many of the speeches you hear on both radio and television have actually been recorded beforehand.)

SUPPLEMENTARY READINGS

Abbot, Waldo, and Richard L. Rider, *Handbook of Broadcasting*, 4th ed., McGraw-Hill, 1957, chap. 6, "Radio and Television Speaking"; chap. 8, "Articulation, Intonation, Rhythm."

Baird, A. Craig, and Franklin H. Knower, *General Speech: An Introduction*, 2nd ed., McGraw-Hill, 1957, pp. 327–336.

Bryant, Donald C., and Karl R. Wallace, *Fundamentals of Public Speaking*, 3rd ed., Appleton-Century-Crofts, 1960, pp. 237–245.

Chester, Giraud, and Garnet R. Garrison, *Television and Radio: An Introduction*, Appleton-Century-Crofts, 1956, chap. 19, "Talking on the Air."

Gilman, Wilbur E., Bower Aly, and Loren Reid, *The Fundamentals of Speaking*, Macmillan, 1951, chap. 21, "Talking to the Audience of Television and Radio."

Hudson, Hoyt H., "The Field of Rhetoric," *Quarterly Journal of Speech*, April, 1923, 9: 167–180.

Lawton, Sherman P., *The Modern Broadcaster: The Station Book*, Harper, 1961, pp. 261–270.

Lindsley, Charles Frederick, *Radio and Television Communication*, McGraw-Hill, 1952, chap. 10, "The Radio Talk and the Radio Speaker."

Reid, Loren, *First Principles of Public Speaking*, Artcraft, 1960, chap. 16, "Manuscript Speaking: Impromptu Speaking."

Weaver, Andrew Thomas, and Ordean Gerhard Ness, *The Fundamentals and Forms of Speech*, Odyssey, 1957, chap. 16, "Radio and Television Speaking."

White, Eugene E., and Clair R. Henderlider, *Practical Public Speaking*, Macmillan, 1954, part II, chap. 15, "The Manuscript Speech."

Woolbert, Charles H., "The Audience," *Psychological Monographs*, 1916, 21: 37–54.

25

Using Language
for Clarity

Once you have made your analysis of the occasion and the audience, determined your purpose, and assembled and organized your material, your next problem is to put the speech into words—into language. Much of your success in speaking will depend on your effective use of language.

When we speak of communicating ideas or conveying thoughts to other people, we are speaking figuratively, for thoughts cannot be really conveyed from one to another; ideas cannot actually be communicated to anyone else. Despite occasional reports of mental telepathy or extrasensory perception, there is at present no known way for one person to transmit thoughts reliably and consistently to another. In the normal speaking situation nothing passes from the speaker to the listener but sound waves and light waves. In the present chapter we shall be concerned primarily with the first of these, sound waves as utilized in the audible aspects of speech. These sound waves do not convey thought; they only stir up thoughts in the listener.

THE BASIS OF WORD MEANING

By repeatedly hearing certain vocal sound patterns in close association with things, actions, events, or qualities while you were learning to speak, you learned to use those patterns yourself as substitutes for the nonverbal occurrences. The sounds came to stand for them, to be symbols for them, to *mean* them. When they were used in your hearing, they called to your mind the things for which they had come to stand; you yourself learned to use them for the same purpose. Others had learned, in the same way you had, that these sound patterns could be used to symbolize or "mean" the things with which they had been so often and so closely associated. These patterns, which may now be called *words* (or, often, word combinations or phrases), you and those about you could now use in "speaking" whenever you wanted to refer to the things for which they stand, without bringing up the objects themselves or demonstrating the action. Our entire structure of language is made up of just such patterns, or words and phrases, so arranged and so systematized as to have highly complex meanings.

To put it briefly, language has meaning for you and those around you solely on the basis of the associations which have been built up between the sound patterns and the things for which they have come to stand. Meaning for you is thus based entirely on your own individual experiences in associating symbol, that is, word or phrase, with object.[1]

For your listeners meaning is likewise based on their individual experiences. Since those experiences can never be the same for

[1] The word *object* is used here to refer to any nonverbal fact or experience. We do, however, learn meanings (or rather, definitions) of words by relating them to other words whose meanings we have learned through direct association. The ultimate basis of word meanings is still the associations established between sound pattern and nonverbal experience.

different persons, no word can have exactly the same meaning for two or more individuals. And since our experiences and associations are constantly changing and thus meanings are also constantly developing, no word can have exactly the same meaning for the same person over a period of time; nor will words have identical meanings for any group of people (so far as that is at all possible) from one time, say, one generation, to another time or generation.

Communication between individuals is possible only because those associations are sufficiently similar, both for different individuals and for the same individual at different times, to permit more or less common and consistent meanings to be aroused or stimulated by the symbols.

As we study different subjects we discover that words and word combinations are not the only type of symbol that can be used to communicate. Quite early in school children learn the symbols indicating the fundamental arithmetical processes expressed in the words *plus, minus, times,* and *divided by,* and in the symbols associated with them in print. Later they will learn the significance and use of symbols for more complicated processes and relationships. They will learn how to use maps of different kinds and blueprints and schematic designs essential in the understanding and study of many of the sciences, both theoretical and applied. These codes of symbols constitute "languages" just as truly as do words and the ways they are put together. It might be suggested that such symbolic systems are likely to have more consistent meanings to different persons, and over a longer period of time, than are the words we use in our daily communication.

Since the ideas which other people get from you come through the symbols you use and the ways you use them—whether you are giving a public speech or submitting an architectural blueprint or a circuit diagram for some electronic instrument—it is evident that their understanding is largely dependent upon your use of those symbols. Since our present interest is in speaking, let us concentrate our attention on the symbolizations of speech, or verbal language.

Obviously, if you are really impelled by what we have been calling the *urge to communicate,* you must choose your language with extreme care. The wrong use of a word, the use of a wrong word, or a sentence poorly phrased may completely destroy the meanings you want to arouse. You must be sure first of all that you understand clearly and definitely the language you are using; then you must see to it that your language is as clear and definite for your listeners, so that you and they get approximately the same meanings from your language.

OBJECTIVES IN THE USE OF LANGUAGE

When you plan the wording of a speech, therefore, you should work toward three specific objectives: clarity, vividness, and impressiveness.

By *clarity* is meant that attribute in your language which arouses definite and specific meanings. Clarity provides understanding. Your own ideas may often lack clarity because you have never gone to the trouble to put them into language of definite and specific meaning. Not until you have expressed your thoughts in clear, definite language, whatever the system of symbolism of that particular language, have you clarified the thoughts themselves.

Vividness is based primarily on imagery, which in turn arises from concrete experiences. This imagery may be visual, auditory, motor, thermal, or other, or any combination of them. The more definitely and strongly your language recalls such imagery, the more vivid it will be.

Impressiveness refers to emotional coloring, which is an integral aspect of the meaning of most of the language you use. "Meaning for speech," says Woolbert, *"is always twofold. . . .* It is not enough that a speaker use a type of expression that carries only a logical meaning: he must show the hearer *how he himself feels about the matter.* He must not only let the hearer know what the idea is, but how well or ill he himself thinks of it."[2]

In arousing definite logical meanings and securing understanding, you must ensure the attribute of clarity. In stimulating rich and vivid imagery, you seek to provide vividness. In arousing the emotional aspects of meaning, you attempt to achieve impressiveness.

These three objectives are by no means incompatible. It is not only possible, it is usually highly advantageous for you to choose languages that will accomplish all of them at the same time. You won't always be able to do this, but not infrequently a single sen-

[2] Charles Henry Woolbert, *The Fundamentals of Speech,* 2nd ed., Harper, 1927, p. 195.

tence will be at once clear in arousing logical meanings, vivid in the recall of personal experiences, and impressive in the stimulation of emotional attitudes. When you can achieve all three of these, your chance of success in speaking will be more nearly assured. We shall now consider each of these objectives somewhat more in detail.

ACHIEVING CLARITY

In his *Art of Rhetoric* Aristotle had a great deal to say about style, a term which refers to one's use of language which is peculiar to him and by which he may often be distinguished from other writers or speakers. Said Aristotle, ". . . a good style is, first of all, clear."[3] If you would make your own ideas clear to your listeners, you must first of all make them clear to yourself. What we call thinking goes on largely through the use of language. If your own concepts are vague and hazy, it will not only be impossible to make them anything else for your listeners, but you yourself will be going about in a perpetual fog. Clarification of concepts, then, is an absolute essential to clear thinking as well as to clear speaking. A term misunderstood is a term falsified, said a medieval scholar.[4]

Be sure, then, that you have a clear understanding of your own words. Even though you may have to hunt for the concrete facts of experience to which your abstract language refers, your use of word meanings must be true to those facts, and the relationships expressed in that language must correspond to the relationships among the facts of experience themselves. The statement that snow is white is true if and only if snow is actually white.

Finding the Meanings of Words

For many of our words we have little or no difficulty in knowing with sufficient exactness what they mean when we use them. You hear and use such words as *book, horse, automobile* (usually *car*), *credits, football, shoes, walk, write, study, speak, red, cold, hard,* and the like; and with some variations for individual differences in

[3] Lane Cooper, *The Rhetoric of Aristotle,* Appleton-Century-Crofts, 1932, p. 185, 1404b.

[4] Cassiodorus, cited by J. W. H. Atkins, *English Literary Criticism: The Medieval Phase,* Cambridge University Press, 1943, p. 46.

the details of your experiences, they "mean" pretty much the same for college students all over the country. Because they refer to fairly definite things or experiences, because their meanings are recognizably representative of facts, you can use them in an intelligent context with little fear of misunderstanding either on the part of yourself as speaker or on the part of your listeners. They are often called *concrete* terms. But even though the meanings of such terms are on the whole fairly definite, confusion often results from their careless use.

On the other hand, a large number of words have meanings not so easily determined. They come under the classification commonly known as *abstract* terms, because they do not refer to definite, specific things or even classes of things or experiences but to generalized concepts based on a wide variety of experiences. In forming these concepts we *abstract* some significant feature of a large number of experiences in which this particular feature is significant, and to that "persistent constant," as it may be called, we give the term by which we designate it in our communication. The final step in the process of forming these concepts consists in giving this "persistent constant" a name. "Not until we own the symbol do we feel that we hold a key to the immediate knowledge or understanding of the concept."[5]

Although the process of abstracting is not simple, perhaps it can be illustrated fairly simply. The vehicle you drive about the campus (if permitted) is a single, specific object; but there are scores, perhaps hundreds of other vehicles driven by a relatively equal number of students and faculty. They all have sufficient features in common and perform sufficiently similar functions to be grouped under a single classification to which we can give the name *car* or *automobile*. But there are many types of essentially similar vehicles, as well as others that carry not people but goods of all kinds. Furthermore, still other kinds of such equipment travel across the water, in the air, and even underground, as in metropolitan subways. By extracting the common features of all these instruments we can finally arrive at a concept which we can call *traffic* or *transportation*. We can even go beyond these abstractions and group them with such other activities as production and merchandising—whether of raw or manufactured products, coal, oil derivatives, or

[5] Edward Sapir, *Language*, Harcourt, Brace, 1921, p. 17.

anything else that needs moving; we then arrive at a still higher order of abstraction which we designate as *commerce.*

We do not need to stop there in our process of abstracting; we can take yet further elements from other areas, and finally arrive at the concept of *business.* Or we may even consider such things as the country's or the world's *economy.* The abstraction or concept of *economy* may include the production, processing, distribution and utilization of goods and services, so far as these functions apply.

Words of this type may give rise to great indefiniteness and confusion;[6] therefore with these words you must be most careful to ensure that your own understanding is clear, if you are to make your meanings clear to your audience.

Suppose you want to use the term *big business* in a speech. Precisely what does it mean to you? What are the facts of experience to which this term corresponds? How "big" must a business be to come under this classification? Is mere "bigness" the sole criterion, or does the term imply some particular type of organization, like a corporation, a trust, a monopoly—any of which terms may themselves require some explanation? Similarly, you may want to talk some time about "free enterprise," the "welfare state," "social security," "states' rights," or "state sovereignty," or any of a great number of terms that have come into common use during recent years.

Exactly what do these terms mean to you? To what facts of experience do they refer? Or what "persistent constant" can you find among a large number of business organizations of great size that will enable you to form a rational concept to which you can apply the term "big business"?

What exactly is involved in an intelligent understanding of the term "states' rights"? What, for example, is the origin of the concept, if it can be said to have any specific origin. Has the concept changed in meaning since that concept was originally formulated?

If such terms have no clear meanings to you yourself, how are you going to be able to use them intelligently in talking? How, in fact, are you going to be able even to think intelligently about the

---

[6] All words are in a sense abstract, in that it is impossible to know completely the full meaning of any term, any more than Tennyson could know the full meaning of the "Flower in the crannied wall." For a more extended discussion of this principle, see Giles Wilkeson Gray and Claude Merton Wise, *The Bases of Speech,* 3rd ed., Harper, 1959, pp. 503–508. Differences between concrete and abstract terms are mainly of degree.

things for which they stand unless your own ideas about those things are clear? The clarity and honesty of your thinking is largely revealed by the definiteness of meaning of the words in which your ideas are framed. Unless you have a fairly good idea of the meaning of the term *communism*, or even what we call the *American way*, you can't even think intelligently about either, much less talk meaningfully about them.

One might enumerate scores of such words which we use daily without actually having a clear notion of just what they do mean. We have never checked closely their correspondence with any facts of experience or the relationships among those facts. Consequently, not only is our own thinking muddy and indefinite, but because we ourselves do not understand, we find it impossible to make others understand. There is nothing in our discussion for our listeners *to* understand. We have not gone to the trouble of discovering adequately specific meanings for the terms we use.

Deliberate use of language which is not clear either to ourselves or to our listeners does not meet the demand for honest thinking, as discussed in Chapter 4; for honest thinking requires clear thinking. When such language is used for the purpose of concealing thought or confusing the listeners, then such speaking fails to measure up to the requirement of social responsibility.

The Use of Abstractions in Speaking

It is impossible to avoid the use of abstract terms. While words we commonly designate as concrete are very useful—indispensable in fact—on the other hand we have to be able to condense at least the significant aspects of our specific experiences. We have to have convenient terms that will cover the whole range of experiences that may include the particular feature we want to mention. One of the important characteristics of symbolic communication is that by its use we are able to condense these wide ranges into a single abstract expression.

What, for example, is Konrad Adenauer talking about when he discusses "The Berlin Crisis"?[7] The term *crisis* has been used for many years in various contexts. It is applied frequently to the economic situation, the labor situation, the military situation. Edu-

[7] See *Vital Speeches of the Day*, September 15, 1961, **27**: 706–709.

cation now and then faces a *crisis*. A fever, or a severe illness, will reach a *crisis*. What is the common denominator in all these and other areas of struggle and uncertainty, the "persistent constant" to which the term can be applied so that those using or hearing or reading it will not be in the dark about what is meant? Is it a sufficiently common term that it requires no definition whenever it is used?

Thus we can talk about such moral and ethical concepts as truth, honesty, integrity; religious concepts like faith and belief; aesthetic concepts like beauty; political concepts of democracy, communism, and states' rights; mathematical relationships like equations, numbers, vectors, and so on. We do not have to spell out these terms by reference to specific human experience each time we use them.

Remember, however, that the experiences of different people in building up these concepts are far from identical. They vary from generation to generation, from one geographical locality to another, from one educational level to another, from one religious group to the next. Cost of living at one income level "means" something quite different from cost of living in a much higher income bracket. Unless you are certain that your specific listeners' background is sufficiently similar to your own that their understanding is essentially the same as yours, you would do well to translate each new concept you introduce into terms with which they are familiar, experiences which will put you on common ground with them.

Clarity in Continuous Discourse

Clarity in communication involves more than the choice of isolated words; it is perhaps even more definitely a function of the discourse as a whole, the way you put your words into phrases, clauses, and sentences, sentences into paragraphs, and paragraphs into the whole speech. For it is easy to frame words whose meanings may be entirely understandable into a composition which, taken as a whole, simply does not make sense.

The three stanzas which follow illustrate this principle. Read them aloud; they can be read with a great deal of feeling.

> Music of the starshine shimmering o'er the sea,
> Mirror me no longer in the dusk of memory;

Dim and white the rose-leaves drift along the shore.
Wind among the roses, blow no more!

All along the purple creek, lit with silver foam,
Silent, silent voices, cry no more of home!
Soft beyond the cherry-trees, o'er the dim lagoon,
Dawns the crimson lantern of the large, low moon.

Haunted, haunted, haunted—we that mocked and sinned
Hear the vanished voices wailing down the wind,
Watch the ruined rose-leaves drift along the shore.
Wind among the roses, blow no more! [8]

Beautiful, isn't it? Or *is* it? But try to get some sense out of it. It just doesn't mean anything. One wonders whether some of what passes for poetry today may not be equally void of meaning!

Late in the administration of former President Truman the chairman of his Advisory Committee on Management submitted its final report to him. It contained the following paragraph, which was characterized at the time as "one of the finest pieces of gobbledygook ever to be placed before a president":

The general rationale underlying all of these moves has been to try to insure, so far as organizational lines can do it, that, while the advantages of specialization are kept, the broadest possible view of all the applicable considerations in any decision is also retained at the lowest point in the hierarchy where that decision can be finally reached—and so to minimize interagency co-ordination problems.

In an effort to clarify the passage, the editor and publisher declared,

There is nothing difficult about the sentence. The "general rationale" means simply that the fundamental justification is as thereafter set forth. It proceeds to delineate by declaring that top level determinations must be made by specialists in the area of thought involved, but they must be supported by generalized considerations constructed on lower levels. In other words, there is a superimposition of specialized thought upon journeyman practice.[9]

[8] "Wind Among the Roses," anonymous; quoted in Charles Henry Woolbert, *The Fundamentals of Speech*, 1st ed., Harper, 1920, p. 227.
[9] George Dixon, "Railroading a Party Bid," New Orleans *Times-Picayune*, January 18, 1953, sec. 2.

But perhaps the finest example of complete obfuscation is found in the following attempt of a top mobilization official during the Korean conflict to describe the defense effort:

We are peaking our program philosophically, but it is naive to assume the allotment program as an equity program unless the allotments are so abysmally low that they permit the agency to relax and allow market determination at percentage of base period, sidetracking the military return with adjustments. This is based on use levels proportionately and is in the market test sense. We now have a quantitative framework with marginal qualitative reallocations to formalize the procedure for the further refining and implementing of our objectives.[10]

And an inspired headline writer topped the paragraph with "Now You Know."

You cannot allow your audiences to become bogged down with a superfluity of verbiage in bewildering array of scintillating nonsense. Ninety years ago Herbert Spencer, the English philosopher, wrote, "As we do not think in generals but in particulars—as, whenever any class of things is referred to, we represent it to ourselves by calling to mind individual members of it; it follows that when an abstract word is used, the hearer or reader has to choose from his stock of images, one or more, by which he may figure to himself the genus mentioned."[11]

At the same time, according to Adams Sherman Hill, general rather than specific words are sometimes used by those "who wish, for good reasons, to disarm opposition or to veil unpleasant facts; but too frequently they are a resource for those who try to hide their poverty of thought in pompous language, to give obscurity an air of cleverness or shallowness the dignity of an oracle, to cover the fact of having said nothing with the appearance of having said much."[12]

Revealing Your Meanings to Your Listeners

There are a number of methods by which you can reveal the meanings of your words to your hearers—or, for that matter, to

[10] *Newsweek*, March 24, 1952, p. 95.
[11] Herbert Spencer, *The Philosophy of Style*, Appleton-Century-Crofts, 1871, p. 15.
[12] Adams Sherman Hill, *Beginnings of Rhetoric and Composition Including Practical Exercises in English*, American Book, 1902, p. 396.

yourself. All of these have to do with the application of the fundamental determinants of meaning. Some are available to both speaker and writer, and some are useful only to the speaker.

Finding the referent.   Much has already been made of the necessity of finding the events, objects, qualities, and so on for which the word is made to stand. A few specific procedures are helpful in discovering the referent, as it may be called, to yourself, and in revealing it to the audience (that is, in finding for yourself what the term refers to, and in letting your hearers know).

Explanation

Explanation is illustrated by the typical definition found in any dictionary. It consists essentially in finding one word or set of words to explain the meaning of another word, or so much of it as can be condensed into a brief statement. But the words used to define must themselves be understood if the definition and the words being defined are to be intelligible. The definition of the word *metal* in the *American College Dictionary* would be quite unintelligible to one who does not know the meanings of all the words: "any of a class of elementary substances, as gold, silver, copper, etc., all of which are characterized by opacity, ductility, conductivity, and a peculiar luster when freshly fractured."

Sometimes these verbal definitions are the only kind available. The dictionary is a very useful work, and its frequent use is to be encouraged. But if you seek your definitions in dictionaries, be sure you understand all the terms used in those definitions. Similarly, if you try to explain to your listeners the meaning of some term, be very sure that your explanation itself is understandable.

Classification

The meanings of words can often be made clear by a process of classification and differentiation. This process is usually combined with explanation. The thing (object, action, quality, relationship, etc.) is first indicated as belonging to a large class of more or less similar objects and then is shown to differ in certain respects from others in that class. An automobile, according to the *American College Dictionary*, is classed as a vehicle, but differentiated from other vehicles by (1) being especially for carrying passengers, (2) carrying its own power-generating and propelling mechanism, and (3) being for travel on ordinary roads.

Synonyms

Often a word may be satisfactorily defined by using another single word or phrase, known as a *synonym*, which is so close to the word being defined that a clear understanding is obtained. Thus, to *alter* is to *change*; *illicit* and *unlawful* as well as *illegal* are near enough in meaning usually to permit the use of one in defining the other. *Illicit* is occasionally mistaken for *elicit*, and *vice versa*.

The careful study of synonyms is often valuable in indicating delicate shadings of difference in word meanings. For example, consider such a group of synonyms as *command, order, dictate, regulate, instruct, rule,* and so on; in one rather narrow sense they all have similar meanings. But in more precise senses no two of them could be used interchangeably. Thus you must be careful in using synonyms to explain the meanings of your terms.

For one thing, no two words have precisely the same meaning. If great precision is required to make the sense unmistakable, synonyms alone are not enough; they must be supplemented by other methods. Furthermore, since many of our words may be used in various senses, it is easy to select the wrong sense, so that you can have and convey to your listeners an entirely erroneous understanding of your term.

For example, one of the definitions—a synonym—for *sanguine* is *sanguinary*. But whereas the commonly accepted understanding of the former is hopeful or naturally cheerful, the general understanding of the latter is bloody or bloodthirsty.

Furthermore, the use of synonyms, like other methods of definition, is of no value unless the synonyms themselves serve to clarify the meanings. It will not help to define *turgid* as *tumid* unless your hearers understand the meaning of the latter term. If you use synonyms, therefore, be sure that your listeners as well as yourself know their meanings.

Etymology

Sometimes knowing the derivation of a word, its etymology, will help you understand its meaning and as well make the word intelligible to your audience. Many of our words have interesting histories. *Salary*, for instance, comes from the Latin *salarium* and originally referred to money paid to Roman soldiers for the purchase of salt. The prefix *sal* as in *sal ammoniac* comes from the same origin. There is a suggestion of this original meaning when we say that someone is "not worth his salt." The familiar saying, "It's the exception that proves the rule," does not or did not originally mean that the exceptions establish and make valid a rule. *Prove* comes from the same origin as the German *prüfen* and simply means to test or to examine.

Obviously, therefore, you must use caution in attempting to determine or explain meanings from etymologies. A recognized characteristic of words is that most of them are in a fairly constant process of changing meaning, so that often their original meanings no longer apply. You must take this phenomenon of change into consideration, for many of our words have meanings quite different from those they had originally or even some years ago. *Fond*, for example, which has the general meaning of affectionate or feeling affection for, once meant foolish, and is still used often in the sense of foolishly affectionate, as in *fond mammas*.

Purpose or Effect

The meaning of a term can often be explained by stating its purpose or effect. Thus a league can be defined briefly as a compact or agreement among persons for the purpose of maintaining or promoting mutual interests. A *rhetorical question* is a question asked during a discourse, which may be either oral or written, intended to create a specific attitude of inquiry in the minds of the listeners or readers but not intended to be answered verbally. Similarly, the *Frasch process* may be defined as a process for extracting sulfur from the ground by forcing superheated steam (or water) into the subterranean bed of solid sulfur, and thereby forcing the molten element through pipes to the surface.

Many words in our language can be similarly translated into the experiences of our listeners by telling, in terms they will understand, the purpose of the referent.

Negation

An understanding of the meaning of a word may often be made clear by telling what the word does *not* mean. Usually a negative statement is coupled directly or indirectly with a positive definition: "Not this, but that." For example, *conscience*, as Shakespeare used the word in the line, "Thus conscience does make cowards of us all," referred not to a sense of guilt or remorse and a fear of future punishment, as it does today (negative), but to thoughtful meditation (positive).[13] "Liberty," says Judge Florence E. Allen, "does not mean the license to commit cruel murder 'for kicks.' Liberty means that you and I live unregimented, unrepressed, unbrainwashed, with freedom to choose our calling of profession, to choose our place of living, to choose our friends, with the right to develop ourselves just as plants grow in the sun."[14]

Contrast

Closely allied to negation as a method of definition, and often supplementary to it, is contrast. If one term is already understood, another may be explained by indicating points of both similarity and difference in the meanings. For example, in "defining" the different major American dialects, we might describe all three in some detail, but ". . . only those characteristics are recorded for a given dialect which contrast with corresponding characteristics of the other dialects. Features common to all are omitted."[15]

Direct Experiences

Many of our words are difficult if not impossible to define in any of the ways here described. Our own understanding of them has grown up with our direct experiences, and we have never been forced to frame into words any adequate brief statement which would clarify them for anyone who has not had similar experiences. For example, you would have considerable difficulty in explaining to an Asian the meaning of *hot dog*, familiar as you are with the term and what it refers to. The best way to clarify its meaning for such a person would be to take him down to the hot-dog stand and buy him one so that he could experience it directly.

No American boy or girl has to be told what the game of baseball is; but it is doubtful if any of them could describe the game

---

[13] Charles Hubbard Judd, *The Psychology of Social Institutions*, Macmillan, 1926, p. 205. Cf. Gray and Wise, *op. cit.*, p. 516.

[14] Florence E. Allen, "Challenge to the Citizen," commencement address at the University of Utah, August 26, 1960. In Lester Thonssen, ed., *Representative American Speeches*, 1960–1961, H. W. Wilson, 1961, pp. 100–114. Judge Allen is Senior United States Circuit Judge.

[15] Gray and Wise, *op. cit.*, Chapter V, "The Phonetic Basis of Speech," especially, p. 264.

meaningfully to anyone who did not already know it. At the same time, a great many American adults do not understand what the game of straightrail or three-cushion billiards is all about. An observer watching a game of billiards one day asked what the purpose of the game was. "You see on the table," he was told, "two white balls and one red. With his 'cue,' or stick, the player strikes one of the white balls in such a way that it will hit both the others." "I see. Then what do you do?"

If we could get many more of our meanings, even for abstract terms, from direct experiences, our thinking and speaking about the things they stand for would be less vague and indistinct. If we do not know how to apply the processes of abstraction, we ourselves cannot fully grasp the meanings of such abstract terms as democracy. Even though we live in the midst of the circumstances the term stands for, too many of us fail to avail ourselves of opportunities to learn the meaning of the term by close observation of or participation in the processes involved.

Experience through participation is often the only effective method of acquiring meanings. The more directly our understanding of these meanings comes from experiences and from actually associating the word with the "thing," the more complete and exact that understanding will be. Clearly, then, when the opportunity for such direct experience is wholly lacking, we must derive our meanings by other methods, such as those discussed above.

Establishing community of reference. Finding the referent, as already explained, is the first of the fundamental determinants of meanings of teams as they are applicable in communication. But, as we have seen, it is not enough that the speaker know what he means when he uses certain language; there must be a community of reference between speaker and audience. It is not enough that you as speaker have a clear understanding of the meanings of your words; your listeners must also understand them. If there is not enough similarity in the associations which you and your hearers have attached to your language to make it mutually intelligible, then no communication is possible.

Either your words must come within the vocabulary of your audience or you must provide enough of a definition, using one or more of the methods described above, to make your words understandable. You cannot talk about democracy unless and until you and your hearers are in some agreement regarding the referent for the term.

When Manual Prado, President of the Republic of Peru, addressed a joint session of Congress in Washington on the subject of "Nonintervention," he made clear not only to the United States but to the peoples of the Western Hemisphere just what he meant by the term so there would be no misunderstanding of his meaning.

> Now with regard to nonintervention. The principle is being badly misrepresented by some who would invoke it to permit the destruction of the inter-American system of free republics by an outside power—namely international communism. The doctrine of nonintervention is designed to prevent interference by one nation in the foreign and domestic affairs of another, whether this interference be done through infiltration, through propaganda or through the abuse of diplomatic privileges. . . .
>
> A state which interferes in the internal affairs of another by subversion and by provoking uprisings and disturbances is in no position to claim for itself the benefits of the very principle of nonintervention which it is violating. Any other interpretation would be illogical and would destroy the true meaning of the sound American doctrine of nonintervention.
>
> I say to you therefore, . . . that the democratic, law-abiding republics of the Western Hemisphere have no obligation to submit to subversive, vicious antidemocratic propaganda, or other abuse from any nation of the Americas which for the time being may become the creature of a foreign ideology.[16]

Be sure, then, that your listeners know the sense in which you are using a given word, especially if there is likely to be any question about its meaning. The first requisite of language is that it clarify meanings rather than obscure them. A good criterion to observe in choosing language for clarity is to use terms, as Dewey suggests, which "convey meaning so directly that no effort at translation is needed."[17]

Using contexts. Many if not most of the words in our language have more than one definition. Some words are difficult to explain, classify, or define in specific terms. In such cases it is often helpful

[16] Manuel Prado, "Nonintervention," delivered September 21, 1961; in *Vital Speeches of the Day*, October 15, 1961, **28:** 18–19.

[17] John Dewey, *How We Think*, Heath, 1910, p. 136.

to put them into *context*, which is a third of the five determinants of meaning. By this procedure we put them into phrases or sentences in which the meaning is easily understood. Moreover, since so many of our words are used in different senses, the context aids in determining which of these senses is intended. To inquire what the simple word *cast* means, for example, may elicit a number of answers, even when written; if the spoken word is offered, it will also include *caste,* which would make still more definitions possible.

Misunderstandings are bound to arise when you use words of multiple definition unless you make it abundantly clear the particular sense in which you are using the term. *Integration,* for example, is an indispensable term in sociological theory; it has come to have a much more highly specified connotation, even denotation, in the discussion of race relations. In using one of the various concepts that have developed around the word—including integration as a pedagogical principle—one needs to designate clearly how it is meant. When a noted sociologist, lecturing not long ago to an audience of Southern school administrators, introduced the principle of "integration of the curriculum," a member of the audience rose to his feet and announced, "I would like to tell the speaker that we don't use that word down here." And in order to show the effect of paresis on the patient's speech, a psychiatrist in a mental hospital asked the patient to say, among other things, "Methodist Episcopal." "I won't do it," was the angry reply; "I'm a Catholic." Emotional coloring can become so strongly attached to a word in one sense that the possibility of its being used in another sense is not recognized.

Conveying your personal attitude.   A fourth determinant of meaning, as words are used in communication, is your particular personal attitude toward the subject of discussion or the specific language you are using at the time. You will recall that meanings in speech are always twofold: one expresses both what the speaker thinks about the matter under consideration, and how he feels about it (Chapter 4). Your feelings are almost certain to color your meanings in the language you use—perhaps in the choice of words and the way those words are put together, but most positively in the fifth and last of the determinants of meaning, merely referred to here because it is discussed somewhat extensively in Chapter 6, "General Principles of Delivery," and in Chapters 28 and 29, "Vocal Aspects of Delivery" and "Visible Aspects of Delivery." This determinant may be designated as your *manner of utterance*, which as we have pointed out, has a much greater effect on our meanings than we are likely to realize.

SPECIAL TYPES OF TERMS

In discussing the use of language for clarity, the development has seemed to center about units of words, phrases, and the like under the more or less general rubric of *terms*. A few special types of language units have come to be used in certain senses, and these need to be discussed briefly.

Multiple Terms

If the terms used in speaking and writing were always composed of single words, the difficulties in understanding language might be considerably lessened. Often, however, our terms are combinations of words which cannot be understood merely by combining the meanings of the separate word elements. The term *big business* mentioned before is not to be defined by adding the definition of *big* to that of *business,* any more than one can describe sodium chloride in chemistry by adding the chemical attributes of sodium to those of chlorine. Both *big business* and *sodium chloride* have come to mean something more than the sum of the two respective word elements. Similarly, the term *labor union* cannot be understood by first defining *union* and then *labor,* or in reverse order, and putting the two together. Whenever multiple terms are used as single concepts, their definitions must refer to the combinations as wholes, and your understanding must be of the whole. In speaking of them, you must consider them as single concepts.

Further examples of such multiple terms, which you might be interested in attempting to define as wholes, are suggested on page 461. A few others which are familiar because of frequent use are *laissez-faire, hillbilly, fellow traveler, left wing, base hit, down payment, rock 'n' roll, town hall,* and so on.

We do not mean to suggest that such multiple terms are generally to be avoided or that there is anything reprehensible in their use. Carr has shown the wide prevalence of word-compounding in American speech, pointing out that "Although a single, completely new word is rarely coined, a cleverly contrived compound appears rather frequently."[18] These combinations are usually useful locutions, condensing into a single brief, pointed expression a broader and sometimes deeper meaning than could easily be put into a more involved term.

The elements need not be written together, or even hyphenated, in order to represent a single concept. A *down payment* is such a single concept, and is so understood whether it is written or spoken. So is *base hit* or *town hall*, though neither may even be hyphenated. *Cape Canaveral, New York*, and *Baton Rouge* are not dual localities as are Cocoa and Rockledge, near Cape Canaveral; they are integral places with indivisible names which can no more be thought of as separable concepts than the places themselves. *Table linen* and *tablecloth*, as the terms are ordinarily used, are both single concepts, however they may appear on the printed page. Either element in either word, like the elements of practically all compounds, can be used separately in other contexts; but when used as single concepts they are inseparable whether written so or not. While they can cause confusion to the writer, who may be in a quandary until he consults a dictionary about whether the elements of a combination are written as a single word, a hyphenated compound, or two separate words, they are taken in stride by the speaker, who seldom stops to consider just how they are to be written.[19]

Technical Terms

Every specialized field of thought has its own peculiar vocabulary or set of terms used in senses restricted to that particular discipline or occupation. Many of these terms are also used in ordinary everyday discourse. For example, when you say that you have made up your mind, you are not using the term *mind* as the psychologist uses it, but in what has often been thought of as the common everyday

---

[18] Elizabeth Carr, "Word-Compounding in American Speech," *Speech Monographs*, March, 1959, **26**, 1–20.

[19] Louis B. Salomon, "The Game of Words," *Harper's Magazine*, November, 1961, **223**: 40–42.

language—the vernacular. If you insist that you have work to do, you are not using *work* according to its meaning in physics.

Specialists are not as a rule good speakers.[20] For one reason, being so familiar with the specialized vocabulary of their own profession, they forget that to the uninitiated much of the language they are using has no meaning because there is no community of reference. The sign of the integral in mathematics is just as unintelligible to people who have not studied calculus as Greek is to those who have not studied that language. Not all of your speaking will be to people in your own special field of interest. You will also have to address people who are quite unfamiliar with your technical language. Aside from any other requirements of good speaking, you need to know how to translate your technical terms into language that will be intelligible to the layman.

Medical subjects are on the whole quite technical, and the layman usually has difficulty understanding them when they are discussed in the language of medicine. But when Dr. Charles Watkins, head of the Department of Neurology and Psychiatry in the Louisiana State University School of Medicine, discussed the topic of "Tranquilizers and Energizers" on a television broadcast on July 30, 1961, he spoke in terms that everyone could understand. The broadcast was in the form of an interview. The following is illustrative:

Q. Dr. Watkins, in the absence of actual physical illness, just what is the danger of taking pills such as the tranquilizers for nervous tension?

A. Because actually the tranquilizer alone is no more effective in treating a severe psychiatric disorder than is morphine in treating appendicitis. Morphine relieves the pain of appendicitis, for example, just as enough tranquilizers will relieve the discomfort that you get with a psychiatric illness. So we have a drug that, because of its effectiveness—and certainly in many cases they are extremely effective—is dangerous in that it may mask the progress of an illness; in other words, the individual feels fine while he is getting crazier and crazier. I am much in favor of having a paranoid schizophrenic who thinks that people are trying to poison him be tranquilized, because that way he is not going to kill somebody. On the other hand, if the problem is simply that you cannot get along with your wife, I am not certain that taking tranquilizers is going to settle the problems.[21]

[20] James A. Winans, *Speech-Making,* Appleton-Century-Crofts, 1938, p. 183.
[21] One of a series of programs presented over Station WBRZ-TV, under the general heading of "Pursuit of Learning," by the Station in cooperation with Louisiana State University.

Astronomy is perhaps one of the most abstruse subjects in the combined realm of mathematics and physics. Yet Dr. Harlow Shapley can hold a lay audience spellbound for over an hour with his highly comprehensible lecture on "The Expanding Universe."

Mysticism in some fields of thought may be deeply impressive, but it contributes nothing to clarity, to understanding. Whether or not the words you use technically are also used in a nontechnical sense, you must be sure that you yourself have a clear understanding of the sense in which you are using them at the moment, and you must see to it that the audience understands them in that same sense. *Invention* does not mean at all the same thing in the field of rhetoric as it does in the field of mechanics, and you would not use it in the rhetorical sense if you were speaking to a group of industrialists hunting for new kinds of machinery for doing certain things.

Stereotypes

Our conversation as well as much of the public speech that we hear contains many terms or expressions whose meanings have a high emotional but often a very low logical component. That is, they have come to have for us meanings which are vague as to understanding but nevertheless effective in arousing strong emotional responses. They summon up some picture or image, pleasant or unpleasant according to the connotations of the terms, about which we are not called upon to think; all we are expected to do is to feel. In fact, because most of us *think* we know what they mean, without ever having clarified our concepts, they may be used also to give the impression of reasoning without actually stimulating the rational processes at all. Thus it is not necessary to specify who or what is indicated by the term *selfish interests*; whatever or whoever they may be, mere mention is often enough to generate vigorous opposition.

The use of such terms may not be wholly reprehensible; sometimes they stimulate entirely praiseworthy attitudes which in turn may be carried over into eminently worthwhile undertakings. In the stimulating speech, for example, in which the goal is to intensify attitudes already held, the occasional use of expressions which carry a heavy load of emotional meaning may be entirely permissible. But such terms should not be used as a substitute for thinking. They are too often used not to stimulate thought but to furnish ready-made judgments without giving the listeners the opportunity of making their own judgments. Such expressions are often designated as *stereotypes;* often they are clichés.

Many of our stereotypes have developed out of beliefs which arise from oversimplifying solutions to problems or answers to questions that may be a little more difficult than we are willing to undertake. The unthinking generalizations characteristic of primitive taboos are not confined to the primitive mind. We generalize often before we have examined the problems adequately to make the generalization valid. From what we may have heard about a few Scotsmen we conclude that all Scots are miserly and therefore tack that label on every individual Scot. To many people, all college professors are "visionary," all corporations are predaceous, all labor leaders dictatorial. To those who oppose it, the Taft-Hartley Law is a "slave-labor" law. These and other labels we use to stimulate either approval or disapproval without examining a sufficient number of cases or gathering a sufficient body of evidence on which to base a rational judgment.

Test your terms before you take them into your own thinking and thence into your speaking vocabulary. Determine whether they represent objectively ascertainable fact or merely a subjective evaluation. Does a given term arouse an emotional reaction only, or does it refer you and your listeners to direct objective experience?

If you want to base your argument on sound reasoning, honest thinking, then avoid slogans, which are typical stereotypes, as part of your argument. The typical advertising slogan often means very little by way of proof. Many radio advertisers apparently believe that if a statement is repeated often enough and long enough and loudly enough, it will be believed. Hitler, you will recall, incorporated that belief into his *Mein Kampf.* Whether the name of some product is another word spelled backward has nothing to do with the efficacy of the product itself.

In deploring the slogan "Asia for Asians," the late President Magsaysay of the Philippine Islands pointed out that "We must not try to fit the many and changing needs of national welfare into a strait jacket of a slogan."[22] And former Governor G. Mennen Wil-

[22] Baton Rouge *Morning Advocate,* May 31, 1954, p. 4-A.

liams contributed nothing to the solution of the problems in Africa by his slogan "Africa for the Africans."

BREVITY

As a rule, long, involved sentences are to be avoided in speaking, and brief, concise statements favored. Aristotle writes of making speeches "obscure through wordiness."[23] Superficial impressiveness achieved through verbosity is no substitute for clarity; if you can say what needs to be said in five words, do not use fifteen. You will often find that brevity itself has not only clarity but an impressiveness because of its directness.

Now and then, however, one hears something like the following examples, which are intended to illustrate the point of view some apparently hold that ". . . brevity is the mark of a Very Unimportant Person." The samples present the "right" and the "wrong" way of making statements according to this point of view.

Politician Available for Office

Wrong: "I'd like to be elected."
Right: "While I am not, and never have been, beset with ambitions to aspire to this high office, I am deeply conscious of the necessity, duty, and obligation of acceding to the people's wishes in the event that these wishes may be summarized as a desire that I make clear my availability. I shall not, therefore, raise obstacles to the consummation of this wish."

Company Unable To Fill Orders

Wrong: "We can't make billipers fast enough."
Right: "The current crisis in the billiper industry is a manifestation of the law of supply and demand, in that the public's desire to obtain billipers is thwarted by our present inability to supply the demand within the time at our disposal. When a point is reached where the volume of billipers equals the quantity demanded by potential customers, it is our considered opinion that this situation should terminate." [24]

In choosing your language for clarity, then, you must take every precaution to ensure that you yourself have a clear, definite un-

---

[23] Cooper, *op. cit.*, p. 191.
[24] Parke Cummings, "How to Make Statements to the Newspapers," *Saturday Evening Post,* March 25, 1950, p. 44.

derstanding of the meanings of the terms you use. Otherwise not only will your own thinking be vague, but you will be entirely unable to stimulate your intended meanings in the thinking of your audience. Speak in familiar terms; use concrete, specific language; be simple, direct, and brief.

QUESTIONS AND TOPICS FOR STUDY AND REVIEW

1. With reference to the use of language, define the terms *clarity, vividness,* and *impressiveness.* Illustrate the differences among them.
2. What is the ultimate basis of word meaning? Why is it that no word can have the same meaning to two or more people or to the same person twice?
3. Explain the relation between clarity of concepts and honesty of thinking.
4. What is the difference between what are known as concrete words and abstract words? Give several examples of each. In what sense are all words abstract?
5. State, explain, and illustrate the different methods of determining and explaining the meanings of words.
6. "Specialists are not as a rule good speakers." Why?
7. Discuss some of the risks one runs in determining meaning (a) by synonym; (b) by etymology; (c) by negation.
8. Define and illustrate, by examples from outside the text, multiple terms, technical terms, stereotypes, and clichés.
9. What is involved in "community of reference"? Why is it important?
10. It was said that the verses on page 463f do not "mean" anything. Do they in fact establish any kind of "mood"? Can they in any sense be said to have "emotional" aspects of meaning? Or do they have *for you* also some ideational aspects of meaning? Explain.
11. Find in the dictionary four words each of which has widely different definitions. Use these words in different contexts so as to reveal those differences in meaning.
12. Study the etymologies of four or five words whose meanings as they have developed are quite different from that derived from their original elements. To what degree does the etymology help convey their present meaning?
13. List a number of words (outside the field of games and athletics) for which definitions would be quite different, but whose meanings have been derived from experience, and which are generally understood.

PROJECTS

1. Select a passage from some speech (as in *Vital Speeches of the Day*) and determine the techniques used in achieving clarity; or point out in what ways the speaker failed to achieve clarity or might have succeeded.
2. Set down ten of the most nearly concrete terms you can think of. Now study these words, and discover to what degree they are actually abstract or represent abstractions.
3. Put into intelligent context the following words:

precedent	except	affinity
precedence	accept	infinity
admittance	collision	annular
admission	collusion	annual
anomalous	barnacle	podiatry
anonymous	binnacle	pediatrics
excess	injunction	euphoria
access	mandate	euthanasia

   Add to this list any others which you may discover, whose meanings need clarification by use.
4. Make a list of ten words you have recently encountered whose meanings were not clear to you. Find the meanings according to the context in which you discovered them.
5. Select one of the words mentioned in this chapter, as having meanings which are often confused, and give the class a clear definition in a three- to five-minute speech. Use two or more of the techniques of definition described in the chapter. Do not discuss the various ways in which the word may be used; give one extended explanation of one of the senses in which it actually is used.
6. Select a two-word term now in current use, and give a statement of its meaning. Several such terms are suggested in this chapter.
7. Select some technical term and explain its meaning to a group of uninitiated listeners. Make them understand the term as nearly as possible as it is used in its technical sense.
8. Select a group of words of similar meanings (synonyms, approximately), and differentiate their meanings and connotations.
9. Give the etymology of some word of interest, showing how its meaning has developed and changed since the original use of the source word.
10. Study some speech, from *Vital Speeches of the Day* or some other source, and list the stereotypes to be found there.

11. In order to be able to discuss some matters intelligently, agreement is necessary on accepted meanings of terms. Such agreement may often be arrived at through the processes of discussion. Organize a series of symposiums of five members and a chairman each, which will attempt to frame in specific language a definition of some commonly used terms on which there may be no common agreement. Work toward smoothing out differences. Emphasize common understandings at first rather than divergences, eliminating as many of the latter as possible, and attempt to arrive at a statement on which all can agree. The following are examples of terms that may be used:

elocution	liberal
group dynamics	fall out
hillbilly	discipline (academic)
free enterprise	freedom of speech
"right-to-work" (law)	conservative
integration	civil defense

12. Where the facilities are available, make a recording on wire or tape of one of your speeches of this group of projects. Listen to it critically, studying it for ideas, organization, and language. Revise wherever it seems neecssary for greater effectiveness. Record again and listen. When you are satisfied that you can make no more improvement yourself, present it to the class.

SUPPLEMENTARY READINGS

Babcock, C. Merton, *The Harper Handbook of Communication Skills*, Harper, 1957, chap. 10, "Adapt to Your Subject and Purpose."

Baird, A. Craig, and Franklin H. Knower, *General Speech: An Introduction*, 2nd ed., McGraw-Hill, 1957, chap. 9, "Using Effective Language."

Blair Hugh, *Lectures on Rhetoric and Belles Lettres*, Hayes & Zell (Philadelphia), 1854, Lecture X, "Style—Perspicuity and Precision." There are many editions of this famous work, first published in 1783. Any of them will be satisfactory in this reference.

Brigance, William Norwood, *Speech: Its Techniques and Disciplines in a Free Society*, 2nd ed., Appleton-Century-Crofts, 1961, chap. 15, "Using Words."

Bryant, Donald C., and Karl R. Wallace, *Fundamentals of Public Speaking*, 3rd ed., Appleton-Century-Crofts, 1960, chap. 16, "The Language of the Speech."

Gray, Giles Wilkeson, and Claude Merton Wise, *The Bases of Speech*,

3rd ed., Harper, 1959, chap. 7, pp. 441–450, "The Relation Between Language and Thought"; chap. 7, pp. 450–454, "Language and Culture"; chap. 9, pp. 499–523, "The Determinants of Meaning."

McBurney, James H., and Ernest J. Wrage, *Guide to Good Speech*, 2nd ed., Prentice-Hall, 1960, chap. 12, "Language and Style."

Reid, Loren, *First Principles of Public Speaking*, Artcraft, 1960, chap. 13, "Improving Your Use of Words."

Sarett, Lew, William Trufant Foster, and Alma Johnson Sarett, *Basic Principles of Speech*, 3rd ed., Houghton Mifflin, 1958, chap. 11, "Integrating the Skills: Style."

Soper, Paul L., *Basic Public Speaking*, 2nd ed., Oxford, 1956, chap. 13, "Language."

Thonssen, Lester, and A. Craig Baird, *Speech Criticism*, Ronald, 1948, chap. 15, "The Style of Public Address." This work discusses the problem of language and style largely from a historical and theoretical point of view. It will offer much to the inquiring student.

26

Achieving Vividness

To secure understanding, as explained in the previous chapter, you must give your language clarity; to arouse and maintain interest and attention, you must give it vividness. The primary sources of vividness lie in the sense imagery you are able to arouse in the minds of your listeners. "Vividness," says Brigance, "is the *sine qua non* of spoken style."[1]

This is not to imply that vividness and clarity are necessarily separate and distinct. On the contrary, in order to achieve vividness you must first of all be clear; clarity is the first step to vividness. If you are giving instruction, for instance, you will need to be clear

[1] William Norwood Brigance, *Speech Composition,* 2nd ed., Appleton-Century-Crofts, 1958, p. 218.

in your verbal explanation; you will also need to make your listeners see, at least in imagination, the details of the subject matter. The chief advantage of visual aids, as well as of the other visual forms of support discussed in an earlier chapter, lies in their potency in providing an experience which forms the basis for arousing clear, vivid imagery. It is this imagery which makes possible both immediate understanding of the points being discussed and later recall of the experience itself.

But imagery provides more than clarity. We have all experienced the rise of interest and attention when the speaker introduces the phrase "To illustrate" or "For example," or when he draws some striking word picture to enable us to see mentally what he is talking about. They are almost as effective in recapturing the attention as the expression "In conclusion." Vividness, created by copious use of imagery, has as one of its main values, in addition to clarity, the holding of attention and interest. This chapter, then, can easily be studied in connection with Chapter 11, "Attention and Interest."

IMAGERY

Imagery as Recall

While the exact nature of images and of imagery are not fully known, the phenomenon itself is a familiar one. In one sense, imagery is a form of recall. We cannot relive actual experiences; we can bring them back into consciousness only through some form of imagery. It is not important for our present purposes that we understand fully just what goes on in the individual to produce what is called imagery, but we should understand something of its importance in thinking.

Much of our thinking goes on in the form of recall of past experiences, and the organization of those experiences into new combinations. It is the reliving of these experiences, their recall in terms of the sensory avenues by which the data of experience became known to us in the first place, that constitutes imagery. If, for example, you have attended a symphony concert, you may relive that experience by recalling how the orchestra appeared on the stage, the graceful movements of the conductor as he drew the performers out, the

unison bowing of the first violin section, the movements of the hands
of the harpist as she plucked the strings of her instrument. Your
renewal of the visual experience constitutes your visual imagery. At
the same time, you may recall also the sounds you heard: the exquisite blending of the tones from the different sections, the development of the motif of the symphony, the crashing of the cymbals or
the blare of the brasses, the plaintive nasality of the oboes or the
tinkle of the celesta. Your reliving of that auditory experience constitutes your auditory imagery.

Have you ever taken a boat ride when the waves caused the ves-
sel to rock noticeably? For a time after you landed, what were your
sensations? Did you not relive that rocking for some time? Did you
not have a distinct imagery of shifting of balance, of movement?

Verbal Imagery

Many people have considerable difficulty in arousing a strong
sense image; they have, however, a strong imagery for *words*. A
former professor of one of the present writers was, by his own admission, very weak in visual imagery. He said one day in a graduate
seminar, in which the subject of imagery was under discussion, that
he could not recall a mental picture of his own mother's face. Moreover, there are many abstractions for which no direct experience can
be recalled and for which there is no immediate sense imagery. As
we hear and use such terms as *justice, truth, beauty, honor, charity,*
and scores of other abstract ideas, we find it difficult to visualize
such generalizations. There is nothing to see, to hear, to sense directly. The words, however, are of the greatest importance in the
thinking process, for we can and do use them in the formulation of
ideas; we use them, first, in referring directly and specifically to
things of sense, thereby calling up the direct imagery of those
things; we use them, second, quite as often for those abstractions
for which it is difficult to recall direct experience. We combine
words into new combinations, put them into new relationships, and
develop new ideas. But in these new relationships and new ideas
we must be sure that the things for which the words stand, even
abstractly, can by themselves be combined into the new relationships
indicated by the new word combinations. Word relations which
have no correspondence to fact relationships simply do not make

sense outside of fairy tales and fantasy. As Roderigo said to Iago, ". . . your words and performances are no kin together."[2]

Forms of verbal imagery. Verbal imagery can take various forms. The words in which we think may come to us through the auditory sense as though we hear them spoken, through the visual sense as if they appeared on a page, kinesthetically as if we pronounced them or even were pounding them out on a typewriter, or through any other mechanism by which we symbolize. Verbal imagery of the deaf may be through manual symbols, but it may also be visual.

In whatever form it occurs, verbalization thus provides the imagery in which most of our thinking goes on, mainly for the reason that so much of the thinking process involves abstract concepts for which the only method of recall we have is verbal imagery. These concepts are so general and so removed through the processes of abstraction from direct experience that clear, vivid imagery of the generalization itself is impossible. Imagery is specific: we do not recall abstract beauty, we recall things that are beautiful. We have no experience of truth as such, we know directly only those things which are true. All we have of any of these generalizations is a *concept* of beauty, of harmony, of truth, in the formulation of which the *word* is the final step, and the word itself is concrete. The only way in which we can recall the concepts is through the imagery of the words which have come to stand for the generalizations. The concepts themselves are made up of innumerable specific instances of direct experiences, for any one or combination of which we might easily call up a rich imagery. Thus verbal imagery plays a major role in memory itself.

Because abstractions are so difficult to interpret in terms of actual experience, your listeners will soon tire of an unbroken succession of such generalized ideas. Their interest and attention will waver unless you can find a way to bring these abstractions to life and put them into language that will be more directly related to the audience's experiences. Vividness in language demands imagery, which is aroused by concrete terms. You will not be able to avoid abstract terms entirely, but your listeners' understanding of such terms will be made clearer, the ideas will be more vivid, if you express the abstractions in terms that will arouse specific images. George Wil-

---

[2] *Othello*, IV, ii.

liam Curtis might have spoken in general terms of the patriotism that fired the men of the Revolution, but instead, he gave a vivid picture: "The inspiring statue of the Minute Man at Concord . . . commemorates the spirit that left the plow standing in the furrow, that drew Nathanael Green from his anvil and Esek Hopkins from his farm."[3]

Imagery and Imagination

Simple imagery is a simple act of recall, an act of memory. When the sense images are combined into new arrangements, often quite logical but sometimes fantastic, the process is known as imagination. James Watt, seeing the force of steam raise the lid of a teakettle, combined these elements into new relationships with other known elements, "saw" the steam moving a piston in a cylinder—and the steam engine was born. Every new invention is the result of an active imagination. Every new relationship is a product of old images in new combinations. It is these new combinations of old elements that the speaker describes whenever he proposes something different from what is already known.

Types of Images

Generally speaking, authorities recognize seven principal and common types of imagery, each corresponding to one of the physical senses.[4]

1. *Visual:* the recall of things and events that have come into our awareness through the sense of vision, such as familiar scenes, faces, happenings, localities, pictures.
2. *Auditory:* the recollection of impressions that have entered our experience through the sense of hearing, such as the voices of friends, musical melodies or harmonies, the noise of crowds, the roar of the waves, the gentle drip of rain.
3. *Gustatory:* the recollection of impressions reaching our conscious-

[3] George William Curtis, "The Leadership of Educated Men," in James Milton O'Neill, ed., *Classified Models of Speech Composition,* Century, 1921, pp. 816–828.
[4] See also William Phillips Sandford and Willard Hayes Yaeger, *Principles of Effective Speaking,* 5th ed., Ronald, 1950, p. 228.

ness through the sense of taste, such as the tartness of lemon juice, the richness of pecan pie, the bitter of quinine, the salt of sea water, the flavor of a well-cooked steak.

4. *Olfactory:* the recall of impressions that have come to us through the sense of smell, such as the fragrance of new-mown hay or freshly ploughed land, the heaviness of Cape Jasmine (gardenia), the aroma of breakfast coffee or of cooking cabbage (if you like it; *stench* if you don't!), the freshness of the air after a summer rain, the pungency of onions.

5. *Kinesthetic:* the memory of sensations of movement, such as running or strolling, driving a golf ball, striking a tennis ball, kicking a football, paddling a canoe, deftly (or otherwise) tossing a dry fly on the surface of a quiet pool, driving over the mountains or through heavy traffic.

6. *Tactile:* the remembrance of things felt through the sense of touch, such as the smoothness of silk, the roughness of an unshaven chin, the wind across the forehead, the sleekness of fine fur.

7. *Thermal:* the recall of impressions of temperatures, such as the extreme heat or cold of an August or January day, the cooling breeze from the Gulf or the freezing winds across the prairie, hot coffee for breakfast or a cold coke in midafternoon.[5]

These are not all the avenues by which impressions may enter our awareness. Several other senses are generally recognized by psychologists, each of which gives rise to an additional kind of imagery. Among these are hunger, thirst, pain, nausea, fatigue, pressure, balance, to all of which there may be a related imagery just as vivid as that based on those listed above, and to all of which the speaker can appeal in his effort to get vividness into his descriptions.

When the listener hears you give a description or use a word or phrase involving one or more of these types of imagery, he bases the images thus aroused upon his own past experiences involving sense impressions similar to those represented in the words. Upon the basis of those experiences, he constructs in his own consciousness an image pattern through which he tends to relive mentally, if only for a fleeting instant, his original experience. In that process

---

[5] Notice that each of these more or less detailed descriptions calls up other types of imagery than the particular one being described.

he is creating for *himself* a vivid reconstruction of his own experiences and is himself materially aiding you in achieving vividness in your descriptions. Listening thus becomes in a very real sense a creative process. Notice the sense images aroused by this excerpt:

A defective automobile can mean poor tires, bad brakes, or a faulty steering mechanism, among other things. These are things which can easily be controlled, and if they are not, they can just as easily create tragedy. Of these, probably the worst offender is poor brakes. Have you ever seen a trailer loaded with one or two long utility poles? If you have, you remember that these poles extend back behind the trailer a distance of 10 to 20 feet. If you had ever seen one of these poles extending back through an automobile like an apple on a sword, you would never again take a chance on driving a car with poor brakes. Just as impressive and also just as tragic was the fellow who pushed his radiator into the front seat of his car. It was a little late, but he finally learned that a car with 60,000 miles on it should be checked for loose nuts, screws and bolts. His wasn't, and when a tie rod came loose, he learned that so far as he was concerned, a large oak tree is a pretty immovable object. Defects? These are just a few. Poor tires cause blowouts that in turn cause an unbelievable number of accidents. I have seen blowouts cause the driver to lose control and strike other cars, strike other objects, and overturn. The pitiful thing about accidents caused by poor tires is that you don't have to be a mechanic to look at tires occasionally to see if they are worn.[6]

Although any or all of the types of imagery may be strong and vivid, it is generally believed that for most people visual imagery is stronger and more vivid than any other type. Word pictures, then, that recall visual experiences or images would seem to stand the greatest chance of being effective for the greatest number of listeners. Notice how Grady made use of the visual in his moving description of the Confederate soldier at the close of the Civil War:

Let me picture to you the footsore Confederate soldier, as, buttoning up in his faded gray jacket the parole which was to bear testimony to his children of his fidelity and faith, he turned his face southward from Appomattox in April, 1865. Think of him as ragged, half-starved, heavy-

[6] J. T. Nason, "Some People Learn the Hard Way," student speech in Speech 103, Advanced Public Speaking, at Louisiana State University; in Waldo W. Braden and Mary Louise Gehring, *Speech Practices: A Resource Book for the Student of Public Speaking*, Harper, 1958, pp. 31–32.

hearted, enfeebled by want and wounds; having fought to exhaustion, he surrenders his gun, wrings the hands of his comrades in silence, and, lifting his tear-stained and pallid face for the last time to the graves that dot the old Virginia hills, pulls his gray cap over his brow and begins the slow and painful journey.[7]

Visual is not by any means, of course, the only type of imagery in the passage.

Although visual imagery seems to be strongest for most people, many are especially strong in auditory imagery and have little difficulty in recalling the various sounds that have come into their experience. Patrick Henry uses the appeal to the auditory in this passage from his famous "liberty or death" speech delivered in 1775: "The next gale that sweeps from the north will bring to our ears the clash of resounding arms!" Also, in his repeated use of such terms as "a snare to your feet," "subjugation," "bind and rivet upon us those chains which the British Ministry have been so long forging," "we have been spurned, with contempt, from the foot of the throne," "until our enemies have bound us hand and foot," he arouses a strong kinesthetic imagery of coercion, of forcible restraint from an outside agency.

Some people are apparently able to call up vivid imagery of many types; others insist that their entire imaginal experience is very weak, that they are able to call up any imagery at all only with extreme difficulty, and even that tends to be faint and indistinct. They do respond, as we said, to language or verbal imagery, which seems to serve in lieu of imagery based on the senses. Yet, as pointed out, even verbal imagery depends on other types, such as auditory, visual, kinesthetic, and so on. It is probable that people who lack a considerable amount of imagery of one kind or another are extremely rare.

CHOOSING WORDS FOR VIVIDNESS

"No style can be vivid," says Brigance, "which is not clear, yet clearness alone cannot give vividness for there must be the added quality of force."[8] Whatever has been said with respect to the use

[7] Henry W. Grady, "The New South,' 'in William Norwood Brigance, *Classified Speech Models*, F. S. Crofts, 1928, pp. 287–297.

[8] Brigance, *Speech Composition, op. cit.*, p. 218.

of language and the choice of words for clarity, therefore, applies with equal potency to their importance in developing vividness. Language has a few attributes, however, which contribute especially to vividness. The chief one of these is concreteness.

Concreteness

In the previous chapter, "Using Language for Clarity," we saw that whereas abstract words are remote in their reference to experience, concrete terms, on the other hand, lead much more directly back to the actual associations which gave original meaning to the terms themselves. The meanings of these terms are therefore much more definite and clear than are the meanings of abstract terms. Since they are far more likely to arouse specific imagery, they contribute to vividness to a much greater degree. Thus, *parliamentary procedure,* with which many people have had direct, concrete experience, may have a more specific meaning than *democracy,* although they are based on identical philosophies and are put into practice through the functioning of identical principles. Churchill made the severity of the coming struggle highly vivid when he promised the British people nothing but "blood, toil, tears, and sweat."

In his *The Philosophy of Style* Herbert Spencer explains the force of "specific" as compared with "generic" words on the basis of economy of effort.

This superiority of specific expressions is clearly due to a saving of the effort required to translate words into thoughts. As we do not think in generals but in particulars—as, whenever any class of things is referred to, we represent it to ourselves by calling to mind individual members of it; it follows that when an abstract word is used, the hearer or reader has to choose from his stock of images, one by one, by which he may figure to himself the genus mentioned. In doing this, some delay must arise—some force be expended; and if, by employing a specific term, an appropriate image can be at once suggested, an economy is achieved, and a more vivid impression produced.[9]

One implication at least of this statement is that your listeners simply will not go to the trouble and effort to trace the reference in abstract

[9] Herbert Spencer, *The Philosophy of Style,* Appleton-Century-Crofts, 1871, p. 15.

words to original experiences, with the result that meanings for them continue to be hazy, vague, and indefinite. "Eloquence," says Emerson, "is *the power to translate a truth into language perfectly intelligible to the person to whom you speak.*"[10] "Instant intelligibility" is the goal set by Winans.[11]

Instead of using general terms, then, whenever possible, use words and expressions that will stimulate definite sense imagery. Remember that your listeners can have no image of abstract beauty; they will recall with any degree of vividness only *things* that are beautiful. Therefore, don't say that a certain scene was beautiful; point out its specific elements of beauty—the rolling hills, the green pastures with grazing cattle, the acres of ripening wheat waving in the breeze, the pattern of well-marked fields that lie spread out before you from your vantage point on a high hill. These are all descriptive details which require, in Spencer's terms, a minimum of translation into "thoughts" in order to establish vividness.

The fables of Aesop, the parables of Jesus, the stories of Lincoln are all powerful examples of the specific, the concrete, as compared with the generalized or abstract. They all make their point because they were taken directly from the lives and experiences of the people who heard them.

Mark Twain concluded his after-dinner speech on "New England Weather" with an effective description of a winter scene, in which the element of vividness is achieved through the use of concrete terms.

If we had not our own bewitching autumn foliage, we should still have to credit the weather with one feature which compensates for all its bullying vagaries, the ice-storm—when a leafless tree is clothed with ice from the bottom to the top—ice that is as bright and clear as crystal; every bough and twig is strung with ice-beads, frozen dewdrops; and the whole tree sparkles, cold and white, like the Shah of Persia's diamond plume. Then the wind waves the branches, and the sun comes out and turns all those myriads of beads and drops to prisms, that glow and hum and flash with all manner of colored fires, which change and change

---

[10] Ralph Waldo Emerson, "Eloquence," *Letters and Social Aims,* vol. VIII of *The Complete Works of Ralph Waldo Emerson* (centenary ed.), Houghton Mifflin, 1904, p. 130. Italics are in the original.

[11] James A. Winans, *Speech Making,* Appleton-Century-Crofts, 1938, p. 180.

again, with inconceivable rapidity, from blue to red, from red to green, and green to gold; the tree becomes a sparkling fountain, a very explosion of dazzling jewels; and it stands there the acme, the climax, the supremest possibility in art or nature of bewildering, intoxicating, intolerable magnificence. One cannot make the words too strong.[12]

The above quotation illustrates the effective use of descriptive words in achieving concreteness and thereby vividness. Mark Twain did not say merely that the ice storm is beautiful; he chose his details, and then used his descriptive words to give a series of vivid images that impress us with their beauty. Unfortunately, those who have had no experience with the elements that are woven into this description will find it difficult to construct for themselves, out of the details Mark Twain gave, the picture which he evidently witnessed over and over again.

Similarly, in the passage from Grady quoted on pages 490–491, observe that nowhere did the speaker use a term intended to describe in general the returning soldier; instead he chose his particular details and, by selecting his words for their descriptive value, created an effect which could not have been achieved with a less skillful use of language. Every one of those details stands out in vivid imagery: "footsore," "faded gray jacket," "turned his face southward," "ragged, half-starved, heavy-hearted, enfeebled," "fought to exhaustion," and so on. Note the effect of the statements "wrings the hands of his comrades in silence," "lifting his tear-stained and pallid face for the last time to the graves that dot the old Virginia hills," "begins the slow and painful journey." The picture is as vivid as if it had been painted, and it is made so by the skillful use of descriptive words, which give concreteness and arouse strong imagery.

Familiarity

A second attribute of words that contribute to vividness is familiarity. Whenever possible use words that are well within the vocabulary of your listeners. If, as Spencer suggests, you must use

---

[12] Samuel L. Clemens, "New England Weather," in Ashley Thorndike, ed., *Modern Eloquence*, Modern Eloquence Corp., I 288–292. This speech also appears in the writings of Samuel L. Clemens in the volume *Tom Sawyer Abroad*, Harper, 1896, pp. 364–376, under the less familiar title, "Speech on the Weather."

new, strange terms, be sure to translate them yourself. Do not make it necessary for your listeners to translate your language for themselves. ". . . the more time and attention it takes to receive and understand each sentence," says Spencer, "the less time and attention can be given to the contained idea; and the less vividly will that idea be conceived."[13]

Shades of Meaning

Much of the clarity and vividness of your language will depend on your careful use of fine shades of meaning. No two words are identical in meaning; between every two words, however closely related they may be, there is some slight distinction that can make the difference between ordinary language and vivid usage.

About 2400 years ago an old Greek by the name of Prodicus attempted to point out shades of meaning in such groups of words as *bravery, boldness, rashness, courage,* and *fearlessness; adversary, opponent, antagonist,* and *enemy; argue* and *wrangle; esteem* and *praise; gratify* and *please; will* and *wish,* and so on. Even at that early date he recognized the importance of choosing the right word to give the exact shade of meaning desired and to add vividness as well as clarity to the language.

A careful study of the dictionary or some good thesaurus, such as Roget's or Crabbe's *Synonyms,* will produce a great number of these word groups, that is, groups of words having somewhat similar meanings yet sufficiently different to justify great care in selecting the right ones. It could make quite a difference in vividness which word you chose in the following groups:

detriment	have	gaudy	complete	firm
harm	hold	flashy	entire	hard
damage	own	garish	intact	solid
injury	occupy	tawdry	perfect	stiff
little	melt	refuse	hint	rectify
diminutive	thaw	decline	insinuate	remedy
minute	fuse	reject	suggest	correct
small	dissolve	spurn	intimate (v.)	reform
				amend

[13] Spencer, *op. cit.,* p. 11.

compete	map	fate	irony	ease
contend	chart	destiny	satire	comfort
contest	graph	doom	sarcasm	
brave	ripe	meaning	modify	break
courageous	mellow	purport	qualify	crush
fearless	mature	sense	temper (v.)	shatter
gallant		significance		smash
		import		

Do your windows have *curtains, shades, shutters, blinds,* or *drapes?* Is your way of doing things a matter of *custom, habit, wont,* or *practice?* In your social relations are you merely *civil,* or are you *affable, genial, courteous,* or *polite?* Was the murder described in this morning's paper *premeditated, voluntary, intentional, deliberate?*

Textile manufacturers and dyers are continually bringing out new shades of old colors, to each of which a new name is given. Those who deal in fabrics learn these names and are able to discuss them knowingly. There are large numbers of reds, blues, greens, and yellows and many shades, hues, and tints made up of combinations of the primary colors, each with its own designation. In cases where the precise shading is significant, learn these differences and be able to use them.

To the person keenly interested in such things, these differences are important. Hester Prynne wore a *scarlet* letter, not one of *carmine* or *crimson.* Fine differences in human relations are just as important as differences in colors, perhaps even more so; the terms that are used to designate them are likewise important in giving your language both vividness and clarity. The merchant must know the difference between the *cost,* the *price,* the *worth,* and the *value* of his goods. It has been said that a personal photograph, when given, is *priceless;* when purchased, it is *worthless.*

In your speaking you will be dealing not only in material things but in human relations as well. In these relations are many fine shadings. The perception of and response to these shadings may be said to constitute part of that elusive human quality known as refinement. "To be refined,' says Woolbert, "is to be able to make fine distinctions."[14] It was Oscar Wilde who said there were people who knew the price of everything but the value of nothing.

[14] Charles Henry Woolbert, *The Fundamentals of Speech,* 2nd ed., Harper, 1927, p. 46.

Simple Words

Short, simple words ordinarily lend themselves more readily than long ones to translation into imagery and hence to vividness. Lincoln's "Gettysburg Address" contains only twelve different words of more than two syllables. Of these twelve, one, *dedicate(d)*, is used six times, and two others, *consecrate* and *devotion*, twice each. None of these or the other nine can be thought of as anything but plain, simple words.

Often your choice will be not so much between short and long words as between simple, easily understood phrasing and long, complex conceptions that are difficult to translate. The words must not only be in good usage; they must be so familiar to the listener that they facilitate rather than retard translation into concrete imagery. Length is often of less importance than intelligibility. Do not attempt the restricted idiom of a relatively small section of the country unless you are thoroughly familiar with it.

Winston Churchill used a complex conception and then translated it himself: ". . . profound scientific, social and philosophical issues . . . are to be examined . . . not only in their integrity but in their relationship, meaning thereby not only one by one but all together."[15]

There is a great difference between simplicity and floridity. Generally the latter refers to a type of language, a style, exalted far beyond any fitness to the speaker, the audience, the subject, or the occasion. An experienced speaker who is known to be widely read, speaking on some highly important subject on a great, formal occasion, might use language that would be entirely out of place for a younger speaker on a less exalted subject on an informal occasion. An exalted style, a part of which consists in the use of words that would rarely be used in conversation, will be appropriate on some occasions; but the occasion must call for that style. Even then, it can easily be overdone.

FIGURES OF SPEECH

Not all vividness of language comes from single words, although they are in themselves important. Probably more comes from the ways in which we put words together into expressions that arouse

[15] Winston Churchill, "United We Stand Secure," in A. Craig Baird, ed., *Representative American Speeches: 1948–1949*, H. W. Wilson, 1949, pp. 36–50.

definite, sharp images. In addition to direct literal narrative and description, certain indirect methods of giving vividness to language are often even more effective because they are indirect. Our language is filled with words and phrases that originated as figures of speech but have become so deeply embedded in daily usage that we no longer think of them as figurative at all. We all once heard much about the *New Horizons;* we *ruminate* on a subject, *drive a hard bargain,* weigh our *arguments, ponder* a situation; a campaign speaker *takes the stump; brass hats* or just *brass* is a term familiar to everyone. The *Iron Curtain* separating Eastern from Western Europe has been replaced in Berlin by the *Concrete Curtain.* Such expressions are especially effective mainly because they suggest rather than state outright. They arouse imagery but leave the details of the images for the listener to supply out of his own background of experience.

Simile and Metaphor

Probably the two most useful figures for the speaker are the simile and the metaphor. They resemble each other in that both are comparisons of things essentially unlike; they differ in that the former *states* that a likeness exists while the latter simply *implies* it.[16]

Churchill made use of a simile when he said, "The blockade of Berlin . . . is like a contest in endurance between two men, one of whom sits quietly grinning in his arm chair while the other stands on his head hour after hour to show how much he is in earnest."[17] But when he said that he "foresaw . . . that the armies of democracy would melt in the sunlight of victory,"[18] he used metaphor, as did the then General Eisenhower when he said that "serious differences [between America and England] must be beaten out on the anvil of logic and justice."[19]

[16] A simple statement of likeness between two similar things is known as a comparison. When General Eisenhower in his "Inaugural Address" at Columbia University said, ". . . or your republic will be as fearfully plundered and laid waste by barbarians in the twentieth century as the Roman Empire was in the fifth . . . ," he was using a simple comparison rather than a simile.

[17] Winston Churchill, "Peace Rests Upon Strength," in *Vital Speeches of the Day,* November 1, 1948, **15:** 44–46. The speech was given October 8, 1948.

[18] *Ibid.*

[19] Dwight D. Eisenhower, "The Challenge of Our Time," an address before the English-Speaking Union in London, July 3, 1951; in Harold F. Harding, ed., *The Age of Danger: Major Speeches on American Problems,* Random House, 1952, pp. 529–534.

Dorothy Thompson used a mixture of metaphor and personification, described below, in the title of a commencement address "Freedom's Back Is Against the Wall."[20] Although the expression was by no means original, President Roosevelt's metaphorical phrase "stab in the back" was peculiarly appropriate in the context in which it was used. President Eisenhower, speaking before the General Assembly of the United Nations, pointed out, "We must guard jealously against those who in alternating moods look upon the United Nations as an instrument for use or abuse. The United Nations was not conceived as an Olympian organ to amplify the propaganda tunes of member nations."[21] And again, the very title of Charles Talbott Garland's address to the Sertoma Club of Washington, D.C., October 10, 1961, is a good illustration of figurative language; he spoke on "Civilization's Nuclear Countdown to Barbarism."[22]

Herbert Hoover spoke of "the frozen class barriers of Europe" and "the hurricanes of social and economic destruction that have swept the world."[23] Daniel Webster, in his famous Knapp-White murder case speech, referred to "the key which unlocks the whole mystery."[24] George William Curtis called Patrick Henry "that Virginian tongue of flame," and referred to a sermon preached in 1750 by Jonathan Mayhew as "the morning gun of the Revolution."[25]

The excerpts below contain good examples of metaphors and similes.

A monarchy is a man-of-war, stanch, iron-ribbed, resistless when under full sail; yet a single hidden rock sends her to the bottom. Our republic is a raft, hard to steer, and your feet always wet; but nothing can sink her.[26]

[20] Dorothy Thompson, "Freedom's Back Is Against the Wall," in Lew Sarett and William Trufant Foster, eds., *Modern Speeches on Basic Issues,* Houghton Mifflin, 1939, pp. 185–199.

[21] Dwight D. Eisenhower, speech delivered September 22, 1960; in Lester Thonssen, ed., *Representative American Speeches, 1960–1961,* H. W. Wilson, 1961, pp. 55–70.

[22] In *Vital Speeches of the Day,* November 1, 1961, 28: 36–38. Dr. Garland is president of the American Society of Living History, Alexandria, Virginia.

[23] Herbert Hoover, "The Meaning of America," in A. Craig Baird, ed., *Representative American Speeches, 1948–1949,* H. W. Wilson, 1949, pp. 89–95.

[24] Daniel Webster, "Prosecution in the Knapp-White Case," in O'Neill, *op. cit.,* pp. 3–47.

[25] George William Curtis, "The Leadership of Educated Men," in O'Neill, *op. cit.,* pp. 816–828.

[26] Fisher Ames, as quoted in Wendell Phillips, "The Scholar in a Republic," in O'Neill, *op. cit.,* pp. 795–816.

Fifteen years ago we hung by our eyelashes over the precipice of the police state.[27]

. . . there arises the question of how and whether Communism should be "taught." Of course it should be. There is a considerable difference between teaching and preaching a doctrine. We do not condone malaria by discussing the anopheles mosquito.[28]

A more extended meptahor used by Henry Watterson in his after-dinner speech on "The Puritan and the Cavalier" gives an unusually clear, vivid pattern of imagery: "Grady told us, and told us truly, of that typical American who . . . in Abraham Lincoln's actuality, had already come. . . . from that rugged trunk, drawing its sustenance from gnarled roots, interlocked with Cavalier sprays and Puritan branches deep beneath the soil, shall spring, is springing, a shapely tree—symmetric in all its parts—under whose sheltering boughs this nation shall have the new birth of freedom Lincoln promised it, and mankind the refuge which was sought by the forefathers when they fled from oppression."[29]

In speaking on "The First Asian Republic," Chiang Kai-Shek said in part, "The sacred charter of [The United Nations] is written in the blood of innumerable freedom fighters, including 3,600,000 servicemen and civilians of the Republic of China who fell in the last world war."[30]

Personification

Another figure of speech useful in achieving vividness is *personification*, in which things or ideas are treated as living beings, endowed with the attributes or characteristics of people or sometimes animals. Here is an example: "The first responsibility of science is to shout from the housetops whenever it sees science and technology being used in the dangerous ways in which they have been used in

[27] Ruth Alexander, "Which Way America," in Baird, *op. cit.* (1949), pp. 145–154.

[28] Rufus Carrollton Harris, former president of Tulane University, *Report of the President, 1948–1949*, p. 4.

[29] Henry Watterson, "The Puritan and the Cavalier," in William Norwood Brigance, ed., *Classified Speech Models*, Appleton-Century-Crofts, 1928, pp. 297–302.

[30] Chiang Kai-Shek, speech delivered to the nation on the fiftieth anniversary of the Chinese Republic, October 19, 1961; in *Vital Speeches of the Day*, November 1, 1961, **28**: 34–36.

the past."[31] And Erwin D. Canham, editor of the *Christian Science Monitor,* after referring to the first "great lie" of communism, dialectical materialism, made the statement, "The second great lie of Communism walks hand in hand with the first. It is that there is no God."[32] "While business has talked, labor has acted," said Harry R. Hall.[33] "The Communists," according to Admiral Arleigh Burke, USN (Ret.), "have probed the soul of the Free World. . . ."[34]

In setting up a program for the improvement of broadcasting, LeRoy Collins, president of the National Association of Broadcasters, said regarding the national rating systems, "And yet, NAB has no check-rein or oversee-status whatever over what the raters do, or how they do it. Broadcasting is, therefore, allowing an outsider to become master of its own house, and does not even check his health card."[35]

Using Figures of Speech

A judicious use of figures of speech adds greatly to vividness, as it often does also to clarity. A few precautions must be observed, however, in order that the effect not be ludicrous or otherwise unfortunate.

1. *Whether you use similes, metaphors, personifications, or other figures, they must not be farfetched.* The imagery aroused by their use must not be grotesque or ludicrous, unless that is the specifically intended effect. Occasionally a humorous effect is intended and is entirely permissible; but take care that its use does not destroy a prevailingly serious mood.

2. *The figures must not offend; they must be in good taste.* As in working for clarity, avoid the cheap, the off-color, the risqué, the

---

[31] Francis B. Sayre, "Major Problems in the United States Foreign Policies," in Baird, *op. cit.* (1949), pp. 51–63.

[32] "The Authentic Revolution," commencement address at Lehigh University, June 19, 1950; Harding, *op. cit.*, pp. 517–528.

[33] "The Need for Politically Sophisticated Managers," delivered in Ann Arbor, Michigan, September 19, 1961, at a management conference; in *Vital Speeches of the Day,* November 1, 1961, 28: 51–54. Mr. Hall is executive vice-president of the Michigan State Chamber of Commerce, Lansing.

[34] Arleigh Burke, "The Fate of Our Country," delivered before the National Press Club, Washington, D.C., August 3, 1961; in *Vital Speeches of the Day,* September 15, 1961, 27: 713–716.

[35] Speech made February 10, 1961, at Mr. Collin's first meeting with the NAB Board of Directors; in Thonssen, *op. cit.*, pp. 178–188.

repulsive, and the disgusting. On the other hand, language does not need to be exalted to be on a high plane.

3. *Your figures must be consistent.* Incongruous or mixed metaphors usually arise from the failure on the part of the speaker himself to visualize the particular things which are being used as a basis for comparison. For instance, a candidate for a political office recently promised the voters to "clear up this cesspool of corruption, and let the chips fall where they may." One of the most famous mixed metaphors is considered by some scholars as really a chain of figures which, when understood, is not mixed at all. It is that of Shakespeare who has Hamlet considering whether he should "take arms against a sea of troubles."

The New Yorker has located in various publications a number of prime examples of mixed metaphors, and published them from time to time:

The critics of Hollywood rushed into print to announce that movies had "come of age" and that if the American industry did not keep its ear to the ground it would surely fall on its face. [December 17, 1960, p. 164.]

Senator Goldwater is playing the cat and mouse game. . . . If he can't hold the reins, at least he wants to be the lead horse. [January 21, 1961, p. 86.]

Catch the tax delinquents, of course, but the money shaken out of their shoes is peanuts compared to what could be saved by a little earnest effort to squeeze the water out of Federal spending. [September 9, 1961, p. 111.]

. . . I think the greenhorns have put their shoulders to the wheel and have the good ship Milwaukee moving at a pretty good clip. [September 23, 1961, p. 154.]

4. *The figures must be in keeping with the tone of the context.* If subject and treatment are plain and simple, the figures too must be plain. Such simplicity was one of the sources of effectiveness in Lincoln's use of the homely anecdote to carry a point.

5. *Do not overdo the use of figures.* There are occasions when direct language is more effective than the indirect language of figures. Your listeners will sometimes want and demand facts and straightforward statements without embellishment. Under such con-

ditions it is best to use figures of speech sparingly or not at all. Objectionable floridity, which is composed of inappropriately exalted language, also is often guilty of excessive use of figures, employing them chiefly for their ornamental value rather than for their illuminating significance.

QUESTIONS AND TOPICS FOR STUDY AND REVIEW

1. What is the place of imagery in achieving vividness?
2. To what extent can you identify or associate the factor of memory with imagery?
3. How does verbal imagery differ from other forms of sensory imagery? What are its forms? How can the speaker make use of verbal imagery?
4. Describe and illustrate the forms of sensory imagery. Can you suggest some not mentioned in the text? How can the speaker make use of these? What types are most likely to be useful?
5. What are shades of meaning? Put the words of at least two of the groups on page 494f into meaningful context that will reveal the shadings of meaning involved.
6. Differentiate between simplicity and floridity.
7. What are figures of speech? Name and illustrate five. There are many more than those discussed in your text.
8. State a few precautions to be observed in the use of figures of speech.

PROJECTS

1. Listen to several sports broadcasters announcing different kinds of sports events. Discuss them on the basis of these points:
   a. What makes some sportscasters "better" than others? (1) Is it their fluency, their ability to keep up a constant flow of description and comment? (2) Is it their ability to make you "see" what is going on?
   b. Compare the announcers' ability to give you vivid imagery of the event that is taking place.
   c. To what extent are they able to arouse in you something of the excitement, suspense, response to conflict?
   d. Do you agree with what many people have insisted, that they get more out of hearing a game broadcast than out of actually seeing it played? Is that attitude stimulated by all the sportscasters under consideration?
   e. What devices of speech have your announcers used in order to give you a more satisfactory experience of the game?
2. Read a short poem (such as "Trees," "Crossing the Bar," "The Wolf Cry," "The Loon," "Cupid Swallowed," "Abou Ben Adhem") and

determine the different kinds of imagery aroused. To what extent did your reading actually arouse vivid imagery? To what extent do such images as were aroused contribute to your understanding or appreciation of the poem?

3. Study some good speech (in *Vital Speeches of the Day, Representative American Speeches,* or some other collection) and analyze the imagery aroused. What different types? What is the preponderant type? Would you say that the speaker is mainly of one type or another? In your reading of the speech, how vivid was the imagery in your own mind? Did it contribute to your understanding and appreciation of the speech?

4. Give a three-minute talk in which you differentiate among the words of one of the groups on page 494, or any other group of not fewer than three words. Make use of imagery-arousing language in order to make your differentiation vivid.

5. Bring to class and be prepared to discuss the use which some speaker has made of figures of speech in making his ideas vivid. To what extent has the speaker avoided the pitfalls discussed in the chapter? Was his use of figures effective?

6. Find in the speeches of Winston Churchill (or some other acceptable speaker) five examples each of simile, personification, and metaphor. What figures not discussed in the text do you find?

7. Give a three- to five-minute speech in which you make specific use of three or more specific techniques for securing vividness. Be able to identify the techniques you have used.

SUPPLEMENTARY READINGS

Brigance, William Norwood, *Speech Composition,* 2nd ed., Appleton-Century,Crofts, 1953, pp. 218–272, "Vividness."

Brigance, William Norwood, *Speech: Its Techniques and Disciplines in a Free Society,* 2nd ed., Appleton-Century-Crofts, 1961, pp. 175–176; 299–313.

Overstreet, H. A., *Influencing Human Behavior,* Norton, 1925, chap. 3, "The Problem of Vividness."

Quintilian, *Institutes of Oratory,* bk. VIII, chap. 3, "Concerning the Embellishments of Style"; chap. VI, "Concerning Tropes."

Reid, Loren, *First Principles of Public Speaking,* Artcraft, 1960, pp. 194–198.

Sanford, William Phillips, and Willard Hayes Yeager, *Principles of Effective Speaking,* 4th ed., Ronald, 1942, pp. 193–196.

Sarett, Lew, William Trufant Foster, and Alma Johnson Sarett, *Basic Principles of Speech,* 3rd ed., Houghton Mifflin, 1958, pp. 349–355.

27

Achieving
Impressiveness

We have already said several times that you must do more than make your ideas intelligible to your audience. Your listeners must know not only what you think about your subject, but also how you feel about it. You must create or intensify attitudes as well as provide understanding. You must, in other words, go beyond the logical development of your subject; you must stimulate the emotional component associated with that subject in the minds of your audience.

Impressiveness is important also because of its contribution to retention and recall. Psychologists tell us that learning, and hence the power of recall, depends mainly on three factors: recency of the stimulus or response, frequency of occurrence (repetition), and intensity of the stimulus or response. That is, we remember most easily occurrences of the immediate past, those which have taken place repeatedly, and those which have involved an intense or all-over response, such as a profound emotional reaction. It would seem, then, that whatever adds to the intensity of the stimulus or to its emotional coloring would also add to one's ability to recall that experience.

These emotional responses can be stimulated in your listener by the use of language which will make your ideas so impressive that they will be readily recalled, and when recalled will have a strong emotional coloring. When demanded by the situation, therefore, use language that can easily be translated into experience to which a strong emotional component is attached.

Still another reason for making your language impressive is the fact that, in the very nature of the speaking situation, the listener has no time for reflection; he must grasp your idea immediately. A reader can go over an obscure passage as many times as necessary to grasp its full significance. He can stop entirely if he feels like it and meditate for as long as he pleases before reading further. The need for making an instant impression is thus not vital for the writer. As a speaker, however, you must create your impression at once. There is no time for meditation; your listeners have no opportunity to go back and listen again to a point you have just made. If you are to make your impression at all, you must do it as you proceed. Impressiveness is a means of getting the point across to the audience instantaneously and making it "stick." (See also Chapter 7 "Listening.")

IMPRESSIVENESS, VIVIDNESS, AND CLARITY

Clarity is not an essential in achieving impressiveness, though both clarity and vividness may be used to intensify it. Conversely, your speech may be perfectly clear without being either vivid or impressive; a classroom lecture may be quite intelligible and yet, because it is neither vivid nor impressive, be utterly dull. A speech to instruct or inform, lacking the spark of impressiveness, clear though it may be, is likely to be most uninteresting. The fact that a group of people has assembled to hear your discussion or that a class of students is under a certain degree of compulsion to listen to your lecture, does not mean that you are therefore justified in assuming that they will listen attentively to a dull, unimpressive enumeration of unadorned facts.

On the other hand, to an uncritical audience a speech may be highly impressive without actually meaning a great deal if it consists of a succession of vague, emotional ideas strung together, none of which when analyzed has a close reference to any reality. The verses on page 463f, for example, may be very impressive; they may even arouse a certain amount of vivid imagery. But in clarity—in understanding of what they are all about—they are signally lacking. A highly dramatic description of deplorable conditions in some faraway land may sound impressive without corresponding in any detail to conditions as they actually exist. Descriptions of American life published in *Izvestia* and read by the Russian people contain little that bears any resemblance to reality.

Much of the gobbledygook of official and diplomatic language sounds very impressive; but translated as Spencer suggests[1] into intelligible language, when and if it can be, it adds up to little more than nonsense. Someone has described much of what goes by the name of oratory as "the art of making deep rumblings from the chest sound like deep thoughts from the brain." The ideal use of language achieves clarity or clear ideas, vividness or strong imagery, *and* impressiveness through emotional coloring—all three.

METHODS OF ACHIEVING IMPRESSIVENESS

Some of the methods for achieving clarity and vividness are also helpful in achieving impressiveness. The use of many of the figures of speech, for instance, contributes to all three characteristics of language. Hill points out that ". . . many of the principles of selection which render language clear also render it forcible. The unequivocal, brief, specific, and familiar word will, in the great majority of cases, be the forcible word; for though men may admire language they do not understand, they will not be influenced by it."[2]

---

[1] Herbert Spencer, *The Philosophy of Style*, Appleton-Century-Crofts, 1871, pp. 11–12.

[2] Adams Sherman Hill, *The Principles of Rhetoric*, Harper, 1885, pp. 85–86.

Ideas are made impressive [says Woolbert] by being made to live again. Old truths lie dormant and then blaze into liveliness when brought out into the light. In many ways "Old things are best." This reviving of the long beloved can be done in the following ways:

Recall vivid and concrete pictures of old experiences, old descriptions, old impressions of all kinds; stir up concrete mental imagery.

Relate old and lively adventures, escapades, dramatic moments, crises, incidents charged with emotion.

Quote old and reliable authorities, opinions of authors, leaders, heroes, divinities, anyone especially beloved; especially poetry and "holy writ."[3]

In his *The Philosophy of Rhetoric*, first published in 1775, George Campbell used the following passages to show the effectiveness of the specific word as compared with the general:

Consider the lilies how they grow; they toil not, they spin not; and yet I say unto you, that Solomon in all his glory was not arrayed like one of these. If, then, God so clothe the grass which to-day is in the field and to-morrow is cast into the oven, how much more will he clothe you? (Luke xii: 27, 28.)

Consider the flowers how they gradually increase in their size; they do no manner of work, and yet I declare to you that no king whatever, in his most splendid habit, is dressed up like them. If, then, God in his providence doth so adorn the vegetable productions which continue but a little time on the land, and are afterward put into the fire, how much more will he provide clothing for you?[4]

The two passages are equally clear, but the reference to a specific flower and a specific king, rather than to flowers in general and rulers as a class, impresses us with the belief that whatever is true for this particular individual is true as well for all, whether it be flowers, kings, or people in general. Campbell himself stated the broad principle thus: "The more general the terms are, the picture is the fainter; the more special they are, it is the brighter. The same sentiments may be expressed with equal justness, and even perspicuity [clarity], in the former way as in the latter; but as the colouring

[3] Charles Henry Woolbert, *The Fundamentals of Speech*, Harper, 2nd ed., 1927, p. 358.
[4] George Campbell, *The Philosophy of Rhetoric*, Harper, new ed., 1846, pp. 307–308.

will in that case be more languid, it cannot give equal pleasure to the fancy, and, by consequence, will not contribute so much either to fix the attention or to impress the memory."[5]

Again, an unimaginative writer might have told us simply, but without the "colouring" which Campbell mentions, that "It is evening; the cows are coming in from the pasture, and the tired farmer is going home from his fields." It took Thomas Gray, with his rich appreciation of imaginary detail, to phrase the picture differently:

> The curfew tolls the knell of parting day,
> The lowing herd winds slowly o'er the lea,
> The plowman homeward plods his weary way,
> And leaves the world to darkness and to me.

Here is a further example: instead of flatly stating that Karl Marx was wrong in his economic and social theories and actually had contributed little or nothing to human welfare, Samuel B. Pettengill makes telling use of specific language to achieve impressiveness:

Was the conquest of starvation a humanitarian thing? What conquered it? Who conquered it? Karl Marx? *No.*

The time in the field required to raise a bushel of wheat in America has gone down from 60 hours of human labor to 2 hours or less today. What did it? The steel plow, the tractor, the harvester, better fertilizer and seed, the conquest of insects and plant diseases, and cheap transportation. American wheat now feeds millions today in the Europe that is adopting the philosophy of Karl Marx.

Aluminum was so expensive in 1870 that Napoleon III of France had an aluminum table set for state dinners, more valuable then than gold. Today aluminum is found in the American kitchen.

. . . The answer [to the problem of improving conditions] is to substitute slaves of iron and steel for the sweat and toil of human backs.[6]

The electrical wizard, Steinmetz, dramatized his new 60,000 kilowatt alternating current generator by showing that it would produce more energy, day and night, day in and day out, than the 4,700,000 slave population in 1860 could produce.[7]

[5] *Ibid.*

[6] Samuel B. Pettengill, "Where Karl Marx Went Wrong," in *Vital Speeches of the Day,* May 1, 1949, **15:** 442–444.

[7] Floyd Miller, "The Hunchbacked Genius of Liberty Hall," *Reader's Digest,* June, 1962 (Book Section), p. 227.

Characteristic Relations and Traits

General ideas can often be made more impressive by using figures of speech in which a word having one referent is used for another. This may take the form of using the name of one object for some other object, the two being so closely related that mention of one in a given context suggests the other. It may take the form of a part being named for the whole or the whole for the part. In any case, the language itself cannot be taken literally. For example, to say that the thermometer is dropping is not literally true; the statement simply means that the temperature, as indicated by the thermometer, is getting lower. We are told that "man shall live by the sweat of his brow," and that "man shall not live by bread alone." We speak of *the bar*, referring to the legal profession (someone has recently been "admitted to the bar"); in parliamentary proceedings we address the *chair*, and thereby *obtain the floor* or the privilege of speaking. We say we are reading *Milton* or *Hemingway* or *Faulkner*, or are taking a course in *Shakespeare*. A singer may be *in good voice*, and a baseball player wields *a powerful bat*.

Byron could write,

> There was a sound of revelry by night,
> And Belgium's capital had gathered there
> Her Beauty and Her Chivalry, . . .

The passage also illustrates personification. He could also write, in his "Apostrophe to the Ocean,"

> Ten thousand fleets sail over thee in vain.

Our language is full of such expressions. "Use your head," we say, or a person is "all eyes." We attribute certain emotions to the heart, though the heart is no more the seat of emotion than is the stomach. However, such expressions give concreteness to our language, and aid in achieving impressiveness.

Allusions

Often an idea which might need several words or sentences to present, and even then might be flat and uninteresting, can be made more impressive by the use of an appropriate allusion to something already known, toward which certain attitudes have been built up. Such allusions may be direct or indirect, literal or figurative, historical, literary, Biblical, or legendary.

Typical of the historical allusion, for example, is "The march of civilization is as romantic as the Crusades."[8] We hear and read often that certain proposals for some proposed ideal social organization are Utopian, the allusion being to Sir Thomas More's description of a mythical island which enjoyed perfection in every aspect of human society. The famous Zenger trial in 1733–1734, a landmark in the history of freedom of the press, was referred to recently by Admiral Arleigh Burke in speaking before the National Press Club in Washington on "The Fate of Our Country."[9]

An allusion may also be a figure of speech. Excessive love of wealth is often designated as the *"worship of mammon,"*[10] and we are told, furthermore, that "the love of money is the root of all evil."[11]

Be sure when you use allusions that your audience will understand the reference. Many people are accustomed to reading the Bible; allusions to Biblical sources will be readily understood. Others are widely familiar with general literature; literary allusions therefore will be useful. Still others are familiar with historical events and personalities. A wide range in your choice of sources for allusions will give you a better likelihood of reaching a wide range of interests among your listeners. But if your listeners do not understand the reference or if it is not in keeping with the general atmosphere of the situation, your allusion will add little to impressiveness.

Probably the only aspect of speaking that might be enhanced by your use of unfamiliar references is the audience's impression of your own learning; but that will be of little help to you in getting the idea and the audience together. Instead of making the idea impressive, such usage serves only to make you yourself impressive, and that can hardly be thought of as ethical speaking. Use allusions, then, that are within the understanding of your listeners and will probably arouse or deepen the attitude you want to establish. So used, they can add greatly to the impressiveness of the speech. It should be

---

[8] Edwin P. Morrow, "The Cost of Heritage," in William Norwood Brigance, ed., *Classified Speech Models*, Appleton-Century-Crofts, 1928, pp. 279–287.

[9] See *Vital Speeches of the Day*, September 15, 1961, **27**: 713–716.

[10] Matt. 6:24; Luke 16:9, 11, 13.

[11] I Tim. 6:10.

unnecessary to add that you should of course be thoroughly familiar with the significance of your reference in relation to the point you are trying to make; otherwise you are likely to make yourself ridiculous. The problem has been pointed out in the classical writings on rhetoric, the distinction between giving effectiveness to the *speaker* and giving effectiveness to *truth*. It was over-emphasis on the former that contributed to the low esteem to which "rhetoric" fell in the attitude of many scholars.

Quotations

In one sense, quotations may be thought of as extended allusions. Frequently you can use a familiar passage from some well-known writing to increase impressiveness and hold interest. These quotations may be from any recognized source, and will be especially effective if the source itself is highly regarded. Henry W. Grady opened his address before the New England Society of New York on "The New South" with a quotation from Benjamin H. Hill and closed it with one from Daniel Webster, both highly esteemed in New England.

Winston Churchill expressed his faith in the future of the human race in the following passage from Tennyson's "Locksley Hall":

> Men, my brothers, Men, the workers, ever reaping something new;
> That which they have done but earnest of the things that they shall do.[12]

Biblical passages are often used as the basis for speeches by laymen as well as by ministers of the church. The late Dr. Karl T. Compton chose for the thesis of his baccalaureate address to the class of 1937 at the Massachusetts Institute of Technology the parable of the talents, putting special stress on the verse, "Well done, thou good and faithful servant; thou hast been faithful over a few things, I will make thee ruler over many things; enter thou into the joy of thy Lord."[13] This reference is also an excellent example

[12] Winston Churchill, "United We Stand Secure," in A. Craig Baird, ed., *Representative American Speeches, 1948–1949,* H. W. Wilson, 1949, pp. 35–50.

[13] Karl T. Compton, "The Stuff of Life: Our Talents and Their Care," in Lew Sarett and William Trufant Foster, eds., *Modern Speeches on Basic Issues,* Houghton Mifflin, 1939, pp. 13–21. Dr. Compton, 1887–1954, famous as a physicist, was president of the Massachusetts Institute of Technology. This quotation is also a good example of a Biblical allusion.

of Biblical allusion. It is no sacrilege to say that Biblical quotations are almost always effective, provided they are appropriate to the subject and the occasion.

Even in a lawyer's address to a jury in the courtroom, quotations are occasionally used to secure impressiveness. Jeremiah S. Black, in his famous "Right to Trial by Jury," delivered before the Supreme Court of the United States, made frequent use of quotations throughout the speech, some of them from the Constitution, some from the Bible, some from secular literary sources. Each one introduced made the argument more impressive.[14]

Repetition

Some of the techniques of speech which are useful in creating certain effects also achieve other effects at the same time. For example, we discussed repetition as useful in securing attention and interest. With a little adaptation, it can also be used to make ideas impressive. Sometimes a single word will be repeated, sometimes a phrase, sometimes an entire clause. Shortly after the Spanish American War, when the United States had suddenly acquired more territory than it knew what to do with, Senator Albert J. Beveridge, spokesman of the "imperialists," raised in his "March of the Flag" speech the stirring question and challenge, "Who will haul down that flag?" He was answered by John Sharp Williams, who repeated the question several times, each time answering it himself by insisting that the American people themselves would "haul down that flag" because it was the sensible thing to do.[15]

In his radio speech to the American people on December 9, two days after the bombing of Pearl Harbor, former President Roosevelt made use of the technique of repetition both to maintain high interest and to achieve the maximum of impressiveness.

The course that Japan has followed for the past ten years in Asia has paralleled the course of Hitler and Mussolini in Europe and in Africa. Today it has become far more than a parallel. It is collaboration—actual collaboration—so well calculated that all the continents of the world, and

---

[14] Jeremiah S. Black, "In Defense of the Right of Trial by Jury," in Brigance, *op. cit.*, pp. 101–136.

[15] John Sharp Williams, "Who Will Haul Down That Flag?" in Brigance, *op. cit.*, pp. 206–208.

all the oceans, are now considered by the Axis strategists as one gigantic battlefield.

In 1931, ten years ago, Japan invaded Manchukuo—without warning.

In 1935, Italy invaded Ethiopia—without warning.

In 1938, Hitler occupied Austria—without warning.

In 1939, Hitler invaded Czechoslovakia—without warning.

Later in 1939, Hitler invaded Poland—without warning.

In 1940, Hitler invaded Norway, Denmark, The Netherlands, Belgium and Luxembourg—without warning.

In 1940, Italy attacked France and later Greece—without warning.

And this year, in 1941, the Axis powers attacked Yugoslavia and Greece and they dominated the Balkans—without warning.

In 1941 also, Hitler invaded Russia—without warning.

And now Japan has attacked Malaya and Thailand—and the United States—without warning.

It is all of one pattern.[16]

Repetition was used with strong effect also in Dr. George Hedley's refutation of the well-known statement of Karl Marx, that religion is the "opium of the people." After quoting directly from the writings of Marx, Dr. Hedley declared that "from the very beginning religion had been, and has continued to be, a vital force of social criticism, social protest, and social change; that the great leaders of religion, so far from being defenders of the *status quo*, were one after another revolutionaries. . . ." He then went on to name many of the great leaders, introducing each one with a challenging question:

Will you grant that Moses was a religious leader?
Were the prophets Amos and Micah religious leaders?
Was the prophet Jesus, of Nazareth in Galilee, a religious leader?
Was St. Paul a religious leader?
Was St. Francis of Assisi a religious leader?
Was John Bunyan a religious leader?
Was John Wesley a religious leader?
Was John Woolman a religious leader?[17]

[16] Franklin Delano Roosevelt, "America Accepts the Challenge," radio address December 9, 1941, in A. Craig Baird, ed., *Representative American Speeches, 1941–1942*, H. W. Wilson, 1942, pp. 30–39.

[17] George Hedley, "Religion: What It Isn't, and Is," in *Vital Speeches of the Day*, December 15, 1947, 14: 148–152.

In his Madison Square Garden address during the 1948 presidential campaign, former President Truman used the technique of repetition with great effectiveness in playing repeatedly on the proposition that, although his opponent had followed him in his itinerary, he would not follow him into the White House. Over and over again he repeated that his opponent could follow him into Framingham, Massachusetts, into Cleveland, into Chicago, Boston, and elsewhere, but he would not follow in raising minimum wages, in broadening the base of social security, in providing for health insurance, for federal aid to education, or in any of the other issues which the President was placing before the American voters.[18]

Similarly, in his speech accepting the nomination of the Progressive Party for the presidency, Henry A. Wallace introduced each plank of his platform with the introductory phrase, "I am committed . . ." Twice this formula is broken by "I am pledged . . ."[19]

Howard Appling, secretary of state of Oregon, used essentially the same technique in a recent address to the Downtown Kiwanis Club of Portland. His subject was "Let's Get out of the Rut." Having referred to the great material progress America has made, he inquires, "But where are we *really* in some other respects?" and proceeds to take stock: "We're at a point, for example, where to be a businessman today makes one a little suspect and the concept of profit is one which requires apology and rather labored explanation. We're at a point where state governments are forced in many cases to sugarcoat their tax climate propaganda in an effort to lure industries that have become almost totally discouraged in some other state." Six times the speaker introduces with the statement "We're at a point where . . ." some aspect of political and economic life that should be called into question. "It used to be permissible," he says, "to stand up for some of our time-tested values and to have a healthy reaction to a situation . . . but now one is a 'reactionary,' and that, too, is somehow a nasty thing."[20]

These examples should be enough to indicate some of the ways repetition can be used to make your ideas impressive. The repeated

[18] Harry Truman, "Madison Square Garden Address," in Baird, *op. cit.* (1949), pp. 112–121.
[19] Henry A. Wallace, "Progressive Party Commitments," in Baird, *op. cit.* (1949), pp. 123–133.
[20] Howard Appling, "Let's Get out of the Rut," in *Vital Speeches of the Day,* December 1, 1959, **26:** 118–121.

idea need not always be in identical language, though a short phrase can be repeated verbatim. Be sure not to overdo the practice; once you have made your point, go on to the next idea.

Use of Facts

You may not need to resort to any of the techniques described above in order to make your ideas impressive if your facts themselves are sufficiently significant. There is some validity to the old saying, "Truth is stranger than fiction." Plain, unvarnished facts are often so striking that they need no embellishment or figures of speech to dress them up. The startling statement, the believe-it-or-not technique can make a statement of fact impressive. An excellent illustration of such a method is the opening of Gordon L. Hostetter's speech on "Human Liberty." "Of all the people who have ever lived on the earth's surface only about 3 percent have ever known freedom, and only as they have been free politically have they been relatively free from the most elemental pang of human nature—hunger."[21]

It is an impressive fact that more people have been killed in America in automobile accidents than in all the wars we have ever fought, beginning with the Revolution. Some years ago the *Reader's Digest* carried an article which had to do with the immediate results of many fatal traffic accidents. Many of these effects were described quite without emotional coloring, as simple, straightforward facts, without elaboration. The descriptions were so detailed and so realistic that hundreds of drivers felt the full impact of the pictures. Shortly after that particular issue appeared on the stands, one student used as her speech a résumé of the article, "And Sudden Death."[22] Although such résumés are discouraged and sometimes prohibited, the speaker was permitted to continue. Her presentation of this particular subject was so impressive that when she sat down her listeners drew a sigh of relief, and one young man was heard to say, as if to himself, "I've had enough of that!" Incidentally, the title of the article itself is an effective quotation, probably not recognized as such by many who use it or hear it.

[21] Gordon Hostetter, "Human Liberty," in *Vital Speeches of the Day*, November 15, 1948, **15**: 83–87.

[22] Joseph Chamberlain Furnas, "And Sudden Death," in Theodore Roosevelt and Staff, eds., *Reader's Digest Reader*, Doubleday, Doran, 1941, pp. 295–300.

It is another impressive fact that the teaching of speech goes back almost to the time of the building of the Great Pyramid of Khufu. It is an impressive fact that the theater in the South flourished all through the Confederacy. It is likewise an impressive fact that the radio program "The Voice of America," according to the evidence, is penetrating the Iron Curtain, and with highly desirable results, so far as can be ascertained.

Facts in themselves, then, may be highly impressive. Ripley's "Believe It Or Not" series, which ran for years, together with several similar series such as "This Curious World" and "Strange As It Seems," is evidence that the unusual has both attention value and the quality of impressiveness.

Statistics

You may be surprised at what can be done with statistics to make your ideas impressive. Quantitative comparisons need not be dull and uninteresting; they will not be if they are chosen because they represent wide departures from the usual or the expected and if they can be related to human interests.[23] For example, a recent survey of attitudes toward principles that Americans have always apparently held in highest regard and more specifically toward the Bill of Rights, reported as follows: "A seven-year survey of 10,000 high school students by Purdue University shows that 34 percent would abolish the right to circulate petitions, 37 percent favor third-degree police methods, 43 percent do not oppose curbs on free speech, and 34 percent oppose school integration."[24]

In an effort to impress his listeners with the terrific slaughter of modern warfare, the Reverend Edward D. Gates said:

From the year 1900 to 1950 this world of ours has witnessed warfare on a scale that has outslaughtered all previous history. Do you realize that if tonight every man, woman, and child within the continental limits

[23] For an illustration of the interpretative use of statistics in written discourse, see the editorial "Statistics and the National Association," *Quarterly Journal of Speech*, October, 1939, **25**: 462–464.

[24] William C. Lang, dean of Iowa State Teachers College, "The Bold Go Toward Their Time," in Lester Thonssen, ed., *Representative American Speeches, 1960–1961*, H. W. Wilson, 1961, pp. 71–82. The speech was delivered at the midwinter commencement of the State University of Iowa. February 4, 1961.

of these United States were suddenly wiped off the earth, their number would be less than the number of human beings who have died in war, or by causes directly resulting from war, during the 50 years from 1900 to 1950! Recent studies by Professor Quincy Wright of the University of Chicago inform us that during the first 30 years of our century European nations alone fought 74 wars, the average war four years long, or wars lasting a total of 297 years. From the eleventh to the twentieth century, during those 900 years, war casualties amounted to about 18 million. But in the first 30 years only of this century from 1900 to 1930, there were killed by warfare 33⅓% more human beings than in all those previous 900 years! And this does not include five continents and World War II and its immediate prelude.[25]

Lowell B. Mason, former member of the Federal Trade Commission, reminded the American Hardware Manufacturers of the growth of their business with these words:

A decade ago the so-called "value added" to our economy by your operations in the hardware industry was about $728 millions. Today it is up in the $2 billions—over a 300 percent rise.

When I talked to you in 1948 you had 131,000 employees in your industry. Today you have 147,000—an increase of more than 12 percent.

In 1948 there were 97,000 stores handling your products. Now there [are] well over 105,000—an increase of some 8 to 10 percent.

A decade ago your market in the United States was 146 million people. Today it is 178 million people—an approximate increase of 22 percent.

In 1948 our Gross National Production was $254 billions. Today our GNP is $436 billions—an increase of 72 percent. So you can see the great material advance and progress in our nation to which your industry has contributed.[26]

In supporting the point that "the evolution of our economic life is leading toward larger concentrations of economic power with in-

[25] Rev. Edward D. Gates, "Time is Running Out," in Harold F. Harding, ed., *The Age of Danger: Major Speeches on American Problems*, Random House, 1952, pp. 472–480. This sermon, delivered at the First Presbyterian Church of Peoria, Illinois, September 17, 1950, was awarded first place in the sermons category of the annual Freedoms Foundation Awards for outstanding contributions to freedom in 1950.

[26] Lowell B. Mason, "The Language of Dissent," in *Vital Speeches of the Day*, December 15, 1959, **26:** 144–147. The subtitle of the speech is, "We Have Lost 27½% of our Protections to Liberty." The date of the speech was October 6, 1959; Mr. Mason had addressed the same group in 1948.

stitutions—power based not on the ownership of wealth but on the control of wealth," James P. Mitchell, former Secretary of Labor, said:

> These institutions are various: corporations, of which 500 now account for two-thirds of our total industry; pension and trust funds, already totaling some $40 billion and growing at the rate of $4 billion annually; labor unions, supported by 16 million members; mutual funds, trusts, insurance and banking firms and so on.
>
> It has been estimated that 50 million citizens are now sharing in the profits of the 500 largest corporations, directly and indirectly. Since 1952, the number of direct stockholders in public corporations has risen from 6.5 millions to 12.5 million. . . .
>
> A comparison of the average annual increase in hourly earnings between the steel and other major settlements shows the following: Aluminum, 5.2 percent; can, 4.5 percent; Kaiser, 3.82 percent; steel, 3.75 percent.[27]

Senator Joseph S. Clark of Pennsylvania, comparing federal and state finances, presents these figures: "Since 1946, Federal revenues have risen by 74 percent, which is considerably less than the economy has grown. But State and local revenues have more than tripled. The Federal Government still collects 63 percent of all tax revenues—but this is down from 77 percent in 1946. Federal tax rates are high, but State and local tax rates have risen steadily, while Federal taxpayers have enjoyed tax reductions—the last one in 1954. Since 1946 Federal indebtedness has risen 5 percent. But State and local debt has risen 309 percent—or 62 times as fast."[28]

You can make your statistics more impressive if you relate them to things your listeners already understand, a principle which applies to the use of any of your supporting materials. A word of caution should be given here. We have referred before to the epigram, "Figures don't lie, but liars figure." Your figures in the form of statistics should not be juggled or slanted to make your point, even though you can make them more impressive by so doing. If statistical

---

[27] James P. Mitchell, "The Steel Strike Settlement," delivered at the Economic Club, Detroit, on January 11, 1960, in *Vital Speeches of the Day*, February 1, 1960, 26: 231–233.

[28] Sen. Joseph S. Clark, "Toward National Federalism," delivered March 28, 1960, at George Washington University; in *Vital Speeches of the Day*, May 15, 1960, 26: 472–476.

analysis will not support your point, either use other forms of support that may balance out the figures or drop the point, if you want to retain the honesty that should characterize all your speaking.

Often the mere presentation of the data themselves is sufficiently impressive that they need no elaboration. In many of the subjects you will want to talk about you may find startling facts, items of simple numerical information that are so divergent from the expected or the usual that they arouse instant attention and keen interest. A single statistical item may be so striking as to draw attention; but its impressiveness can be greatly enhanced if it is supplemented by further data of the same general type, so that the factor of cumulation becomes operative. If isolated facts are impressive, a mass of fact, should give additional weight to the point you are trying to make. But it is possible to accumulate such an overpowering mass of statistics that the point that those data are supposed to support is entirely lost.

Detailed Description

Often the best way to make your ideas impressive is detailed description, adding one descriptive item after another, so that a complete picture is created in fine detail. In recasting the actual crime for which Knapp was being tried, Webster went into such a minute description of every movement that the incident became both exceedingly vivid and deeply impressive:

Deep sleep had fallen on the destined victim, and on all beneath his roof. A healthful old man, to whom sleep was sweet, the first sound slumbers of the night held him in their soft but strong embrace. The assassin enters, through the window already prepared, into an unoccupied apartment. With noiseless foot he paces the lonely hall, half lighted by the moon. He winds up the ascent of the stairs, and reaches the door of the chamber. Of this he moves the lock, by soft and continued pressure, till it turns on its hinges without noise, and he enters, and beholds his victim before him. The room is uncommonly open to the admission of light. The face of the innocent sleeper is turned from the murderer, and the beams of the moon, resting on the gray locks of his aged temple, show him where to strike. The fatal blow is given, and the victim passes, without a struggle or a motion, from the repose of sleep to the repose of death! It is the assassin's purpose to make sure work; and he plies the dagger, though it is obvious that life has been destroyed by the blow of the bludgeon. He even raises the aged arm, that he may not fail in his aim at the heart, and replaces it again over the wounds of the poniard! To finish the picture, he explores the wrist for the pulse! He feels for it, and ascertains that it beats no longer! It is accomplished. The deed is done. He retreats, retraces his steps to the window, passes out through it as he came in, and escapes.[29]

Not all descriptions, needless to say, are of the "horror" type. Many are effective in giving clear information, stimulating vivid imagery, and arousing an appreciation of the things described, thereby achieving all three of the objectives in the use of language. Such is the description in the following student talk on "Party Games":

Old style fun-making still survives in many sections of back country of Arkansas. This institution is strictly American, and democratic in the broadest sense of the word.

Sometimes these frolics are held in the district school house, more often at a home or in a vacant cabin. The back rooms are provided for the very old or the very young; the fore-room is cleared of all furnishings and rugs, and the walls are lined with chairs and benches. Fun-makings usually begin after sundown as soon as the chores are done. They last sometimes until sunup, and very often the folks get home just in time to begin the chores again. These activities take strong constitutions, for during the frolic season a young man or young woman may go for as long as a week with little sleep.

One type of play party is a square dance without fiddles or other instrumental music. The merrymakers sing their own songs and provide their own mirth as they go along. . . .

Not too long ago, the fun-makings were havens for the dudes of the hills, who "dressed fit to kill." We no longer see the stiff collars and loud ties. We no longer hear those ivory cuff buttons clicking in celluloid cuffs either. And it once was the sign of a real "cat" to see the trouser leg tucked down into the top of the boots.

The creation of the folk people is free and spontaneous. Their stories and songs have luckily been passed on to us for our enjoyment.[30]

[29] Daniel Webster, "Prosecution in the Knapp-White Case," in James Milton O'Neill, ed., *Classified Models of Speech Composition*, Century 1921, pp. 3–47.

[30] Peggy Taylor, talk presented in Speech 60, Mississippi Southern College; in Waldo W. Braden and Mary Louise Gehring, *Speech Practices: A Resource Book for the Student of Public Speaking*, Harper, 1958, pp. 122–123.

Loaded Words

Another technique by which you can often make your ideas impressive is the use of words or phrases which are so rich in connotation that they immediately arouse an emotional response: the affective, or emotional, component in the meaning is so strong that for the moment it outweighs whatever there may be of logical meaning. Webster, in the Knapp-White case previously quoted, spoke of "extraordinary guilt, exquisite wickedness, the high flights and poetry of crime," and "murder; deliberate, concerted, malicious murder"; and again in the same speech, "What is innocence? How deep stained with blood, how reckless in crime, how deep in depravity may it be, and yet retain innocence?"

Henry B. DuPont, referring to criticism of "Big Business" merely on the ground of size, pointed out that "These criticisms have, in the main, come from the lips of many people in politics, bureaucrats, irresponsible labor elements and, unfortunately, also from many well-meaning but uninformed people, and they have been fanned by the radical section of the press and radio. The little businessman has been depicted as a poor little fellow living and working in a continual state of oppression at the hands of Big Business."[31]

It is not difficult to pick out of this passage a number of words which carry logical meaning but also have strong emotional connotations. The intent is obviously to create an attitude unfavorable to the criticism of "Big Business" which comes from prejudiced sources.

The use of loaded words may be somewhat like the use of the "hidden persuaders," about which Packard writes. Listeners are hardly aware of the significance of a single word of this kind injected into an otherwise objective discussion of a given subject. They may not even be conscious of the effect of several words having emotional components above the normal. But the impact is cumulative, so that the final result is the creation, first, of a doubt of the validity of one's own point of view, and second, of at least a tentative acceptance of the speaker's attitude. Just as the ethics of "hidden persuaders" has been brought sharply into question, so can extensive use of loaded words be examined very closely. Such a use can be just as pernicious

[31] Henry B. DuPont, "That No Man Shall Be Poor," in *Vital Speeches of the Day*, July 15, 1948, 14: 587–590.

as the theory that the basis of persuasion is attention: maintain the attention of the audience on a given proposal, without once permitting any alternative or negative suggestion to enter into their awareness.

If you want to impress your listeners with the superiority of your argument, then in all honesty and fairness you must let them know just what it is superior to.

SUMMARY

For their maximum effect most speeches will require a certain amount of impressiveness, the degree being determined by the occasion and the purpose of the speaker. Only such colorless reports as the minutes of meetings, intended to present nothing more than the bare record of proceedings, can be devoid of this particular characteristic. In most of your speaking you will want to do more than present cold, barren, colorless fact. Even the report of an especially interesting bit of research may be made impressive by pointing up its significance, its departure from commonly held theories, its distinctive contribution to the field of knowledge.

QUESTIONS AND TOPICS FOR STUDY AND REVIEW

1. What is the importance of impressiveness in the use of language? What other terms have been used for the same attribute of language? Differentiate these various terms, showing the shades of meaning among them.
2. Illustrate aad explain the relation between impressiveness and retention. What value has the element of impressiveness in the informative speech?
3. Show the relationships among the elements of clarity, vividness, and impressiveness.
4. How can the factor of impressiveness be related to ethical speaking?
5. What techniques of achieving impressiveness are illustrated in the text? Your text discusses eight. Give an example of each.
6. Relate the factor of impressiveness to interest and attention.
7. Give examples of the different types of allusion. What types can you find other than those discussed?
8. Give a specific illustration of the use of facts for the purpose of impressiveness. What characteristics should facts have in order to be impressive?

9. What are "loaded words"? Why are they useful in achieving impressiveness? How could their use conflict with ethical speaking?
10. Find the source of the Byron quotations on page 509 and identify other figures of speech found in them.
11. What is significant in the reference to the Zenger trial by Admiral Burke? Identify the other men mentioned in the same paragraph of his speech, with reference to their part in national development.

PROJECTS

1. Bring to class one example of each of the specific techniques of impressiveness discussed in the chapter, taken from some speech or speeches.
2. Select some general term the meanings of which are very broad and indefinite, and list not fewer than ten words having specific, concrete meanings related to that of the general term.
3. Find five to ten illustrations of allusion in a speech, and give a talk discussing the references in each one.
4. Summarize in a single word a particular trait of some individual, like the example of General Bolivar as a "Casanova."
5. Give a two- or three-minute talk in which you make use, for the purpose of impressiveness, of at least three quotations.
6. Prepare a talk based on a passage from a well-known source which is highly regarded by your audience.
7. Give a three- to five-minute speech in which you make use of (a) impressive facts, (b) impressive statistics, or (c) a combination of the two.
8. Select from a recent speech in *Vital Speeches of the Day* not fewer than ten examples of loaded words. Analyze the effect of these terms with reference to impressiveness.
9. Write a speech which will take you approximately ten minutes to deliver in which you make use of at least five specific techniques of impressiveness. Do not neglect in your writing the principles of clarity and vividness. Keep constantly in mind how the speech will sound when read aloud to an audience, rather than how it will appeal to one reading it to himself. Record the speech, and make corrections before presenting it to the class.
10. Organize a symposium of from five to seven members of the class as participants. Select one of your members to serve as spokesman for the group in presenting a point of view on an argument, or in submitting a set of important facts. The symposium is to consider how those facts can be made more impressive through the applica-

tion of specific techniques. The spokesman will then give the finished speech on behalf of the group. Each participant should bring to the discussion material emphasizing the use of one of the specific techniques.

SUPPLEMENTARY READINGS

Bryant, Donald C., and Karl R. Wallace, *Fundamentals of Public Speaking*, 3rd ed., Appleton-Century-Crofts, 1960, pp. 270–276.

Gilman, Wilbur E., Bower Aly, and Loren Reid, *The Fundamentals of Speaking*, Macmillan, 1951, chap. 14, "Impressing."

Overstreet, H. A., *Influencing Human Behavior*, Nelson, 1925, chap. 7.

Quintilian, *Institutes of Oratory*, bk. VIII, chap. 3, "Concerning the Embellishments of Style"; bk. IX, chap. 1, "Of Figures. . . ."

Reid, Loren, *First Principles of Public Speaking*, Artcraft, 1960, pp. 194–198.

Sarett, Lew, William Trufant Foster, and Alma Johnson Sarett, *Basic Principles of Speech*, 3rd ed., Houghton Mifflin, 1958, pp. 264–268.

Thonssen, Lester, and A. Craig Baird, *Speech Criticism*, Ronald, 1948, pp. 431–432.

Whately, Richard, *Elements of Rhetoric*, Sheldon & Co. (New York), 1871, part III, chap. II, "Of Energy." There are many editions of this old text, first published in 1828, any of which will be satisfactory in this reference. The work had a wide influence in the nineteenth century particularly.

PART VII  DELIVERY

28

Vocal Aspects
of Delivery

Although speech is an overall activity, as we have pointed out, and delivery involves the whole bodily mechanism, it is still possible, for the sake of convenience, to separate the two principal aspects of delivery—voice and action. In this chapter, therefore, we shall consider the voice and its various aspects in relation to the delivery of your speech and the meanings you want to arouse.

Keep constantly in mind that the way you use your voice is an integral part of your speech, as important as the words themselves. The *spoken* word is a different phenomenon from the *written* word. Both have to do with communicating ideas, as we have come to understand the process; actually, the voice and the word can no more be separated in speech than can the notes and the melody or harmony of music.

Former President Hoover has pointed out that "Propaganda, even when it sticks to facts, can be slanted by the magic of the human voice. All of which can be accomplished by emotion and emphasis on words and phrases." But what Mr. Hoover does not recognize is that when the "facts" are so slanted, propaganda is not sticking to facts.[1]

We can consider the vocal or audible aspects of speech somewhat as we consider the production and modification of any sound: there must be some source of energy which initiates a vibration in some elastic body. This vibration produces sound which, when modified and amplified, creates all the effects of which the voice is capable. Intensive investigation of these many aspects of voice is a study in itself, worthy of many years of inquiry. The meager information on the anatomy, physiology, and physics of voice that could be given here would certainly not be of much assistance in helping you to improve your own speech. A few principles, however, should be helpful.

BREATHING

It has long been held that, for the greatest effectiveness of voice, for the greatest volume (loudness), and for the best tone quality, it is necessary to breathe in a certain definite way, with maximum expansion of the torso around the region just above the belt line. This method of breathing is ordinarily called the diaphragmatic or abdominal, on the theory that it is produced by a downward movement of the diaphragm in inhalation and by the action of the abdominal muscles in exhalation. It has even been suggested that the diaphragm gives an upward thrust to help force the air out of the lungs in exhalation. Unfortunately for the theory, the general respiratory apparatus is so closely tied up neurologically that it functions pretty much as a unit and is not easy to control in its separate parts. Furthermore, you cannot inhale *without* using your diaphragm, and you cannot exhale actively *without* using your abdominal muscles,

[1] Herbert Hoover, "Radio Gets a Policeman," in "The Early Hours of Radio," *American Heritage*, August, 1955, **VI**: 73–76.

since, in the latter case, there are no others to use. Of the different types of breathing the so-called abdominal or diaphragmatic is the least susceptible of conscious control; and even if one could control it, there would be no advantage whatever so far as more effective voice production is concerned.[2]

Does this mean that one should pay no attention whatever to breathing? Probably not. The purpose of breathing, so far as speech is concerned, is (1) to set and keep the vocal bands vibrating, (2) to produce through modification the "voiced" sounds,[3] and (3) to direct a stream of air through the throat and oral passages where it can produce the "voiceless" sounds.[4] For good breathing three requirements seem to be necessary.

1. The breath stream must have adequate pressure back of it so that the sounds will be plainly audible as far as your voice is intended to carry. It is possible for you to be heard in a whisper for a surprising distance if your sounds have sufficient pressure and distinctness back of them. Adequate pressure will make your consonants clearer and more distinct and give your vowels more carrying power so that your voice can be heard more easily over greater distances. Unfortunately, the prevalent use of microphones and public address systems seems to have minimized the importance of developing strong carrying voices. With an adequate voice there should be no need of mechanical and electrical speech aids for an audience of fewer than several hundred in an auditorium with fair acoustics.

2. Maintain an adequate reserve of breath at all times so that your speech will not trail off into inaudibility. Do not speak with your lungs either entirely full or almost empty. In ordinary speaking you actually need only a little breath at any one time: the average amount expelled between inhalations is only about thirty cubic inches, or approximately one pint. Your natural tendency is to take a short breath at each short pause and a full breath at the long

---

[2] Wesley A. Wiksell, "An Experimental Study of Controlled and Uncontrolled Types of Breathing," in Giles Wilkeson Gray, ed., *Studies in Experimental Phonetics*, University Studies No. 27, Louisiana State University Press, 1936, pp. 99–164. Doctoral dissertation, 1935.

[3] "Voiced" sounds are those in whose production the vocal bands are vibrating. They include all the vowels and such consonants as *b, d, g, l, m, n, ng, r, v, w, z,* and others.

[4] "Voiceless" sounds are those which do not require for their formation the vibration of the vocal bands. Among these are *p, t, k, s, sh, f, wh,* and *h.*

pauses. With these short "catches" of breath you should ordinarily be able to speak or read a sentence of any length without running out of breath. Whenever you come to a full stop in speaking or reading, as at the ends of sentences, take a full breath (*not* your maximum capacity), whether that full stop comes at the end of a sentence or not. If your sentence divisions (phrases) are well worked out and you replenish your breath with every short pause, you should have no difficulty maintaining an adequate reserve of breath in your lungs at all times.

3. Control your breath so as to produce a steady pressure of air against the vocal bands, tongue, teeth, and lips. These are the originators and modifiers of voice which enable you to produce all the various sounds and tonal effects of speech. Steadiness does not mean constant uniformity of pressure, for you will want to vary it to produce changes in loudness and for accent and emphasis. But your voice should not be wavering or jerky, now booming and now fading into a whisper. Changes in loudness should be because the meaning demands them rather than because you are unable to maintain a smooth, steady tone.

If your breathing enables you to have adequate pressure of breath, an adequate reserve of breath, and a steadiness and smoothness of breath pressure, you are not likely to experience great difficulty with your voice production in speaking so far as respiration is concerned.

VOICE PRODUCTION

If you will gently stroke down the front of your neck with your fingers you will come to a somewhat rounded projection about half-way down. This little projection, commonly called the *Adam's apple* is ordinarily somewhat more prominent in men than in women. It is the foremost part of the *larynx*, which is a most important organ in the production of voice. It has other uses, too, but we are not concerned with them here. The larynx contains two narrow tendinous edges called the *vocal bands* or *voice lips*. Through the operation of a number of pairs of the muscles of the larynx these vocal bands can be brought together (approximated) or spread apart at one end so as to form a sort of V, with the apex at the point of the Adam's apple, very much as you can spread the first and second fingers of your open hand apart and bring them together again. In fact, by blowing strongly between the fingers thus brought together, you can produce a sound of sorts.

The vocal bands can also be tensed and relaxed; they can even be made to vibrate in only a portion of their length. Of course we are not conscious of, nor can we consciously control, these movements in themselves, but we can feel and hear the effects, and through controlling the effects we are controlling the mechanisms that produce them.

When the two vocal bands are brought together just enough to form the proper resistance to the outward passage of breath from the lungs but not tightly enough to close off the breath entirely, and the breath stream is forced between them, they can be made to vibrate in somewhat the same way a trumpet player makes his lips vibrate on the mouthpiece of his instrument.[5] This oscillation of the vocal bands sets up in turn a vibration in the air cavities between the bands themselves and the lips and nares of the speaker; between the two, in some way that is not as yet fully understood, a sound is produced.

Through tensing and relaxing the vocal bands, varying the pressure of the breath stream, and movements of the several organs in the mouth and throat (tongue, lips, soft palate, lower jaw, teeth), this sound can be modified, changed, raised and lowered in pitch, made louder or weaker, and formed into any of the more than two score different sounds that enter into our daily speech. In the formation of words these sounds are combined into well-nigh countless ways to give us an English vocabulary that runs into the hundreds of thousands of words without beginning to use up all the possible combinations. Furthermore, these words in turn can be uttered in an almost infinite number of ways by changes in the tone of the voice, producing a great variety of effects highly important in the meanings that we want to express.

Through these variations we can produce subtle changes in our vocal patterns which stimulate in our listeners equally subtle changes in meanings, without their actually being aware of what is happening. The pernicious possibilities of these techniques, particularly in the use of spoken language, are discussed extensively by Vance Packard in his book *Hidden Persuaders*.

The tones thus produced (quite apart from the words) can be

[5] Engineers will understand the analogy when such a vibration is compared to a relaxation oscillation. The Bernouille principle may also be operative here.

described in terms of four basic attributes, which have been given various names but ordinarily are called *quality, force, time,* and *pitch.* Let us consider each of these in turn.

QUALITY

Quality is the term usually given to that characteristic of sound (tone) which enables one to identify it as coming from a certain type of source. Another term often used in the same sense is *timbre,* given either the French or the Anglicized pronunciation. Thus you recognize a friend's voice even over the telephone by its individual quality or timbre. Similarly, you are able to hear the tone from a given instrument in the orchestra, the oboe, for instance, by the peculiar "nasal" timbre of its tone. One piano may have a soft, smooth, "velvety" tone, while another has a bright, brilliant, "hard" tone.

The term *quality* is often used to refer also to the subjective evaluation of a sound, whether it is pleasant or unpleasant, good or poor. We say that the tone from a cheap "fiddle" would have a poor quality, whereas that from a Stradivarius would have a beautiful quality; but both would be recognized as violin tones by their characteristic timbre. Your own voice has an individual timbre which distinguishes it from other voices, but that does not mean that its quality is necessarily either pleasant or unpleasant.

A good quality, if you do not already possess it in your voice, is not to be acquired overnight or in a few easy lessons. If your voice is definitely unpleasant, you should certainly enroll in a course in which more emphasis is placed on voice training than can be given in this one. However, under the guidance of your instructor, you can do certain things to eliminate some of your most noticeable faults of voice quality.

Principal Faults of Voice Quality

Nasality.   Nasality is generally caused by allowing too much of the tone to go out through the nasal passages.[6] Theoretically, only three sounds of English or American speech are properly nasal, the

---

[6] There are a number of theories as to what causes nasality. The one given here probably explains the great majority of cases.

m, the *n*, and the *ng*. As you utter these sounds, notice that in each instance you close off your breath and tone in your mouth and permit them, by dropping your soft palate away from the back wall of your pharynx, to go up and through your nasal cavities. Actually, vowels preceding any of these three in the same syllable are also nasalized in anticipation of the following consonant. The fault of nasality lies in allowing sounds which are not so connected with a nasal consonant also to go up through the nose.

Pronounce the following pairs of words. The two words in each pair should and probably will sound different; but while the first of the two will have a definite nasal component because of the nasal consonant, the second should have no trace of nasality.

ban	bad	candy	caddy	pain	paid	sank	sack
bin	bid	come	cup	pawn	pawl	some	sup
Ben	bed	crank	crack	plunk	pluck	think	thick
blank	black	dandy	daddy	ring	rig	trunk	truck
boon	boot	fan	fat	rink	rick	window	widow
brink	brick	flank	flack	rung	rug	wind	wide
bunk	buck	home	hope	Sam	sap	whine	white
came	cape	moon	mood	sang	sag	whimper	whipper

As a partial test of your own nasality, pronounce the first word of each pair a number of times in succession, alternately closing the nostrils by gently pressing in with the forefingers from both sides and then releasing them. The word should sound markedly different when the nostrils are closed and when they are open. Now pronounce the second of each pair similarly, alternately closing and releasing the nostrils. Since these sounds are not normally nasal, it should make no difference whether the nose is closed or not.[7] If there is such a difference, then your voice is nasal, and the degree of your nasality probably bears a direct relation to the amount of difference. Practice on these and other words having no nasal consonants until they sound approximately the same with the nostrils closed and open. When they do, it will mean that only a negligible amount of tone is passing through the nasal cavities.

Make up short sentences without any nasal consonants, and practice on them until they also sound the same with the nostrils closed and open. The following are illustrative.

[7] A slight degree of nasal resonance is probably not serious. Some investigators believe that it is neither possible nor desirable to get rid of it entirely.

1. Sister threw out the dishwater.
2. A little boy ate a piece of buttered bread with sugar.
3. Set the hook hard to catch your big fish.
4. Prices today are far above average levels for the past decade.
5. Books will add greatly to your culture if read assiduously.
6. Electric power is a chief requisite to true prosperity.
7. Life without drudgery would be delightful.
8. "Swift as the boreal light which flies. . . ."
9. "The bride kissed the goblet."
10. Puppies are able to sleep at the stable.
11. "Bless the Lord, all ye his works."

Huskiness.   Huskiness may be caused by various factors. It may be the result of foreign substances or growths on the vocal bands, which in turn may be the effect of overuse or of a pathological development. The best procedure is to visit a doctor and have the growth removed if in his judgment it should be. Often such growths can be reduced or removed entirely by judicious and well-directed exercises under the guidance of a competent instructor. If the huskiness is the result of a cold, the obvious procedure is to get the cold cleared up as soon as possible. While the throat is inflamed, it is best not to put great strain on the vocal bands. When blood vessels are distended their walls are stretched very thin. Under such conditions the stress put on them by excessive use can easily rupture those thin walls, resulting in a huskiness that does not subside as soon as the cold disappears but holds on until the tissues are repaired.

Huskiness, which is often described as hoarseness, may also be caused by too great relaxation of the vocal bands, to such a degree that they lack the proper tonus for clear tones. Such relaxation is probably not localized but is more likely to be simply one aspect of an overall relaxation or general lassitude. The remedy in such a case is to build up the general bodily tonus. Since overrelaxation is often the result of some acquired attitude, as of ennui or boredom, another and probably more effective remedy is to change the attitude.

A fourth possible cause of huskiness or hoarseness is the attempt to lower the pitch of the voice far below the normal range. In fact one study[8] reached the conclusion that this is by far the most common cause. When the voice is brought up to the normal range, the hoarseness tends to disappear of its own accord.

[8] Arleigh B. Williamson, "Diagnosis and Treatment of Seventy-Two Cases of Hoarse Voice," *Quarterly Journal of Speech*, April, 1945, **31**: 189–202.

Muffled tones. Muffled tones are usually associated with low pitch, a nearly closed mouth, and loose or flabby lips and tongue. The voice seems not to be permitted to emerge clearly and cleanly. It seems dull, and the whole speech is lifeless. Ordinarily the difficulty can be remedied by opening the mouth wider to let the tone out, raising the pitch to its normal level, and putting greater liveliness into the movements of the tongue, jaw, and lips. Both in practice and in speaking emphasize the consonants, particularly those formed near the front of the mouth, that is, with the lips and the front part of the tongue: *p, b, t, d, f, v, l, sh, zh, s,* and *z*. In a later section in this chapter the formation of these sounds is described in somewhat more detail.

Thinness. Thinness is a weakness, a feebleness of tone, a seeming lack of "body." The tone has neither carrying power nor fullness. It gives the impression of being too high-pitched, although it may not actually be pitched any higher than normal. It is often associated with illness or weakness and, if heard in a man's voice, with effeminacy.

Thinness in the voice seems to be the result of misplaced resonance. There seems to be too much resonance in the front part of the oral cavity and too little in the back part. It is sometimes a help to try to make yourself heard in larger areas—big rooms, open spaces —but be careful not to put a heavy strain on your voice mechanism. Practicing relaxation of the throat musculature may also aid in developing the "back resonances" that seem to be missing. It might be pointed out that this voice characteristic is much less obvious in the feminine voice than in the masculine, probably because the former is naturally somewhat higher than the latter. Try speaking at a somewhat lower pitch.

In the matter of voice improvement, as in other aspects of speech development, there is no adequate substitute for a well-trained instructor. In Chapter 1 (pp. 13–14) we pointed out the advantages of classroom study. These advantages extend to voice improvement as much as to other phases of speech development. No amount of printed instruction can take the place of direct classroom or even individual guidance in the improvement of certain aspects of your speech, voice quality among them.

Having your voice recorded on a tape recorder and played back so that, again under the guidance of a competent instructor, you can hear for yourself what you are doing should be of great assistance in revealing to you just what your voice sounds like.

Stridency. In a sense stridency is hardly a fault of quality. It is often little more than a booming loudness, but is often associated with harshness; it may be almost raucous. It has the effect of almost overpowering the listener. People who have such voices bellow their way through life with no regard for a sense of fitness; their voices are as loud and intrusive in private conversation (they never, in fact, hold any conversation privately) as in the largest gathering. They are often known as "leather-lunged"; they frequently act as outdoor announcers at sporting events, but one hears them everywhere.

The usual cause of such a quality is hypertension, which again is an overall condition and not merely a matter of the vocal mechanism. The remedy is relaxation, working toward smoother and easier social adaptation, together perhaps with some readjustment of social attitudes. Possibly, too, some personality readjustment may be necessary. Such stridency may sometimes be the effect of an attempt to overcompensate for an unrecognized feeling of inadequacy or inferiority. On the other hand, it may arise from an exaggerated sense of superiority, although such a cause is probably less often encountered than the former.

Breathiness. Some voices have a sort of "featheredge" rather than "knife edge" quality. There is a sort of fuzziness about them; you seem to hear about as much breath as voice. This breathiness is probably caused by failure to bring the vocal bands together closely enough to set all the breath stream into vibration; some of the breath thus escapes without being vocalized. The defect may sometimes develop from the frequent and persistent efforts of parents to soften the childish clarion of their children's voices, with a resultant semi-whisper. It is not as a rule heard among people who are alert, animated, and vivacious mentally and physically.

Quality and Personality

An agreeable voice quality is an asset in any form of speaking, whether it be public speaking, reading from a printed page, acting, or conference and private conversation. Much of the impression which people get of you is due to the quality of your voice; certainly your voice creates one of the earliest impressions, one which may be difficult to change later. In fact, much of what is often called your personality arises from the impressions you create by the quality and other attributes of your voice.

Your personality is basically the way you affect other people, whether they react favorably or unfavorably to you. There is no mysterious essence emanating from your organism to which the label *personality* can be attached. The only way you can make an impression of any kind upon others is through what you let them see and hear you doing. If you want to create a favorable impression, that is, if you want to exhibit a pleasing personality, then you must do those things to which others react favorably. Certainly a voice which is extremely nasal, shrill, muffled, hoarse, or strident or which possesses any other unpleasant quality does not contribute to a favorable impression. One of the ways in which social friction can be lessened is to cultivate a voice that others enjoy hearing, just for the sound of it if for no other reason.

FORCE

The term *force* is not too well chosen, because it can be interpreted in so many ways. With respect to voice and its production it refers to the element of loudness, which is correlated with what is called intensity in the physics of sound. For our present purposes we can think of force as manifesting itself in three ways, all of which may need some study by the aspiring public speaker.

Accent

Accent refers to the slight stress or increased loudness one gives to certain syllables in a word. It is discussed further under pronunciation. Stress is more often used among linguists than accent.

Emphasis

Just as you stress one syllable of a word a little harder to make that syllable stand out and give the word its correct rhythmic pattern and hence its correct pronunciation, so you can stress one or more words in the sentence a little more to make them stand out and give the sentence meaning. Such stress laid on words in the sentence is known as *emphasis*. The early elocutionists, in distinguishing between accent and emphasis, pointed out that, whereas the former had to do with correctness in the pronunciation of the word, the latter had to do with the sense of the passage. "Emphasis," said William Scott more than 150 years ago, "points out the precise meaning of a sentence, shows in what manner one idea is connected with and rises out of another, marks the several clauses of a sentence, gives to every part its proper sound, and thus conveys to the mind of the reader the full import of the whole."[9]

The differentiation has some foundation, but emphasis (as well as accent) should not be thought as entirely a matter of increased force; it involves usually a change in pitch as well. An increase in force for either accent or emphasis is characteristically accompanied by a rise in pitch, although there are occasional deviations from the general pattern.[10]

For example, take the sentence, "This is the house that Jack built," and note how the meaning changes as you read it stressing successively the separate words:

> *This* (not another) is the house that Jack built.
> This *is* (believe it or not) the house that Jack built.
> This is *the* (it's the only one) house that Jack built.
> This is the *house* (not a garage or barn) that Jack built.
> This is the house *that* (not some other Jack) Jack built.
> This is the house that *Jack* (not Tom or Henry) built.
> This is the house that Jack *built* (he didn't buy it; he *built* it).

Note too that as you emphasize these successive words you give them not only added force but a different inflectional pattern from that given when they are unstressed. Furthermore, emphasizing the different words also changes the stress and inflectional pattern throughout the whole sentence. When these and other changes are made in the manner of utterance, the entire meaning of the sentence is also changed.

---

[9] William Scott, *Essay on Elocution*, Lincoln and Gleason, 1809, p. 37. This is not the first edition of Scott's *Essay*, by any means.

[10] See Dwight L. Bollinger, "Inhibited and Uninhibited Stress," *Quarterly Journal of Speech*, April, 1945, **31**: 202–207.

General Loudness

Different occasions call for different degrees of loudness. In a small room it is not only unnecessary, it would be out of place for you to speak with as much general force as you would use in a large auditorium. The degree of force you need to use is determined mainly by the distance you need to project your voice, modified by the interferences (conflicting noises, acoustic peculiarities, and the like) encountered in the process. It is a mistake to feel that you must always speak above the audience noise. Sometimes by using a somewhat softer voice, yet one which *could* be heard if the listeners were quiet, you will be able to draw their attention and induce them to be quiet in order to hear at all.

In general, animated speakers, those who are keenly interested in their subjects and who have the urge to communicate, are more inclined to speak forcefully than are the less enthusiastic. A degree of spontaneous force in the voice is a fairly accurate indication of the speaker's interest and sincerity. However, avoid shouting which superficial speakers often resort to as a substitute for sound material and honest thinking. With force, as with the other attributes of delivery, it is variety which gives the voice its effectiveness.

TIME

The factor of time as an attribute of vocal tone, having its effect on meaning, is manifested in three principal ways: quantity, length of phrase, and length of pause between phrases. These three together make up the general *rate* of speech.

Elements of Time

Quantity. The term *quantity* refers to the length of time a given sound or word is held. It makes a difference, for example, whether you say simply, "all night long" or "a-a-a-all ni-i-i-ght lo-o-o-ng." Lengthening a sound or a whole word often makes it more impressive; it intensifies meaning which otherwise might seem quite casual. On the other hand, by clipping a word short you can give it an incisive, definite, final quality it would not otherwise have.

Length of phrase.   If you will observe closely, you will notice that you speak not in isolated words but in phrases, which normally are comprised of the words making up a "sense unit." Thus, the opening words of the "Gettysburg Address" form sense units in this manner: Not "Four / score / and / seven / years / ago," with the words separated just as many of us learned to read "I / see / a / cat," but "Fourscoreandsevenyearsago / ourfathersbroughtforth / uponthiscontinent / anewnation / conceivedinliberty / anddedicatedtotheproposition / thatallmen / arecreatedequal."

It would be possible to vary the length of the phrases here, for example, by combining the second and third/ourfathersbroughtforthuponthiscontinent / and the last two / thatallmenarecreatedequal, which would tend to speed up the total time a little.

When the phrases are too short, so that the "sense units" themselves are broken up, the speech sounds choppy, especially if the pauses between the phrases are also too short. Phrasing the above passage thus, "Fourscore / andsevenyearsago / ourfathers / broughtforth / uponthiscontinent / anewnation / conceived / inliberty / anddedicated / totheproposition / thatallmen / arecreated / equal," while it might make some sense, would make the whole utterance jerky. However, if you want to make this passage very impressive, you will read it in short phrases, especially at the beginning, each of these phrases being a sense unit. But within each phrase you must also lengthen the words somewhat in quantity so that the whole rate of utterance will be much slower. The whole phrasal pattern in this case would probably be different from that indicated above in this paragraph.

Sense units are not fixed and rigid; in any extended passage they can be shortened or expanded. Two or more can sometimes be combined to form a larger unit, or a long one can be broken up into two or three. Much will depend on the effect you want to create. But be sure that your phrases, whether long or short, consist of one sense unit and do not break over from one into the next, for it often happens that the specific phrasing determines the exact meaning. It makes a difference whether one says "The professor insists / the student is lazy," or "The professor / insists the student / is lazy."

In determining the sense units in written material, either your own or another's, do not depend on the punctuation, which is primarily a matter of grammar. Phrasing is entirely a matter of meaning, except for the occasional necessity for catching one's breath. The first sentence of the "Gettysburg Address" is punctuated differently in different texts, usually with commas only after *nation* and *liberty,* thus: "Fourscore and seven years ago our fathers brought forth upon this continent a new nation, conceived in liberty, and dedicated to the proposition that all men are created equal." These commas, however, do not necessarily set off sense units; certainly they do not set off all of them. These are more adequately indicated by such phrasing as that in the illustrations given a little earlier. Styles in punctuation change; the same statement cannot be made of the phrasal unit, which is not a matter of style.

As a rule, the more important and weighty the subject matter, the shorter the phrases and the slower the general rate. As a former prominent professor of speech used to say, "Bodies of great weight always start slowly." Speakers often start out very slowly and gather momentum and speed as they proceed, thus giving the impression of a great mass which accelerates slowly. The famous "locomotive yell" so familiar to thousands of students, was created by a professor of speech.

Length of pause. In varying the length of phrase, we obviously also vary the number of pauses or periods of silence between phrases. But the general rate may also be affected through varying the *length* of the pauses. As a rule, in smooth, even speech short phrases are accompanied by relatively long pauses, the whole impression being one of weight, importance, and dignity, as suggested above. By lengthening the pauses and using more of them, you obviously slow down the rate; by shortening them and using fewer, you speed up your utterance.

Time values are very subtle, for the reason that it takes only slight variations to be significant. These variations may be measured in units of only a few hundredths of a second, in some instances even a few thousandths. Short as they are, however, they have their effects.

Dramatic pause. Occasionally, when you have just finished some particularly impressive passage and have risen to a climax of thought and utterance, you can add significantly to the impressiveness by suddenly stopping completely and remaining silent for a few seconds while the full import of what you have just said sinks in. One can imagine the effect if William Pitt had made use of such a dramatic pause immediately after his powerful climax: "If I were an American, as I am an Englishman, while a foreign troop were landed in my country, I would never lay down my arms—never—*never*—NEVER!" He may, in fact, have used such a pause.

Another situation in which this dramatic pause can be used with telling effect arises when, after giving your hearers a strong build-up, you suddenly stop for a moment of dead silence before uttering your final words, to which you have actually been building all the time. Henry W. Grady may have used this technique in the following passage from "The New South": "But from the union of these colonist Puritans and Cavaliers, from the straightening of their purposes and the crossing of their blood, slow perfecting through a century, came he who stands as the first typical American, the first who comprehended within himself all the strength and gentleness, all the majesty and grace of this Republic—Abraham Lincoln.

Rate

The elements of quantity, phrase, and pause together make up the general rate at which you speak. There is no optimum rate or average number of words per minute for speech; it may vary from somewhere near 90 words for very slow speech to 200 or more for rapid speech. Instances have been reported of rates of utterance of more than 600 words per minute, but the reports say nothing of the intelligibility of the resulting speech.

The general rate will vary somewhat with the type of material and the total situation. Ponderous themes and weighty matters, rendered with deep impressiveness, seem to call for slower rates; lighter moods will permit more rapid rates. Large auditoriums, especially if they have a long reverberation time, require slow utterance; small rooms, with negligible reverberation, place no limit on the rate of speech. On most occasions your best rate will probably be from 130 to 150 words per minute.

Such a statement does not mean that every minute you are uttering so many words, no more and no less, say, 140, nor that every 30 seconds you will have spoken 70 words. Rate of utterance is an overall average. You can estimate that, if your tendency is to speak only fairly rapidly, in ten minutes you should be able to utter approximately 1500 words; if you are a slow speaker, you may not be able to utter more than 1000 or 1200.

PITCH

The fourth attribute of voice which influences the meanings of words as we utter them is pitch and its variations. Pitch may be defined as the "highness" or "lowness" of a tone as compared with the notes of a musical scale. It is exhibited in the voice in three particular ways in what have been called *key, step,* and *slide* or *inflection.*

Key

Key refers to the general pitch level at which we speak, whether it is high, low, or medium. The term is not used with anything like the specificity that it is in music, the three ranges being very broad and general. Furthermore, what would be a high pitch for one might be only a normal pitch for another.

Optimum pitch.   For each voice there is a general pitch level which seems to be the norm above and below which that voice moves. Voices are somewhat like musical instruments in that each one is constructed to play within a certain range, some high, some low, some medium, and is most effective when being played within that range. This level for the voice is not fixed; the principle simply means that, when a speaker finds the general level at which his voice is easiest and most effective, he has probably found his optimum pitch. This pitch, according to Fairbanks, is about one-fourth the way up from your lowest to your highest singing note, including your falsetto.[11]

The general principle of optimum pitch does not mean that you are limited in your pitch range to that particular level. Some moods call for a low pitch, others for normal, or medium, and still others for fairly high pitches. Deep solemnity, awe, reverence, grief—those moods which seem to inhibit vigorous bodily action—require as a rule low pitches and narrow ranges; one can hardly imagine Byron's well-known "Apostrophe to the Ocean" being read in other than a low pitch: "Roll on, thou deep and dark blue ocean, roll . . . ."

[11] Grant Fairbanks, *Voice and Articulation Drillbook,* 2nd ed., Harper, 1960, chap. 11, "Pitch," especially pp. 125–129.

At the other extreme, moods of gaiety, excitement, keen pleasure —those that tend to incite bodily activity—call in general for higher pitches and wider ranges, sometimes rising to the upper limit of one's vocal range.

Probably most of your speaking will be in a medium key, that is to say, rising above and falling below your normal or optimum pitch level as a median. It is important for the sake of your own vocal expression as well as to avoid strain on your vocal organs that you find your most favorable level. At the same time it is also important that you be able to adapt your pitch level to the mood you want to establish. You would not tell ghost stories in the same tone you would use in telling a lively, humorous anecdote.

Step

Although step is one manifestation of the attribute of pitch, you will probably not need to pay much attention to its variations. The term refers to those changes which occur *between* words or syllables when the voice skips, so to speak, from one pitch to another, either up or down. It is comparable to singing the notes D and G (or G and D) successively without sliding from one to the other. If the general pitch level of the voice is used effectively and the inflectional patterns are meaningful, the steps will probably pretty much take care of themselves.

On the other hand, proper use of steps is a requisite to the best use of inflectional patterns. In the conclusion of Patrick Henry's famous speech before the Virginia Convention on March 23, 1775, steps are well illustrated.

Normally, the first clause will be spoken in a constantly rising pitch, in which the voice must drop back down to pick up the next clause beginning with *or*. This drop between the final syllable of *liberty* to the succeeding *or* constitutes a downward step. Such changes occur between unstressed and stressed syllables of a word, and usually between adjacent words of successive phrases. If you read the preceding sentence aloud, you will probably put a step between *ad* and *ja* in the word *adjacent*. Other illustrations will be found in the exercises in connection with the various aspects of pitch.

Slide or Inflection

By far the most meaningful use of pitch in the voice is to be found in the inflections and the manifold patterns that are made possible by the slides of the voice. The term *inflection* refers to those pitch changes which are accomplished by means of continuous slides or glides from one pitch to another, through a wide or narrow range. These patterns may be rising inflections, falling inflections, or various combinations of rising-falling or falling-rising, and may cover ranges from as narrow as one semitone or even less to more than a full octave. It is in these variations that the most noticeable aspects of vocal flexibility are to be observed; yet they do not follow the specific intervals of the musical scale. They are indefinite as to range, except that they may be narrow or wide or any degree between.

Although extremely narrow pitch ranges may be employed occasionally to express strong emotional attitudes, a habitually narrow range, when not expressive of specific moods calling for a low pitch level, may denote generally an overall lassitude, a lack of animation, an indifference, or even mental dullness. It is often accompanied by an inactive articulatory apparatus, muffled tones, and indistinct utterance, which are further evidences of the same emotional attitude. Extremely wide habitual patterns, on the other hand, may suggest excitability, hypersensitivity to both external and internal stimuli, and in extreme cases, especially when coupled with other phenomena, certain types of manic neuroticism. For the speaker these extremes are useful in the expression of strong emotional attitudes and in stimulating such attitudes in listeners. Special care should be taken, however, not to overdo these patterns to the point where your listeners get so used to them that they no longer have any effect.

In your voice development, cultivate the ability to use the particular inflectional patterns that will express the specific meaning you intend. Learn to listen to what your own voice is doing, both when you speak and as it is recorded for playback. The following exercises may give you something of an idea of inflections; they will also give you practice in flexibility. If you have the opportunity, record them, study them, listen for errors, and try to determine the degree to which you are able to make your voice do what you want it to do or what you think it is doing. Practice on these expressions, giving them the inflections indicated. A line slanting upward (/) indicates a rising inflection; one slanting downward (\ ) indicates a falling inflection.

/ No	\ Well, / now	/ Oh, \ yes	/ / All day	\ \ Why, then
\ No	\ Well, \ now	\ \ Indeed	/ \ All day	/ \ Do you, / really?
\ Oh	\ Oh, / yes	/ \ Indeed	\ / Why, then	/ / Do you, \ really?
/ Sure	\ What, / again?	\ That's / why	/ That's \ why	\ \ Here you / are

/ \ /
The queen, my lord, is dead

\ / \
The queen, my lord, is dead

/ \ \ /
No, that's not right

/ \
There is a man

\ /
There is a man

/ / / \
No, that's not right

These four elements, then—quality, force, time, and pitch—are important because their proper use adds variety to the voice and contributes significantly to the meanings suggested by the words. Meanings, you will remember, are twofold: they have a logical or intellectual content and a personal or emotional content. No effective utterance is wholly one or the other; that is, no good speech is either entirely intellectual or entirely emotional. The latter is necessary to give life and feeling to speech and to establish or strengthen attitudes; the former is needed to give direction and control, and to add the rational element which distinguishes man from the lower animals. There must be something of both. As we said earlier, you must not only *express* ideas, you must also let your listeners know how you *feel* about those ideas.

So far as vocal effects are concerned, your ability to communicate these two aspects of meaning is dependent upon your effective use of changes or variety in the four attributes of vocal tone described above. Your language, of course, and your bodily activity also make heavy contributions to that communication. In general, changes in voice quality seem to have more to do with stimulating the emotional aspects of meaning than the logical.[12] In most of your speaking you probably will not be greatly concerned with changes of quality, though they may be useful in some situations calling for short characterizations. Changes in the middle ranges of pitch apparently have most to do, though not entirely, with the intellectual component of meaning. Extreme changes in any of the four, whether extremely narrow or extremely wide, are essentially emotional. Variety in force and in time has to do about equally with the intellectual and the emotional, with the extremes again being expressive primarily of the latter.

LISTENING TO YOUR VOICE

We have mentioned listening to what your voice is doing. The time for that is in your practice periods and not when you are before an audience. When you are in an actual speaking situation the most important thing is getting your idea and audience together; forget your voice then. "Consciously selective conduct," says Palmer, "is elementary and inferior. People distrust it, or rather they distrust him who exhibits it."[13] If you have been working on flexibility as you practice, your voice should at other times take care of itself. Practice, therefore, on various kinds of changes so that you can make your voice do what you want it to do. Learn, if you do not already know, how to place the proper accent or stress in words of more than one syllable (consult your dictionary). Learn to make your voice take a rising or falling inflection, or a combination of the rising-falling or falling-rising, whenever you want it to. Study your phrasing—the sense units of your speaking—and make your pauses correspond to those units. Only by conscious attention to what your voice is doing and by practice in making it do the various things you want it to do will you develop a voice of maximum flexibility and expressiveness which can stimulate in the minds of your audience the meanings you intend.

With a voice of adequate power you should not need microphones

---

[12] Charles Henry Woolbert, *The Fundamentals of Speech*, 2nd ed., Harper, 1927, chap. X, "Voice and Meaning."

[13] George Herbert Palmer, *Self-Cultivation in English*, Houghton Mifflin, 1908, p. 15.

and public address systems for audiences of normal size. Before the advent of such electromechanical boosters to the voice, speakers like Chauncey M. Depew, William Jennings Bryan, Albert J. Beveridge, and scores of others could address audiences of several thousand listeners and make themselves heard. The public address systems commonly in use today distort the voice and take from it much of its natural quality, making it sound mechanical. Work to make your voice audible to as large audiences as you reasonably can without having to strain or shout.

With a voice of adequate flexibility you should be able to avoid such vocal atrocities as "quote-unquote" in introducing and ending quoted material. You should be able to indicate either by your voice or by the wording, or both, just when you begin your quotation and just when you resume your own wording. One does not read semicolons, commas, periods, or question marks; they are intended for the eye. Quotation marks are also intended only for the eye.

ARTICULATION

Carefully conducted experiments show that the greater part of the carrying power of voice is in the vowel sounds; the intelligibility of speech is mainly a matter of the distinctness of consonants. For speech that can easily be understood for any distance, therefore, you must attend to both your vowels and your consonants—in other words, to your entire utterance. If the quality of your voice is developed so that the faults described earlier in this chapter have been eliminated and if you have developed adequate breath supply, ample reserve, and steady pressure, the vowels and, hence, the carrying power should largely take care of themselves. It will be worth while to examine the consonants in order to understand their importance in distinctness and to form a basis for improvement in articulation.

Consonant Formation[14]

Each speech sound is formed by the modification of the vocal tone or of the breath stream as it passes through the mouth or nasal

[14] See Giles Wilkeson Gray, "Speech Sound Formation," in Lee Edward Travis, ed., *Handbook of Speech Pathology*, Appleton-Century-Crofts, 1957, chap. 4.

cavities or both. Many of these sounds include both vocal tones and breath, and in a few cases both the mouth and the nasal cavities are involved. Sometimes this modification is achieved by shaping the oral cavities, mainly by movements of the tongue and lips and to some extent by movements of other organs with which we are somewhat less familiar. These modifications by which the timbre of the vocal tone is altered produce all the different vowels and some of the so-called consonants. Sometimes the modification consists of putting partial or complete blockages or bars in the way of the emission of voice or breath or both, producing most of what are commonly called consonants. It is with the latter that we are primarily concerned here, though there is no generally accepted basis upon which a consistent division of vowels and consonants can be made.

For example, if you close your lips tightly, raise the soft palate at the back of the throat, build up a breath pressure back of the closed lips, and then suddenly release the lips, you produce a sound which is easily recognizable as *p*. Now, if while building up the breath pressure behind the closed lips you start your vocal bands vibrating, you find on releasing your lips that you have produced a clear *b*.

If you slide the tip of your tongue back along the roof of the mouth, you will notice perhaps a half inch or so behind the base of the upper teeth a sort of rounded ridge. Bring the front part of the tongue (not the extreme tip, but just back of it) up against this ridge, again closing off the passage so the breath cannot get through, again build up the pressure and suddenly pull the tongue away, and you will discover that you have made a very respectable *t*. Addition of the vocal-band vibration to this sound will give you a good *d*.

The *k* and *g* (as in *go*) are similarly produced by raising the back of the tongue to the palate just about where the hard and soft palates are joined, building up pressure, and again releasing. The *g* differs from the *k* primarily in that it contains the addition of voice, in the same way that *b* differs from *p* and *d* from *t*.

Did you notice the exact places where the dam was made to prevent the escape of breath? Now, if you form the dam again with your lips and hum, allowing the sound to go out through the nasal passages, what sound is produced? It should be *m*. Forming the dam in the same place as for the *t* and the *d* and humming should give you an *n*. The consonant similarly corresponding to the *k* and the *g* should be that ordinarily spelled with *ng* as in *sing*. Notice that this *ng* sound actually has no more of a *g* in it than *m* has a *b* in it or the *n* a *d*.

Let us try some different kinds of sounds. If you simply stick the tip (no more) of your tongue between your teeth and blow, the resulting sound should be the initial consonant in *thin* or *thick*. In fact, you don't have to protrude your tongue through; just partially close the opening between the upper and lower teeth with the tip and blow. Add the vocal-band vibration to it, and you get the initial sound in *this* and *that* (unless you say *dis* and *dat!*).

We do not intend to give a detailed description here of the formation of all the consonant sounds. These examples illustrate certain important points, given below, with respect to distinct utterance, particularly with reference to the production of consonants.

1. Every consonant is best produced and is most distinct when the complete or partial closure for the breath or tone is formed in the right place. In the English language, the *t* and the *d* are correctly formed *only* when the front of the tongue closes off the breath at the "teeth ridge," or as it is more technically called, the *alveolar ridge*. For every consonant there is a correct place of articulation, and if the sound is formed at that place and other factors are present, only the one sound can result. After one has learned correct habits of forming sounds, some latitude may develop in their production in various phonetic contexts, that is, as the sounds are connected with different sounds in word production.

2. For a good, distinct consonant the position or movement must be adequately formed. That is, there must be a strong, firm muscular action of tongue or lips. For such sounds as *p*, *d*, and the like, for instance, the closure must be firm, positive, and complete. All the organs of articulation should have good tonus.

3. The breath pressure back of the partial or complete closure must be strong, the degree of pressure being determined by the necessity for more or less incisive speech. For your speech to be understood approximately as far as your voice can be heard, as in a large auditorium, the pressure must be stronger than in a small room, for the same reason that the whole utterance must be louder.

4. The release called for by the formation of the sound and its context must be clean and sharp. The *t*, for example, is not complete in most instances without such a release. When it precedes another

consonant, as in *utmost*, no "explosion" is heard for the first *t;* there should be one for the final sound, and it should be distinctly heard.

Consonants may occupy one of four positions in words: initial, medial, final, or in a consonant combination, in which case the last sound of the group may be in a final position. These positions cannot always be determined by the place of the sound in the isolated word; the place in the *phrase* governs whether it is initial, medial, or final. When the phrase "Fourscore and seven years ago" is spoken as a sense unit, there is only one initial consonant and no final one; all the rest are medial or in combination.

The criteria for well-formed consonants are equally valid for all these positions: the sound must be correctly (*accurately*) formed; it must be *adequately* formed; and it must have *sufficient breath pressure* back of it, and a *clean and sharp release,* when demanded.

Consonant Combinations

Not all consonants occur singly; they are found frequently in combinations of many kinds. Some of these are relatively easy to produce, but some of them, mainly through force of habit, are badly slurred. The way you handle your consonant combinations will set you off as a careful, distinct speaker, one whom it is easy to understand—or the opposite.

The following words illustrate some of the more common types of consonant combinations which often cause difficulty. A common tendency is to slur or omit entirely the second consonant of the pair, except in the case of such words as *help*, in which the *l* is often omitted (*he'p*). Be sure to pronounce the *st, lp, sp, kt, pt, nd, vd,* and other combinations, giving each sound its proper value.[15]

Two-Consonant Combinations

help	least	frost	flask	wrapped	lacked
clasp	first	priest	task	around	correct
crisp	lest	field	risk	fact	exact
east	cast	yield	wept	respect	lived
fast	toast	pulled	apt	waked	arrived
wrist	waste	cold	swept	looked	bribed

[15] *Lacked, correct, looked,* and *exact* do not look as if the final sounds were *kt*, nor does *wrapped* look as if the final sound were *t* (*pt*); but those are actually the sounds.

The usual error in the combinations below is to omit either the middle element (as in *cas's, wris's, Pic's, cryp's, as't, correc's, fiel's*) or in some cases, the final one (as in *cask', pest', ask'*, etc.).

Three- and Four-Consonant Combinations

casks	wisps	yields	accepts	fixed
asks	basked	folds	adopts	boxed
hasps	posts	molds	thanked	addled
rasps	costs	pumped	yanked	muddled
tasks	wrists	corrects	bunked	jingled
tusks	pests	Picts	pinked	mingled
whisks	waists	crypts	conked	mangled
asked	fields	battled	mixed	befuddled

There are many other such combinations, all of which need to be perfectly pronounced. Not every sound in every such combination is to be heard; but if you want your speech to be clear and distinct, you will have to learn just what sounds are supposed to be heard. In all such combinations every consonant which is to be pronounced at all must receive its proportionate value. Clarity of utterance is as vital as clarity of language; it is to speech as legibility is to writing.

Nineteenth-century elocutionists took great pleasure in practicing the following and other archaic consonant combinations, taken from old forms of the verb in the second person singular:

exist'st	(stst)	mixedst	(kstst)	yankedst	(nktst)
yield'st	(ldst)	ask'st	(skst)	heardst	(rdst)
correct'st	(ktst)	askedst	(sktst)	fearedst	(rdst)
accept'st	(ptst)	battledst	(tldst)	governedst	(rndst)
claspedst	(sptst)	jingledst	(ngldst)	earnedst	(rndst)

Whatever has been said about the exaggerations of which those speakers and readers were guilty, at least there was never any question of the distinctness of their utterance; they could be understood.

PRONUNCIATION

Correct pronunciation is different from distinct articulation, and the two aspects of utterance are cultivated for different reasons. Whereas articulation is basic to intelligibility and comprehension, pronunciation is primarily a matter of convention, something that people have come to agree upon.

By way of analogy, if you cannot read someone's writing, you get no idea of what he is trying to say. Or he may spell atrociously, and while you call him illiterate, you may still be able to understand clearly; he simply has not learned how good writers spell. Similarly, if someone's speech is unintelligible to you, the communicative effort is a total loss; if his pronunciation deviates widely from accepted standards, you may call him ignorant, but you can still understand him.

Good pronunciation can be defined as giving to the sounds of a word their proper sequence and values and to the syllables their proper stress. "Proper" here is no more than a matter of general agreement; there is no inherently right or wrong way to pronounce any word in the language. We pronounce as we do for no other reason than that it is the way most if not all careful speakers pronounce their words. True, there is some historical basis for our pronunciations, but even that goes back finally to a matter of general agreement. The processes by which these accepted ways are determined are too involved to be described here; but they have been evolved by dictionary makers and others over a period of more than 300 years and can be discovered by reading the fine-print introduction to a good dictionary. However determined, though, it is universally recognized that wherever the language is spoken a pronunciation that follows some accepted convention, some admitted standard, is one of the criteria of an educated person.

Standards of Pronunciation

What constitutes a "standard of pronunciation"—or a "standard pronunciation"? How can one determine what mode of pronunciation to follow with any degree of assurance that his speech will be acceptable? These are some of the questions that inevitably arise to plague the student who is seriously attempting to improve his speech. The answers are not always easy to find, but perhaps a few suggestions will be helpful.

First of all, a "standard of pronunciation" consists broadly of a set of criteria by which it may be determined approximately whether a given pronunciation is "acceptable" or not. Essentially these criteria are determined by the dictates of usage and by the prestige of speakers whose pronunciation is considered good and is therefore taken as a basis for comparison. It is not difficult to understand why authorities, in trying to evaluate these criteria and in weighing the prestige of different speakers, all equally eminent, occasionally disagree on the predominant pronunciation of a given word. The simple fact is that for a large number of our words there is no single accepted pronunciation, though in recording those words our dictionaries follow these "standards of pronunciation" as rigorously as possible.

Where does all this divergence of opinion, this seeming confusion, leave you who are interested in learning how to use words and use them correctly? It can safely be said that even though there may be no inherently "correct" pronunciation of any word in our language, dictionary makers have performed a remarkably scholarly task in discovering those pronunciations which are widely accepted as correct.[16] Therefore, any pronunciation you find in any reputable up-to-date dictionary is placed there because the makers of that dictionary found ample evidence that it was being widely used by careful, educated speakers, and you are quite justified in using such a pronunciation yourself.

It is a lamentable but unavoidable fact that dictionaries, even the latest editions, are usually from five to ten years behind the times in the matter of indicating word usage. The real language of any people is not to be found in their writings but in their speech. This speech is constantly changing, and has been changing since man first began to speak. If Benjamin Franklin were to be "time-machined" forward to the middle of the twentieth century, we should have difficulty in understanding him, and our speech would be jargon to him. Speech is constantly changing; pronunciations are constantly changing. By the time the makers of an unabridged dictionary get around to compiling a new edition, with the new pronunciations indicated, those pronunciations may already have been in extensive use for several years. It takes time to assemble all the necessary information that goes into a new edition of a dictionary.

Despite the time lag between actual usage and the dictionary's recognition of it, your safest course is to follow recommended pronunciations. In using a pronunciation that may be in fairly wide use but which you cannot find indicated in any standard dictionary, it

[16] See Thomas A. Knott, "How the Dictionary Determines What Pronunciations To Use," *Quarterly Journal of Speech*, February, 1935, **21**: 1–10.

is possible that you may be right; but if you use those recorded by authorities, you are sure to be right.

Regional Variants

It is a matter of common observation, and occasionally some amusement, that different modes of speech are heard in the various sections of the country. What is known as Eastern speech is heard mainly in a narrow strip of country along the Atlantic Coast north of Long Island Sound. What is often called Southern speech is commonly heard south of the Mason and Dixon Line, up the Potomac and down the Ohio Rivers, and cutting across southeast Texas— roughly the area that made up the old Confederacy. All the rest of the country, with a few local variations, uses a fairly uniform mode of speech—at least with so few variations that it may be thought of as one "dialect." This is commonly known as general American speech.[17]

Even within these large divisions pronunciation is by no means consistent; because of increased facilities for travel and more or less permanent migrations, the three major forms are now so widely distributed that regional characteristics are rapidly breaking down. About all one can say is that in some sections of the country certain forms of speech are heard somewhat more frequently than they are in others.

Comparative Merits of Regional Variants

The question is often raised, which of these modes of pronunciation is correct? Or, which is the *best* of these forms? Some years ago a fond mother was personally entering her daughter in the university, with the intention of having the girl major in speech. During the interview with a member of the faculty the mother asked, "And what do you do about Southern speech?" "What do you mean, what do we do about it?" "Don't you try to correct it?" "No, madam, not if it is good Southern speech."

There is, of course, no possible answer to the question as to which pronunciation is "correct," or which is the "best" of the three, or even

[17] See Claude Merton Wise, *Applied Phonetics*, Prentice-Hall, 1957, chap. 6, "Speech Regions of America."

of possible others. No one pronunciation can be considered as *the* correct one when good speakers freely and without embarrassment use other pronunciations. There are equally cultured people, equally careful speakers whose usage carries equal prestige in all sections of the country, so that no one speech can be set up as *the* standard for the rest of the country to follow. Any effort to establish a uniform mode of pronunciation in this country is futile nonsense.[18]

If, therefore, you use good speech modeled on that of the Northeast section of the country, centering perhaps in Boston and its environs, continue to use it with the full assurance that there is no better speech to be heard anywhere. If your speech is that of the South Atlantic section or the Gulf States, you have no cause to develop an inferiority complex. Similarly, if you have learned your pronunciation somewhere in the Middle West or along the Pacific Coast—or at points between—you may rest assured that your speech, if it is good speech for that area, will be accepted anywhere you go. Any mode of speech that is good in one of the broad, general sections is "legal tender" wherever the English language is spoken.

"Acceptable" Pronunciation

Do not interpret the foregoing to mean that you are free to use any pronunciation you please. There are, even with all possible variations, pronunciations that are acceptable and those that are not. Within each general section of the country typical errors are often heard, though no general type of error is local. They are all heard everywhere. Make every effort to check your own pronunciations; look up words about which there is the slightest doubt, and learn how to interpret dictionary systems of indicating acceptable pronunciations. Familiarize yourself with the dictionary; it will tell you many interesting things about words, not the least important of which is pronunciation.

Types of Mispronunciation

Judging from the many words we hear mispronounced, it would be easy to think that there are countless types of error that can be

---

[18] See Giles Wilkeson Gray, "American Modes of Speech," in Stewart Morgan, ed., *Opinions and Attitudes*, rev. ed., Nelson, 1938, pp. 220–232; and "Sidelights on the Pronunciation of English," *Quarterly Journal of Speech*, November, 1932, **18**: 546–560.

committed. Actually, there are very few, perhaps a half dozen or so. Furthermore, one type of error often leads to another. Note, too, that some pronunciations considered unacceptable a few years ago are recognized now by most authorities. The principal types of errors are discussed below.

Misplaced accent. This error consists in placing the accent on a syllable other than the one usually recommended. Often the shifting of the accent results in changing some of the sounds in the word. Illustrative of this type of error are the following, the accepted pronunciation being given first:

mis chiev ous	Often the accent is placed on the second syllable, resulting in a different vowel in that syllable, and the introduction of an additional syllable before the *ous,* as mis *chiev* i ous.
i *de* a	Often the accent is put on the first syllable, with the third syllable omitted entirely.
mu *nic* i pal	Sometimes a complete change in syllabication occurs as mu ni *cip* al.
lam en ta ble	Often the second syllable is accented.
pref er a ble	Not pre *fer* a ble.
se *cret* ive	Not *sec* re tive.

In some sections of the South, notably in Louisiana, the tendency in many words has been to shift the accent forward, so that Monroe (the city) becomes *Mun* roe, police becomes *po* lice, Vermont *Ver* mont, and so on.

Many words are stressed differently according to the part of speech they represent; that is, the same word may be stressed one way as one part of speech and another way as another. For example, the noun *accent,* according to the *American College Dictionary,* is *ac* cent; when used as a verb it may be either *ac* cent or ac *cent.* Desert, when a noun, is *des* ert, but when a verb it is de *sert.* One's visits to a given spot may be *fre* quent, but he may be said to fre *quent* that place. A *min* ute is a very mi *nute* space of time. *Ref* use is usually thrown away as rubbish; but we would re *fuse* to accept something we don't want.

Foreign students have difficulty sometimes in learning the shift in stress that often occurs in derivatives of a word. For example, con *trib* ute is not difficult; but con tri *bu* tion often causes confusion.

As we have said, in the case of many words certain pronunciations not acceptable a few years ago are recognized today as quite good: ad *dress, ad* dress; al *ly, al* ly; a *dult, ad* ult; al *loy, al* loy; ab *do* men, *ab* do men, and so on.

In case of doubt, check with the dictionary. If your preferred accentuation is recognized, you are free to use it.

Omission of sounds. Mispronunciation resulting from omission of sounds has been partially described under our discussion of articulation, which should be reviewed here; but there are additional errors of this type. When the accent in *idea* is shifted to the first syllable, for example, the fourth sound, represented by the *a*, is usually omitted. Omissions may be of either vowels or consonants. In the list below, the examples of omitted sounds appear on the right of each pair.

help	he'p	least	leas'
film	fi'm	tolerable	tol'a'ble
family	fam'ly	Saturday	Sad'dy
company	comp'ny	student	stu'ent
asked	as't	Louisiana	Lou'z'ana

Addition of extra sounds. Often extra sounds are put into words. Sometimes this error arises from what is known as "spelling pronunciation," in which each letter that appears in the spelling of a word is pronounced; actually, quite a number of words in our language contain letters that represent no sound at all. In other instances extra sounds are simply inserted or added. The following are illustrative.

a'mond	not al*mond*	drown	not drown*d*
pa'm	not pa*l*m (but pal *met* to)	column	not col*y*um
yo'k	not yo*l*k	drowned	not drownd*ed*
of'en	not of*t*en	World's Series	not World's Ser*ious*
athlete	not ath*a*lete	mischievous	not mischie*vious*
elm	not el*em*	twice	not twice*t*
across	not acros*t*	close	not close*t*
idea	not idea*r*	once	not once*t*
film	not fil*em*	realtor	not real*a*tor

In speech think what the word should *sound* like, not what it *looks* like on the page. What adds frequently to confusion is that many sounds can be represented by a number of spellings, and the same letter or letter combination can represent several different sounds. If you take the *u* from *busy* and the *gh* from *cough*, then *ugh* can be made to represent the same sound pattern as *if;* that is, it can be made to spell *if*. The *ou* which represents one sound in *cough* represents also the different sounds in th*ou*gh, thr*ou*gh, en*ou*gh, and s*ou*nd. Spelling is often quite unreliable in determining how a word is to be pronounced in English.

Inversion of sounds. In inversion the right sounds may all be included, but some of them are in the wrong order. Many people do not distinguish between the following pronunciations:

Right	Wrong	Right	Wrong
cavalry	Calvary	prefer	perfer
larynx	larnyx	asked	axed, ast
children	childern	pretty	purty
perspiration	prespiration	hundred	hunderd
perforation	preforation	modern	modren

A student from Puerto Rico some years ago always spoke of the "Thous" instead of the "South." "Casual" and "causal" are often confused because of a letter inversion which results in a combination of sound addition and substitution.

Sound substitution. Sometimes the persistent substitution of one sound for another is classified as a speech defect. Most substitutions, however, are like most mispronunciations, the result of early habits, and can be corrected by building up new habits. There are many types of substitution, both of vowels and of consonants, of which the following are among the most common:

yit for *yet; git* for *get; tin* for *ten; fince* for *fence,* and so on
form for *farm* (where *farm* is intended)
len'th for *length; stren'th* for *strength*
champeen for *champion*
talkin' for *talking; goin'* for *going; writin'* for *writing,* and so on
lugzury for *luxury*
stomp for *stamp*

wether for *whether* (acceptable in some localities)
simular for *similar*
substantuate for *substantiate* (heard among debaters)
interputation for *interpretation* (this from a debate director!)
particalar for *particular*
Chewsday for *Tuesday*

General elisions. Words are often mispronounced by generally slurring over the sounds. This is so closely related to faulty articulation that little further needs to be said about it than was said under the general heading of articulation.

Reasons for Mispronunciation

It can be said with reasonable certainty that, assuming normal hearing, there are four general reasons for mispronunciation, no one of which is irremediable:

1. Not knowing what the correct pronunciation is.
2. Too indifferent to look up the correct pronunciation.
3. Not knowing how to find the correct pronunciation or how to interpret the symbols.
4. Too indifferent to apply what knowledge one has or can obtain.

Most mistakes in pronunciation are the result of either ignorance or carelessness, neither of which is an admirable trait of personality.[19] Again it must be recognized that such a broad statement must make exceptions for those with pronounced hearing losses.

Learning Good Pronunciation

After all this discussion of the various types of mispronunciation, your logical inquiry would be, how and where can I learn how to pronounce my words correctly? In general there are three basic sources for learning good pronunciation.

1. Listen to good speakers. As we said earlier the use of language,

---

[19] For a more complete description of substandard deviations from standard regional modes of pronunciation, see Giles Wilkeson Gray and Claude Merton Wise, *The Bases of Speech*, 3rd ed., Harper, 1959, pp. 268–281, 287–299, 309–314; also see pp. 56–57.

including the ability to pronounce it fluently and correctly without exaggeration or affectation, is one of the marks of an educated person. It must be admitted that many otherwise admirable people, even many who are considered to be highly educated and cultured, do make gross errors in their use of language. Sometimes these errors are localized; some areas have their own peculiarities of pronunciation which identify the native of those sections. The antidote to being misled by such relatively isolated speech traits is to listen to speakers from many different localities and try to discover how they pronounce. You will probably settle for the general mode of speech you have grown up with or in which you will spend most of your life, eliminating any errors that have crept into your own version of it. If you change your habitat, you will probably find your habitual speech changing slightly—and usually unconsciously—in the direction of the speech of your new location. Such changes are to be neither deplored nor hailed with joy; they are one of the factors of linguistic change. So long as your speech meets the best standards of your linguistic area, you have nothing to apologize for.

2. Study under some competent instructor who can point out your errors or deviations from the acceptable and help you correct them. You should not need constant supervision if you learn, first, to recognize your own mistakes and, second, to know when you are making the correction successfully. Practice and then practice more. You may sound stilted to yourself when you attempt to maintain what you know to be good pronunciation, but if you get the habit of correcting yourself each time you recognize an error, it will not be long before you will have eliminated most mistakes. However, do not extend this critical tendency and your habit of correcting to the speech of your friends and acquaintances! It is an excellent way to "lose friends and alienate people." Besides, since many words have different pronunciations, they too may be right.

3. Get in the habit of consulting a good dictionary, one that indicates pronunciations as well as meanings and other items of interest and significance. Different dictionaries use different methods of indicating pronunciation; you will have to learn the system of whichever one you use. Any one of them, if you understand its symbols, will give you all the essential information you need to find the correct pronunciations of words.

The two most widely used systems are the diacritical markings of

Webster and most other dictionaries, and the International Phonetic Alphabet, used in two or three of the most modern pronouncing dictionaries such as Daniel Jones's, which gives the pronunciations of southern British,[20] and the Kenyon-Knott *Dictionary*,[21] which records American pronunciations. Each has its faults and its merits. For several generations every child at home or in school who has studied the dictionary at all has become familiar with the Webster system of diacritical marks. Most other general dictionaries use similar systems, with a few deviations. The *American College Dictionary*[22] uses diacritical marks for general guidance in pronunciation, but for the troublesome unaccented vowel which is almost characterless—as in fin*a*l, inf*a*nt, or*a*tor, comm*a*—it uses the International Phonetic Alphabet's symbol known as *schwa* (ə). This makes for more precise pronunciation, especially of many unstressed syllables in which the essential character of the vowel is not retained, as it is in orb*i*t, fam*i*sh, det*e*r, and so on. However, on an early page (xxvii) the *American College Dictionary* does give a complete table of the equivalent values of the diacritical system and the International Phonetic Alphabet.

The International Phonetic Alphabet also has its advantages. It permits and even requires a more specific interpretation of its symbols, since each symbol represents one and only one sound. It makes definite the regional variants, as most diacritical systems do not, and it also makes it possible to learn the pronunciation of any language or dialect if one is familiar with the symbols.

If you are interested only in pronunciations, a dictionary with a specific system of symbolization, like the International Phonetic Alphabet or a set of diacritical marks well correlated with it, is probably preferable. If you want all the other information usually given by dictionaries, you will need something more than a pronouncing dictionary alone. For most of your purposes the "college" or "desk" editions are entirely satisfactory. In many circles, however, unabridged editions are still the ultimate authority. The prevalence of mispronunciation and the general lack of familiarity with words today is probably less the result of the inadequacy of the usual sys-

[20] Daniel Jones, *An English Pronouncing Dictionary*, 5th ed., Dutton, 1943.
[21] John S. Kenyon and Thomas A. Knott, *A Pronouncing Dictionary of American English*, Merriam, 1944.
[22] Clarence L. Barnhart, ed., *The American College Dictionary*, text ed., Harper, 1948.

tems of indicating correct usage and acceptable pronunciations than of the decreased emphasis at the lower school levels on the use of the ones we have.

FLUENCY

One further aspect of the use of voice in speaking should be considered, and that is fluency. The term comes from a Latin word meaning to flow. Fluent speech does just that: it flows. It moves along without hesitation, without grouping for words, exhibiting no uncertainty in either ideas or language.

Do not mistake fluency for rapidity of utterance. You can be just as fluent at a speed of 130 words per minute as at 200. Fluency is not speed. Although speech should move without hesitation, this does not mean that it should move continuously without breaks or pauses. You can and should break your speech up into phrases, separating them by pauses of appropriate length. You can and should make the fullest use of variations in quantity. You can make use of all the variations in rate of utterance and still be fluent.

The essential requirements for achieving a fluency are (1) a thorough knowledge of the points you intend to present and the order in which you intend to present them, (2) an equally thorough knowledge of the supporting materials with which you are going to develop those ideas, (3) a sufficient command of vocabulary to avoid groping for words in which to clothe those ideas and the support details, (4) avoidance of such expressions as *uh, ah, and-a,* and other superfluous vocalizations that often occur when you are groping for the next idea or word, (5) enough self-confidence in your knowledge not to be overcome by the occasion, and (6) much practice and experience in speaking to *audiences.*

QUESTIONS AND TOPICS FOR STUDY AND REVIEW

1. What are the requirements for good breathing in voice production? Explain each briefly.
2. Explain the general structure and functioning of the voice mechanism.
3. Name the four basic attributes of vocal tone. Define each.
4. Describe six faults of voice quality. Describe each and tell how it may be overcome.

5. Discuss the relation between voice and "personality."
6. What are the three ways in which "force" may manifest itself? Explain each.
7. What is the importance of good phrasing in speaking? In what three ways is the time element manifested?
8. Discuss the importance of the "slide" or "inflection" in vocal utterance. To what exent can you make your voice rise or fall at will? Describe your experience in practicing the patterns on page 546.
9. Describe the manner in which you form the consonants in speaking. State the principles necessary in distinct utterance.
10. Describe your experience in practicing the consonant combinations on pages 551 and 552, and the tongue twisters in project 7, page 565.
11. What is meant by a standard of pronunciation? By standard pronunciation?
12. Discuss the problem of regional dialects in pronunciation.
13. Illustrate six types of mispronunciation.
14. What steps can one take to learn good pronunciation? What is meant by the term "good pronunciation" or "correct pronunciation"? What is really meant by the term *correct* as applied to pronunciation?
15. Describe the two general methods of indicating pronunciations in use in modern dictionaries. Evaluate these methods.
16. Describe your experience in attempting to carry out the instructions in project 7 on page 565.
17. How may one acquire fluency in speaking? (Your text mentions six ways.)

PROJECTS

1. Read a passage in as nearly a normal conversational manner as possible. Count the number of words in the passage, and then time your reading. Calculate the speed of your reading. Repeat for two or three more passages of different lengths, and find your average rate.
2. Select an interesting passage that will take approximately two minutes to read. Estimate from your findings in project 1 how many words you will need. Divide this entire passage into sense units, and mark these off by short vertical or slanting lines. Now read the passage, making pauses only where you have marked. Does this exercise give you a better idea of phrasing? Be sure to take a short inhalation at short pauses, with a full inhalation at complete stops.
3. Write out an original paragraph, marking off the phrases as in the above exercise. Read the passage once with no effort to phrase it,

and a second time pausing at the end of each phrase. What is the effect on the meaning of the paragraph?

4. Record the words and phrases on page 546, with the inflectional patterns as indicated. Listen to them as they are played back, and try to discover your errors. To what extent were you able to make your voice move up or down as indicated?

5. Read aloud a short sentence of perhaps a dozen words, and try to plot with slanting lines the inflectional patterns you use. Now arbitrarily reverse some of these patterns and read again. Report on the differences in meaning that you observed.

6. Pronounce very slowly the following words: *pat, bad, plod, blot, flat, bleed, nob, knot, nod, gold, cold, shove, azure, path, bathe, very, ferry, valid, yes, yet, wait, wade.* Describe as accurately as you can the positions of the tongue, lips, and other organs of articulation in pronouncing each word.

7. For clearness in consonant combinations practice the following:

> Amidst the mists and fiercest frosts,
> With barest wrists and stoutest boasts,
> He thrusts his fists against the posts,
> And still insists he sees the ghosts.

He first asked the postmistress exactly how the clasps should be wrapped around the casks before the tasks were completed.

The Picts waked in their crypts, looked across the fields, and wept because from the first they had lacked the correct respect.

The crisp clasp on the wrist fixed the pesky pest.

The molds were in fact at last boxed with the casts, but the costs swept skyward.

8. Give a talk in which you describe, in terms of the material of this chapter, the voice of some speaker you have recently heard. Give some illustrations of a few of his mannerisms, if any.

SUPPLEMENTARY READINGS

Akin, Johnnye, *And So We Speak: Voice and Articulation,* Prentice-Hall, 1958.

Baird, A. Craig, and Franklin H. Knower, *General Speech: An Introduction,* 2nd ed., McGraw-Hill, 1957, chap. 11, "The Speaking Voice"; chap. 12, "Articulation and Pronunciation."

Brigance, William Norwood, *Speech: Its Techniques and Disciplines in a Free Society,* 2nd ed., Appleton-Century-Crofts, 1961, chap. 17, "Improving Voice Quality and Variety"; chap. 18, "Being Heard and Understood."

Brown, Charles T., *Introduction to Speech*, Houghton Mifflin, 1955, chap. 15, "The Speaking Voice"; chap. 16, "The Meaning of the Voice"; chap. 17, "The Faults of Voice and Their Correction."

Fairbanks, Grant, *Voice and Articulation Drillbook*, 2nd ed., Harper, 1960.

Gray, Giles Wilkeson, and Claude Merton Wise, *The Bases of Speech*, 3rd ed., Harper, 1959, chap. 3, "The Physiological Basis of Speech"; chap. 5, "The Phonetic Basis of Speech."

Hahn, Elise, *et al.*, *Basic Voice Training for Speech*, 2nd ed., McGraw-Hill, 1957.

Karr, Harrison M., *Developing Your Speaking Voice*, Harper, 1953.

Van Dusen, C. Raymond, *Training the Voice for Speech*, McGraw-Hill, 1953.

Van Riper, Charles, and John Irwin, *Voice and Articulation*, Prentice-Hall, 1958.

Woolbert, Charles Henry, *The Fundamentals of Speech*, 2nd ed., Harper, 1927, sec. III, "Voice," especially chap. 8, "Improving the Voice"; chap. 9, "Pronunciation and Enunciation"; chap. 10, "Voice and Meaning." 3rd ed., with Joseph F. Smith, 1934. III "Voice," especially chap. 8, "Voice and Meaning," chap. 9, "Improving the Voice"; IV, "Language," chap. 15, "Pronunciation and Enunciation."

29

Visible Aspects
of Delivery

A great deal of speaking today is still being done over the radio, by which only the voice can be carried. Yet it is highly significant that vast amounts of time, money, and effort are being spent in developing the means of carrying to the broadcasting listener the final element in the complete process of speech, namely, the visible aspects of delivery. The increasing use of television in mass communciations emphasizes the *visible* aspects of speaking; otherwise it would not come so closely to supplanting the radio entirely.

The language one uses is of the utmost importance in communication; as you have now seen, the manner in which that language is uttered also has a bearing on the meanings stimulated. That language is even more meaningful when the speaker can also be seen.

CONFRONTATION

Almost 5000 years ago the wise old sage of the Fifth Egyptian Dynasty referred to in Chapter 1 told his children, "If you would judge a friend's character, do not depend on the evaluations of others; seek him out at a mutually agreeable time, and hold discussions with him; 'test his heart in an occasion of speech.' Hear him to the end without interruption, if he wants to open his heart to you, and avoid seeming to be scornful, or withdrawing from him. He will thus give you the opportunity of passing a fair judgment."[1]

What makes speech pre-eminent as a means of communication is this factor of *confrontation*,[2] the face-to-face directness which permits the simultaneous giving and receiving of stimuli: the speaker receives stimuli from his listeners at the same time that he is giving visible and audible stimuli to them. Our everyday conversations are our most familiar example of the operation of the principle of confrontation. This is the factor that impels business firms to hold frequent conferences, professional organizations to meet in periodic conventions, and nations to assign diplomatic missions to other nations.

Because confrontation is lacking in any form of communication other than direct speech, no other form can quite take its place. Radio, television, the motion pictures, excellent as they all may be technically, do not and cannot permit the simultaneous giving and receiving of stimuli which is the essential ingredient of direct speech. When a candidate for public office wants to make an effective campaign, he does not let the voters merely listen to him over the radio or see him on a television screen; he goes out before them, where he can see them as well as be seen by them, where he can get their reactions *even while he is speaking*—an impossibility in any other type of speaking situation.

[1] See Giles Wilkeson Gray, "'The Precepts of Kagemni and Ptah-Hotep,'" *Quarterly Journal of Speech*, December, 1946, **32**: 446–454.
[2] See Giles Wilkeson Gray and Claude Merton Wise, *The Bases of Speech*, 3rd ed., Harper, 1959, pp. 21–24.

The speaker is something more than a person to be heard; he is more than a user of words. In the normal and most effective speaking situation he is also a person to be seen. Despite an increasing amount of speaking into the microphone, there is still a vast amount of face-to-face speaking, in which the visible aspect of delivery makes its contribution to the effectiveness of the communication. It is important, therefore, for us to examine the question of visible bodily action to determine what principles will enable us to make that contribution even more significant.

No Actionless Speaking

When you are facing your audience directly there is no such thing as actionless speaking. It is even doubtful whether there is any actionless speaking before the microphone. Visible actions of course contribute nothing directly over the radio, although they may have an influence on the speaker's voice. But so long as you are within sight of your hearers as a speaker, what they see you doing is of interest and significance to them. "Every little movement has a meaning all its own," ran a popular song many years ago. That is particularly true in a speaking situation in which confrontation is a factor.

It is therefore no solution to the problem of what to do with your hands, your arms, or your feet to do nothing at all, since even doing nothing, as we have already pointed out, is in itself significant. And if you do nothing so vigorously that your muscles become all tense and knotted, it is likely to mean to your listeners most of all that you are a scared and nervous speaker! You cannot hide from your audience so long as you stand before them. The more you try to conceal your movements from them, the more noticeable they become.

Subliminal and Supraliminal Stimuli

People are often affected by impressions of which they are totally unaware. They respond, peculiarly enough, to stimuli too faint to be sensed. You must often have become suddenly aware that you have been hearing for some time a faint sound that has only at the moment entered your consciousness. Sometimes you can tell whether a certain element is present in a given stimulus pattern or not, even though that element would be too weak to be sensed at all if it stood alone.

In a similar way you are influenced by little things you see and hear your friends do, even though you are not actually conscious of just what it is that makes the impression on you. It may be an imperceptible tension of a facial muscle, a slight inflectional turn in the voice, a twitch of a finger. Football scouts are trained to detect telltale actions of opposing players and are often able to spot some slight movement, a shift of weight by a player, for example, that gives a play away completely. A boxer may not even consciously see the punch that he "instinctively" blocks.

Those aspects of the stimulus of which you are quite unaware, because they are below the threshold or *limen* of perception, yet to which you nevertheless respond, are known as *subliminal* stimuli. Those of which you are aware, because they are strong enough to be above the lower limit of perception, are called *supraliminal.*

The converse to the principle stated above is that the individual himself is also quite unaware that he is giving out such imperceptible stimuli. He is totally unconscous of the faint movements of his own facial muscles, the inflectional turns of his own voice, the twitch of his own finger. In other words, you yourself are constantly presenting stimulus patterns containing elements well above the threshold of perception for both you and those about you. But you are also presenting patterns containing elements *below* your own limit of perception as well as theirs, yet which are strongly influential in creating the impressions that others form of you.

That these subliminal stimuli actually have subtle persuasive influence is discussed at considerable length by Packard. According to his account, extensive studies by social and other psychologists in the field of motivational research as well as in relation to advertising and other forms of merchandising have fully verified the existence and use of such an influence. Certain moral and ethical problems are raised, however, which seem to suggest that extensive use of subliminal persuasive techniques can be both morally and ethically indefensible. "The most serious offense many of the depth manipulators commit, it seems to me," Packard concludes, "is that they try to invade the privacy of our minds. It is this right to privacy in our minds—privacy to be either rational or irrational—that I believe we must strive to protect."[3]

Packard's conclusions are based on the belief that "hidden persuaders," as used by those he calls "depth manipulators," constitute quite a new technique in persuasion, and that their effectiveness has been fully verified. The reliability of both these propositions, however, is sharply criticized by Weir, himself an advertising writer for some thirty years.[4] Weir points out that the basic techniques used by the "depth manipulators" have in fact been used in human relations for generations and present nothing essentially new: "Actually, the practice that Mr. Packard names 'hidden persuasion' has been around for a long time and is, I would say, one of the outstanding qualities that distinguish human beings from animals." Furthermore, he adds, "The hidden persuasion of which Mr. Packard writes is . . . certainly nothing capable of bringing about a George-Orwell–Big-Brother situation."[5]

Perhaps the testimony of an English customs officer will illustrate the point being made: "We look at a person's upper lip," he said. "If there is a bead of sweat on his lip, we open *everything*."[6]

There is a further basis for differentiating between the supraliminal and the subliminal. The former, being within the consciousness, is subject to conscious control and to habit formation. It is possible, for example, to control the gross changes in the vocal attributes, such as inflections, phrasing, pauses, loudness; it is also possible to control the larger movements of the body—arms, legs, feet, hands; you gain a measure of consistent control over your facial expression, likewise. It is possible, though not advisable, for you to develop habits of observable behavior quite incompatible with your actual nature. Contrary to the opinion held by many, most criminals neither look nor behave like desperadoes. In short, your habitual, overt behavior provides only a part of the basis for others' judgments of what is called your *personality*.

In a well-motivated person, whose external activities correspond to his underlying impulses and attitudes, there is no conflict between the supra- and the subliminal stimuli which he presents to his listen-

---

[3] Vance Packard, *The Hidden Persuaders*, McKay, 1957, p. 266.

[4] Walter Weir, *On the Writing of Advertising*, McGraw-Hill, 1960, chap. 26, "The Hidden Persuaders."

[5] *Ibid.*, pp. 145–146.

[6] *Reader's Digest*, December, 1961, p. 190.

ers. But when one has cultivated habits that are contrary to his basic nature, then conflicts arise, and the listeners are faced with the necessity of determining which set of patterns is the more authentic, which represents more accurately the man himself. It is significant that, however polished the external form may be, the strongest and most lasting impressions come from the deeper patterns of activity. What you do when you are "off guard" is often of highest significance in the estimates others make of your character; as for the subliminal stimuli, you are *always* "off guard."

If, therefore, you would provide for your hearers what Aristotle called the *ethical proof* for what you say, be sure that those minute, imperceptible movements of which both you and they are quite unaware, and against which you can never raise an adequate guard of habit, do not betray you. The old principle handed down from ancient times, that an orator is a good man skilled in speaking, is sound from both the ethical and the psychological points of view.

None of what has been said should detract from the importance of good delivery, consciously and intentionally developed and consisting of physical attitudes and movements which are entirely obvious to both the speaker and the audience. The important thing to consider, with reference to the subliminal aspects of your behavior, is that, if your speaking is to have its maximum effectiveness, there must be no conflict between these unconscious, unintentional aspects and the conscious, controllable phases of delivery. ". . . unless our public utterances and our moral character are in accord," said Philostratus, "we shall seem, like flutes, to speak with a tongue that is not our own."[7] It will be worth while to consider those aspects of delivery over which we have some measure of control.

Visible bodily activity is usually considered in four divisions or aspects: posture, movement, gesture, and facial expression.

POSTURE

The first thing an audience observes when you appear before it, after noting your general appearance, size, and general proportions, is the way you carry yourself—your carriage, bearing, the way you

---

[7] Philostratus and Eunapius, *The Lives of the Sophists*, with an English translation by Wilmer Cave Wright, New York, G. P. Putnam's Sons, 1922. Loeb Classical Library, p. 49.

hold your shoulders and your arms, how you carry your head—in other words, your general posture. Since this is what gives an audience its first impression, and since first impressions are often difficult to change, you should take pains to ensure that this one is favorable.

Posture, like other aspects of bodily behavior, is an overall matter creating a total impression. It involves the position of the feet, the distribution of weight, the set of the shoulders, the position of the head, the "hang" of the arms when not in use. All parts of the body must work as a unit. Your audience does not see these separate parts or the contribution they make to the total impression; it sees you "all in one piece." However, for purposes of analysis and study, it is convenient to consider separately the different parts of the body and their effect on the total pattern.

Position of the Feet

Let it be said at the outset that there is no "orator's position." Many good speakers are so active before their audiences that they do not take any position for more than a few seconds at a time. There is, then, no specific position the feet should take simply because it is the thing to do. Efforts have been made in the past to describe such positions and to prescribe them for certain attitudes of the speaker, but the rules were too rigid; they became so entirely mechanical that they were finally discarded altogether.

That does not mean that any position in which you may want to put your feet will be acceptable. One can be quite awkward primarily on account of ungraceful positions of the feet. A few elementary principles govern these positions in general:

1. The most flexible position your feet can take is for one foot to be a little in advance of the other, with the heel of the advanced foot turned in at any comfortable angle toward the other. From this basic position you can advance, withdraw, step forward as if to approach your audience, shift your weight from one foot to the other as you turn from one side of the audience to address the other side, or as the idea itself calls for a shift.

By recommending such a position we do not mean that as you advance to your place before the audience you should place your feet just so, deliberately and mechanically; that would be worse than anything else you might do with your feet. Practice the position in your room, whenever you stop for a moment, and discover for yourself how flexible it really is. It can serve as the basic position from which all others are departures. Moreover, we do not mean to suggest that, once having assumed such a position, you should maintain it throughout the speech. On the contrary, move about. But you will find that, with all your movement, the suggested position is the easiest and the most comfortable to come back to.

Such advice is not a reversion to the practices of late nineteenth-century elocutionists, many of whom made a speech into an exhibition rather than an act of communication. The point we are making is that, as a basic position, the one just described is at once the easiest to assume and the most flexible.

2. Do not hesitate to shift your foot positions, but vary the type of shift as well as the specific position. Some attitudes call for placing the feet close together, others for a broader stance, either of which can be achieved without getting too far away from the basic position.

3. Turning from one side of the audience to the other, as you will do from time to time, can be accomplished (a) by simply turning the upper part of the body, (b) by total movement, that is, by walking from one side of the platform to the other, or (c) by turning on the balls of your feet, swinging the heels around. Turning on the heels, swinging the toes around, is not so good.

Distribution of Weight

If you are at all animated in your speaking and move about the platform, the problem of weight distribution will for the most part take care of itself, just as foot positions do. You will often, however, stand for some time without changing your position at all. At such times the question of weight distribution may become of some importance. The principles of foot position just discussed will not alone enable you to achieve poise or to avoid appearing awkward and ill at ease; you will never acquire good posture or position if you limit your attention to the position of the feet. What you do with the rest of your body also contributes to the total impression as well as to your own comfort. Woolbert even says, "Get the weight of the whole in the right place, and the feet, if they have any sense at all, have to take care of themselves."[8] The positions of the feet just described, when combined with proper weight distribution, will contribute most to an effective, graceful, flexible posture.

Actually, there are only a few possibilities for placing the weight of the body:

The ball of either foot
The heel of either foot
The ball *and* heel of either foot
The balls of both feet
The heels of both feet
The balls and heels of both feet

With the general basic position of the feet described above, any of these six distributions is possible. Which one is actually used will depend on the idea to be expressed, the intensity of the attitude to be established, and the strength of your attitude toward the audience and toward the very act of communication.

A further analysis of the relation between the positions of the feet and the distribution of weight reveals the fact that, of the first three possibilities listed above, the weight can easily and appropriately be placed on either the ball or the heel, or both ball and heel, of either the advanced or rear foot. None of the last three cases in the above list requires that the feet be placed close together, with the heels on the same line; any type of weight distribution can be achieved with one foot advanced. It is quite obvious, then, that there is great latitude in the matter of both foot position and weight distribution.

For attitudes of aggressiveness, of advancing, of reaching out to the audience, throw the weight forward. It makes little difference on which foot it rests; you will soon change anyway. For attitudes of retirement, submission, of casualness, indifference, or for the stronger attitude of defiance, put the weight backward on the heels.

So far as weight distribution is concerned, the latitude is so great that it is easier to suggest a few things not to do than to recommend what can or should be done.

1. Avoid a position of rigid military "attention." As a matter of fact, an experienced Army man can stand at attention and yet be quite

[8] Charles Henry Woolbert and Joseph F. Smith, *The Fundamentals of Speech,* 3rd ed., Harper, 1934, p. 114.

relaxed. It is usually the "rookie" who draws himself up with every muscle tense.

2. Avoid placing the feet at an exact angle—any precise angle—intentionally or with the heels tight together.
3. Do not allow the positions of your feet and the distribution of your weight to come into conflict.
4. Avoid placing all your weight on one leg held firmly under you, with the other thrust forward like the brace on a telephone pole. Keep your feet fairly close together for the most part; it looks better and gives you more flexibility.
5. Avoid constantly shifting your weight back and forth, forward and back on toe and heel or to and fro sidewise from one foot to the other. Keep your position steady until you have reason to change.
6. On the other hand, avoid holding one position constantly from the beginning of your speech to the end; it will be equally tiresome to you and to your audience.

The Set of Your Body and Shoulders

Your carriage, which is revealed largely by the way you hold your shoulders, indicates to your audience much of your attitude toward yourself, toward them, and toward your relations with them. Maintain an erect posture with stomach drawn in and chest up, which will exhibit to your audience a decent self-respect. You can as a rule look for much the same degree of respect from your listeners that you show for yourself, and little more. Therefore, your general bearing before them should grow out of a reasonable self-confidence in your own knowledge and skill and in your own integrity—your *ethical proof.*

Avoid overdoing such a carriage, however, for exaggeration will create an impression of overconfidence, of conceit, even of arrogance and condescension, attitudes which are certain to arouse unfavorable or antagonistic reactions. But it is equally important that you avoid seeming to be apologetic when you have nothing for which to apologize. There are few occasions when you need to apologize to your audience; on those occasions do it openly, frankly, just as you would any time. It is the habitually apologetic attitude which you should avoid.

Hold yourself erect, but do not draw yourself up rigidly, with every muscle tense, shoulder blades pulled back so far they almost touch, and all arm movement prevented. Relax, but don't sag; don't let your shoulders droop forward and your whole body slump. Don't allow yourself to assume the "question mark in parentheses" posture. The ideal is a mixture of *strength* and *ease,* the basis of gracefulness. This involves a balance of relaxation and tension—enough tension to give you alertness and enough relaxation to permit easy control of your whole expressive mechanism.

The Hands and Arms

What to do with the hands and arms is always a problem. It is little help to suggest that you do nothing, for doing nothing, even when possible, is in reality one of the most difficult and least effective things you can do on the platform. You will want to do something with them.

Probably the best thing you can do with your arms when you are not using them is simply let them hang from the shoulders. In your practice, determine where they should hang by letting them swing like pendulums, and if they are quite relaxed, they will come to rest at about the right place. But don't let them swing like that while you are speaking. There are a few things you cannot do; the occasion will determine some of the limits. On an informal occasion, you may now and then put your hand in your pocket—but don't keep it there. You may for a short while put your arms behind you, but don't allow them to get locked there; get them out where you can use them. If you have a reading stand, you may rest your hands lightly on its edges for a time; you may even lean your weight on the stand momentarily. But unless you are using a manuscript, get out now and then from behind the stand. There are many things you can do with your hands and arms; probably the best thing after all is to use them, as explained a little later in this chapter.

The Head and Neck

What has been said of the body and shoulders is equally applicable to the head and neck. The important thing is that you hold your head up so that you can establish and maintain eye contact with the audience and let your voice get out to them. Even when you are speaking from manuscript, have the paper so placed that you can still hold your head up and not have to be bobbing it up and down constantly as you shift attention from manuscript to listeners. If the manuscript is not properly placed you will probably finally give up and devote your whole attention to the paper. Thus the listeners are relegated to a secondary position—a status they will not relish very long.

On the other hand, audiences are inclined to be long-suffering, at least in America. If they have come to hear a speaker because of his reputation or to hear him discuss something they are really interested in, they will put up with an amazing amount of poor speaking. It hardly seems fair to abuse their patience.

Hold your head up so that your eyes can look straight out; but don't let the whole musculature about the neck go tense. Move your head about, turning from one part of the audience to another, without, however, setting up anything like a rhythmic pattern.

MOVEMENT

However good your posture may be, you will want to vary your position, to move about to give yourself some change and to afford some variety to your listeners. Furthermore, movement often helps you to make a point clearer or more emphatic. Finally, movement is one of the most effective remedies that can be prescribed for the ills resulting from nervousness.

That movement provides variety to yourself and to the audience needs no elaboration or explanation. You can easily become tired of just standing in one spot and will want to move about as a matter of relief. The audience gets tired of having to look constantly in one direction and will welcome the opportunity to move their eyes a little.

Movement may also be instrumental in indicating shifts in thought, in which case it serves somewhat as paragraph indentation does in writing. It furthermore serves to emphasize or to symbolize for the eye the verbal concepts of *but, on the other hand, still, however, therefore,* and so on.

Amount of Movement

You will probably be concerned with the problem of how much and what sort of movement to use. Again, the answer depends on the nature of the occasion and the audience and the type of response you are seeking from your listeners.

Sedentary audiences, that is, those whose occupations have accustomed them to relatively inactive existences, are likely to prefer the speaker who uses little movement, whereas those who habitually engage in active pursuits will respond better to more extensive and vigorous movement. Those whose interests call for fine distinctions are likely to appreciate smaller, more discriminating actions on the part of the speaker. Occasions calling for highly emotional speaking, particularly when excitatory emotional attitudes are involved, will likewise call for a large amount of movement; inhibitory emotional attitudes will demand the greatest reserve in the matter of movement.

Develop a keen sensitivity to the nature of the situation, and then learn to control the amount and type of movement to fit the occasion. Some of you will undoubtedly continue to use more than others; but there are no absolutes, no prescriptions. But whether your tendency is to use much or little, you can and should learn to govern your movements according to the demands of the situation.

GESTURE

The term *gesture* commonly refers to movements of the hands and arms which often accompany the verbal aspects of speech. However, since in speaking, as in other activities of the human mechanism, the body tends to act as a whole and is most efficient when acting as a whole, gesture properly involves the hands and arms, the head and eyes, the shoulders, body, legs, and feet, all parts of a coordinated whole. Although it is possible to describe a gesture as a matter primarily of the arms from the shoulders down to the fingers, actually with each such movement the head and eyes also move, the shoulders turn, the balance of weight shifts with the body, and the legs and feet change to allow for the shifted weight. One can almost say that in a well-coordinated gesture the whole body follows hands and arms; what the arm and hand do is only a part of the whole. The actual movement begins with the shoulders and as a rule is in a curved line from the center outward.

Functions of Gesture

Gesture serves both the speaker and the listener in the clarification of imagery. Distances, locations, dimensions, and even abstractions can often be clarified through imagery set up by gesture, which is also of value to the speaker as an aid in the development of his own thought.

But gestures do more than clarify thought; they also help to intensify and make more impressive the attitudes the speaker is trying to build up. It is generally recognized that the more sensory avenues utilized in entering consciousness, the more impressive the effect will be. Visible action in the form of communicative gestures provides one more sensory appeal.

Empathic Responses

Gestures help build up what is known as empathic responses on the part of the hearers. You have all noticed when watching a football game how you tend to push in the direction your team is driving; or how, when you are watching a high jumper, you try to raise yourself off the ground as if to clear the bar yourself or at least to assist the jumper. Many of you are familiar with the "body English" often used by billiard and pool players. These responses to observed actions, in which we tend to imitate the movement we are observing, are what are called *empathic responses.*

Many such responses are conscious; at least, as in the instances just cited, they are easily observable, even though they are not intentionally made. But much as in the case of subliminal stimuli, we also respond unconsciously to many types of movement, line, mass, balance; and the feeling we derive from our own responses determines whether the observed movement is pleasant or unpleasant. If you see someone perched precariously atop an unstable, swaying ladder, you yourself are uncomfortable because you feel the imbalance, the lack of stability, the possibility of falling. Similarly, a massive superstructure suppported by thin, reedlike columns is as unpleasant as a light, lacy structure supported by thick, heavy pillars. Compare the effect produced by pictures of the massive columns of the ancient Egyptian Temple of Karnak with those of the Parthenon. The perfectly proportioned columns of ancient Greek architecture were designed to give a balance of height and thickness in relation to the mass they were supporting. The towering spires which surmounted the medieval cathedral as well as many modern churches achieve their effect through empathic response.

What has all this to do with gesture? Just this: listeners tend, however unconsciously, to follow the actions and movements of the speaker, to enter into what he is doing; in following his behavior, they experience with him his emotions and feelings. Once you have aroused these attitudes, you have succeeded in large part in getting the response you set out to get in the first place.

Types of Gesture

Gestures may generally be divided or classified into four main types: gestures of location, gestures of description, gestures of emphasis, and gestures of symbolism.

Gestures of location. In gestures of location you point out the exact or approximate locations of the things you are talking about, placing them in space for your listeners. You place various objects in spatial relations with each other. You indicate directions, sizes, and areas. You visualize these spatial relations for your audience.

In gestures of location you will need to distinguish between the literal and the figurative. You will no doubt have occasion to describe scenes and actions that are not within the vision of your audience or within the physical limits of your immediate locality. Place them somewhere out in front of you, and let the imagination of the listeners fill in the details. As Winans suggests, you do not need to be literally exact in referring to points of the compass, but you do need to be consistent.[9]

[9] James A. Winans, *Speech-Making*, Appleton-Century-Crofts, 1938, pp. 444–445.

If your object is at a distance, indicate that distance by elevating your arm above the horizon and by letting your eyes look off beyond the confines of the auditorium in which you are speaking. Lowering the level of your arm and letting your eyes focus on a point about where you are placing the object will give the idea of nearness. Do not look at your hands—look at the place where the object is supposed to be.

If you want to suggest great distances as covered in some extensive movement, such as from the Atlantic Coast to the Pacific, do not place the two terminals directly opposite with yourself in the middle; let the extent of your own movement be sufficiently broad and sweeping from one side to the other to create the suggestion of the vast distance covered. Great distances can be indicated by an extended sweep of one or both arms; small distances can be suggested by delicate, fine movements of your hands and fingers.

Develop the ability to suggest locations, movements, and positions. Once you have located an object in one position, keep it there, unless in your discussion a change is indicated. In describing a scene, keep yourself out of it; do not build the scene with yourself as center. Place it outside of you—out in front—and build it up through suggestion and imagination. Your audience will complete the picture from their own imaginations and probably get a better one than you can draw for them.

Gestures of description.   You will often be faced with the necessity of giving descriptive details of some object which you do not have with you. You can frequently supply enough detail to give your listeners a satisfactorily accurate picture for the immediate purpose. You can indicate sizes and shapes; you can suggest the type of movement involved, if any, and the relative location of significant parts. In this respect, gestures of description are somewhat similar to those of location.

In this type of gesture, as in that of location, both literal and figurative (imaginative or suggestive) gestures can be used. In describing sizes and shapes, the literal will probably be most useful; that is, you will attempt actually to indicate the size and shape unless, of course, the size is beyond your reach, in which case you will resort to suggestion.

In representing type of action, you will probably find figurative or suggestive gestures more appropriate. As a rule, attempts to imitate the action or type of action you are describing should be made with extreme caution, if at all. Suppose you are telling about an old man tottering down the street, as in the first stanza of "The Last Leaf":

> I saw him once before,
> As he passed by the door
>   And again
> The pavement stones resound
> As he totters o'er the ground
>   With his cane.

If you demonstrated the tottering, you would be describing that action in your own individuality and not that of the old man. You cannot, even in imagination, *be* the old man and yourself at the same time. If you were telling about Stephen Leacock's knight and trying at the same time to imitate him, you would, as we said before, certainly encounter difficulties, for you will remember that he mounted his horse and rode off in all directions!

On the other hand, if you are clearly demonstrating some action or movement, such as a dance step or a golf or tennis stroke, you would certainly give an illustration of the movements involved. Then, too, imitation may often be used for humorous effects, although in such cases it should be essentially exaggerated suggestion. As in so many of the techniques of speech, much depends on your purpose and on the effect you want to create.

The public speaker retains at all times his own individuality, and does not take on that of another. He is himself and no one else. Impersonation is an art in itself: the speaker—or reader—assumes the character he is portraying for the duration of his performance, and steps out of his own personality. If you are reading Browning's "The Last Duchess" you will impersonate the duke, and for the time being will no longer be yourself. In other words, to inject such a reading into a public speech is to try to be two people at the same time.

It is much easier to introduce a short passage of interpretation into a speech, but it should not be extended to the point that the esssential nature of the speech itself is lost. There is no reason why the speaker cannot include a short passage of literature in his speech, so long as the passage furthers the development of his "argument." In this text are a number of short literary passages which have been introduced for the sole reason that they make some points clear, vivid, or impressive.

In any case, the central thought of your speech is the heart of your speech. Anything that interferes with the process of bringing that central thought to your listeners is to be avoided. Impersonation almost certainly will; interpretation, if used skillfully and with restraint, may contribute to your achieving the desired responses from your listeners.

Gestures of emphasis. If you speak with due regard to giving proper emphasis to your language, you will find yourself placing more stress on some words than on others. If you are permitting the rest of your communicative mechanism to make its contribution to the speaking act, not all of this emphasis will be vocal. Part of it will be visible; it will consist of certain definite strokes of the hand and arm which accompany the emphatic word or phrase. These strokes are helpful also in creating vocal emphasis, for it is well-nigh impossible to give a strong, vigorous movement of the clenched hand, for instance, without increasing the force with which the accompanying word is uttered.

Most gestures of simple emphasis consist of such downward strokes, sometimes of the open hand, sometimes of the index finger, sometimes of the clenched fist. Pounding the lectern or stamping the foot for emphasis generally are not to be recommended.

Gestures of emphasis consist of three separate parts, all blended together to make one unified whole: the *approach,* the *stroke* or *ictus,* and the *return* or *recovery.* In the approach you move into the position for the essential part of the gesture, the stroke. Often this is done unobtrusively, though not secretively; it can be made a significant part of the whole. The stroke or ictus is, as the term indicates, a short, sudden movement of the hand or finger coming exactly on the word or phrase to be emphasized; it embodies the significance of the gesture. On the return the hand and arm are permitted to go back unnoticed to some neutral position, or they may make the approach to the next gesture.

All this sounds as if it might be thoroughly mechanical. In practicing these gestures and parts of gestures, it *will* be mechanical, and it should. Just as in learning any skill, you must pass through a stage in which every aspect of each movement is consciously and carefully controlled. That is the only way in which you can ever learn good form for doing anything involving skill. You must pass through a mechanical period; there is no short cut.

But it is only in your practice that you should be conscious of all your movements. In your actual speaking, when you are attempting to influence your audiences, let the situation take care of itself. Do your practicing before you take the platform, not while you are addressing your audience.

Gestures of symbolism. Gestures of location and description for the most part represent concrete ideas. Gestures of emphasis are somewhat more abstract: Gestures of symbolism are for the most part abstract, although they are based on quite understandable physical reactions to various stimuli.

In presenting an idea, for example, you may use a gesture much like presenting a book or some other object. If you ask a question, you may hold out your hand as if, having asked for a gift, you reach out to receive it. A balance of ideas may be suggested by extending both hands, as if you were either presenting one idea with each hand or comparing the weights of two objects. Aversion may be indicated by turning away or by an outward thrust of the hands with the palms turned outward; benediction by extending the hands up and in front of you with the palms down. The same position with the palms up may suggest supplication.

It is impossible to suggest all the possible movements and positions of the hands and arms that can be used to symbolize attitudes and even simple ideas having a minimum of emotional content. As a rule, the stronger the emotional component of meaning, the more vigorous and intense the gesture; the stronger the logical component, the more restricted, discriminating, and controlled the gesture.

FACIAL EXPRESSION

You may have formed the impression from what we have said about the importance of posture, movement, and gesture that your listeners are going to be watching closely every movement, every gesture that you make, that they will be conscious of each step you take, each raising of the hand, each change of position. In short, you may by now feel that everything you do will be reviewed in detail and that the success or failure of your speech will depend on what your audience thinks of your physical behavior on the platform.

The sober truth is that, if these actions are what they should be, namely, a part of the total communicative process, your listeners will not notice specifically and consciously just what you are doing. They are far more likely to notice what you are doing if your physical actions are *not* what they ought to be. Your behavior on the platform partakes somewhat of the nature of the subliminal stimuli discussed earlier in this chapter. Your audience will not be watching your hands, your arms, your feet; these parts of your expressive mechanism, if they are functioning effectively, will be relegated to the fringes of consciousness. They will have their effect; make no mistake about that. But they will make their impression as a part of the *total communicative process.*

Audience Contact (Rapport)

Through the eyes perhaps more than through any other agency is contact with the audience established and maintained. It would be absurd for us to insist that you must keep your eyes constantly on the audience and estimate your degree of *rapport* with your hearers by counting the number of times you look away. Looking off over the heads of your listeners, up at the ceiling, out the window, and down at the floor can all be done without breaking audience contact, provided that you do them only occasionally, for a definite purpose or effect, and that you quickly turn again to the audience. Looking now and then at individual members of the audience often gives them the feeling that you are interested in them and in imparting to them what you have to say. It is especially appropriate when there is a measure of audience participation involved. Do not overdo this selection, however; it may be embarrassing to the person so singled out, and it may make others feel that you are practicing some discrimination.

It is often effective to look straight at specific sections of the audience, shifting from one to another, until you have in effect covered the whole audience. Even though you may not fix your gaze on any particular individuals in the auditorium, you will have given most of them the feeling that you have been talking directly to them. You may not remember, in fact, that you have seen a familiar face during the whole speech.

Eye Movement

Shift your glance from one part of the audience to another, so that you will within a short time have recognized the presence of every section. Let them feel that you have seen them and are addressing your speech to them as much as to anyone else. At the same time, avoid giving the impression of "shifty" eyes. Do not let your eyes move constantly, apparently never meeting other eyes and never remaining even momentarily fixed on some portion of the audience. In giving the impression of thinking through some solution, you may even fix your eyes on some indefinite spot in space. Generally, however, let your eyes rest occasionally now on one, now on another general area, the movement from one to the other being definite and purposeful. Shifty eyes in a speaker create at least two impressions: first, of doubtful personal integrity, and second, of vagueness of thought and purpose. They suggest an unwillingness to meet possible opposition on comparable terms.

Reflection of Mood

Your entire face should mirror the general mood or attitude. It has been said that your face should wear a genial expression. If the mood is one of geniality, well and good; but sometimes the mood you want has little of the genial in it. You may be deadly serious. You may even be solemn. Your face then has no business looking genial. If the situation calls for seriousness, *look* serious. If it calls for merriment, don't be a "sourpuss."

Do not try, as a rule, to assume the expression of a mood that you cannot feel. Essentially, this means that your expression should be a sincere reflection of your mood. There will be occasions when you are under obligation to speak even though you do not feel like it at the moment. If it is an occasion worthy of your time and attention, though, make every effort to meet the general temper of the situation.

Avoid, too, allowing your face to assume a dead-pan expression, without life or animation. A masklike, expressionless face is about as uninspiring and uninteresting as a lump of putty; it has no character, no communicativeness, nothing that will stimulate or sustain the interest of the audience. It indicates a dull, sluggish, uninterested and uninteresting person back of it. Let your entire facial expression be alive, alert, responsive to the constantly shifting moods of the speech. Avoid anything resembling a set expression—one which is assumed at the outset and maintained throughout so that it becomes nothing more than a mask. Keep in mind that what serves as a stimulus is change, variety, deviation from a more or less constant background; the principle is just as valid for facial expression as it is for any other type of stimulus.

Facial Exercise

The essential requirements for effective facial expression are, first, responsiveness to the changing emotional aspects of the total stimulus pattern, and second, mobility of facial muscles. The first of these has already been discussed. For mobility the facial muscles, especially those about the eyes and mouth, need plenty of exercise.

Practice moving your eyes themselves up and down, sidewise, and in a rotary motion clockwise and counterclockwise, in order to strengthen the muscles. Practice also focusing them at different distances—far away, close at hand, and at intermediate points. Your audience will be able to tell whether you are looking "a mile or so away" or here, close at hand, by the focus of your eyes. Therefore you will need to be able to adjust your focus just as you do in viewing near and distant objects.

Exercise also your eyebrow, eyelid, and forehead muscles in order to tone them up, for that region makes the face particularly expressive. The muscles about your mouth also, which should be very active in the process of articulation, are important in contributing to the expressiveness of the lower part of your face. Strengthening them, therefore, will add to facility of expression and to sharpness of articulation and distinctness of utterance at the same time. Do not be afraid to use the musculature of your lips and tongue vigorously; in practice exaggerate their movements, so that in actual speaking they will tone down somewhat and be just about right.

You may find it helpful as well as interesting simply to stand before a mirror and make all manner of faces at yourself. Do not be afraid of wrinkles. The face which arrives at an advanced degree of maturity without having acquired a few is likely to be a vapid, expressionless, characterless visage, evidence of an individual who has never felt deeply. Wrinkles acquired as a result of honest thinking, the satisfaction of worthy motives, the experiencing of wholesome emotions, and the labor engaged in to advance the welfare of human society are an indication of a life well spent. We are told,

. . . whereas Demosthenes himself did not succeed in his first attempts, through his having neglected to study action, he arrived afterwards at such a pitch in that faculty, that when the people of Rhodes expressed in high terms their admiration of his famous oration for Ctesiphon, upon hearing it read with a very sweet and strong voice by Aeschines, whose banishment it had procured, that great and candid judge said to them, How would you have been affected, had you seen him speak it! For he that *only hears* Demosthenes loses much the better part of the oration.[10]

QUESTIONS AND TOPICS FOR STUDY AND REVIEW

1. What is meant by confrontation? What is its importance? Illustrate by example how it functions in various speaking situations.
2. Differentiate supraliminal and subliminal stimuli. Why are the latter of such importance? What is the relation between subliminal stimuli and ethical proof or ethical appeal?
3. What are the elements of good posture? Explain and illustrate each.
4. What principles should govern the positions of the feet?
5. State the actions or positions to be avoided in the matter of weight distribution.
6. Describe and demonstrate an effective set of the shoulders.
7. What are the functions of gesture? Explain the principle of "all-in-one-piece" as related to bodily action.
8. What are emphatic responses? Illustrate. How do they function in a speaking situation? To what extent do they contribute to the factors of clarity, vividness, and impressiveness?
9. Name and describe the types of gesture. Give an example of each type, with an appropriate verbal accompaniment.
10. What is the importance of facial expression in speaking? Should one always have a genial expression? Explain and illustrate your answer.

[10] Fordyce, "Ancient Eloquence," in *The American Orator,* by Increase Cooke, New Haven, 1819, pp. 137–139 (Sec. XIV).

11. To what extent should the audience be permitted to be aware of the speaker's visible activity? Of his vocal technique? Of his specific techniques in the use of language or any other medium of communication? Explain and justify your answer.

12. Many techniques of delivery, both vocal and visible, were emphasized by the elocutionists of the latter part of the nineteenth and early part of the twentieth centuries. To what extent, if any, did these techniques have a rational basis? Can the study and practice of techniques of delivery be placed on such a foundation today?

PROJECTS

1. Examine your own posture with a view to improving it. Practice correcting faults in general bearing, such as slumping, draping yourself over the reading stand, drawing yourself up too rigidly, locking your arms behind you, or any other things you may do to make your posture ineffective.

2. Practice positions of the feet and various distributions of weight until they seem quite natural, that is, until they become habitual. Observe whether any of these general postures seem to be associated with any particular emotional attitude.

3. While imagining that you are standing before an audience, practice moving about, changing foot positions and weight distribution, even complete changes of position, seldom turning much more than one-quarter away from any major portion of your audience.

4. Study various possible positions of the arms and hands, extending them vertically from straight downward up through various angles to directly overhead. Note whether the different angles seem to suggest different attitudes.

5. Add to the various arm positions described in project 4 various hand positions—palm down, palm up, palm vertical, palm turned away from the body. Observe and report on any differences you can sense in these diffeernt positions. In connection with these positions, be sure to achieve, balance with the entire body.

6. Bring to class some object which you will use to demonstrate the construction, operation, or product of an operation. Be sure that (a) the article is large enough for everyone to see; (b) it is simple enough for everyone to see all the significant parts, and (c) the demonstration itself is communicative.

7. Give a descriptive speech in which you make use of your hands to present the descriptive details.

8. Describe a scene, placing it imaginatively out in front of you and placing by gestures of location the various important details of the scene.

9. Tell a story or describe a situation by means of pantomime only. Use no words even as an introduction. Try to make your pantomime so clear that the class will have no difficulty identifying what you are trying to do.

SUPPLEMENTARY READINGS

Baird, A. Craig, and Franklin H. Knower, *General Speech: An Introduction,* 2nd ed., McGraw-Hill, 1957, chap. 12, "Physical Activity and Visual Aids."

Black, John W., and Wilbur E. Moore, *Speech: Code, Meaning, and Communication,* McGraw-Hill, 1955, chap. 11, "The Speaker's Gestures and Bearing."

Brigance, William Norwood, *Speech: Its Techniques and Disciplines in a Free Society,* 2nd ed., Appleton-Century-Crofts, 1961, chap. 16, "Being Seen."

Brown, Charles T., *Introduction to Speech,* Houghton Mifflin, 1955, chap. 14, "Visible Speech: Movement and Gesture."

Bryant, Donald C., and Karl R. Wallace, *Fundamentals of Public Speaking,* 3rd ed., Appleton-Century-Crofts, 1960, chap. 12, "Delivery: Methods of Development"; chap. 15, "Further Study of Delivery."

Gilman, Wilbur E., Bower Aly, and Loren Reid, *The Fundamentals of Speaking,* Macmillan, 1951, chap. 12, "Bodily Action in Effective Speaking."

Reid, Loren, *First Principles of Public Speaking,* Artcraft, 1960, chap. 10, "The Body in Speech Making."

Ruesch, Jurgen, and Weldon Kees, *Nonverbal Communication,* University of California Press, 1956.

Sarett, Lew, William Trufant Foster, and Alma Johnson Sarett, *Basic Principles of Speech,* 3rd ed., Houghton Mifflin, 1958, chap. 10, "Communicating Meaning Through Action."

Weaver, Andrew Thomas, and Ordean Gerhard Ness, *The Fundamentals and Forms of Speech,* Odyssey, 1957, chap. 6, "The Visible Speech Code."

White, Eugene E., and Clair R. Henderlider, *Practical Public Speaking,* Macmillan, 1954, chap. 10, "Using the Body in Delivering the Speech."

Winans, James A., *Speech-Making,* Appleton-Century-Crofts, 1938, chap. 2, "Conversing with an Audience"; chap. 20, "Further Study of Delivery"; chap. 21, "Gesture."

Woolbert, Charles Henry, *The Fundamentals of Speech,* 2nd ed., Harper, 1927, chap. 6, "Total Bodily Action"; chap. 7, "Posture, Movement, Gesture"; 3rd ed., with Joseph F. Smith, 1934, chap. 6, "Total Bodily Action and the Speaker"; chap. 7, "Gesture and the Audience."

INDEX

Speaker's, faults, listening and the, 115; notebook, 207–208
Speaking, two-way process, 107; general preparation for, 50–51; requires broad knowledge, 48–52; situation, the, 5
Specialization, 49
Special preparation, 51–52
Specific preparation, 51–52
Specific instances, argument from, 299–300
See also Examples
Speech activities, approach to, 18; outlining the, 245–252; planning the, 21–26, 34–37; practicing the, 32–34; preparation, overview of, 234–235; the speaking situation, 5, 123–125; training in democratic living, 11
Spencer, Herbert, 465, 491, 494, 506
Spontaneous group audience, 137
Stage fright: among athletes, 69; among other performers, 68–70; among students, 69; and musicians, 71; and muscular tonus, 70–71; approaches to, 65–66; bodily changes in, 73–74; causes of, 71–73; characteristics of, 68; Cicero's testimony, 69; complete relaxation and, 71; Demosthenes, 69; free and open discussion of, 66; ignoring, 65–66; "personality" and, 66; prevalence of, 68–69; remedial measures for, 74–82; specific procedures for, 77–82; symptoms of, 68; "take a course" for, 79; terminology, 66; types of bodily change in, 74; various names for, 67
See also Tonus
Stagner, Ross, 182
Statistics, as proof, 294–297; testing, 295–297
Steinhaus, Arthur H., 338–339
Step, as pitch change, 544
Stereotypes, 476–478
Stevens, Leonard A., 102, 103
Stevenson, Adlai, 344
Stimulating speech, audience for, the, 381; essential steps in, 387–392; nature of the, 380–383; persuasive speech, compared, 360–361; response sought, 381

Stimulation, as end in listening, 105–106
Stinnett, T. M., 294, 297
Stimuli, subliminal and supraliminal, 569–572
Stoddard, George D., 51
Stridency, description, cause and therapy, 537
Step chart, 326
Structure of a speech outline, logical, 251–252
Struggle, in relation to attention and interest, 195
Studio behavior in radio and television speaking, 451–452
Study of principles required, 46–48
Subject, an aspect of the speaking situation, 5; finding a, 209–211; general background and speech, 204–207; in relation to the speech situation, 211; listeners' attitude toward, 230; selecting a, 19–21, 203–204; testing the, 211–215
Summary in conclusion, 279–280
Sumner, G. Lynn, 399–400
Supporting materials, 286–315; example or specific instance, 298; gathering, 28–29; inference, 299–309; purposes of, 287–312; to amplify, 309–312; to clarify, 287–291; to prove, 309–312
Suspense, in relation to attention and interest, 194–195
Symposium, 418–419
Synonyms in definition, 467

Talmadge, Thomas DeWitt, 28
Target group, the, 146–147
Tavolga, W. N., 9
Taylor, Peggy, 520
Tensions, delivery and excessive, 95–96
Terms, special, 473–478; technical, 474–476
Testimony, testing the sources of, 292–293
Testing the subject, 211–215
Thinness in voice quality, 535–536
Thomas, Lowell, 53
Thomas, Norman, 144
Thompson, Dorothy, 498
Thonssen, Lester, 58, 290

Composed by Brown Brothers, Linotypers, Inc.
Format by Jeanne Ray
Set in Linotype Caledonia
Printed by The Haddon Craftsmen, Inc.
Bound by The Haddon Craftsmen, Inc.
HARPER & ROW, PUBLISHERS, INCORPORATED